P9-ECS-228

Every so often, an author comes along who offers us something extraordinary. Martin Plamondon's *Lewis and Clark Trail Maps* is just such an extraordinary work. With his eye for detail, his understanding of the Corps of Discovery story, and his abilities as a cartographer, Plamondon has given us a gift of immense importance. It complements Dr. Gary Moulton's edited thirteen-volume series, *The Journals of the Lewis and Clark Expedition.*

Every so often, a publisher comes along with the courage to try something new and different. Washington State University Press is to be commended for their courage, their foresight, and their exquisite work. The partnership between the WSU Press and Plamondon is something akin to that of the great partnership between Meriwether Lewis and William Clark.

—Barb Kubik, Chair, Governor's Washington Lewis and Clark Trail Committee, and former President, Lewis and Clark Trail Heritage Foundation

LEWIS *and* CLARK
Trail Maps

LEWIS *and* CLARK *Trail Maps*

A Cartographic Reconstruction, Volume II

Beyond Fort Mandan (North Dakota/Montana) to Continental Divide and Snake River (Idaho/Washington)—Outbound 1805; Return 1806.

Martin Plamondon II

Washington State University Press
Pullman, Washington

Washington State University Press
PO Box 645910
Pullman, Washington 99164-5910
Phone: 800-354-7360
Fax: 509-335-8568
E-mail: wsupress@wsu.edu
Web site: www.wsu.edu/wsupress

First printing 2001

Library of Congress Cataloging-in-Publication Data

Plamondon, Martin.
Lewis and Clark trail maps, a cartographic reconstruction, Volume II Beyond Fort Mandan (North Dakota/Montana) to Continental Divide and Snake River (Idaho/Washington)—Outbound 1805; return 1806 / by Martin Plamondon II.
p. cm.
Includes bibliographical references and index.
ISBN 0-87422-242-7 (hdb.)—ISBN 0-87422-243-5 (pbk.)—ISBN 0-87422-244-3 (spiral)
1. Lewis and Clark National Historic Trail—Maps. 2. Lewis and Clark Expedition (1804–1806)—Maps. 3. Cartography—Northwestern States—History—Maps. I. Title.

G1417.L4 P5 2001
912.78—dc21 v. 2

Cover art: John Ford Clymer, *Up the Jefferson,* 1978.
Courtesy of Doris Clymer and the Clymer Museum of Art, Ellensburg, Washington.

The WSU Press acknowledges the assistance provided to Martin Plamondon II by the Lewis and Clark Trail Heritage Foundation, the Governor's Washington Lewis and Clark Trail Committee, two anonymous grants in the name of the Columbia Gorge Interpretive Center (Stevenson, Washington), Captain and Mrs. J.P. Brooks (Washougal, Washington), and VIAs Multimedia Productions (Lolo, Montana).

Contents

Index Maps and Legend, Volume II

Lewis and Clark Trail Maps, Volume II

Indexes, Volume II

Dedication

William Clark, the Explorer, and Evelyn Plamondon

Volume I of the *Lewis and Clark Trail Maps* was dedicated to "General" William Clark. That volume, published in the year 2000, included 153 maps depicting the Corps of Discovery's route from near St. Louis up the Missouri River to the Fort Mandan area, where the expedition spent the winter of 1804–05. In later years, it was in this eastern Great Plains country that Clark's work as Indian agent, general of the Louisiana militia, and governor of Missouri came to be well known. Consequently, *Volume I* was dedicated to William Clark, the General.

Volume II of the *Lewis and Clark Trail Maps* consists of 180 maps extending from near Fort Mandan in North Dakota to the junction of the Snake and Columbia rivers in the state of Washington. It was in the western Great Plains, Rockies, and the Columbia Plateau that the Corps of Discovery truly stepped into the unknown geography of the West. Again, it is the survey notes recorded by William Clark that have allowed for a modern reconstruction of the famous exploration in these regions. In recognition of these facts, *Volume II* is dedicated to William Clark, the Explorer.

The cartographic work in *Volume II* has been extremely complicated because in 1805–06 the expedition often broke up into detachments to investigate waterways, judge alternate routes, seek Indian tribes, acquire provisions, or explore a broader range of territory. Furthermore, during the long journey the main party itself proceeded and returned over much of the same terrain. For example, the main group and one significant detachment passed over a western portion of the Lolo Trail on "five" different occasions in 1805–06. And as another example, at times during their return in the summer of 1806 the Corps was broken down into no less than "four" widely dispersed detachments in the Yellowstone and Missouri watersheds.

Due to this complexity, many were the times when this cartographer wanted nothing more than to give up—it seemed there was no end to the problem solving. However, going on little more than a desperate prayer and my wife's calming words and her constant faith in my ability, I got it done. For that reason, *Volume II* is dedicated to Evelyn as well. My gratitude to Evelyn has no end.

Acknowledgments

As we—the author, the editor, and the WSU Press staff—wrap up the final details of *Volume II* with one last edit, collect a final piece of artwork, find the perfect shade of blue for the cover, review the computer-scanned maps one last time, and confirm if "North Fork" the community and "North Fork" the stream are both listed in the index, we ask: "Have we missed anything?" It is a time of stress, but it is a time of release too. We have finally reached the point that there no longer is anything else to do. The manuscript now will find its way to the university pressmen, who create their magic with ink and paper. Soon, our thoughts will move on to compiling and completing *Volume III*.

There are people that I wish to thank regarding *Volume II*. I will begin with my wife, Evelyn, who has helped me keep a steady hand on the tiller. Evelyn and I spent nine days in Idaho and Montana this past summer looking here and there, and interviewing people about the Lewis and Clark route. Perhaps I talked far too much about the explorers, but she never complained. Thanks also to my daughter, Monica, for spending another seven days in Idaho and western Montana. And, to my father for accompanying me on a four-day trip to southeast Washington, Idaho's Clearwater country, and the Lemhi and Beaverhead areas in Montana and Idaho.

Special thanks go to my mother for her constant support, until she passed away in late March. I miss her phone calls, and the quiet hours sitting with her toward the end.

Acknowledgment goes to Dr. John Greves for monitoring my health and allowing me to keep my hands drafting.

Gratitude at least as big as the great Palouse Empire is due to my editor, Glen Lindeman. I never thought that working with an editor could be so easy or so enjoyable. And, I certainly want to mention business director Mary Read, marketing coordinator Sue Emory, editor-typesetter Nancy Grunewald, coordinator-proofreader Jean Taylor, order fulfillment coordinator Jenni Lynn, and cover designer Diana Whaley. These people make for a really fine team to work with; each and every one of them has my undying gratitude.

Of course, there are many other people to acknowledge in the university's publishing department, including those who do the actual printing, move books through the binders, and then warehouse them. These people work with knowledge and skill, and their pride in seeing a book printed is every bit as great as that of the author's. People in lithography prepare negatives for the presses; and, there are people who mail the books out, including my youngest son, Gordon, a working senior at Washington State University.

I wish to acknowledge the members of the Governor's Washington Lewis and Clark Trail Committee, all of whom have taken keen interest in this project and never fail to ask me about it. Thanks, likewise, to all of the others working in various Lewis and Clark organizations that have provided support, including the staffs at the Great Falls and Columbia Gorge interpretive centers.

A thank you also is due to all of the people who have called, written, or e-mailed to express their interest, support, and encouragement. I am grateful to those I met in my travels this last year, including Curly Bear Wagner of the Blackfeet Nation, Viola Anglin of Tendoy, Idaho, and Joe Mussulman of Lolo, Montana, who is a best friend and is always ready to listen and help.

Likewise, a special thank-you goes to Larry and Bonnie Cook of Missouri River Outfitters. A note on Map 221 tells about the vandalism that destroyed the rock formation known as The Eye of the Needle. Larry related the story: The Needle had been important to him. It was a place of solitude where he went to contemplate life. Larry is still upset all these years later over how people could do such a senseless act.

A massive project of this nature demands a constant supply of funds for purchasing drafting tools, ink cartridges, map paper, research materials, and all the rest. A number of people and organizations have provided essential assistance in this regard. Special gratitude is due to Ludd A. Trozpek and the Grants Committee of the Lewis and Clark Trail Heritage Foundation, the Governor's Washington Lewis and Clark Trail Committee (the only continuously active state committee since its creation), two anonymous individuals who gave funds in the name of the Columbia Gorge Interpretive Center, Captain and Mrs. J.P. Brooks of Washougal, Washington, and VIAs Multimedia Productions of Lolo, Montana. I doubt that the *Lewis and Clark Trail Maps* could be completed without the financial support and encouragement of these people.

If I have forgotten anyone, I fully apologize—my most sincere appreciation goes to each and every one of you too.

Martin Plamondon II
Vancouver, Washington
October 26, 2001

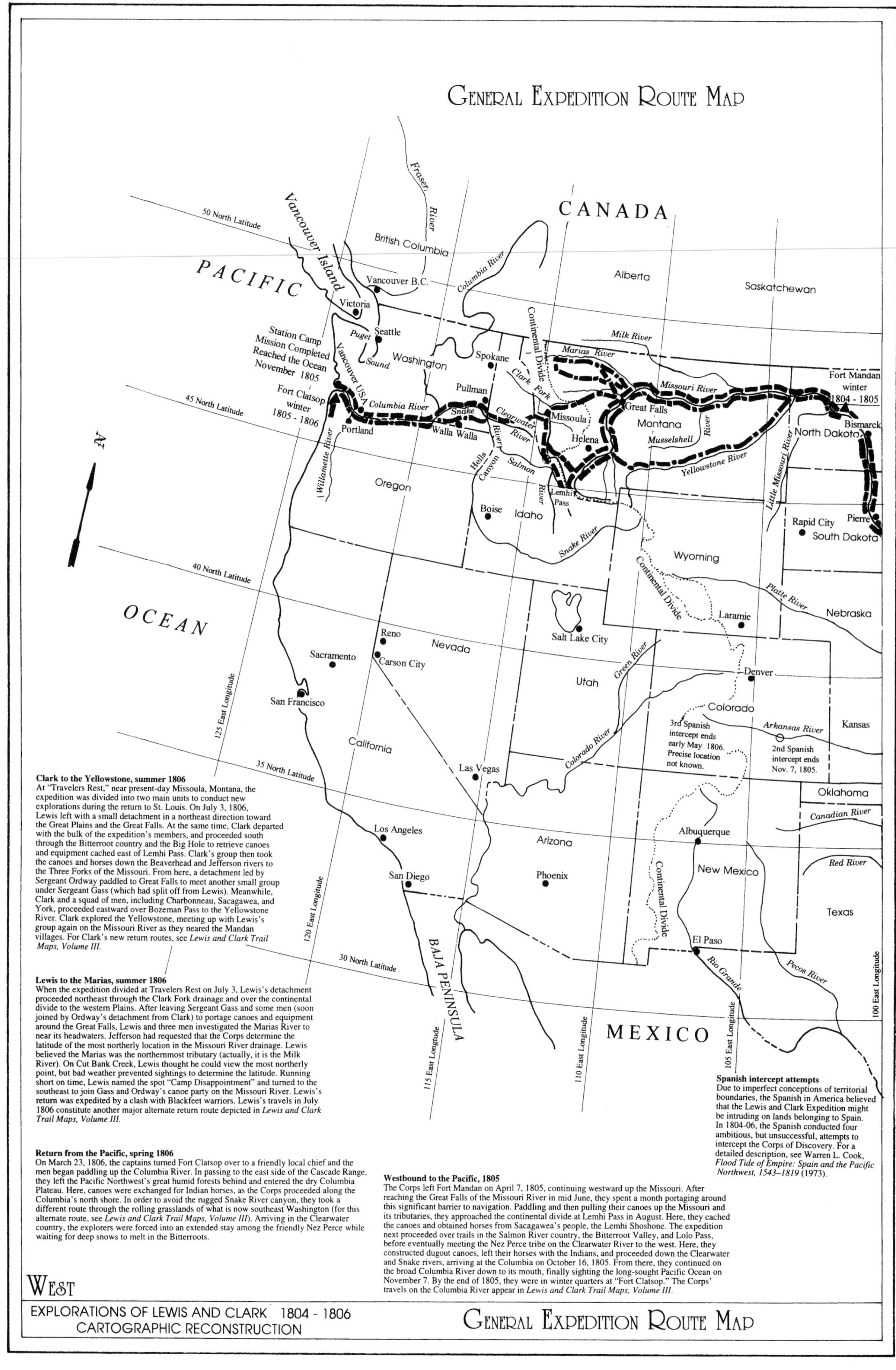
General Expedition Route Map
CANADA
PACIFIC
OCEAN
MEXICO
Vancouver Island
Fraser River
British Columbia
Columbia River
Alberta
Saskatchewan
Vancouver B.C.
Victoria
Seattle
Puget Sound
Washington
Spokane
Continental Divide
Milk River
Marias River
Missouri River
Fort Mandan winter 1804 - 1805
Station Camp Mission Completed Reached the Ocean November 1805
Fort Clatsop winter 1805 - 1806
Vancouver USA
Columbia River
Pullman
Snake
Clearwater River
Clark Fork
Missoula
Great Falls
Montana
Musselshell
River
Helena
Bismarck
North Dakota
Little Missouri River
Yellowstone River
50 North Latitude
45 North Latitude
40 North Latitude
35 North Latitude
30 North Latitude
Portland
Walla Walla
Willamette River
Hells Canyon
River
Salmon River
Lemhi Pass
Oregon
Boise
Idaho
Snake River
Rapid City
Pierre
South Dakota
Wyoming
Continental Divide
Platte River
Nebraska
Laramie
Salt Lake City
Reno
Nevada
Carson City
Sacramento
San Francisco
Green River
Utah
Denver
Colorado
Kansas
3rd Spanish intercept ends early May 1806. Precise location not known.
Arkansas River
2nd Spanish intercept ends Nov. 7, 1805.
California
Las Vegas
Colorado River
Oklahoma
Canadian River
Los Angeles
Arizona
Albuquerque
New Mexico
Red River
San Diego
Phoenix
Continental Divide
Texas
El Paso
Rio Grande
Pecos River
BAJA PENINSULA
125 East Longitude
120 East Longitude
115 East Longitude
110 East Longitude
105 East Longitude
100 East Longitude
N

Clark to the Yellowstone, summer 1806
At "Travelers Rest," near present-day Missoula, Montana, the expedition was divided into two main units to conduct new explorations during the return to St. Louis. On July 3, 1806, Lewis left with a small detachment in a northeast direction toward the Great Plains and the Great Falls. At the same time, Clark departed with the bulk of the expedition's members, and proceeded south through the Bitterroot country and the Big Hole to retrieve canoes and equipment cached east of Lemhi Pass. Clark's group then took the canoes and horses down the Beaverhead and Jefferson rivers to the Three Forks of the Missouri. From here, a detachment led by Sergeant Ordway paddled to Great Falls to meet another small group under Sergeant Gass (which had split off from Lewis). Meanwhile, Clark and a squad of men, including Charbonneau, Sacagawea, and York, proceeded eastward over Bozeman Pass to the Yellowstone River. Clark explored the Yellowstone, meeting up with Lewis's group again on the Missouri River as they neared the Mandan villages. For Clark's new return routes, see Lewis and Clark Trail Maps, Volume III.

Lewis to the Marias, summer 1806
When the expedition divided at Travelers Rest on July 3, Lewis's detachment proceeded northeast through the Clark Fork drainage and over the continental divide to the western Plains. After leaving Sergeant Gass and some men (soon joined by Ordway's detachment from Clark) to portage canoes and equipment around the Great Falls, Lewis and three men investigated the Marias River to near its headwaters. Jefferson had requested that the Corps determine the latitude of the most northerly location in the Missouri River drainage. Lewis believed the Marias was the northernmost tributary (actually, it is the Milk River). On Cut Bank Creek, Lewis thought he could view the most northerly point, but bad weather prevented sightings to determine the latitude. Running short on time, Lewis named the spot "Camp Disappointment" and turned to the southeast to join Gass and Ordway's canoe party on the Missouri River. Lewis's return was expedited by a clash with Blackfeet warriors. Lewis's travels in July 1806 constitute another major alternate return route depicted in Lewis and Clark Trail Maps, Volume III.

Return from the Pacific, spring 1806
On March 23, 1806, the captains turned Fort Clatsop over to a friendly local chief and the men began paddling up the Columbia River. In passing to the east side of the Cascade Range, they left the Pacific Northwest's great humid forests behind and entered the dry Columbia Plateau. Here, canoes were exchanged for Indian horses, as the Corps proceeded along the Columbia's north shore. In order to avoid the rugged Snake River canyon, they took a different route through the rolling grasslands of what is now southeast Washington (for this alternate route, see Lewis and Clark Trail Maps, Volume III). Arriving in the Clearwater country, the explorers were forced into an extended stay among the friendly Nez Perce while waiting for deep snows to melt in the Bitterroots.

Spanish intercept attempts
Due to imperfect conceptions of territorial boundaries, the Spanish in America believed that the Lewis and Clark Expedition might be intruding on lands belonging to Spain. In 1804-06, the Spanish conducted four ambitious, but unsuccessful, attempts to intercept the Corps of Discovery. For a detailed description, see Warren L. Cook, Flood Tide of Empire: Spain and the Pacific Northwest, 1543–1819 (1973).

Westbound to the Pacific, 1805
The Corps left Fort Mandan on April 7, 1805, continuing westward up the Missouri. After reaching the Great Falls of the Missouri River in mid June, they spent a month portaging around this significant barrier to navigation. Paddling and then pulling their canoes up the Missouri and its tributaries, they approached the continental divide at Lemhi Pass in August. Here, they cached the canoes and obtained horses from Sacagawea's people, the Lemhi Shoshone. The expedition next proceeded over trails in the Salmon River country, the Bitterroot Valley, and Lolo Pass, before eventually meeting the Nez Perce tribe on the Clearwater River to the west. Here, they constructed dugout canoes, left their horses with the Indians, and proceeded down the Clearwater and Snake rivers, arriving at the Columbia on October 16, 1805. From there, they continued on the broad Columbia River down to its mouth, finally sighting the long-sought Pacific Ocean on November 7. By the end of 1805, they were in winter quarters at "Fort Clatsop." The Corps' travels on the Columbia River appear in Lewis and Clark Trail Maps, Volume III.

West
EXPLORATIONS OF LEWIS AND CLARK 1804 - 1806
CARTOGRAPHIC RECONSTRUCTION
General Expedition Route Map

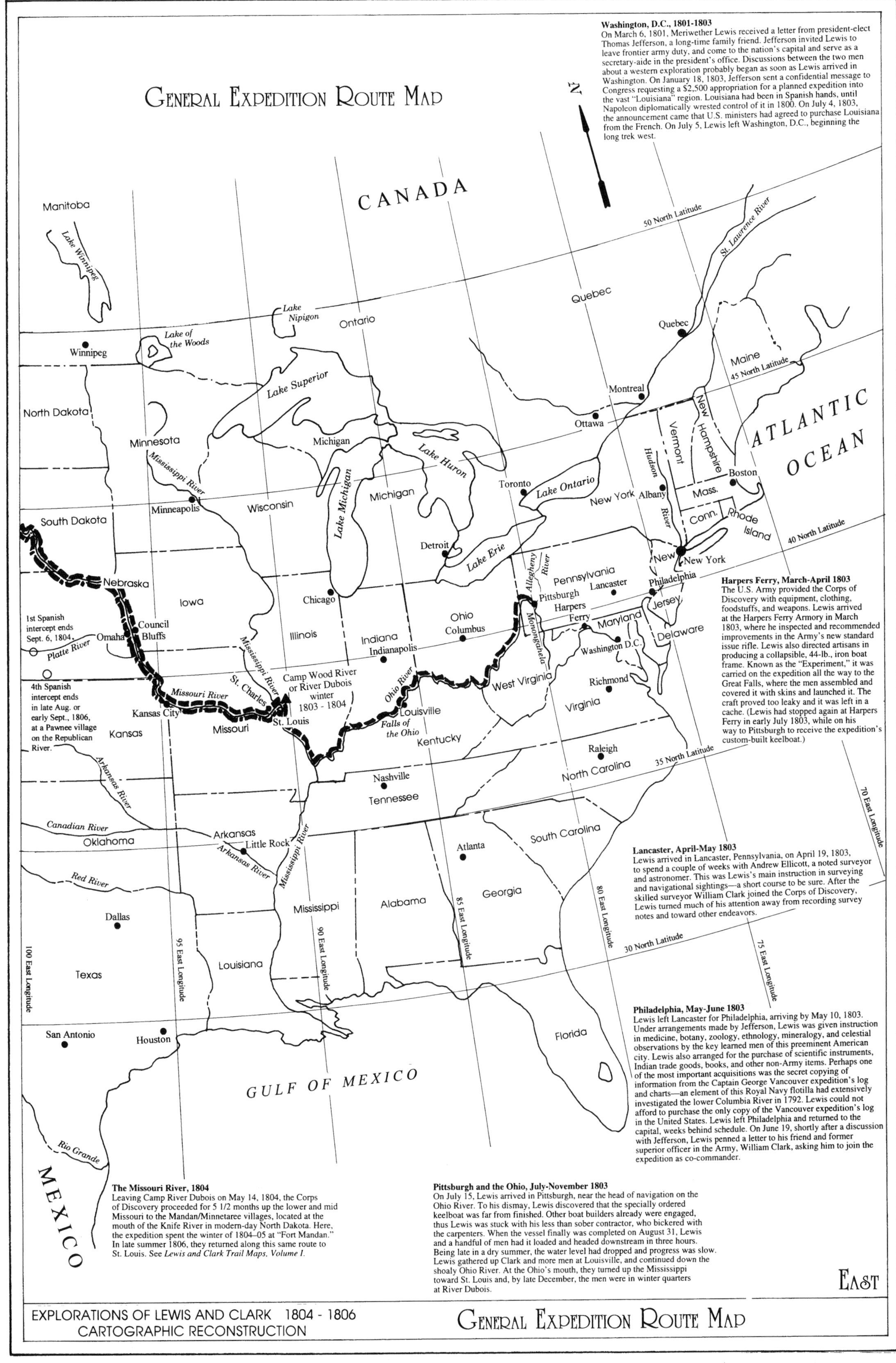

General Expedition Route Map
Washington, D.C., 1801-1803
On March 6, 1801, Meriwether Lewis received a letter from president-elect Thomas Jefferson, a long-time family friend. Jefferson invited Lewis to leave frontier army duty, and come to the nation's capital and serve as a secretary-aide in the president's office. Discussions between the two men about a western exploration probably began as soon as Lewis arrived in Washington. On January 18, 1803, Jefferson sent a confidential message to Congress requesting a $2,500 appropriation for a planned expedition into the vast "Louisiana" region. Louisiana had been in Spanish hands, until Napoleon diplomatically wrested control of it in 1800. On July 4, 1803, the announcement came that U.S. ministers had agreed to purchase Louisiana from the French. On July 5, Lewis left Washington, D.C., beginning the long trek west.
N
CANADA
Manitoba
Lake Winnipeg
50 North Latitude
St. Lawrence River
Quebec
Lake Nipigon
Ontario
Quebec
Lake of the Woods
Winnipeg
Lake Superior
Maine
45 North Latitude
Montreal
North Dakota
Ottawa
Minnesota
Michigan
Lake Huron
New Hampshire
Vermont
ATLANTIC OCEAN
Mississippi River
Hudson River
Boston
Toronto
Lake Ontario
Mass.
Minneapolis
Wisconsin
Lake Michigan
Michigan
New York
Albany
South Dakota
Conn.
Rhode Island
40 North Latitude
Detroit
Lake Erie
New Jersey
New York
Nebraska
Allegheny River
Pennsylvania
Lancaster
Philadelphia
Iowa
Chicago
Pittsburgh
Harpers Ferry
Harpers Ferry, March-April 1803
The U.S. Army provided the Corps of Discovery with equipment, clothing, foodstuffs, and weapons. Lewis arrived at the Harpers Ferry Armory in March 1803, where he inspected and recommended improvements in the Army's new standard issue rifle. Lewis also directed artisans in producing a collapsible, 44-lb., iron boat frame. Known as the "Experiment," it was carried on the expedition all the way to the Great Falls, where the men assembled and covered it with skins and launched it. The craft proved too leaky and it was left in a cache. (Lewis had stopped again at Harpers Ferry in early July 1803, while on his way to Pittsburgh to receive the expedition's custom-built keelboat.)
1st Spanish intercept ends Sept. 6, 1804.
Council Bluffs
Omaha
Platte River
Illinois
Indiana
Indianapolis
Ohio
Columbus
Monongahela
Maryland
Delaware
Washington D.C.
4th Spanish intercept ends in late Aug. or early Sept., 1806, at a Pawnee village on the Republican River.
Missouri River
St. Charles
Camp Wood River or River Dubois winter 1803 - 1804
Ohio River
West Virginia
Richmond
Kansas City
Missouri
St. Louis
Louisville
Falls of the Ohio
Virginia
Kansas
Kentucky
Raleigh
Arkansas River
35 North Latitude
North Carolina
Nashville
Tennessee
70 East Longitude
Canadian River
Oklahoma
Arkansas
Little Rock
Arkansas River
Mississippi River
South Carolina
Atlanta
Lancaster, April-May 1803
Lewis arrived in Lancaster, Pennsylvania, on April 19, 1803, to spend a couple of weeks with Andrew Ellicott, a noted surveyor and astronomer. This was Lewis's main instruction in surveying and navigational sightings—a short course to be sure. After the skilled surveyor William Clark joined the Corps of Discovery, Lewis turned much of his attention away from recording survey notes and toward other endeavors.
Red River
Mississippi
Alabama
Georgia
80 East Longitude
85 East Longitude
Dallas
100 East Longitude
95 East Longitude
90 East Longitude
30 North Latitude
75 East Longitude
Texas
Louisiana
Philadelphia, May-June 1803
Lewis left Lancaster for Philadelphia, arriving by May 10, 1803. Under arrangements made by Jefferson, Lewis was given instruction in medicine, botany, zoology, ethnology, mineralogy, and celestial observations by the key learned men of this preeminent American city. Lewis also arranged for the purchase of scientific instruments, Indian trade goods, books, and other non-Army items. Perhaps one of the most important acquisitions was the secret copying of information from the Captain George Vancouver expedition's log and charts—an element of this Royal Navy flotilla had extensively investigated the lower Columbia River in 1792. Lewis could not afford to purchase the only copy of the Vancouver expedition's log in the United States. Lewis left Philadelphia and returned to the capital, weeks behind schedule. On June 19, shortly after a discussion with Jefferson, Lewis penned a letter to his friend and former superior officer in the Army, William Clark, asking him to join the expedition as co-commander.
San Antonio
Houston
Florida
GULF OF MEXICO
Rio Grande
MEXICO
The Missouri River, 1804
Leaving Camp River Dubois on May 14, 1804, the Corps of Discovery proceeded for 5 1/2 months up the lower and mid Missouri to the Mandan/Minnetaree villages, located at the mouth of the Knife River in modern-day North Dakota. Here, the expedition spent the winter of 1804–05 at "Fort Mandan." In late summer 1806, they returned along this same route to St. Louis. See Lewis and Clark Trail Maps, Volume I.
Pittsburgh and the Ohio, July-November 1803
On July 15, Lewis arrived in Pittsburgh, near the head of navigation on the Ohio River. To his dismay, Lewis discovered that the specially ordered keelboat was far from finished. Other boat builders already were engaged, thus Lewis was stuck with his less than sober contractor, who bickered with the carpenters. When the vessel finally was completed on August 31, Lewis and a handful of men had it loaded and headed downstream in three hours. Being late in a dry summer, the water level had dropped and progress was slow. Lewis gathered up Clark and more men at Louisville, and continued down the shoaly Ohio River. At the Ohio's mouth, they turned up the Mississippi toward St. Louis and, by late December, the men were in winter quarters at River Dubois.
East
EXPLORATIONS OF LEWIS AND CLARK 1804 - 1806
CARTOGRAPHIC RECONSTRUCTION
General Expedition Route Map

A Typical Sample from William Clark's Traverse Notes

For Trail Maps 199 and 200

Course & Distance May 14th 1805

	mile	
S. 55°. W.	1	on the Lar[d] Side swift water
S. 35°. W	½	allong the Lar[d] Side ops[d]. the lower point of an Is[d]. in a bind to St[d]. Side.
S. 20°. W.	½	allong the Lar[d] Side passed the h[d] of the Is[d]. ops[d]. to which a large creek falls in on the St[d] Side. Gibson Creek
S. 12°. E.	3	to a point of timber on the St[d]. Side high hills on the Lar[d] Side
S. 20°. W	2½	to a point of timbered land on the St[d] Side, a bluff on Lar[d] Side
S. 80°. W	3	to a point of timbered land on the Lar[d]. Side, pass[d]. a point of wood land on the St[d] Side at 1 mile
S. 85°. W	2½	to a point of timbered land on Lar[d]. s[d] Pass[g]. Yellow Bear Defeat creek 40 yds wide
S. 62°. W	3½	to a point of wood land on the Star[d] Side, at which place one perogue like to have been lost & we camped
	16½	

[Source: Reuben Gold Thwaites, ed., *Original Journals of the Lewis and Clark Expedition, 1804–1806*, Volume Two (1904), 38.]

Introduction

Overview of *Volume II*

This is the second atlas in the three-volume set, *Lewis and Clark Trail Maps: A Cartographic Reconstruction.* In *Volume I,* 153 maps depict the Lewis and Clark National Historic Trail from the Missouri-Mississippi junction to the Fort Mandan locality in central North Dakota—a distance of some 1,400 miles, and entirely on the Missouri River.

Volume II continues the trek from where *Volume I* ends. It includes 180 trail maps taking the Corps of Discovery further up the Missouri past the mouths of the Yellowstone, Milk, Musselshell, Judith, and Marias rivers. It then depicts the expedition's difficult month-long portage of canoes and equipment around the Great Falls of the Missouri, and, not long after, their passage through the first gaps in the several Rocky Mountain ridges that they encountered. The maps continue with the trek up the Jefferson and Beaverhead rivers, and the crossing of the continental divide at Lemhi Pass. Here, they were befriended by the Lemhi (Agaideka), who supplied the horses that allowed the Corps to continue toward the Pacific Ocean.

In passing over the continental divide, the expedition had left U.S. territory (acquired by the 1803 Louisiana Purchase), and entered a vast area claimed by Great Britain, Russia, Spain, and the United States. This disputed region soon would be known as the Oregon Country. After investigating the westward flowing Salmon River canyon and finding it impassable by boat or on foot, the Corps set out with their pack string of horses northward through the mountains to the Bitterroot Valley. They found the mountain trails obstructed by rocks, windfall, and brush, while early snowfall appeared on the peaks. Unlike the bountiful Great Plains, game was scarce in this region. The mention of short rations and hunger would become common in the journals.

Proceeding quickly through the broad, magnificent Bitterroot Valley, where travel was easy, they turned west toward rugged Lolo Pass. Experiencing both frigid early season snows and sultry autumnal heat, the Corps struggled on through the broad, tangled Bitterroot Range. The party's strength deteriorated due to exposure, exertion, and hunger, and sometimes they resorted to eating tallow candles and Lewis's dried soup, which had been specially prepared in the East and brought along in canisters as emergency supplies.

The expedition eventually reached the beautiful Clearwater country and met the Nez Perce, a noble people who generously supplied provisions and hospitality. On the Clearwater River, the Corps constructed a small fleet of canoes and set off downstream, after caching much of their equipment and leaving the horses and other accoutrements with the Nez Perce. The Corps' pine dugout canoes quickly took them down the Clearwater to the Snake (or "Lewis") River.

With the season getting late, they continued on the Snake, struggling to get their canoes through the many rapids. The Corps finally reached the long sought Columbia River on October 16, 1805. Here, their Nez Perce guides introduced them to the several Indian nations occupying this locality. *Volume II* ends with the Corps of Discovery camped for two nights on the north side of the Snake River's mouth, where they anxiously made preparations to set out down the Columbia for the Pacific.

(*Volume III* depicts the Corps of Discovery's travels on the Columbia River in 1805–06, their investigations at the river's mouth, and the winter spent at Fort Clatsop. Also covered in *Volume III* are the Corps' new explorations during the return in 1806, particularly the main party's overland routes in southeast Washington and a nearby part of Idaho, William Clark's investigation of the Big Hole, Gallatin Valley, and Yellowstone River, and Meriwether Lewis's travels in the Clark Fork watershed and the western Great Plains, including the Marias journey.)

In *Volume II,* two new themes are apparent—(1) important detachments often are sent out from the main group, and (2) the explorers encounter great topographical diversity as they proceed westward.

Detachments

In 1804 (i.e., *Volume I*), while coming up the lower and middle Missouri, the expedition frequently had sent out hunters, both individually or in small groups, and sometimes for days at a time. Also, one of the captains, mainly Lewis, at times walked on shore, usually to observe the local topography and collect floral, faunal, or geological specimens. Generally, there is sparse information in the journals about where the hunters or Lewis foraged. Often, they went off the boundaries of the areas depicted in the *Lewis and Clark Trail Maps.* To avoid confusion (and too much speculation), this cartographer decided to leave off the assumed trails taken by hunters. This generally is the case for all of the *Lewis and Clark Trail Maps* volumes.

During the voyage of 1804 (i.e., *Volume I*), the expedition generally proceeded en masse up the Missouri as one party. In the area covered by *Volume II,* however, Lewis, Clark, the sergeants, and others in 1805–06 often left the main body of men and led detachments on important assignments. At the Marias-Missouri junction, for instance, Lewis and Clark each led small parties to explore and determine which stream was the main branch. In the process, Lewis explored the lower Marias, and he later found the Great Falls of the Missouri. Shortly, other detachments were assigned to cut wooden wheels for portage vehicles and to haul the boats and baggage around the Great Falls. These and similar tracks for special detachments are depicted in *Volume II.*

Continuing in this vein, upon entering the Rocky Mountains, Clark and a small party proceeded ahead, seeking the Lemhi Shoshone. The captains feared that Sacagawea's people would take fright at the size of the main party or the reports of the hunters' guns. Clark hoped that his small group's approach would be non-threatening. However, he did not encounter any tribesmen.

After Clark's detachment rejoined the main group at the Three Forks of the Missouri, Lewis took over the search, proceeding ahead up the Beaverhead River and over Lemhi Pass to Columbia waters, where he successfully met the Lemhi. Here, various detachments of the Corps bartered for horses, cached equipment and boats, moved on foot and horseback, and scouted the Salmon River.

As the expedition crossed the Lolo Trail in the Bitterroot Range, Clark went on ahead with a small detachment to acquire desperately needed provisions for the main party coming along behind. Further divisions occurred in the Nez Perce lands of the Clearwater country.

During the return trip in 1806, other longer, significant separations occurred when the Corps retrieved canoes and equipment in caches on the Beaverhead and at the Great Falls, and explored new areas of the Intermountain West and the Great Plains. These divisions, too, are indicated in *Volume II*, and especially in *Volume III.*

During the preparation of *Volume II*, the depiction of the routes taken by the detachments and their campsites added an element of complexity to the map making. Detachments seldom, if ever, recorded adequate traverse notes. Consequently, the routes of the detachments and the locations of their camps usually have been determined as best as possible by a close examination of the journals, Clark's various sketch maps, and by calculating the estimated pace of travel for the parties. The goal was to identify all of this activity and still provide an attractive and clearly understandable set of maps in *Volume II.* Often, the use of large directional arrows with hatching, and special Cartographer's Notes, seemed most applicable for the task of tracking the detachments. When appropriate, the notes also indicate where a detachment's trek connected to the new return routes depicted in *Volume III.*

Topographical Diversity

The second new theme in *Volume II* involves the diversity of landscapes that the Corps encountered as they penetrated the western Great Plains, the Rockies, and the Inland Northwest. *Volume II* depicts approximately 1,400 miles of the expedition's trails. Massive geological forces, differing soil patterns, rugged relief, elevation differences, prevailing weather patterns, and snow and rainfall variances had created landscapes that were mostly unfamiliar to the oft-amazed explorers from the east.

Tall Grass Plains

Leaving Fort Mandan on April 7, 1805, the Corps of Discovery initially noted a topography little changed from what they had seen in the previous autumn. The Missouri Valley was narrower, but it had bottomlands that would be sufficient for small farms. The bottoms were fertile, thanks to the springtime flooding. Eroded gulches lacerated the valley walls, making a climb up to the prairie somewhat difficult.

Short Grass Plains

As the Corps proceeded, the tall grass prairie had quickly diminished, replaced by a drier, short-grass topography resulting from the rain shadow effect caused by the distant Rocky Mountains. As the expedition left the frequented hunting grounds of the Knife River tribes, game animals became more numerous, particularly buffalo and elk. As spring passed into summer, the overall fitness and appearance of these animals improved remarkably.

On April 25, 1805, just before leaving what is today North Dakota, the Corps reached the Yellowstone River where it discharges into the Missouri. The bottomlands increase in size at this major confluence. (Once, it was proposed that a large, shallow lake be scraped out in these bottoms. The lake was to be shaped in the silhouettes of Meriwether Lewis and William Clark's portraits, and large enough to be seen from space.) Here again, the bottomlands appeared to be excellent for farming and grazing, but the scenery would quickly change as the expedition pushed further west.

Badlands

The Corps entered the badlands about April 29, 1805. Modern Americans usually recognize this kind of terrain as typifying the Theodore Roosevelt and Badlands national parks in the Dakotas, and by the triangle of territory bordered by the Yellowstone and Missouri rivers in eastern Montana. Other sections of badlands, however, are found elsewhere in Montana, the western Dakotas, and, indeed, in a number of other localities throughout the western United States.

Rocky, nearly barren, and deeply eroded gullies, buttes, tablelands, and streambeds characterize the badlands. The often-colorful formations are composed of fine-grained rock and gravelly deposits that are easily eroded and carved by wind and rain, and which are susceptible to flash flooding. Ground vegetation is scant and trees are few in these lightly watered and quickly drained localities. In eastern Montana, the expedition observed rugged badlands extending for miles in either direction from the river bottom.

Missouri River Breaks

The spectacular and highly eroded Missouri River Breaks differ in degree from other badlands because this formation lay

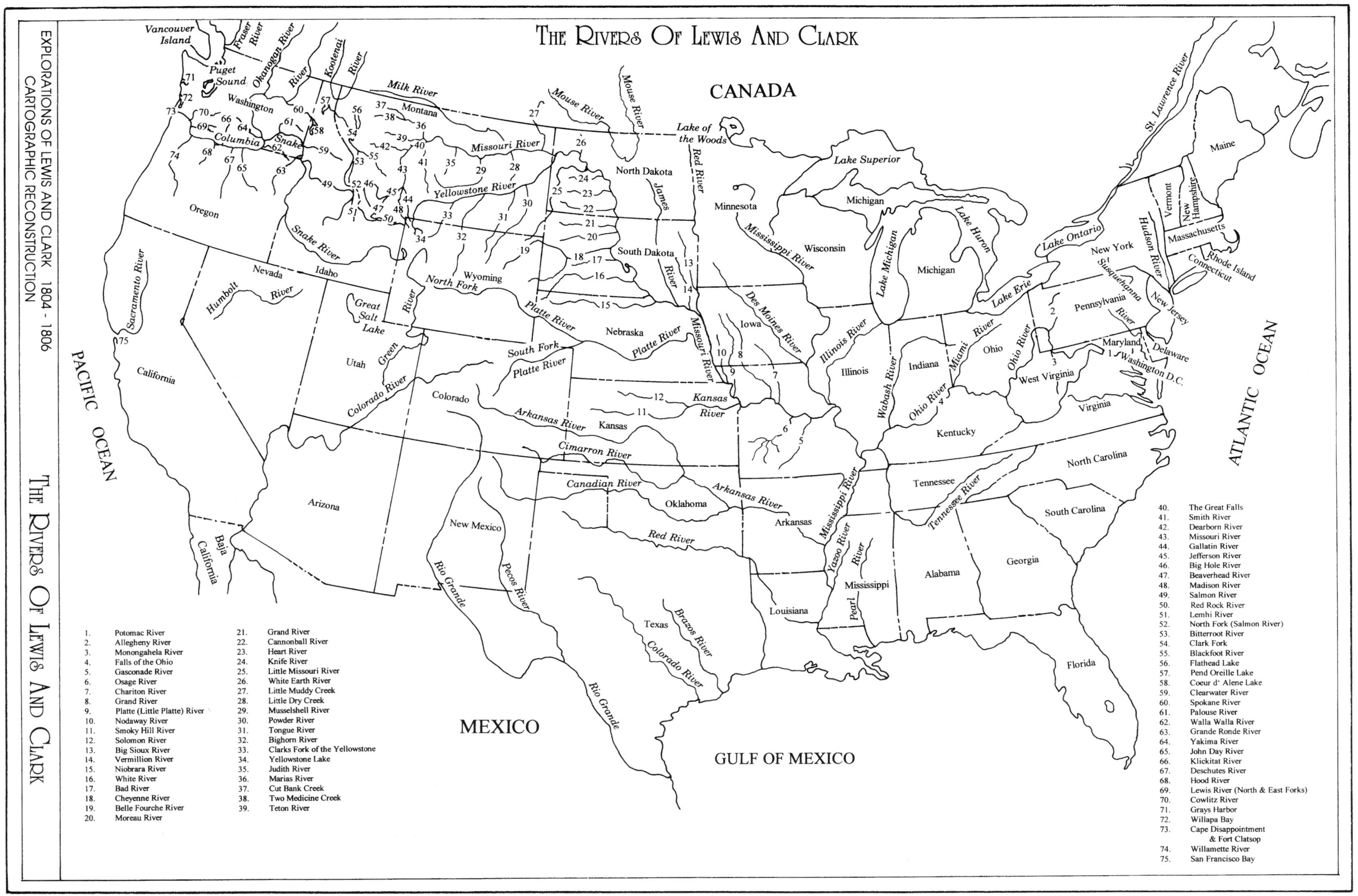

The Rivers Of Lewis And Clark
CANADA
PACIFIC OCEAN
ATLANTIC OCEAN
MEXICO
GULF OF MEXICO
Vancouver Island
Puget Sound
Washington
Oregon
California
Baja California
Nevada
Idaho
Montana
Utah
Arizona
Wyoming
Colorado
New Mexico
North Dakota
South Dakota
Nebraska
Kansas
Oklahoma
Texas
Minnesota
Iowa
Missouri River
Arkansas
Louisiana
Wisconsin
Michigan
Illinois
Indiana
Ohio
Kentucky
Tennessee
Mississippi
Alabama
Georgia
Florida
South Carolina
North Carolina
Virginia
West Virginia
Pennsylvania
Maryland
Washington D.C.
Delaware
New Jersey
New York
Vermont
New Hampshire
Maine
Massachusetts
Rhode Island
Connecticut
Fraser River
Okanogan River
Kootenai River
Milk River
Mouse River
Lake of the Woods
Red River
Lake Superior
Lake Michigan
Lake Huron
Lake Erie
Lake Ontario
St. Lawrence River
Hudson River
Susquehanna River
Columbia
Snake
Snake River
Missouri River
Yellowstone River
North Fork
Platte River
South Fork
Great Salt Lake
Green River
Colorado River
Humbolt River
Sacramento River
James River
Mississippi River
Des Moines River
Illinois River
Wabash River
Miami River
Ohio River
Kansas River
Arkansas River
Cimarron River
Canadian River
Red River
Tennessee River
Yazoo River
Pearl River
Brazos River
Colorado River
Pecos River
Rio Grande
1. Potomac River
2. Allegheny River
3. Monongahela River
4. Falls of the Ohio
5. Gasconade River
6. Osage River
7. Chariton River
8. Grand River
9. Platte (Little Platte) River
10. Nodaway River
11. Smoky Hill River
12. Solomon River
13. Big Sioux River
14. Vermillion River
15. Niobrara River
16. White River
17. Bad River
18. Cheyenne River
19. Belle Fourche River
20. Moreau River
21. Grand River
22. Cannonball River
23. Heart River
24. Knife River
25. Little Missouri River
26. White Earth River
27. Little Muddy Creek
28. Little Dry Creek
29. Musselshell River
30. Powder River
31. Tongue River
32. Bighorn River
33. Clarks Fork of the Yellowstone
34. Yellowstone Lake
35. Judith River
36. Marias River
37. Cut Bank Creek
38. Two Medicine Creek
39. Teton River
40. The Great Falls
41. Smith River
42. Dearborn River
43. Missouri River
44. Gallatin River
45. Jefferson River
46. Big Hole River
47. Beaverhead River
48. Madison River
49. Salmon River
50. Red Rock River
51. Lemhi River
52. North Fork (Salmon River)
53. Bitterroot River
54. Clark Fork
55. Blackfoot River
56. Flathead Lake
57. Pend Oreille Lake
58. Coeur d' Alene Lake
59. Clearwater River
60. Spokane River
61. Palouse River
62. Walla Walla River
63. Grande Ronde River
64. Yakima River
65. John Day River
66. Klickitat River
67. Deschutes River
68. Hood River
69. Lewis River (North & East Forks)
70. Cowlitz River
71. Grays Harbor
72. Willapa Bay
73. Cape Disappointment & Fort Clatsop
74. Willamette River
75. San Francisco Bay
EXPLORATIONS OF LEWIS AND CLARK 1804 - 1806
CARTOGRAPHIC RECONSTRUCTION
The Rivers Of Lewis And Clark

close to an area where mountain building had occurred. Tremendous subterranean forces had caused numerous layers of rock to twist, tilt, and fold. Weather sculpting then further altered these sandstone outcroppings into all sorts of unique contours. Here, the explorers' imaginations saw natural rock features resembling castle walls, minarets, battlements, and ancient ruins.

Today, there are few roads crossing the primitive, but beautiful, Missouri River Breaks. Below Fort Benton, a long stretch of the Missouri through the White Cliffs and adjoining badlands has been designated as a National Wild and Scenic River. One of the best ways to view these wonders is by canoe or raft trip.

Marias River and the High Plains

At this upriver locality, the badlands are significantly diminished and grassy hills and level prairie dominate the landscape. Extensive river bottomlands lay adjacent to where the Marias, a major stream, flows into the Missouri. The bottomland continues along the Missouri shore, which provided an ideal habitat for prairie dog "towns."

When the explorers reached this junction in early June 1805, the north branch (the Marias) was filled by spring runoff and appeared to be as large as the south branch (the Missouri). The Indians in the Knife River villages had failed to tell the captains about the Marias during the previous winter. Before the Corps could move on, they had to determine which stream—the south branch or the north branch—was the main stem of the Missouri. A week was spent exploring here before the captains concluded that the southerly branch was the Missouri proper.

Great Falls of the Missouri

Lewis led a small detachment ahead of the main party and discovered a series of spectacular cascades—the Great Falls. Buffalo, grizzly bear, and wolves abounded in the area. The Giant Spring, another nearby feature observed by the expedition, is as awe inspiring today as it was two centuries ago.

When summer showers fell in this locality, the hard baked ground quickly turned to mud, which hampered the men's efforts to portage the canoes and baggage over an 18-mile route around the falls. On the flats, the hooves of passing buffalo deepened and pockmarked the mud. When the sun came out again, it quickly hardened the ground into sharp points of flinty soil that tore through the men's moccasins. Perhaps causing even more misery for the men was the abundant prickly pear cactus growing in the area. Dust, dirt, and gravel covered much of the low-lying cacti, and consequently it was frequently stepped on. Even double-soled moccasins were no match for the spines, which worked their way through heavy leather in seconds.

Lewis's special prefabricated canoe proved unworkable when launched above the falls. Consequently, the expedition was forced to seek timber to build two additional canoes, but the few sparse cottonwoods growing in the area were barely acceptable. The expedition's craftsmen, however, were able to cobble together two serviceable craft.

Mountains were visible in the far distance where the High Plains terminated. As the party continued up the Missouri, they occasionally encountered fertile bottomlands of significant size in the river valley.

The Rocky Mountains

The magnificent Rockies—frequently snow-capped even in midsummer—were higher peaks than any ever seen before by the expedition members, excepting Sacagawea. Upon entering the first outlying range in their path (the Big Belt Mountains), the expedition passed through a spectacular gorge, which they named the Gates of the Mountains.

Continuing beyond, they entered a long, dry, broad valley surrounded on all sides by high country. Reaching the Three Forks of the Missouri, the Corps proceeded up the Jefferson River through yet another deep mountain gorge, and again entered a lengthy, broad valley (the Beaverhead). This kind of terrain—i.e., extensive, open valleys interspersed between long, rugged, and frequently alpine-topped mountain ridges—also typified much of the Rocky Mountain region through which they later traveled, particularly the Lemhi and Bitterroot valleys.

The men paddled, and then began pulling, their dugout boats in the clear, cold, and ever swifter and shallower Beaverhead River. Cottonwood, willow, and lesser vegetation lined the shore, but the expansive valley floor was dry prairie and sagebrush plains, with some swamplands. Bands of evergreen forests were visible on the far-off flanks of the highest mountains. Gone were the huge herds of the Great Plains; hunters now sighted only an occasional buffalo, deer, elk, antelope, big horn, or wolf. By late summer, the evenings were cold with many frosty mornings.

Originally, the captains had expected to find a conveniently short portage over the Rocky Mountain divide, perhaps of only a half-day's labor, that would take them from the Missouri headwaters to a westward flowing stream presumably in the Columbia River drainage. At the previous winter camp of 1804–05, however, the Knife River tribes had told the captains that there was no easy portage. Instead, they would encounter mighty peaks and a series of barrier ranges.

In light of this information, it became apparent to the captains that they must find Sacagawea's people, the Lemhi, and trade for horses in order to proceed over a rocky pass. They did, in fact, accomplish this aim, but another hope—a wistful one as it turned out—was that a navigable stream would be discovered a short distance west of the continental divide on which they could construct and launch dugout canoes and float to the Pacific Ocean. Instead, they soon discovered that their journey on foot and horseback would be a long one.

The Bitterroots

Located primarily west of the Lemhi and Bitterroot valleys, the Bitterroot Range is a seemingly endless jumble of thick

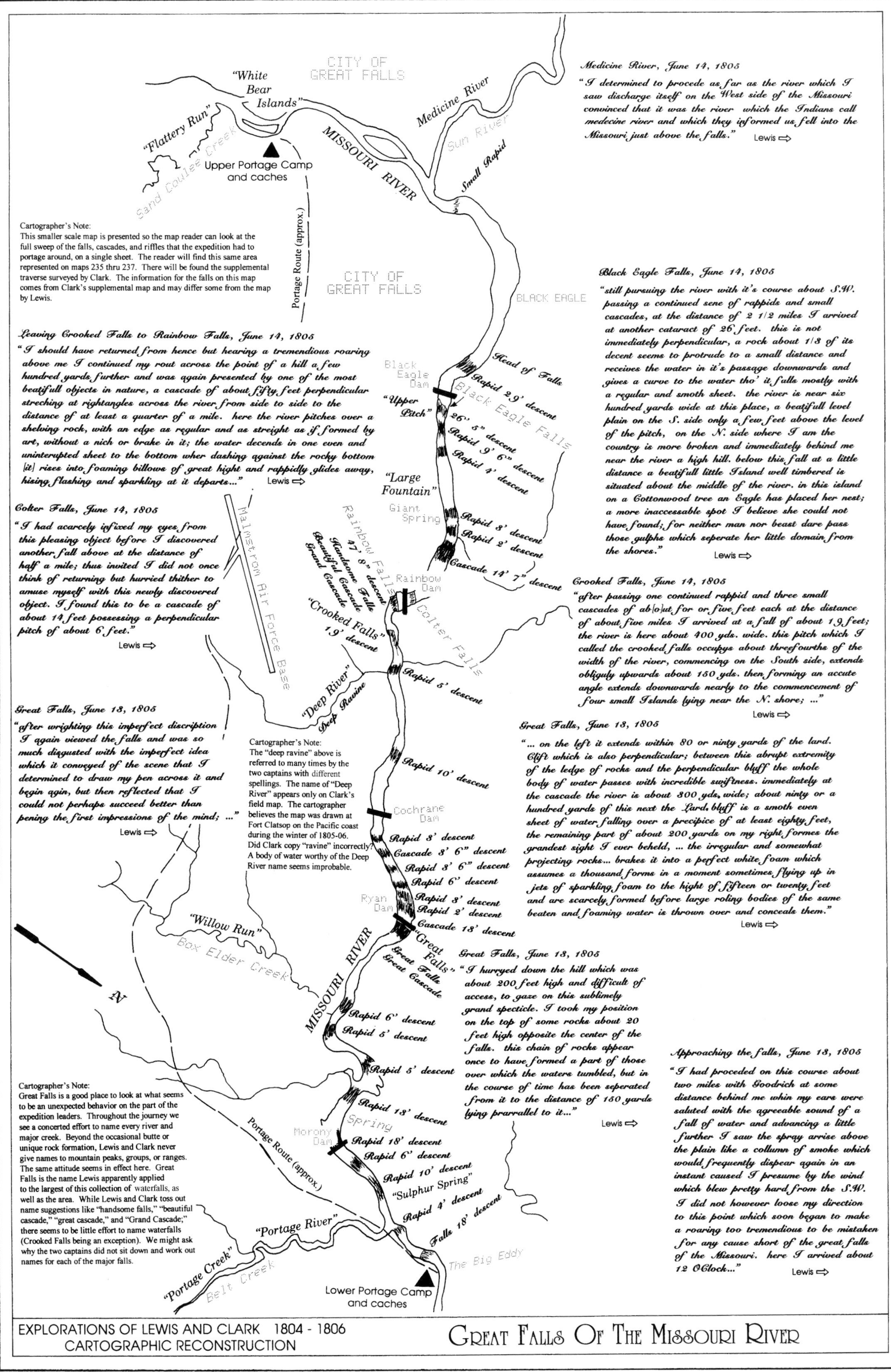
CITY OF GREAT FALLS
"White Bear Islands"
"Flattery Run"
Sand Coulee Creek
Upper Portage Camp and caches
MISSOURI RIVER
Medicine River
Sun River
Small Rapid
Medicine River, June 14, 1805
"I determined to procede as far as the river which I saw discharge itself on the West side of the Missouri convinced that it was the river which the Indians call medecine river and which they informed us fell into the Missouri just above the falls." Lewis ⇨
Cartographer's Note:
This smaller scale map is presented so the map reader can look at the full sweep of the falls, cascades, and riffles that the expedition had to portage around, on a single sheet. The reader will find this same area represented on maps 235 thru 237. There will be found the supplemental traverse surveyed by Clark. The information for the falls on this map comes from Clark's supplemental map and may differ some from the map by Lewis.
Portage Route (approx.)
CITY OF GREAT FALLS
BLACK EAGLE
Black Eagle Falls, June 14, 1805
"still pursuing the river with it's course about S.W. passing a continued sene of rappids and small cascades, at the distance of 2 1/2 miles I arrived at another cataract of 26 feet. this is not immediately perpendicular, a rock about 1/3 of its decent seems to protrude to a small distance and receives the water in it's passage downwards and gives a curve to the water tho' it falls mostly with a regular and smoth sheet. the river is near six hundred yards wide at this place, a beatifull level plain on the S. side only a few feet above the level of the pitch, on the N. side where I am the country is more broken and immediately behind me near the river a high hill. below this fall at a little distance a beatifull little Island well timbered is situated about the middle of the river. in this island on a Cottonwood tree an Eagle has placed her nest; a more inaccessable spot I believe she could not have found; for neither man nor beast dare pass those gulphs which seperate her little domain from the shores." Lewis ⇨
Leaving Crooked Falls to Rainbow Falls, June 14, 1805
"I should have returned from hence but hearing a tremendious roaring above me I continued my rout across the point of a hill a few hundred yards further and was again presented by one of the most beatifull objects in nature, a cascade of about fifty feet perpendicular streching at rightangles across the river from side to side to the distance of at least a quarter of a mile. here the river pitches over a shelving rock, with an edge as regular and as streight as if formed by art, without a nich or brake in it; the water decends in one even and uninterupted sheet to the bottom wher dashing against the rocky bottom [it] rises into foaming billows of great hight and rappidly glides away, hising flashing and sparkling at it departs..." Lewis ⇨
Head of Falls
Black Eagle Dam
Black Eagle Falls
Rapid 29' descent
"Upper Pitch"
26' 5" descent
Rapid 9' 6" descent
Rapid 4' descent
"Large Fountain"
Giant Spring
Rapid 8' descent
Rapid 2' descent
Cascade 14' 7" descent
Colter Falls, June 14, 1805
"I had scarcely infixed my eyes from this pleasing object before I discovered another fall above at the distance of half a mile; thus invited I did not once think of returning but hurried thither to amuse myself with this newly discovered object. I found this to be a cascade of about 14 feet possessing a perpendicular pitch of about 6 feet." Lewis ⇨
Malmstrom Air Force Base
Rainbow Falls
47' 8" descent
Handsome Falls
Beautiful Cascade
Grand Cascade
Rainbow Dam
"Crooked Falls" 19' descent
Colter Falls
Crooked Falls, June 14, 1805
"after passing one continued rappid and three small cascades of ab[o]ut for or five feet each at the distance of about five miles I arrived at a fall of about 19 feet; the river is here about 400 yds. wide. this pitch which I called the crooked falls occupys about threefourths of the width of the river, commencing on the South side, extends obliquly upwards about 150 yds. then forming an accute angle extends downwards nearly to the commencement of four small Islands lying near the N. shore; ..." Lewis ⇨
Rapid 5' descent
"Deep River"
Deep Ravine
Great Falls, June 13, 1805
"after wrighting this imperfect discription I again viewed the falls and was so much disgusted with the imperfect idea which it conveyed of the scene that I determined to draw my pen across it and begin agin, but then reflected that I could not perhaps succeed better than pening the first impressions of the mind; ..." Lewis ⇨
Cartographer's Note:
The "deep ravine" above is referred to many times by the two captains with different spellings. The name of "Deep River" appears only on Clark's field map. The cartographer believes the map was drawn at Fort Clatsop on the Pacific coast during the winter of 1805-06. Did Clark copy "ravine" incorrectly? A body of water worthy of the Deep River name seems improbable.
Great Falls, June 13, 1805
"... on the left it extends within 80 or ninty yards of the lard. Clift which is also perpendicular; between this abrupt extremity of the ledge of rocks and the perpendicular bluff the whole body of water passes with incredible swiftness. immediately at the cascade the river is about 300 yds. wide; about ninty or a hundred yards of this next the Lard. bluff is a smoth even sheet of water falling over a precipice of at least eighty feet, the remaining part of about 200 yards on my right formes the grandest sight I ever beheld, ... the irregular and somewhat projecting rocks... brakes it into a perfect white foam which assumes a thousand forms in a moment sometimes flying up in jets of sparkling foam to the hight of fifteen or twenty feet and are scarcely formed before large roling bodies of the same beaten and foaming water is thrown over and conceals them." Lewis ⇨
Rapid 10' descent
Cochrane Dam
Rapid 8' descent
Cascade 3' 6" descent
Rapid 3' 6" descent
Rapid 6' descent
Rapid 3' descent
Rapid 2' descent
Ryan Dam
Cascade 18' descent
"Willow Run"
Box Elder Creek
N
MISSOURI RIVER
"Great Falls"
Great Falls
Great Cascade
Great Falls, June 13, 1805
"I hurryed down the hill which was about 200 feet high and difficult of access, to gaze on this sublimely grand specticle. I took my position on the top of some rocks about 20 feet high opposite the center of the falls. this chain of rocks appear once to have formed a part of those over which the waters tumbled, but in the course of time has been seperated from it to the distance of 150 yards lying prarrallel to it..." Lewis ⇨
Rapid 6' descent
Rapid 5' descent
Rapid 5' descent
Approaching the falls, June 13, 1805
"I had proceded on this course about two miles with Goodrich at some distance behind me whin my ears were saluted with the agreeable sound of a fall of water and advancing a little further I saw the spray arrise above the plain like a collumn of smoke which would frequently dispear again in an instant caused I presume by the wind which blew pretty hard from the S.W. I did not however loose my direction to this point which soon began to make a roaring too tremendious to be mistaken for any cause short of the great falls of the Missouri. here I arrived about 12 OClock..." Lewis ⇨
Cartographer's Note:
Great Falls is a good place to look at what seems to be an unexpected behavior on the part of the expedition leaders. Throughout the journey we see a concerted effort to name every river and major creek. Beyond the occasional butte or unique rock formation, Lewis and Clark never give names to mountain peaks, groups, or ranges. The same attitude seems in effect here. Great Falls is the name Lewis apparently applied to the largest of this collection of waterfalls, as well as the area. While Lewis and Clark toss out name suggestions like "handsome falls," "beautiful cascade," "great cascade," and "Grand Cascade;" there seems to be little effort to name waterfalls (Crooked Falls being an exception). We might ask why the two captains did not sit down and work out names for each of the major falls.
Rapid 13' descent
Spring
Portage Route (approx.)
Morony Dam
Rapid 18' descent
Rapid 6' descent
Rapid 10' descent
"Sulphur Spring"
Rapid 4' descent
Falls 18' descent
"Portage River"
"Portage Creek"
Belt Creek
The Big Eddy
Lower Portage Camp and caches
EXPLORATIONS OF LEWIS AND CLARK 1804 - 1806
CARTOGRAPHIC RECONSTRUCTION
GREAT FALLS OF THE MISSOURI RIVER

forests, long ridges, rugged peaks, and deep canyons. Encompassing most of today's central and northern Idaho, this vast wilderness literally is impassable in places. It clearly was the most formidable barrier that the explorers encountered.

Shortly after crossing the continental divide at Lemhi Pass, a detachment under Clark had sought a navigable waterway (unsuccessfully as it turned out) through the Bitterroots. The impassable, rapid-strewn, Salmon River canyon thwarted them. Nearly a month later, the expedition again attempted to penetrate the Bitterroots, this time successfully, via Lolo Pass to the north.

By now, the expedition had left the buffalo ranges far behind, and deer and elk were hard to find in the mountains. In places, passage through jungle-like undergrowth and brush was accomplished only with the greatest effort. Thick groves of western red cedar stood in the wet, darker places, while Ponderosa and lodgepole pine covered the sunnier locations and upper slopes. Also interspersed in these forests were fir, white pine, tamarack, and other evergreens. This was the largest timber that the expedition had seen to date.

Fallen trees, due to high winds, disease, or fire, lay like jackstraws in places, blocking the route. With difficulty, horses and men picked their way through the logs; they could not spare the time to hand-cut a trail. The Indian tribes had long ago determined that the best way to proceed through these mountains was by following along the tops of major ridges where the terrain was somewhat more open, particularly with less underbrush and, sometimes, with sizeable meadows. Even so, travel proved very difficult when passing over the steep peaks and saddles of the ridgelines.

Clearwater Country

As expedition members came out of the Bitterroots, they found themselves traveling along broad, plateau-like ridges covered by beautiful grassy meadows and intermittent groves of timber. Over time, streams in the Clearwater drainage had cut deep canyons into these wide flat benches.

The dietary mainstays of the tribes living in this region principally included roots growing in vast amounts in the prairies, the great runs of migratory Pacific salmon in the rivers, and, in most years, a seemingly endless supply of mountain huckleberries ripened by the summer sun. The first Nez Perces that the Corps encountered here were, as might be expected, digging camas root at Weippe Prairie, situated some 1,500 feet above the Clearwater River.

After replenishment, the party made its way across the flat meadows and then down steep, lightly timbered canyon walls to the banks of the Clearwater. At last they had reached navigable waters that would take them to the Pacific Ocean. Finding large Ponderosa pine trees, they commenced constructing dugout canoes. The waters of the Clearwater were crystal clear and the climate in the Clearwater canyon was pleasant and warm—sometimes even a little too hot for men who recently had spent so much time in the mountains.

Snake River and the Palouse

Near the junction of the Clearwater and Snake rivers, the forested and grassy plateaus of the Clearwater country opened out into broad, hilly plains covered by bunchgrass and wildflowers—an area known as the Palouse. No buffalo herds roamed here (though modern paleontologists and archaeologists have determined that they once did thousands of years ago). In Lewis and Clark's time, only an occasional antelope or deer could be seen, along with large herds of Indian horses owned by the Nez Perce, Palouse, and other Plateau tribes. In fact, the name for the famous "Appaloosa" horse breed is derived from the expression, "A Palouse" horse. The Palouse country, with its small streams, lush grasslands, and relatively mild winters was one of the ideal habitats in the West for raising Indian horses.

The rich soils in this region were formed mainly by the disintegration of the underlying basaltic rock, combined with wind-blown loess from ice-age glaciers that retreated northward thousands of years ago, and by ash carried in on prevailing winds from Cascade Range volcanoes. Today, the loess soils of the semi-humid grasslands of the eastern Palouse make it one of the most productive grain growing regions in the world (mainly lentils, and especially wheat). When Lewis and Clark glimpsed the rolling Palouse hills, however, they missed the potential for great agricultural fertility that was before them.

Some pines and cottonwoods line the stream bottoms in the eastern Palouse, but these quickly dissipate in the semi-arid sagebrush plains to the west near the Snake-Columbia junction. When paddling down the Snake River, the explorers had been concerned primarily with negotiating the many rapids and finding firewood in the nearly treeless bottoms. The Indians themselves, of course, gathered up driftwood brought down from the mountains by the spring runoff, but they also journeyed to the Clearwater country to cut and gather wood for building purposes and firewood, and floated it downstream on rafts. *Volume II* concludes with Lewis and Clark camping at the Snake-Columbia confluence on October 16–17, 1805; not a single tree was visible to them anywhere in the nearby dry plains.

Magnetic Declination

In his instructions to Lewis in 1803, President Thomas Jefferson directed that sightings and calculations be taken during the expedition to determine magnetic declination in western North America. Because of Jefferson's orders, many people today assume that Clark must have considered magnetic declination when recording his bearings. This cartographer contends that this was not so.

The "magnetic" north and south poles of the Earth do not correspond to the "true" geographic north and south poles. In fact, they are many, many miles apart in the case of each pole. Depending on where you are on the globe, a compass sighting with very few exceptions will read at least a few degrees off from the true geographical pole. This difference is called magnetic declination. Often, the angle of declination varies as much as a dozen or more degrees from true north or true south. This was, of course, the case in Lewis and Clark's era, as it remains so in our own time for surveyors, mountaineers, the military, and others who rely on maps and compass readings.

In simple terms, magnetic declination is caused by the massive amount of iron in the Earth's makeup. The deepest interior of our planet appears to consist of a solid inner core surrounded by a somewhat fluid outer core—both of these cores consist mainly of iron, representing a quarter to a third of the Earth's mass. The outer part of the planet, on the other hand, includes the "upper" mantle (and the earth's crust), beneath which is a liquid "lower" mantle, always on the move. It is made up of silicate, containing large quantities of iron and magnesium. Thus, the great amount of iron within the planet creates a magnetic or electrical force field that encompasses the entire planet, connecting both poles. It even extends in great loops into space where it deflects and dissipates much of the sun's harmful radiation.

The magnetic force reaches through the inside of the planet, too, connecting at two opposite points on the earth's surface (i.e., near the north and south poles, but not at "true" north or south). Over time, there have been frequent changes in the locations of the magnetic poles due to the flux of iron in the Earth's interior. Consequently, the magnetic poles move, and certainly have done so in the past two centuries.

It is likely that Jefferson, when instructing Lewis to take sightings, did not intend to have the explorers actually determine declinations in the daily traverse notes. This sort of application would have required an expert far more accomplished in mathematics than either of our explorers. In 1702, English astronomer Edmund Halley had compiled the first type of world map that attempted to provide a guide for determining declination. It is doubtful that Lewis and Clark had access to the map. At any rate, its lengthy and complicated instructions, and in fact, its hypotheses, would have been much too complicated to be of any practical use to the explorers.

This cartographer has tried to determine declinations from two centuries ago, but due to complications far too lengthy to explain here, the attempt was dropped. However, Map 197 includes a note indicating an attempt at computing an angle of magnetic declination, approximately 20 degrees east, in Lewis and Clark's time. Having later returned to that note to rework the data, this cartographer is not confident at the outcome. At any rate, this note has been left in Map 197 as a reminder to the reader of the complications of magnetic declination. (True north is indicated on all of the Trail Maps.)

Early on in the preparation of the *Lewis and Clark Trail Maps*, it became apparent that Clark was anything but accurate when it came to recording the daily traverse distances. He made calls that were too long—but fortunately he did so at a "consistent" rate. Also, in the traverse notes at times he rounded off directional figures to five or ten degrees. Recognizing these patterns and making adjustments for them were important in the preparation of the *Lewis and Clark Trail Maps*, and normally did not provide any difficulties whatsoever.

During the cartographic reconstruction, Clark's methods and performance and the terrain over which he traveled were constantly checked. The expedition's journal entries and the traverse notes were thoroughly investigated until a known beginning point and an identifiable ending point were located and marked on modern USGS topographic maps, which served as a base. These identified landmarks or other topographical features usually were a stream mouth, an ox-bow bend, a prominent butte, etc. Next, Clark's traverse was plotted to see how accurately it fit on the map. The fit always required rotation, which indicated that Clark did not consider declination when recording his traverse. Also as already explained, Clark's "consistently" long distances needed shortening, and some bearings or directions that did not correlate accurately had to be adjusted. For the cartographer, it quickly became evident that the cartographic work for the *Lewis and Clark Trail Maps* proceeded best if declination was ignored, as Clark himself had done.

Latitude and Longitude

Some may ask why latitude and longitude are not indicated throughout the *Lewis and Clark Trail Maps*, except when "full" degrees of latitude and longitude are shown, such as on Map 158. The answer is that latitude, and especially longitude, are extremely difficult to plot. As one proceeds farther north using this system, distances continually decrease between the ever-narrowing longitudinal lines. Working this on to flat, rectangular pieces of map paper, rather than on a globe, is truly problematical.

On the other hand, the Universal Transverse Mercator Mapping Grid System, or UTM, proved to be of far more practical use in preparing the *Lewis and Clark Trail Maps*. The UTM system indicates precise coordinates for every location on the planet in 60 zones between latitudes 84 degrees north and 80 degrees south. The Lewis and Clark trail fits nicely within a half-dozen zones of this system. Supplementally, this cartographer studied State Plane Coordinate Systems. Difficulties arose with these because they were for small areas, and some states had at least two systems. Jumping from one system to another can be confusing. In summary, the UTM system proved most practical, and highly satisfactory, for this cartographic reconstruction.

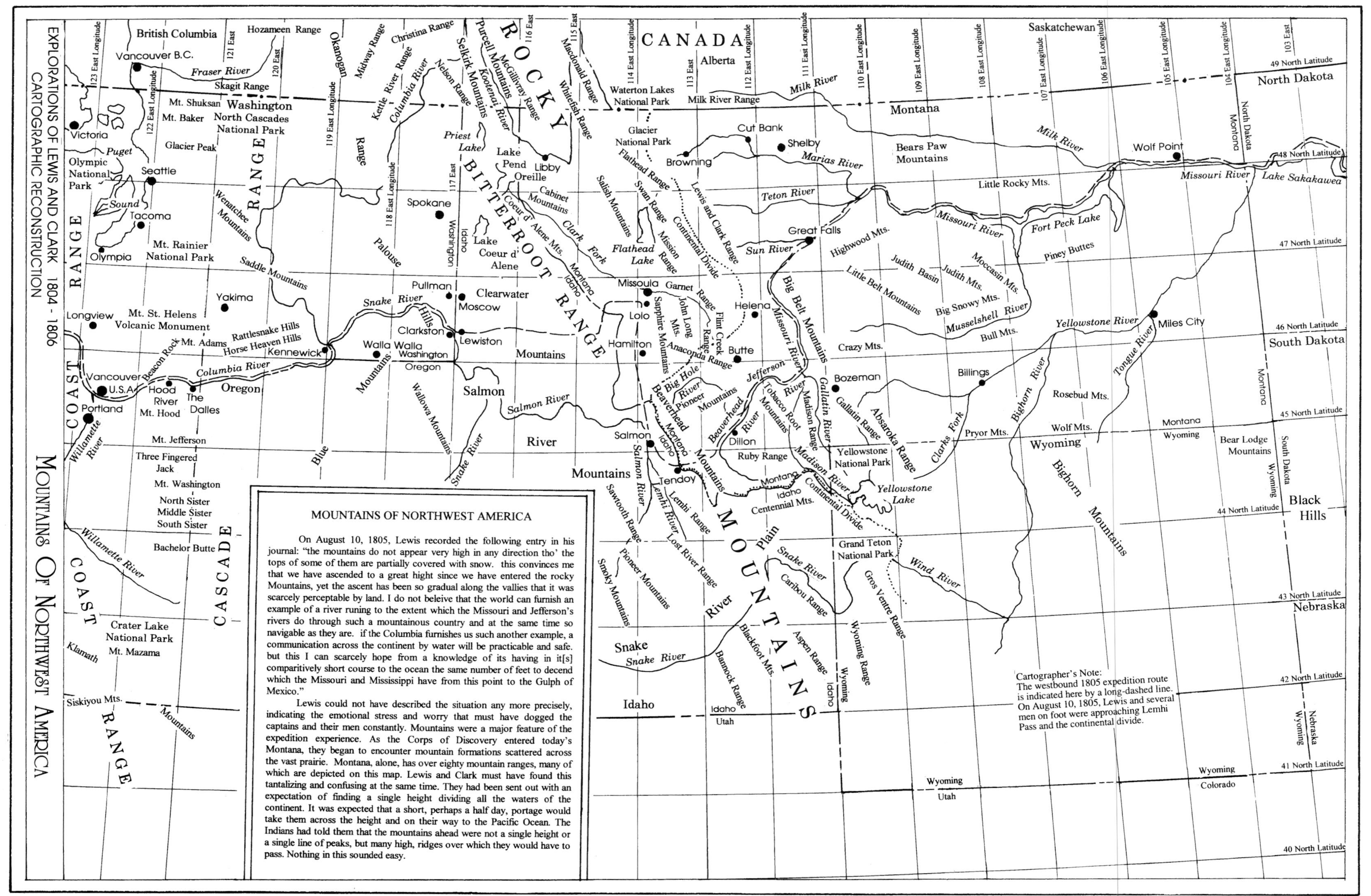

MOUNTAINS OF NORTHWEST AMERICA

On August 10, 1805, Lewis recorded the following entry in his journal: "the mountains do not appear very high in any direction tho' the tops of some of them are partially covered with snow. this convinces me that we have ascended to a great hight since we have entered the rocky Mountains, yet the ascent has been so gradual along the vallies that it was scarcely perceptable by land. I do not beleive that the world can furnish an example of a river runing to the extent which the Missouri and Jefferson's rivers do through such a mountainous country and at the same time so navigable as they are. if the Columbia furnishes us such another example, a communication across the continent by water will be practicable and safe. but this I can scarcely hope from a knowledge of its having in it[s] comparitively short course to the ocean the same number of feet to decend which the Missouri and Mississippi have from this point to the Gulph of Mexico."

Lewis could not have described the situation any more precisely, indicating the emotional stress and worry that must have dogged the captains and their men constantly. Mountains were a major feature of the expedition experience. As the Corps of Discovery entered today's Montana, they began to encounter mountain formations scattered across the vast prairie. Montana, alone, has over eighty mountain ranges, many of which are depicted on this map. Lewis and Clark must have found this tantalizing and confusing at the same time. They had been sent out with an expectation of finding a single height dividing all the waters of the continent. It was expected that a short, perhaps a half day, portage would take them across the height and on their way to the Pacific Ocean. The Indians had told them that the mountains ahead were not a single height or a single line of peaks, but many high, ridges over which they would have to pass. Nothing in this sounded easy.

Index Maps and Legend, Volume II

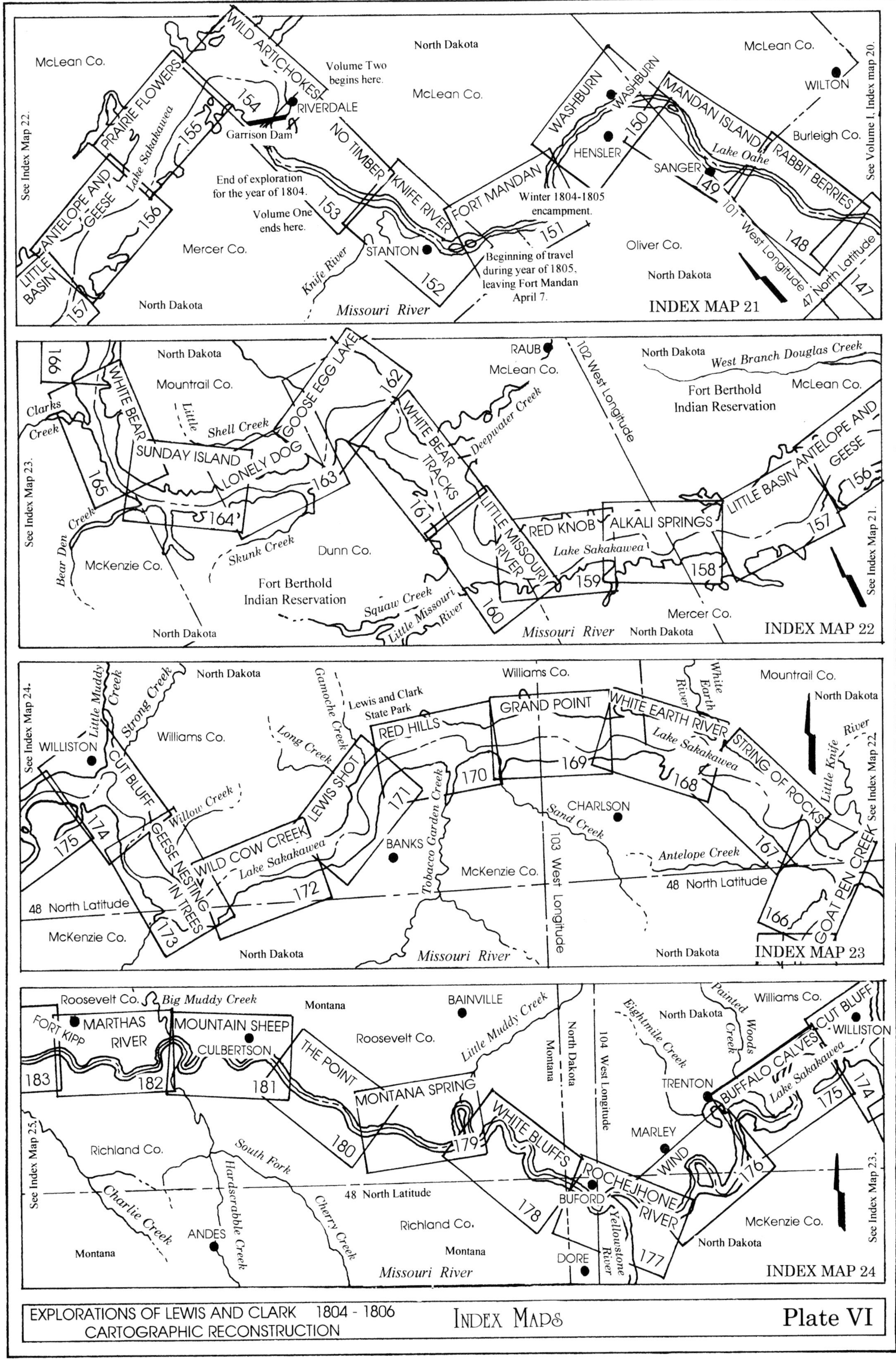

EXPLORATIONS OF LEWIS AND CLARK 1804 - 1806
CARTOGRAPHIC RECONSTRUCTION

INDEX MAPS

Plate VI

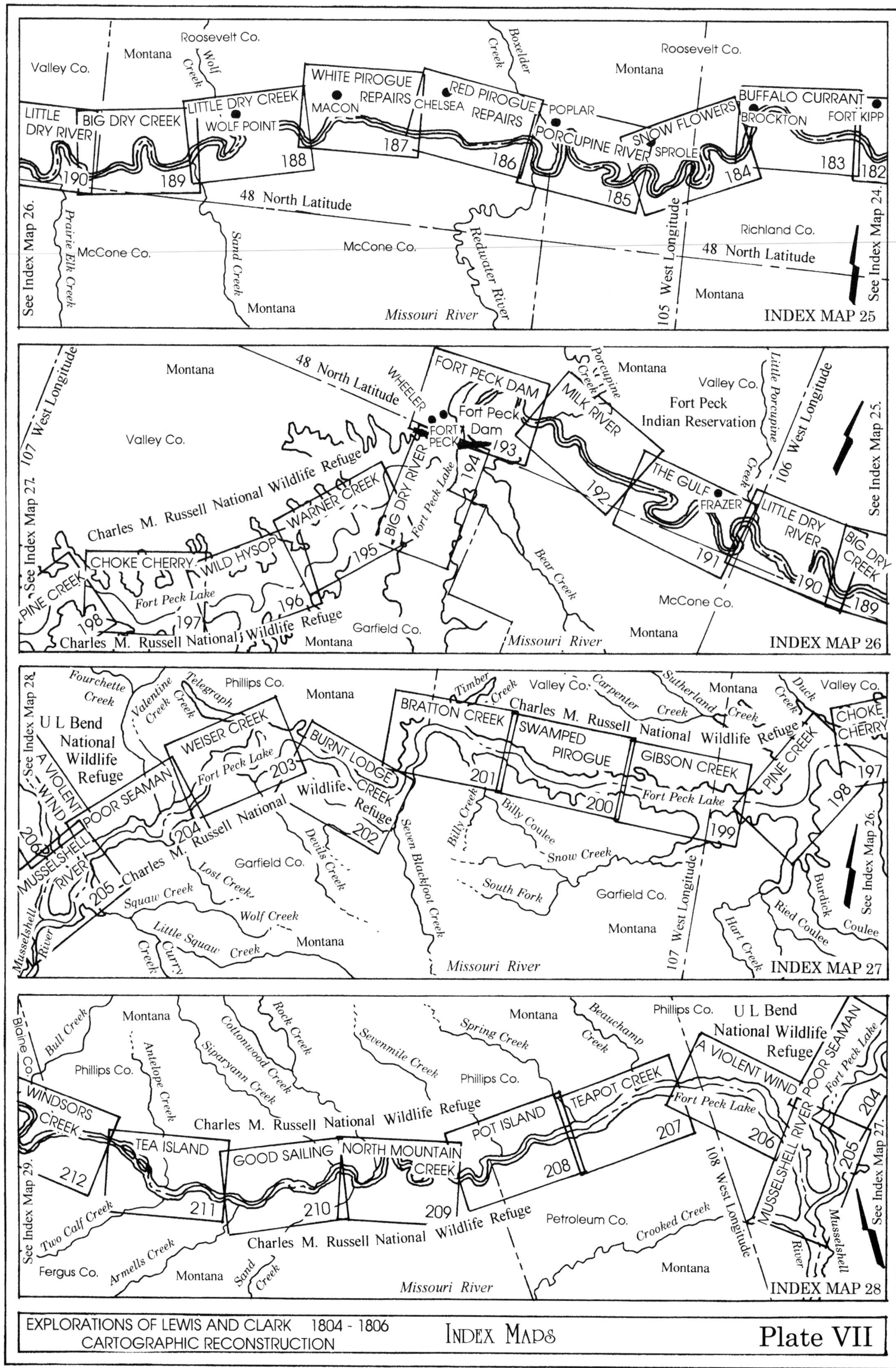

EXPLORATIONS OF LEWIS AND CLARK 1804 - 1806
CARTOGRAPHIC RECONSTRUCTION

INDEX MAPS

Plate VII

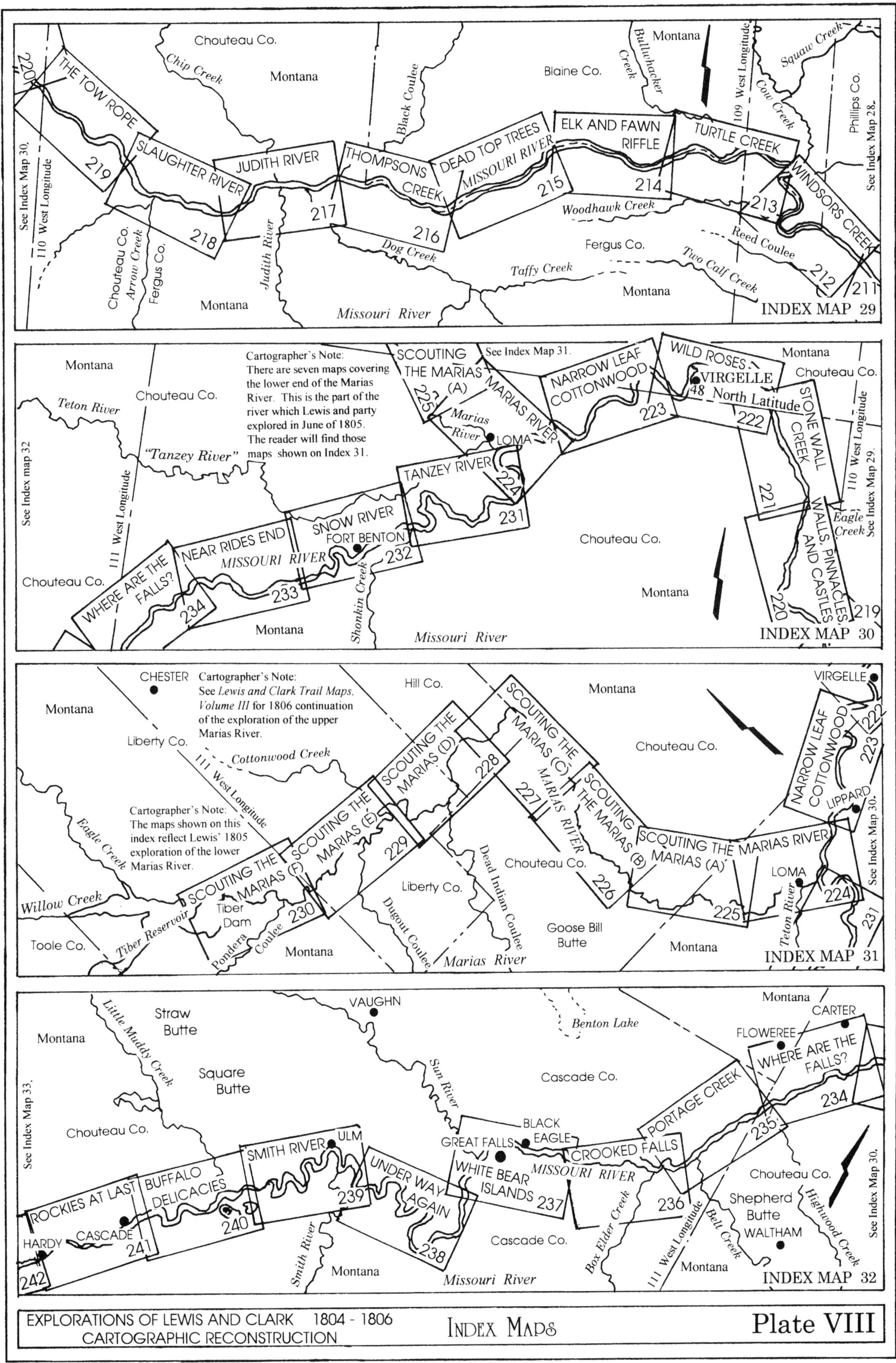
INDEX MAP 29
THE TOW ROPE
SLAUGHTER RIVER
JUDITH RIVER
THOMPSONS CREEK
DEAD TOP TREES
ELK AND FAWN RIFFLE
TURTLE CREEK
WINDSORS CREEK
Chouteau Co.
Montana
Blaine Co.
Fergus Co.
Phillips Co.
Chip Creek
Black Coulee
Bullwhacker Creek
Squaw Creek
Cow Creek
Missouri River
Woodhawk Creek
Reed Coulee
Two Calf Creek
Taffy Creek
Dog Creek
Judith River
Arrow Creek
See Index Map 30.
110 West Longitude
109 West Longitude
See Index Map 28.
INDEX MAP 30
SCOUTING THE MARIAS (A)
MARIAS RIVER
NARROW LEAF COTTONWOOD
WILD ROSES
VIRGELLE
48 North Latitude
STONE WALL CREEK
WALLS, PINNACLES AND CASTLES
TANZEY RIVER
SNOW RIVER
FORT BENTON
NEAR RIDES END
MISSOURI RIVER
WHERE ARE THE FALLS?
LOMA
Teton River
"Tanzey River"
Shonkin Creek
Eagle Creek
See Index map 32
111 West Longitude
110 West Longitude
See Index Map 29.
See Index Map 31.
Cartographer's Note: There are seven maps covering the lower end of the Marias River. This is the part of the river which Lewis and party explored in June of 1805. The reader will find those maps shown on Index 31.
INDEX MAP 31
CHESTER
Cartographer's Note: See Lewis and Clark Trail Maps, Volume III for 1806 continuation of the exploration of the upper Marias River.
Cartographer's Note: The maps shown on this index reflect Lewis' 1805 exploration of the lower Marias River.
Hill Co.
Liberty Co.
Toole Co.
Chouteau Co.
Cottonwood Creek
Eagle Creek
Willow Creek
Tiber Reservoir
Tiber Dam
Pondera Coulee
Dugout Coulee
Dead Indian Coulee
Goose Bill Butte
Marias River
SCOUTING THE MARIAS (F)
SCOUTING THE MARIAS (E)
SCOUTING THE MARIAS (D)
SCOUTING THE MARIAS (C)
SCOUTING THE MARIAS (B)
SCOUTING THE MARIAS RIVER
SCOUTING THE MARIAS (A)
NARROW LEAF COTTONWOOD
LIPPARD
LOMA
Teton River
See Index Map 30.
INDEX MAP 32
VAUGHN
Straw Butte
Square Butte
Little Muddy Creek
Benton Lake
Cascade Co.
Sun River
BLACK EAGLE
GREAT FALLS
FLOWEREE
CARTER
WHERE ARE THE FALLS?
PORTAGE CREEK
CROOKED FALLS
WHITE BEAR ISLANDS
MISSOURI RIVER
UNDER WAY AGAIN
SMITH RIVER
ULM
BUFFALO DELICACIES
ROCKIES AT LAST
CASCADE
HARDY
Smith River
Box Elder Creek
Belt Creek
Highwood Creek
Shepherd Butte
WALTHAM
See Index Map 33.
See Index Map 30.
EXPLORATIONS OF LEWIS AND CLARK 1804 - 1806
CARTOGRAPHIC RECONSTRUCTION
INDEX MAPS
Plate VIII

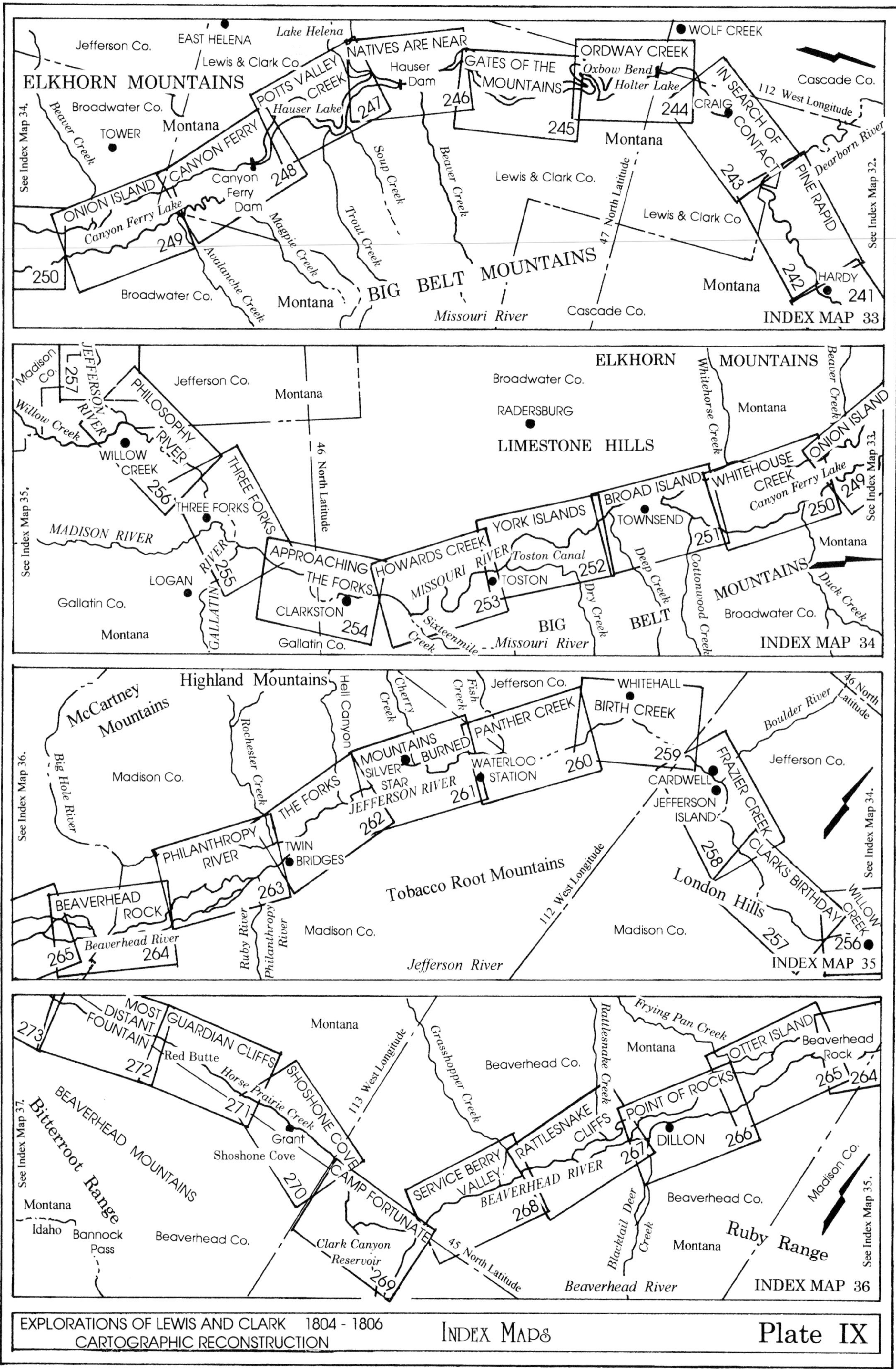

EXPLORATIONS OF LEWIS AND CLARK 1804 - 1806
CARTOGRAPHIC RECONSTRUCTION

INDEX MAPS

Plate IX

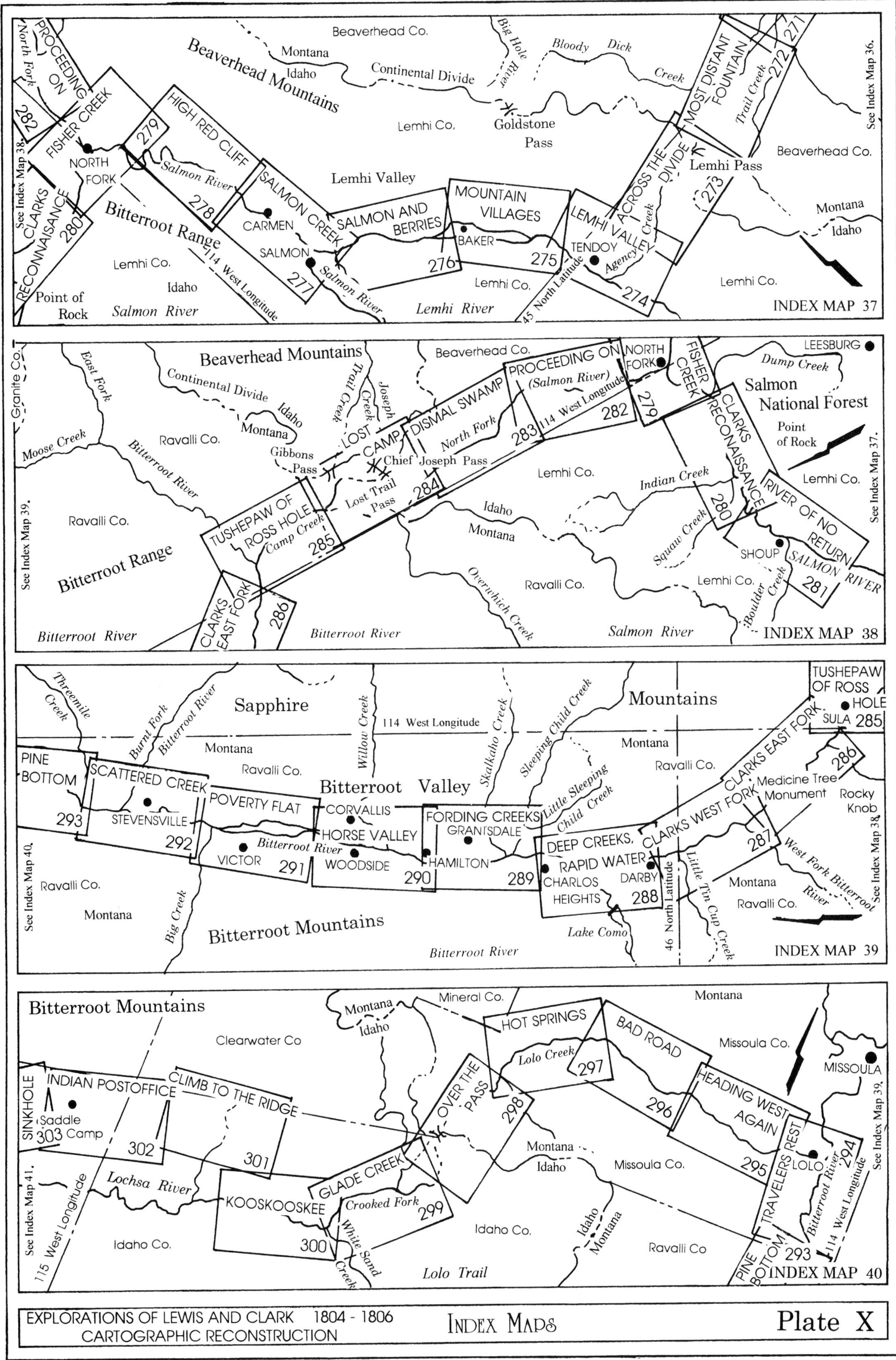
INDEX MAP 37
INDEX MAP 38
INDEX MAP 39
INDEX MAP 40
EXPLORATIONS OF LEWIS AND CLARK 1804 - 1806
CARTOGRAPHIC RECONSTRUCTION
INDEX MAPS
Plate X

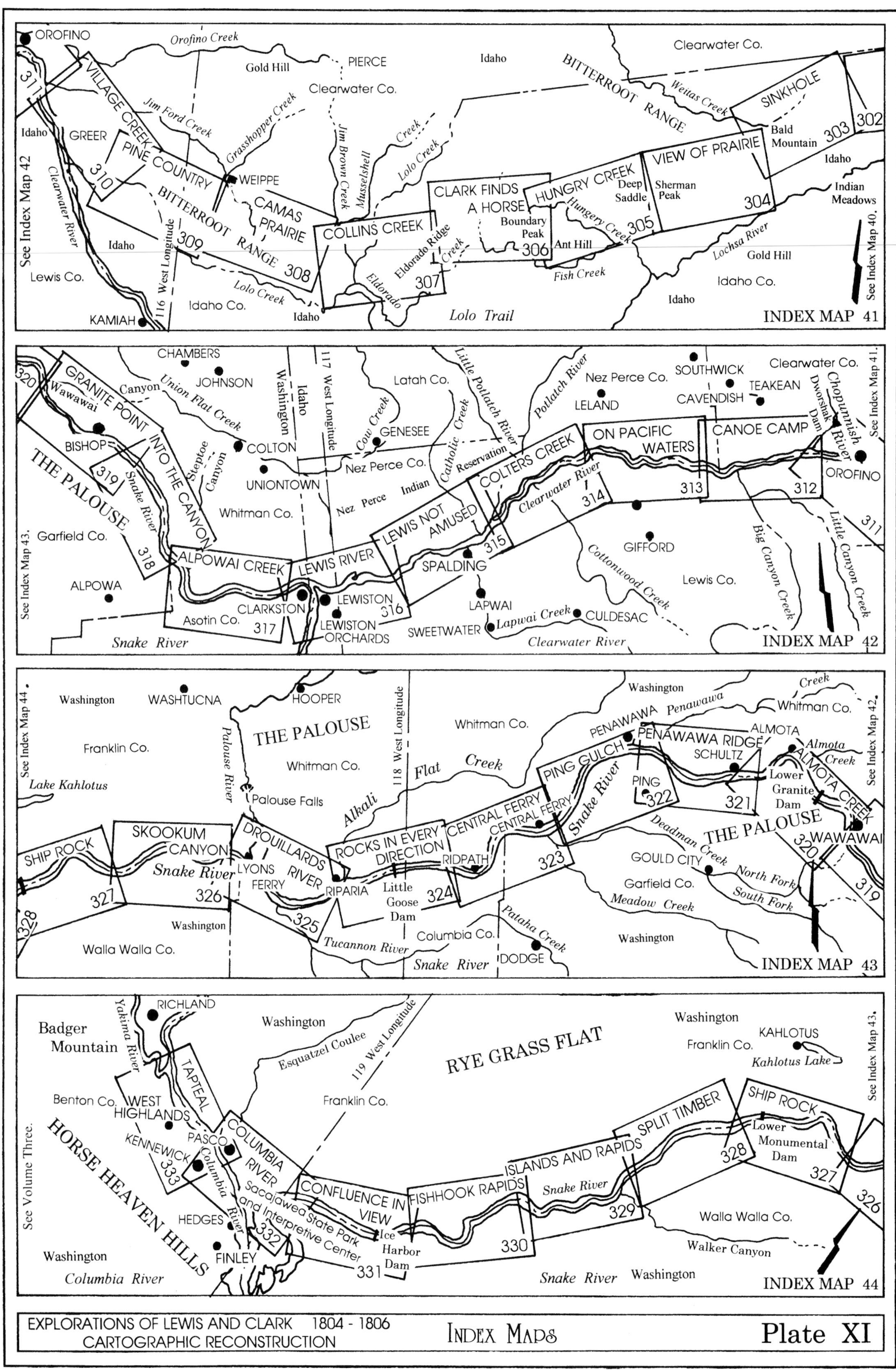
INDEX MAP 41
INDEX MAP 42
INDEX MAP 43
INDEX MAP 44
EXPLORATIONS OF LEWIS AND CLARK 1804 - 1806
CARTOGRAPHIC RECONSTRUCTION
INDEX MAPS
Plate XI

LEGEND

Lines

Water boundary 1804 - 1806

Small stream 1804 - 1806

Water boundary or stream, modern

Water boundary for reservoir (normal pool elevation)

Principal parallel or meridian

State boundary line

County, reservation, or other jurisdictional boundary

Major highway, modern

Contour line (historically reconstructed)

Depression in topography

Shading lines 1804 - 1806 (water bodies only)

Symbols

Interstate highway shield with number

Federal highway shield with number

State or local highway

Airport or landing strip

Bridge

Dam (small)

Spring

Cave

Falls

Rapid

Point of interest

Surveyed Traverse Symbol
End of one bearing/distance and beginning of next. Direction and distance as stated in Clark's journal. Traverse corrected for magnetic declination and adjusted to fit topography. Unusual deviation of bearing is noted.

Universal Transverse Mercator
Mapping grid. Grid tics are shown at 1,000 meter intervals along map border. Larger number in notation indicates thousands of meters, smaller number indicates hundreds of thousands of meters.

Fonts

Various font styles have been used to relate certain types of information.

Century Font *Century Font*

The Century font is used to denote feature names existing at the time of Lewis and Clark. Vertical for land features. Italicized for water features. Quotation marks about the name indicate that Lewis and Clark gave the name.

Dot Matrix Font

The Dot Matrix font is used for all notations relating to modern or post Lewis and Clark information. Notations relevant to water are italicized.

Script Roundhand Font

Script Roundhand font is used to convey information from the journals. Short notes that have been altered slightly to fit mapping standards do not have quotation marks. Direct quotes from the journals are enclosed in quotation marks. They are followed by the name of the journal writer and an arrow indicating whether the quote comes from the Outbound travel (⇨) or Return journey (⇦). See further explanation Maps 1 and 2.

Advance Font

The Advance font is used to denote information related to the story but not addressed adequately in the journals.

Cartographer's Note:

Generally an explanation of a mapping detail, a mapping decision, a major adjustment to the surveyed traverse, or an explanation of events as viewed by the cartographer.

All north arrows on The Trail Maps, as well as the index sheets, indicate True North.

Campsite Notations

Camp
May 6, 1805
Outbound Camp with date of the evening camp. Corps left camp on morning following last date.

Return Camp
June 23, 1806
Home Bound Camp with date of the evening camp. Corps left camp on morning following last date.

Camp Station
Nov. 18 - 22, 1805
Named Camp. Important enough to be named by the explorers along with date of encampment.

Notations

453 — Lewis and Clark mileposts. Mileposts based on traverse distances. Distances are not scaleable. Outbound and alternate return routes only.

+398 — Corrected mileposts. Outbound only.

N 23 W 2 MILES — Traverse notations. Traverse bearings (directions) based on magnetic north, 1804 1806. Notations are from Clark's journal and have been adjusted to fit topography.

VANCOUVER — City or town. Position of note indicates location of town.

American Grizzly Bear (Ursus horribilis horribilis) — Flora and fauna. New to science, first described by Lewis and Clark, or significant mention by journalist. Common name followed by scientific or Latin name in parentheses.

Title Block Notations

Approximate date(s) for post Expedition data shown on map.

Visual Scale.

Dates for which the Expedition was in an area covered by a map. Outbound and return dates are shown.

Project Title.

Map sheet title.

Universal Transverse Mercator (UTM) zone number.

Map sheet number.

Map covers portions of these states.

Contour interval information.

EXPLORATIONS OF LEWIS AND CLARK 1804 - 1806
CARTOGRAPHIC RECONSTRUCTION

Lewis and Clark Trail Maps, Volume II

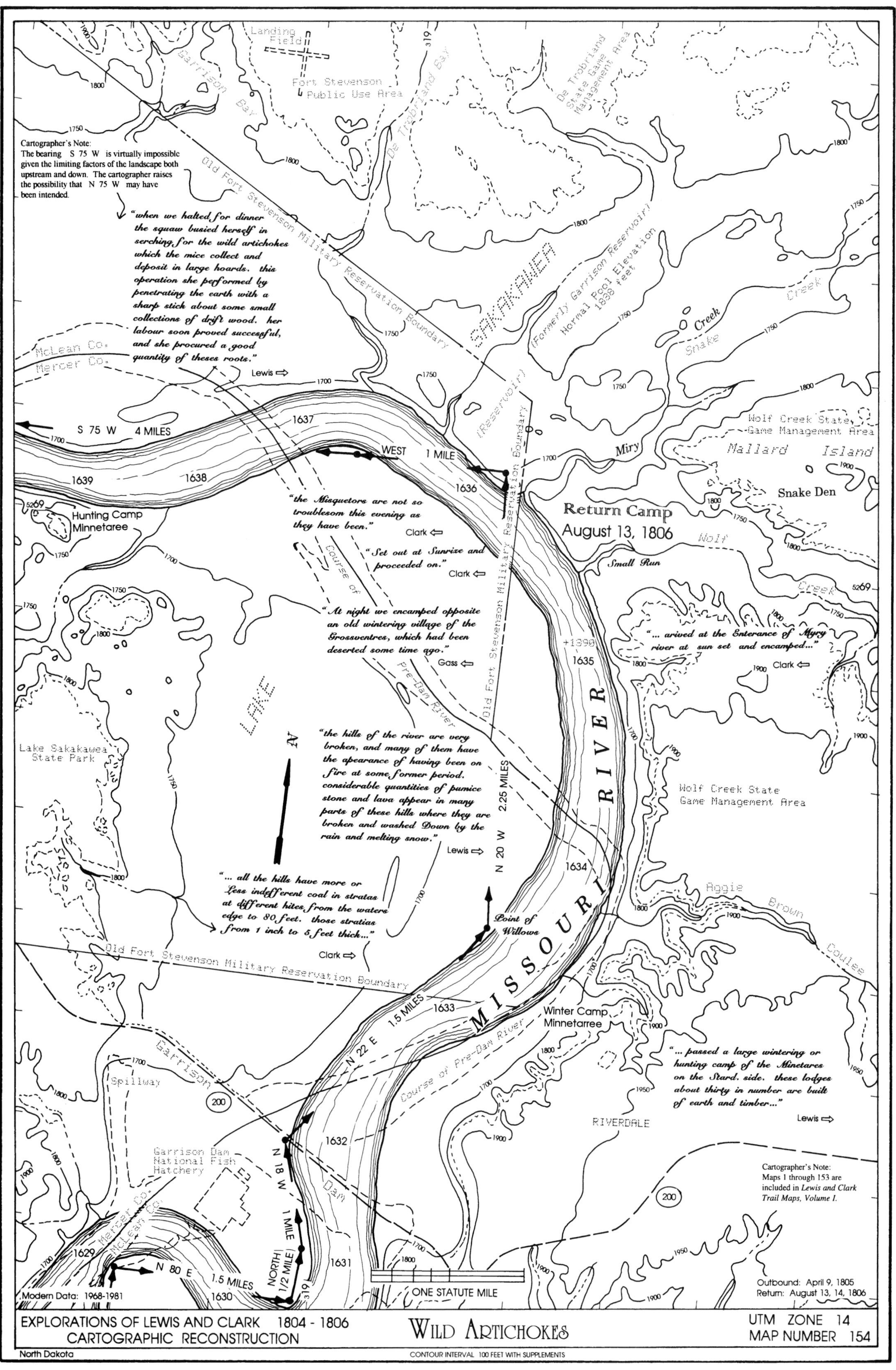
Cartographer's Note:
The bearing S 75 W is virtually impossible given the limiting factors of the landscape both upstream and down. The cartographer raises the possibility that N 75 W may have been intended.
"when we halted for dinner the squaw busied herself in serching for the wild artichokes which the mice collect and deposit in large hoards. this operation she performed by penetrating the earth with a sharp stick about some small collections of drift wood. her labour soon proved successful, and she procured a good quantity of theses roots."
Lewis
"the Misquetors are not so troublesom this evening as they have been."
Clark
"Set out at Sunrize and proceeded on."
Clark
"At night we encamped opposite an old wintering village of the Grossventres, which had been deserted some time ago."
Gass
"the hills of the river are very broken, and many of them have the apearance of having been on fire at some former period. considerable quantities of pumice stone and lava appear in many parts of these hills where they are broken and washed Down by the rain and melting snow."
Lewis
"... all the hills have more or Less indefferent coal in stratas at different hites from the waters edge to 80 feet. those stratias from 1 inch to 5 feet thick..."
Clark
"... arived at the Enterance of Myry river at sun set and encamped..."
Clark
"... passed a large wintering or hunting camp of the Minetares on the Stard. side. these lodges about thirty in number are built of earth and timber..."
Lewis
Return Camp
August 13, 1806
Hunting Camp Minnetaree
Winter Camp Minnetarree
Point of Willows
Small Run
Miry
Snake Den
Snake Creek
Wolf Creek
Mallard Island
Aggie Brown Coulee
Wolf Creek State Game Management Area
Lake Sakakawea State Park
LAKE SAKAKAWEA (Formerly Garrison Reservoir) Normal Pool Elevation 1838 feet
MISSOURI RIVER
Old Fort Stevenson Military Reservation Boundary
Fort Stevenson Public Use Area
Landing Field
Garrison Bay
De Trobriand Bay
De Trobriand State Game Management Area
Course of Pre-Dam River
Garrison Dam National Fish Hatchery
Garrison Dam
Spillway
RIVERDALE
McLean Co.
Mercer Co.
S 75 W 4 MILES
WEST 1 MILE
N 20 W 2.25 MILES
N 22 E 1.5 MILES
N 18 W 1 MILE
NORTH 1/2 MILE
N 80 E 1.5 MILES
ONE STATUTE MILE
Cartographer's Note: Maps 1 through 153 are included in Lewis and Clark Trail Maps, Volume I.
Outbound: April 9, 1805
Return: August 13, 14, 1806
Modern Data: 1968-1981
EXPLORATIONS OF LEWIS AND CLARK 1804 - 1806
CARTOGRAPHIC RECONSTRUCTION
WILD ARTICHOKES
UTM ZONE 14
MAP NUMBER 154
North Dakota
CONTOUR INTERVAL 100 FEET WITH SUPPLEMENTS

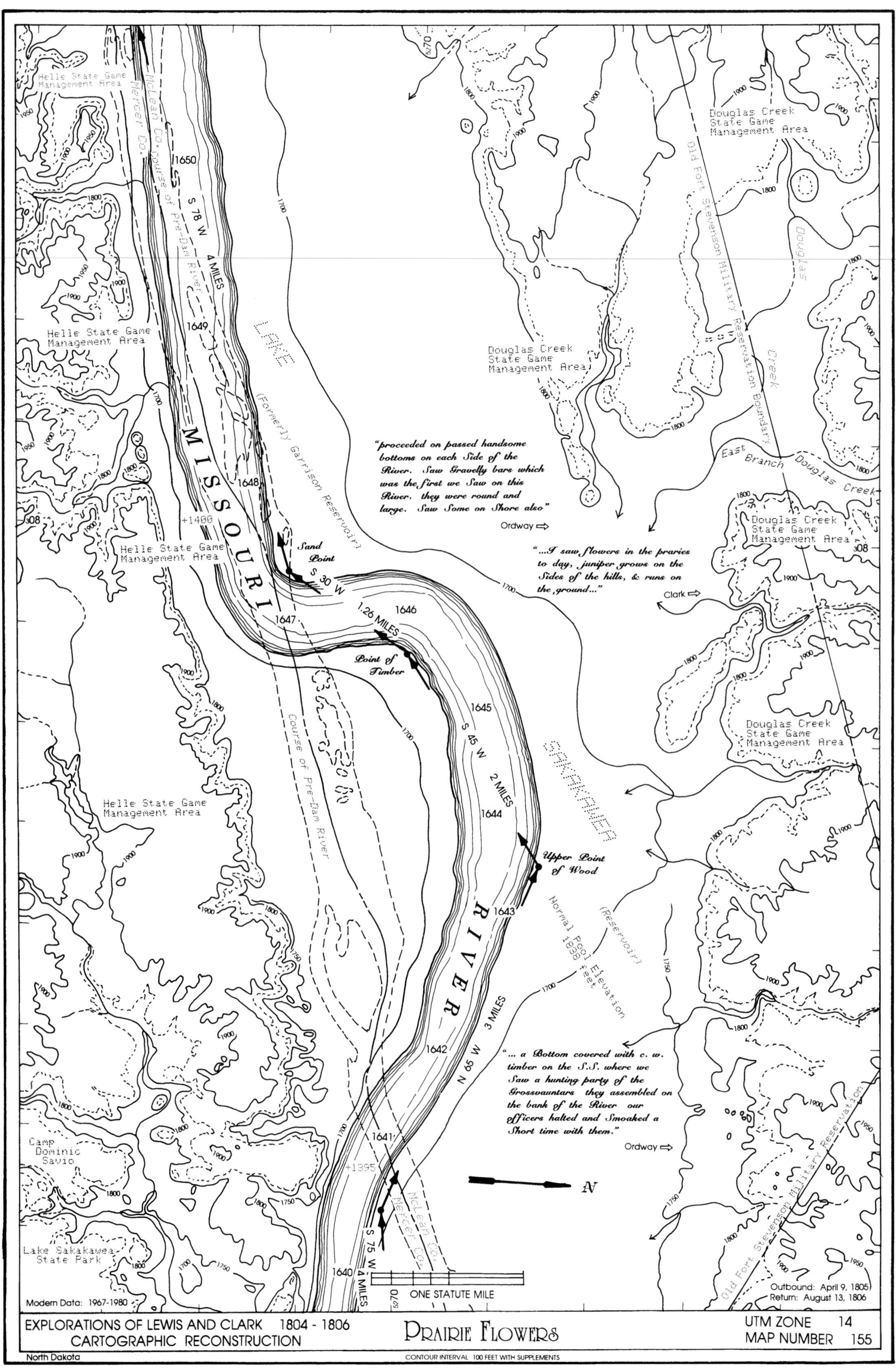
"proceeded on passed handsome bottoms on each Side of the River. Saw Gravelly bars which was the first we Saw on this River. they were round and large. Saw Some on Shore also"
Ordway
"...I saw flowers in the praries to day, juniper grows on the Sides of the hills, & runs on the ground..."
Clark
"... a Bottom covered with c. w. timber on the S.S. where we Saw a hunting party of the Grossvauntars they assembled on the bank of the River our officers halted and Smoaked a Short time with them."
Ordway
MISSOURI RIVER
LAKE SAKAKAWEA
(Formerly Garrison Reservoir)
Normal Pool Elevation 1838 feet
Sand Point
Point of Timber
Upper Point of Wood
S 78 W 4 MILES
S 30 W
1.26 MILES
S 45 W 2 MILES
N 65 W 3 MILES
S 75 W 4 MILES
Course of Pre-Dam River
McLean Co.
Mercer Co.
Helle State Game Management Area
Douglas Creek State Game Management Area
Douglas Creek
East Branch Douglas Creek
Old Fort Stevenson Military Reservation Boundary
Camp Dominic Savio
Lake Sakakawea State Park
N
ONE STATUTE MILE
Modern Data: 1967-1980
Outbound: April 9, 1805
Return: August 13, 1806
EXPLORATIONS OF LEWIS AND CLARK 1804 - 1806
CARTOGRAPHIC RECONSTRUCTION
PRAIRIE FLOWERS
UTM ZONE 14
MAP NUMBER 155
North Dakota
CONTOUR INTERVAL 100 FEET WITH SUPPLEMENTS

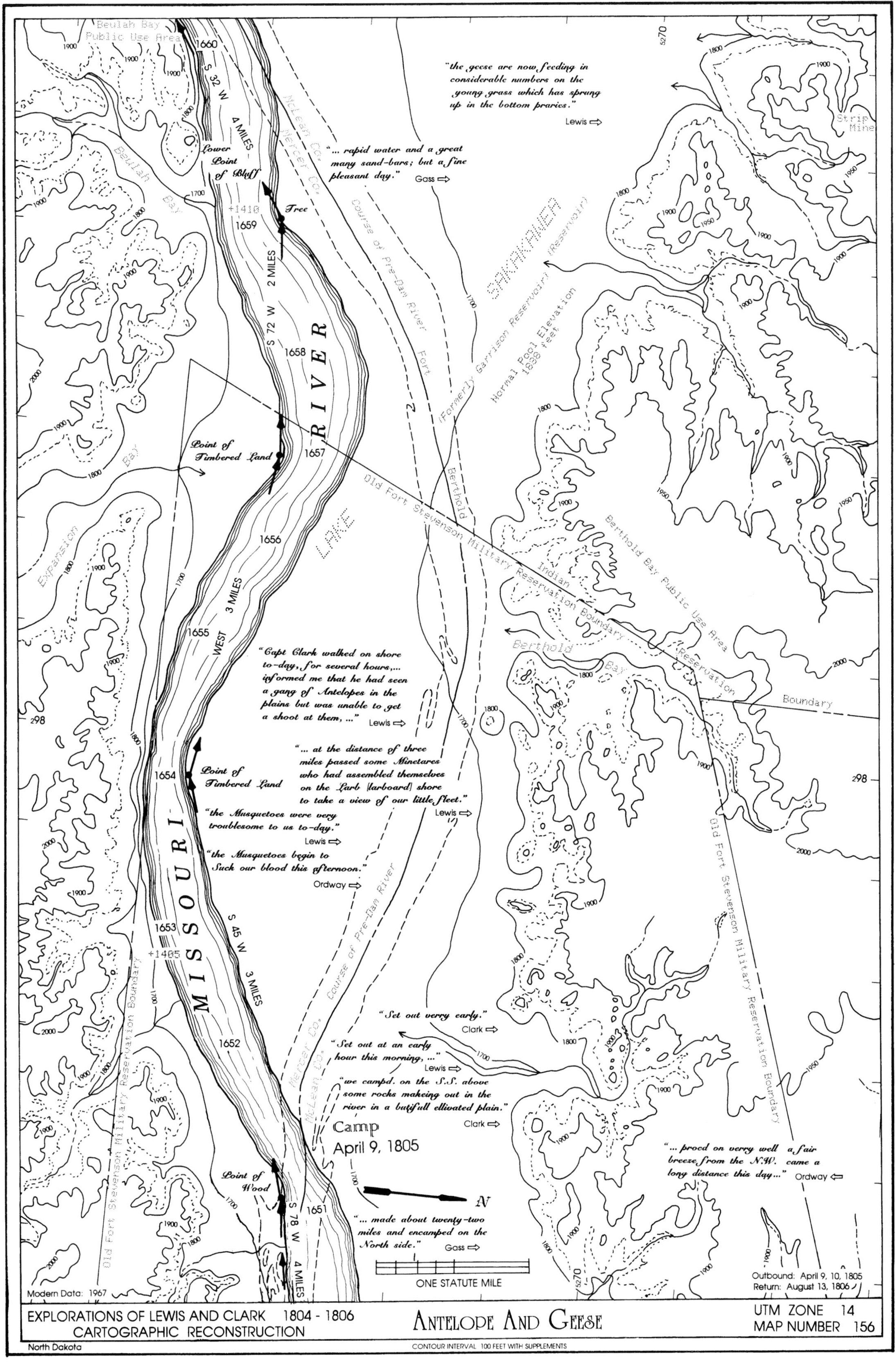
Beulah Bay Public Use Area
"the geese are now feeding in considerable numbers on the young grass which has sprung up in the bottom praries."
Lewis ⇨
Strip Mine
"... rapid water and a great many sand-bars; but a fine pleasant day."
Gass ⇨
Lower Point of Bluff
S 32 W
4 MILES
1660
McLean Co.
Mercer Co.
Beulah Bay
+1410
1659
Tree
2 MILES
S 72 W
Course of Pre-Dam River
SAKAKAWEA
(Formerly Garrison Reservoir) (Reservoir)
Normal Pool Elevation 1838 feet
1658
RIVER
Fort
Point of Timbered Land
1657
Bay
Old Fort Stevenson Military Reservation Boundary
Berthold
LAKE
Expansion
1656
Indian
Berthold Bay Public Use Area
3 MILES
WEST
1655
Berthold Bay
Reservation
Boundary
"Capt Clark walked on shore to-day, for several hours,... informed me that he had seen a gang of Antelopes in the plains but was unable to get a shoot at them, ..."
Lewis ⇨
298
"... at the distance of three miles passed some Minetares who had assembled themselves on the Larb [larboard] shore to take a view of our little fleet."
Lewis ⇨
Point of Timbered Land
1654
"the Musquetoes were very troublesome to us to-day."
Lewis ⇨
"the Musquetoes begin to Suck our blood this afternoon."
Ordway ⇨
MISSOURI
Course of Pre-Dam River
Old Fort Stevenson Military Reservation Boundary
1653
+1405
S 45 W
3 MILES
"Set out verry early."
Clark ⇨
1652
"Set out at an early hour this morning, ..."
Lewis ⇨
Mercer Co.
McLean Co.
"we campd. on the S.S. above some rocks makeing out in the river in a butifull ellivated plain."
Clark ⇨
Camp
April 9, 1805
"... proceed on verry well a fair breeze from the N.W. came a long distance this day..."
Ordway ⇦
Point of Wood
N
1651
S 78 W
4 MILES
"... made about twenty-two miles and encamped on the North side."
Gass ⇨
ONE STATUTE MILE
5270
Outbound: April 9, 10, 1805
Return: August 13, 1806
Modern Data: 1967
EXPLORATIONS OF LEWIS AND CLARK 1804 - 1806
CARTOGRAPHIC RECONSTRUCTION
ANTELOPE AND GEESE
UTM ZONE 14
MAP NUMBER 156
North Dakota
CONTOUR INTERVAL 100 FEET WITH SUPPLEMENTS

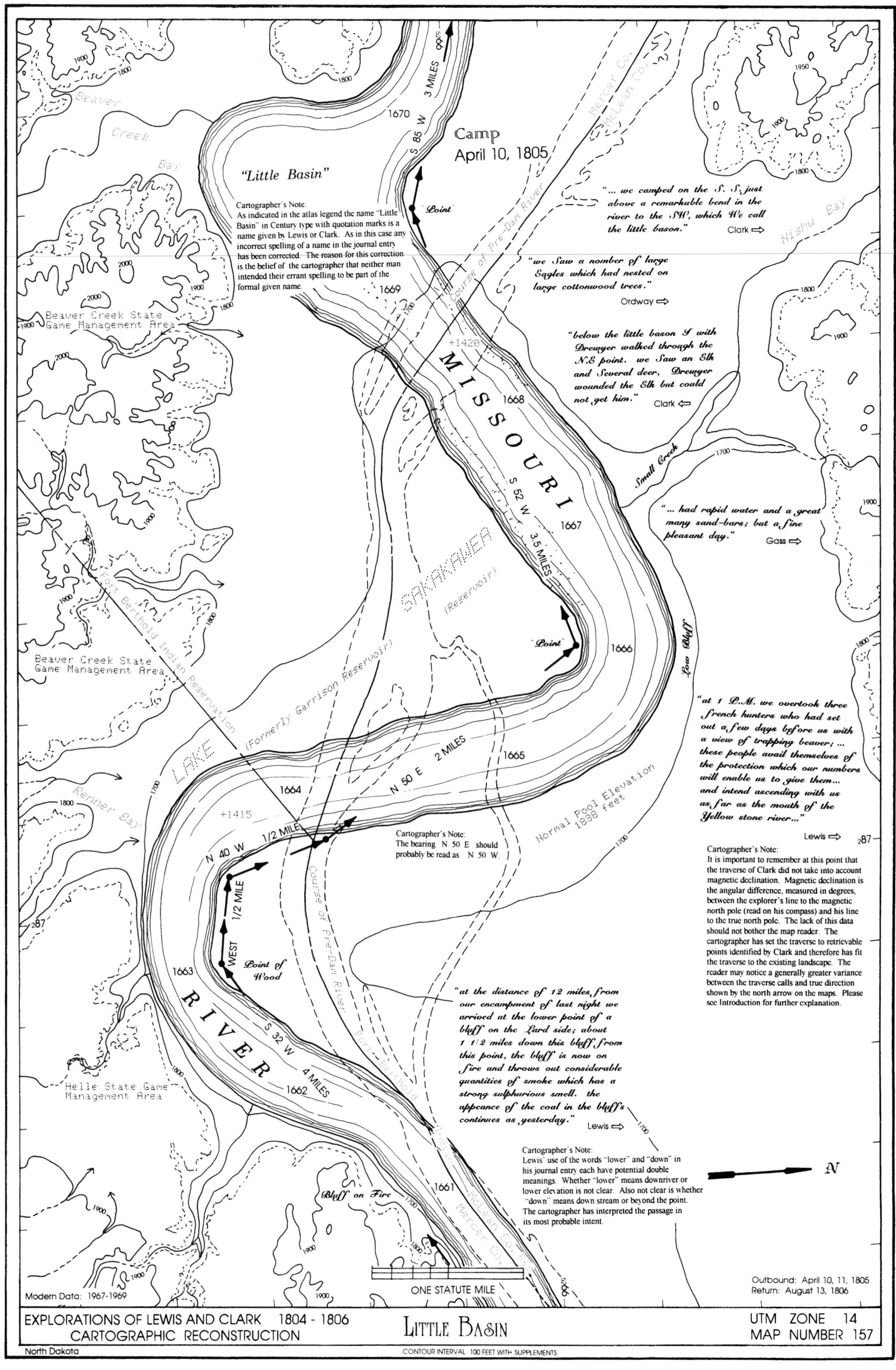
"Little Basin"
Cartographer's Note:
As indicated in the atlas legend the name "Little Basin" in Century type with quotation marks is a name given by Lewis or Clark. As in this case any incorrect spelling of a name in the journal entry has been corrected. The reason for this correction is the belief of the cartographer that neither man intended their errant spelling to be part of the formal given name.
Camp
April 10, 1805
"... we camped on the S. S. just above a remarkable bend in the river to the SW, which We call the little bason."
Clark ⇨
"we Saw a nomber of large Eagles which had nested on large cottonwood trees."
Ordway ⇨
"below the little bason I with Drewyer walked through the N.E point. we Saw an Elk and Several deer, Drewyer wounded the Elk but could not get him."
Clark ⇦
"... had rapid water and a great many sand-bars; but a fine pleasant day."
Gass ⇨
"at 1 P.M. we overtook three french hunters who had set out a few days before us with a view of trapping beaver; ... these people avail themselves of the protection which our numbers will enable us to give them... and intend ascending with us as far as the mouth of the Yellow stone river..."
Lewis ⇨
Cartographer's Note:
It is important to remember at this point that the traverse of Clark did not take into account magnetic declination. Magnetic declination is the angular difference, measured in degrees, between the explorer's line to the magnetic north pole (read on his compass) and his line to the true north pole. The lack of this data should not bother the map reader. The cartographer has set the traverse to retrievable points identified by Clark and therefore has fit the traverse to the existing landscape. The reader may notice a generally greater variance between the traverse calls and true direction shown by the north arrow on the maps. Please see Introduction for further explanation.
Cartographer's Note:
The bearing N 50 E should probably be read as N 50 W.
"at the distance of 12 miles from our encampment of last night we arrived at the lower point of a bluff on the Lard side; about 1 1/2 miles down this bluff from this point, the bluff is now on fire and throws out considerable quantities of smoke which has a strong sulphurious smell. the appeance of the coal in the bluffs continues as yesterday."
Lewis ⇨
Cartographer's Note:
Lewis' use of the words "lower" and "down" in his journal entry each have potential double meanings. Whether "lower" means downriver or lower elevation is not clear. Also not clear is whether "down" means down stream or beyond the point. The cartographer has interpreted the passage in its most probable intent.
MISSOURI
RIVER
LAKE (Formerly Garrison Reservoir)
SAKAKAWEA (Reservoir)
Beaver Creek Bay
Beaver Creek State Game Management Area
Beaver Creek State Game Management Area
Renner Bay
Nishu Bay
Helle State Game Management Area
Fort Berthold Indian Reservation
Course of Pre-Dam River
Course of Pre-Dam River
Mercer Co.
McLean Co.
Normal Pool Elevation 1838 feet
Small Creek
Low Bluff
Bluff on Fire
Point
Point
Point of Wood
S 85 W 3 MILES
S 52 W 3.5 MILES
N 50 E 2 MILES
N 40 W 1/2 MILE
1/2 MILE
WEST
S 32 W 4 MILES
1661
1662
1663
1664
1665
1666
1667
1668
1669
1670
+1420
+1415
N
ONE STATUTE MILE
Modern Data: 1967-1969
Outbound: April 10, 11, 1805
Return: August 13, 1806
EXPLORATIONS OF LEWIS AND CLARK 1804 - 1806
CARTOGRAPHIC RECONSTRUCTION
LITTLE BASIN
UTM ZONE 14
MAP NUMBER 157
North Dakota
CONTOUR INTERVAL 100 FEET WITH SUPPLEMENTS

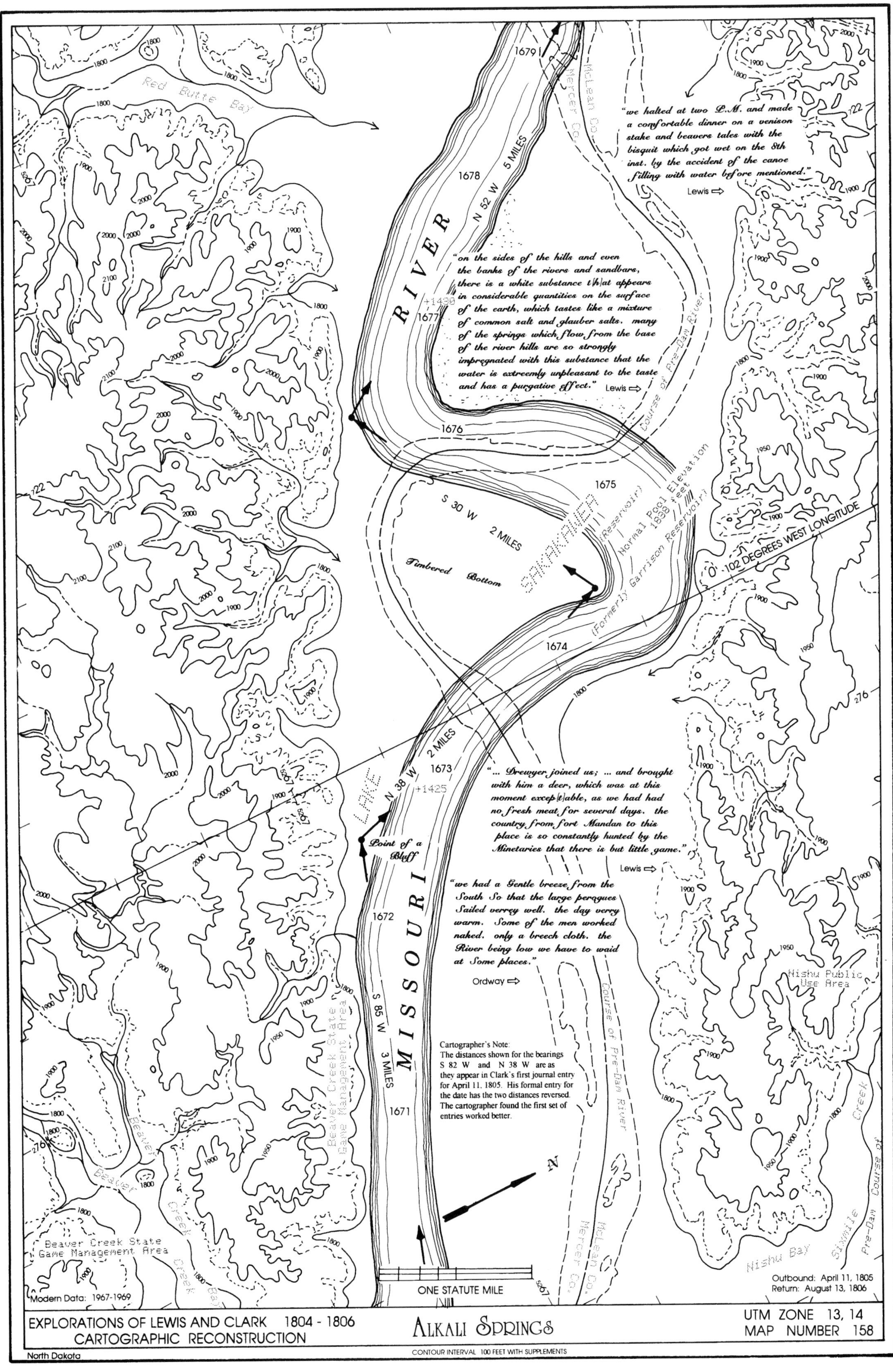

Red Butte Bay
"we halted at two P.M. and made a comfortable dinner on a venison stake and beavers tales with the bisquit which got wet on the 8th inst. by the accident of the canoe filling with water before mentioned."
Lewis ⇨
Mercer Co.
McLean Co.
N 52 W 5 MILES
RIVER
"on the sides of the hills and even the banks of the rivers and sandbars, there is a white substance t[h]at appears in considerable quantities on the surface of the earth, which tastes like a mixture of common salt and glauber salts. many of the springs which flow from the base of the river hills are so strongly impregnated with this substance that the water is extreemly unpleasant to the taste and has a purgative effect."
Lewis ⇨
Course of Pre-Dam River
S 30 W 2 MILES
Timbered Bottom
SAKAKAWEA (Reservoir)
Normal Pool Elevation 1838 feet
(Formerly Garrison Reservoir)
102 DEGREES WEST LONGITUDE
N 38 W 2 MILES
LAKE
"... Drewyer joined us; ... and brought with him a deer, which was at this moment excep[t]able, as we had had no fresh meat for several days. the country from fort Mandan to this place is so constantly hunted by the Minetaries that there is but little game."
Lewis ⇨
Point of a Bluff
"we had a Gentle breeze from the South So that the large perogues Sailed verrey well. the day verry warm. Some of the men worked naked. only a breech cloth. the River being low we have to waid at Some places."
Ordway ⇨
MISSOURI
S 85 W 3 MILES
Nishu Public Use Area
Cartographer's Note:
The distances shown for the bearings S 82 W and N 38 W are as they appear in Clark's first journal entry for April 11, 1805. His formal entry for the date has the two distances reversed. The cartographer found the first set of entries worked better.
Beaver Creek State Game Management Area
Beaver Creek
N
Nishu Bay
Pre-Dam Course of Sixmile Creek
ONE STATUTE MILE
Modern Data: 1967-1969
Outbound: April 11, 1805
Return: August 13, 1806
EXPLORATIONS OF LEWIS AND CLARK 1804 - 1806
CARTOGRAPHIC RECONSTRUCTION
ALKALI SPRINGS
UTM ZONE 13, 14
MAP NUMBER 158
North Dakota
CONTOUR INTERVAL 100 FEET WITH SUPPLEMENTS

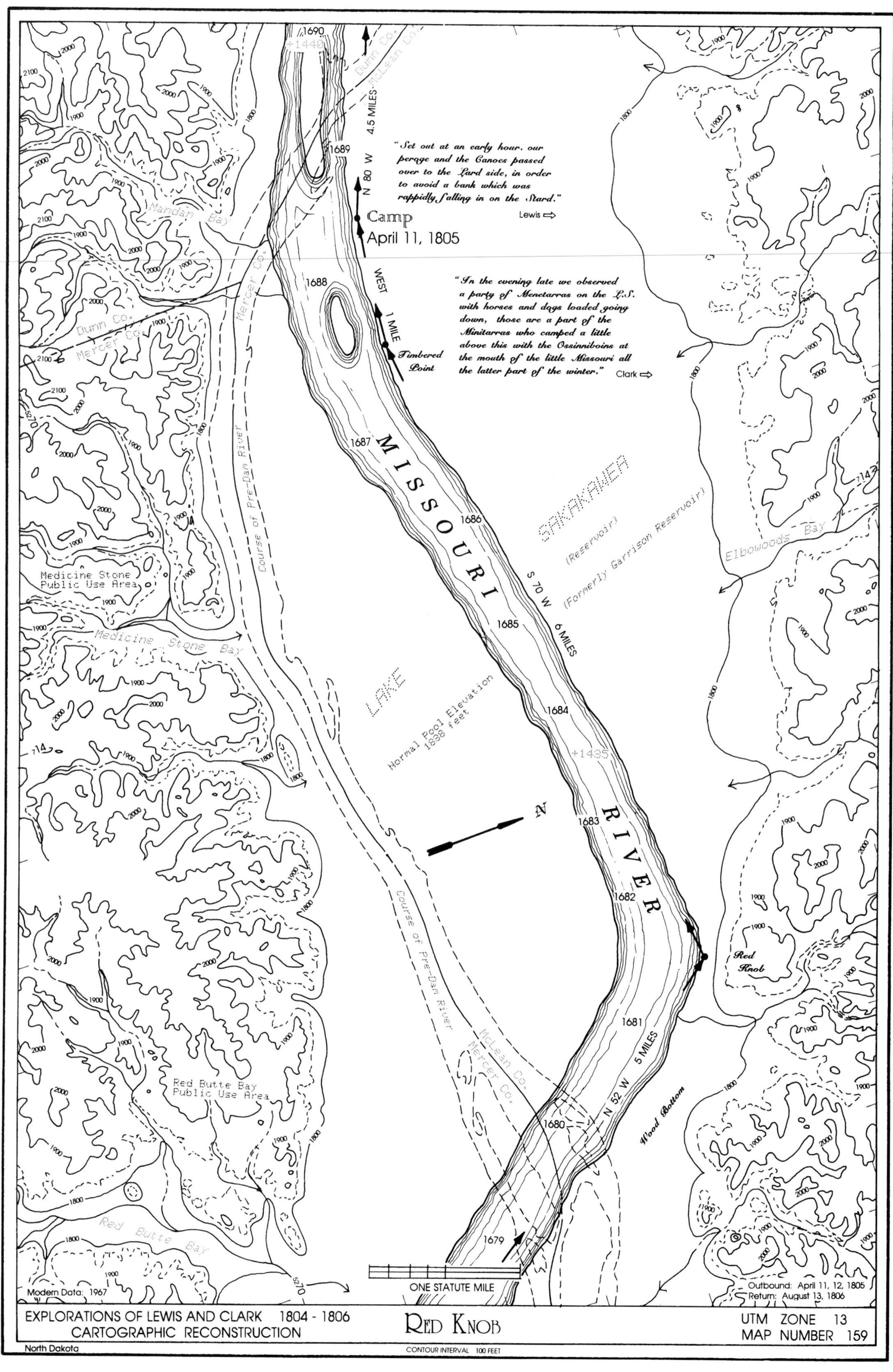
"Set out at an early hour. our peroge and the Canoes passed over to the Lard side, in order to avoid a bank which was rappidly falling in on the Stard."
Lewis
Camp
April 11, 1805
"In the evening late we observed a party of Menetarras on the L.S. with horses and dogs loaded going down, those are a part of the Minitarras who camped a little above this with the Ossinniboins at the mouth of the little Missouri all the latter part of the winter."
Clark
Timbered Point
MISSOURI RIVER
SAKAKAWEA
(Reservoir)
(Formerly Garrison Reservoir)
LAKE
Normal Pool Elevation 1838 feet
Mandan Bay
Medicine Stone Public Use Area
Medicine Stone Bay
Red Butte Bay Public Use Area
Red Butte Bay
Elbowoods Bay
Red Knob
Wood Bottom
Course of Pre-Dam River
Dunn Co.
Mercer Co.
McLean Co.
N 80 W 4.5 MILES
WEST 1 MILE
S 70 W 6 MILES
N 52 W 5 MILES
ONE STATUTE MILE
Modern Data: 1967
Outbound: April 11, 12, 1805
Return: August 13, 1806
EXPLORATIONS OF LEWIS AND CLARK 1804 - 1806
CARTOGRAPHIC RECONSTRUCTION
RED KNOB
UTM ZONE 13
MAP NUMBER 159
North Dakota
CONTOUR INTERVAL 100 FEET

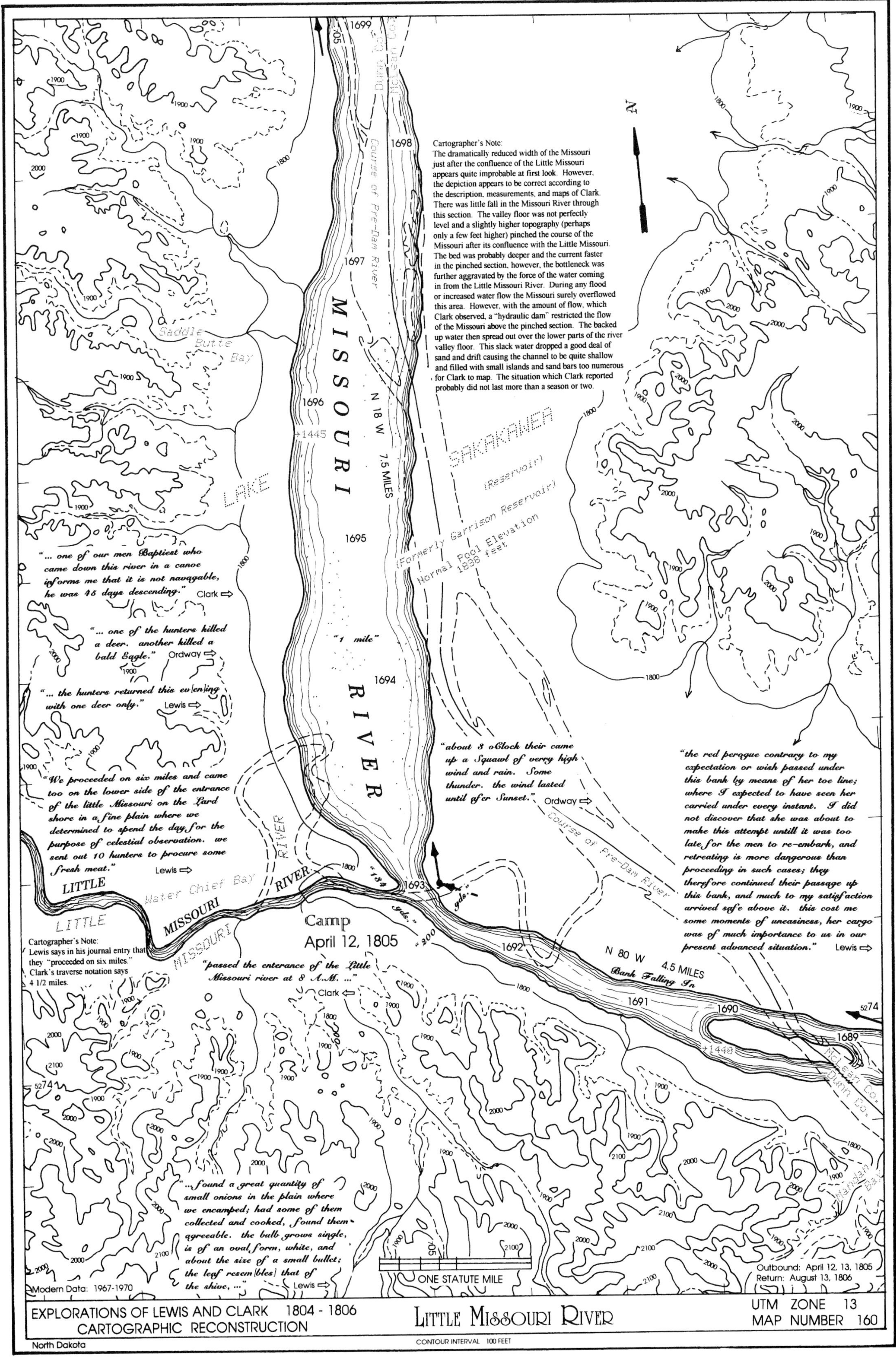

Cartographer's Note:
The dramatically reduced width of the Missouri just after the confluence of the Little Missouri appears quite improbable at first look. However, the depiction appears to be correct according to the description, measurements, and maps of Clark. There was little fall in the Missouri River through this section. The valley floor was not perfectly level and a slightly higher topography (perhaps only a few feet higher) pinched the course of the Missouri after its confluence with the Little Missouri. The bed was probably deeper and the current faster in the pinched section, however, the bottleneck was further aggravated by the force of the water coming in from the Little Missouri River. During any flood or increased water flow the Missouri surely overflowed this area. However, with the amount of flow, which Clark observed, a "hydraulic dam" restricted the flow of the Missouri above the pinched section. The backed up water then spread out over the lower parts of the river valley floor. This slack water dropped a good deal of sand and drift causing the channel to be quite shallow and filled with small islands and sand bars too numerous for Clark to map. The situation which Clark reported probably did not last more than a season or two.
N
MISSOURI
RIVER
Course of Pre-Dam River
Dunn Co.
McLean Co.
N 18 W
7.5 MILES
Saddle Butte Bay
LAKE
SAKAKAWEA
(Reservoir)
(Formerly Garrison Reservoir)
Normal Pool Elevation 1838 feet
"... one of our men Baptiest who came down this river in a canoe informs me that it is not navagable, he was 45 days descending." Clark ⇨
"... one of the hunters killed a deer. another killed a bald Eagle." Ordway ⇨
"... the hunters returned this ev[en]ing with one deer only." Lewis ⇨
"We proceeded on six miles and came too on the lower side of the entrance of the little Missouri on the Lard shore in a fine plain where we determined to spend the day for the purpose of celestial observation. we sent out 10 hunters to procure some fresh meat." Lewis ⇨
"1 mile"
"about 3 oClock their came up a Squawl of verry high wind and rain. Some thunder. the wind lasted until af er Sunset." Ordway ⇨
"the red perogue contrary to my expectation or wish passed under this bank by means of her toe line; where I expected to have seen her carried under every instant. I did not discover that she was about to make this attempt untill it was too late for the men to re-embark, and retreating is more dangerous than proceeding in such cases; they therefore continued their passage up this bank, and much to my satisfaction arrived safe above it. this cost me some moments of uneasiness, her cargo was of much importance to us in our present advanced situation." Lewis ⇨
Course of Pre-Dam River
LITTLE MISSOURI RIVER
Water Chief Bay
LITTLE MISSOURI
RIVER
Camp
April 12, 1805
Cartographer's Note:
Lewis says in his journal entry that they "proceeded on six miles." Clark's traverse notation says 4 1/2 miles.
"passed the enterance of the Little Missouri river at 8 A.M. ..." Clark ⇦
N 80 W
4.5 MILES
Bank Falling In
Mandan Bay
"...found a great quantity of small onions in the plain where we encamped; had some of them collected and cooked, found them agreeable. the bulb grows single, is of an oval form, white, and about the size of a small bullet; the leaf resem[bles] that of the shive, ..." Lewis ⇨
ONE STATUTE MILE
Outbound: April 12, 13, 1805
Return: August 13, 1806
Modern Data: 1967-1970
EXPLORATIONS OF LEWIS AND CLARK 1804 - 1806
CARTOGRAPHIC RECONSTRUCTION
LITTLE MISSOURI RIVER
UTM ZONE 13
MAP NUMBER 160
North Dakota
CONTOUR INTERVAL 100 FEET

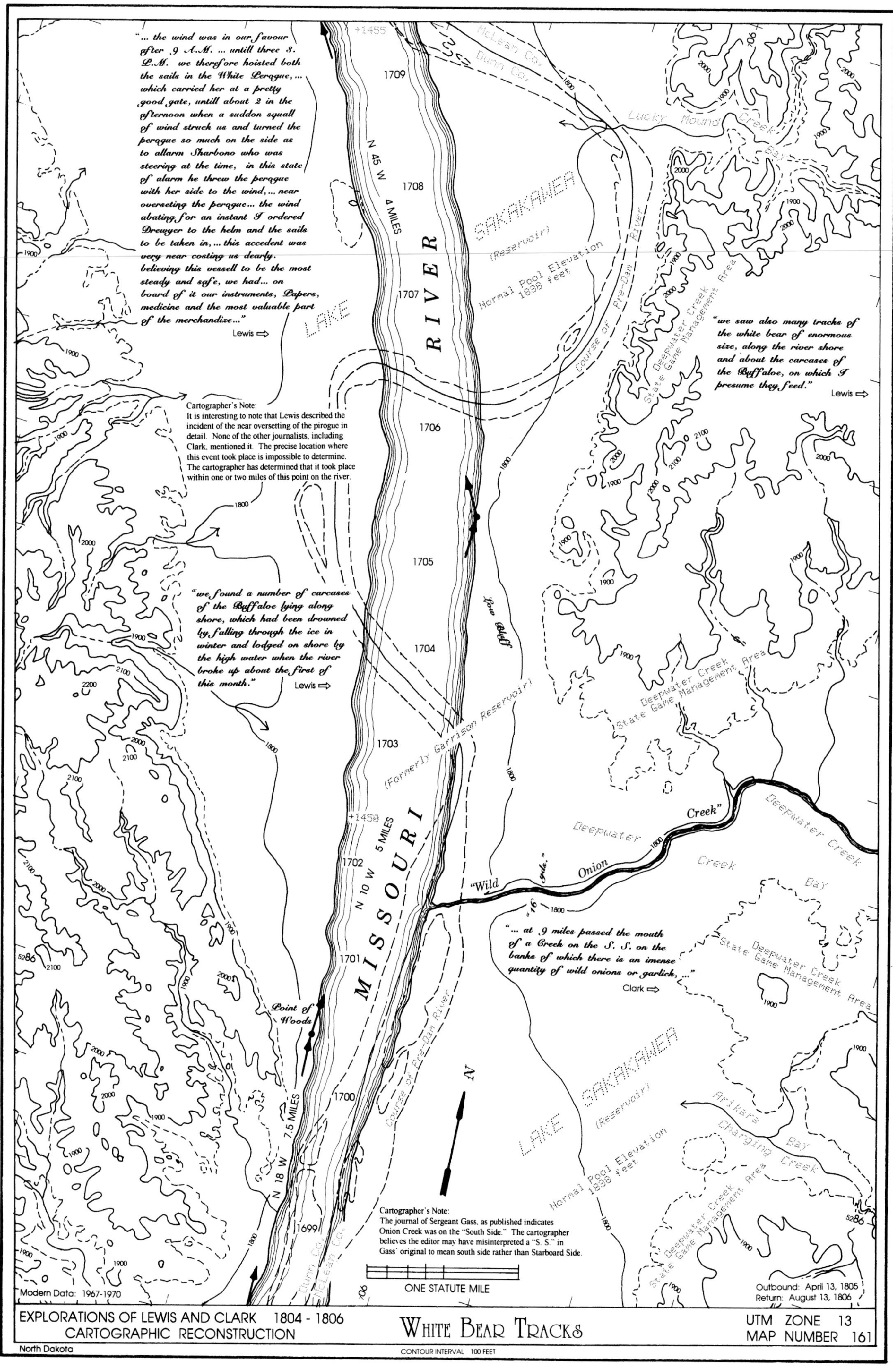

"... the wind was in our favour after 9 A.M. ... untill three 3. P.M. we therefore hoisted both the sails in the White Perogue, ... which carried her at a pretty good gate, untill about 2 in the afternoon when a suddon squall of wind struck us and turned the perogue so much on the side as to allarm Sharbono who was steering at the time, in this state of alarm he threw the perogue with her side to the wind, ... near overseting the perogue... the wind abating for an instant I ordered Drewyer to the helm and the sails to be taken in, ... this accedent was very near costing us dearly. believing this vessell to be the most steady and safe, we had... on board of it our instruments, Papers, medicine and the most valuable part of the merchandize..."
Lewis ⇨
Cartographer's Note:
It is interesting to note that Lewis described the incident of the near oversetting of the pirogue in detail. None of the other journalists, including Clark, mentioned it. The precise location where this event took place is impossible to determine. The cartographer has determined that it took place within one or two miles of this point on the river.
"we found a number of carcases of the Buffaloe lying along shore, which had been drowned by falling through the ice in winter and lodged on shore by the high water when the river broke up about the first of this month."
Lewis ⇨
"we saw also many tracks of the white bear of enormous size, along the river shore and about the carcases of the Buffaloe, on which I presume they feed."
Lewis ⇨
"... at 9 miles passed the mouth of a Creek on the S. S. on the banks of which there is an imense quantity of wild onions or garlick, ..."
Clark ⇨
Cartographer's Note:
The journal of Sergeant Gass, as published indicates Onion Creek was on the "South Side." The cartographer believes the editor may have misinterpreted a "S. S." in Gass' original to mean south side rather than Starboard Side.
MISSOURI RIVER
LAKE SAKAKAWEA (Reservoir)
Normal Pool Elevation 1838 feet
(Formerly Garrison Reservoir)
Course of Pre-Dam River
McLean Co.
Dunn Co.
Lucky Mound Creek Bay
Deepwater Creek State Game Management Area
Deepwater Creek Bay
"Wild Onion Creek"
Low Bluff
Point of Woods
Arikara Charging Creek Bay
N 45 W 4 MILES
N 10 W 5 MILES
N 18 W 7.5 MILES
1709
1708
1707
1706
1705
1704
1703
1702
1701
1700
1699
+1455
+1450
N
ONE STATUTE MILE
Modern Data: 1967-1970
Outbound: April 13, 1805
Return: August 13, 1806
EXPLORATIONS OF LEWIS AND CLARK 1804 - 1806
CARTOGRAPHIC RECONSTRUCTION
WHITE BEAR TRACKS
UTM ZONE 13
MAP NUMBER 161
North Dakota
CONTOUR INTERVAL 100 FEET

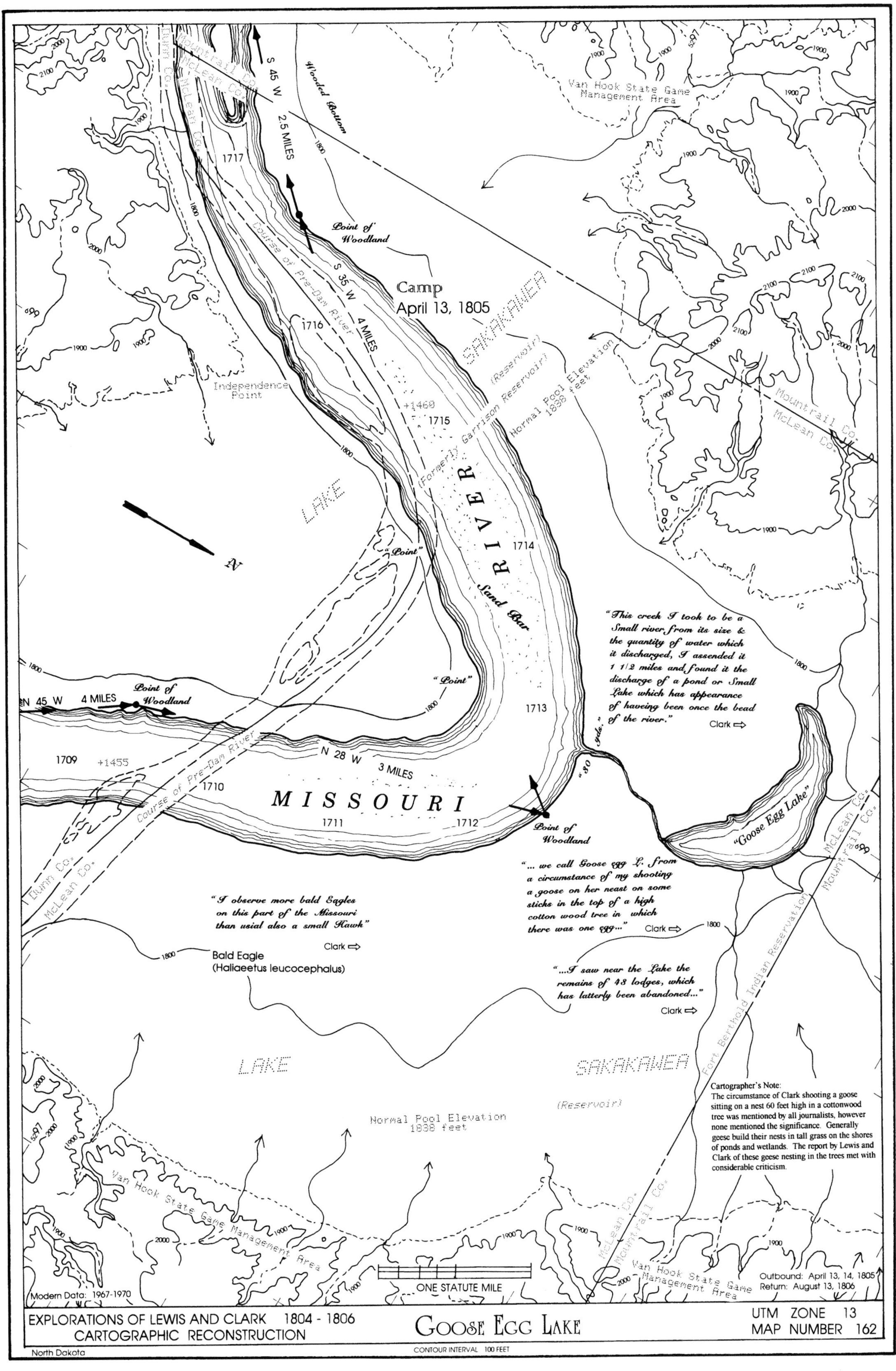
Camp
April 13, 1805
S 45 W
2.5 MILES
Wooded Bottom
Point of Woodland
S 35 W
4 MILES
Course of Pre-Dam River
Van Hook State Game Management Area
Independence Point
SAKAKAWEA
(Reservoir)
(Formerly Garrison Reservoir)
Normal Pool Elevation 1838 feet
LAKE
Mountrail Co.
McLean Co.
Dunn Co.
"Point"
RIVER
Sand Bar
N 45 W
4 MILES
Point of Woodland
N 28 W
3 MILES
MISSOURI
Point of Woodland
"80 yds."
"Goose Egg Lake"
"This creek I took to be a Small river from its size & the quantity of water which it discharged, I assended it 1 1/2 miles and found it the discharge of a pond or Small Lake which has appearance of haveing been once the bead of the river."
Clark ⇨
"... we call Goose egg L. from a circumstance of my shooting a goose on her neast on some sticks in the top of a high cotton wood tree in which there was one egg..."
Clark ⇨
"I observe more bald Eagles on this part of the Missouri than usial also a small Hawk"
Clark ⇨
Bald Eagle
(Haliaeetus leucocephalus)
"...I saw near the Lake the remains of 48 lodges, which has latterly been abandoned..."
Clark ⇨
Fort Berthold Indian Reservation
LAKE
SAKAKAWEA
(Reservoir)
Normal Pool Elevation
1838 feet
Cartographer's Note:
The circumstance of Clark shooting a goose sitting on a nest 60 feet high in a cottonwood tree was mentioned by all journalists, however none mentioned the significance. Generally geese build their nests in tall grass on the shores of ponds and wetlands. The report by Lewis and Clark of these geese nesting in the trees met with considerable criticism.
ONE STATUTE MILE
Modern Data: 1967-1970
Outbound: April 13, 14, 1805
Return: August 13, 1806
EXPLORATIONS OF LEWIS AND CLARK 1804 - 1806
CARTOGRAPHIC RECONSTRUCTION
GOOSE EGG LAKE
UTM ZONE 13
MAP NUMBER 162
North Dakota
CONTOUR INTERVAL 100 FEET

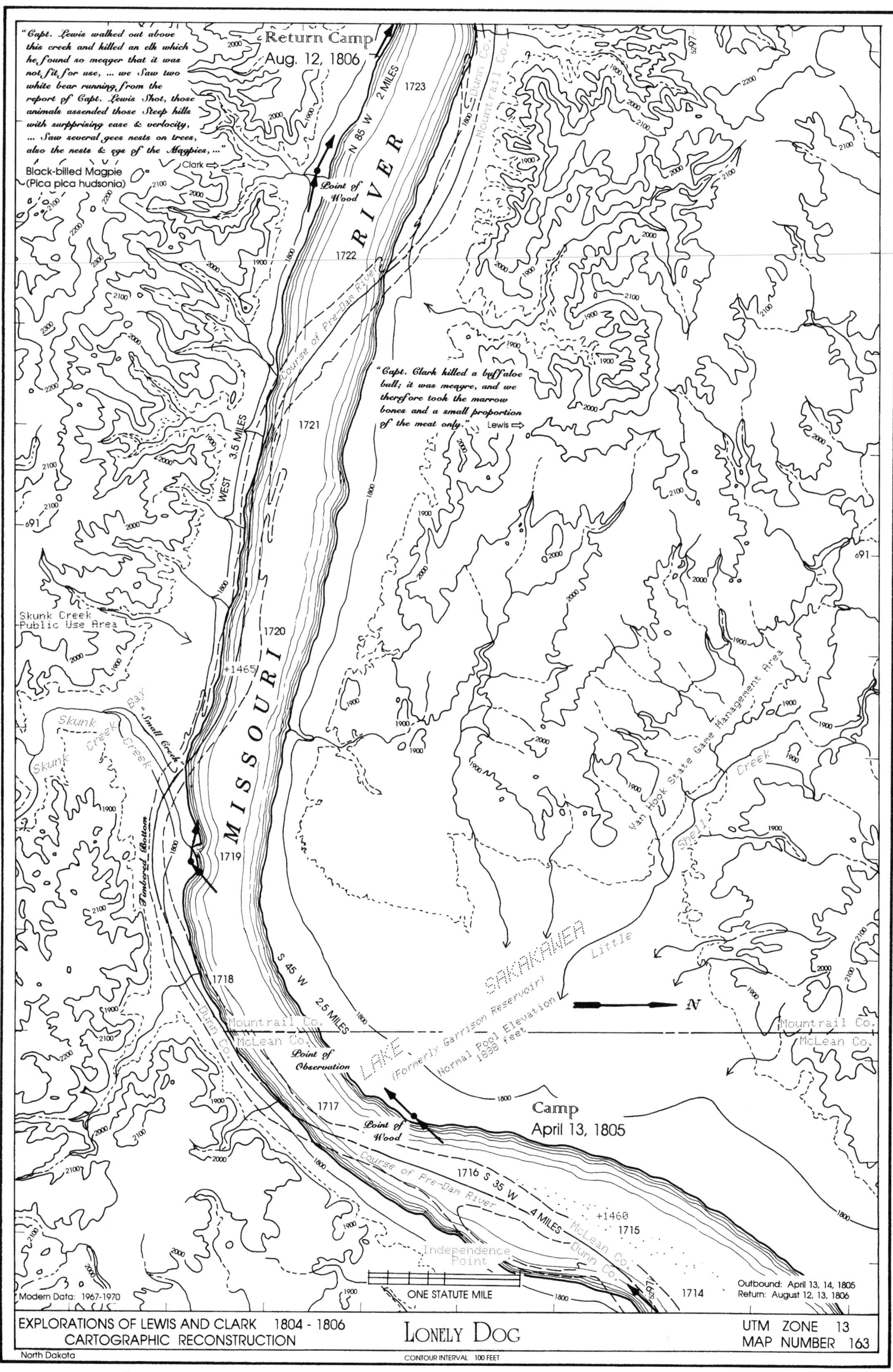
"Capt. Lewis walked out above this creek and killed an elk which he found so meager that it was not fit for use, ... we Saw two white bear running from the report of Capt. Lewis Shot, those animals assended those Steep hills with surpprising ease & verlocity, ... Saw several gees nests on trees, also the nests & egs of the Magpies, ..."
Clark ⇨
Black-billed Magpie (Pica pica hudsonia)
Return Camp
Aug. 12, 1806
N 85 W
2 MILES
1723
Point of Wood
RIVER
1722
Course of Pre-Dam River
"Capt. Clark killed a buffaloe bull; it was meagre, and we therefore took the marrow bones and a small proportion of the meat only." Lewis ⇨
1721
WEST
3.5 MILES
Skunk Creek
Public Use Area
1720
+1465
MISSOURI
Skunk
Skunk
Creek
Creek
Bay
Small Creek
Timbered Bottom
1719
Van Hook State Game Management Area
Shell
Creek
Little
SAKAKAWEA
LAKE
(Formerly Garrison Reservoir)
Normal Pool Elevation
1838 feet
N
S 45 W
2.5 MILES
1718
Mountrail Co.
McLean Co.
Dunn Co.
Point of Observation
Camp
April 13, 1805
1717
Point of Wood
1716 S 35 W
4 MILES
Course of Pre-Dam River
+1460
1715
Independence Point
McLean Co.
Dunn Co.
1714
ONE STATUTE MILE
Modern Data: 1967-1970
Outbound: April 13, 14, 1805
Return: August 12, 13, 1806
EXPLORATIONS OF LEWIS AND CLARK 1804 - 1806
CARTOGRAPHIC RECONSTRUCTION
North Dakota
LONELY DOG
CONTOUR INTERVAL 100 FEET
UTM ZONE 13
MAP NUMBER 163

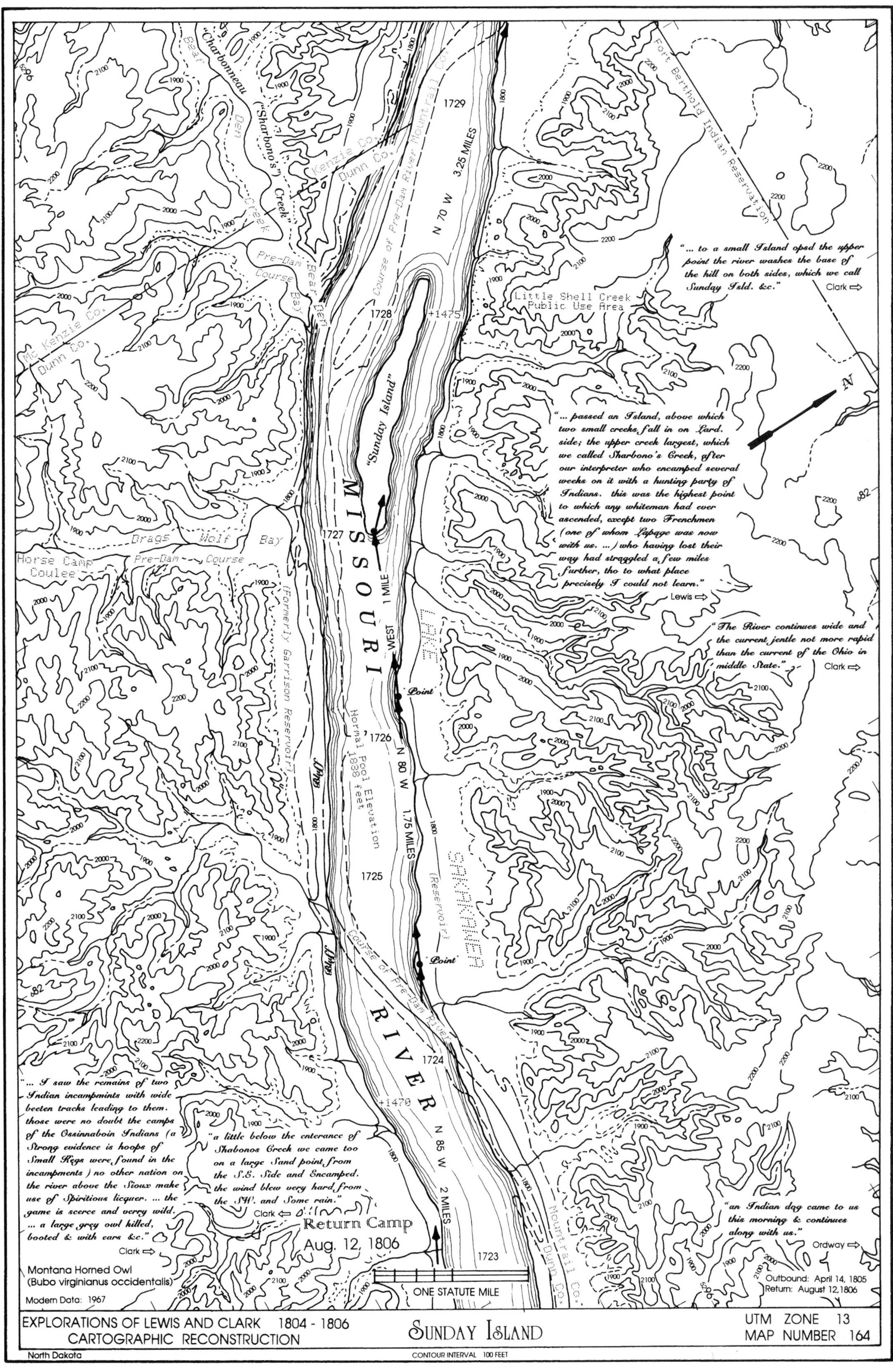

"... to a small Island opsd the upper point the river washes the base of the hill on both sides, which we call Sunday Isld. &c." Clark
"... passed an Island, above which two small creeks fall in on Lard. side; the upper creek largest, which we called Sharbono's Creek, after our interpreter who encamped several weeks on it with a hunting party of Indians. this was the highest point to which any whiteman had ever ascended, except two Frenchmen (one of whom Lapage was now with us. ...) who having lost their way had straggled a few miles further, tho to what place precisely I could not learn." Lewis
"The River continues wide and the current jentle not more rapid than the current of the Ohio in middle State." Clark
"... I saw the remains of two Indian incampmints with wide beeten tracks leading to them. those were no doubt the camps of the Ossinnaboin Indians (a Strong evidence is hoops of Small Kegs were found in the incampments) no other nation on the river above the Sioux make use of Spiritious licquer. ... the game is scerce and verry wild. ... a large grey owl killed, booted & with ears &c." Clark
"a little below the enterance of Shabonos Creek we came too on a large Sand point from the S.E. Side and Encamped. the wind blew very hard from the SW. and Some rain." Clark
"an Indian dog came to us this morning & continues along with us." Ordway
Return Camp
Aug. 12, 1806
Montana Horned Owl
(Bubo virginianus occidentalis)
Modern Data: 1967
Outbound: April 14, 1805
Return: August 12,1806
"Charbonneau ("Sharbono's") Creek"
Bear Den Creek
Pre-Dam Bear Den Course Bay
Mc Kenzie Co.
Dunn Co.
Course of Pre-Dam River Mountrail Co.
Fort Berthold Indian Reservation
Little Shell Creek Public Use Area
"Sunday Island"
Drags Wolf Bay
Horse Camp Coulee
Pre-Dam Course
(Formerly Garrison Reservoir)
MISSOURI RIVER
SAKAKAWEA LAKE (Reservoir)
Normal Pool Elevation 1838 feet
N 70 W 3.25 MILES
1 MILE WEST
N 80 W 1.75 MILES
N 85 W 2 MILES
Point
Bluffs
Mountrail Co.
Dunn Co.
N
ONE STATUTE MILE
EXPLORATIONS OF LEWIS AND CLARK 1804 - 1806
CARTOGRAPHIC RECONSTRUCTION
SUNDAY ISLAND
UTM ZONE 13
MAP NUMBER 164
North Dakota
CONTOUR INTERVAL 100 FEET

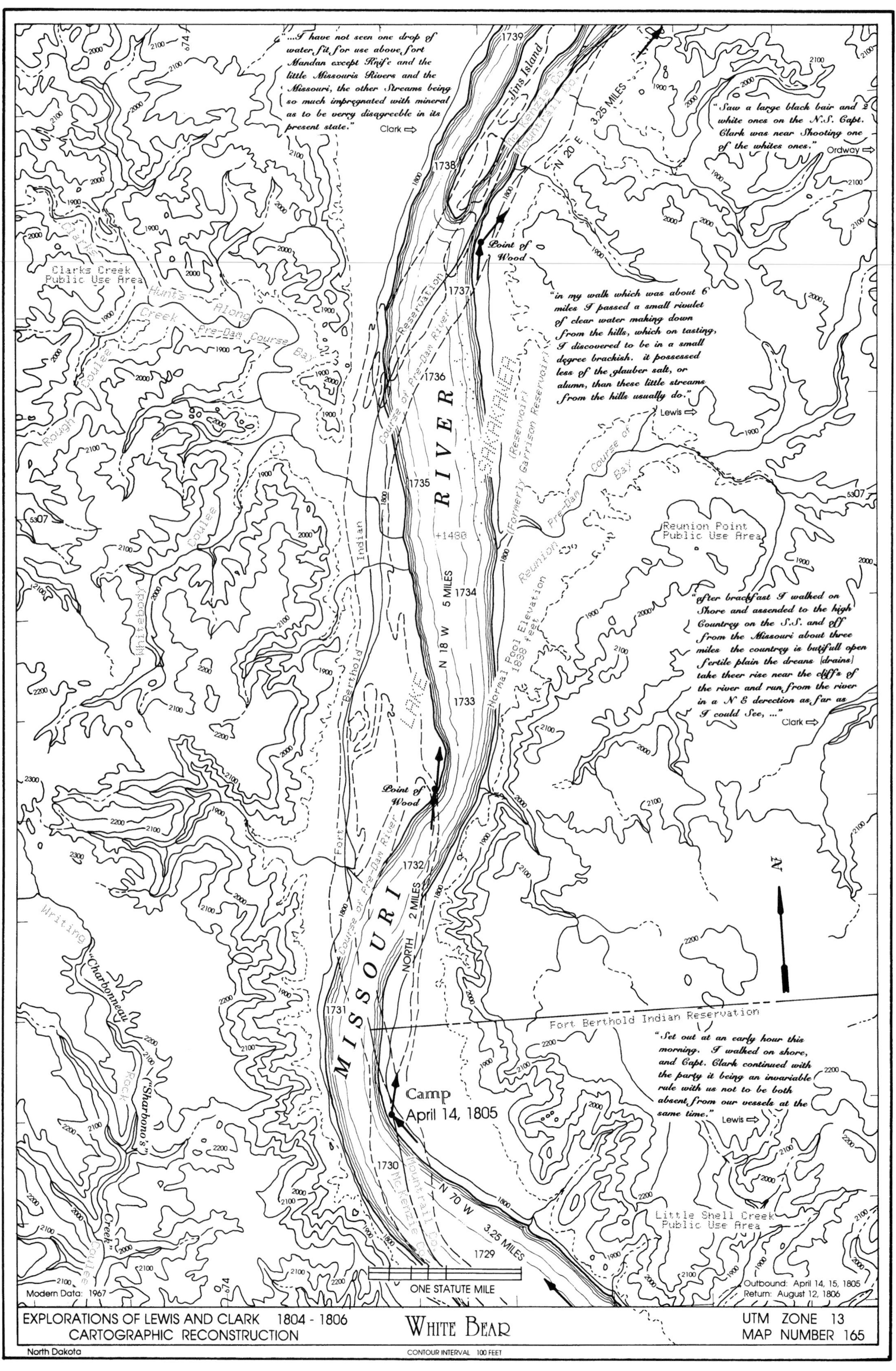
"...I have not seen one drop of water fit for use above fort Mandan except Knife and the little Missouris Rivers and the Missouri, the other Streams being so much impregnated with mineral as to be verry disagreeble in its present state." Clark ⇨
"Saw a large black bair and 2 white ones on the N.S. Capt. Clark was near Shooting one of the whites ones." Ordway ⇨
"in my walk which was about 6 miles I passed a small rivulet of clear water making down from the hills, which on tasting, I discovered to be in a small degree brackish. it possessed less of the glauber salt, or alumn, than these little streams from the hills usually do." Lewis ⇨
"after brackfast I walked on Shore and assended to the high Countrey on the S.S. and off from the Missouri about three miles the countrey is butifull open fertile plain the dreans [drains] take theer rise near the cliffs of the river and run from the river in a N E derection as far as I could See, ..." Clark ⇨
"Set out at an early hour this morning. I walked on shore, and Capt. Clark continued with the party it being an invariable rule with us not to be both absent from our vessels at the same time." Lewis ⇨
Jims Island
McKenzie Co.
Mountrail Co.
N 20 E 3.25 MILES
Point of Wood
Clarks Creek Public Use Area
Hunts Along Creek
Pre-Dam Course
Bay
Rough Coulee
Whitebody Coulee
Indian Reservation
Course of Pre-Dam River
MISSOURI RIVER
LAKE
SAKAKAWEA (Reservoir) (Formerly Garrison Reservoir)
Normal Pool Elevation 1838 feet
Pre-Dam Course of Bay
Reunion Bay
Reunion Point Public Use Area
+1460
N 18 W 5 MILES
Fort Berthold
Point of Wood
Writing Rock
Charbonneau ("Sharbono's") Creek Coulee
NORTH 2 MILES
Fort Berthold Indian Reservation
Camp April 14, 1805
N 70 W 3.25 MILES
Little Shell Creek Public Use Area
1729
1730
1731
1732
1733
1734
1735
1736
1737
1738
1739
N
Modern Data: 1967
ONE STATUTE MILE
Outbound: April 14, 15, 1805
Return: August 12, 1806
EXPLORATIONS OF LEWIS AND CLARK 1804 - 1806
CARTOGRAPHIC RECONSTRUCTION
WHITE BEAR
UTM ZONE 13
MAP NUMBER 165
North Dakota
CONTOUR INTERVAL 100 FEET

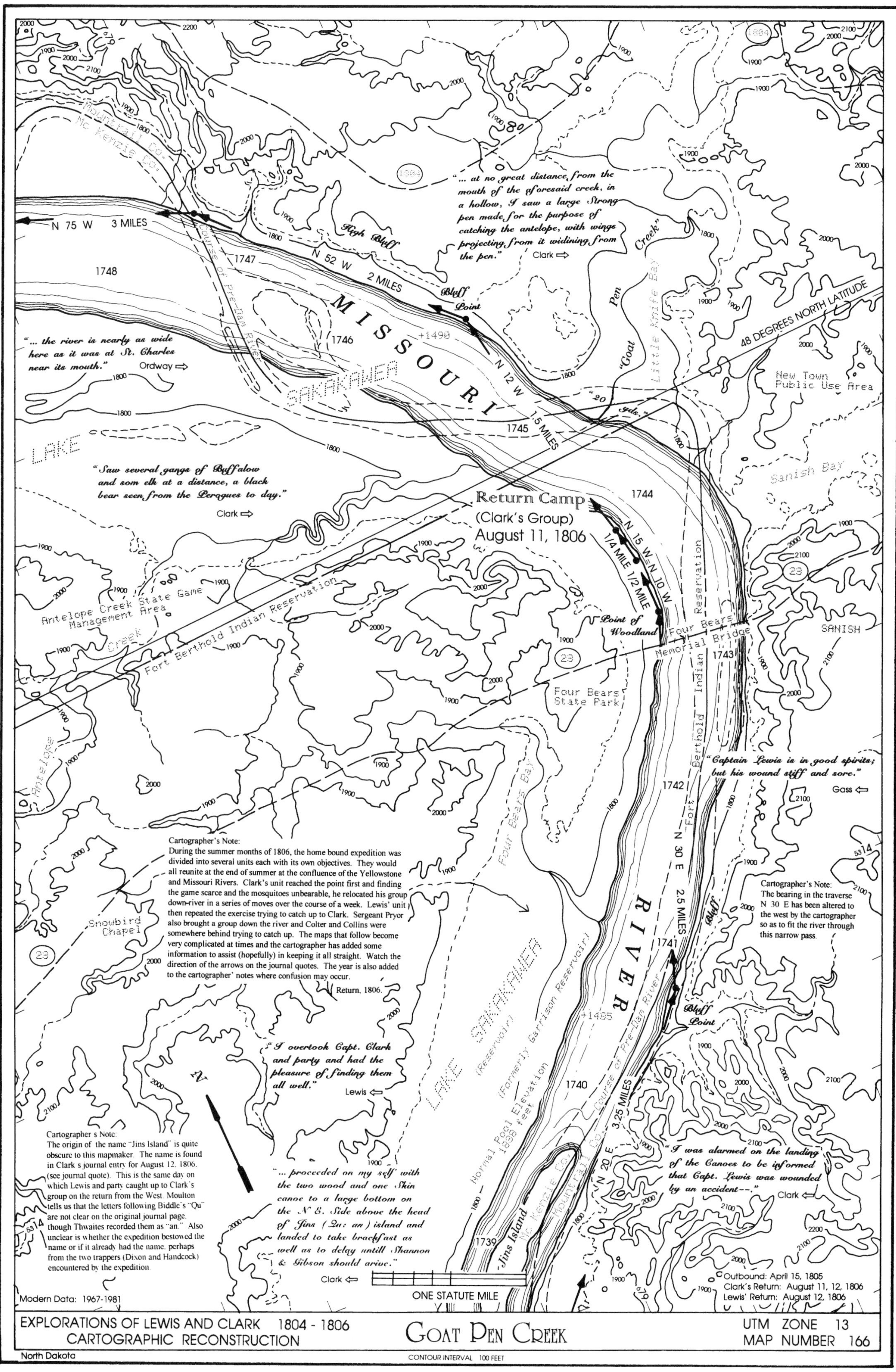

"… at no great distance from the mouth of the aforesaid creek, in a hollow, I saw a large Strong pen made for the purpose of catching the antelope, with wings projecting from it widening from the pen."
Clark ⇨
High Bluff
N 75 W 3 MILES
N 52 W 2 MILES
Bluff Point
MISSOURI
N 12 W 1.5 MILES
"Goat Pen Creek"
Little Knife Bay
48 DEGREES NORTH LATITUDE
New Town Public Use Area
Mountrail Co.
Mc Kenzie Co.
Course of Pre-Dam River
"… the river is nearly as wide here as it was at St. Charles near its mouth."
Ordway ⇨
SAKAKAWEA
LAKE
"20 yds."
"Saw several gangs of Buffalow and som elk at a distance, a black bear seen from the Perogues to day."
Clark ⇨
Sanish Bay
Return Camp
(Clark's Group)
August 11, 1806
N 15 W 1/4 MILE
N 10 W 1/2 MILE
Point of Woodland
Four Bears Memorial Bridge
Fort Berthold Indian Reservation
Antelope Creek State Game Management Area
Antelope Creek
SANISH
Four Bears State Park
"Captain Lewis is in good spirits; but his wound stiff and sore."
Gass ⇦
Four Bears Bay
N 30 E 2.5 MILES
RIVER
Bluff
Cartographer's Note:
During the summer months of 1806, the home bound expedition was divided into several units each with its own objectives. They would all reunite at the end of summer at the confluence of the Yellowstone and Missouri Rivers. Clark's unit reached the point first and finding the game scarce and the mosquitoes unbearable, he relocated his group down-river in a series of moves over the course of a week. Lewis' unit then repeated the exercise trying to catch up to Clark. Sergeant Pryor also brought a group down the river and Colter and Collins were somewhere behind trying to catch up. The maps that follow become very complicated at times and the cartographer has added some information to assist (hopefully) in keeping it all straight. Watch the direction of the arrows on the journal quotes. The year is also added to the cartographer' notes where confusion may occur.
Return, 1806.
Cartographer's Note:
The bearing in the traverse N 30 E has been altered to the west by the cartographer so as to fit the river through this narrow pass.
Snowbird Chapel
Bluff Point
LAKE SAKAKAWEA
(Reservoir)
(Formerly Garrison Reservoir)
Normal Pool Elevation 1838 feet
"I overtook Capt. Clark and party and had the pleasure of finding them all well."
Lewis ⇦
N
N 20 E 3.25 MILES
"I was alarmed on the landing of the Canoes to be informed that Capt. Lewis was wounded by an accident—."
Clark ⇦
Cartographer's Note:
The origin of the name "Jins Island" is quite obscure to this mapmaker. The name is found in Clark's journal entry for August 12, 1806, (see journal quote). This is the same day on which Lewis and party caught up to Clark's group on the return from the West. Moulton tells us that the letters following Biddle's "Qu" are not clear on the original journal page, though Thwaites recorded them as "an." Also unclear is whether the expedition bestowed the name or if it already had the name, perhaps from the two trappers (Dixon and Handcock) encountered by the expedition.
"… proceeded on my self with the two wood and one Skin canoe to a large bottom on the N. E. Side above the head of Jins (Qu: an) island and landed to take brackfast as well as to delay untill Shannon & Gibson should arive."
Clark ⇦
Jins Island
ONE STATUTE MILE
Outbound: April 15, 1805
Clark's Return: August 11, 12, 1806
Lewis' Return: August 12, 1806
Modern Data: 1967-1981
EXPLORATIONS OF LEWIS AND CLARK 1804 - 1806
CARTOGRAPHIC RECONSTRUCTION
GOAT PEN CREEK
UTM ZONE 13
MAP NUMBER 166
North Dakota
CONTOUR INTERVAL 100 FEET

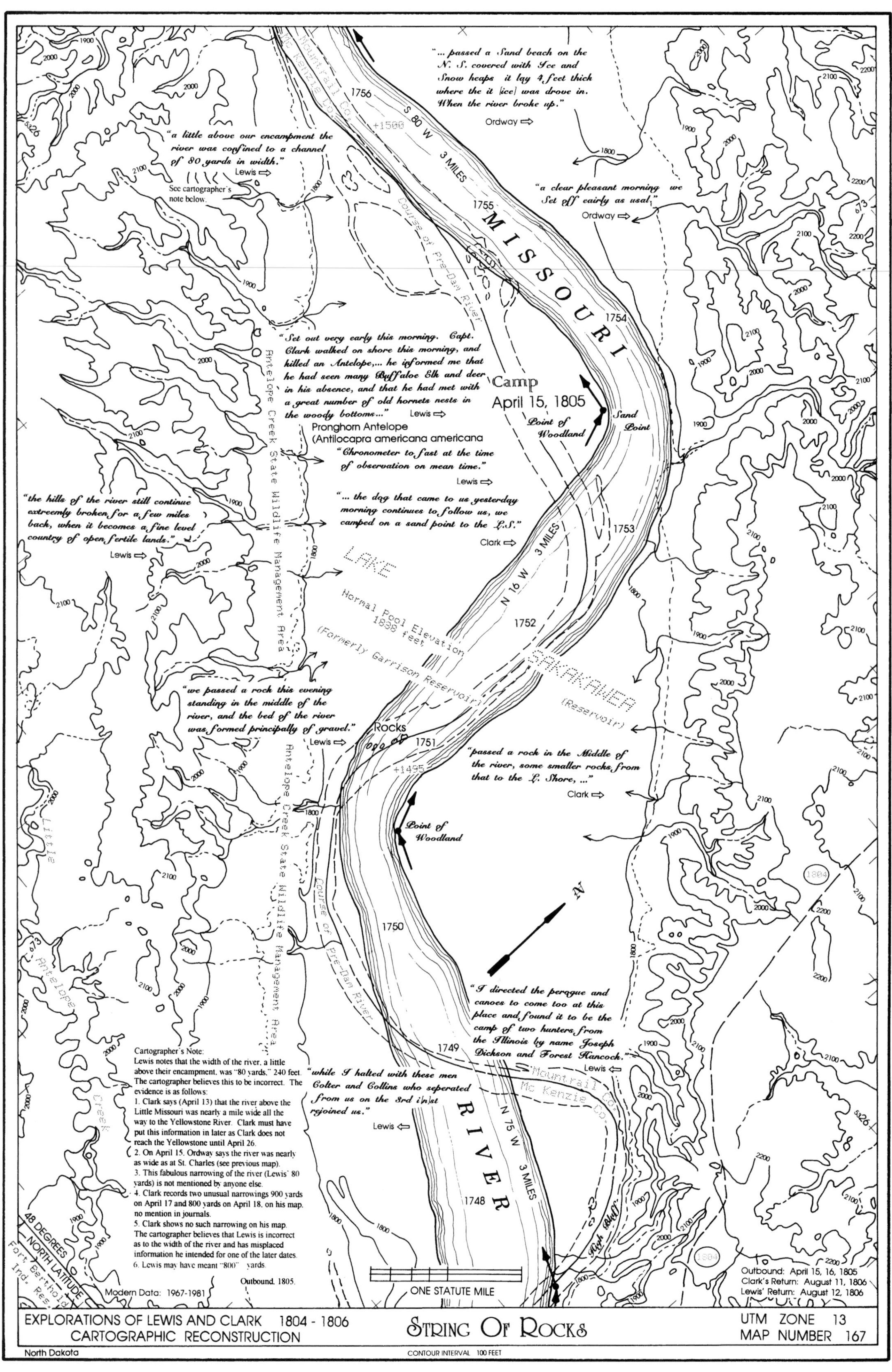

"... passed a Sand beach on the N. S. covered with Ice and Snow heaps it lay 4 feet thick where the it [ice] was drove in. When the river broke up."
Ordway ⇨
"a little above our encampment the river was confined to a channel of 80 yards in width."
Lewis ⇨
See cartographer's note below.
"a clear pleasant morning we Set off eairly as usal,"
Ordway ⇨
MISSOURI
RIVER
Mc Kenzie Co.
Mountrail Co.
Course of Pre-Dam River
S 80 W 3 MILES
N 16 W 3 MILES
N 75 W 3 MILES
1756
1755
1754
1753
1752
1751
1750
1749
1748
+1500
+1495
"Set out very early this morning. Capt. Clark walked on shore this morning, and killed an Antelope,... he informed me that he had seen many Buffaloe Elk and deer in his absence, and that he had met with a great number of old hornets nests in the woody bottoms..."
Lewis ⇨
Camp
April 15, 1805
Point of Woodland
Sand Point
Pronghorn Antelope
(Antilocapra americana americana)
"Chronometer to fast at the time of observation on mean time."
Lewis ⇨
"the hills of the river still continue extreemly broken for a few miles back, when it becomes a fine level country of open fertile lands."
Lewis ⇨
"... the dog that came to us yesterday morning continues to follow us, we camped on a sand point to the L.S."
Clark ⇨
Antelope Creek State Wildlife Management Area
LAKE
SAKAKAWEA
(Reservoir)
Normal Pool Elevation 1838 feet
(Formerly Garrison Reservoir)
"we passed a rock this evening standing in the middle of the river, and the bed of the river was formed principally of gravel."
Lewis ⇨
Rocks
"passed a rock in the Middle of the river, some smaller rocks from that to the L. Shore, ..."
Clark ⇨
Point of Woodland
Little
Antelope
Creek
N
"I directed the perogue and canoes to come too at this place and found it to be the camp of two hunters from the Illinois by name Joseph Dickson and Forest Hancock."
Lewis ⇦
"while I halted with these men Colter and Collins who seperated from us on the 3rd i[n]st rejoined us."
Lewis ⇦
High Bluff
Cartographer's Note:
Lewis notes that the width of the river, a little above their encampment, was "80 yards," 240 feet. The cartographer believes this to be incorrect. The evidence is as follows:
1. Clark says (April 13) that the river above the Little Missouri was nearly a mile wide all the way to the Yellowstone River. Clark must have put this information in later as Clark does not reach the Yellowstone until April 26.
2. On April 15, Ordway says the river was nearly as wide as at St. Charles (see previous map).
3. This fabulous narrowing of the river (Lewis' 80 yards) is not mentioned by anyone else.
4. Clark records two unusual narrowings 900 yards on April 17 and 800 yards on April 18, on his map, no mention in journals.
5. Clark shows no such narrowing on his map. The cartographer believes that Lewis is incorrect as to the width of the river and has misplaced information he intended for one of the later dates.
6. Lewis may have meant "800" yards.
Outbound, 1805.
48 DEGREES NORTH LATITUDE
Fort Berthold Ind. Res.
Modern Data: 1967-1981
ONE STATUTE MILE
Outbound: April 15, 16, 1805
Clark's Return: August 11, 1806
Lewis' Return: August 12, 1806
1804
EXPLORATIONS OF LEWIS AND CLARK 1804 - 1806
CARTOGRAPHIC RECONSTRUCTION
STRING OF ROCKS
UTM ZONE 13
MAP NUMBER 167
North Dakota
CONTOUR INTERVAL 100 FEET

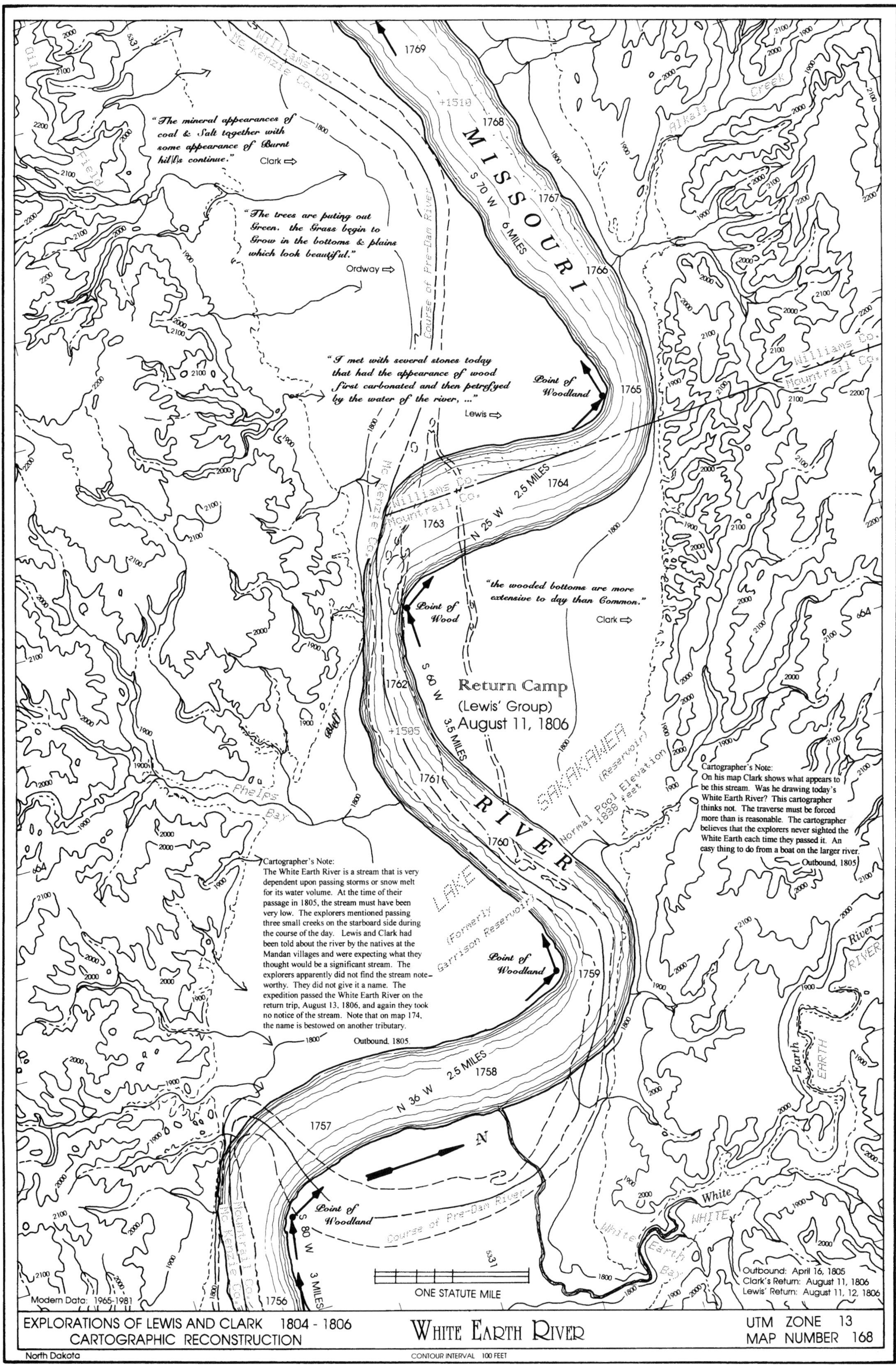
"The mineral appearances of coal & Salt together with some appearance of Burnt hil(l)s continue."
Clark ⇨
"The trees are puting out Green. the Grass begin to Grow in the bottoms & plains which look beautiful."
Ordway ⇨
"I met with several stones today that had the appearance of wood first carbonated and then petrefyed by the water of the river, ..."
Lewis ⇨
"the wooded bottoms are more extensive to day than Common."
Clark ⇨
MISSOURI
RIVER
S 70 W 6 MILES
N 25 W 2.5 MILES
S 60 W 3.5 MILES
N 36 W 2.5 MILES
S 80 W 3 MILES
Point of Woodland
Point of Wood
Return Camp
(Lewis' Group)
August 11, 1806
McKenzie Co.
Williams Co.
Mountrail Co.
Course of Pre-Dam River
Alkali Creek
Phelps Bay
SAKAKAWEA (Reservoir)
Normal Pool Elevation 1838 feet
LAKE (Formerly Garrison Reservoir)
White Earth River
WHITE EARTH RIVER
White Earth Bay
Cartographer's Note:
On his map Clark shows what appears to be this stream. Was he drawing today's White Earth River? This cartographer thinks not. The traverse must be forced more than is reasonable. The cartographer believes that the explorers never sighted the White Earth each time they passed it. An easy thing to do from a boat on the larger river.
Outbound, 1805
Cartographer's Note:
The White Earth River is a stream that is very dependent upon passing storms or snow melt for its water volume. At the time of their passage in 1805, the stream must have been very low. The explorers mentioned passing three small creeks on the starboard side during the course of the day. Lewis and Clark had been told about the river by the natives at the Mandan villages and were expecting what they thought would be a significant stream. The explorers apparently did not find the stream noteworthy. They did not give it a name. The expedition passed the White Earth River on the return trip, August 13, 1806, and again they took no notice of the stream. Note that on map 174, the name is bestowed on another tributary.
Outbound, 1805.
N
ONE STATUTE MILE
Outbound: April 16, 1805
Clark's Return: August 11, 1806
Lewis' Return: August 11, 12, 1806
Modern Data: 1965-1981
EXPLORATIONS OF LEWIS AND CLARK 1804 - 1806
CARTOGRAPHIC RECONSTRUCTION
WHITE EARTH RIVER
UTM ZONE 13
MAP NUMBER 168
North Dakota
CONTOUR INTERVAL 100 FEET

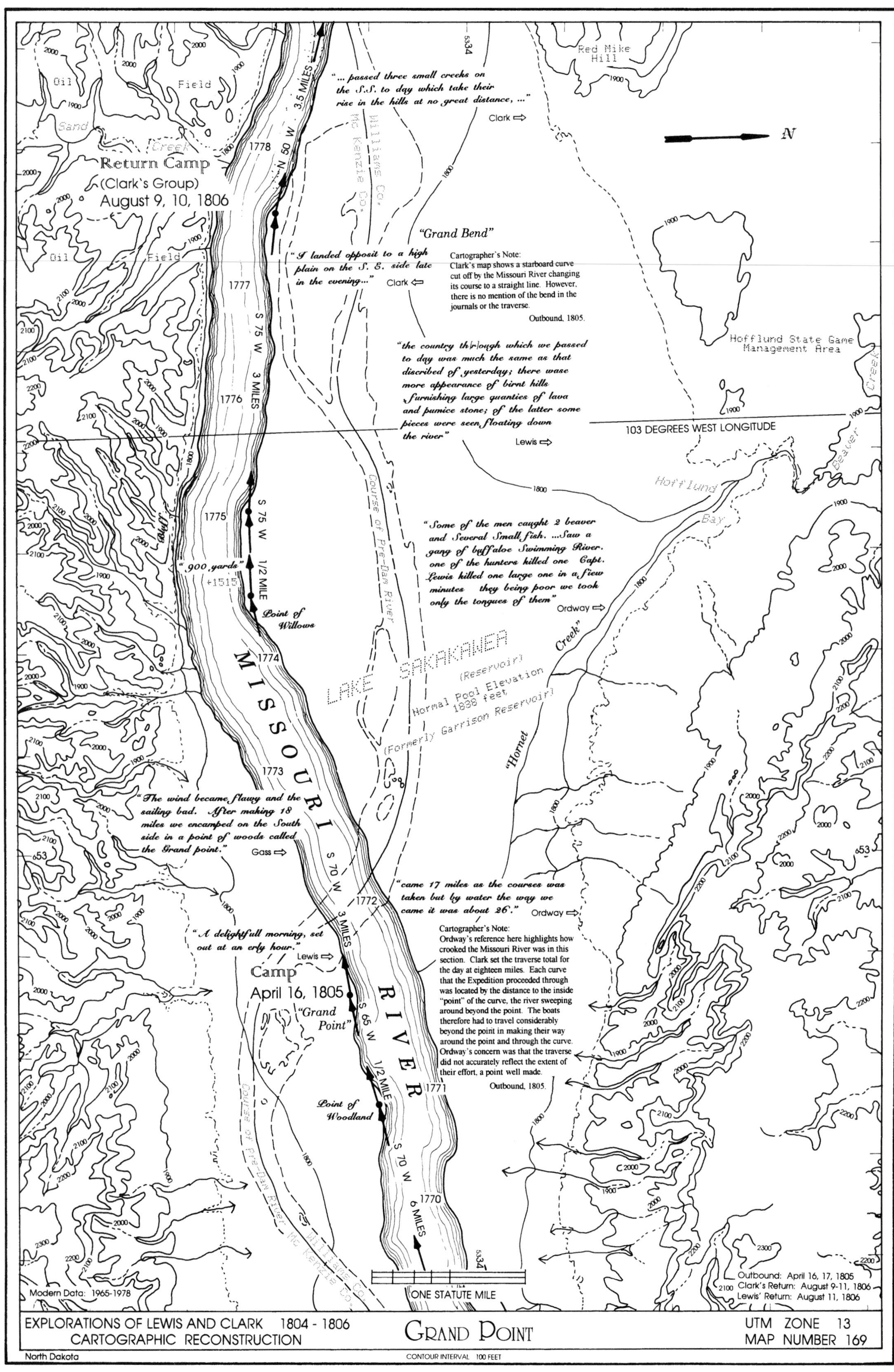

"... passed three small creeks on the S.S. to day which take their rise in the hills at no great distance, ..."
Clark ⇨
N
Red Mike Hill
Oil Field
Sand Creek
Return Camp (Clark's Group) August 9, 10, 1806
N 50 W 3.5 MILES
McKenzie Co. Williams Co.
"Grand Bend"
"I landed opposit to a high plain on the S. E. side late in the evening..."
Clark ⇦
Cartographer's Note:
Clark's map shows a starboard curve cut off by the Missouri River changing its course to a straight line. However, there is no mention of the bend in the journals or the traverse.
Outbound, 1805.
S 75 W 3 MILES
Hofflund State Game Management Area
"the country th[r]ough which we passed to day was much the same as that discribed yesterday; there wase more appearance of birnt hills furnishing large quanties of lava and pumice stone; of the latter some pieces were seen floating down the river"
Lewis ⇨
103 DEGREES WEST LONGITUDE
Hofflund Bay
Beaver Creek
Bluff
"900 yards"
S 75 W 1/2 MILE
Course of Pre-Dam River
"Some of the men caught 2 beaver and Several Small fish. ...Saw a gang of buffaloe Swimming River. one of the hunters killed one Capt. Lewis killed one large one in a fiew minutes they being poor we took only the tongues of them"
Ordway ⇨
Point of Willows
MISSOURI RIVER
LAKE SAKAKAWEA (Reservoir) Normal Pool Elevation 1838 feet (Formerly Garrison Reservoir)
"Hornet Creek"
"The wind became flawy and the sailing bad. After making 18 miles we encamped on the South side in a point of woods called the Grand point."
Gass ⇨
S 70 W 3 MILES
"came 17 miles as the courses was taken but by water the way we came it was about 26."
Ordway ⇨
Cartographer's Note:
Ordway's reference here highlights how crooked the Missouri River was in this section. Clark set the traverse total for the day at eighteen miles. Each curve that the Expedition proceeded through was located by the distance to the inside "point" of the curve, the river sweeping around beyond the point. The boats therefore had to travel considerably beyond the point in making their way around the point and through the curve. Ordway's concern was that the traverse did not accurately reflect the extent of their effort, a point well made.
Outbound, 1805.
"A delightfull morning, set out at an erly hour."
Lewis ⇨
Camp April 16, 1805
"Grand Point"
S 65 W 1/2 MILE
Point of Woodland
S 70 W 6 MILES
ONE STATUTE MILE
Modern Data: 1965-1978
Outbound: April 16, 17, 1805
Clark's Return: August 9-11, 1806
Lewis' Return: August 11, 1806
EXPLORATIONS OF LEWIS AND CLARK 1804 - 1806
CARTOGRAPHIC RECONSTRUCTION
GRAND POINT
UTM ZONE 13
MAP NUMBER 169
North Dakota
CONTOUR INTERVAL 100 FEET

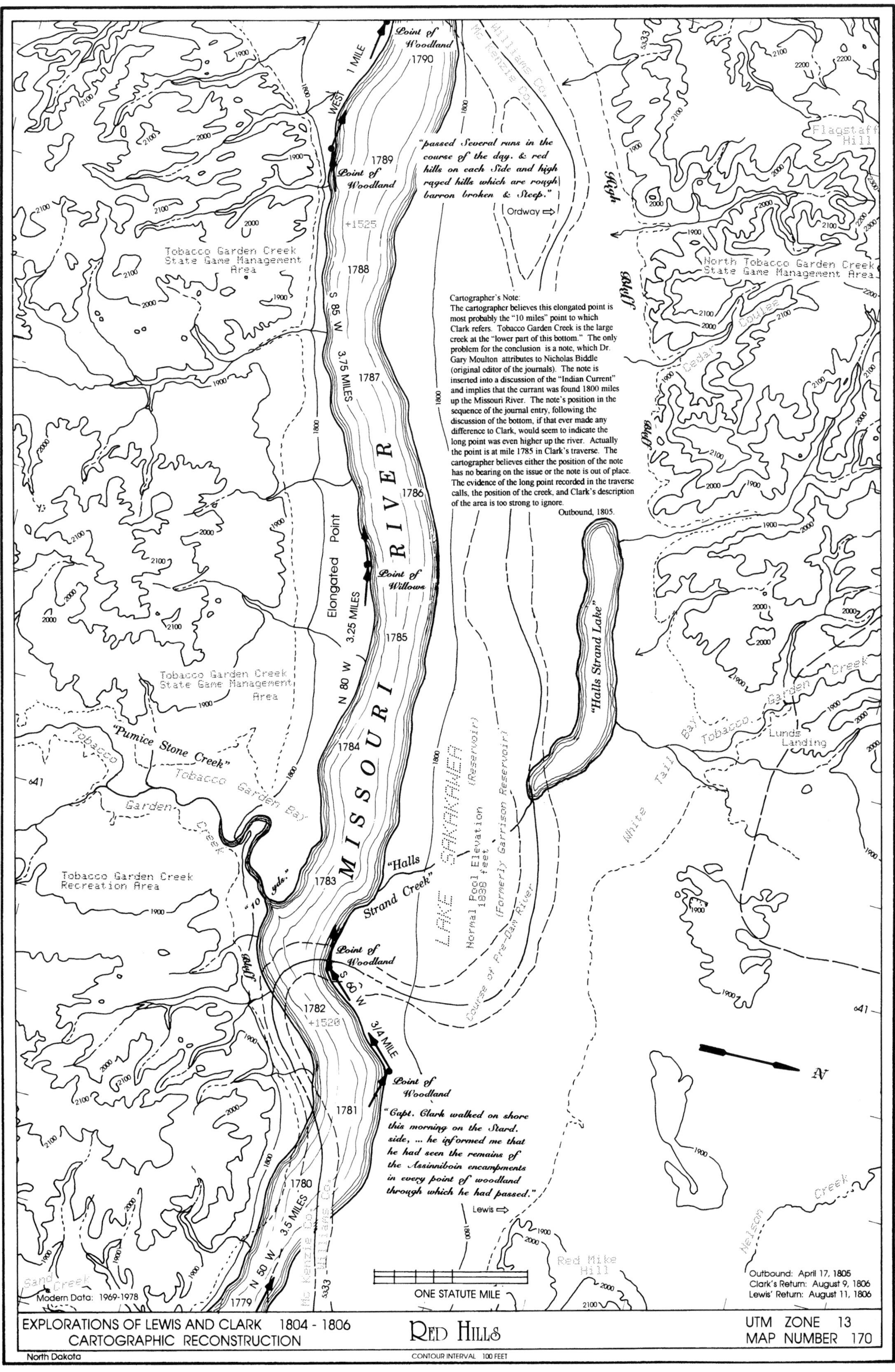

Point of Woodland
1790
WEST 1 MILE
Mc Kenzie Co.
Williams Co.
"passed Several runs in the course of the day. & red hills on each Side and high raged hills which are rough barron broken & Steep."
Ordway ⇨
1789
Point of Woodland
+1525
High
Flagstaff Hill
Tobacco Garden Creek State Game Management Area
1788
North Tobacco Garden Creek State Game Management Area
S 85 W
3.75 MILES
Bluff
Cedar Coulee
Cartographer's Note:
The cartographer believes this elongated point is most probably the "10 miles" point to which Clark refers. Tobacco Garden Creek is the large creek at the "lower part of this bottom." The only problem for the conclusion is a note, which Dr. Gary Moulton attributes to Nicholas Biddle (original editor of the journals). The note is inserted into a discussion of the "Indian Current" and implies that the currant was found 1800 miles up the Missouri River. The note's position in the sequence of the journal entry, following the discussion of the bottom, if that ever made any difference to Clark, would seem to indicate the long point was even higher up the river. Actually the point is at mile 1785 in Clark's traverse. The cartographer believes either the position of the note has no bearing on the issue or the note is out of place. The evidence of the long point recorded in the traverse calls, the position of the creek, and Clark's description of the area is too strong to ignore.
Outbound, 1805.
1787
1786
Bluff
MISSOURI RIVER
Elongated Point
Point of Willows
3.25 MILES
1785
N 80 W
"Halls Strand Lake"
Tobacco Garden Creek State Game Management Area
Tobacco Garden Creek
Lunds Landing
Tobacco Garden Bay
"Pumice Stone Creek"
Tobacco Garden Bay
Garden Creek
1784
LAKE SAKAKAWEA (Reservoir)
Normal Pool Elevation 1838 feet
(Formerly Garrison Reservoir)
Course of Pre-Dam River
White Tail Bay
Tobacco Garden Creek Recreation Area
"10 yds."
1783
"Halls Strand Creek"
Bluff
Point of Woodland
S 60 W
1782
+1520
3/4 MILE
Point of Woodland
N
1781
"Capt. Clark walked on shore this morning on the Stard. side, ... he informed me that he had seen the remains of the Assinniboin encampments in every point of woodland through which he had passed."
Lewis ⇨
1780
3.5 MILES
N 50 W
Mc Kenzie Co.
Williams Co.
Nelson Creek
Red Mike Hill
Sand Creek
Modern Data: 1969-1978
1779
ONE STATUTE MILE
Outbound: April 17, 1805
Clark's Return: August 9, 1806
Lewis' Return: August 11, 1806
EXPLORATIONS OF LEWIS AND CLARK 1804 - 1806
CARTOGRAPHIC RECONSTRUCTION
RED HILLS
UTM ZONE 13
MAP NUMBER 170
North Dakota
CONTOUR INTERVAL 100 FEET

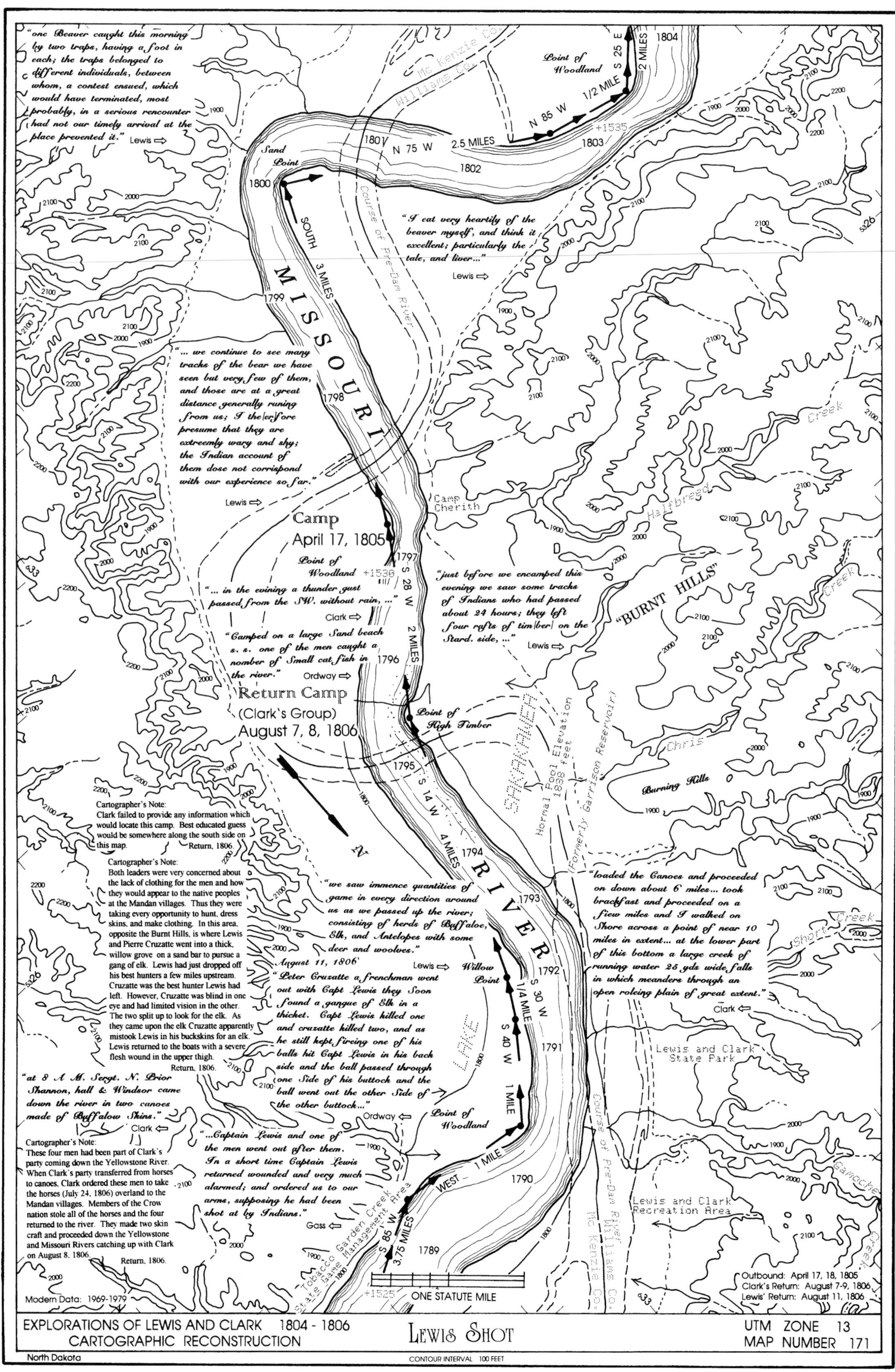
"one Beaver caught this morning by two traps, having a foot in each; the traps belonged to different individuals, between whom, a contest ensued, which would have terminated, most probably, in a serious rencounter had not our timely arrival at the place prevented it." Lewis ⇨
Point of Woodland
1804
S 25 E
2 MILES
1/2 MILE
N 85 W
+1535
1803
McKenzie Co.
Williams Co.
1801
N 75 W
2.5 MILES
1802
Sand Point
1800
SOUTH
3 MILES
Course of Pre-Dam River
"I eat very heartily of the beaver myself, and think it excellent; particularly the tale, and liver..." Lewis ⇨
1799
MISSOURI
"... we continue to see many tracks of the bear we have seen but very few of them, and those are at a great distance generally runing from us; I the[er]fore presume that they are extreemly wary and shy; the Indian account of them dose not corrispond with our experience so far." Lewis ⇨
1798
Creek
Camp Cherith
Halfbreed
Camp
April 17, 1805
1797
Point of Woodland +1530
S 28 W
"... in the evining a thunder gust passed from the SW. without rain, ..." Clark ⇨
"just before we encamped this evening we saw some tracks of Indians who had passed about 24 hours; they left four rafts of tim[ber] on the Stard. side, ..." Lewis ⇨
"BURNT HILLS"
Creek
"Camped on a large Sand beach s. s. one of the men caught a nomber of Small cat fish in the river." Ordway ⇨
2 MILES
1796
Return Camp
(Clark's Group)
August 7, 8, 1806
Point of High Timber
SAKAKAWEA
Normal Pool Elevation 1838 feet
(Formerly Garrison Reservoir)
Chris
Burning Hills
1795
S 14 W
4 MILES
N
Cartographer's Note:
Clark failed to provide any information which would locate this camp. Best educated guess would be somewhere along the south side on this map. Return, 1806.
Cartographer's Note:
Both leaders were very concerned about the lack of clothing for the men and how they would appear to the native peoples at the Mandan villages. Thus they were taking every opportunity to hunt, dress skins, and make clothing. In this area, opposite the Burnt Hills, is where Lewis and Pierre Cruzatte went into a thick, willow grove on a sand bar to pursue a gang of elk. Lewis had just dropped off his best hunters a few miles upstream. Cruzatte was the best hunter Lewis had left. However, Cruzatte was blind in one eye and had limited vision in the other. The two split up to look for the elk. As they came upon the elk Cruzatte apparently mistook Lewis in his buckskins for an elk. Lewis returned to the boats with a severe flesh wound in the upper thigh. Return, 1806.
1794
RIVER
"we saw immence quantities of game in every direction around us as we passed up the river; consisting of herds of Buffaloe, Elk, and Antelopes with some deer and woolves." Lewis ⇨
"loaded the Canoes and proceeded on down about 6 miles... took brackfast and proceeded on a fiew miles and I walked on Shore across a point of near 10 miles in extent... at the lower part of this bottom a large creek of running water 25 yds wide falls in which meanders through an open roleing plain of great extent." Clark ⇦
1793
Short Creek
August 11, 1806
"Peter Cruzatte a frenchman went out with Capt Lewis they Soon found a gangue of Elk in a thicket. Capt Lewis killed one and cruzatte killed two, and as he still kept fireing one of his balls hit Capt Lewis in his back side and the ball passed through one Side of his buttock and the ball went out the other Side of the other buttock..." Ordway ⇦
Willow Point
1792
S 30 W
1/4 MILE
LAKE
S 40 W
1791
Lewis and Clark State Park
"at 8 A M. Sergt. N. Prior Shannon, hall & Windsor came down the river in two canoes made of Buffalow Skins." Clark ⇦
1 MILE
Point of Woodland
Cartographer's Note:
These four men had been part of Clark's party coming down the Yellowstone River. When Clark's party transferred from horses to canoes, Clark ordered these men to take the horses (July 24, 1806) overland to the Mandan villages. Members of the Crow nation stole all of the horses and the four returned to the river. They made two skin craft and proceeded down the Yellowstone and Missouri Rivers catching up with Clark on August 8, 1806. Return, 1806.
"...Captain Lewis and one of the men went out after them. In a short time Captain Lewis returned wounded and very much alarmed; and ordered us to our arms, supposing he had been shot at by Indians." Gass ⇦
1 MILE
WEST
1790
Course of Pre-Dam River
Williams Co.
McKenzie Co.
Lewis and Clark Recreation Area
Tobacco Garden Creek
State Game Management Area
S 85 W
3.75 MILES
1789
Garrison
Creek
Outbound: April 17, 18, 1805
Clark's Return: August 7-9, 1806
Lewis' Return: August 11, 1806
+1525
ONE STATUTE MILE
Modern Data: 1969-1979
EXPLORATIONS OF LEWIS AND CLARK 1804 - 1806
CARTOGRAPHIC RECONSTRUCTION
LEWIS SHOT
UTM ZONE 13
MAP NUMBER 171
North Dakota
CONTOUR INTERVAL 100 FEET

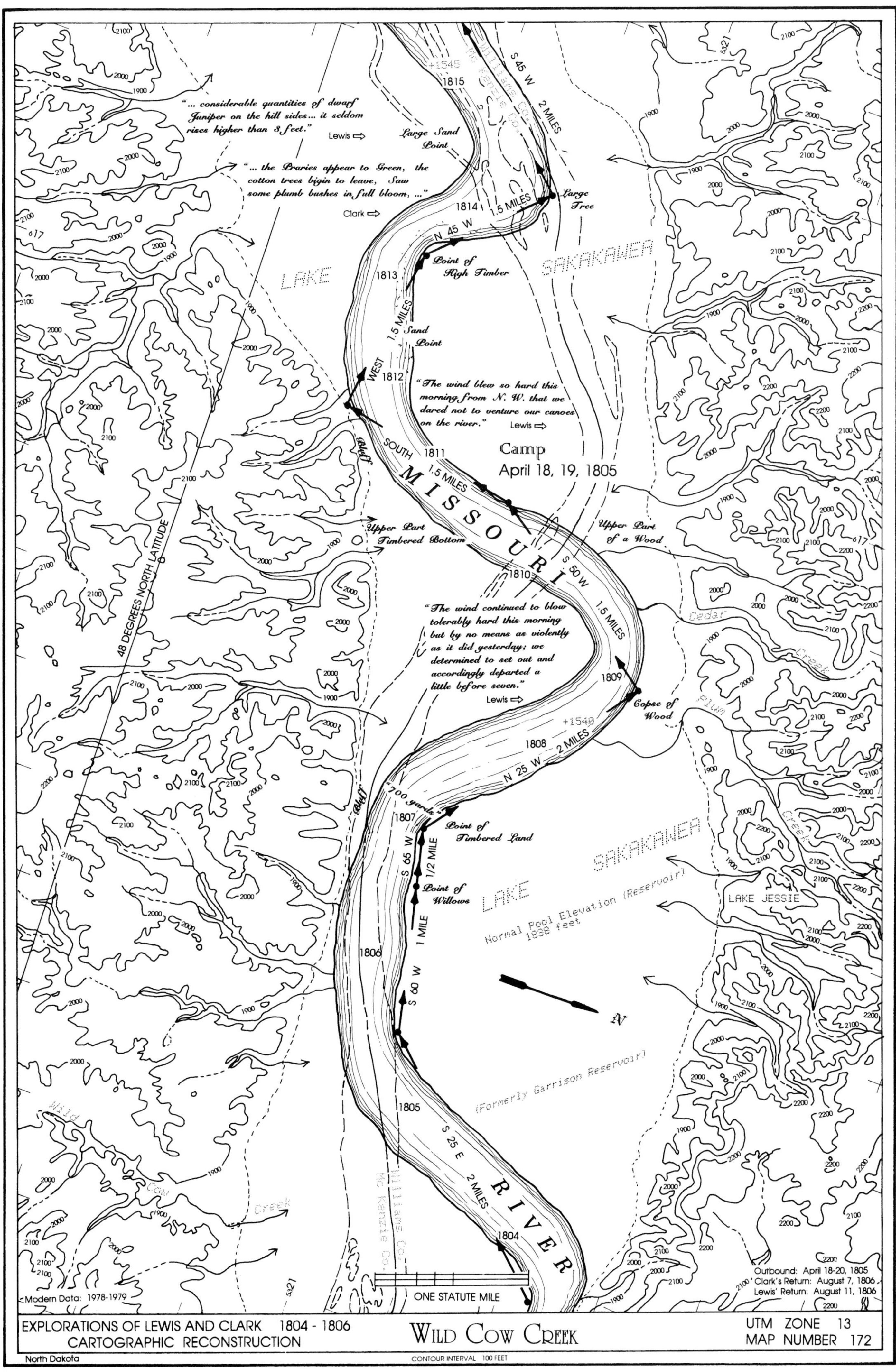
"... considerable quantities of dwarf Juniper on the hill sides... it seldom rises higher than 3 feet."
Lewis ⇨
Large Sand Point
"... the Praries appear to Green, the cotton trees bigin to leave, Saw some plumb bushes in full bloom, ..."
Clark ⇨
Large Tree
Point of High Timber
Sand Point
"The wind blew so hard this morning from N. W. that we dared not to venture our canoes on the river."
Lewis ⇨
Camp
April 18, 19, 1805
Upper Part Timbered Bottom
Upper Part of a Wood
"The wind continued to blow tolerably hard this morning but by no means as violently as it did yesterday; we determined to set out and accordingly departed a little before seven."
Lewis ⇨
Copse of Wood
"700 yards"
Point of Timbered Land
Point of Willows
LAKE SAKAKAWEA
Normal Pool Elevation (Reservoir) 1838 feet
(Formerly Garrison Reservoir)
LAKE JESSIE
Cedar Creek
Plum Creek
Wild Cow Creek
MISSOURI RIVER
48 DEGREES NORTH LATITUDE
Mc Kenzie Co.
Williams Co.
S 45 W 2 MILES
1.5 MILES
N 45 W
1.5 MILES
WEST
SOUTH
1.5 MILES
S 50 W 1.5 MILES
N 25 W 2 MILES
S 65 W 1/2 MILE
1 MILE
S 60 W
S 25 E 2 MILES
ONE STATUTE MILE
Outbound: April 18-20, 1805
Clark's Return: August 7, 1806
Lewis' Return: August 11, 1806
Modern Data: 1978-1979
EXPLORATIONS OF LEWIS AND CLARK 1804 - 1806
CARTOGRAPHIC RECONSTRUCTION
WILD COW CREEK
UTM ZONE 13
MAP NUMBER 172
North Dakota
CONTOUR INTERVAL 100 FEET

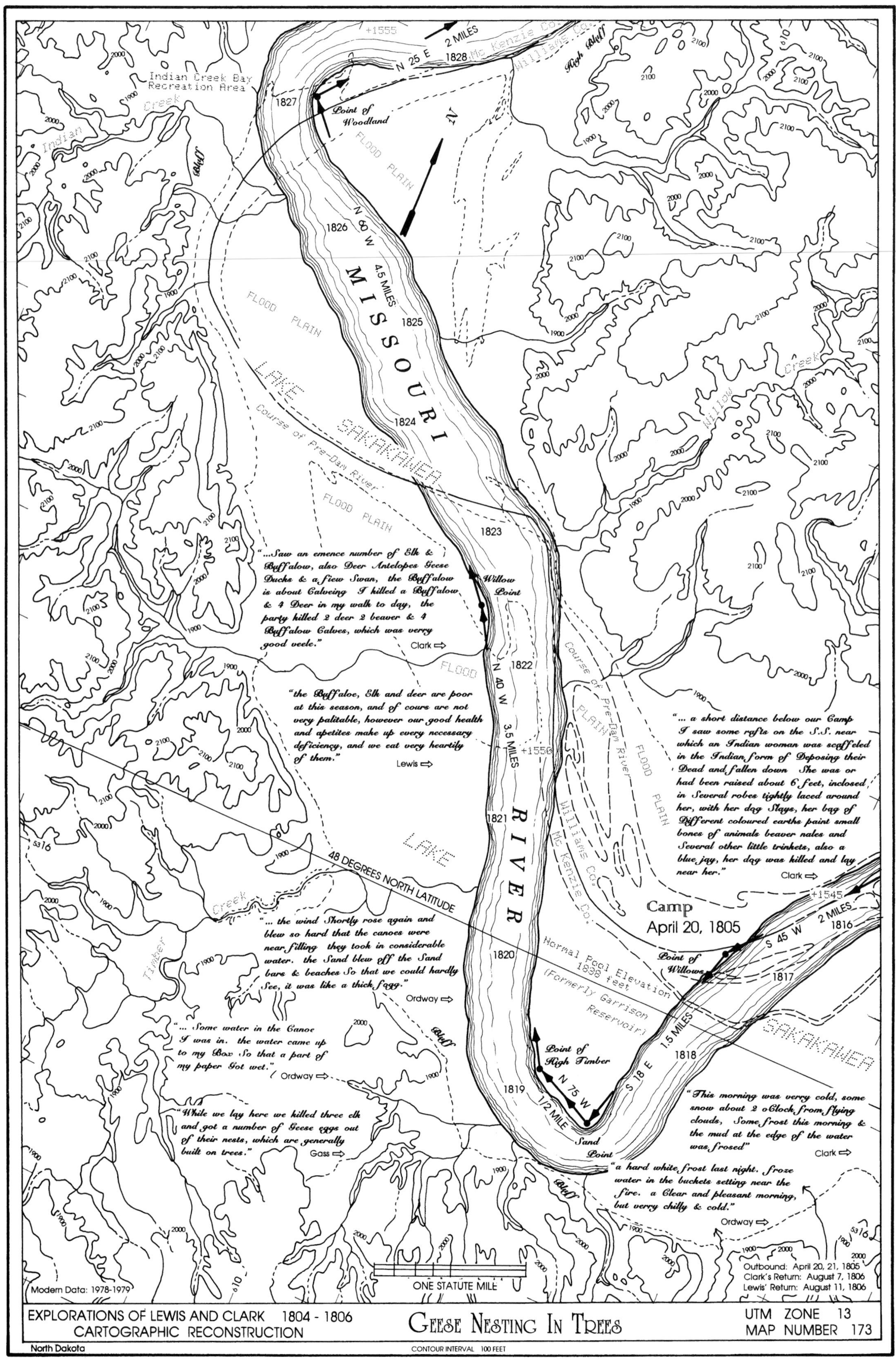

Indian Creek Bay Recreation Area
Indian Creek
High Bluff
Mc Kenzie Co.
Williams Co.
N 25 E 2 MILES
Point of Woodland
FLOOD PLAIN
N 60 W 4.5 MILES
MISSOURI RIVER
LAKE SAKAKAWEA
Course of Pre-Dam River
"...Saw an emence number of Elk & Buffalow, also Deer Antelopes Geese Ducks & a fiew Swan, the Buffalow is about Calveing I killed a Buffalow, & 4 Deer in my walk to day, the party killed 2 deer 2 beaver & 4 Buffalow Calves, which was very good veele." Clark
Willow Point
"the Buffaloe, Elk and deer are poor at this season, and of cours are not very palitable, however our good health and apetites make up every necessary deficiency, and we eat very heartily of them." Lewis
N 40 W 3.5 MILES
"... a short distance below our Camp I saw some rafts on the S.S. near which an Indian woman was scaffeled in the Indian form of Deposing their Dead and fallen down She was or had been raised about 6 feet, inclosed in Several robes tightly laced around her, with her dog Slays, her bag of Different coloured earths paint small bones of animals beaver nales and Several other little trinkets, also a blue jay, her dog was killed and lay near her." Clark
48 DEGREES NORTH LATITUDE
Camp April 20, 1805
S 45 W 2 MILES
Point of Willows
"... the wind Shortly rose again and blew so hard that the canoes were near filling they took in considerable water. the Sand blew off the Sand bars & beaches So that we could hardly See, it was like a thick fogg." Ordway
Normal Pool Elevation 1838 feet (Formerly Garrison Reservoir)
Timber Creek
"... Some water in the Canoe I was in. the water came up to my Box So that a part of my paper Got wet." Ordway
Point of High Timber
N 75 W 1/2 MILE
S 18 E 1.5 MILES
Sand Point
Bluff
"While we lay here we killed three elk and got a number of Geese eggs out of their nests, which are generally built on trees." Gass
"This morning was verry cold, some snow about 2 oClock from flying clouds, Some frost this morning & the mud at the edge of the water was frosed" Clark
"a hard white frost last night. froze water in the buckets setting near the fire. a Clear and pleasant morning, but verry chilly & cold." Ordway
ONE STATUTE MILE
Modern Data: 1978-1979
Outbound: April 20, 21, 1805
Clark's Return: August 7, 1806
Lewis' Return: August 11, 1806
EXPLORATIONS OF LEWIS AND CLARK 1804 - 1806
CARTOGRAPHIC RECONSTRUCTION
GEESE NESTING IN TREES
UTM ZONE 13
MAP NUMBER 173
North Dakota
CONTOUR INTERVAL 100 FEET

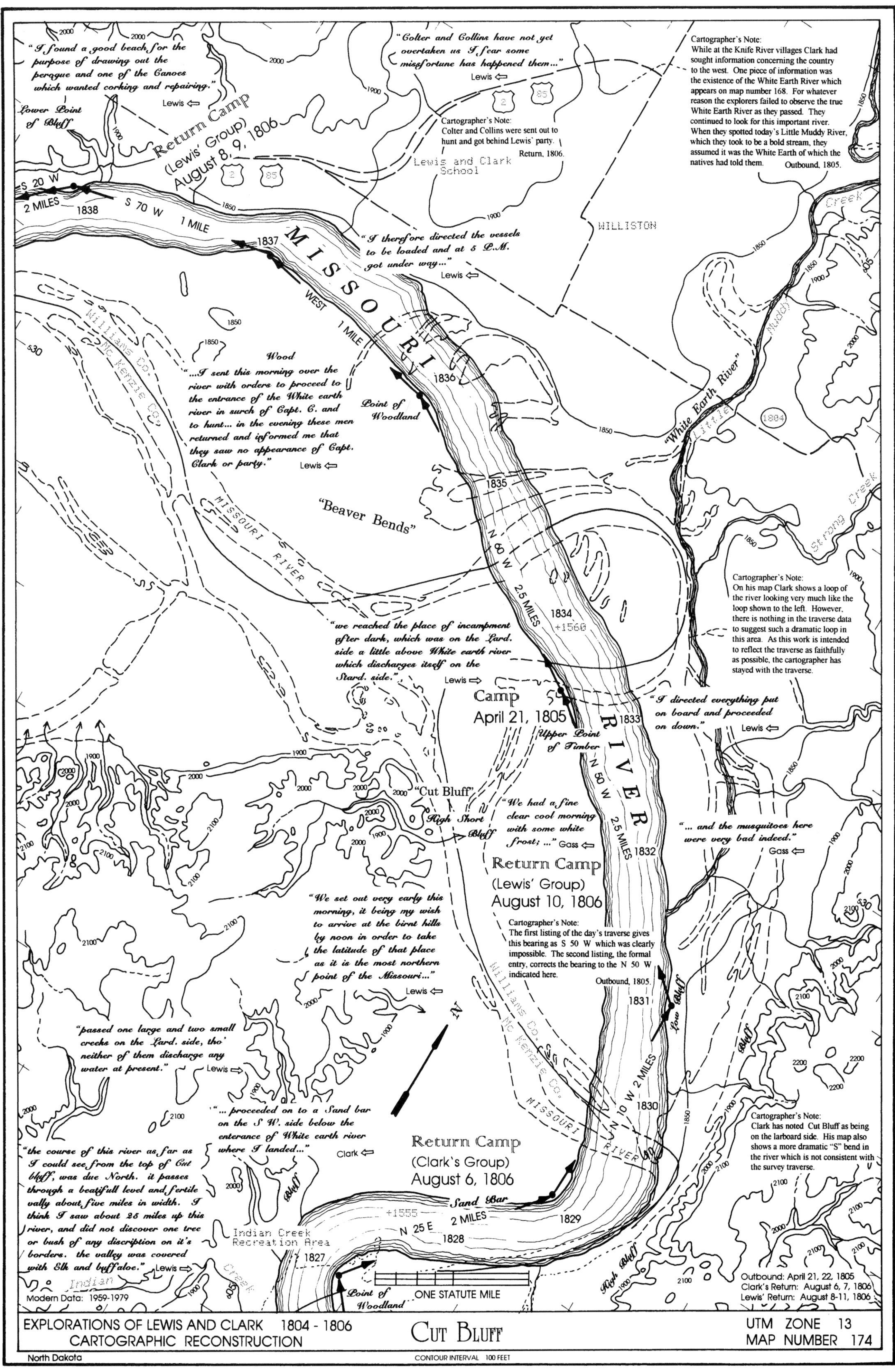

"I found a good beach for the purpose of drawing out the perogue and one of the Canoes which wanted corking and repairing." Lewis ⇦
Lower Point of Bluff
Return Camp (Lewis' Group) August 8, 9, 1806
"Colter and Collins have not yet overtaken us I fear some missfortune has happened them..." Lewis ⇦
Cartographer's Note: Colter and Collins were sent out to hunt and got behind Lewis' party. Return, 1806.
Lewis and Clark School
Cartographer's Note: While at the Knife River villages Clark had sought information concerning the country to the west. One piece of information was the existence of the White Earth River which appears on map number 168. For whatever reason the explorers failed to observe the true White Earth River as they passed. They continued to find this important river. When they spotted today's Little Muddy River, which they took to be a bold stream, they assumed it was the White Earth of which the natives had told them. Outbound, 1805.
WILLISTON
S 20 W
2 MILES
1838
S 70 W
1 MILE
1837
MISSOURI
"I therefore directed the vessels to be loaded and at 5 P.M. got under way..." Lewis ⇦
WEST
1 MILE
Williams Co.
Mc Kenzie Co.
Wood
"...I sent this morning over the river with orders to proceed to the entrance of the White earth river in surch of Capt. C. and to hunt... in the evening these men returned and informed me that they saw no appearance of Capt. Clark or party." Lewis ⇦
Point of Woodland
1836
Little Muddy Creek
"White Earth River"
1835
"Beaver Bends"
MISSOURI RIVER
N 60 W
2.5 MILES
1834
+1560
Strong Creek
Cartographer's Note: On his map Clark shows a loop of the river looking very much like the loop shown to the left. However, there is nothing in the traverse data to suggest such a dramatic loop in this area. As this work is intended to reflect the traverse as faithfully as possible, the cartographer has stayed with the traverse.
"we reached the place of incampment after dark, which was on the Lard. side a little above White earth river which discharges itself on the Stard. side." Lewis ⇨
Camp April 21, 1805
Upper Point of Timber
1833
RIVER
"I directed everything put on board and proceeded on down." Lewis ⇦
"Cut Bluff"
High Short Bluff
"We had a fine clear cool morning with some white frost; ..." Gass ⇦
N 50 W
2.5 MILES
1832
"... and the musquitoes here were very bad indeed." Gass ⇦
Return Camp (Lewis' Group) August 10, 1806
"We set out very early this morning, it being my wish to arrive at the birnt hills by noon in order to take the latitude of that place as it is the most northern point of the Missouri..." Lewis ⇦
Cartographer's Note: The first listing of the day's traverse gives this bearing as S 50 W which was clearly impossible. The second listing, the formal entry, corrects the bearing to the N 50 W indicated here. Outbound, 1805.
1831
Low Bluff
N
"passed one large and two small creeks on the Lard. side, tho' neither of them discharge any water at present." Lewis ⇨
N 10 W 2 MILES
1830
Bluff
"... proceeded on to a Sand bar on the S W. side below the enterance of White earth river where I landed..." Clark ⇦
Cartographer's Note: Clark has noted Cut Bluff as being on the larboard side. His map also shows a more dramatic "S" bend in the river which is not consistent with the survey traverse.
"the course of this river as far as I could see from the top of Cut bluff, was due North. it passes through a beatifull level and fertile vally about five miles in width. I think I saw about 25 miles up this river, and did not discover one tree or bush of any discription on it's borders. the valley was covered with Elk and buffaloe." Lewis ⇨
Return Camp (Clark's Group) August 6, 1806
Sand Bar
+1555
N 25 E
2 MILES
1829
1828
1827
Indian Creek Recreation Area
Indian Creek
Point of Woodland
ONE STATUTE MILE
High Bluff
Modern Data: 1959-1979
Outbound: April 21, 22, 1805
Clark's Return: August 6, 7, 1806
Lewis' Return: August 8-11, 1806
EXPLORATIONS OF LEWIS AND CLARK 1804 - 1806
CARTOGRAPHIC RECONSTRUCTION
CUT BLUFF
UTM ZONE 13
MAP NUMBER 174
North Dakota
CONTOUR INTERVAL 100 FEET

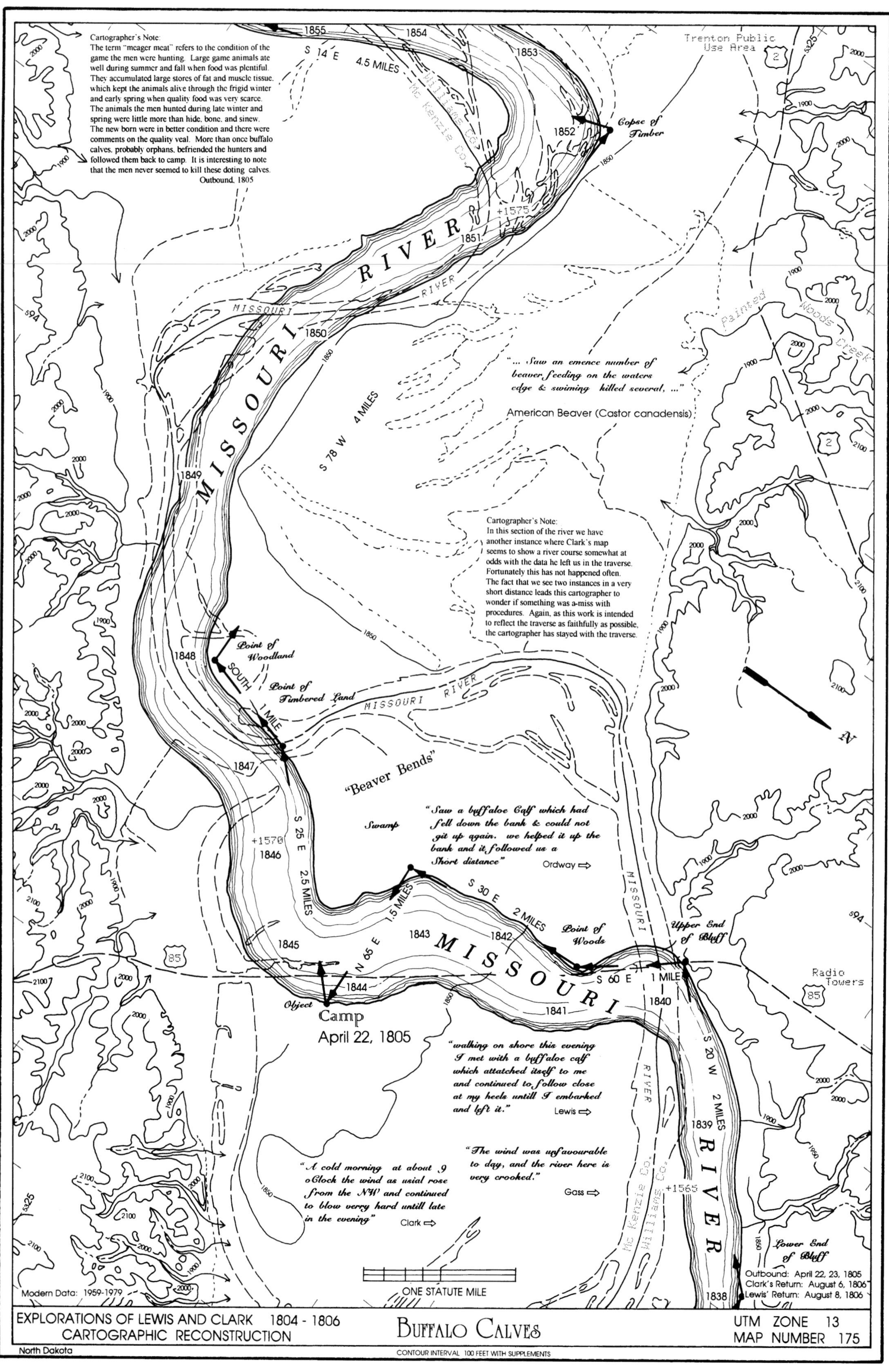
Cartographer's Note:
The term "meager meat" refers to the condition of the game the men were hunting. Large game animals ate well during summer and fall when food was plentiful. They accumulated large stores of fat and muscle tissue, which kept the animals alive through the frigid winter and early spring when quality food was very scarce. The animals the men hunted during late winter and spring were little more than hide, bone, and sinew. The new born were in better condition and there were comments on the quality veal. More than once buffalo calves, probably orphans, befriended the hunters and followed them back to camp. It is interesting to note that the men never seemed to kill these doting calves.
Outbound, 1805
Trenton Public Use Area
Copse of Timber
MISSOURI RIVER
Painted Woods Creek
"... Saw an emence number of beaver feeding on the waters edge & swiming killed several, ..."
American Beaver (Castor canadensis)
Cartographer's Note:
In this section of the river we have another instance where Clark's map seems to show a river course somewhat at odds with the data he left us in the traverse. Fortunately this has not happened often. The fact that we see two instances in a very short distance leads this cartographer to wonder if something was a-miss with procedures. Again, as this work is intended to reflect the traverse as faithfully as possible, the cartographer has stayed with the traverse.
Point of Woodland
Point of Timbered Land
"Beaver Bends"
Swamp
"Saw a buffaloe Calf which had fell down the bank & could not git up again. we helped it up the bank and it followed us a Short distance"
Ordway ⇨
Point of Woods
Upper End of Bluff
Radio Towers
Object
Camp
April 22, 1805
"walking on shore this evening I met with a buffaloe calf which attatched itself to me and continued to follow close at my heels untill I embarked and left it."
Lewis ⇨
"The wind was unfavourable to day, and the river here is very crooked."
Gass ⇨
"A cold morning at about 9 oClock the wind as usial rose from the NW and continued to blow verry hard untill late in the evening"
Clark ⇨
Mc Kenzie Co.
Williams Co.
Lower End of Bluff
Outbound: April 22, 23, 1805
Clark's Return: August 6, 1806
Lewis' Return: August 8, 1806
ONE STATUTE MILE
Modern Data: 1959-1979
EXPLORATIONS OF LEWIS AND CLARK 1804 - 1806
CARTOGRAPHIC RECONSTRUCTION
BUFFALO CALVES
UTM ZONE 13
MAP NUMBER 175
North Dakota
CONTOUR INTERVAL 100 FEET WITH SUPPLEMENTS

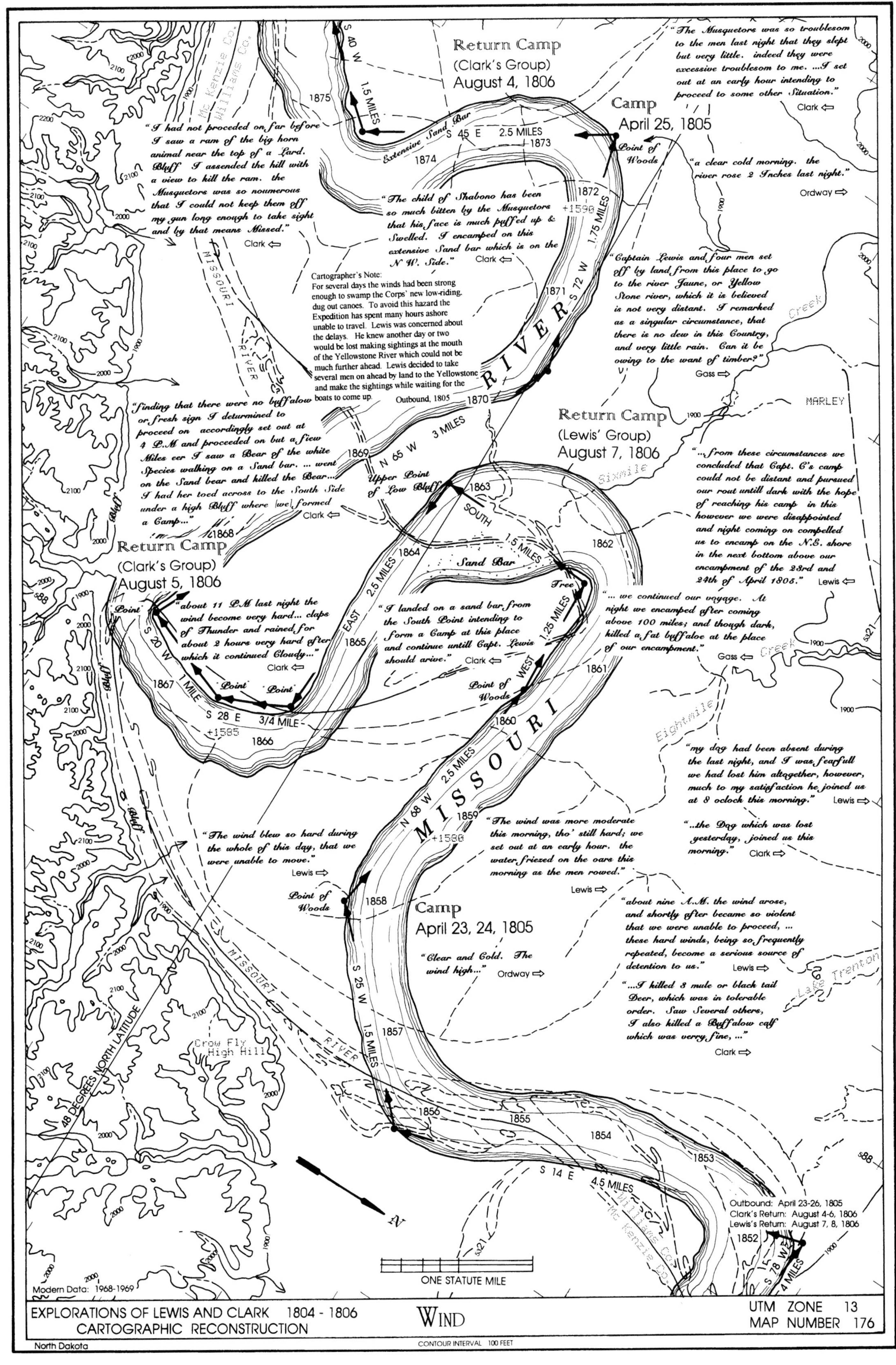

Return Camp
(Clark's Group)
August 4, 1806
"The Musquetors was so troublesom to the men last night that they slept but very little. indeed they were excessive troublesom to me. ...I set out at an early hour intending to proceed to some other Situation."
Clark ⇦
Camp
April 25, 1805
Point of Woods
"a clear cold morning. the river rose 2 Inches last night."
Ordway ⇨
"I had not proceeded on far before I saw a ram of the big horn animal near the top of a Lard. Bluff I assended the hill with a view to kill the ram. the Musquetors was so noumerous that I could not keep them off my gun long enough to take sight and by that means Missed."
Clark ⇦
"The child of Shabono has been so much bitten by the Musquetors that his face is much puffed up & Swelled. I encamped on this extensive Sand bar which is on the N. W. Side."
Clark ⇦
Extensive Sand Bar
S 45 E 2.5 MILES
S 40 W 1.5 MILES
1.75 MILES
S 72 W
Cartographer's Note:
For several days the winds had been strong enough to swamp the Corps' new low-riding, dug out canoes. To avoid this hazard the Expedition has spent many hours ashore unable to travel. Lewis was concerned about the delays. He knew another day or two would be lost making sightings at the mouth of the Yellowstone River which could not be much further ahead. Lewis decided to take several men on ahead by land to the Yellowstone and make the sightings while waiting for the boats to come up.
Outbound, 1805
"Captain Lewis and four men set off by land from this place to go to the river Jaune, or Yellow Stone river, which it is believed is not very distant. I remarked as a singular circumstance, that there is no dew in this Country, and very little rain. Can it be owing to the want of timber?"
Gass ⇨
RIVER
MISSOURI RIVER
MARLEY
Creek
"finding that there were no buffalow or fresh sign I deturmined to proceed on accordingly set out at 4 P.M and proceeded on but a fiew Miles eer I saw a Bear of the white Species walking on a Sand bar. ... went on the Sand bear and killed the Bear... I had her toed across to the South Side under a high Bluff where [we] formed a Camp..."
Clark ⇦
N 65 W 3 MILES
Upper Point of Low Bluff
SOUTH
Return Camp
(Lewis' Group)
August 7, 1806
Sixmile
"...from these circumstances we concluded that Capt. C's camp could not be distant and pursued our rout untill dark with the hope of reaching his camp in this however we were disappointed and night coming on compelled us to encamp on the N.E. shore in the next bottom above our encampment of the 23rd and 24th of April 1805."
Lewis ⇦
Return Camp
(Clark's Group)
August 5, 1806
Point
"about 11 P.M last night the wind become very hard... claps of Thunder and rained for about 2 hours very hard after which it continued Cloudy..."
Clark ⇦
EAST 2.5 MILES
1.5 MILES
Sand Bar
Tree
"I landed on a sand bar from the South Point intending to form a Camp at this place and continue untill Capt. Lewis should arive."
Clark ⇦
1.25 MILES
WEST
"... we continued our voyage. At night we encamped after coming above 100 miles; and though dark, killed a fat buffaloe at the place of our encampment."
Gass ⇦
Creek
S 20 W
1 MILE
Point
Point
S 28 E 3/4 MILE
Point of Woods
Bluff
Eightmile
"my dog had been absent during the last night, and I was fearfull we had lost him altogether, however, much to my satisfaction he joined us at 8 oclock this morning."
Lewis ⇨
"..the Dog which was lost yesterday, joined us this morning."
Clark ⇨
N 68 W 2.5 MILES
MISSOURI
"The wind blew so hard during the whole of this day, that we were unable to move."
Lewis ⇨
"The wind was more moderate this morning, tho' still hard; we set out at an early hour. the water friezed on the oars this morning as the men rowed."
Lewis ⇨
Point of Woods
Camp
April 23, 24, 1805
"Clear and Cold. The wind high..."
Ordway ⇨
"about nine A.M. the wind arose, and shortly after became so violent that we were unable to proceed, ... these hard winds, being so frequently repeated, become a serious source of detention to us."
Lewis ⇨
"...I killed 3 mule or black tail Deer, which was in tolerable order. Saw Several others, I also killed a Buffalow calf which was verry fine, ..."
Clark ⇨
Lake Trenton
S 25 W
1.5 MILES
Crow Fly High Hill
MISSOURI RIVER
48 DEGREES NORTH LATITUDE
S 14 E 4.5 MILES
Williams Co.
Mc Kenzie Co.
N
Outbound: April 23-26, 1805
Clark's Return: August 4-6, 1806
Lewis's Return: August 7, 8, 1806
S 78 W
4 MILES
ONE STATUTE MILE
Modern Data: 1968-1969
EXPLORATIONS OF LEWIS AND CLARK 1804 - 1806
CARTOGRAPHIC RECONSTRUCTION
WIND
UTM ZONE 13
MAP NUMBER 176
North Dakota
CONTOUR INTERVAL 100 FEET

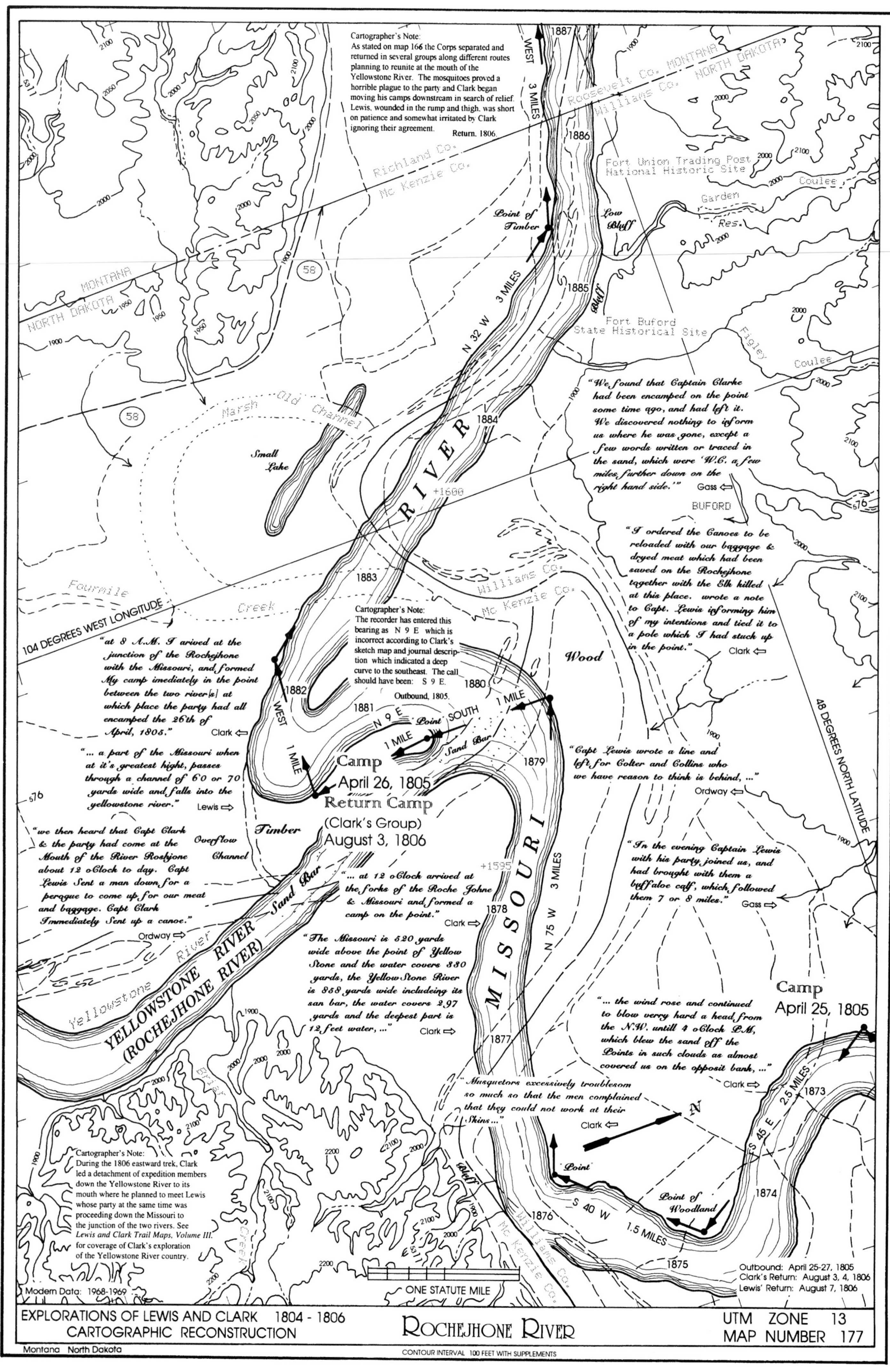

Cartographer's Note:
As stated on map 166 the Corps separated and returned in several groups along different routes planning to reunite at the mouth of the Yellowstone River. The mosquitoes proved a horrible plague to the party and Clark began moving his camps downstream in search of relief. Lewis, wounded in the rump and thigh, was short on patience and somewhat irritated by Clark ignoring their agreement. Return. 1806.
WEST
3 MILES
1887
1886
1885
1884
1883
1882
1881
1880
1879
1878
1877
1876
1875
1874
1873
Roosevelt Co. MONTANA
Williams Co. NORTH DAKOTA
Richland Co.
Mc Kenzie Co.
Fort Union Trading Post
National Historic Site
Garden
Coulee
Res.
Point of Timber
Low Bluff
Bluff
MONTANA
NORTH DAKOTA
58
N 32 W 3 MILES
Fort Buford
State Historical Site
Figley
Coulee
Marsh
Old Channel
Small Lake
RIVER
+1600
"We found that Captain Clarke had been encamped on the point some time ago, and had left it. We discovered nothing to inform us where he was gone, except a few words written or traced in the sand, which were 'W.C. a few miles further down on the right hand side.'" Gass
BUFORD
"I ordered the Canoes to be reloaded with our baggage & dryed meat which had been saved on the Rochejhone together with the Elk killed at this place. wrote a note to Capt. Lewis informing him of my intentions and tied it to a pole which I had stuck up in the point." Clark
Fourmile
Creek
Williams Co.
Mc Kenzie Co.
104 DEGREES WEST LONGITUDE
48 DEGREES NORTH LATITUDE
Cartographer's Note:
The recorder has entered this bearing as N 9 E which is incorrect according to Clark's sketch map and journal description which indicated a deep curve to the southeast. The call should have been: S 9 E.
Outbound, 1805.
Wood
"at 8 A.M. I arived at the junction of the Rochejhone with the Missouri, and formed My camp imediately in the point between the two river[s] at which place the party had all encamped the 26th of April, 1805." Clark
N 9 E
Point
SOUTH
1 MILE
1 MILE
Sand Bar
WEST
1 MILE
"... a part of the Missouri when at it's greatest hight, passes through a channel of 60 or 70 yards wide and falls into the yellowstone river." Lewis
Camp
April 26, 1805
Return Camp
(Clark's Group)
August 3, 1806
"Capt Lewis wrote a line and left for Colter and Collins who we have reason to think is behind, ..." Ordway
"we then heard that Capt Clark & the party had come at the Mouth of the River Roshjone about 12 oClock to day. Capt Lewis Sent a man down for a perogue to come up for our meat and baggage. Capt Clark Immediately Sent up a canoe." Ordway
Timber
Overflow Channel
"... at 12 oClock arrived at the forks of the Roche Johne & Missouri and formed a camp on the point." Clark
+1595
MISSOURI
3 MILES
N 75 W
"In the evening Captain Lewis with his party joined us, and had brought with them a buffaloe calf, which followed them 7 or 8 miles." Gass
Sand Bar
YELLOWSTONE RIVER
(ROCHEJHONE RIVER)
Yellowstone River
"The Missouri is 520 yards wide above the point of Yellow Stone and the water covers 330 yards, the Yellow Stone River is 858 yards wide includeing its san bar, the water covers 297 yards and the deepest part is 12 feet water, ..." Clark
Camp
April 25, 1805
"... the wind rose and continued to blow very hard a head from the N.W. untill 4 oClock P.M. which blew the sand off the Points in such clouds as almost covered us on the opposit bank, ..." Clark
S 45 E 2.5 MILES
"Musquetors excessively troublesom so much so that the men complained that they could not work at their Skins..." Clark
N
Point
S 40 W 1.5 MILES
Point of Woodland
Cartographer's Note:
During the 1806 eastward trek, Clark led a detachment of expedition members down the Yellowstone River to its mouth where he planned to meet Lewis whose party at the same time was proceeding down the Missouri to the junction of the two rivers. See Lewis and Clark Trail Maps, Volume III. for coverage of Clark's exploration of the Yellowstone River country.
Bluff
Creek
Mc Kenzie Co.
Williams Co.
Modern Data: 1968-1969
ONE STATUTE MILE
Outbound: April 25-27, 1805
Clark's Return: August 3, 4, 1806
Lewis' Return: August 7, 1806
EXPLORATIONS OF LEWIS AND CLARK 1804 - 1806
CARTOGRAPHIC RECONSTRUCTION
ROCHEJHONE RIVER
UTM ZONE 13
MAP NUMBER 177
Montana North Dakota
CONTOUR INTERVAL 100 FEET WITH SUPPLEMENTS

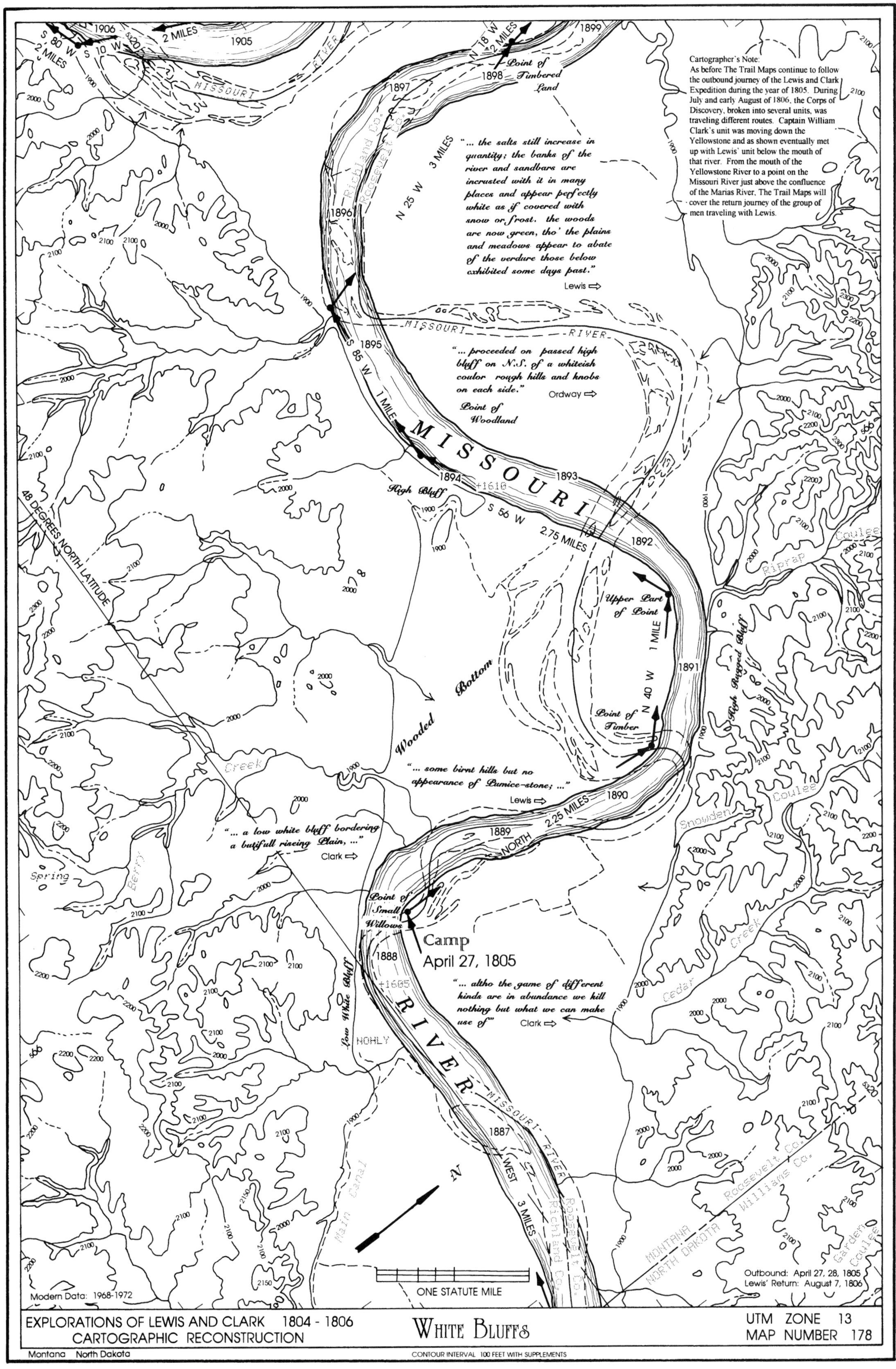
Cartographer's Note:
As before The Trail Maps continue to follow the outbound journey of the Lewis and Clark Expedition during the year of 1805. During July and early August of 1806, the Corps of Discovery, broken into several units, was traveling different routes. Captain William Clark's unit was moving down the Yellowstone and as shown eventually met up with Lewis' unit below the mouth of that river. From the mouth of the Yellowstone River to a point on the Missouri River just above the confluence of the Marias River, The Trail Maps will cover the return journey of the group of men traveling with Lewis.
"... the salts still increase in quantity; the banks of the river and sandbars are incrusted with it in many places and appear perfectly white as if covered with snow or frost. the woods are now green, tho' the plains and meadows appear to abate of the verdure those below exhibited some days past."
Lewis ⇨
"... proceeded on passed high bluff on N.S. of a whiteish coulor rough hills and knobs on each side."
Ordway ⇨
"... some birnt hills but no appearance of Pumice-stone; ..."
Lewis ⇨
"... a low white bluff bordering a butifull riseing Plain, ..."
Clark ⇨
"... altho the game of different kinds are in abundance we kill nothing but what we can make use of"
Clark ⇨
Camp
April 27, 1805
Point of Timbered Land
Point of Woodland
High Bluff
Upper Part of Point
Point of Timber
Wooded Bottom
High Rugged Bluff
Point of Small Willows
Low White Bluff
MISSOURI RIVER
48 DEGREES NORTH LATITUDE
Riprap Coulee
Snowden Coulee
Cedar Creek
Berry Spring Creek
Main Canal
Garden Coulee
Richland Co.
Roosevelt Co.
Williams Co.
MONTANA
NORTH DAKOTA
ONE STATUTE MILE
Outbound: April 27, 28, 1805
Lewis' Return: August 7, 1806
Modern Data: 1968-1972
EXPLORATIONS OF LEWIS AND CLARK 1804 - 1806
CARTOGRAPHIC RECONSTRUCTION
WHITE BLUFFS
UTM ZONE 13
MAP NUMBER 178
Montana North Dakota
CONTOUR INTERVAL 100 FEET WITH SUPPLEMENTS

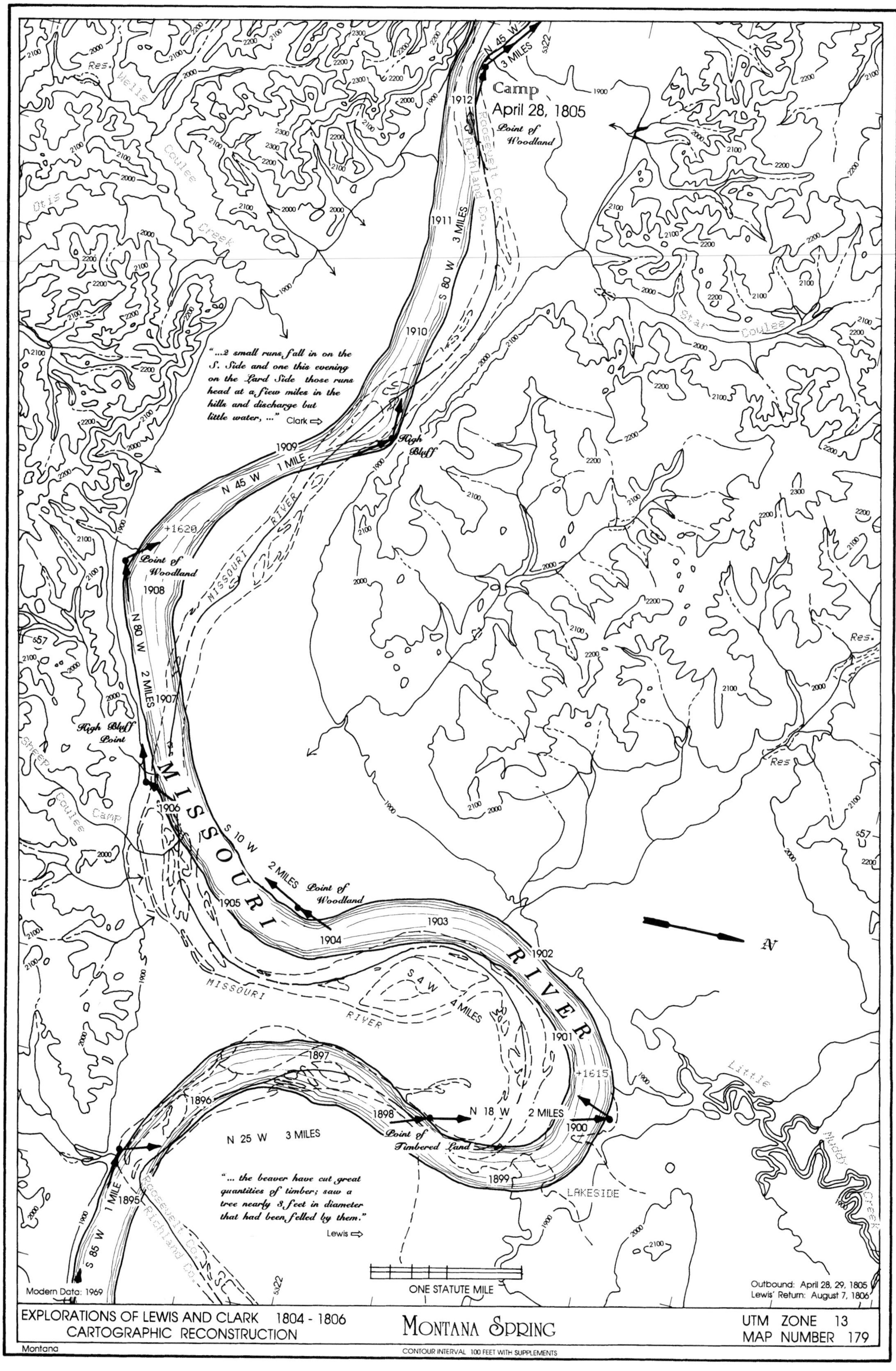
Camp
April 28, 1805
Point of Woodland
"...2 small runs fall in on the S. Side and one this evening on the Lard Side those runs head at a fiew miles in the hills and discharge but little water, ..." Clark ⇨
High Bluff
N 45 W 1 MILE
Point of Woodland
N 80 W 2 MILES
High Bluff Point
Camp
MISSOURI
S 10 W 2 MILES
Point of Woodland
RIVER
S 4 W 4 MILES
N 18 W 2 MILES
Point of Timbered Land
N 25 W 3 MILES
S 85 W 1 MILE
N 45 W 3 MILES
S 80 W 3 MILES
"... the beaver have cut great quantities of timber; saw a tree nearly 3 feet in diameter that had been felled by them." Lewis ⇨
LAKESIDE
Little Muddy Creek
Star Coulee
Otis Creek
Wells Coulee
Sheep Coulee
Roosevelt Co.
Richland Co.
ONE STATUTE MILE
Modern Data: 1969
Outbound: April 28, 29, 1805
Lewis' Return: August 7, 1806
EXPLORATIONS OF LEWIS AND CLARK 1804 - 1806
CARTOGRAPHIC RECONSTRUCTION
MONTANA SPRING
UTM ZONE 13
MAP NUMBER 179
Montana
CONTOUR INTERVAL 100 FEET WITH SUPPLEMENTS

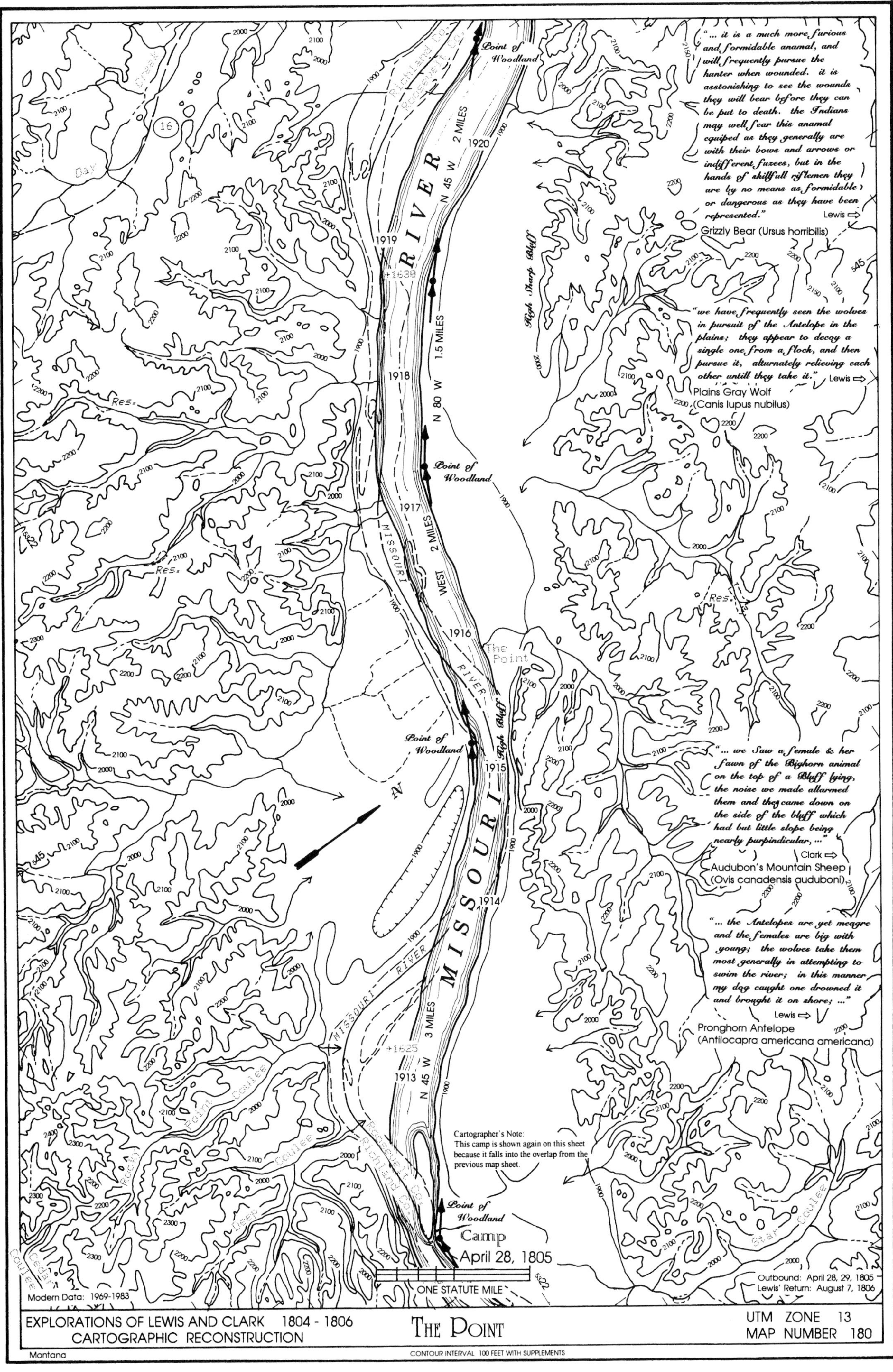
"... it is a much more furious and formidable anamal, and will frequently pursue the hunter when wounded. it is asstonishing to see the wounds they will bear before they can be put to death. the Indians may well fear this anamal equiped as they generally are with their bows and arrows or indifferent fuzees, but in the hands of skillfull riflemen they are by no means as formidable or dangerous as they have been represented."
Lewis
Grizzly Bear (Ursus horribilis)
"we have frequently seen the wolves in pursuit of the Antelope in the plains; they appear to decoy a single one from a flock, and then pursue it, alturnately relieving each other untill they take it."
Lewis
Plains Gray Wolf (Canis lupus nubilus)
"... we Saw a female & her fawn of the Bighorn animal on the top of a Bluff lying, the noise we made allarmed them and they came down on the side of the bluff which had but little slope being nearly purpindicular, ..."
Clark
Audubon's Mountain Sheep (Ovis canadensis auduboni)
"... the Antelopes are yet meagre and the females are big with young; the wolves take them most generally in attempting to swim the river; in this manner my dog caught one drowned it and brought it on shore; ..."
Lewis
Pronghorn Antelope (Antilocapra americana americana)
Point of Woodland
Richland Co.
Roosevelt Co.
Creek
Day
Res.
RIVER
MISSOURI
N 45 W 2 MILES
N 80 W 1.5 MILES
WEST 2 MILES
N 45 W 3 MILES
High Sharp Bluff
High Bluff
The Point
Point Coulee
Rocky Coulee
Deep Coulee
Cedar Coulee
Star Coulee
Cartographer's Note: This camp is shown again on this sheet because it falls into the overlap from the previous map sheet.
Camp
April 28, 1805
ONE STATUTE MILE
Modern Data: 1969-1983
Outbound: April 28, 29, 1805
Lewis' Return: August 7, 1806
EXPLORATIONS OF LEWIS AND CLARK 1804 - 1806
CARTOGRAPHIC RECONSTRUCTION
THE POINT
UTM ZONE 13
MAP NUMBER 180
Montana
CONTOUR INTERVAL 100 FEET WITH SUPPLEMENTS

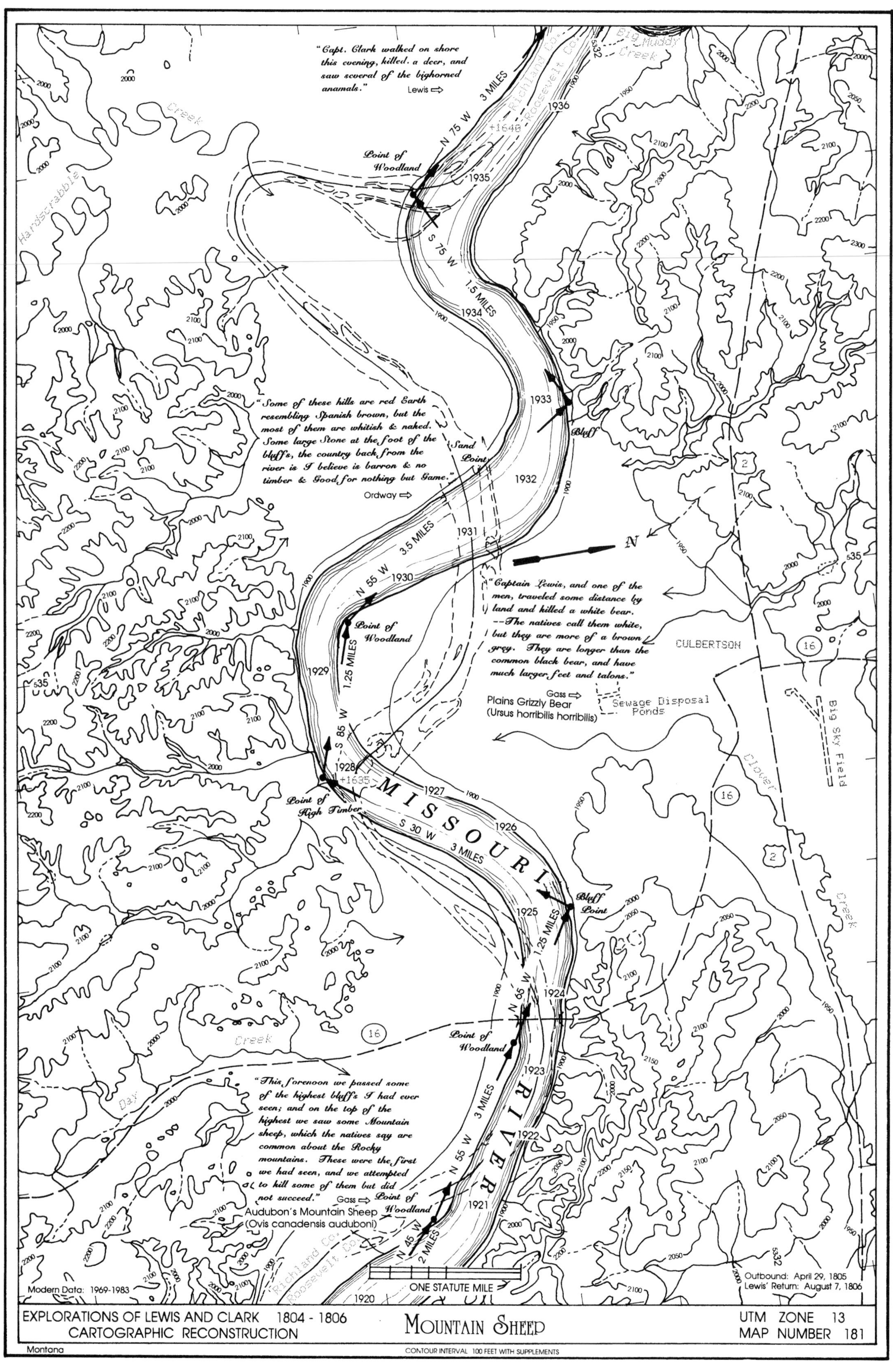
"Capt. Clark walked on shore this evening, killed a deer, and saw several of the bighorned anamals."
Lewis ⇨
Big Muddy Creek
Richland Co.
Roosevelt Co.
Hardscrabble Creek
N 75 W 3 MILES
Point of Woodland
S 75 W 1.5 MILES
"Some of these hills are red Earth resembling Spanish brown, but the most of them are whitish & naked. Some large Stone at the foot of the bluffs, the country back from the river is I believe is barron & no timber & Good for nothing but Game."
Ordway ⇨
Sand Point
Bluff
N 55 W 3.5 MILES
N
"Captain Lewis, and one of the men, traveled some distance by land and killed a white bear. --The natives call them white, but they are more of a brown grey. They are longer than the common black bear, and have much larger feet and talons."
Gass ⇨
Plains Grizzly Bear
(Ursus horribilis horribilis)
CULBERTSON
Sewage Disposal Ponds
Big Sky Field
Clover Creek
Point of Woodland
1.25 MILES
S 85 W
Point of High Timber
MISSOURI
S 30 W 3 MILES
Bluff Point
1.25 MILES
N 65 W
Point of Woodland
RIVER
Day Creek
"This forenoon we passed some of the highest bluffs I had ever seen; and on the top of the highest we saw some Mountain sheep, which the natives say are common about the Rocky mountains. These were the first we had seen, and we attempted to kill some of them but did not succeed."
Gass ⇨
Audubon's Mountain Sheep
(Ovis canadensis auduboni)
Point of Woodland
N 55 W 3 MILES
N 45 W 2 MILES
ONE STATUTE MILE
Modern Data: 1969-1983
Outbound: April 29, 1805
Lewis' Return: August 7, 1806
EXPLORATIONS OF LEWIS AND CLARK 1804 - 1806
CARTOGRAPHIC RECONSTRUCTION
MOUNTAIN SHEEP
UTM ZONE 13
MAP NUMBER 181
Montana
CONTOUR INTERVAL 100 FEET WITH SUPPLEMENTS

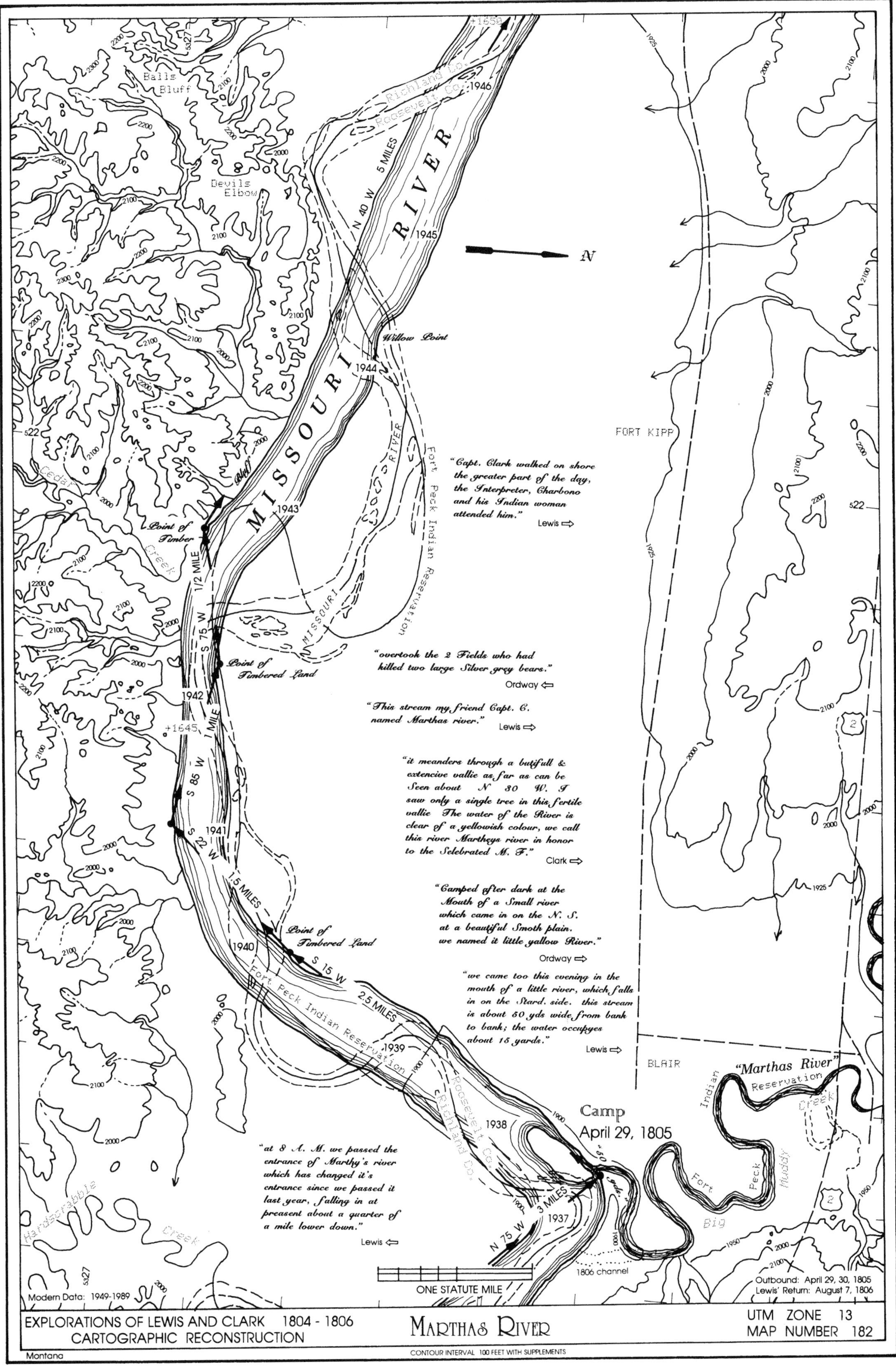

"Capt. Clark walked on shore the greater part of the day, the Interpreter, Charbono and his Indian woman attended him." Lewis
"overtook the 2 Fields who had killed two large Silver grey bears." Ordway
"This stream my friend Capt. C. named Marthas river." Lewis
"it meanders through a butifull & extencive vallie as far as can be Seen about N 30 W. I saw only a single tree in this fertile vallie The water of the River is clear of a yellowish colour, we call this river Martheys river in honor to the Selebrated M. F." Clark
"Camped after dark at the Mouth of a Small river which came in on the N. S. at a beautiful Smoth plain. we named it little yallow River." Ordway
"we came too this evening in the mouth of a little river, which falls in on the Stard. side. this stream is about 50 yds wide from bank to bank; the water occupyes about 15 yards." Lewis
"at 8 A. M. we passed the entrance of Marthy's river which has changed it's entrance since we passed it last year, falling in at preasent about a quarter of a mile lower down." Lewis
MISSOURI RIVER
Balls Bluff
Devils Elbow
Willow Point
Bluff
Point of Timber
Point of Timbered Land
Point of Timbered Land
Cedar Creek
Hardscrabble Creek
Richland Co.
Roosevelt Co.
Fort Peck Indian Reservation
FORT KIPP
BLAIR
"Marthas River"
Big Muddy Creek
Camp
April 29, 1805
N 40 W 5 MILES
1/2 MILE
S 75 W
1 MILE
S 85 W
S 22 W
1.5 MILES
S 15 W
2.5 MILES
3 MILES
N 75 W
50 yds
1806 channel
N
ONE STATUTE MILE
Modern Data: 1949-1989
Outbound: April 29, 30, 1805
Lewis' Return: August 7, 1806
EXPLORATIONS OF LEWIS AND CLARK 1804 - 1806
CARTOGRAPHIC RECONSTRUCTION
MARTHAS RIVER
UTM ZONE 13
MAP NUMBER 182
CONTOUR INTERVAL 100 FEET WITH SUPPLEMENTS
Montana

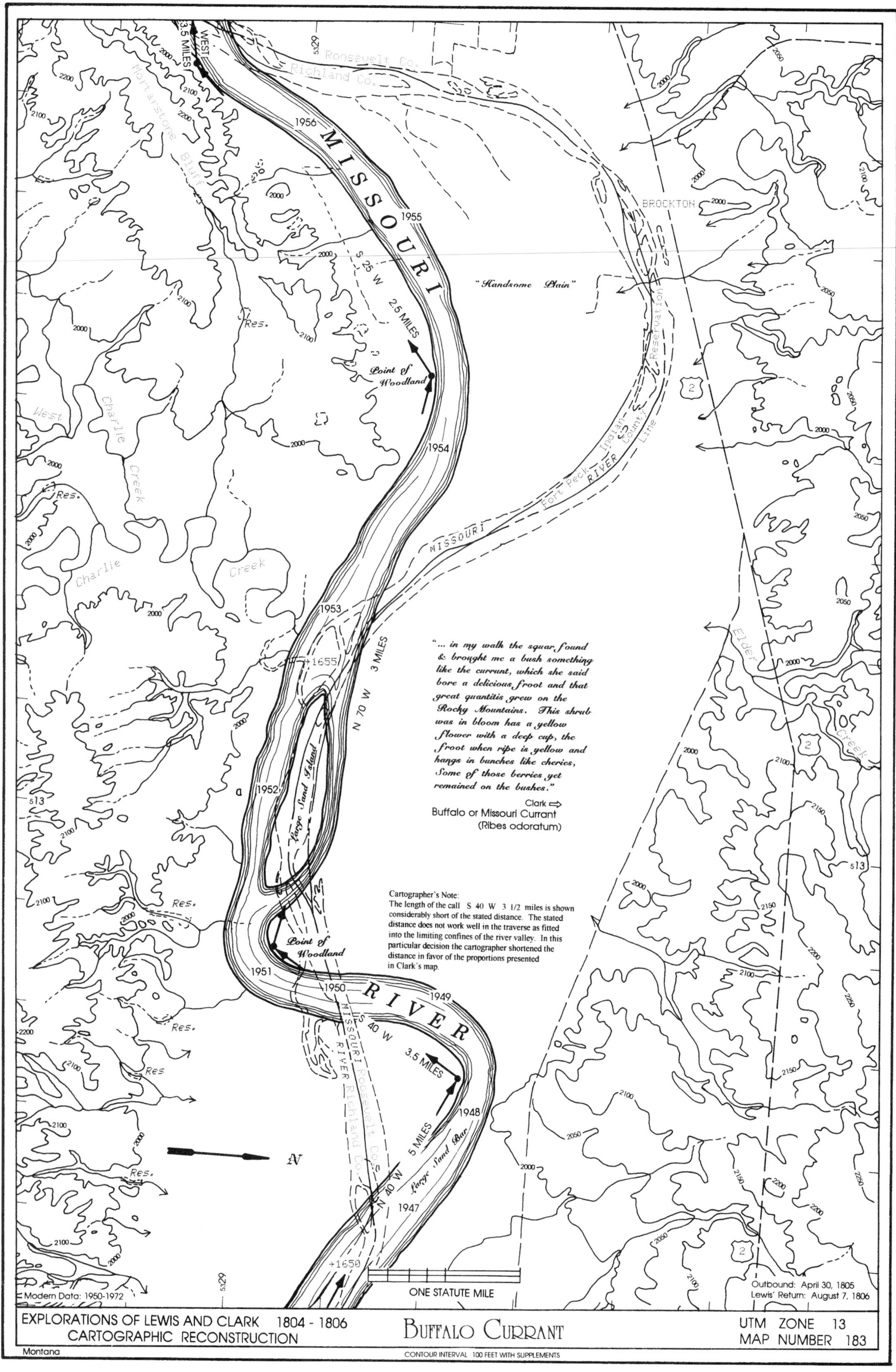

WEST
3.5 MILES
Roosevelt Co.
Richland Co.
Mortarstone Bluff
MISSOURI
1956
1955
1954
1953
1952
1951
1950
1949
1948
1947
BROCKTON
"Handsome Plain"
S 25 W
2.5 MILES
Point of Woodland
Res.
West Charlie Creek
Charlie Creek
Fort Peck Indian Reservation
MISSOURI RIVER
County Line
+1655
N 70 W 3 MILES
Large Sand Island
Elder Creek
"... in my walk the squar found & brought me a bush something like the currunt, which she said bore a delicious froot and that great quantitis grew on the Rocky Mountains. This shrub was in bloom has a yellow flower with a deep cup, the froot when ripe is yellow and hangs in bunches like cheries, Some of those berries yet remained on the bushes."
Clark ⇨
Buffalo or Missouri Currant
(Ribes odoratum)
Cartographer's Note:
The length of the call S 40 W 3 1/2 miles is shown considerably short of the stated distance. The stated distance does not work well in the traverse as fitted into the limiting confines of the river valley. In this particular decision the cartographer shortened the distance in favor of the proportions presented in Clark's map.
Point of Woodland
RIVER
S 40 W
3.5 MILES
5 MILES
Large Sand Bar
N 40 W
MISSOURI RIVER
Roosevelt Co.
Richland Co.
N
+1650
ONE STATUTE MILE
Modern Data: 1950-1972
Outbound: April 30, 1805
Lewis' Return: August 7, 1806
EXPLORATIONS OF LEWIS AND CLARK 1804 - 1806
CARTOGRAPHIC RECONSTRUCTION
BUFFALO CURRANT
UTM ZONE 13
MAP NUMBER 183
Montana
CONTOUR INTERVAL 100 FEET WITH SUPPLEMENTS

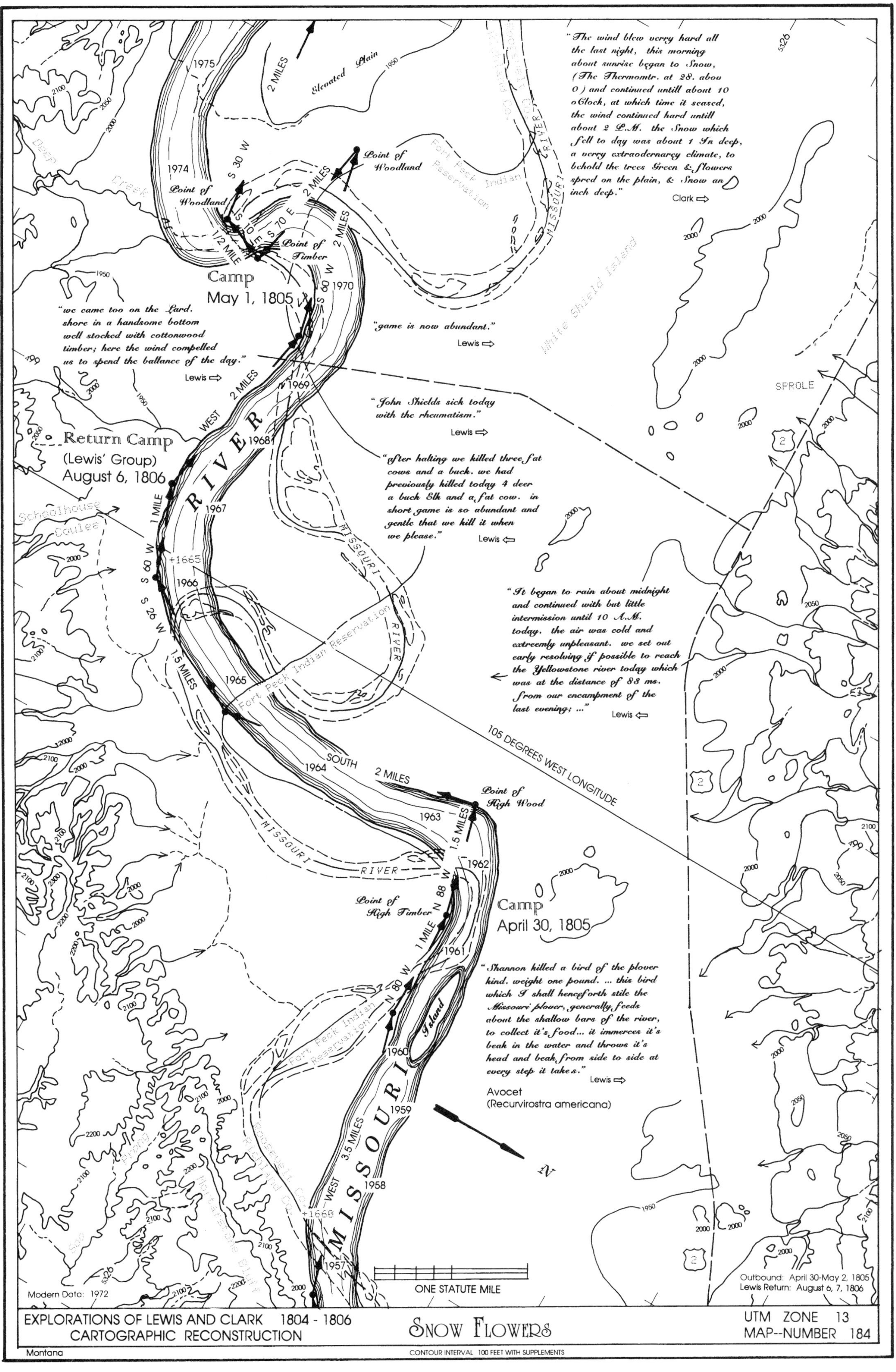

"The wind blew verry hard all the last night, this morning about sunrise began to Snow, (The Thermomtr. at 28. abov 0) and continued untill about 10 oClock, at which time it seased, the wind continued hard untill about 2 P.M. the Snow which fell to day was about 1 In deep, a verry extraodernarey climate, to behold the trees Green & flowers spred on the plain, & Snow an inch deep."
Clark ⇨
Elevated Plain
2 MILES
Deep Creek
Point of Woodland
Point of Woodland
S 30 W
S 10 E
S 70 E
2 MILES
1/2 MILE
Point of Timber
Fort Peck Indian Reservation
Roosevelt Co.
Richland Co.
MISSOURI RIVER
White Shield Island
Camp
May 1, 1805
"we came too on the Lard. shore in a handsome bottom well stocked with cottonwood timber; here the wind compelled us to spend the ballance of the day."
Lewis ⇨
"game is now abundant."
Lewis ⇨
"John Shields sick today with the rheumatism."
Lewis ⇨
SPROLE
Return Camp
(Lewis' Group)
August 6, 1806
RIVER
WEST
2 MILES
S 60 W
"after halting we killed three fat cows and a buck. we had previously killed today 4 deer a buck Elk and a fat cow. in short game is so abundant and gentle that we kill it when we please."
Lewis ⇦
Schoolhouse Coulee
1 MILE
S 60 W
S 26 W
+1665
1.5 MILES
MISSOURI RIVER
Fort Peck Indian Reservation
"It began to rain about midnight and continued with but little intermission until 10 A.M. today. the air was cold and extreemly unpleasant. we set out early resolving if possible to reach the Yellowstone river today which was at the distance of 88 ms. from our encampment of the last evening; ..."
Lewis ⇦
105 DEGREES WEST LONGITUDE
SOUTH
2 MILES
Point of High Wood
1.5 MILES
MISSOURI RIVER
N 88 W
Point of High Timber
Camp
April 30, 1805
1 MILE
N 80 W
Island
"Shannon killed a bird of the plover kind. weight one pound. ... this bird which I shall henceforth stile the Missouri plover, generally feeds about the shallow bars of the river, to collect it's food... it immerces it's beak in the water and throws it's head and beak from side to side at every step it takes."
Lewis ⇨
Avocet
(Recurvirostra americana)
Fort Peck Indian Reservation
MISSOURI
3.5 MILES
WEST
+1660
Roosevelt Co.
Richland Co.
Prong
Horseshoe Bluff
N
ONE STATUTE MILE
Modern Data: 1972
Outbound: April 30-May 2, 1805
Lewis Return: August 6, 7, 1806
EXPLORATIONS OF LEWIS AND CLARK 1804 - 1806
CARTOGRAPHIC RECONSTRUCTION
SNOW FLOWERS
UTM ZONE 13
MAP--NUMBER 184
Montana
CONTOUR INTERVAL 100 FEET WITH SUPPLEMENTS

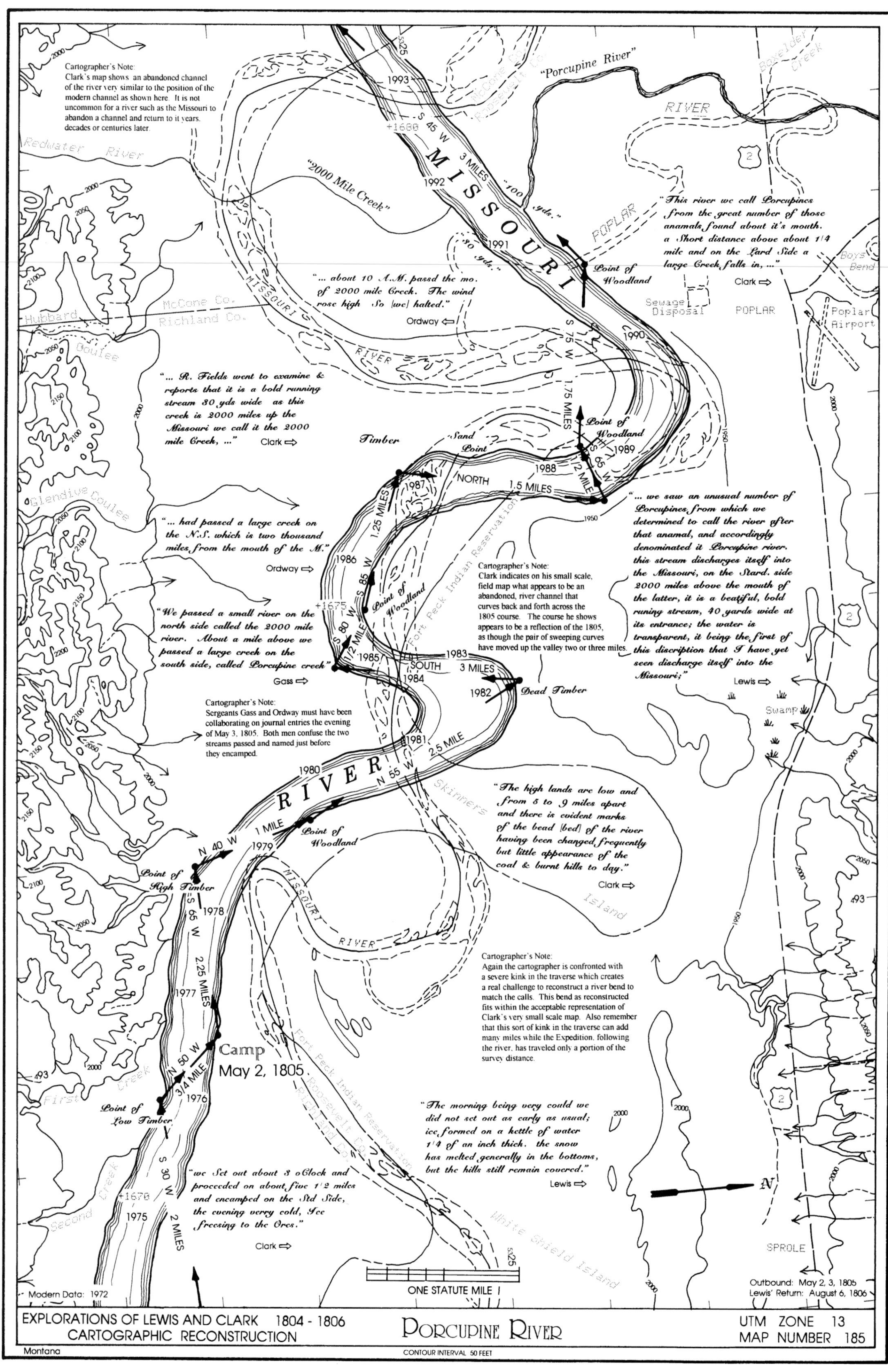

Cartographer's Note:
Clark's map shows an abandoned channel of the river very similar to the position of the modern channel as shown here. It is not uncommon for a river such as the Missouri to abandon a channel and return to it years, decades or centuries later.
"Porcupine River"
MISSOURI
RIVER
"2000 Mile Creek"
"This river we call Porcupine from the great number of those anamals found about it's mouth. a Short distance above about 1/4 mile and on the Lard Side a large Creek falls in, ..."
Clark ⇨
"... about 10 A.M. passd the mo. of 2000 mile Creek. The wind rose high So [we] halted."
Ordway ⇦
"... R. Fields went to examine & reports that it is a bold running stream 80 yds wide as this creek is 2000 miles up the Missouri we call it the 2000 mile Creek, ..."
Clark ⇨
"... had passed a large creek on the N.S. which is two thousand miles from the mouth of the M."
Ordway ⇨
"We passed a small river on the north side called the 2000 mile river. About a mile above we passed a large creek on the south side, called Porcupine creek"
Gass ⇨
Cartographer's Note:
Sergeants Gass and Ordway must have been collaborating on journal entries the evening of May 3, 1805. Both men confuse the two streams passed and named just before they encamped.
"... we saw an unusual number of Porcupines from which we determined to call the river after that anamal, and accordingly denominated it Porcupine river. this stream discharges itself into the Missouri, on the Stard. side 2000 miles above the mouth of the latter, it is a beatiful, bold runing stream, 40 yards wide at its entrance; the water is transparent, it being the first of this discription that I have yet seen discharge itself into the Missouri;"
Lewis ⇨
Cartographer's Note:
Clark indicates on his small scale, field map what appears to be an abandoned, river channel that curves back and forth across the 1805 course. The course he shows appears to be a reflection of the 1805, as though the pair of sweeping curves have moved up the valley two or three miles.
"The high lands are low and from 5 to 9 miles apart and there is evident marks of the bead [bed] of the river having been changed frequently but little appearance of the coal & burnt hills to day."
Clark ⇨
Cartographer's Note:
Again the cartographer is confronted with a severe kink in the traverse which creates a real challenge to reconstruct a river bend to match the calls. This bend as reconstructed fits within the acceptable representation of Clark's very small scale map. Also remember that this sort of kink in the traverse can add many miles while the Expedition, following the river, has traveled only a portion of the survey distance.
"The morning being very could we did not set out as early as usual; ice formed on a kettle of water 1/4 of an inch thick. the snow has melted generally in the bottoms, but the hills still remain covered."
Lewis ⇨
"we Set out about 3 oClock and proceeded on about five 1/2 miles and encamped on the Std Side, the evening very cold, Ice freesing to the Ores."
Clark ⇨
Camp
May 2, 1805
Point of Woodland
Sand Point
Timber
Dead Timber
Point of High Timber
Point of Low Timber
S 45 W
3 MILES
"100 yds."
"80 yds."
S 75 W
1.75 MILES
S 65 W
1/2 MILE
NORTH
1.5 MILES
1.25 MILES
S 85 W
S 80 W
1/2 MILE
SOUTH
3 MILES
N 55 W
2.5 MILE
1 MILE
N 40 W
S 65 W
2.25 MILES
N 50 W
3/4 MILE
S 30 W
2 MILES
Redwater River
Hubbard
McCone Co.
Richland Co.
Roosevelt Co.
Glendive Coulee
Fort Peck Indian Reservation
Skinners Island
White Shield Island
First Creek
Second Creek
Boxelder Creek
POPLAR
Boys Bend
Sewage Disposal
Poplar Airport
Swamp
SPROLE
N
ONE STATUTE MILE
Modern Data: 1972
Outbound: May 2, 3, 1805
Lewis' Return: August 6, 1806
EXPLORATIONS OF LEWIS AND CLARK 1804 - 1806
CARTOGRAPHIC RECONSTRUCTION
PORCUPINE RIVER
UTM ZONE 13
MAP NUMBER 185
Montana
CONTOUR INTERVAL 50 FEET

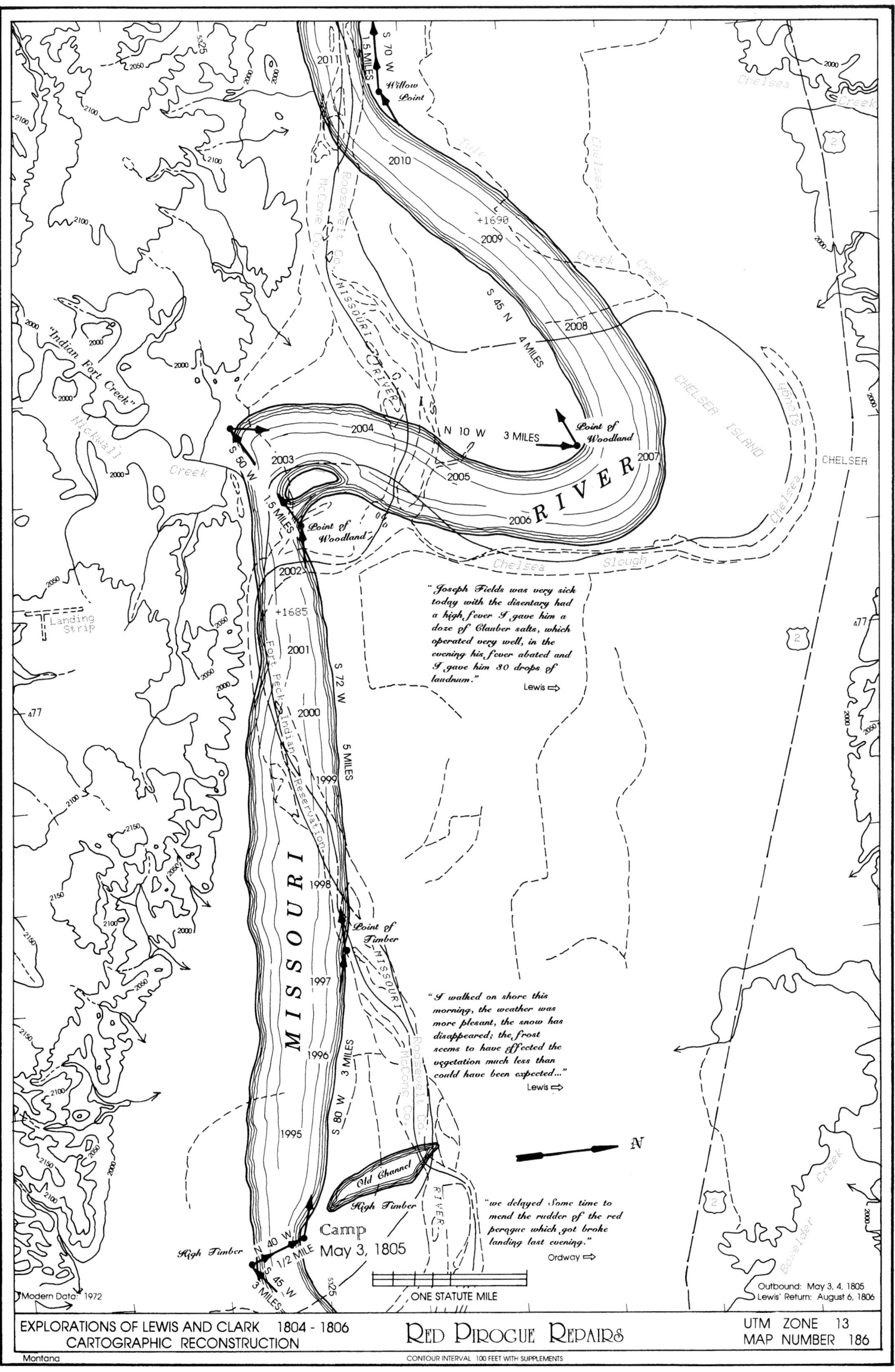
EXPLORATIONS OF LEWIS AND CLARK 1804 - 1806
CARTOGRAPHIC RECONSTRUCTION
RED PIROGUE REPAIRS
UTM ZONE 13
MAP NUMBER 186
Montana
CONTOUR INTERVAL 100 FEET WITH SUPPLEMENTS
Modern Data: 1972
Outbound: May 3, 4, 1805
Lewis' Return: August 6, 1806
ONE STATUTE MILE
N
"Joseph Fields was very sick today with the disentary had a high fever I gave him a doze of Clauber salts, which operated very well, in the evening his fever abated and I gave him 30 drops of laudnum."
Lewis ⇨
"I walked on shore this morning, the weather was more plesant, the snow has disappeared; the frost seems to have effected the vegetation much less than could have been expected..."
Lewis ⇨
"we delayed Some time to mend the rudder of the red perogue which got broke landing last evening."
Ordway ⇨
Camp
May 3, 1805
High Timber
High Timber
Old Channel
Point of Timber
Point of Woodland
Point of Woodland
Willow Point
MISSOURI
RIVER
MISSOURI RIVER
"Indian Fort Creek"
Nickwall Creek
Chelsea Creek
Tule Creek
Chelsea Slough
CHELSEA ISLAND
CHELSEA
Boxelder Creek
Landing Strip
Roosevelt Co.
McCone Co.
Fort Peck Indian Reservation
S 70 W 1.5 MILES
S 45 N 4 MILES
N 10 W 3 MILES
S 50 W 1.5 MILES
S 72 W 5 MILES
S 80 W 3 MILES
N 40 W 1/2 MILE
S 45 W 3 MILES
+1690
+1685

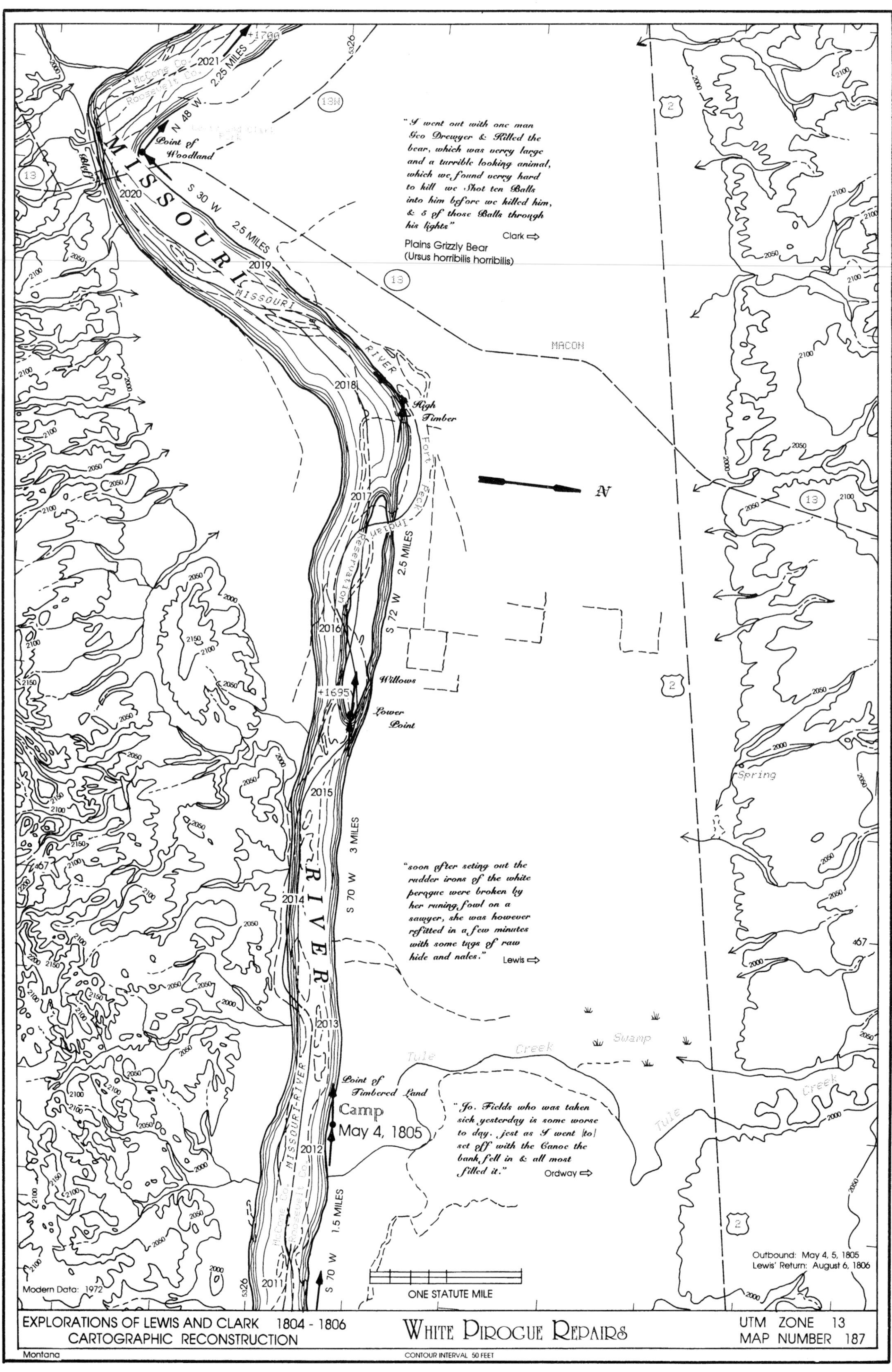
"I went out with one man Geo Drewyer & Killed the bear, which was verry large and a turrible looking animal, which we found verry hard to kill we Shot ten Balls into him before we killed him, & 5 of those Balls through his lights"
Clark ⇨
Plains Grizzly Bear
(Ursus horribilis horribilis)
"soon after seting out the rudder irons of the white perogue were broken by her runing fowl on a sawyer, she was however refitted in a few minutes with some tugs of raw hide and nales."
Lewis ⇨
"Jo. Fields who was taken sick yesterday is some worse to day. jest as I went [to] set off with the Canoe the bank fell in & all most filled it."
Ordway ⇨
MISSOURI
RIVER
Point of Woodland
High Timber
Willows
Lower Point
Point of Timbered Land
Camp
May 4, 1805
N 48 W. 2.25 MILES
S 30 W 2.5 MILES
S 72 W 2.5 MILES
S 70 W 3 MILES
S 70 W 1.5 MILES
MACON
Fort Peck Indian Reservation
Tule Creek
Swamp
Spring
McCone Co.
Roosevelt Co.
Outbound: May 4, 5, 1805
Lewis' Return: August 6, 1806
ONE STATUTE MILE
Modern Data: 1972
EXPLORATIONS OF LEWIS AND CLARK 1804 - 1806
CARTOGRAPHIC RECONSTRUCTION
WHITE PIROGUE REPAIRS
UTM ZONE 13
MAP NUMBER 187
Montana
CONTOUR INTERVAL 50 FEET

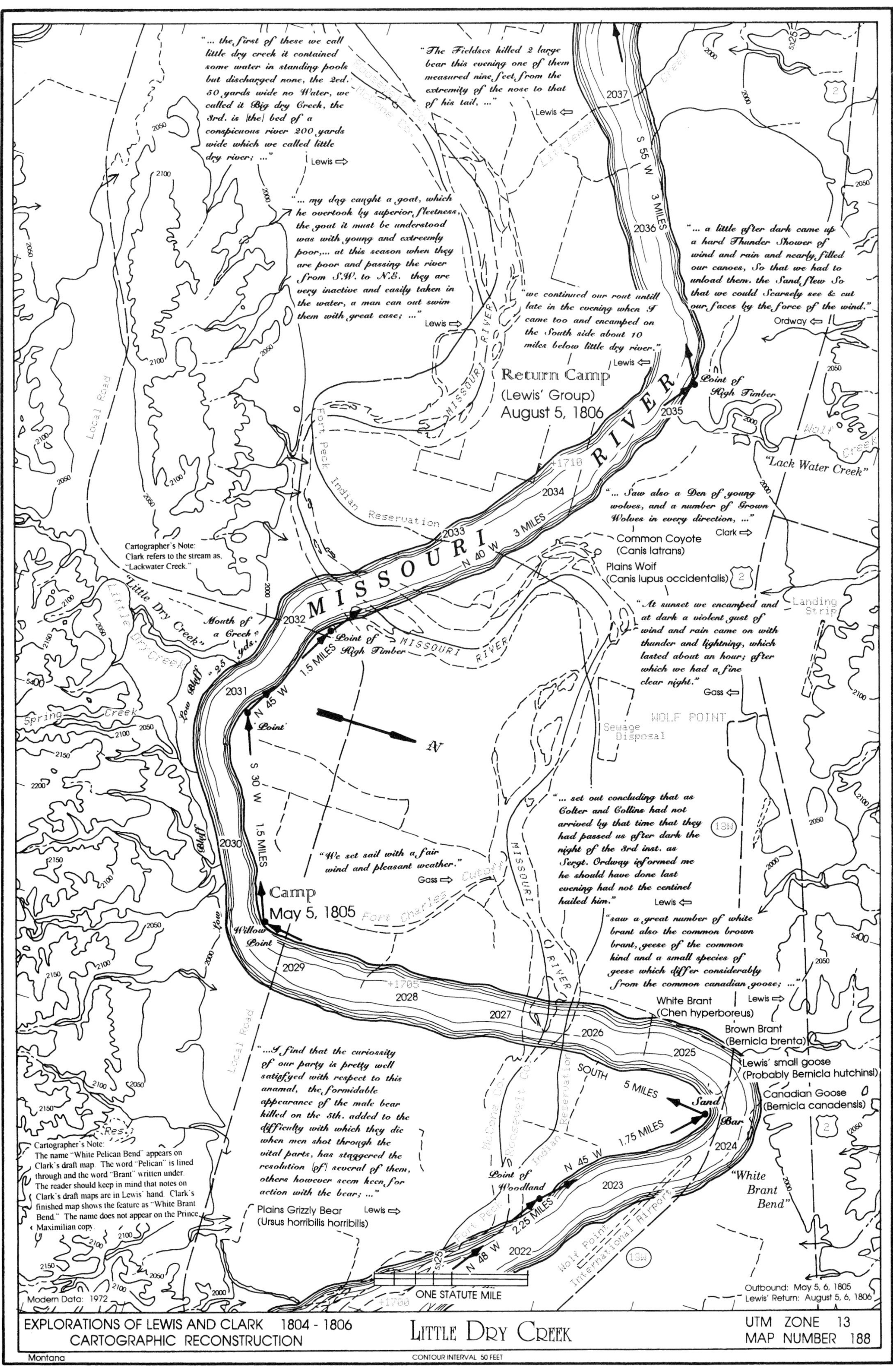

"... the first of these we call little dry creek it contained some water in standing pools but discharged none, the 2ed. 50 yards wide no Water, we called it Big dry Creek, the 3rd. is [the] bed of a conspicuous river 200 yards wide which we called little dry river; ..."
Lewis ⇨
"The Fieldses killed 2 large bear this evening one of them measured nine feet from the extremity of the nose to that of his tail, ..."
Lewis ⇦
"... my dog caught a goat, which he overtook by superior fleetness, the goat it must be understood was with young and extreemly poor,... at this season when they are poor and passing the river from S.W. to N.E. they are very inactive and easily taken in the water, a man can out swim them with great ease; ..."
Lewis ⇨
"we continued our rout untill late in the evening when I came too and encamped on the South side about 10 miles below little dry river."
Lewis ⇦
"... a little after dark came up a hard Thunder Shower of wind and rain and nearly filled our canoes, So that we had to unload them. the Sand flew So that we could Scarsely see & cut our faces by the force of the wind."
Ordway ⇦
Return Camp
(Lewis' Group)
August 5, 1806
Point of High Timber
Wolf Creek
"Lack Water Creek"
"... Saw also a Den of young wolves, and a number of Grown Wolves in every direction, ..."
Clark ⇨
Common Coyote
(Canis latrans)
Plains Wolf
(Canis lupus occidentalis)
Cartographer's Note:
Clark refers to the stream as, "Lackwater Creek."
"Little Dry Creek"
Little Dry Creek
Mouth of a Creek "25 yds."
Spring Creek
Low Bluff
MISSOURI RIVER
S 55 W 3 MILES
N 40 W 3 MILES
N 45 W
1.5 MILES
S 30 W 1.5 MILES
Point of High Timber
"Point"
N
Fort Peck Indian Reservation
Roosevelt Co.
McCone Co.
Littleman Creek
Local Road
Landing Strip
WOLF POINT
Sewage Disposal
"At sunset we encamped and at dark a violent gust of wind and rain came on with thunder and lightning, which lasted about an hour; after which we had a fine clear night."
Gass ⇦
"... set out concluding that as Colter and Collins had not arrived by that time that they had passed us after dark the night of the 3rd inst. as Sergt. Ordway informed me he should have done last evening had not the centinel hailed him."
Lewis ⇦
"We set sail with a fair wind and pleasant weather."
Gass ⇨
Camp
May 5, 1805
Willow Point
Fort Charles Cutoff
MISSOURI RIVER
"saw a great number of white brant also the common brown brant, geese of the common kind and a small species of geese which differ considerably from the common canadian goose; ..."
Lewis ⇨
White Brant
(Chen hyperboreus)
Brown Brant
(Bernicla brenta)
Lewis' small goose
(Probably Bernicla hutchinsi)
Canadian Goose
(Bernicla canadensis)
"...I find that the curiossity of our party is pretty well satisfyed with respect to this anamal, the formidable appearance of the male bear killed on the 5th. added to the difficulty with which they die when men shot through the vital parts, has staggered the resolution [of] several of them, others however seem keen for action with the bear; ..."
Plains Grizzly Bear
(Ursus horribilis horribilis)
Lewis ⇨
SOUTH 5 MILES
Sand Bar
1.75 MILES
N 45 W
Point of Woodland
2.25 MILES
N 48 W
"White Brant Bend"
Wolf Point International Airport
Cartographer's Note:
The name "White Pelican Bend" appears on Clark's draft map. The word "Pelican" is lined through and the word "Brant" written under. The reader should keep in mind that notes on Clark's draft maps are in Lewis' hand. Clark's finished map shows the feature as "White Brant Bend." The name does not appear on the Prince Maximilian copy.
Res.
Modern Data: 1972
ONE STATUTE MILE
Outbound: May 5, 6, 1805
Lewis' Return: August 5, 6, 1806
EXPLORATIONS OF LEWIS AND CLARK 1804 - 1806
CARTOGRAPHIC RECONSTRUCTION
LITTLE DRY CREEK
UTM ZONE 13
MAP NUMBER 188
Montana
CONTOUR INTERVAL 50 FEET

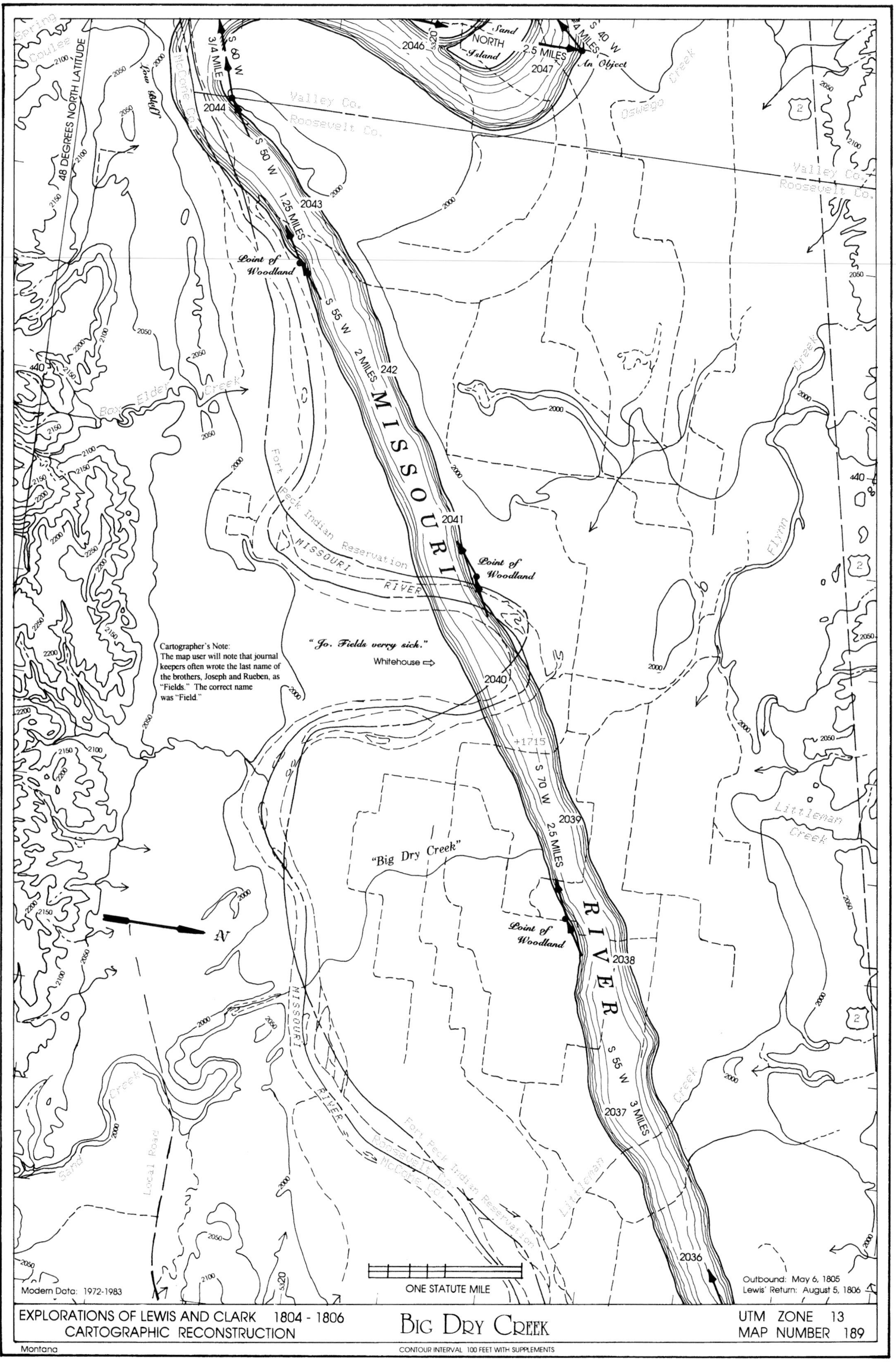

EXPLORATIONS OF LEWIS AND CLARK 1804 - 1806
CARTOGRAPHIC RECONSTRUCTION
BIG DRY CREEK
UTM ZONE 13
MAP NUMBER 189
Montana
CONTOUR INTERVAL 100 FEET WITH SUPPLEMENTS
Modern Data: 1972-1983
ONE STATUTE MILE
Outbound: May 6, 1805
Lewis' Return: August 5, 1806
Cartographer's Note:
The map user will note that journal keepers often wrote the last name of the brothers, Joseph and Rueben, as "Fields." The correct name was "Field."
"Jo. Fields verry sick."
Whitehouse
"Big Dry Creek"
MISSOURI RIVER
48 DEGREES NORTH LATITUDE
Point of Woodland
Sand Island
NORTH
An Object
S 60 W
3/4 MILE
S 40 W
4 MILES
2.5 MILES
S 50 W
1.25 MILES
S 55 W
2 MILES
S 70 W
2.5 MILES
S 55 W
3 MILES
Valley Co.
Roosevelt Co.
McCone Co.
Fort Peck Indian Reservation
Box Elder Creek
Spring Coulee
Oswego Creek
Flynn Creek
Littleman Creek
Sand Creek
Local Road
N

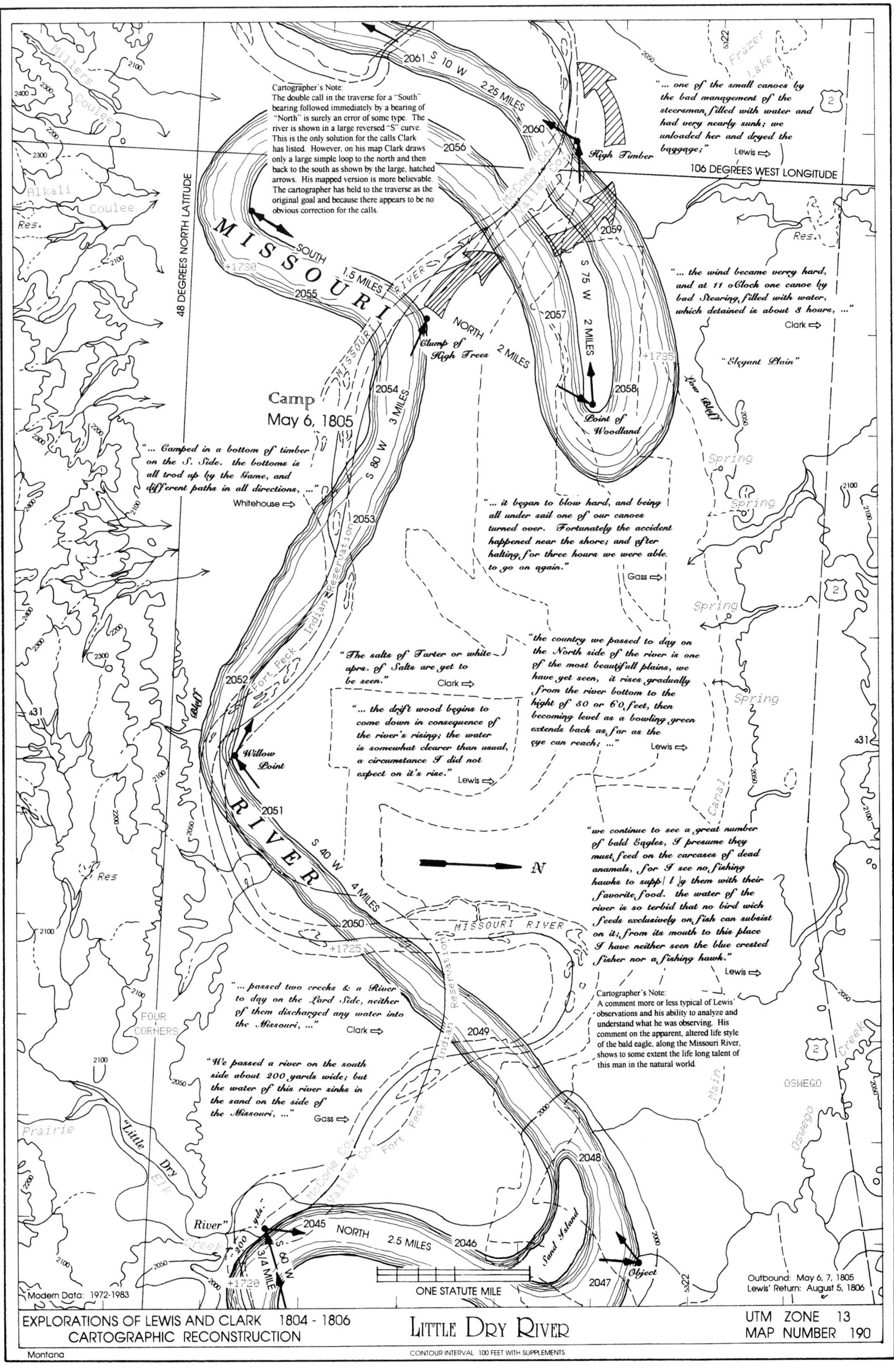
Cartographer's Note:
The double call in the traverse for a "South" bearing followed immediately by a bearing of "North" is surely an error of some type. The river is shown in a large reversed "S" curve. This is the only solution for the calls Clark has listed. However, on his map Clark draws only a large simple loop to the north and then back to the south as shown by the large, hatched arrows. His mapped version is more believable. The cartographer has held to the traverse as the original goal and because there appears to be no obvious correction for the calls.
"... one of the small canoes by the bad manqgement of the steersman, filled with water and had very nearly sunk; we unloaded her and dryed the baggage;"
Lewis ⇨
106 DEGREES WEST LONGITUDE
48 DEGREES NORTH LATITUDE
S 10 W
2.25 MILES
High Timber
MISSOURI
SOUTH
1.5 MILES
NORTH
2 MILES
S 75 W
2 MILES
Clump of High Trees
Point of Woodland
"... the wind became verry hard, and at 11 o Clock one canoe by bad Stearing, filled with water, which detained is about 3 hours, ..."
Clark ⇨
"Elegant Plain"
Low Bluff
Camp
May 6, 1805
S 80 W
3 MILES
"... Camped in a bottom of timber on the S. Side. the bottoms is all trod up by the Game, and different paths in all directions, ..."
Whitehouse ⇨
"... it began to blow hard, and being all under sail one of our canoes turned over. Fortunately the accident happened near the shore; and after halting for three hours we were able to go on again."
Gass ⇨
"The salts of Tarter or white aprs. of Salts are yet to be seen."
Clark ⇨
"the country we passed to day on the North side of the river is one of the most beautifull plains, we have yet seen, it rises gradually from the river bottom to the hight of 50 or 60 feet, then becoming level as a bowling green extends back as far as the eye can reach; ..."
Lewis ⇨
"... the drift wood begins to come down in consequence of the river's rising; the water is somewhat clearer than usual, a circumstance I did not expect on it's rise."
Lewis ⇨
Willow Point
Bluff
RIVER
S 40 W
4 MILES
N
"we continue to see a great number of bald Eagles, I presume they must feed on the carcases of dead anamals, for I see no fishing hawks to supp[l]y them with their favorite food. the water of the river is so terbid that no bird wich feeds exclusively on fish can subsist on it; from its mouth to this place I have neither seen the blue crested fisher nor a fishing hawk."
Lewis ⇨
Cartographer's Note:
A comment more or less typical of Lewis' observations and his ability to analyze and understand what he was observing. His comment on the apparent, altered life style of the bald eagle, along the Missouri River, shows to some extent the life long talent of this man in the natural world.
"... passed two creeks & a River to day on the Lard Side, neither of them discharged any water into the Missouri, ..."
Clark ⇨
"We passed a river on the south side about 200 yards wide; but the water of this river sinks in the sand on the side of the Missouri, ..."
Gass ⇨
"Little Dry River"
"200 yds."
S 60 W
3/4 MILE
NORTH
2.5 MILES
Sand Island
Object
ONE STATUTE MILE
Outbound: May 6, 7, 1805
Lewis' Return: August 5, 1806
Modern Data: 1972-1983
EXPLORATIONS OF LEWIS AND CLARK 1804 - 1806
CARTOGRAPHIC RECONSTRUCTION
LITTLE DRY RIVER
UTM ZONE 13
MAP NUMBER 190
Montana
CONTOUR INTERVAL 100 FEET WITH SUPPLEMENTS

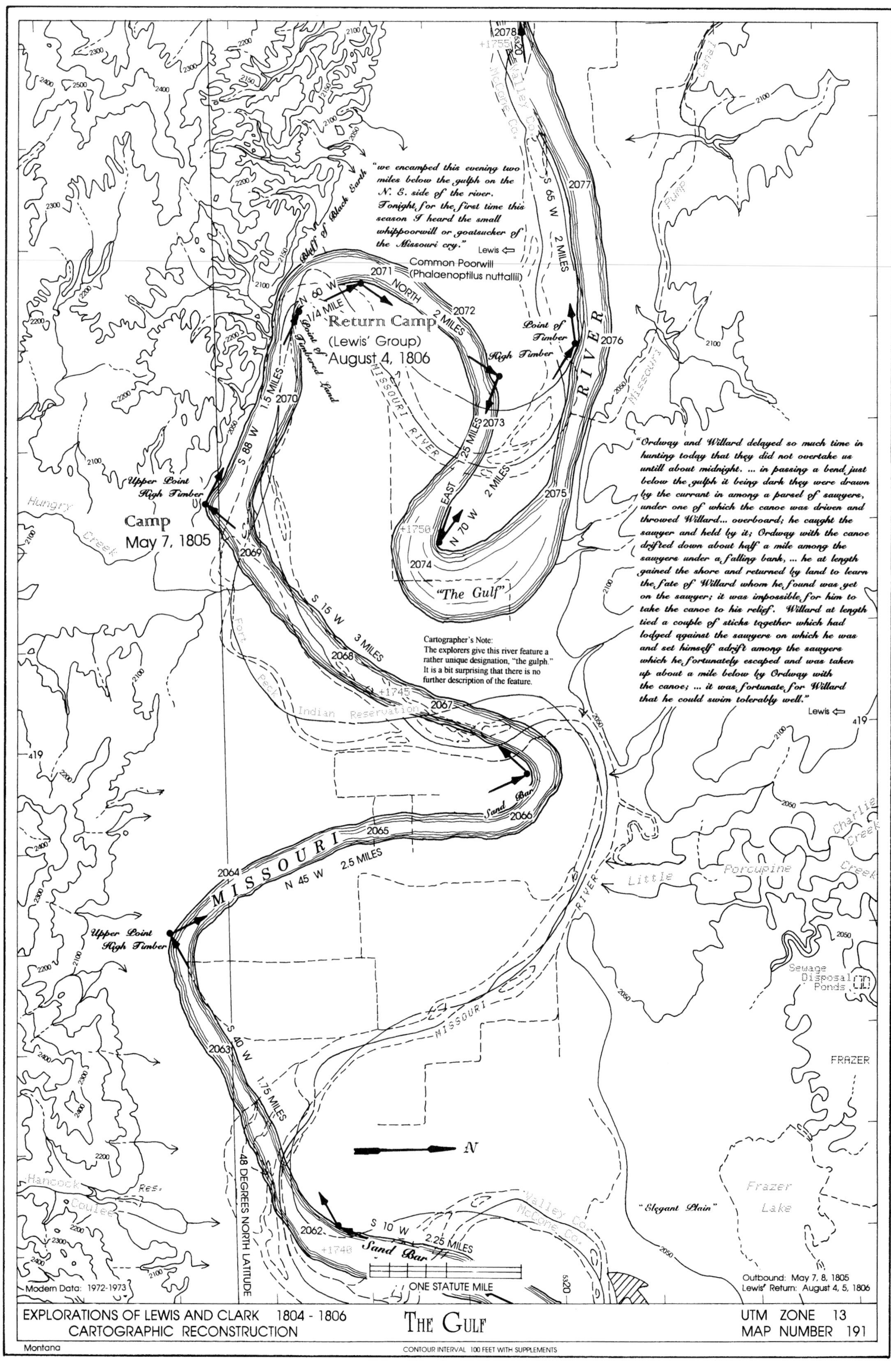
"we encamped this evening two miles below the gulph on the N. E. side of the river. Tonight for the first time this season I heard the small whippoorwill or goatsucker of the Missouri cry."
Lewis
Common Poorwill
(Phalaenoptilus nuttallii)
Bluff of Black Earth
Return Camp
(Lewis' Group)
August 4, 1806
Point of Timbered Land
Point of Timber
High Timber
Upper Point
High Timber
Camp
May 7, 1805
"The Gulf"
MISSOURI RIVER
RIVER
Hungry Creek
Fort Peck Indian Reservation
McCone Co.
Valley Co.
Pump Canal
"Ordway and Willard delayed so much time in hunting today that they did not overtake us untill about midnight. ... in passing a bend just below the gulph it being dark they were drawn by the currant in among a parsel of sawyers, under one of which the canoe was driven and throwed Willard... overboard; he caught the sawyer and held by it; Ordway with the canoe drifted down about half a mile among the sawyers under a falling bank, ... he at length gained the shore and returned by land to learn the fate of Willard whom he found was yet on the sawyer; it was impossible for him to take the canoe to his relief. Willard at length tied a couple of sticks together which had lodged against the sawyers on which he was and set himself adrift among the sawyers which he fortunately escaped and was taken up about a mile below by Ordway with the canoe; ... it was fortunate for Willard that he could swim tolerably well."
Lewis
Cartographer's Note:
The explorers give this river feature a rather unique designation, "the gulph." It is a bit surprising that there is no further description of the feature.
Sand Bar
Charlie Creek
Little Porcupine Creek
Sewage Disposal Ponds
FRAZER
Frazer Lake
"Elegant Plain"
Upper Point
High Timber
Hancock Res.
Coulee
48 DEGREES NORTH LATITUDE
N
Sand Bar
ONE STATUTE MILE
N 60 W
1/4 MILE
NORTH
2 MILES
S 65 W
2 MILES
1.5 MILES
S 88 W
1.25 MILES
2 MILES
EAST
N 70 W
S 15 W
3 MILES
N 45 W
2.5 MILES
S 40 W
1.75 MILES
S 10 W
2.25 MILES
2062
2063
2064
2065
2066
2067
2068
2069
2070
2071
2072
2073
2074
2075
2076
2077
2078
+1740
+1745
+1750
+1755
Modern Data: 1972-1973
Outbound: May 7, 8, 1805
Lewis' Return: August 4, 5, 1806
EXPLORATIONS OF LEWIS AND CLARK 1804 - 1806
CARTOGRAPHIC RECONSTRUCTION
THE GULF
UTM ZONE 13
MAP NUMBER 191
Montana
CONTOUR INTERVAL 100 FEET WITH SUPPLEMENTS

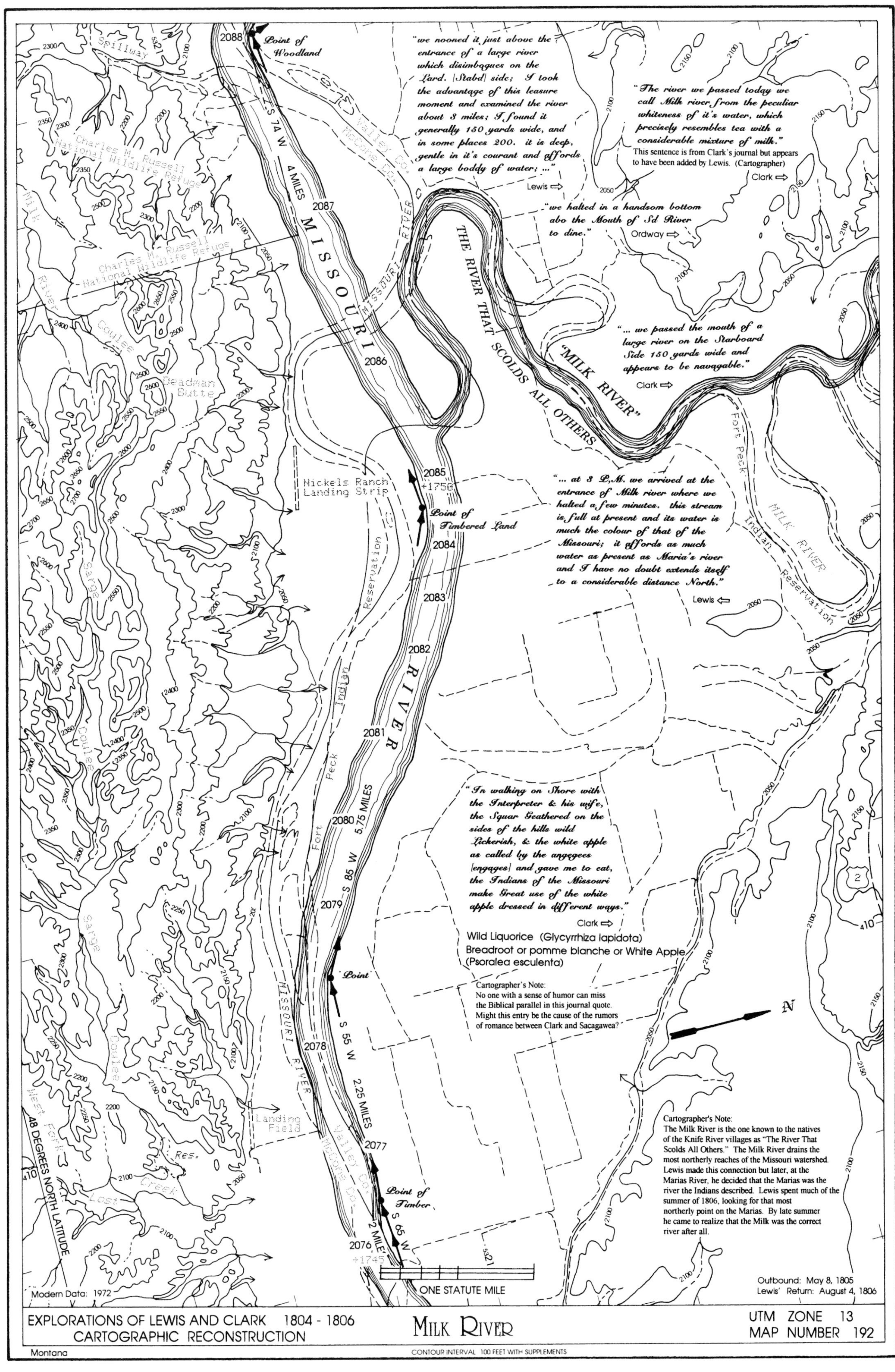

Point of Woodland
"we nooned it just above the entrance of a large river which disimbogues on the Lard. [Stabd] side; I took the advantage of this leasure moment and examined the river about 3 miles; I found it generally 150 yards wide, and in some places 200. it is deep, gentle in it's courant and affords a large boddy of water; ..."
Lewis ⇨
"The river we passed today we call Milk river, from the peculiar whiteness of it's water, which precisely resembles tea with a considerable mixture of milk."
This sentence is from Clark's journal but appears to have been added by Lewis. (Cartographer)
Clark ⇨
"we halted in a handsom bottom abo the Mouth of Sd River to dine."
Ordway ⇨
"... we passed the mouth of a large river on the Starboard Side 150 yards wide and appears to be navagable."
Clark ⇨
"MILK RIVER"
THE RIVER THAT SCOLDS ALL OTHERS
MISSOURI
RIVER
S 74 W
4 MILES
Charles M. Russell National Wildlife Refuge
Deadman Butte
Nickels Ranch Landing Strip
Point of Timbered Land
"... at 3 P.M. we arrived at the entrance of Milk river where we halted a few minutes. this stream is full at present and its water is much the colour of that of the Missouri; it affords as much water as present as Maria's river and I have no doubt extends itself to a considerable distance North."
Lewis ⇦
Fort Peck Indian Reservation
"In walking on Shore with the Interpreter & his wife, the Squar Geathered on the sides of the hills wild Lickerish, & the white apple as called by the angegees [engages] and gave me to eat, the Indians of the Missouri make Great use of the white apple dressed in different ways."
Clark ⇨
Wild Liquorice (Glycyrrhiza lapidota)
Breadroot or pomme blanche or White Apple (Psoralea esculenta)
Point
Cartographer's Note:
No one with a sense of humor can miss the Biblical parallel in this journal quote. Might this entry be the cause of the rumors of romance between Clark and Sacagawea?
S 85 W
5.75 MILES
S 55 W
2.25 MILES
Point of Timber
S 65 W
2 MILES
N
Cartographer's Note:
The Milk River is the one known to the natives of the Knife River villages as "The River That Scolds All Others." The Milk River drains the most northerly reaches of the Missouri watershed. Lewis made this connection but later, at the Marias River, he decided that the Marias was the river the Indians described. Lewis spent much of the summer of 1806, looking for that most northerly point on the Marias. By late summer he came to realize that the Milk was the correct river after all.
48 DEGREES NORTH LATITUDE
Landing Field
Valley Co.
McCone Co.
ONE STATUTE MILE
Modern Data: 1972
Outbound: May 8, 1805
Lewis' Return: August 4, 1806
EXPLORATIONS OF LEWIS AND CLARK 1804 - 1806
CARTOGRAPHIC RECONSTRUCTION
MILK RIVER
UTM ZONE 13
MAP NUMBER 192
Montana
CONTOUR INTERVAL 100 FEET WITH SUPPLEMENTS

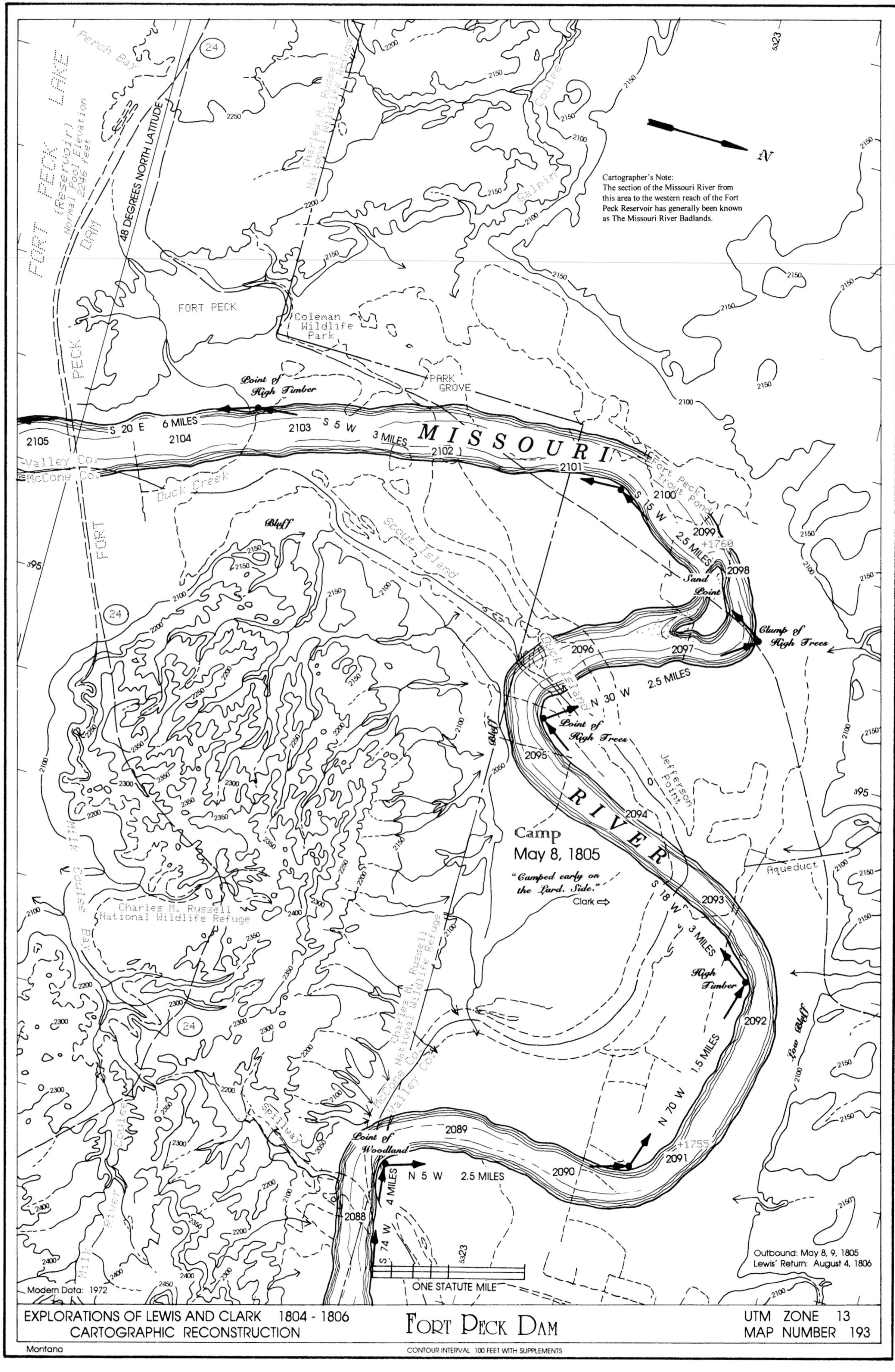
Cartographer's Note:
The section of the Missouri River from this area to the western reach of the Fort Peck Reservoir has generally been known as The Missouri River Badlands.
N
FORT PECK LAKE
(Reservoir)
Normal Pool Elevation 2246 feet
FORT PECK DAM
48 DEGREES NORTH LATITUDE
Charles M. Russell National Wildlife Refuge
FORT PECK
Coleman Wildlife Park
PARK GROVE
Point of High Timber
S 20 E 6 MILES
S 5 W 3 MILES
MISSOURI
RIVER
Valley Co.
McCone Co.
Duck Creek
Scout Island
Fort Peck Trout Pond
S 15 W 2.5 MILES
Sand Point
Clump of High Trees
N 30 W 2.5 MILES
Point of High Trees
Jefferson Point
Bluff
Camp
May 8, 1805
"Camped early on the Lard. Side."
Clark
S 18 W 3 MILES
High Timber
1.5 MILES
N 70 W
Low Bluff
Aqueduct
Spillway
Point of Woodland
N 5 W 2.5 MILES
4 MILES
S 74 W
Coulee
Milk River
Galpin Coulee
Bay
ONE STATUTE MILE
Modern Data: 1972
Outbound: May 8, 9, 1805
Lewis' Return: August 4, 1806
EXPLORATIONS OF LEWIS AND CLARK 1804 - 1806
CARTOGRAPHIC RECONSTRUCTION
FORT PECK DAM
UTM ZONE 13
MAP NUMBER 193
Montana
CONTOUR INTERVAL 100 FEET WITH SUPPLEMENTS

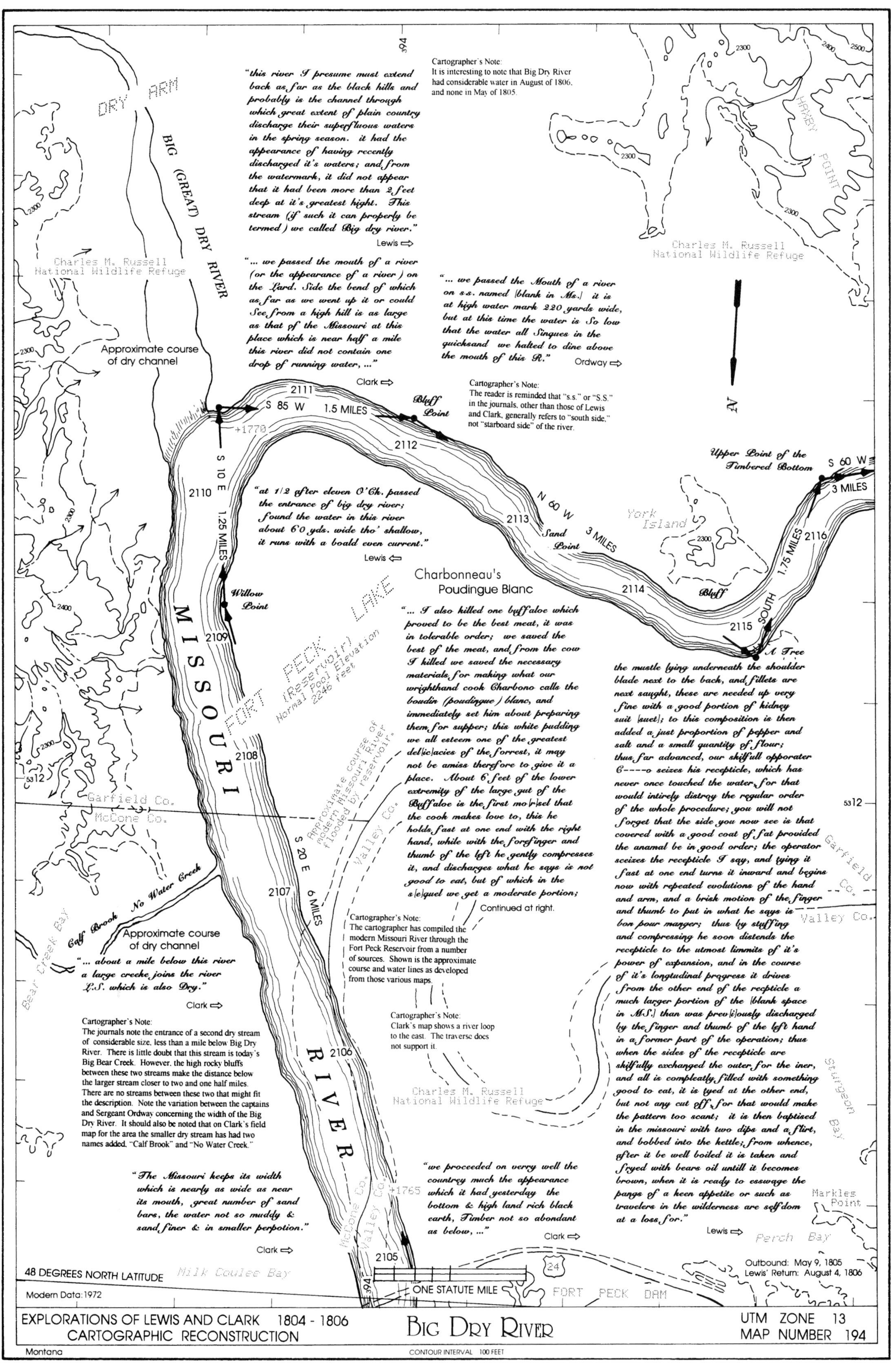

"this river I presume must extend back as far as the black hills and probably is the channel through which great extent of plain country discharge their superfluous waters in the spring season. it had the appearance of having recently discharged it's waters; and from the watermark, it did not appear that it had been more than 2 feet deep at it's greatest hight. This stream (if such it can properly be termed) we called Big dry river."
Lewis ⇨
Cartographer's Note:
It is interesting to note that Big Dry River had considerable water in August of 1806, and none in May of 1805.
"... we passed the mouth of a river (or the appearance of a river) on the Lard. Side the bend of which as far as we went up it or could See from a high hill is as large as that of the Missouri at this place which is near half a mile this river did not contain one drop of running water, ..."
Clark ⇨
"... we passed the Mouth of a river on s.s. named [blank in Ms.] it is at high water mark 220 yards wide, but at this time the water is So low that the water all Singues in the quicksand we halted to dine above the mouth of this R."
Ordway ⇨
Cartographer's Note:
The reader is reminded that "s.s." or "S.S." in the journals, other than those of Lewis and Clark, generally refers to "south side," not "starboard side" of the river.
DRY ARM
BIG (GREAT) DRY RIVER
Charles M. Russell National Wildlife Refuge
HAWBY POINT
Approximate course of dry channel
S 85 W
1.5 MILES
Bluff Point
S 10 E
1.25 MILES
Willow Point
"at 1/2 after eleven O'Ck. passed the entrance of big dry river; found the water in this river about 60 yds. wide tho' shallow, it runs with a boald even current."
Lewis ⇦
N 60 W
3 MILES
Sand Point
York Island
Upper Point of the Timbered Bottom
S 60 W
3 MILES
1.75 MILES
SOUTH
Bluff
A Tree
Charbonneau's Poudingue Blanc
"... I also killed one buffaloe which proved to be the best meat, it was in tolerable order; we saved the best of the meat, and from the cow I killed we saved the necessary materials for making what our wrighthand cook Charbono calls the boudin (poudingue) blanc, and immediately set him about preparing them for supper; this white pudding we all esteem one of the greatest del[ic]acies of the forrest, it may not be amiss therefore to give it a place. About 6 feet of the lower extremity of the large gut of the Buffaloe is the first mo[r]sel that the cook makes love to, this he holds fast at one end with the right hand, while with the forefinger and thumb of the left he gently compresses it, and discharges what he says is not good to eat, but of which in the s[e]quel we get a moderate portion;
Continued at right.
the mustle lying underneath the shoulder blade next to the back, and fillets are next saught, these are needed up very fine with a good portion of kidney suit [suet]; to this composition is then added a just proportion of pepper and salt and a small quantity of flour; thus far advanced, our skilfull opporater C----o seizes his recepticle, which has never once touched the water, for that would intirely distroy the regular order of the whole procedure; you will not forget that the side you now see is that covered with a good coat of fat provided the anamal be in good order; the operator sceizes the recepticle I say, and tying it fast at one end turns it inward and begins now with repeated evolutions of the hand and arm, and a brisk motion of the finger and thumb to put in what he says is bon pour manger; thus by stuffing and compressing he soon distends the recepticle to the utmost limmits of it's power of expansion, and in the course of it's longtudinal progress it drives from the other end of the recpticle a much larger portion of the [blank space in MS.] than was prev[i]ously discharged by the finger and thumb of the left hand in a former part of the operation; thus when the sides of the recepticle are skilfully exchanged the outer for the iner, and all is compleatly filled with something good to eat, it is tyed at the other end, but not any cut off, for that would make the pattern too scant; it is then baptised in the missouri with two dips and a flirt, and bobbed into the kettle; from whence, after it be well boiled it is taken and fryed with bears oil untill it becomes brown, when it is ready to esswage the pangs of a keen appetite or such as travelers in the wilderness are selfdom at a loss for."
Lewis ⇨
MISSOURI
FORT PECK LAKE (Reservoir) Normal Pool Elevation 2246 feet
Approximate course of modern Missouri River flooded by reservoir.
Garfield Co.
McCone Co.
Valley Co.
S 20 E
6 MILES
No Water Creek
Calf Brook
Bear Creek Bay
Approximate course of dry channel
"... about a mile below this river a large creeke joins the river L.S. which is also Dry."
Clark ⇨
Cartographer's Note:
The cartographer has compiled the modern Missouri River through the Fort Peck Reservoir from a number of sources. Shown is the approximate course and water lines as developed from those various maps.
Cartographer's Note:
The journals note the entrance of a second dry stream of considerable size, less than a mile below Big Dry River. There is little doubt that this stream is today's Big Bear Creek. However, the high rocky bluffs between these two streams make the distance below the larger stream closer to two and one half miles. There are no streams between these two that might fit the description. Note the variation between the captains and Sergeant Ordway concerning the width of the Big Dry River. It should also be noted that on Clark's field map for the area the smaller dry stream has had two names added, "Calf Brook" and "No Water Creek."
Cartographer's Note:
Clark's map shows a river loop to the east. The traverse does not support it.
RIVER
Sturgeon Bay
Markles Point
Perch Bay
"The Missouri keeps its width which is nearly as wide as near its mouth, great number of sand bars, the water not so muddy & sand finer & in smaller perpotion."
Clark ⇨
"we proceeded on verry well the countrey much the appearance which it had yesterday the bottom & high land rich black earth, Timber not so abondant as below, ..."
Clark ⇨
Outbound: May 9, 1805
Lewis' Return: August 4, 1806
48 DEGREES NORTH LATITUDE
Milk Coulee Bay
ONE STATUTE MILE
FORT PECK DAM
24
394
Modern Data: 1972
EXPLORATIONS OF LEWIS AND CLARK 1804 - 1806
CARTOGRAPHIC RECONSTRUCTION
BIG DRY RIVER
UTM ZONE 13
MAP NUMBER 194
Montana
CONTOUR INTERVAL 100 FEET

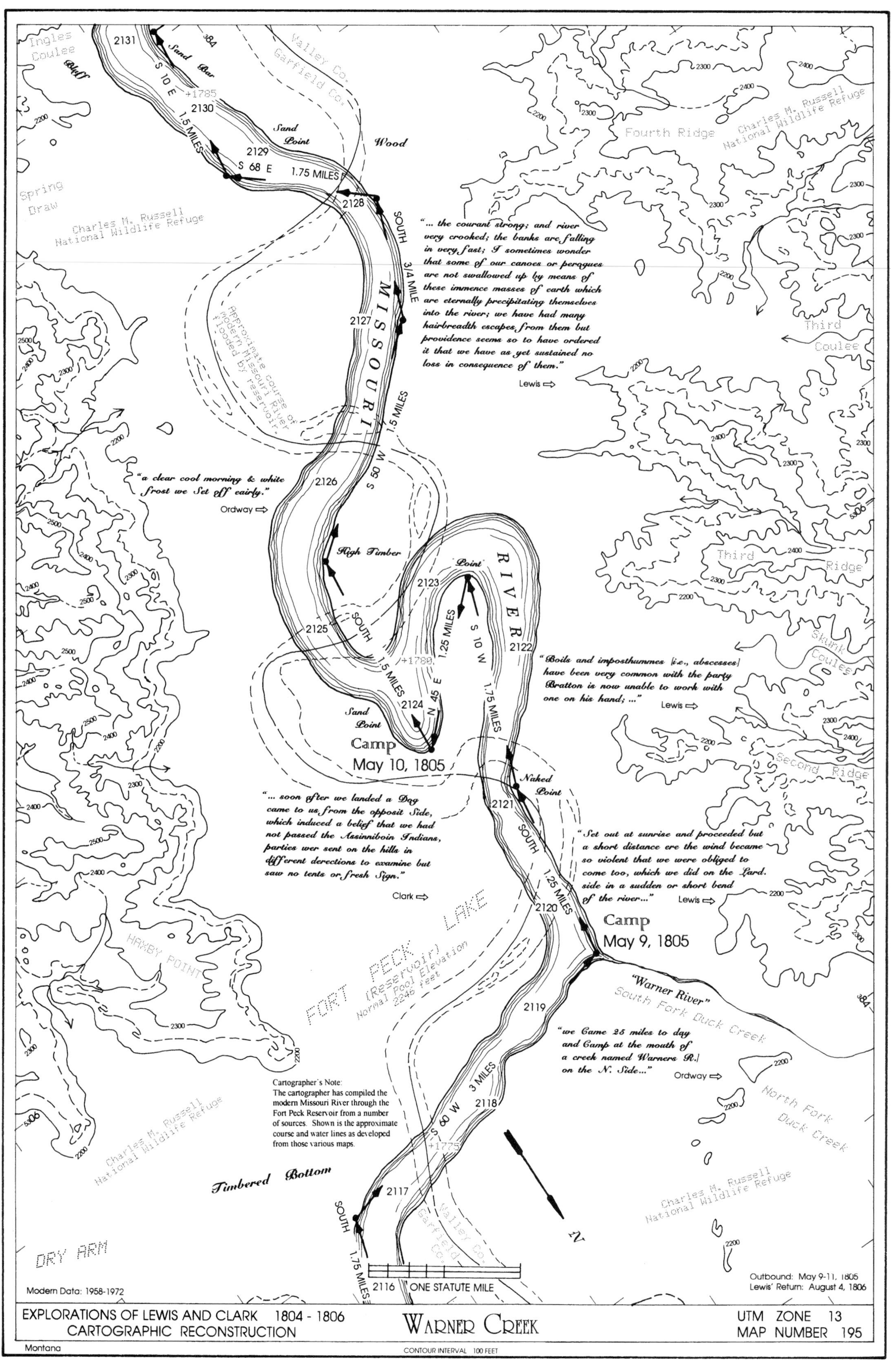
"... the courant strong; and river very crooked; the banks are falling in very fast; I sometimes wonder that some of our canoes or perogues are not swallowed up by means of these immence masses of earth which are eternally precipitating themselves into the river; we have had many hairbreadth escapes from them but providence seems so to have ordered it that we have as yet sustained no loss in consequence of them."
Lewis
"a clear cool morning & white frost we Set off eairly."
Ordway
"Boils and imposthummes [i.e., abscesses] have been very common with the party Bratton is now unable to work with one on his hand; ..."
Lewis
"... soon after we landed a Dog came to us from the opposit Side, which induced a belief that we had not passed the Assinniboin Indians, parties wer sent on the hills in different derections to examine but saw no tents or fresh Sign."
Clark
"Set out at sunrise and proceeded but a short distance ere the wind became so violent that we were obliged to come too, which we did on the Lard. side in a sudden or short bend of the river..."
Lewis
"we Came 25 miles to day and Camp at the mouth of a creek named Warners R.] on the N. Side..."
Ordway
Camp May 10, 1805
Camp May 9, 1805
MISSOURI RIVER
"Warner River"
South Fork Duck Creek
North Fork Duck Creek
FORT PECK LAKE (Reservoir) Normal Pool Elevation 2246 feet
Approximate course of modern Missouri River flooded by reservoir.
Charles M. Russell National Wildlife Refuge
Ingles Coulee
Spring Draw
Fourth Ridge
Third Coulee
Third Ridge
Skunk Coulee
Second Ridge
HAXBY POINT
DRY ARM
Timbered Bottom
Sand Bar
Bluff
Sand Point
Wood
High Timber
Point
Naked Point
Valley Co.
Garfield Co.
Cartographer's Note: The cartographer has compiled the modern Missouri River through the Fort Peck Reservoir from a number of sources. Shown is the approximate course and water lines as developed from those various maps.
ONE STATUTE MILE
Modern Data: 1958-1972
Outbound: May 9-11, 1805
Lewis' Return: August 4, 1806
EXPLORATIONS OF LEWIS AND CLARK 1804 - 1806
CARTOGRAPHIC RECONSTRUCTION
WARNER CREEK
UTM ZONE 13
MAP NUMBER 195
Montana
CONTOUR INTERVAL 100 FEET

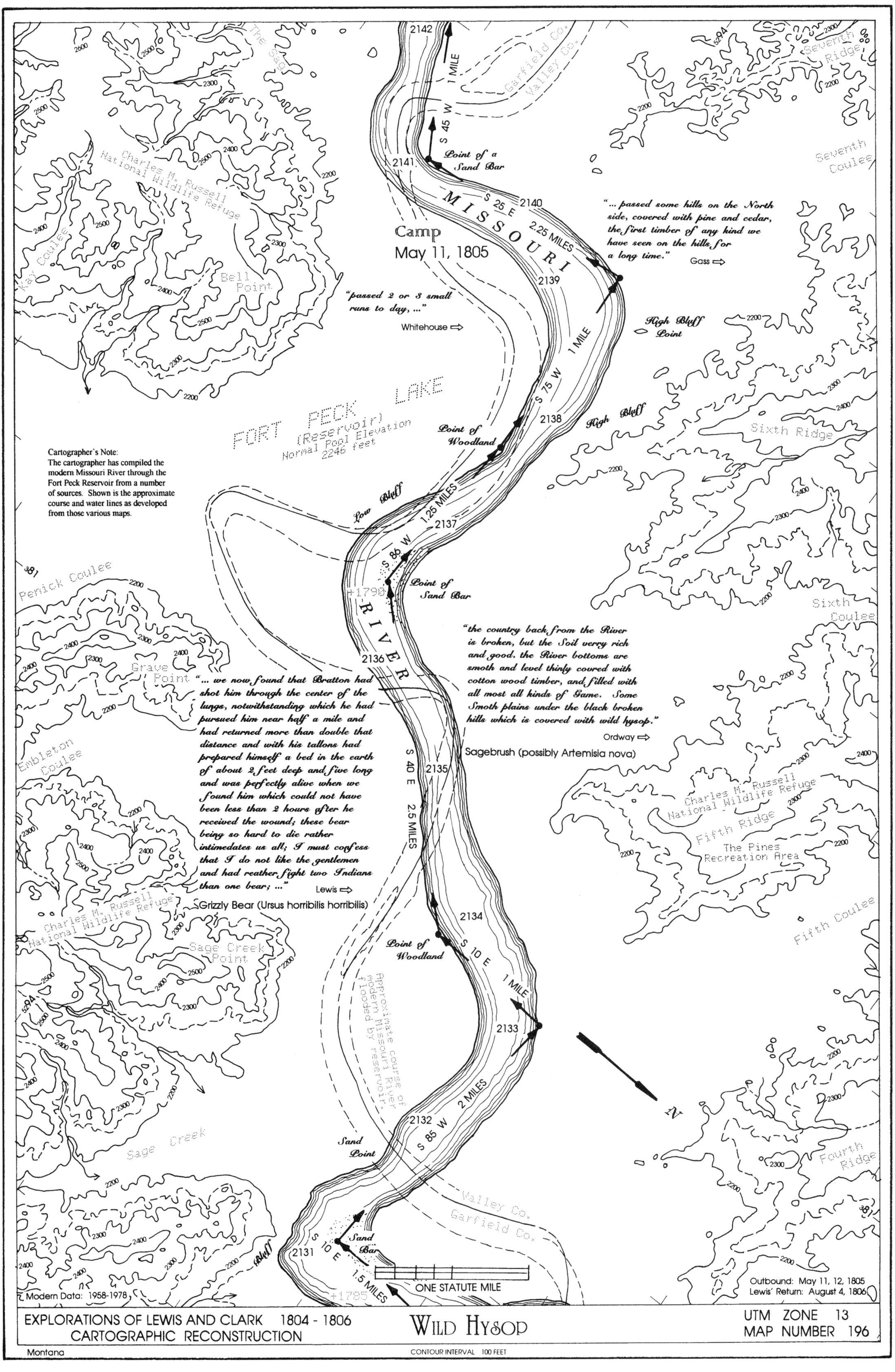
Camp
May 11, 1805
"... passed some hills on the North side, covered with pine and cedar, the first timber of any kind we have seen on the hills for a long time."
Gass ⇨
"passed 2 or 3 small runs to day, ..."
Whitehouse ⇨
FORT PECK LAKE
(Reservoir)
Normal Pool Elevation
2246 feet
Cartographer's Note:
The cartographer has compiled the modern Missouri River through the Fort Peck Reservoir from a number of sources. Shown is the approximate course and water lines as developed from those various maps.
"the country back from the River is broken, but the Soil verry rich and good. the River bottoms are smoth and level thinly covred with cotton wood timber, and filled with all most all kinds of Game. Some Smoth plains under the black broken hills which is covered with wild hysop."
Ordway ⇨
Sagebrush (possibly Artemisia nova)
"... we now found that Bratton had shot him through the center of the lungs, notwithstanding which he had pursued him near half a mile and had returned more than double that distance and with his tallons had prepared himself a bed in the earth of about 2 feet deep and five long and was perfectly alive when we found him which could not have been less than 2 hours after he received the wound; these bear being so hard to die rather intimedates us all; I must confess that I do not like the gentlemen and had reather fight two Indians than one bear; ..."
Lewis ⇨
Grizzly Bear (Ursus horribilis horribilis)
MISSOURI RIVER
Point of a Sand Bar
High Bluff Point
Point of Woodland
High Bluff
Low Bluff
Point of Sand Bar
Sand Point
Sand Bar
Bluff
Charles M. Russell National Wildlife Refuge
Seventh Ridge
Seventh Coulee
Sixth Ridge
Sixth Coulee
Fifth Ridge
Fifth Coulee
Fourth Ridge
The Pines Recreation Area
Bell Point
Penick Coulee
Grave Point
Embleton Coulee
Sage Creek Point
Sage Creek
Garfield Co.
Valley Co.
Approximate course of modern Missouri River flooded by reservoir.
ONE STATUTE MILE
N
Modern Data: 1958-1978
Outbound: May 11, 12, 1805
Lewis' Return: August 4, 1806
EXPLORATIONS OF LEWIS AND CLARK 1804 - 1806
CARTOGRAPHIC RECONSTRUCTION
WILD HYSOP
UTM ZONE 13
MAP NUMBER 196
Montana
CONTOUR INTERVAL 100 FEET

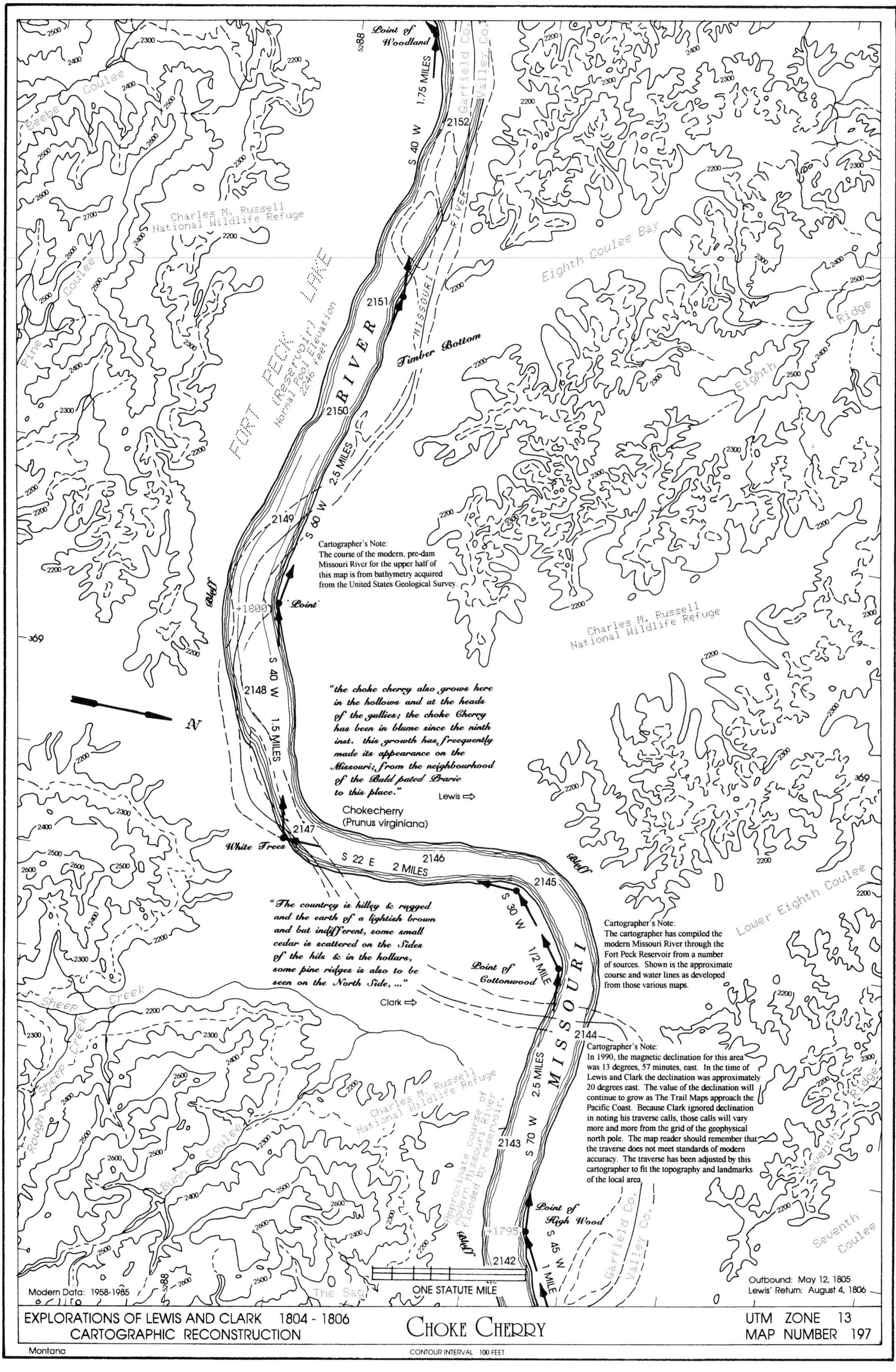

Point of Woodland
1.75 MILES
S 40 W
2152
Garfield Co.
Valley Co.
Beebe Coulee
Charles M. Russell National Wildlife Refuge
Pine Coulee
FORT PECK LAKE
(Reservoir)
Normal Pool Elevation 2246 feet
RIVER
MISSOURI RIVER
2151
2150
Timber Bottom
Eighth Coulee Bay
Eighth Ridge
2.5 MILES
S 60 W
2149
Cartographer's Note:
The course of the modern, pre-dam Missouri River for the upper half of this map is from bathymetry acquired from the United States Geological Survey.
Bluff
Point
+1800
369
S 40 W
2148
1.5 MILES
N
"the choke cherry also grows here in the hollows and at the heads of the gullies; the choke Cherry has been in blume since the ninth inst. this growth has freequently made its appearance on the Missouri; from the neighbourhood of the Bald pated Prarie to this place."
Lewis ⇨
Chokecherry
(Prunus virginiana)
2147
White Trees
S 22 E
2 MILES
2146
Bluff
2145
S 30 W
1/2 MILE
Point of Cottonwood
MISSOURI
"The countrey is hilley & rugged and the earth of a lightish brown and but indifferent, some small cedar is scattered on the Sides of the hils & in the hollars, some pine ridges is also to be seen on the North Side, ..."
Clark ⇨
Cartographer's Note:
The cartographer has compiled the modern Missouri River through the Fort Peck Reservoir from a number of sources. Shown is the approximate course and water lines as developed from those various maps.
Lower Eighth Coulee
Sheep Creek
Rough Sheep Creek
Burn Coulee
2144
2.5 MILES
S 70 W
2143
Cartographer's Note:
In 1990, the magnetic declination for this area was 13 degrees, 57 minutes, east. In the time of Lewis and Clark the declination was approximately 20 degrees east. The value of the declination will continue to grow as The Trail Maps approach the Pacific Coast. Because Clark ignored declination in noting his traverse calls, those calls will vary more and more from the grid of the geophysical north pole. The map reader should remember that the traverse does not meet standards of modern accuracy. The traverse has been adjusted by this cartographer to fit the topography and landmarks of the local area.
Seventh Ridge
Seventh Coulee
Approximate course of modern Missouri River flooded by reservoir.
Point of High Wood
+1795
S 45 W
1 MILE
2142
Bluff
ONE STATUTE MILE
The Sag
Modern Data: 1958-1985
Outbound: May 12, 1805
Lewis' Return: August 4, 1806
EXPLORATIONS OF LEWIS AND CLARK 1804 - 1806
CARTOGRAPHIC RECONSTRUCTION
CHOKE CHERRY
UTM ZONE 13
MAP NUMBER 197
Montana
CONTOUR INTERVAL 100 FEET

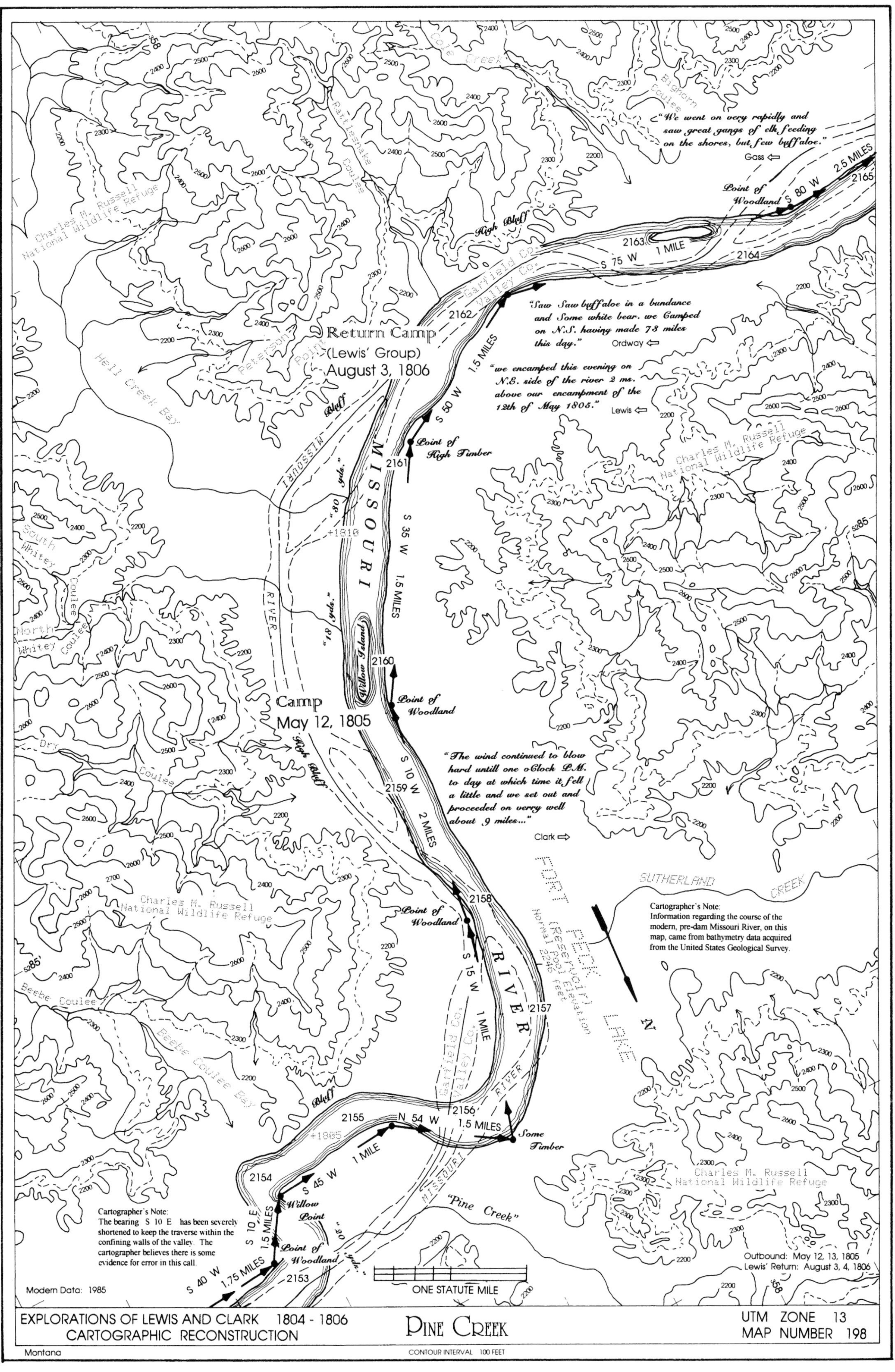

"We went on very rapidly and saw great gangs of elk feeding on the shores, but few buffaloe."
Gass
"Saw Saw buffaloe in a bundance and Some white bear. we Camped on N.S. having made 73 miles this day."
Ordway
"we encamped this evening on N.E. side of the river 2 ms. above our encampment of the 12th of May 1805."
Lewis
"The wind continued to blow hard untill one oClock P.M. to day at which time it fell a little and we set out and proceeded on verry well about 9 miles..."
Clark
Return Camp
(Lewis' Group)
August 3, 1806
Camp
May 12, 1805
MISSOURI
RIVER
Willow Island
Point of Woodland
Point of High Timber
High Bluff
Bluff
Some Timber
Willow Point
"Pine Creek"
FORT PECK (Reservoir) LAKE
Normal Pool Elevation 2246 feet
Charles M. Russell National Wildlife Refuge
Hell Creek Bay
Beebe Coulee Bay
Beebe Coulee
Dry Coulee
North Whitey Coulee
South Whitey Coulee
Rattlesnake Coulee
Cole Creek
Bighorn Coulee
Paterson Point
SUTHERLAND CREEK
Garfield Co.
Valley Co.
Cartographer's Note:
Information regarding the course of the modern, pre-dam Missouri River, on this map, came from bathymetry data acquired from the United States Geological Survey.
Cartographer's Note:
The bearing S 10 E has been severely shortened to keep the traverse within the confining walls of the valley. The cartographer believes there is some evidence for error in this call.
Outbound: May 12, 13, 1805
Lewis' Return: August 3, 4, 1806
Modern Data: 1985
ONE STATUTE MILE
EXPLORATIONS OF LEWIS AND CLARK 1804 - 1806
CARTOGRAPHIC RECONSTRUCTION
PINE CREEK
UTM ZONE 13
MAP NUMBER 198
Montana
CONTOUR INTERVAL 100 FEET

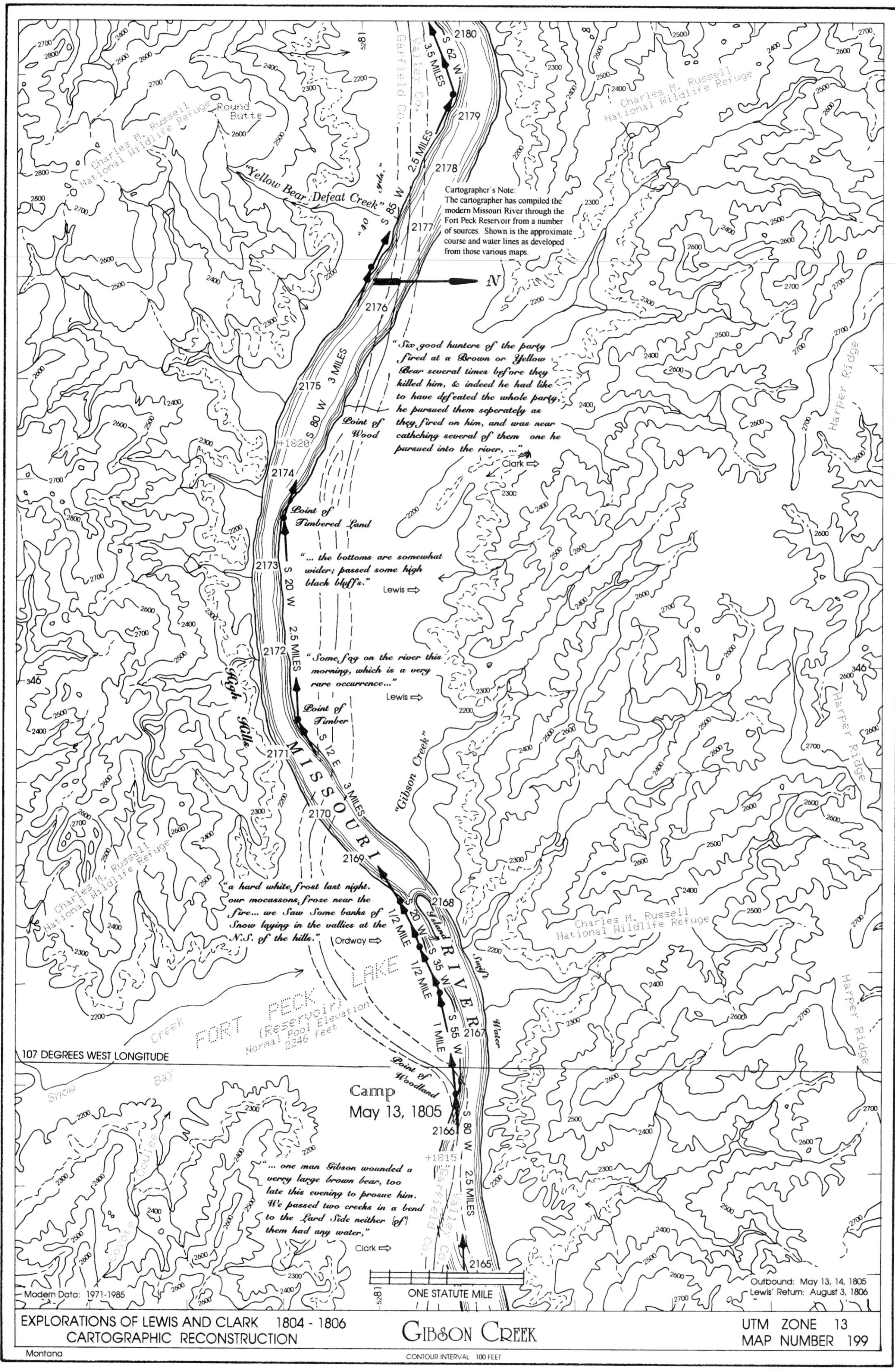

Round Butte
Charles M. Russell National Wildlife Refuge
"Yellow Bear Defeat Creek"
"40 yds."
Cartographer's Note:
The cartographer has compiled the modern Missouri River through the Fort Peck Reservoir from a number of sources. Shown is the approximate course and water lines as developed from those various maps.
N
Garfield Co.
Valley Co.
3.5 MILES
S 62 W
2.5 MILES
S 85 W
3 MILES
S 80 W
Point of Wood
"Six good hunters of the party fired at a Brown or Yellow Bear several times before they killed him, & indeed he had like to have defeated the whole party, he pursued them seperately as they fired on him, and was near cathching several of them one he pursued into the river, ..."
Clark ⇨
Point of Timbered Land
"... the bottoms are somewhat wider; passed some high black bluffs."
Lewis ⇨
S 20 W
2.5 MILES
"Some fog on the river this morning, which is a very rare occurrence..."
Lewis ⇨
Point of Timber
S 12 E
3 MILES
High Hills
Harper Ridge
Gibson Creek
MISSOURI RIVER
Island
Stony Water
"a hard white frost last night. our mocassons froze near the fire... we Saw Some banks of Snow laying in the vallies at the N.S. of the hills."
Ordway ⇨
1/2 MILE
S 20 W
1/2 MILE
S 35 W
1 MILE
S 55 W
FORT PECK LAKE
(Reservoir)
Normal Pool Elevation 2246 feet
Snow Creek
Snow Bay
107 DEGREES WEST LONGITUDE
Point of Woodland
Camp
May 13, 1805
S 80 W
2.5 MILES
Coyote Coulee
"... one man Gibson wounded a verry large brown bear, too late this evening to prosue him. We passed two creeks in a bend to the Lard Side neither [of] them had any water,"
Clark ⇨
ONE STATUTE MILE
Modern Data: 1971-1985
Outbound: May 13, 14, 1805
Lewis' Return: August 3, 1806
EXPLORATIONS OF LEWIS AND CLARK 1804 - 1806
CARTOGRAPHIC RECONSTRUCTION
GIBSON CREEK
UTM ZONE 13
MAP NUMBER 199
Montana
CONTOUR INTERVAL 100 FEET

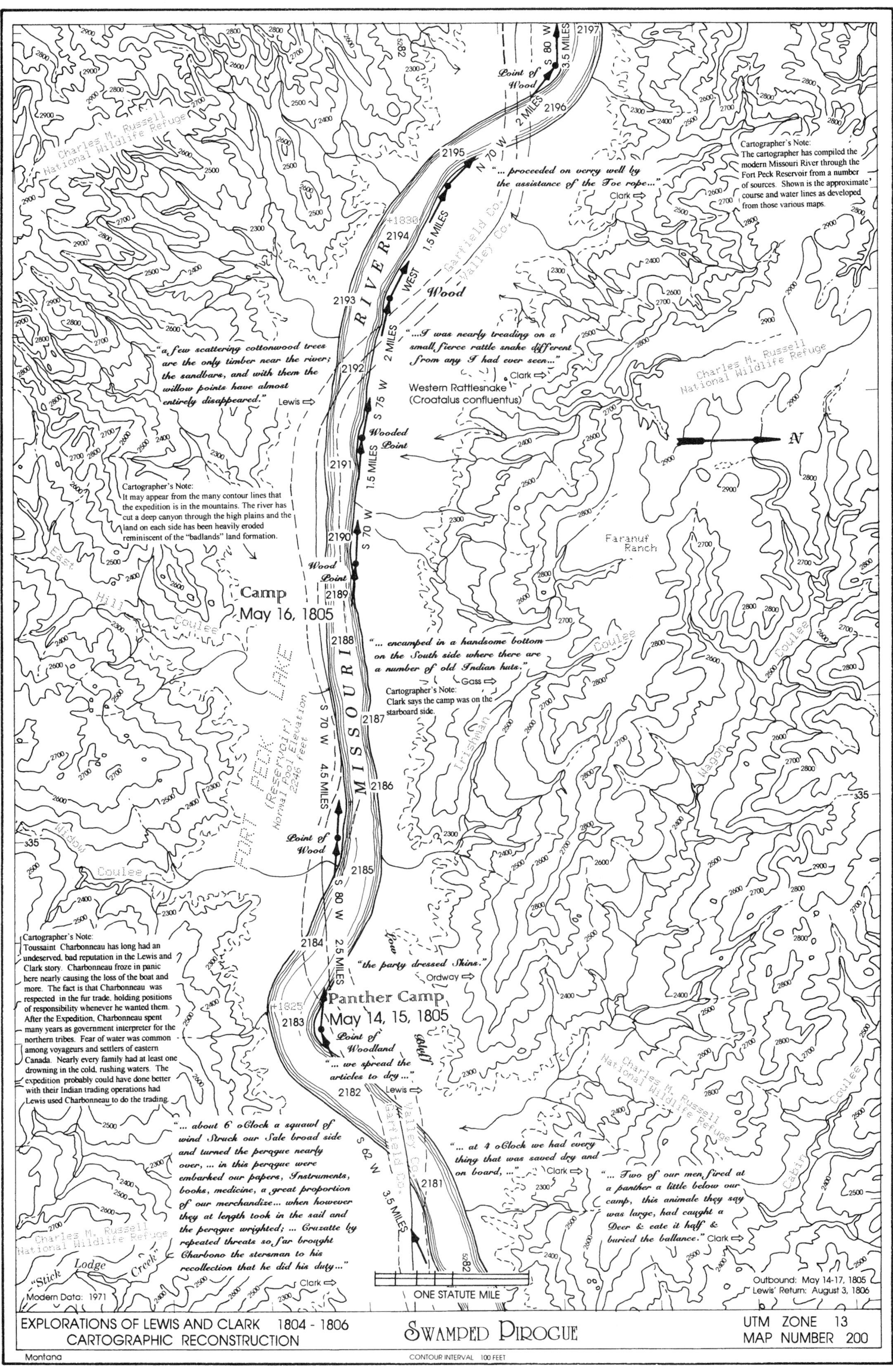
"... proceeded on verry well by the assistance of the Toe rope..." Clark ⇨
Cartographer's Note: The cartographer has compiled the modern Missouri River through the Fort Peck Reservoir from a number of sources. Shown is the approximate course and water lines as developed from those various maps.
Point of Wood
Charles M. Russell National Wildlife Refuge
Garfield Co.
Valley Co.
MISSOURI RIVER
Wood
"...I was nearly treading on a small fierce rattle snake different from any I had ever seen..." Clark ⇨
Western Rattlesnake (Croatalus confluentus)
"a few scattering cottonwood trees are the only timber near the river; the sandbars, and with them the willow points have almost entirely disappeared." Lewis ⇨
Wooded Point
N
Cartographer's Note: It may appear from the many contour lines that the expedition is in the mountains. The river has cut a deep canyon through the high plains and the land on each side has been heavily eroded reminiscent of the "badlands" land formation.
Faranuf Ranch
East Hill Coulee
Wood Point
Camp May 16, 1805
"... encamped in a handsome bottom on the South side where there are a number of old Indian huts." Gass ⇨
Cartographer's Note: Clark says the camp was on the starboard side.
FORT PECK LAKE (Reservoir) Normal Pool Elevation 2246 feet
Irishman
Wagon Coulee
Widow Coulee
Point of Wood
Cartographer's Note: Toussaint Charbonneau has long had an undeserved, bad reputation in the Lewis and Clark story. Charbonneau froze in panic here nearly causing the loss of the boat and more. The fact is that Charbonneau was respected in the fur trade, holding positions of responsibility whenever he wanted them. After the Expedition, Charbonneau spent many years as government interpreter for the northern tribes. Fear of water was common among voyageurs and settlers of eastern Canada. Nearly every family had at least one drowning in the cold, rushing waters. The expedition probably could have done better with their Indian trading operations had Lewis used Charbonneau to do the trading.
Low
"the party dressed Skins." Ordway ⇨
Panther Camp May 14, 15, 1805
Point of Woodland
Bluff
"... we spread the articles to dry..." Lewis ⇨
"... about 6 oClock a squawl of wind Struck our Sale broad side and turned the perogue nearly over, ... in this perogue were embarked our papers, Instruments, books, medicine, a great proportion of our merchandize... when however they at length took in the sail and the perogue wrighted; ... Cruzatte by repeated threats so far brought Charbono the stersman to his recollection that he did his duty..." Clark ⇨
"... at 4 oClock we had every thing that was saved dry and on board, ..." Clark ⇨
"... Two of our men fired at a panther a little below our camp, this animale they say was large, had caught a Deer & eate it half & buried the ballance." Clark ⇨
Cabin Coulee
"Stick Lodge Creek"
Modern Data: 1971
ONE STATUTE MILE
Outbound: May 14-17, 1805
Lewis' Return: August 3, 1806
EXPLORATIONS OF LEWIS AND CLARK 1804 - 1806
CARTOGRAPHIC RECONSTRUCTION
SWAMPED PIROGUE
UTM ZONE 13
MAP NUMBER 200
Montana
CONTOUR INTERVAL 100 FEET

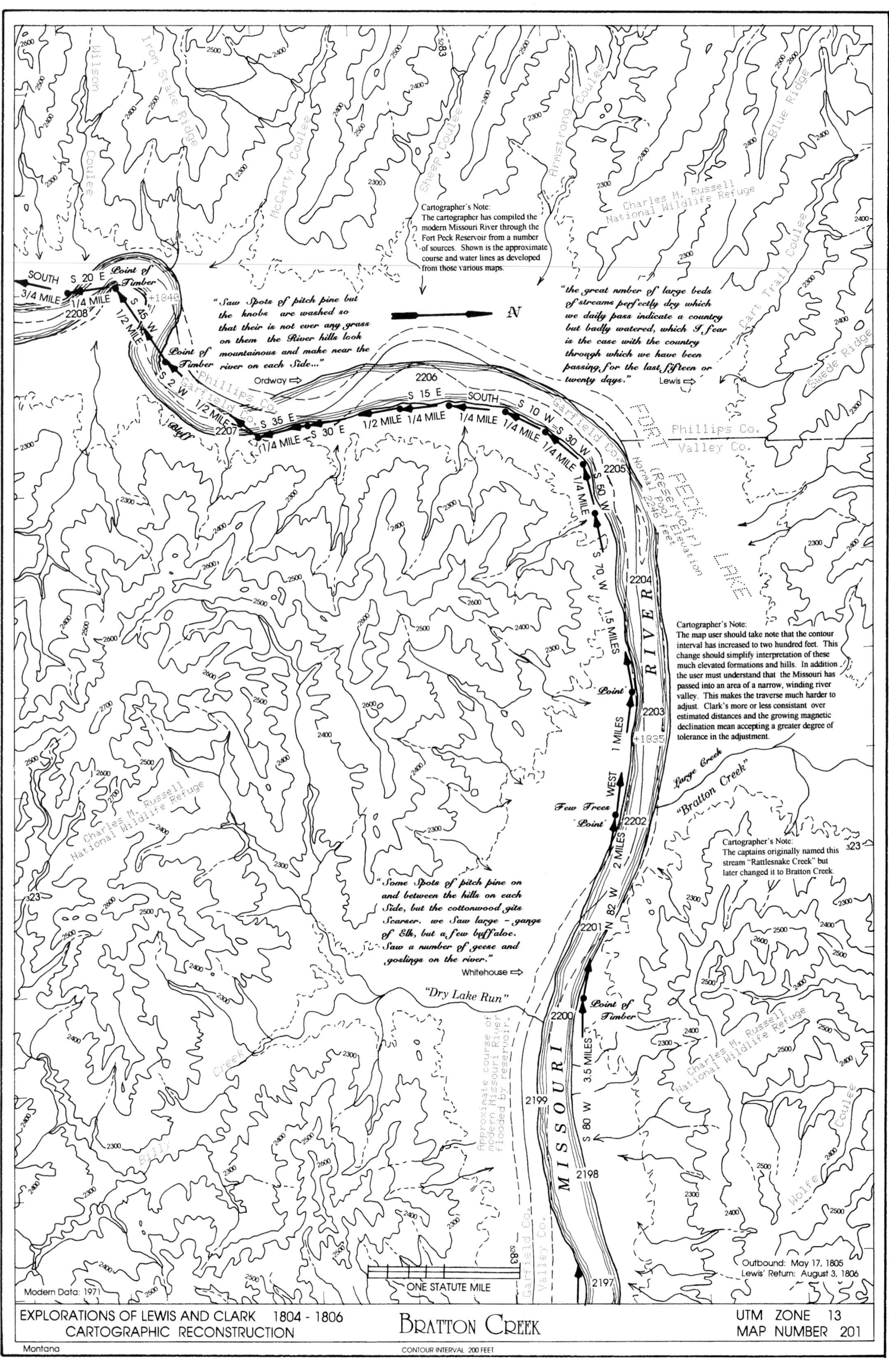

Cartographer's Note:
The cartographer has compiled the modern Missouri River through the Fort Peck Reservoir from a number of sources. Shown is the approximate course and water lines as developed from those various maps.
"Saw Spots of pitch pine but the knobs are washed so that their is not ever any grass on them the River hills look mountainous and make near the river on each Side..."
Ordway ⇨
"the great nmber of large beds of streams perfectly dry which we daily pass indicate a country but badly watered, which I fear is the case with the country through which we have been passing for the last fifteen or twenty days."
Lewis ⇨
Cartographer's Note:
The map user should take note that the contour interval has increased to two hundred feet. This change should simplify interpretation of these much elevated formations and hills. In addition the user must understand that the Missouri has passed into an area of a narrow, winding river valley. This makes the traverse much harder to adjust. Clark's more or less consistant over estimated distances and the growing magnetic declination mean accepting a greater degree of tolerance in the adjustment.
Cartographer's Note:
The captains originally named this stream "Rattlesnake Creek" but later changed it to Bratton Creek.
"Some Spots of pitch pine on and between the hills on each Side, but the cottonwood gits Scarser. we Saw large - gangs of Elk, but a few buffaloe. Saw a number of geese and goslings on the river."
Whitehouse ⇨
"Dry Lake Run"
"Bratton Creek"
Large Creek
FORT PECK LAKE
MISSOURI RIVER
Charles M. Russell National Wildlife Refuge
Phillips Co.
Valley Co.
Garfield Co.
Approximate course of modern Missouri River flooded by reservoir.
Reservoir Elevation Normal Pool 2246 feet
Outbound: May 17, 1805
Lewis' Return: August 3, 1806
Modern Data: 1971
ONE STATUTE MILE
EXPLORATIONS OF LEWIS AND CLARK 1804 - 1806
CARTOGRAPHIC RECONSTRUCTION
BRATTON CREEK
UTM ZONE 13
MAP NUMBER 201
Montana
CONTOUR INTERVAL 200 FEET

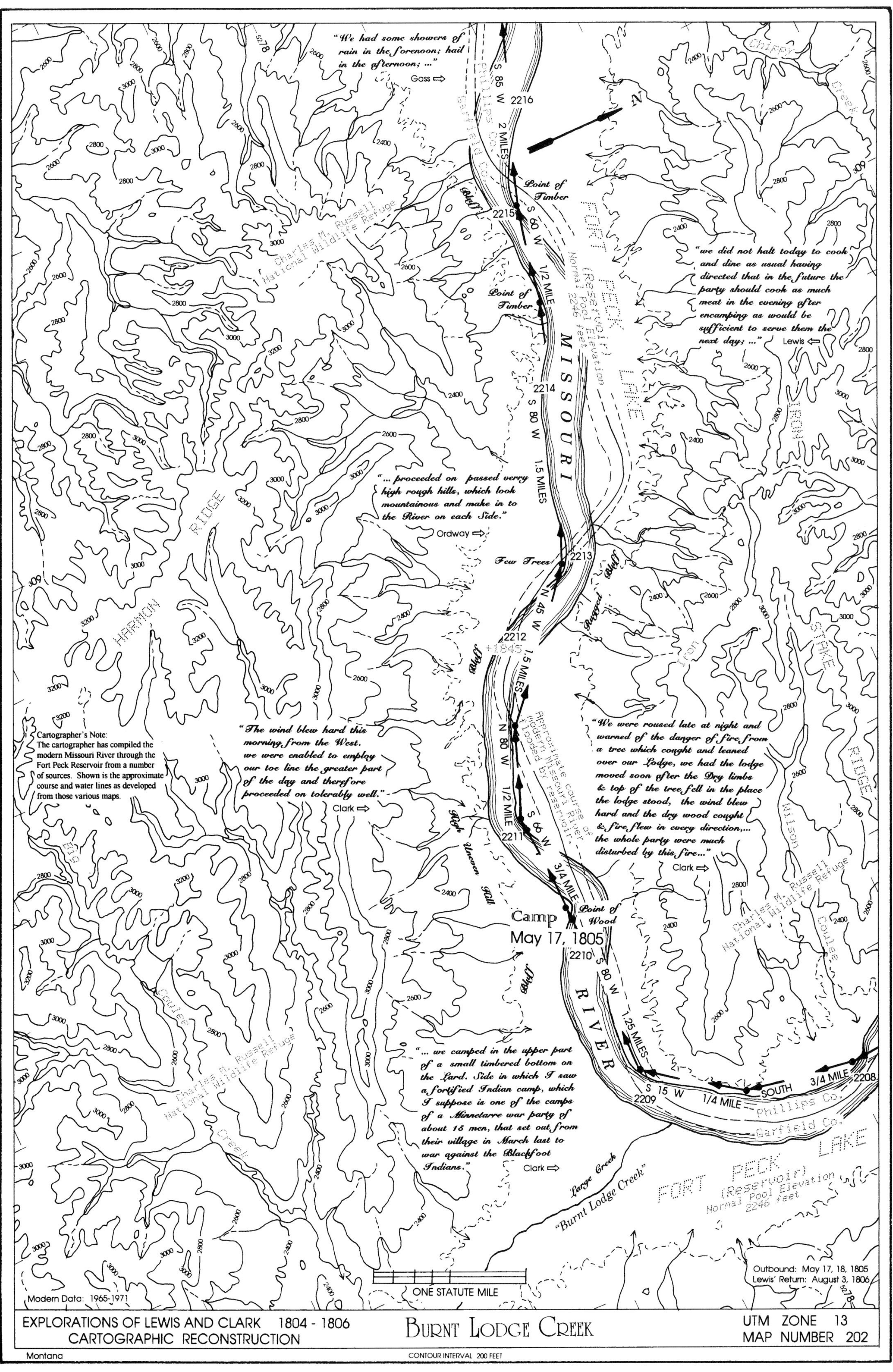
"We had some showers of rain in the forenoon; hail in the afternoon; ..."
Gass ⇨
"we did not halt today to cook and dine as usual having directed that in the future the party should cook as much meat in the evening after encamping as would be sufficient to serve them the next day; ..."
Lewis ⇦
"... proceeded on passed verry high rough hills, which look mountainous and make in to the River on each Side."
Ordway ⇨
Cartographer's Note:
The cartographer has compiled the modern Missouri River through the Fort Peck Reservoir from a number of sources. Shown is the approximate course and water lines as developed from those various maps.
"The wind blew hard this morning from the West. we were enabled to employ our toe line the greater part of the day and therefore proceeded on tolerably well."
Clark ⇨
"We were roused late at night and warned of the danger of fire from a tree which cought and leaned over our Lodge, we had the lodge moved soon after the Dry limbs & top of the tree fell in the place the lodge stood, the wind blew hard and the dry wood cought & fire flew in every direction,... the whole party were much disturbed by this fire..."
Clark ⇨
"... we camped in the upper part of a small timbered bottom on the Lard. Side in which I saw a fortified Indian camp, which I suppose is one of the camps of a Minnetarre war party of about 15 men, that set out from their village in March last to war against the Blackfoot Indians."
Clark ⇨
Camp
May 17, 1805
MISSOURI
RIVER
FORT PECK LAKE
(Reservoir)
Normal Pool Elevation
2246 feet
Approximate course of modern Missouri River flooded by reservoir
Point of Timber
Point of Timber
Few Trees
Point of Wood
Rugged Bluff
High Uneven Hill
Large Creek
"Burnt Lodge Creek"
Charles M. Russell National Wildlife Refuge
Phillips Co.
Garfield Co.
HARMON RIDGE
IRON STAKE RIDGE
Chippy Creek
Wilson Coulee
S 85 W 2 MILES
S 60 W 1/2 MILE
S 80 W 1.5 MILES
N 45 W 1.5 MILES
N 80 W 1/2 MILE
S 66 W 3/4 MILE
S 80 W 1.25 MILES
S 15 W 1/4 MILE
SOUTH 3/4 MILE
2216
2215
2214
2213
2212
2211
2210
2209
2208
N
ONE STATUTE MILE
Outbound: May 17, 18, 1805
Lewis' Return: August 3, 1806
Modern Data: 1965-1971
EXPLORATIONS OF LEWIS AND CLARK 1804 - 1806
CARTOGRAPHIC RECONSTRUCTION
BURNT LODGE CREEK
UTM ZONE 13
MAP NUMBER 202
Montana
CONTOUR INTERVAL 200 FEET

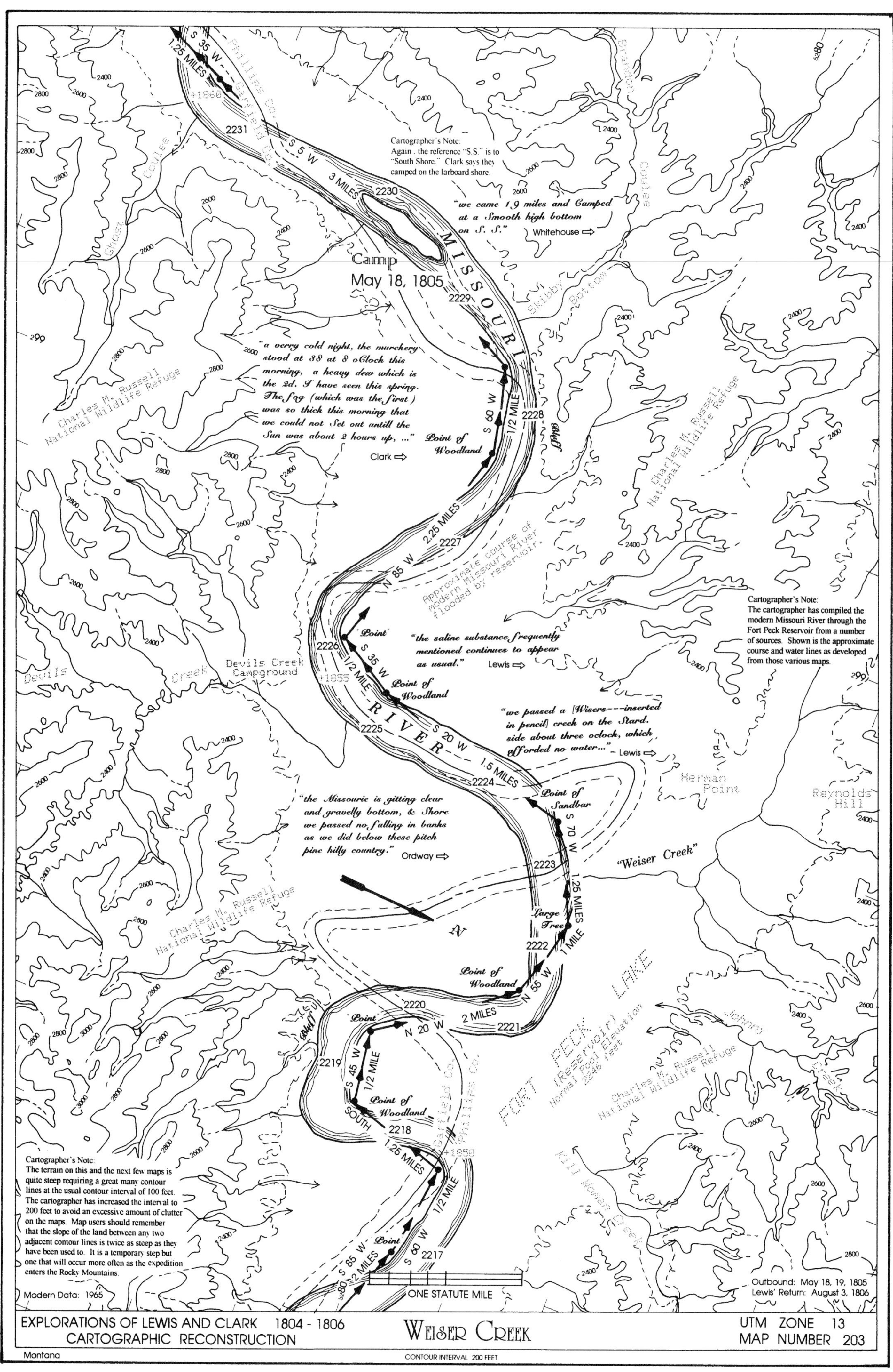
Cartographer's Note:
Again, the reference "S.S." is to "South Shore." Clark says they camped on the larboard shore.
"we came 1 9 miles and Camped at a Smooth high bottom on S. S." Whitehouse ⇨
Camp
May 18, 1805
"a verry cold night, the murckery stood at 38 at 8 oClock this morning, a heavy dew which is the 2d. I have seen this spring. The fog (which was the first) was so thick this morning that we could not Set out untill the Sun was about 2 hours up, ..." Clark ⇨
Point of Woodland
MISSOURI
RIVER
Skibby Bottom
Ghost Coulee
Brandon Coulee
Phillips Co.
Garfield Co.
Charles M. Russell National Wildlife Refuge
Approximate course of modern Missouri River flooded by reservoir.
Cartographer's Note:
The cartographer has compiled the modern Missouri River through the Fort Peck Reservoir from a number of sources. Shown is the approximate course and water lines as developed from those various maps.
"the saline substance frequently mentioned continues to appear as usual." Lewis ⇨
Point
Devils Creek
Devils Creek Campground
"we passed a [Wisers---inserted in pencil] creek on the Stard. side about three oclock, which afforded no water..." - Lewis ⇨
Herman Point
Reynolds Hill
Point of Sandbar
"the Missourie is gitting clear and gravelly bottom, & Shore we passed no falling in banks as we did below these pitch pine hilly country." Ordway ⇨
"Weiser Creek"
Large Tree
N
FORT PECK LAKE
(Reservoir)
Normal Pool Elevation 2246 feet
Johnny Creek
Kill Woman Creek
Bluff
Cartographer's Note:
The terrain on this and the next few maps is quite steep requiring a great many contour lines at the usual contour interval of 100 feet. The cartographer has increased the interval to 200 feet to avoid an excessive amount of clutter on the maps. Map users should remember that the slope of the land between any two adjacent contour lines is twice as steep as they have been used to. It is a temporary step but one that will occur more often as the expedition enters the Rocky Mountains.
Modern Data: 1965
ONE STATUTE MILE
Outbound: May 18, 19, 1805
Lewis' Return: August 3, 1806
EXPLORATIONS OF LEWIS AND CLARK 1804 - 1806
CARTOGRAPHIC RECONSTRUCTION
WEISER CREEK
UTM ZONE 13
MAP NUMBER 203
Montana
CONTOUR INTERVAL 200 FEET

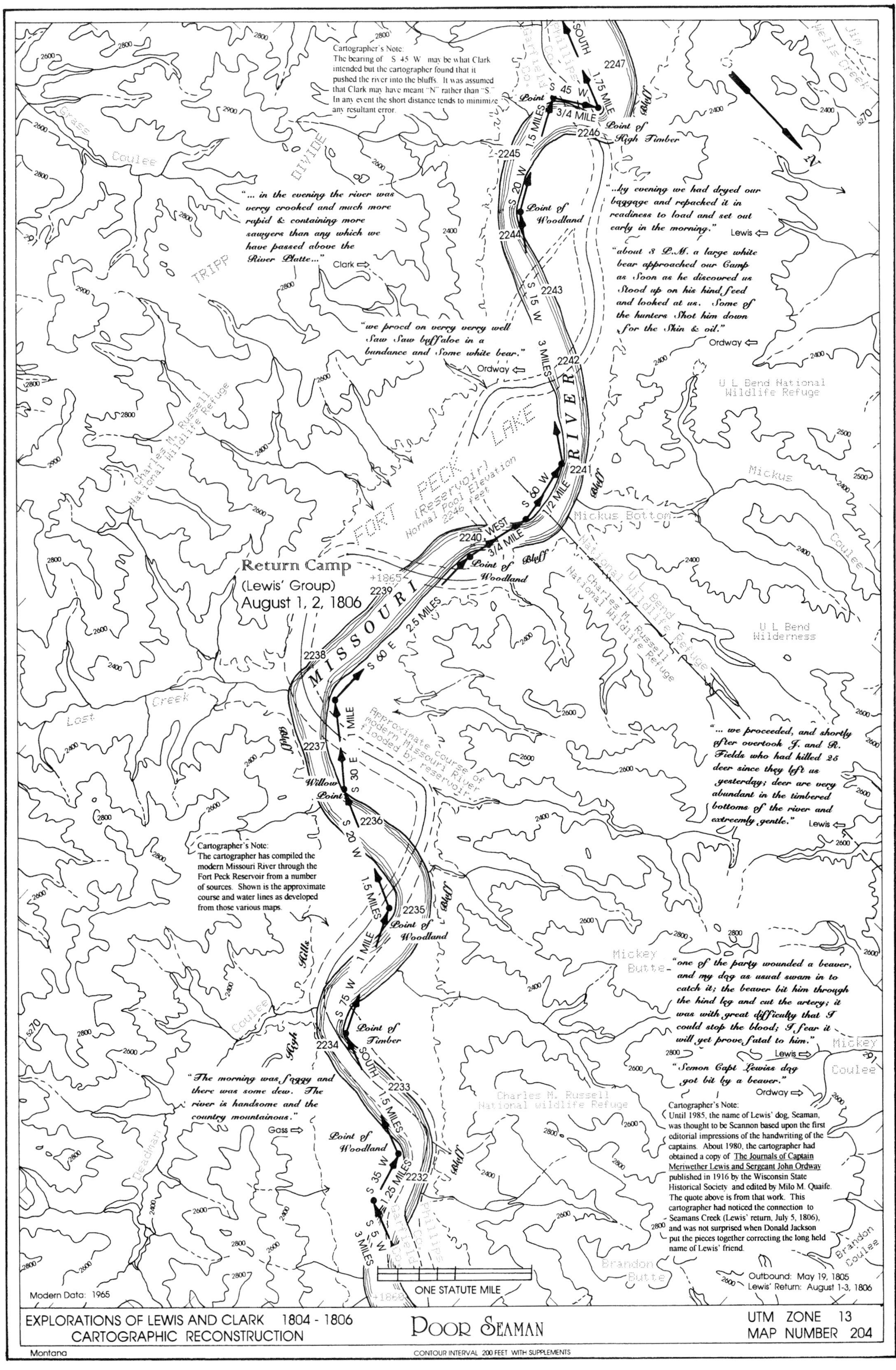
Cartographer's Note:
The bearing of S 45 W may be what Clark intended but the cartographer found that it pushed the river into the bluffs. It was assumed that Clark may have meant "N" rather than "S." In any event the short distance tends to minimize any resultant error.
"... in the evening the river was verry crooked and much more rapid & containing more sawyers than any which we have passed above the River Platte..." Clark ⇨
"...by evening we had dryed our baggage and repacked it in readiness to load and set out early in the morning." Lewis ⇦
"about 3 P.M. a large white bear approached our Camp as Soon as he discovered us Stood up on his hind feed and looked at us. Some of the hunters Shot him down for the Skin & oil." Ordway ⇦
"we procd on verry verry well Saw Saw buffaloe in a bundance and Some white bear." Ordway ⇦
Return Camp
(Lewis' Group)
August 1, 2, 1806
"... we proceeded, and shortly after overtook J. and R. Fields who had killed 25 deer since they left us yesterday; deer are very abundant in the timbered bottoms of the river and extreemly gentle." Lewis ⇦
Cartographer's Note:
The cartographer has compiled the modern Missouri River through the Fort Peck Reservoir from a number of sources. Shown is the approximate course and water lines as developed from those various maps.
"one of the party wounded a beaver, and my dog as usual swam in to catch it; the beaver bit him through the hind leg and cut the artery; it was with great difficulty that I could stop the blood; I fear it will yet prove fatal to him." Lewis ⇨
"Semon Capt Lewiss dog got bit by a beaver." Ordway ⇨
"The morning was foggy and there was some dew. The river is handsome and the country mountainous." Gass ⇨
Cartographer's Note:
Until 1985, the name of Lewis' dog, Seaman, was thought to be Scannon based upon the first editorial impressions of the handwriting of the captains. About 1980, the cartographer had obtained a copy of The Journals of Captain Meriwether Lewis and Sergeant John Ordway published in 1916 by the Wisconsin State Historical Society and edited by Milo M. Quaife. The quote above is from that work. This cartographer had noticed the connection to Seamans Creek (Lewis' return, July 5, 1806), and was not surprised when Donald Jackson put the pieces together correcting the long held name of Lewis' friend.
MISSOURI RIVER
FORT PECK LAKE
(Reservoir)
Normal Pool Elevation 2246 feet
Approximate course of modern Missouri River flooded by reservoir
Charles M. Russell National Wildlife Refuge
U L Bend National Wildlife Refuge
U L Bend Wilderness
Mickus Bottom
Mickey Butte
Brandon Butte
Lost Creek
Grass Coulee
TRIPP DIVIDE
Point of Woodland
Point of High Timber
Willow Point
Point of Timber
Bluff
High Hills
Outbound: May 19, 1805
Lewis' Return: August 1-3, 1806
ONE STATUTE MILE
Modern Data: 1965
EXPLORATIONS OF LEWIS AND CLARK 1804 - 1806
CARTOGRAPHIC RECONSTRUCTION
POOR SEAMAN
UTM ZONE 13
MAP NUMBER 204
Montana
CONTOUR INTERVAL 200 FEET WITH SUPPLEMENTS

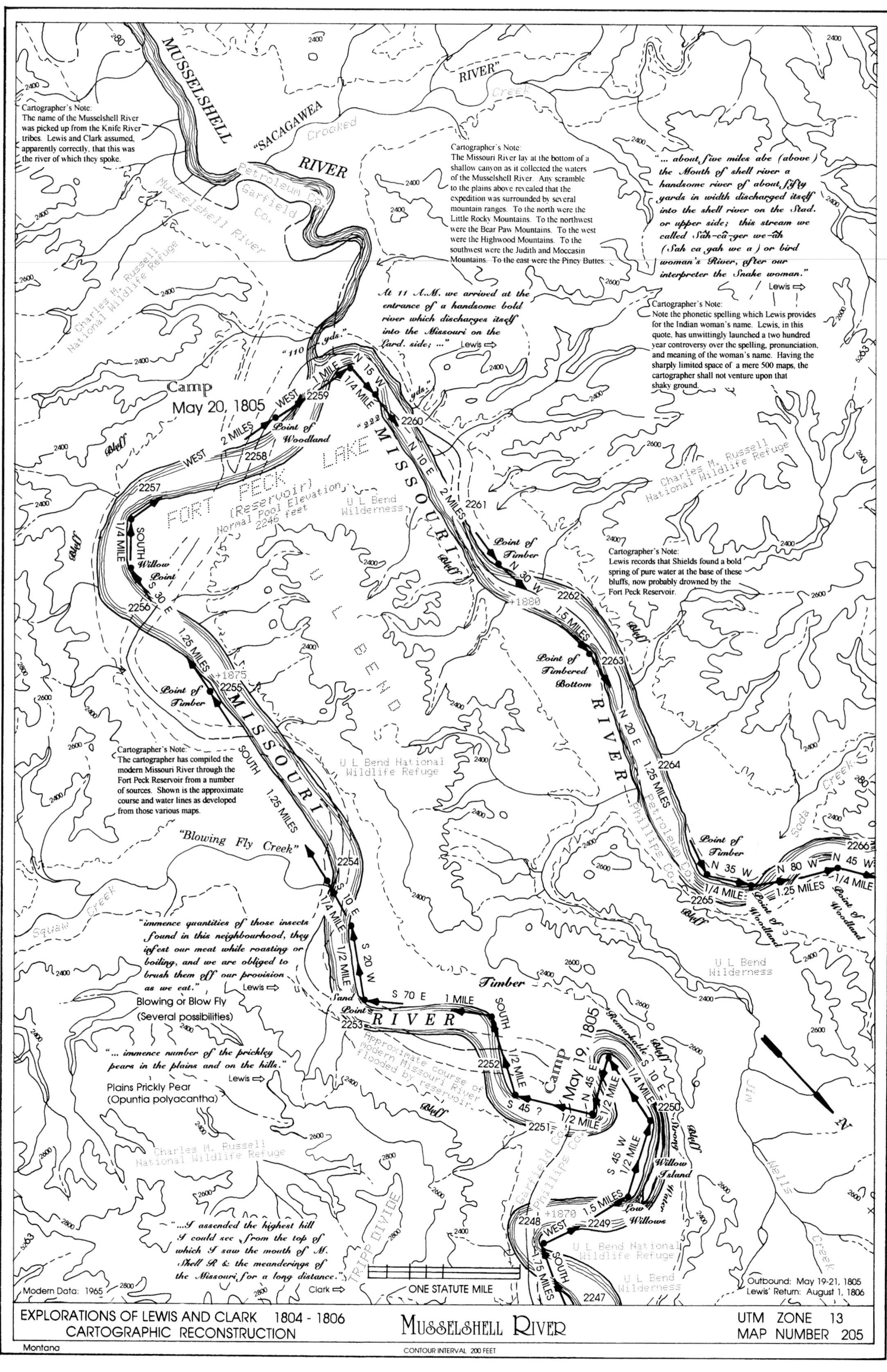
MUSSELSHELL
"SACAGAWEA
RIVER
RIVER"
Cartographer's Note:
The name of the Musselshell River was picked up from the Knife River tribes. Lewis and Clark assumed, apparently correctly, that this was the river of which they spoke.
Cartographer's Note:
The Missouri River lay at the bottom of a shallow canyon as it collected the waters of the Musselshell River. Any scramble to the plains above revealed that the expedition was surrounded by several mountain ranges. To the north were the Little Rocky Mountains. To the northwest were the Bear Paw Mountains. To the west were the Highwood Mountains. To the southwest were the Judith and Moccasin Mountains. To the east were the Piney Buttes.
"... about five miles abe (above) the Mouth of shell river a handsome river of about fifty yards in width discharged itself into the shell river on the Stad. or upper side; this stream we called Sah-ca-ger we-ah (Sah ca gah we a) or bird woman's River, after our interpreter the Snake woman."
Lewis ⇨
Cartographer's Note:
Note the phonetic spelling which Lewis provides for the Indian woman's name. Lewis, in this quote, has unwittingly launched a two hundred year controversy over the spelling, pronunciation, and meaning of the woman's name. Having the sharply limited space of a mere 500 maps, the cartographer shall not venture upon that shaky ground.
At 11 A.M. we arrived at the entrance of a handsome bold river which discharges itself into the Missouri on the Lard. side; ..."
Lewis ⇨
Camp
May 20, 1805
FORT PECK LAKE
(Reservoir)
Normal Pool Elevation 2246 feet
U L Bend Wilderness
Charles M. Russell National Wildlife Refuge
MISSOURI
Cartographer's Note:
Lewis records that Shields found a bold spring of pure water at the base of these bluffs, now probably drowned by the Fort Peck Reservoir.
Cartographer's Note:
The cartographer has compiled the modern Missouri River through the Fort Peck Reservoir from a number of sources. Shown is the approximate course and water lines as developed from those various maps.
U L Bend National Wildlife Refuge
RIVER
"Blowing Fly Creek"
"immence quantities of those insects found in this neighbourhood, they infest our meat while roasting or boiling, and we are obliged to brush them off our provision as we eat."
Lewis ⇨
Blowing or Blow Fly
(Several possibilities)
"... immence number of the prickley pears in the plains and on the hills."
Lewis ⇨
Plains Prickly Pear
(Opuntia polyacantha)
Approximate course of modern Missouri River flooded by reservoir
Camp
May 19, 1805
TRIPP DIVIDE
"...I assended the highest hill I could see from the top of which I saw the mouth of M. Shell R & the meanderings of the Missouri for a long distance."
Clark ⇨
ONE STATUTE MILE
Modern Data: 1965
Outbound: May 19-21, 1805
Lewis' Return: August 1, 1806
EXPLORATIONS OF LEWIS AND CLARK 1804 - 1806
CARTOGRAPHIC RECONSTRUCTION
Montana
MUSSELSHELL RIVER
CONTOUR INTERVAL 200 FEET
UTM ZONE 13
MAP NUMBER 205

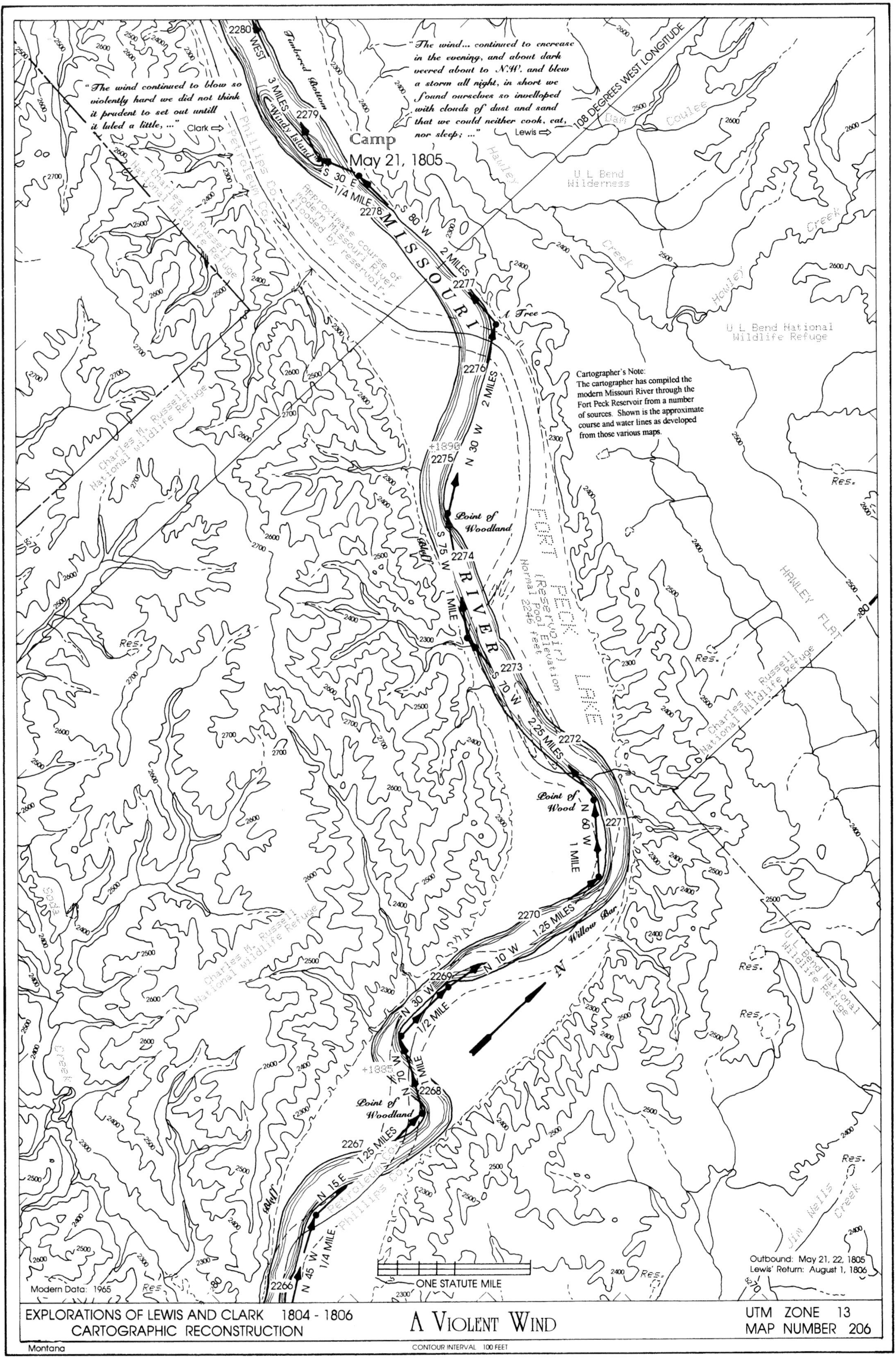
"The wind continued to blow so violently hard we did not think it prudent to set out untill it luled a little, ..." Clark
"The wind... continued to encrease in the evening, and about dark veered about to N.W. and blew a storm all night, in short we found ourselves so invelloped with clouds of dust and sand that we could neither cook, eat, nor sleep; ..." Lewis
Camp
May 21, 1805
Timbered Bottom
Windy Island
MISSOURI RIVER
FORT PECK LAKE
(Reservoir)
Normal Pool Elevation 2246 feet
Approximate course of modern Missouri River flooded by reservoir.
108 DEGREES WEST LONGITUDE
U L Bend Wilderness
U L Bend National Wildlife Refuge
Charles M. Russell National Wildlife Refuge
Phillips Co.
Petroleum Co.
Hawley Creek
Hawley Flat
Dam Coulee
Jim Wells Creek
Res.
A Tree
Point of Woodland
Point of Wood
Willow Bar
Bluff
Cartographer's Note:
The cartographer has compiled the modern Missouri River through the Fort Peck Reservoir from a number of sources. Shown is the approximate course and water lines as developed from those various maps.
WEST
3 MILES
S 30 E
1/4 MILE
S 80 W
2 MILES
N 30 W
2 MILES
S 75 W
1 MILE
S 70 W
2.25 MILES
N 60 W
1 MILE
1.25 MILES
N 10 W
N 30 W
1/2 MILE
N 70 W
1 MILE
1.25 MILES
N 15 E
1/4 MILE
N 45 W
ONE STATUTE MILE
Outbound: May 21, 22, 1805
Lewis' Return: August 1, 1806
Modern Data: 1965
EXPLORATIONS OF LEWIS AND CLARK 1804 - 1806
CARTOGRAPHIC RECONSTRUCTION
A VIOLENT WIND
UTM ZONE 13
MAP NUMBER 206
Montana
CONTOUR INTERVAL 100 FEET

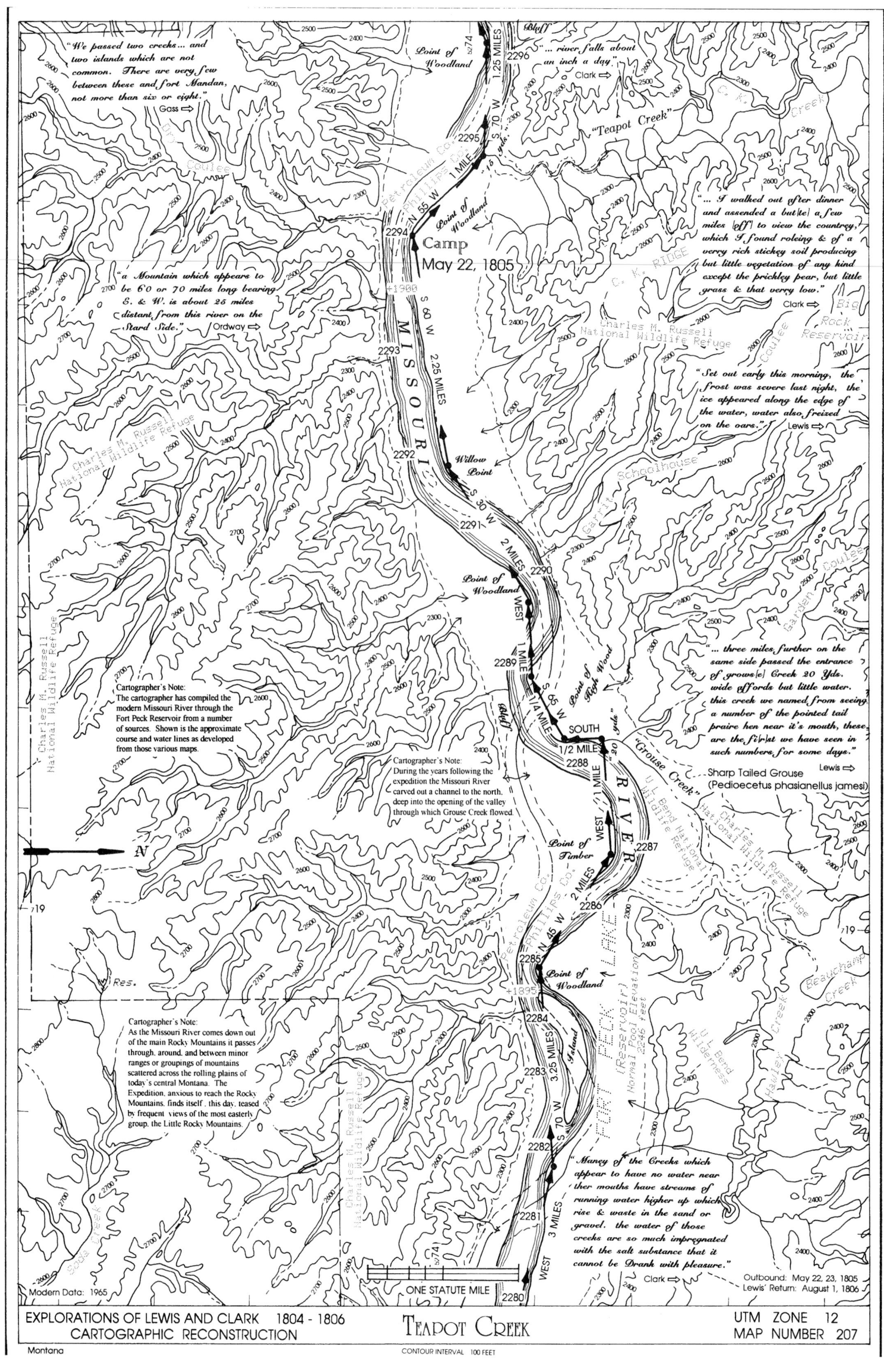
"We passed two creeks... and two islands which are not common. There are very few between these and fort Mandan, not more than six or eight."
Gass ⇨
"... river falls about an inch a day."
Clark ⇨
"Teapot Creek"
Point of Woodland
Bluff
C. K. Creek
Dry Coulee
Phillips Petroleum Co.
"... I walked out after dinner and assended a but[te] a few miles [off] to view the countrey, which I found roleing & of a verry rich stickey soil producing but little vegetation of any kind except the prickley pear, but little grass & that verry low."
Clark ⇨
Camp
May 22, 1805
"a Mountain which appears to be 60 or 70 miles long bearing S. & W. is about 25 miles distant from this river on the Stard Side."
Ordway ⇨
C. K. RIDGE
Charles M. Russell National Wildlife Refuge
Big Rock Reservoir
Coulee
MISSOURI
RIVER
"Set out early this morning, the frost was severe last night, the ice appeared along the edge of the water, water also freized on the oars."
Lewis ⇨
Willow Point
Garrit Schoolhouse
Garden Coulee
Point of Woodland
Point of High Wood
"... three miles further on the same side passed the entrance of grows[e] Creek 20 Yds. wide affords but little water. this creek we named from seeing a number of the pointed tail praire hen near it's mouth, these are the fi[r]st we have seen in such numbers for some days."
Lewis ⇨
Cartographer's Note:
The cartographer has compiled the modern Missouri River through the Fort Peck Reservoir from a number of sources. Shown is the approximate course and water lines as developed from those various maps.
Cartographer's Note:
During the years following the expedition the Missouri River carved out a channel to the north, deep into the opening of the valley through which Grouse Creek flowed.
"Grouse Creek"
Sharp Tailed Grouse
(Pedioecetus phasianellus jamesi)
U. L. Bend National Wildlife Refuge
Point of Timber
N
Point of Woodland
FORT PECK LAKE
(Reservoir)
Normal Pool Elevation 2246 feet
Beauchamp Creek
Res.
Island
U. L. Bend Wilderness
Hawley Creek
Cartographer's Note:
As the Missouri River comes down out of the main Rocky Mountains it passes through, around, and between minor ranges or groupings of mountains scattered across the rolling plains of today's central Montana. The Expedition, anxious to reach the Rocky Mountains, finds itself, this day, teased by frequent views of the most easterly group, the Little Rocky Mountains.
Soda Creek
"Maney of the Creeks which appear to have no water near ther mouths have streams of running water higher up which rise & waste in the sand or gravel. the water of those creeks are so much impregnated with the salt substance that it cannot be Drank with pleasure."
Clark ⇨
Outbound: May 22, 23, 1805
Lewis' Return: August 1, 1806
Modern Data: 1965
ONE STATUTE MILE
EXPLORATIONS OF LEWIS AND CLARK 1804 - 1806
CARTOGRAPHIC RECONSTRUCTION
TEAPOT CREEK
UTM ZONE 12
MAP NUMBER 207
Montana
CONTOUR INTERVAL 100 FEET

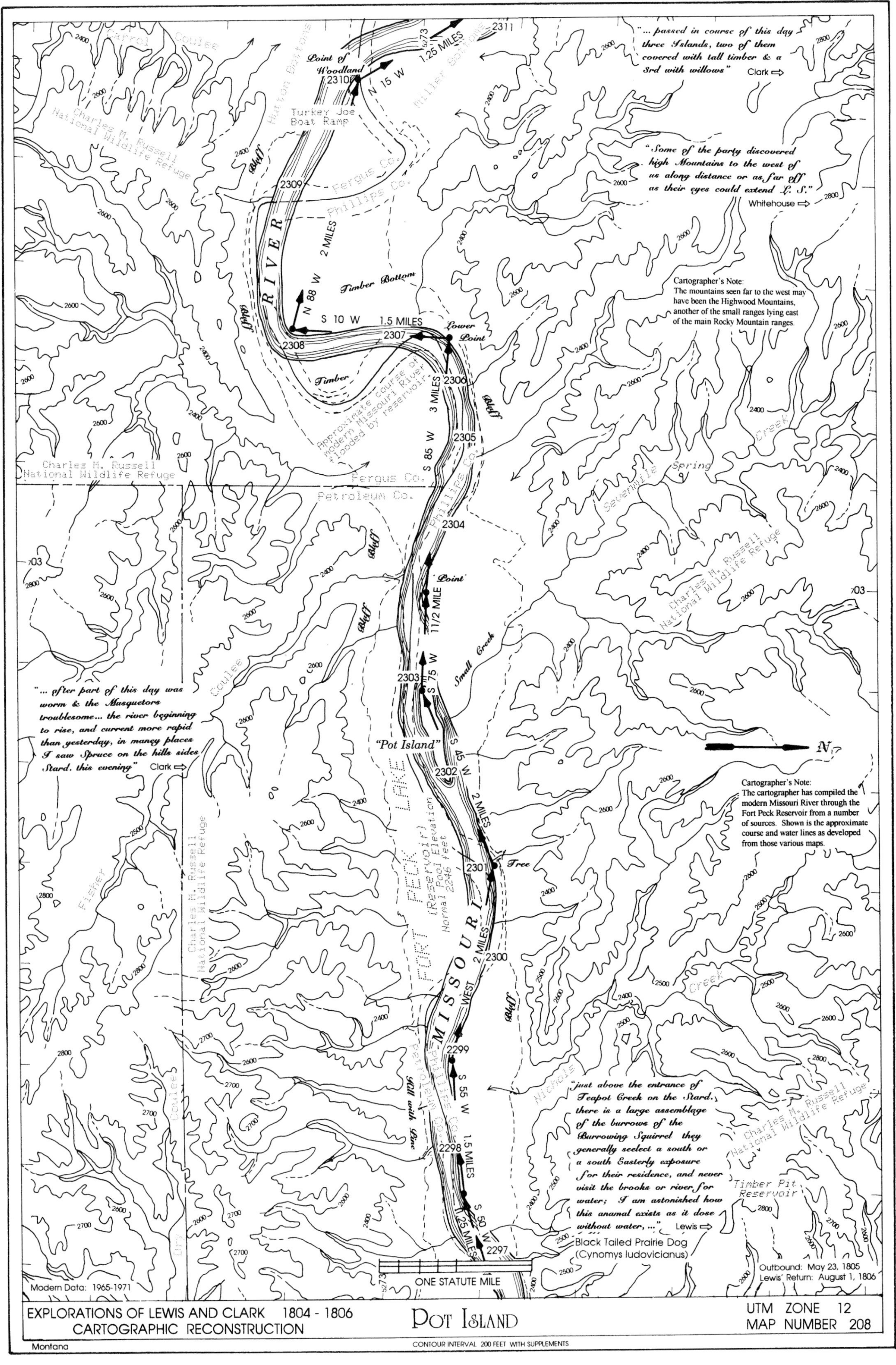
"... passed in course of this day three Islands, two of them covered with tall timber & a 3rd with willows" Clark ⇨
"Some of the party discovered high Mountains to the west of us along distance or as far off as their eyes could extend J. S." Whitehouse ⇨
Cartographer's Note: The mountains seen far to the west may have been the Highwood Mountains, another of the small ranges lying east of the main Rocky Mountain ranges.
"... after part of this day was worm & the Musquetors troublesome... the river beginning to rise, and current more rapid than yesterday, in maney places I saw Spruce on the hills sides Stard. this evening" Clark ⇨
Cartographer's Note: The cartographer has compiled the modern Missouri River through the Fort Peck Reservoir from a number of sources. Shown is the approximate course and water lines as developed from those various maps.
"just above the entrance of Teapot Creek on the Stard. there is a large assemblage of the burrows of the Burrowing Squirrel they generally seelect a south or a south Easterly exposure for their residence, and never visit the brooks or river for water; I am astonished how this anamal exists as it dose without water, ..." Lewis ⇨
Black Tailed Prairie Dog (Cynomys ludovicianus)
"Pot Island"
Point of Woodland
Turkey Joe Boat Ramp
Timber Bottom
Lower Point
Point
Tree
Small Creek
Hill with Pine
MISSOURI RIVER
FORT PECK LAKE (Reservoir) Normal Pool Elevation 2246 feet
Approximate course of modern Missouri River flooded by reservoir
Charles M. Russell National Wildlife Refuge
Fergus Co.
Phillips Co.
Petroleum Co.
Garfield Co.
Hutton Bottoms
Miller Bottoms
Carrol Coulee
Sevenmile Spring
Fisher Coulee
Dry Coulee
Nichols Creek
Timber Pit Reservoir
N 15 W
1.25 MILES
2 MILES
N 88 W
S 10 W
1.5 MILES
3 MILES
S 85 W
11/2 MILE
S 75 W
S 45 W
WEST
S 55 W
S 50 W
2297
2298
2299
2300
230
2302
2303
2304
2305
2306
2307
2308
2309
2310
2311
ONE STATUTE MILE
Modern Data: 1965-1971
Outbound: May 23, 1805
Lewis' Return: August 1, 1806
EXPLORATIONS OF LEWIS AND CLARK 1804 - 1806
CARTOGRAPHIC RECONSTRUCTION
POT ISLAND
UTM ZONE 12
MAP NUMBER 208
Montana
CONTOUR INTERVAL 200 FEET WITH SUPPLEMENTS

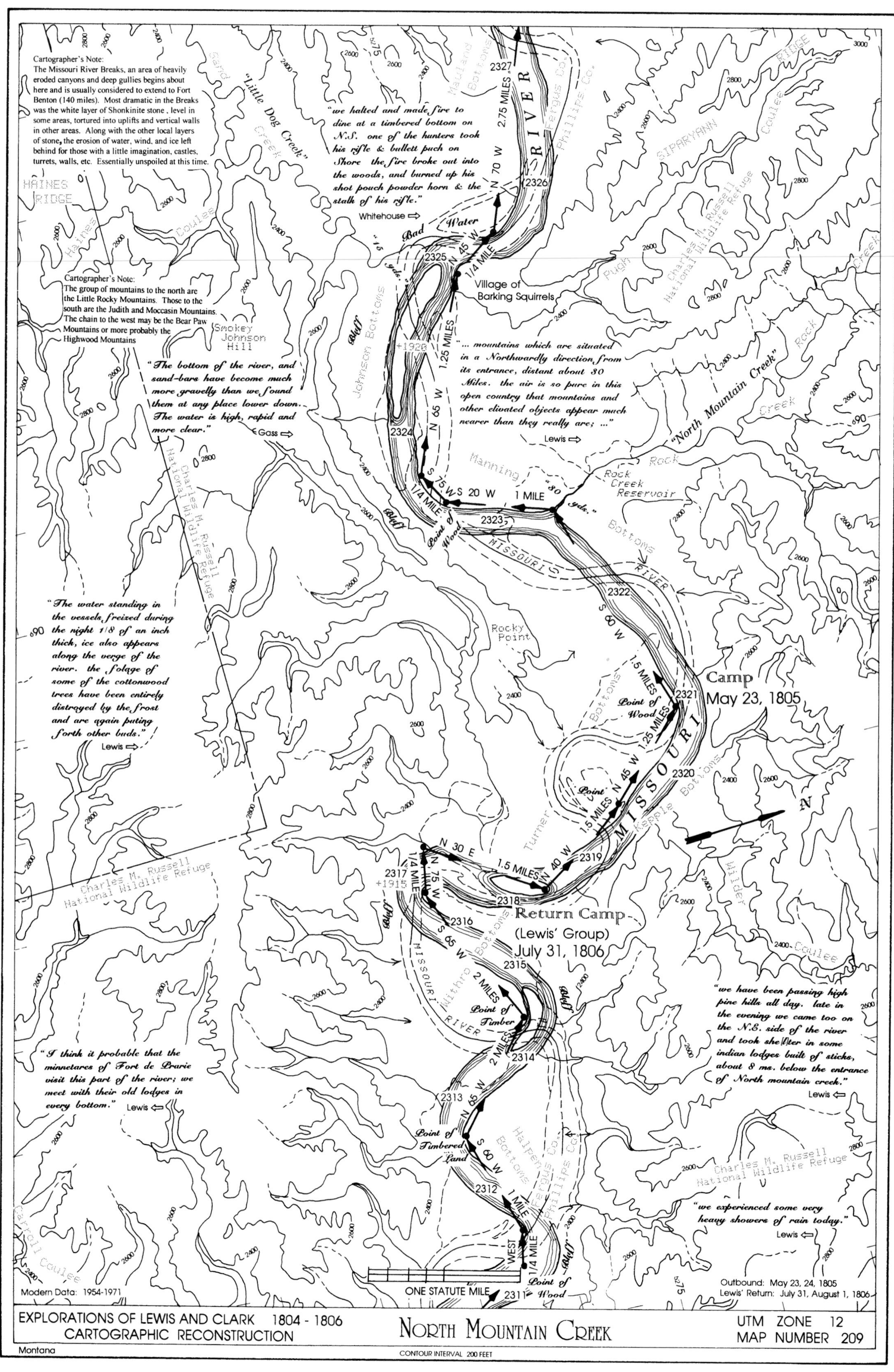
Cartographer's Note:
The Missouri River Breaks, an area of heavily eroded canyons and deep gullies begins about here and is usually considered to extend to Fort Benton (140 miles). Most dramatic in the Breaks was the white layer of Shonkinite stone, level in some areas, tortured into uplifts and vertical walls in other areas. Along with the other local layers of stone, the erosion of water, wind, and ice left behind for those with a little imagination, castles, turrets, walls, etc. Essentially unspoiled at this time.
Cartographer's Note:
The group of mountains to the north are the Little Rocky Mountains. Those to the south are the Judith and Moccasin Mountains. The chain to the west may be the Bear Paw Mountains or more probably the Highwood Mountains
"we halted and made fire to dine at a timbered bottom on N.S. one of the hunters took his rifle & bullett puch on Shore the fire broke out into the woods, and burned up his shot pouch powder horn & the stalk of his rifle."
Whitehouse ⇨
"The bottom of the river, and sand-bars have become much more gravelly than we found them at any place lower down. The water is high, rapid and more clear."
Gass ⇨
"... mountains which are situated in a Northwardly direction from its entrance, distant about 30 Miles. the air is so pure in this open country that mountains and other elivated objects appear much nearer than they really are; ..."
Lewis ⇨
"The water standing in the vessels freized during the night 1/8 of an inch thick, ice also appears along the verge of the river. the folage of some of the cottonwood trees have been entirely distroyed by the frost and are again puting forth other buds."
Lewis ⇨
"I think it probable that the minnetares of Fort de Prarie visit this part of the river; we meet with their old lodges in every bottom."
Lewis ⇦
"we have been passing high pine hills all day. late in the evening we came too on the N.E. side of the river and took shelter in some indian lodges built of sticks, about 8 ms. below the entrance of North mountain creek."
Lewis ⇦
"we experienced some very heavy showers of rain today."
Lewis ⇦
"Little Dog Creek"
"North Mountain Creek"
Village of Barking Squirrels
Camp
May 23, 1805
Return Camp
(Lewis' Group)
July 31, 1806
MISSOURI RIVER
Haines Ridge
Smokey Johnson Hill
Rocky Point
Rock Creek Reservoir
Charles M. Russell National Wildlife Refuge
Fergus Co.
Phillips Co.
Bad Water
Point of Wood
Point of Timber
Point of Timbered Land
Bluff
ONE STATUTE MILE
Modern Data: 1954-1971
Outbound: May 23, 24, 1805
Lewis' Return: July 31, August 1, 1806
EXPLORATIONS OF LEWIS AND CLARK 1804 - 1806
CARTOGRAPHIC RECONSTRUCTION
NORTH MOUNTAIN CREEK
UTM ZONE 12
MAP NUMBER 209
Montana
CONTOUR INTERVAL 200 FEET

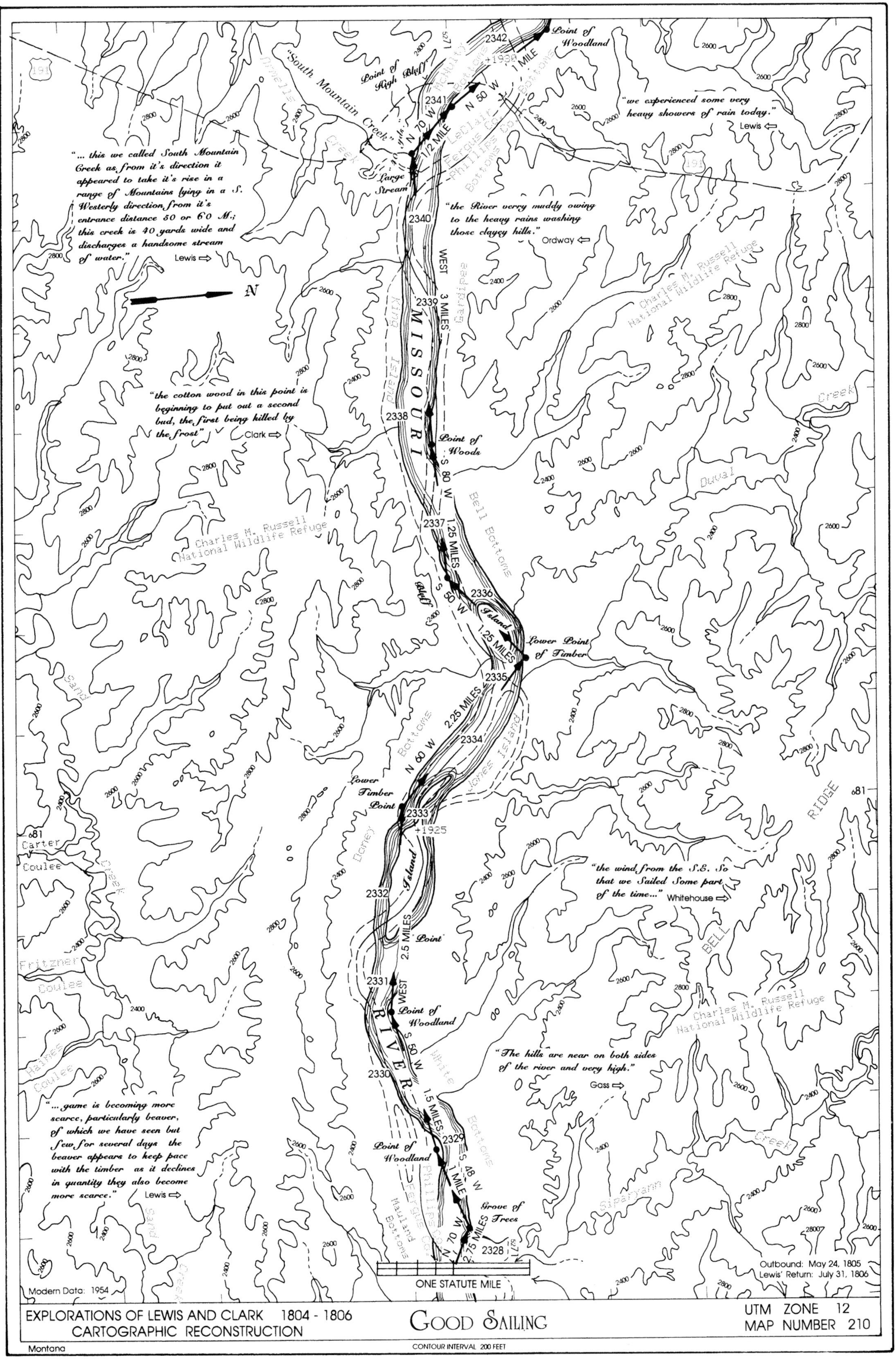

"... this we called South Mountain Creek as from it's direction it appeared to take it's rise in a range of Mountains lying in a S. Westerly direction from it's entrance distance 50 or 60 M.; this creek is 40 yards wide and discharges a handsome stream of water." Lewis
"we experienced some very heavy showers of rain today." Lewis
"the River verry muddy owing to the heavy rains washing those clayey hills." Ordway
"the cotton wood in this point is beginning to put out a second bud, the first being killed by the frost" Clark
"the wind from the S.E. So that we Sailed Some part of the time..." Whitehouse
"The hills are near on both sides of the river and very high." Gass
"... game is becoming more scarce, particularly beaver, of which we have seen but few for several days the beaver appears to keep pace with the timber as it declines in quantity they also become more scarce." Lewis
MISSOURI
RIVER
Point of Woodland
Point of High Bluff
"South Mountain Creek"
Large Stream
Point of Woods
Lower Point of Timber
Lower Timber Point
Point
Grove of Trees
Island
Bluff
Charles M. Russell National Wildlife Refuge
Outbound: May 24, 1805
Lewis' Return: July 31, 1806
ONE STATUTE MILE
Modern Data: 1954
EXPLORATIONS OF LEWIS AND CLARK 1804 - 1806
CARTOGRAPHIC RECONSTRUCTION
GOOD SAILING
UTM ZONE 12
MAP NUMBER 210
Montana
CONTOUR INTERVAL 200 FEET

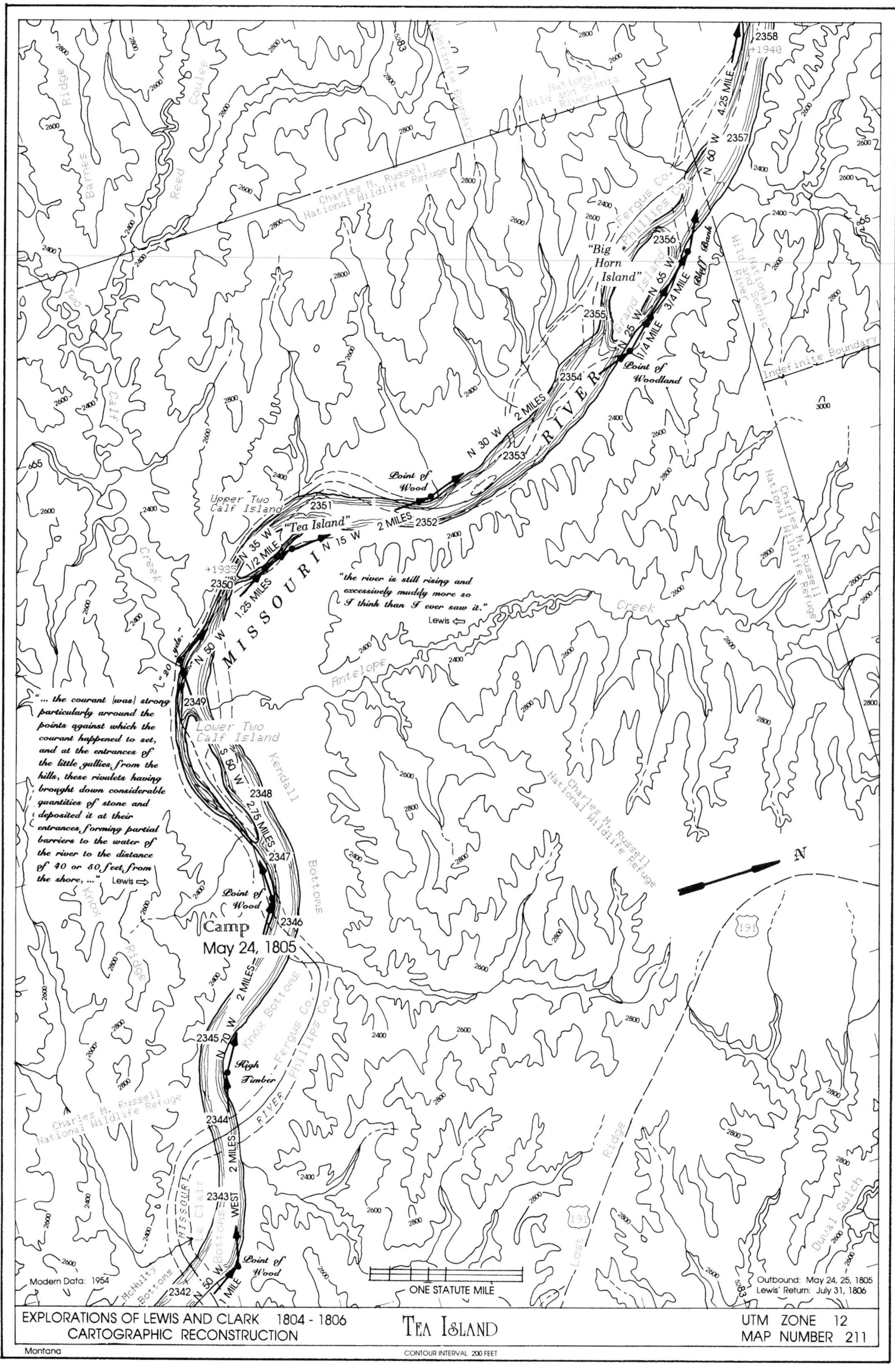
"... the courant [was] strong particularly arround the points against which the courant happened to set, and at the entrances of the little gullies from the hills, these rivulets having brought down considerable quantities of stone and deposited it at their entrances forming partial barriers to the water of the river to the distance of 40 or 50 feet from the shore, ..." Lewis
"the river is still rising and excessively muddy more so I think than I ever saw it." Lewis
MISSOURI RIVER
"Tea Island"
"Big Horn Island"
Grand Island
Upper Two Calf Island
Lower Two Calf Island
Point of Wood
Point of Woodland
Bluff Bank
High Timber
Camp
May 24, 1805
"20 yds."
Charles M. Russell National Wildlife Refuge
National Wild and Scenic River
Indefinite Boundary
Fergus Co.
Phillips Co.
Antelope Creek
Two Calf Creek
Knox Bottoms
Kendall Bottoms
Knox Ridge
Reed Coulee
Barnes Ridge
Lost Ridge
Duval Gulch
McNulty Bottoms
Modern Data: 1954
ONE STATUTE MILE
Outbound: May 24, 25, 1805
Lewis' Return: July 31, 1806
EXPLORATIONS OF LEWIS AND CLARK 1804 - 1806
CARTOGRAPHIC RECONSTRUCTION
TEA ISLAND
UTM ZONE 12
MAP NUMBER 211
Montana
CONTOUR INTERVAL 200 FEET

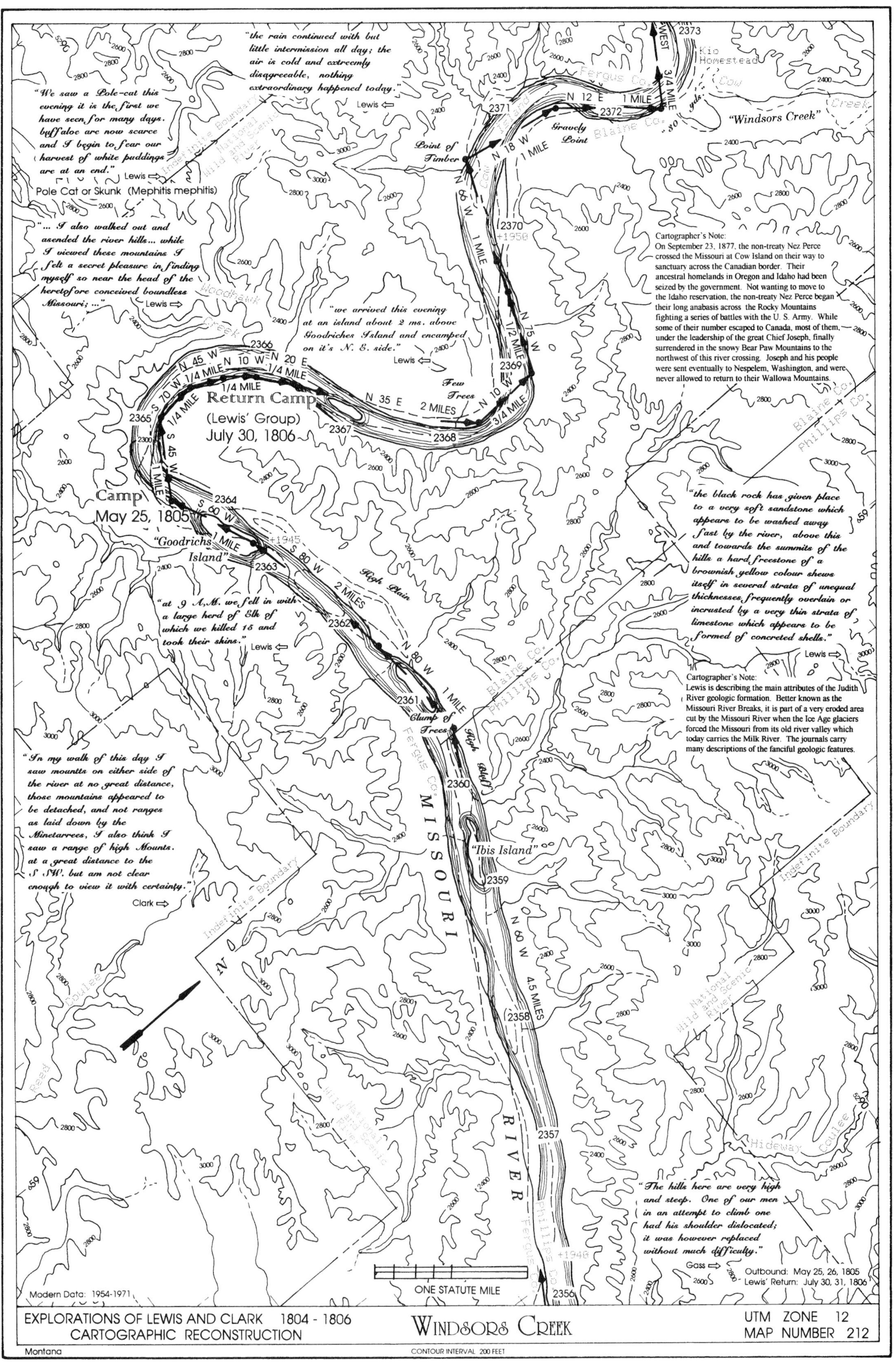

"the rain continued with but little intermission all day; the air is cold and extreemly disagreeable, nothing extraordinary happened today."
Lewis ⇦
"We saw a Pole-cat this evening it is the first we have seen for many days. buffaloe are now scarce and I begin to fear our harvest of white puddings are at an end."
Lewis ⇨
Pole Cat or Skunk (Mephitis mephitis)
"... I also walked out and asended the river hills... while I viewed these mountains I felt a secret pleasure in finding myself so near the head of the heretofore conceived boundless Missouri; ..."
Lewis ⇨
"we arrived this evening at an island about 2 ms. above Goodriches Island and encamped on it's N. E. side."
Lewis ⇦
Cartographer's Note:
On September 23, 1877, the non-treaty Nez Perce crossed the Missouri at Cow Island on their way to sanctuary across the Canadian border. Their ancestral homelands in Oregon and Idaho had been seized by the government. Not wanting to move to the Idaho reservation, the non-treaty Nez Perce began their long anabasis across the Rocky Mountains fighting a series of battles with the U. S. Army. While some of their number escaped to Canada, most of them, under the leadership of the great Chief Joseph, finally surrendered in the snowy Bear Paw Mountains to the northwest of this river crossing. Joseph and his people were sent eventually to Nespelem, Washington, and were never allowed to return to their Wallowa Mountains.
Kio Homestead
"Windsors Creek"
Point of Timber
Gravely Point
Fergus Co.
Blaine Co.
Phillips Co.
Return Camp
(Lewis' Group)
July 30, 1806
Camp
May 25, 1805
"Goodrichs Island"
Few Trees
High Plain
Clump of Trees
High Bluff
"Ibis Island"
MISSOURI RIVER
"the black rock has given place to a very soft sandstone which appears to be washed away fast by the river, above this and towards the summits of the hills a hard freestone of a brownish yellow colour shews itself in several strata of unequal thicknesses frequently overlain or incrusted by a very thin strata of limestone which appears to be formed of concreted shells."
Lewis ⇨
Cartographer's Note:
Lewis is describing the main attributes of the Judith River geologic formation. Better known as the Missouri River Breaks, it is part of a very eroded area cut by the Missouri River when the Ice Age glaciers forced the Missouri from its old river valley which today carries the Milk River. The journals carry many descriptions of the fanciful geologic features.
"at 9 A.M. we fell in with a large herd of Elk of which we killed 15 and took their skins."
Lewis ⇦
"In my walk of this day I saw mountts on either side of the river at no great distance, those mountains appeared to be detached, and not ranges as laid down by the Minetarrees, I also think I saw a range of high Mounts. at a great distance to the S SW. but am not clear enough to view it with certainty."
Clark ⇨
Indefinite Boundary
National Wild and Scenic River
Woodhawk Creek
Reed Coulee
Hideway Coulee
Cow Island
Cow Creek
"The hills here are very high and steep. One of our men in an attempt to climb one had his shoulder dislocated; it was however replaced without much difficulty."
Gass ⇨
Outbound: May 25, 26, 1805
Lewis' Return: July 30, 31, 1806
ONE STATUTE MILE
Modern Data: 1954-1971
EXPLORATIONS OF LEWIS AND CLARK 1804 - 1806
CARTOGRAPHIC RECONSTRUCTION
WINDSORS CREEK
UTM ZONE 12
MAP NUMBER 212
Montana
CONTOUR INTERVAL 200 FEET

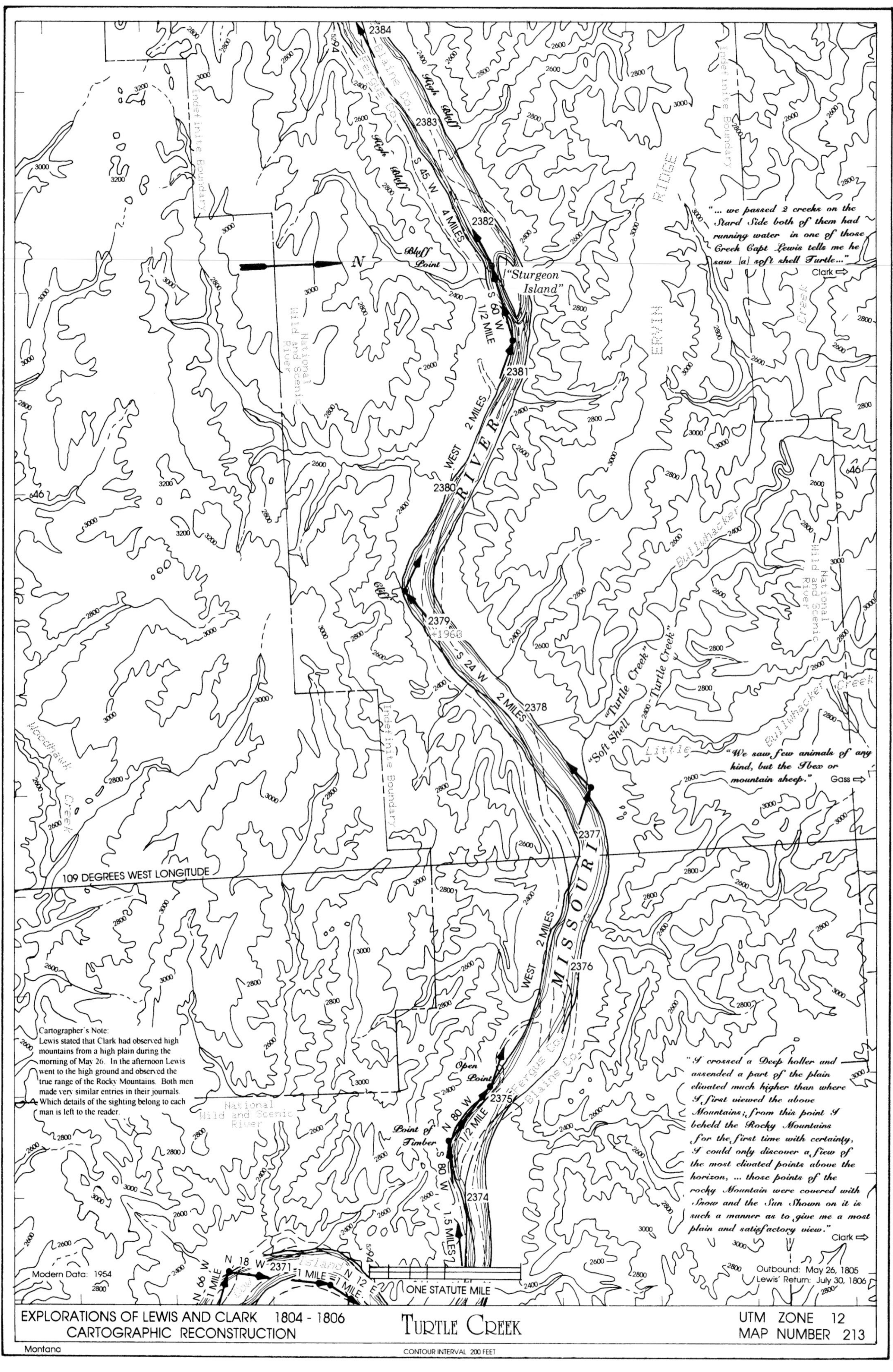
"... we passed 2 creeks on the Stard Side both of them had running water in one of those Creek Capt Lewis tells me he saw [a] soft shell Turtle..."
Clark
"We saw few animals of any kind, but the Ibex or mountain sheep."
Gass
"I crossed a Deep holler and assended a part of the plain elivated much higher than where I first viewed the above Mountains; from this point I beheld the Rocky Mountains for the first time with certainty, I could only discover a fiew of the most elivated points above the horizon, ... those points of the rocky Mountain were covered with Snow and the Sun Shown on it in such a manner as to give me a most plain and satisfactory view."
Clark
Cartographer's Note:
Lewis stated that Clark had observed high mountains from a high plain during the morning of May 26. In the afternoon Lewis went to the high ground and observed the true range of the Rocky Mountains. Both men made very similar entries in their journals. Which details of the sighting belong to each man is left to the reader.
"Sturgeon Island"
Bluff Point
Open Point
Point of Timber
"Soft Shell Turtle Creek"
"Turtle Creek"
MISSOURI
RIVER
109 DEGREES WEST LONGITUDE
Modern Data: 1954
ONE STATUTE MILE
Outbound: May 26, 1805
Lewis' Return: July 30, 1806
EXPLORATIONS OF LEWIS AND CLARK 1804 - 1806
CARTOGRAPHIC RECONSTRUCTION
TURTLE CREEK
UTM ZONE 12
MAP NUMBER 213
Montana
CONTOUR INTERVAL 200 FEET

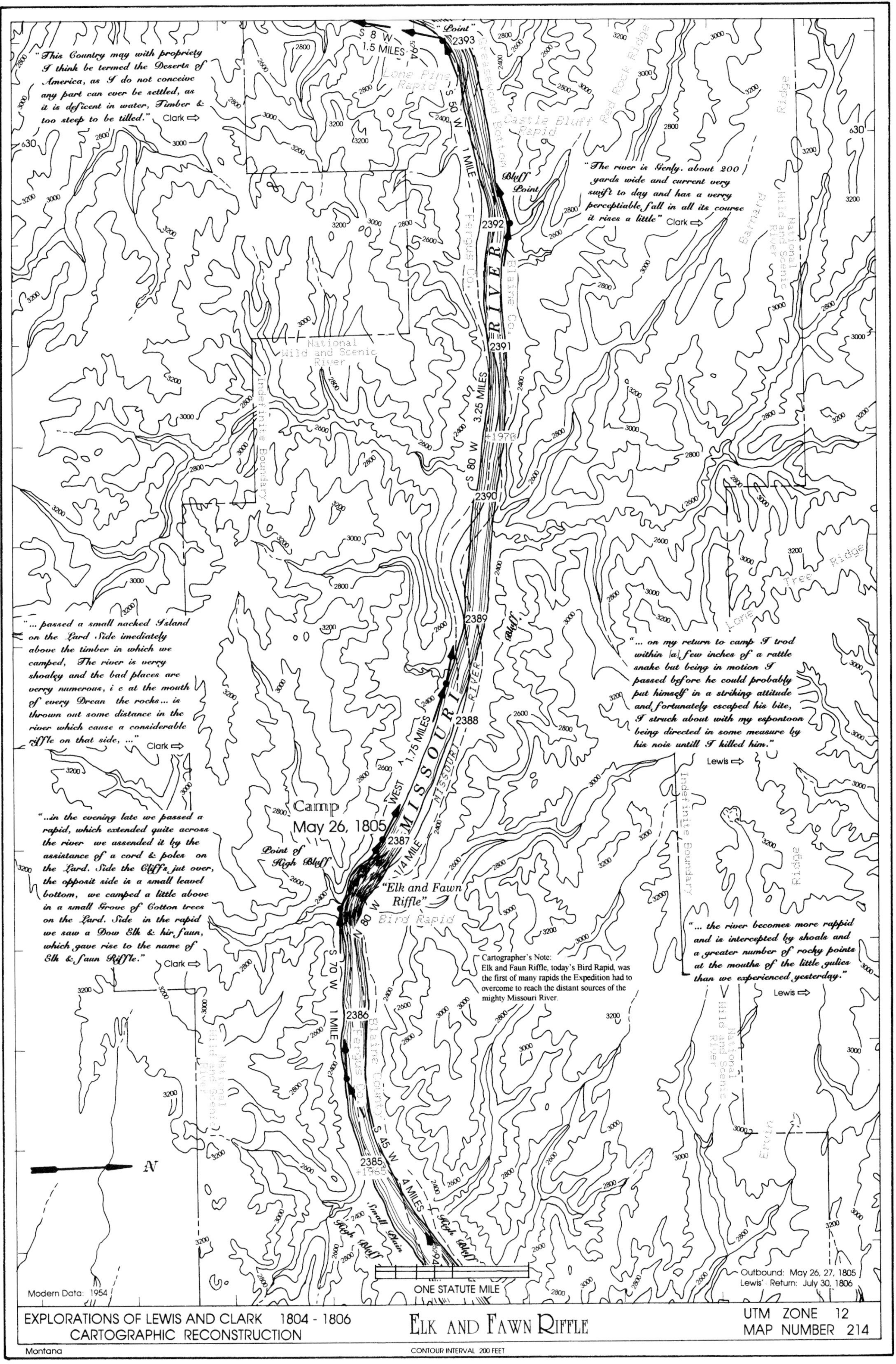
"This Country may with propriety I think be termed the Deserts of America, as I do not conceive any part can ever be settled, as it is deficent in water, Timber & too steep to be tilled." Clark ⇨
"The river is Genly. about 200 yards wide and current very swift to day and has a very perceptiable fall in all its course it rises a little" Clark ⇨
"... passed a small nacked Island on the Lard Side imediately above the timber in which we camped, The river is verry shoaley and the bad places are verry numerous, i e at the mouth of every Drean the rocks... is thrown out some distance in the river which cause a considerable riffle on that side, ..." Clark ⇨
"... on my return to camp I trod within [a] few inches of a rattle snake but being in motion I passed before he could probably put himself in a striking attitude and fortunately escaped his bite, I struck about with my espontoon being directed in some measure by his nois untill I killed him." Lewis ⇨
"..in the evening late we passed a rapid, which extended quite across the river we assended it by the assistance of a cord & poles on the Lard. Side the Cliffs jut over, the opposit side is a small leavel bottom, we camped a little above in a small Grove of Cotton trees on the Lard. Side in the rapid we saw a Dow Elk & hir faun, which gave rise to the name of Elk & faun Riffle." Clark ⇨
"... the river becomes more rappid and is intercepted by shoals and a greater number of rocky points at the mouths of the little gulies than we experienced yesterday." Lewis ⇨
Cartographer's Note:
Elk and Faun Riffle, today's Bird Rapid, was the first of many rapids the Expedition had to overcome to reach the distant sources of the mighty Missouri River.
Camp
May 26, 1805
"Elk and Fawn Riffle"
Bird Rapid
Point of High Bluff
"Point"
Bluff Point
Lone Pine Rapid
Castle Bluff Rapid
Greasewood Bottom
Red Rock Ridge
Barnard Ridge
Lone Tree Ridge
Ervin Ridge
MISSOURI RIVER
Fergus Co.
Blaine Co.
Fergus County
Blaine County
National Wild and Scenic River
Indefinite Boundary
Small Plain
High Bluff
S 8 W 1.5 MILES
S 50 W 1 MILE
S 80 W 3.25 MILES
WEST 1.75 MILES
N 80 W 1/4 MILE
S 70 W 1 MILE
S 45 W 4 MILES
2393
2392
2391
2390
2389
2388
2387
2386
2385
+1970
+1963
N
ONE STATUTE MILE
Modern Data: 1954
Outbound: May 26, 27, 1805
Lewis' Return: July 30, 1806
EXPLORATIONS OF LEWIS AND CLARK 1804 - 1806
CARTOGRAPHIC RECONSTRUCTION
Elk and Fawn Riffle
UTM ZONE 12
MAP NUMBER 214
Montana
CONTOUR INTERVAL 200 FEET

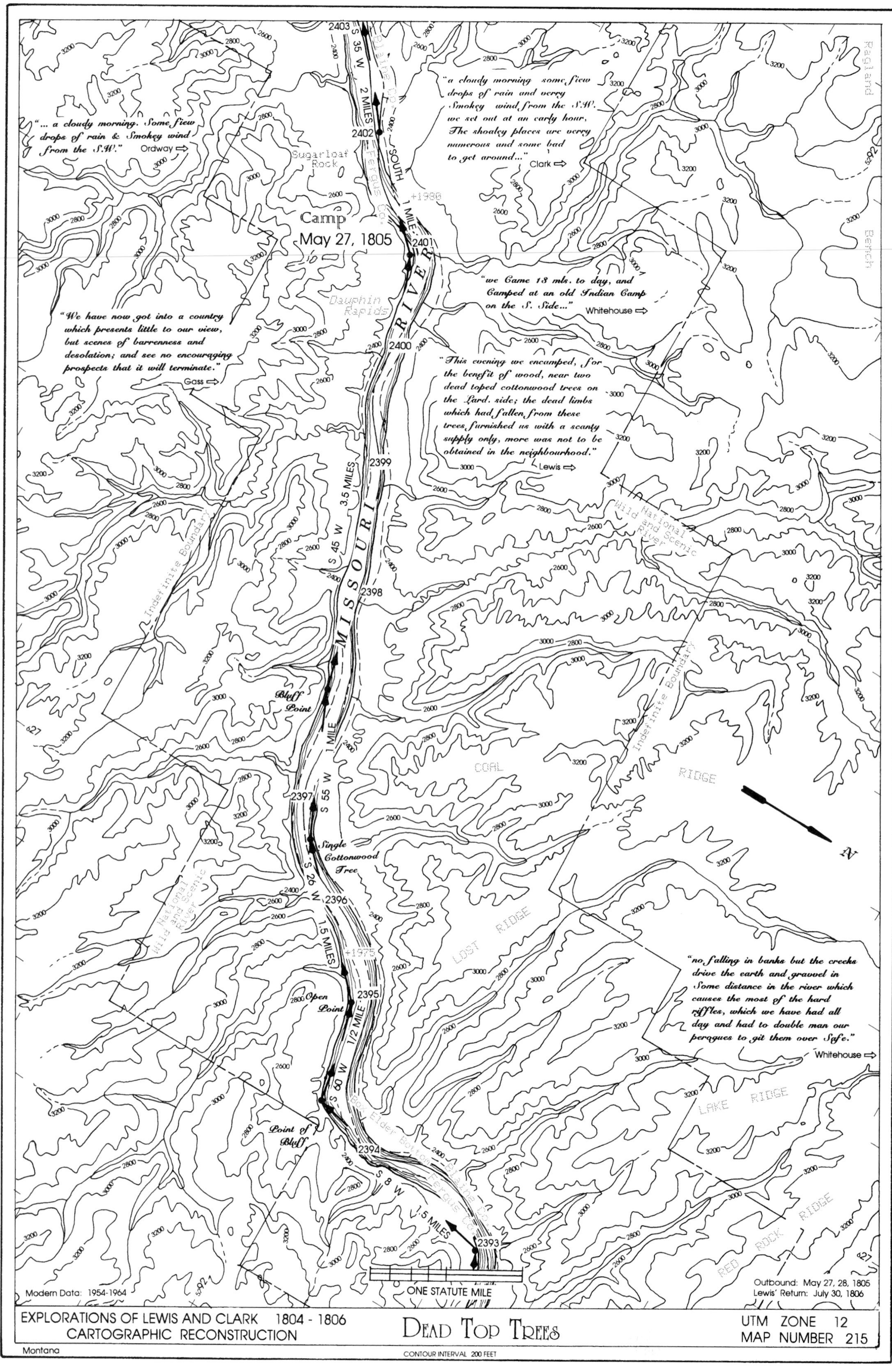

"... a cloudy morning. Some few drops of rain & Smokey wind from the S.W." Ordway ⇨
"a cloudy morning some few drops of rain and verry Smokey wind from the S.W. we set out at an early hour. The shoaley places are verry numerous and some bad to get around..." Clark ⇨
Sugarloaf Rock
Camp
May 27, 1805
Dauphin Rapids
"we Came 13 mls. to day, and Camped at an old Indian Camp on the S. Side..." Whitehouse ⇨
"We have now got into a country which presents little to our view, but scenes of barrenness and desolation; and see no encouraging prospects that it will terminate." Gass ⇨
"This evening we encamped, for the benefit of wood, near two dead toped cottonwood trees on the Lard. side; the dead limbs which had fallen from these trees furnished us with a scanty supply only, more was not to be obtained in the neighbourhood." Lewis ⇨
MISSOURI RIVER
S 35 W 2 MILES
SOUTH 1 MILE
S 45 W 3.5 MILES
S 55 W 1 MILE
S 26 W 1.5 MILES
S 60 W 1/2 MILE
S 8 W 1.5 MILES
Blaine Co.
Fergus Co.
Ragland Bench
National Wild and Scenic River
Indefinite Boundary
Bluff Point
Single Cottonwood Tree
Open Point
Point of Bluff
Box Elder Bottom
COAL RIDGE
LOST RIDGE
LAKE RIDGE
RED ROCK RIDGE
N
"no falling in banks but the creeks drive the earth and gravvel in Some distance in the river which causes the most of the hard riffles, which we have had all day and had to double man our perogues to git them over Safe." Whitehouse ⇨
Modern Data: 1954-1964
ONE STATUTE MILE
Outbound: May 27, 28, 1805
Lewis' Return: July 30, 1806
EXPLORATIONS OF LEWIS AND CLARK 1804 - 1806
CARTOGRAPHIC RECONSTRUCTION
DEAD TOP TREES
UTM ZONE 12
MAP NUMBER 215
Montana
CONTOUR INTERVAL 200 FEET

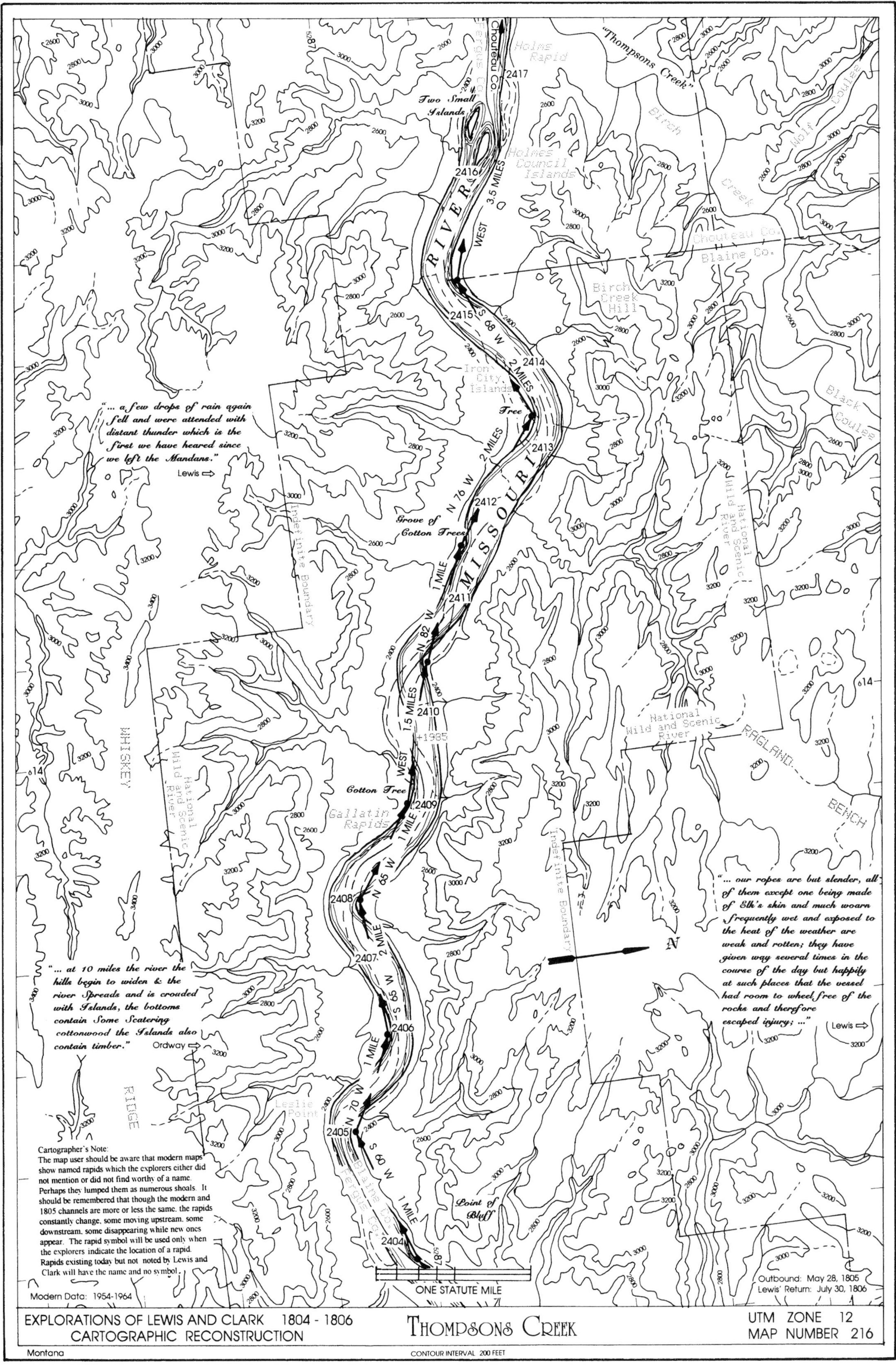
"... a few drops of rain again fell and were attended with distant thunder which is the first we have heared since we left the Mandans."
Lewis ⇨
"... at 10 miles the river the hills begin to widen & the river Spreads and is crouded with Islands, the bottoms contain Some Scatering cottonwood the Islands also contain timber."
Ordway ⇨
"... our ropes are but slender, all of them except one being made of Elk's skin and much woarn frequently wet and exposed to the heat of the weather are weak and rotten; they have given way several times in the course of the day but happily at such places that the vessel had room to wheel free of the rocks and therefore escaped injury; ..."
Lewis ⇨
Cartographer's Note:
The map user should be aware that modern maps show named rapids which the explorers either did not mention or did not find worthy of a name. Perhaps they lumped them as numerous shoals. It should be remembered that though the modern and 1805 channels are more or less the same, the rapids constantly change, some moving upstream, some downstream, some disappearing while new ones appear. The rapid symbol will be used only when the explorers indicate the location of a rapid. Rapids existing today but not noted by Lewis and Clark will have the name and no symbol.
Two Small Islands
Holmes Rapid
Holmes Council Islands
"Thompsons Creek"
Birch Creek
Wolf Coulee
Chouteau Co.
Blaine Co.
Fergus Co.
Birch Creek Hill
Iron City Islands
Tree
Black Coulee
MISSOURI RIVER
Grove of Cotton Trees
Cotton Tree
Gallatin Rapids
Indefinite Boundary
National Wild and Scenic River
WHISKEY RIDGE
RAGLAND BENCH
Leslie Point
Point of Bluff
N
ONE STATUTE MILE
Modern Data: 1954-1964
Outbound: May 28, 1805
Lewis' Return: July 30, 1806
EXPLORATIONS OF LEWIS AND CLARK 1804 - 1806
CARTOGRAPHIC RECONSTRUCTION
THOMPSONS CREEK
UTM ZONE 12
MAP NUMBER 216
Montana
CONTOUR INTERVAL 200 FEET

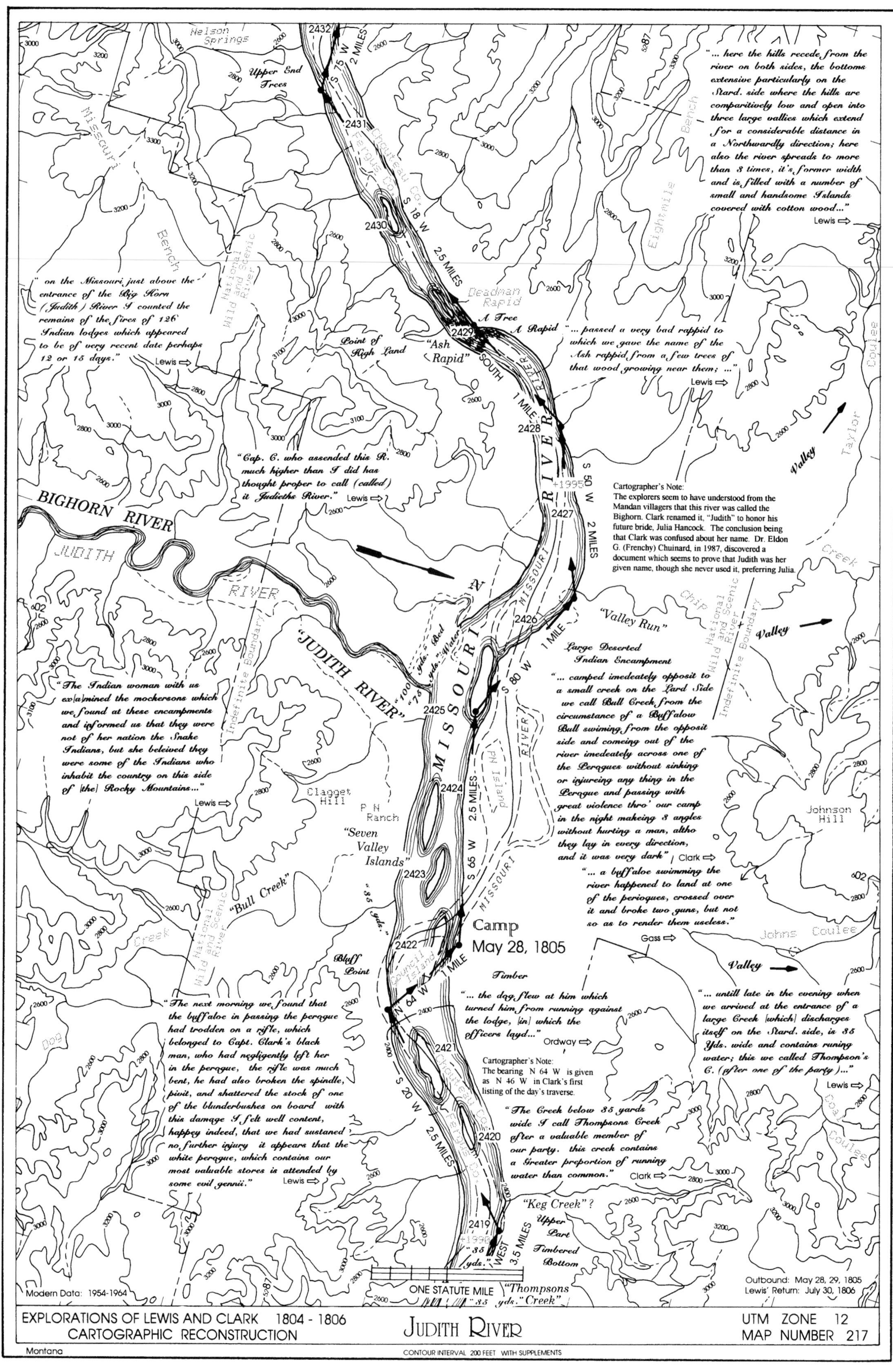

Nelson Springs
Upper End Trees
S 75 W 2 MILES
Missouri
Bench
Choteau Co. Fergus Co.
S 18 W 2.5 MILES
Eightmile Bench
"... here the hills recede from the river on both sides, the bottoms extensive particularly on the Stard. side where the hills are comparitively low and open into three large vallies which extend for a considerable distance in a Northwardly direction; here also the river spreads to more than 3 times, it's former width and is filled with a number of small and handsome Islands covered with cotton wood..."
Lewis ⇨
Deadman Rapid
A Tree
A Rapid
"Ash Rapid"
Point of High Land
SOUTH
1 MILE
RIVER
" on the Missouri just above the entrance of the Big Horn (Judith) River I counted the remains of the fires of 126 Indian lodges which appeared to be of very recent date perhaps 12 or 15 days."
Lewis ⇨
"... passed a very bad rappid to which we gave the name of the Ash rappid from a few trees of that wood growing near them; ..."
Lewis ⇨
Wild National and Scenic River
Coulee
Taylor
Valley
"Cap. C. who assended this R. much higher than I did has thought proper to call (called) it Judieths River."
Lewis ⇨
BIGHORN RIVER
JUDITH RIVER
S 50 W 2 MILES
MISSOURI RIVER
Cartographer's Note:
The explorers seem to have understood from the Mandan villagers that this river was called the Bighorn. Clark renamed it, "Judith" to honor his future bride, Julia Hancock. The conclusion being that Clark was confused about her name. Dr. Eldon G. (Frenchy) Chuinard, in 1987, discovered a document which seems to prove that Judith was her given name, though she never used it, preferring Julia.
N
Chip Creek
"Valley Run"
Valley
1 MILE
S 80 W
Large Deserted Indian Encampment
"JUDITH RIVER"
"100 yds." Bed "75 yds." Water
Indefinite Boundary
MISSOURI
"The Indian woman with us ex[a]mined the mockersons which we found at these encampments and informed us that they were not of her nation the Snake Indians, but she beleived they were some of the Indians who inhabit the country on this side of [the] Rocky Mountains..."
Lewis ⇨
"... camped imedeately opposit to a small creek on the Lard Side we call Bull Creek from the circumstance of a Buffalow Bull swiming from the opposit side and comeing out of the river imedeately across one of the Perogues without sinking or injureing any thing in the Perogue and passing with great violence thro' our camp in the night makeing 3 angles without hurting a man, altho they lay in every direction, and it was very dark"
Clark ⇨
"... a buffaloe swimming the river happened to land at one of the perioques, crossed over it and broke two guns, but not so as to render them useless."
Gass ⇨
Clagget Hill
P N Ranch
PN Island
2.5 MILES
"Seven Valley Islands"
S 65 W
Johnson Hill
"Bull Creek"
"35 yds."
Camp
May 28, 1805
Johns Coulee
Valley
Bluff Point
Council Island
1 MILE
N 64 W
Timber
Dog Creek
"The next morning we found that the buffaloe in passing the perogue had trodden on a rifle, which belonged to Capt. Clark's black man, who had negligently left her in the perogue, the rifle was much bent, he had also broken the spindle, pivit, and shattered the stock of one of the blunderbushes on board with this damage I felt well content, happey indeed, that we had sustaned no further injury it appears that the white perogue, which contains our most valuable stores is attended by some evil gennii."
Lewis ⇨
"... the dog flew at him which turned him from running against the lodge, [in] which the officers layd..."
Ordway ⇨
Cartographer's Note:
The bearing N 64 W is given as N 46 W in Clark's first listing of the day's traverse.
"... untill late in the evening when we arrived at the entrance of a large Creek [which] discharges itself on the Stard. side, is 35 Yds. wide and contains runing water; this we called Thompson's C. (after one of the party)..."
Lewis ⇨
Coal Coulee
S 20 W
2.5 MILES
"The Creek below 35 yards wide I call Thompsons Creek after a valuable member of our party. this creek contains a Greater preportion of running water than common."
Clark ⇨
"Keg Creek"?
Upper Part Timbered Bottom
WEST 3.5 MILES
"35 yds."
Modern Data: 1954-1964
ONE STATUTE MILE
"Thompsons "35 yds." Creek"
Outbound: May 28, 29, 1805
Lewis' Return: July 30, 1806
EXPLORATIONS OF LEWIS AND CLARK 1804 - 1806
CARTOGRAPHIC RECONSTRUCTION
JUDITH RIVER
UTM ZONE 12
MAP NUMBER 217
Montana
CONTOUR INTERVAL 200 FEET WITH SUPPLEMENTS

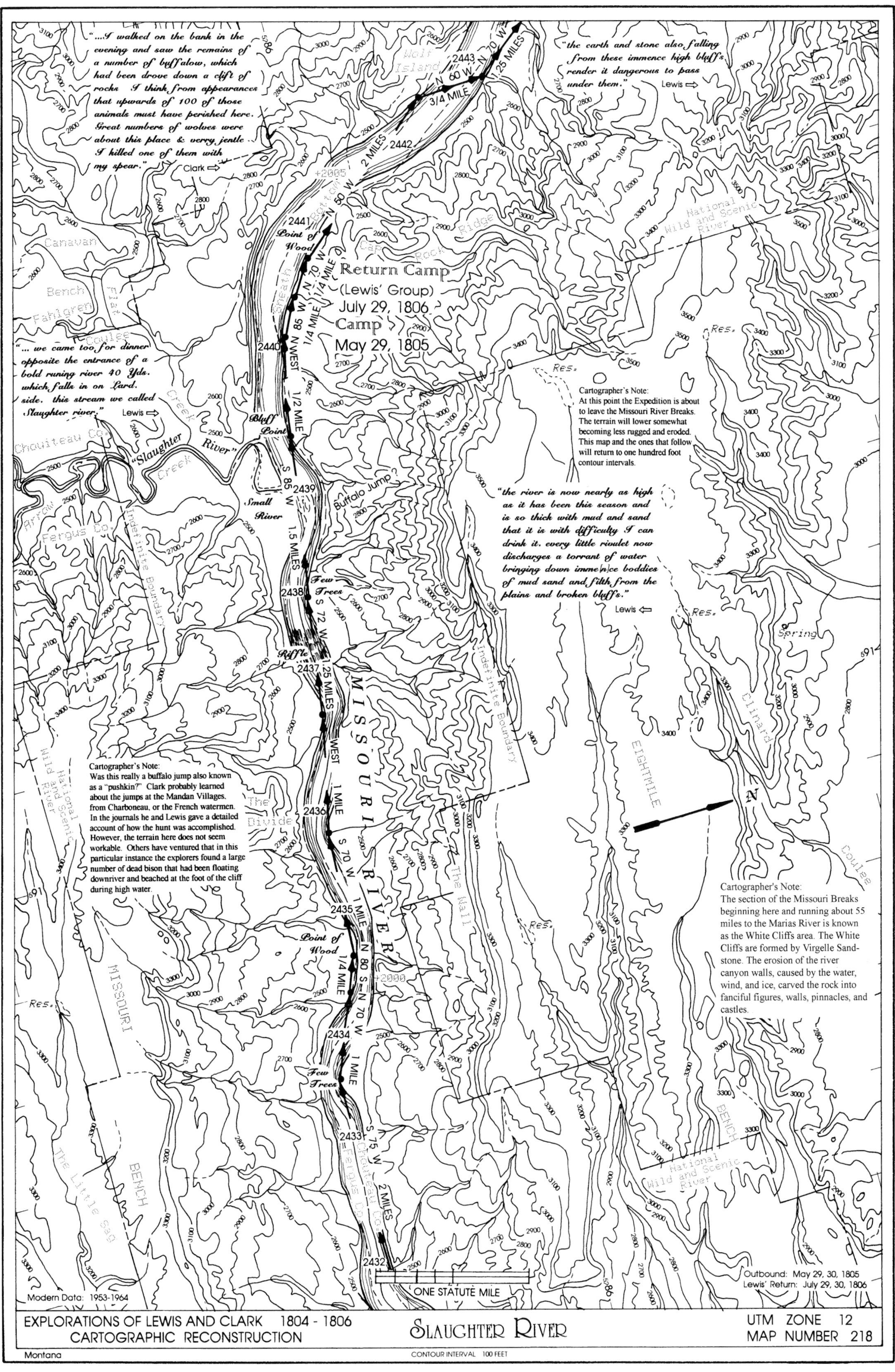
"...I walked on the bank in the evening and saw the remains of a number of buffalow, which had been drove down a clift of rocks. I think from appearances that upwards of 100 of those animals must have perished here. Great numbers of wolves were about this place & verry jentle. I killed one of them with my spear."
Clark ⇨
"the earth and stone also falling from these immence high bluffs render it dangerous to pass under them."
Lewis ⇨
Wolf Island
N 60 W
3/4 MILE
N 70 W
1.25 MILES
2443
2442
2 MILES
N 50 W
2441
Point of Wood
Cap Rock Ridge
Canavan
Bench
Fahlgren Flat
Coulee
Sneath Bottom
Return Camp
(Lewis' Group)
July 29, 1806
Camp
May 29, 1805
N 70 W
1/4 MILE
N 85 W
1/4 MILE
N WEST
2440
"... we came too for dinner opposite the entrance of a bold runing river 40 Yds. which falls in on Lard. side. this stream we called Slaughter river."
Lewis ⇨
1/2 MILE
Bluff Point
Chouiteau Co.
"Slaughter River"
Creek
National Wild and Scenic River
Res.
Cartographer's Note:
At this point the Expedition is about to leave the Missouri River Breaks. The terrain will lower somewhat becoming less rugged and eroded. This map and the ones that follow will return to one hundred foot contour intervals.
S 85 W
2439
Buffalo Jump?
Small River
Arrow
Fergus Co.
Indefinite Boundary
1.5 MILES
"the river is now nearly as high as it has been this season and is so thick with mud and sand that it is with difficulty I can drink it. every little rivulet now discharges a torrant of water bringing down imme[n]ce boddies of mud sand and filth from the plains and broken bluffs."
Lewis ⇦
Few Trees
2438
S 72 W
Riffle
2437
1.25 MILES
WEST
MISSOURI RIVER
Spring
Clinard
EIGHTMILE
Cartographer's Note:
Was this really a buffalo jump also known as a "pushkin?" Clark probably learned about the jumps at the Mandan Villages, from Charboneau, or the French watermen. In the journals he and Lewis gave a detailed account of how the hunt was accomplished. However, the terrain here does not seem workable. Others have ventured that in this particular instance the explorers found a large number of dead bison that had been floating downriver and beached at the foot of the cliff during high water.
The Divide
2436
1 MILE
S 70 W
The Wall
N
Coulee
Cartographer's Note:
The section of the Missouri Breaks beginning here and running about 55 miles to the Marias River is known as the White Cliffs area. The White Cliffs are formed by Virgelle Sandstone. The erosion of the river canyon walls, caused by the water, wind, and ice, carved the rock into fanciful figures, walls, pinnacles, and castles.
2435
1 MILE
Point of Wood
N 80 S
1/4 MILE
N 70 W
MISSOURI
2434
1 MILE
Few Trees
2433
S 75 W
2 MILES
Fergus Co.
Chouteau Co.
The Little Sag
BENCH
2432
ONE STATUTE MILE
Outbound: May 29, 30, 1805
Lewis' Return: July 29, 30, 1806
Modern Data: 1953-1964
EXPLORATIONS OF LEWIS AND CLARK 1804 - 1806
CARTOGRAPHIC RECONSTRUCTION
SLAUGHTER RIVER
UTM ZONE 12
MAP NUMBER 218
Montana
CONTOUR INTERVAL 100 FEET

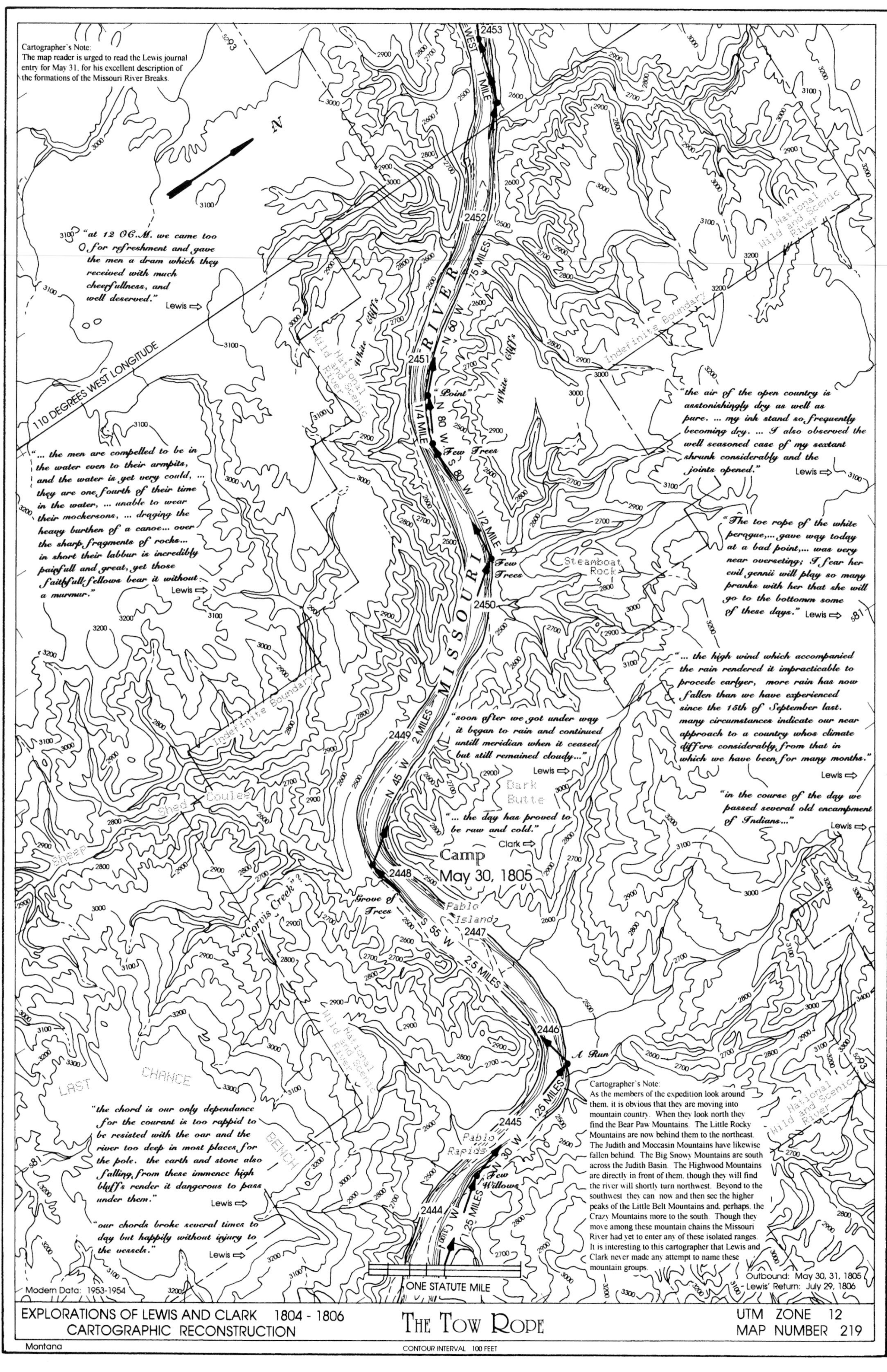

Cartographer's Note:
The map reader is urged to read the Lewis journal entry for May 31, for his excellent description of the formations of the Missouri River Breaks.
N
"at 12 OC.M. we came too for refreshment and gave the men a dram which they received with much cheerfullness, and well deserved." Lewis ⇨
110 DEGREES WEST LONGITUDE
MISSOURI RIVER
White Cliffs
"Point"
Few Trees
National Wild and Scenic River
Indefinite Boundary
"the air of the open country is asstonishingly dry as well as pure. ... my ink stand so frequently becoming dry. ... I also observed the well seasoned case of my sextant shrunk considerably and the joints opened." Lewis ⇨
"... the men are compelled to be in the water even to their armpits, and the water is yet very could, ... they are one fourth of their time in the water, ... unable to wear their mockersons, ... draging the heavy burthen of a canoe... over the sharp fragments of rocks... in short their labbur is incredibly painfull and great, yet those faithfull fellows bear it without a murmur." Lewis ⇨
Steamboat Rock
"The toe rope of the white peroque,... gave way today at a bad point,... was very near oversetting; I fear her evil gennii will play so many pranks with her that she will go to the bottomm some of these days." Lewis ⇨
"... the high wind which accompanied the rain rendered it impracticable to procede earlyer, more rain has now fallen than we have experienced since the 15th of September last. many circumstances indicate our near approach to a country whos climate differs considerably from that in which we have been for many months." Lewis ⇨
"soon after we got under way it began to rain and continued untill meridian when it ceased but still remained cloudy..." Lewis ⇨
Dark Butte
"... the day has proved to be raw and cold." Clark ⇨
Camp May 30, 1805
"in the course of the day we passed several old encampment of Indians..." Lewis ⇨
Sheep Shed Coulee
"Corvis Creek"?
Grove of Trees
Pablo Island
LAST CHANCE BENCH
A Run
Pablo Rapids
Few Willows
"the chord is our only dependance for the courant is too rappid to be resisted with the oar and the river too deep in most places for the pole. the earth and stone also falling from these immence high bluffs render it dangerous to pass under them." Lewis ⇨
"our chords broke several times to day but happily without injury to the vessels." Lewis ⇨
Cartographer's Note:
As the members of the expedition look around them, it is obvious that they are moving into mountain country. When they look north they find the Bear Paw Mountains. The Little Rocky Mountains are now behind them to the northeast. The Judith and Moccasin Mountains have likewise fallen behind. The Big Snowy Mountains are south across the Judith Basin. The Highwood Mountains are directly in front of them, though they will find the river will shortly turn northwest. Beyond to the southwest they can now and then see the higher peaks of the Little Belt Mountains and, perhaps, the Crazy Mountains more to the south. Though they move among these mountain chains the Missouri River had yet to enter any of these isolated ranges. It is interesting to this cartographer that Lewis and Clark never made any attempt to name these mountain groups.
ONE STATUTE MILE
Modern Data: 1953-1954
Outbound: May 30, 31, 1805
Lewis' Return: July 29, 1806
EXPLORATIONS OF LEWIS AND CLARK 1804 - 1806
CARTOGRAPHIC RECONSTRUCTION
THE TOW ROPE
UTM ZONE 12
MAP NUMBER 219
Montana
CONTOUR INTERVAL 100 FEET

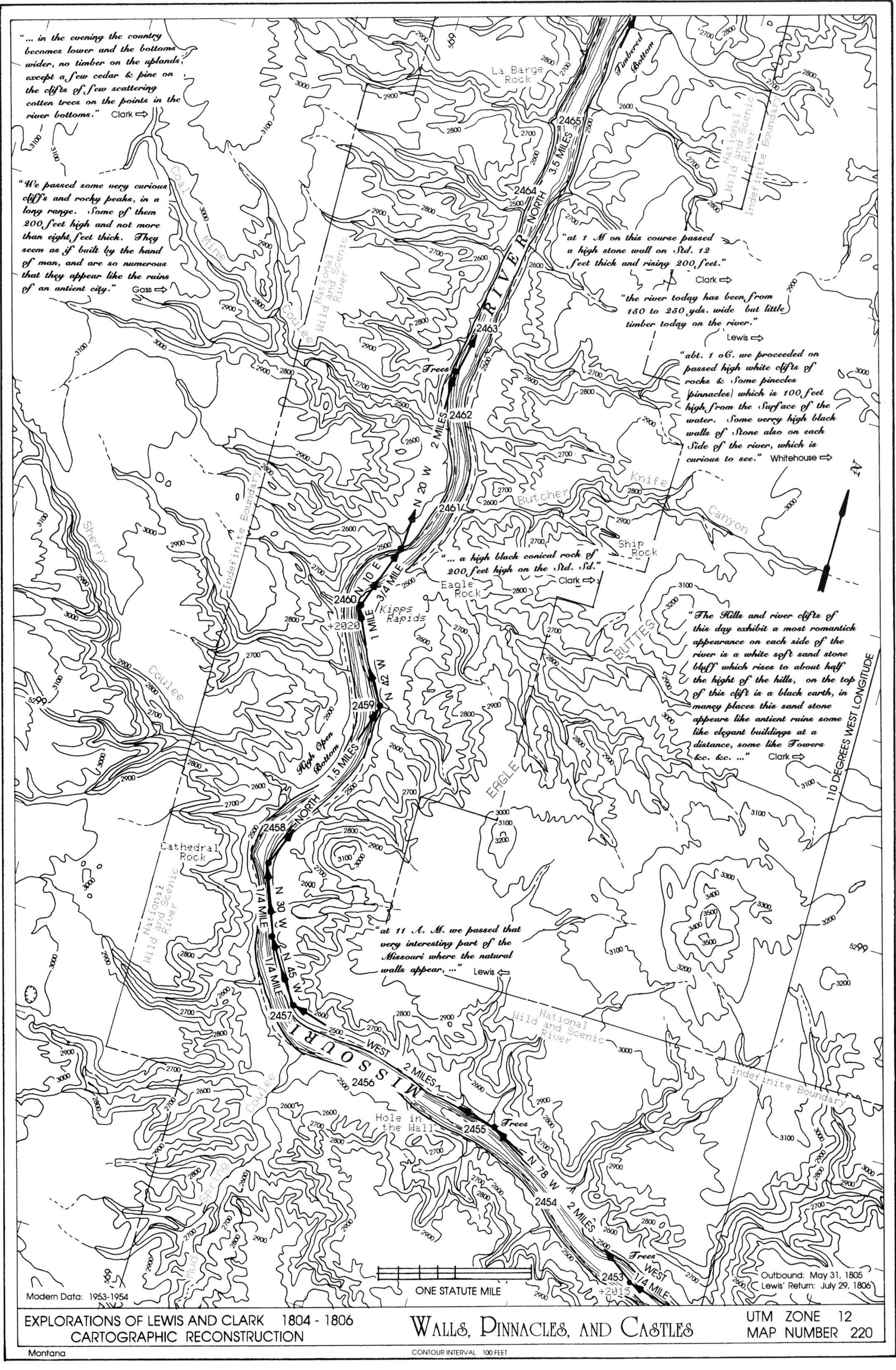
"... in the evening the country becomes lower and the bottoms wider, no timber on the uplands, except a few cedar & pine on the clifts of few scattering cotten trees on the points in the river bottoms." Clark ⇨
"We passed some very curious cliffs and rocky peaks, in a long range. Some of them 200 feet high and not more than eight feet thick. They seem as if built by the hand of man, and are so numerous that they appear like the ruins of an antient city." Gass ⇨
"at 1 M on this course passed a high stone wall on Std. 12 feet thick and rising 200 feet." Clark ⇨
"the river today has been from 150 to 250 yds. wide but little timber today on the river." Lewis ⇨
"abt. 1 oC. we proceeded on passed high white clifts of rocks & Some pinecles [pinnacles] which is 100 feet high from the Surface of the water. Some verry high black walls of Stone also on each Side of the river, which is curious to see." Whitehouse ⇨
"... a high black conical rock of 200 feet high on the Std. Sd." Clark ⇨
"The Hills and river clifts of this day exhibit a most romantick appearance on each side of the river is a white soft sand stone bluff which rises to about half the hight of the hills, on the top of this clift is a black earth, in maney places this sand stone appears like antient ruins some like elegant buildings at a distance, some like Towers &c. &c. ..." Clark ⇨
"at 11 A. M. we passed that very interesting part of the Missouri where the natural walls appear, ..." Lewis ⇦
La Barge Rock
Timbered Bottom
Coal Mine Coulee
National Wild and Scenic River
Indefinite Boundary
MISSOURI RIVER
Butcher Knife Canyon
Ship Rock
Eagle Rock
Kipps Rapids
EAGLE BUTTES
High Open Bottom
Cathedral Rock
Hole in the Wall
Trees
N
110 DEGREES WEST LONGITUDE
Modern Data: 1953-1954
ONE STATUTE MILE
Outbound: May 31, 1805
Lewis' Return: July 29, 1806
EXPLORATIONS OF LEWIS AND CLARK 1804 - 1806
CARTOGRAPHIC RECONSTRUCTION
WALLS, PINNACLES, AND CASTLES
UTM ZONE 12
MAP NUMBER 220
Montana
CONTOUR INTERVAL 100 FEET

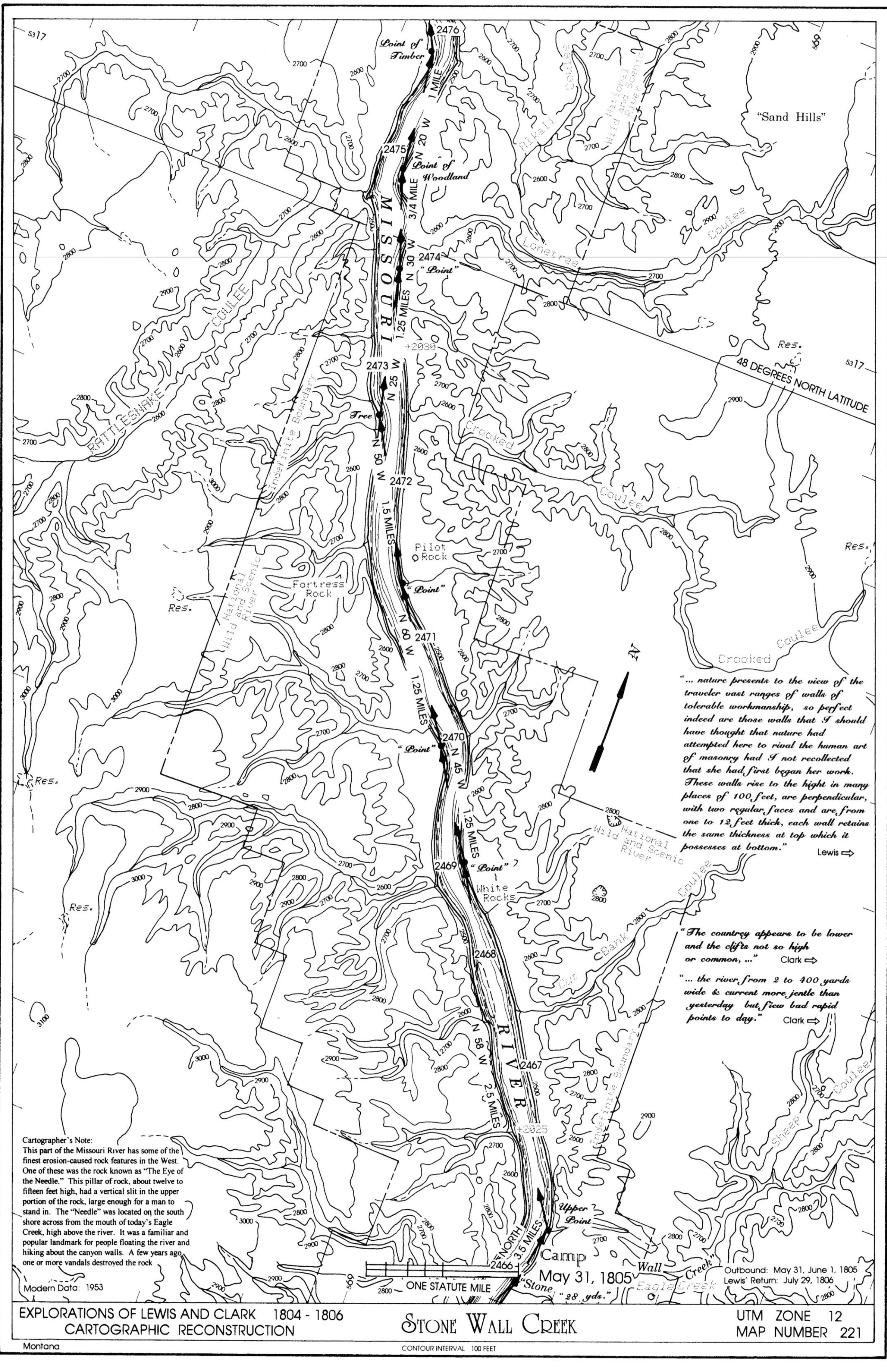

Point of Timber
2476
1 MILE
N 20 W
2475
Point of Woodland
3/4 MILE
MISSOURI
N 30 W
2474
"Point"
1.25 MILES
+2830
2473
N 25 W
Tree
N 50 W
2472
1.5 MILES
Pilot Rock
Fortress Rock
"Point"
N 60 W
2471
1.25 MILES
2470
"Point"
N 45 W
1.25 MILES
2469
"Point"
White Rocks
2468
RIVER
N 58 W
2467
2.5 MILES
+2825
Upper Point
NORTH
3.5 MILES
2466
Camp
May 31, 1805
"Stone Wall Creek"
"28 yds."
Eagle Creek
"Sand Hills"
Alkali Coulee
Lonetree Coulee
Rattlesnake Coulee
Crooked Coulee
Cut Bank Coulee
Sheep Coulee
National Wild and Scenic River
Indefinite Boundary
Res.
48 DEGREES NORTH LATITUDE
N
"... nature presents to the view of the traveler vast ranges of walls of tolerable workmanship, so perfect indeed are those walls that I should have thought that nature had attempted here to rival the human art of masonry had I not recollected that she had first began her work. These walls rise to the hight in many places of 100 feet, are perpendicular, with two regular faces and are from one to 12 feet thick, each wall retains the same thickness at top which it possesses at bottom." Lewis ⇨
"The countrey appears to be lower and the clifts not so high or common, ..." Clark ⇨
"... the river from 2 to 400 yards wide & current more jentle than yesterday but fiew bad rapid points to day." Clark ⇨
Cartographer's Note:
This part of the Missouri River has some of the finest erosion-caused rock features in the West. One of these was the rock known as "The Eye of the Needle." This pillar of rock, about twelve to fifteen feet high, had a vertical slit in the upper portion of the rock, large enough for a man to stand in. The "Needle" was located on the south shore across from the mouth of today's Eagle Creek, high above the river. It was a familiar and popular landmark for people floating the river and hiking about the canyon walls. A few years ago one or more vandals destroyed the rock
Modern Data: 1953
ONE STATUTE MILE
Outbound: May 31, June 1, 1805
Lewis' Return: July 29, 1806
EXPLORATIONS OF LEWIS AND CLARK 1804 - 1806
CARTOGRAPHIC RECONSTRUCTION
STONE WALL CREEK
UTM ZONE 12
MAP NUMBER 221
Montana
CONTOUR INTERVAL 100 FEET

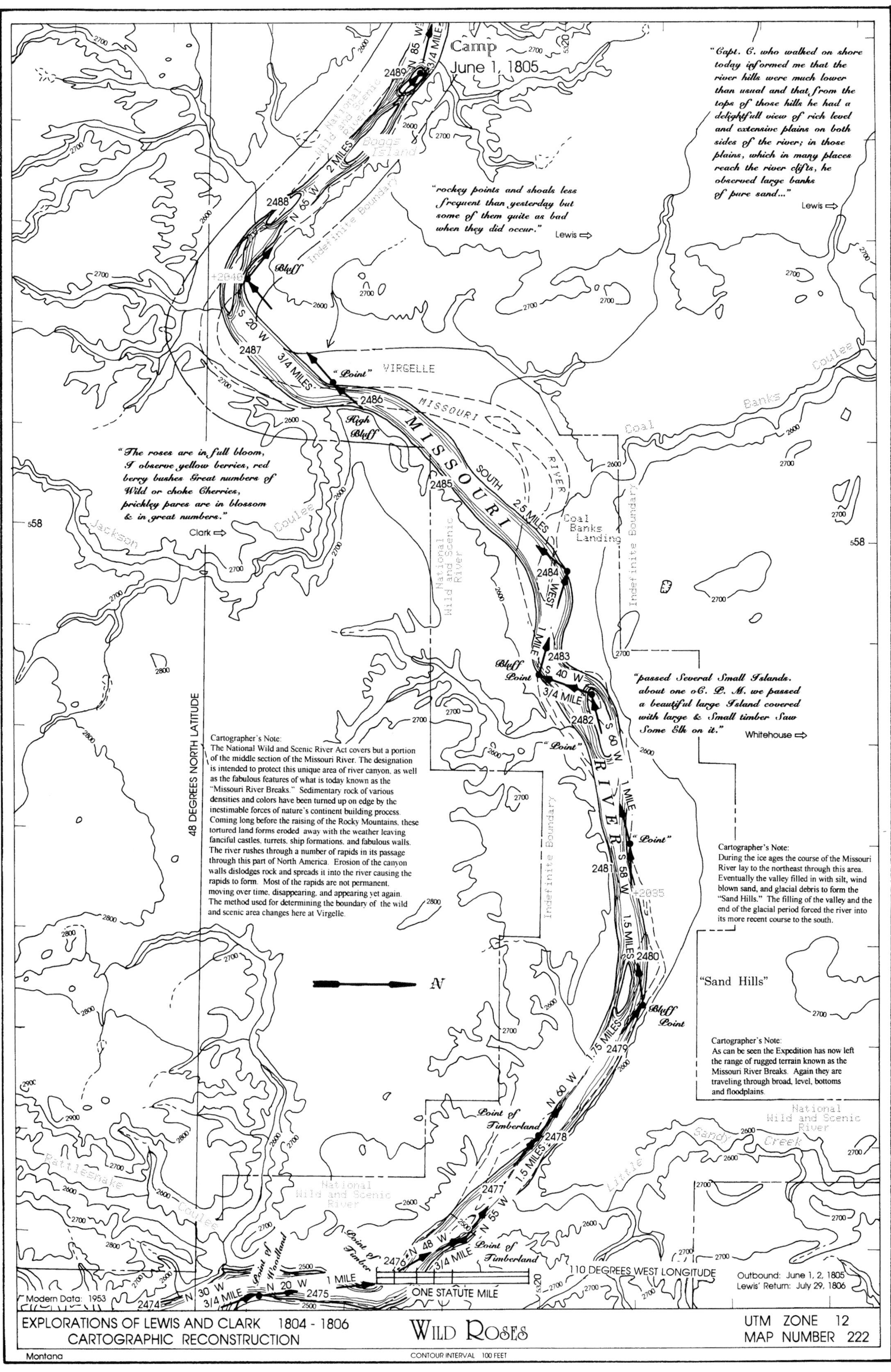
Camp
June 1, 1805
"Capt. C. who walked on shore today informed me that the river hills were much lower than usual and that from the tops of those hills he had a delightfull view of rich level and extensive plains on both sides of the river; in those plains, which in many places reach the river clifts, he observed large banks of pure sand..."
Lewis
"rockey points and shoals less frequent than yesterday but some of them quite as bad when they did occur."
Lewis
"The roses are in full bloom, I observe yellow berries, red berry bushes Great numbers of Wild or choke Cherries, prickley pares are in blossom & in great numbers."
Clark
"passed Several Small Islands. about one oC. P. M. we passed a beautiful large Island covered with large & Small timber Saw Some Elk on it."
Whitehouse
Cartographer's Note:
The National Wild and Scenic River Act covers but a portion of the middle section of the Missouri River. The designation is intended to protect this unique area of river canyon, as well as the fabulous features of what is today known as the "Missouri River Breaks." Sedimentary rock of various densities and colors have been turned up on edge by the inestimable forces of nature's continent building process. Coming long before the raising of the Rocky Mountains, these tortured land forms eroded away with the weather leaving fanciful castles, turrets, ship formations, and fabulous walls. The river rushes through a number of rapids in its passage through this part of North America. Erosion of the canyon walls dislodges rock and spreads it into the river causing the rapids to form. Most of the rapids are not permanent, moving over time, disappearing, and appearing yet again. The method used for determining the boundary of the wild and scenic area changes here at Virgelle.
Cartographer's Note:
During the ice ages the course of the Missouri River lay to the northeast through this area. Eventually the valley filled in with silt, wind blown sand, and glacial debris to form the "Sand Hills." The filling of the valley and the end of the glacial period forced the river into its more recent course to the south.
Cartographer's Note:
As can be seen the Expedition has now left the range of rugged terrain known as the Missouri River Breaks. Again they are traveling through broad, level, bottoms and floodplains.
"Sand Hills"
National Wild and Scenic River
Boggs Island
Indefinite Boundary
VIRGELLE
MISSOURI
SOUTH
RIVER
Coal Banks Landing
Coal Banks Coulee
Jackson Coulee
Little Sandy Creek
Rattlesnake Coulee
Bluff
"Point"
High Bluff
Bluff Point
Point of Timberland
Point of Timber
Point of Woodland
48 DEGREES NORTH LATITUDE
110 DEGREES WEST LONGITUDE
N
ONE STATUTE MILE
Modern Data: 1953
Outbound: June 1, 2, 1805
Lewis' Return: July 29, 1806
EXPLORATIONS OF LEWIS AND CLARK 1804 - 1806
CARTOGRAPHIC RECONSTRUCTION
WILD ROSES
UTM ZONE 12
MAP NUMBER 222
Montana
CONTOUR INTERVAL 100 FEET

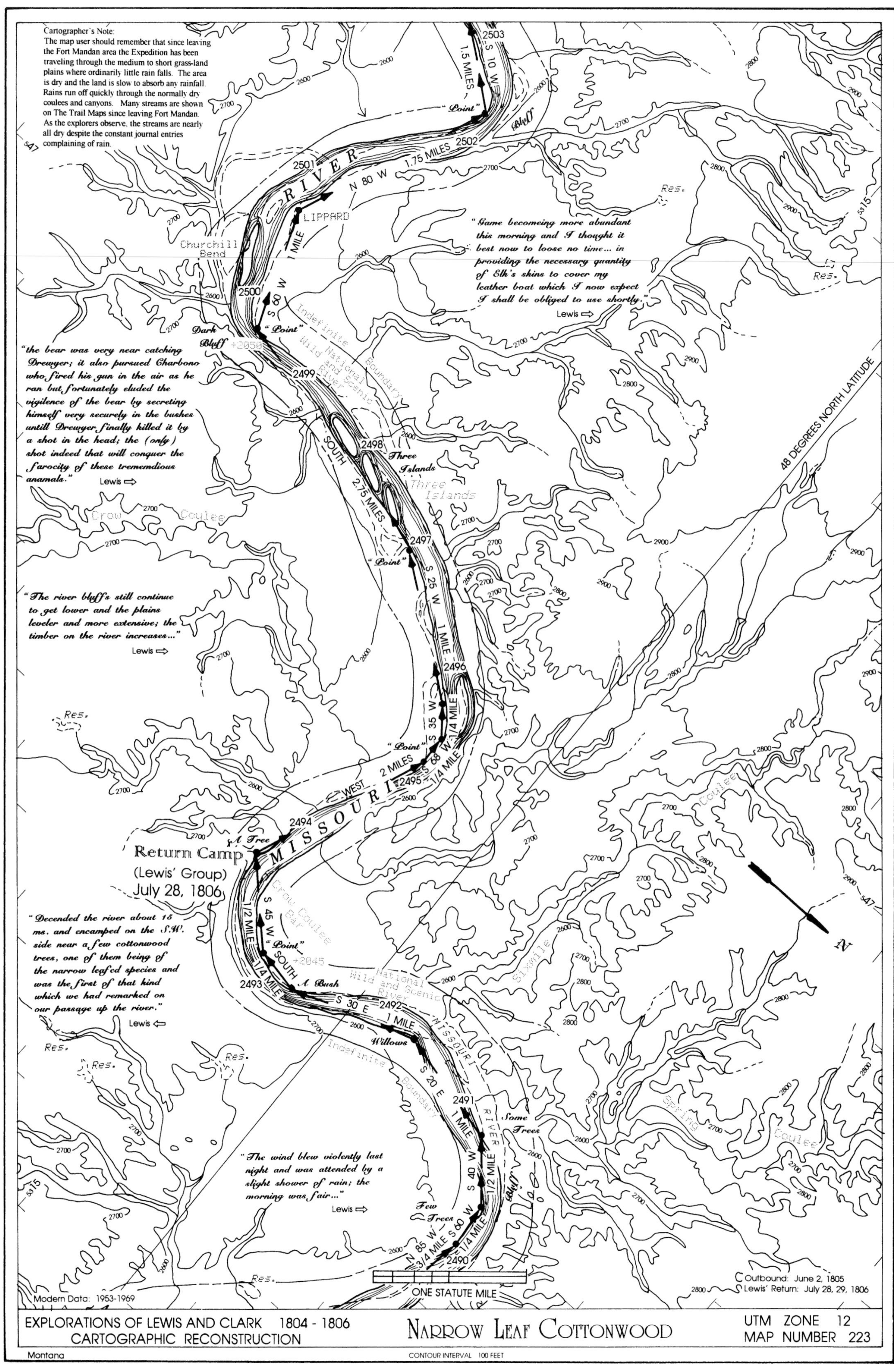

Cartographer's Note:
The map user should remember that since leaving the Fort Mandan area the Expedition has been traveling through the medium to short grass-land plains where ordinarily little rain falls. The area is dry and the land is slow to absorb any rainfall. Rains run off quickly through the normally dry coulees and canyons. Many streams are shown on The Trail Maps since leaving Fort Mandan. As the explorers observe, the streams are nearly all dry despite the constant journal entries complaining of rain.
"Game becomeing more abundant this morning and I thought it best now to loose no time... in providing the necessary quantity of Elk's skins to cover my leather boat which I now expect I shall be obliged to use shortly."
Lewis
"the bear was very near catching Drewyer; it also pursued Charbono who fired his gun in the air as he ran but fortunately eluded the vigilence of the bear by secreting himself very securely in the bushes untill Drewyer finally killed it by a shot in the head; the (only) shot indeed that will conquer the farocity of these tremendious anamals."
Lewis
"The river bluffs still continue to get lower and the plains leveler and more extensive; the timber on the river increases..."
Lewis
"Decended the river about 15 ms. and encamped on the S.W. side near a few cottonwood trees, one of them being of the narrow leafed species and was the first of that kind which we had remarked on our passage up the river."
Lewis
"The wind blew violently last night and was attended by a slight shower of rain; the morning was fair..."
Lewis
Return Camp
(Lewis' Group)
July 28, 1806
MISSOURI RIVER
Churchill Bend
LIPPARD
Dark Bluff
Three Islands
Crow Coulee
Crow Coulee Bar
Indefinite National Wild and Scenic River Boundary
48 DEGREES NORTH LATITUDE
Sixmile Coulee
Spring Coulee
Res.
A Tree
A Bush
Willows
Some Trees
Few Trees
Bluff
"Point"
N
ONE STATUTE MILE
Outbound: June 2, 1805
Lewis' Return: July 28, 29, 1806
Modern Data: 1953-1969
EXPLORATIONS OF LEWIS AND CLARK 1804 - 1806
CARTOGRAPHIC RECONSTRUCTION
NARROW LEAF COTTONWOOD
UTM ZONE 12
MAP NUMBER 223
Montana
CONTOUR INTERVAL 100 FEET

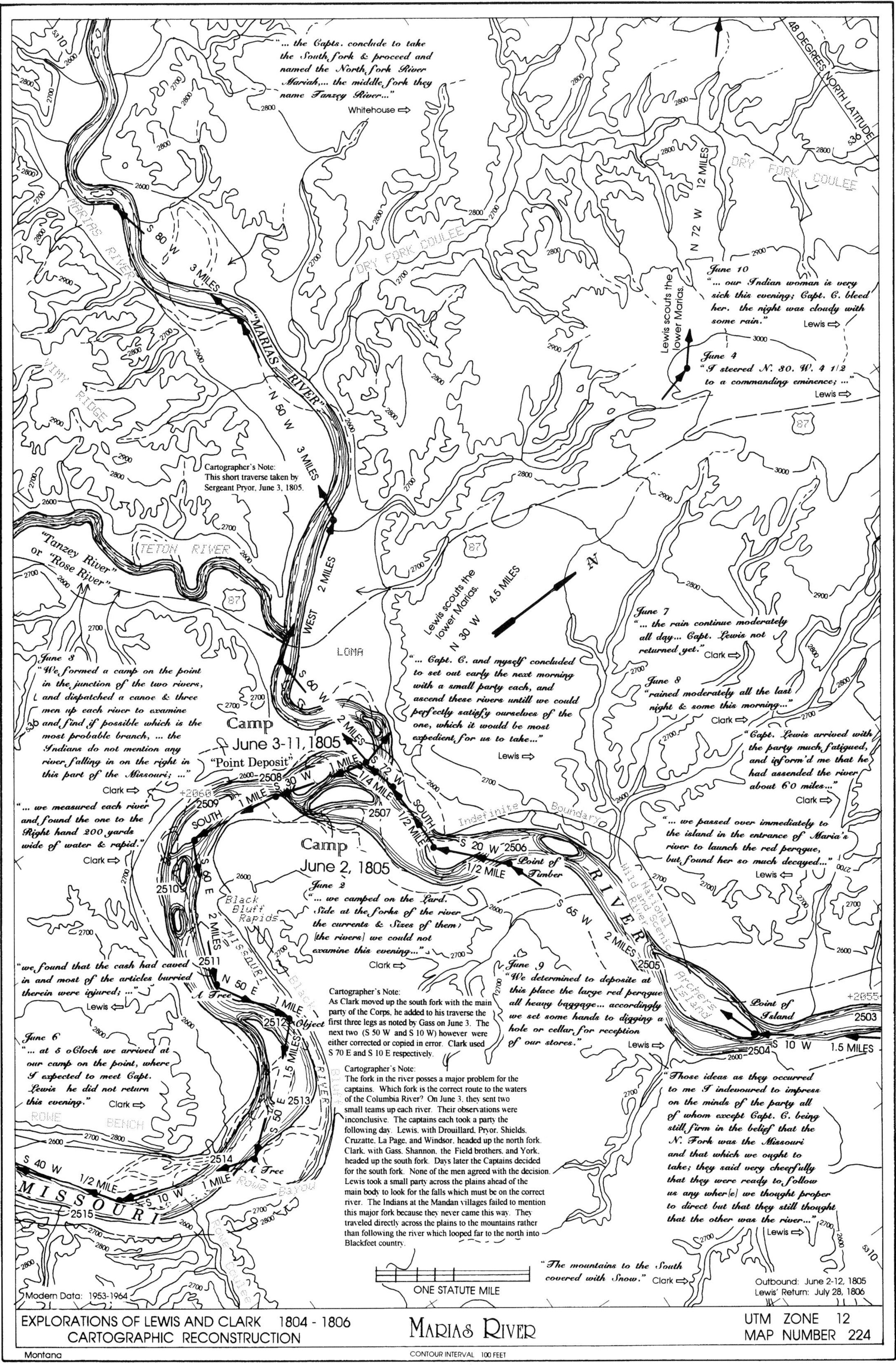
"... the Capts. conclude to take the South fork & proceed and named the North fork River Mariah,... the middle fork they name Tanzey River..."
Whitehouse ⇨
48 DEGREES NORTH LATITUDE
DRY FORK COULEE
MARIAS RIVER
"MARIAS RIVER"
S 80 W
3 MILES
N 50 W
3 MILES
N 72 W 12 MILES
Lewis scouts the lower Marias.
June 10
"... our Indian woman is very sick this evening; Capt. C. bleed her. the night was cloudy with some rain."
Lewis ⇨
June 4
"I steered N. 30. W. 4 1/2 to a commanding eminence; ..."
Lewis ⇨
VIMY RIDGE
Cartographer's Note:
This short traverse taken by Sergeant Pryor, June 3, 1805.
"Tanzey River" or "Rose River"
TETON RIVER
2 MILES
WEST
Lewis scouts the lower Marias.
N 30 W 4.5 MILES
N
LOMA
S 60 W
June 7
"... the rain continue moderately all day... Capt. Lewis not returned yet."
Clark ⇨
June 3
"We formed a camp on the point in the junction of the two rivers, and dispatched a canoe & three men up each river to examine and find if possible which is the most probable branch, ... the Indians do not mention any river falling in on the right in this part of the Missouri; ..."
Clark ⇨
"... Capt. C. and myself concluded to set out early the next morning with a small party each, and ascend these rivers untill we could perfectly satisfy ourselves of the one, which it would be most expedient for us to take..."
Lewis ⇨
June 8
"rained moderately all the last night & some this morning..."
Clark ⇨
Camp
June 3-11, 1805
"Point Deposit"
2 MILES
1 MILE
S 72 W
1/4 MILE
S 30 W
1 MILE
SOUTH
1/2 MILE
"Capt. Lewis arrived with the party much fatigued, and inform'd me that he had assended the river about 60 miles..."
Clark ⇨
"... we measured each river and found the one to the Right hand 200 yards wide of water & rapid."
Clark ⇨
SOUTH
Camp
June 2, 1805
S 20 W
1/2 MILE
Point of Timber
Indefinite Boundary
"... we passed over immediately to the island in the entrance of Maria's river to launch the red perogue, but found her so much decayed..."
Lewis ⇦
S 60 E
Black Bluff Rapids
June 2
"... we camped on the Lard. Side at the forks of the river the currents & Sizes of them (the rivers) we could not examine this evening..."
Clark ⇨
RIVER
National Wild and Scenic River
S 65 W
2 MILES
2 MILES
"we found that the cash had caved in and most of the articles burried therein were injured; ..."
Lewis ⇦
N 50 E
A Tree
1 MILE
Object
MISSOURI
Black Bluff
Cartographer's Note:
As Clark moved up the south fork with the main party of the Corps, he added to his traverse the first three legs as noted by Gass on June 3. The next two (S 50 W and S 10 W) however were either corrected or copied in error. Clark used S 70 E and S 10 E respectively.
June 9
"We determined to deposite at this place the large red perogue all heavy baggage... accordingly we set some hands to digging a hole or cellar for reception of our stores."
Lewis ⇨
Archers Island
Point of Island
S 10 W
1.5 MILES
June 6
"... at 5 oClock we arrived at our camp on the point, where I expected to meet Capt. Lewis he did not return this evening."
Clark ⇨
1.5 MILES
Cartographer's Note:
The fork in the river posses a major problem for the captains. Which fork is the correct route to the waters of the Columbia River? On June 3, they sent two small teams up each river. Their observations were inconclusive. The captains each took a party the following day. Lewis, with Drouillard, Pryor, Shields, Cruzatte, La Page, and Windsor, headed up the north fork. Clark, with Gass, Shannon, the Field brothers, and York, headed up the south fork. Days later the Captains decided for the south fork. None of the men agreed with the decision. Lewis took a small party across the plains ahead of the main body to look for the falls which must be on the correct river. The Indians at the Mandan villages failed to mention this major fork because they never came this way. They traveled directly across the plains to the mountains rather than following the river which looped far to the north into Blackfeet country.
"Those ideas as they occurred to me I indevoured to impress on the minds of the party all of whom except Capt. C. being still firm in the belief that the N. Fork was the Missouri and that which we ought to take; they said very cheerfully that they were ready to follow us any wher(e) we thought proper to direct but that they still thought that the other was the river..."
Lewis ⇨
ROWE BENCH
S 50 E
A Tree
S 40 W
1/2 MILE
S 10 W
1 MILE
Rowe Bayou
MISSOURI
Rowe Coulee
"The mountains to the South covered with Snow."
Clark ⇨
ONE STATUTE MILE
Outbound: June 2-12, 1805
Lewis' Return: July 28, 1806
Modern Data: 1953-1964
EXPLORATIONS OF LEWIS AND CLARK 1804 - 1806
CARTOGRAPHIC RECONSTRUCTION
MARIAS RIVER
UTM ZONE 12
MAP NUMBER 224
Montana
CONTOUR INTERVAL 100 FEET

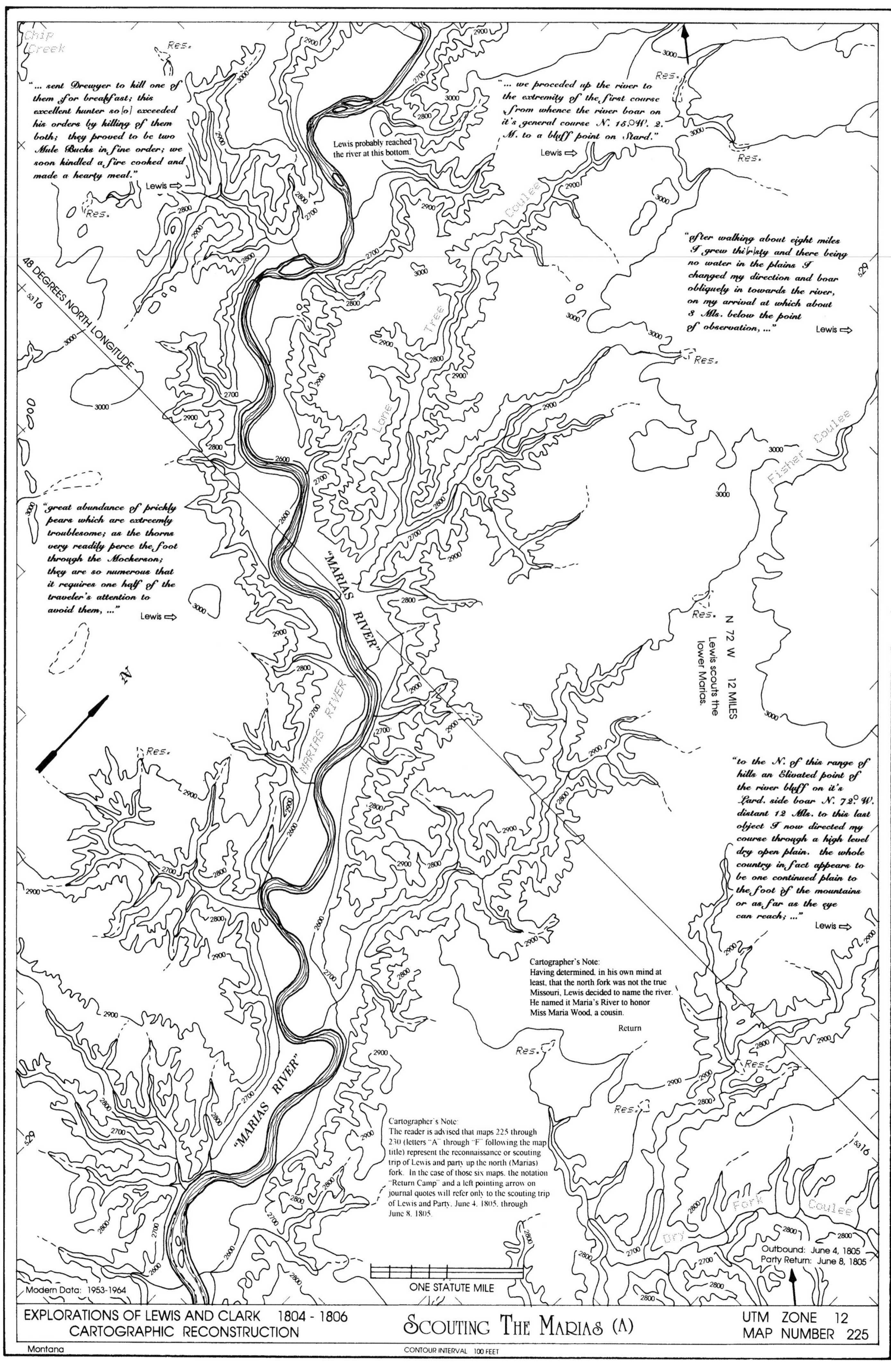
Chip Creek
Res.
"... sent Drewyer to kill one of them for breakfast; this excellent hunter so[o] exceeded his orders by killing of them both; they proved to be two Mule Bucks in fine order; we soon kindled a fire cooked and made a hearty meal."
Lewis ⇨
Lewis probably reached the river at this bottom.
"... we proceeded up the river to the extremity of the first course from whence the river boar on it's general course N. 15.°W. 2. M. to a bluff point on Stard."
Lewis ⇨
Coulee
"after walking about eight miles I grew thi[r]sty and there being no water in the plains I changed my direction and boar obliquely in towards the river, on my arrival at which about 8 Mls. below the point of observation, ..."
Lewis ⇨
48 DEGREES NORTH LONGITUDE
Lone Tree
Fisher Coulee
"great abundance of prickly pears which are extreemly troublesome; as the thorns very readily perce the foot through the Mockerson; they are so numerous that it requires one half of the traveler's attention to avoid them, ..."
Lewis ⇨
"MARIAS RIVER"
MARIAS RIVER
N 72 W 12 MILES
Lewis scouts the lower Marias.
N
"to the N. of this range of hills an Elivated point of the river bluff on it's Lard. side boar N. 72.° W. distant 12 Mls. to this last object I now directed my course through a high level dry open plain. the whole country in fact appears to be one continued plain to the foot of the mountains or as far as the eye can reach; ..."
Lewis ⇨
Cartographer's Note:
Having determined, in his own mind at least, that the north fork was not the true Missouri, Lewis decided to name the river. He named it Maria's River to honor Miss Maria Wood, a cousin.
Return
"MARIAS RIVER"
Cartographer's Note:
The reader is advised that maps 225 through 230 (letters "A" through "F" following the map title) represent the reconnaissance or scouting trip of Lewis and party up the north (Marias) fork. In the case of those six maps, the notation "Return Camp" and a left pointing arrow on journal quotes will refer only to the scouting trip of Lewis and Party, June 4, 1805, through June 8, 1805.
Dry Fork Coulee
Outbound: June 4, 1805
Party Return: June 8, 1805
ONE STATUTE MILE
Modern Data: 1953-1964
EXPLORATIONS OF LEWIS AND CLARK 1804 - 1806
CARTOGRAPHIC RECONSTRUCTION
SCOUTING THE MARIAS (A)
UTM ZONE 12
MAP NUMBER 225
Montana
CONTOUR INTERVAL 100 FEET

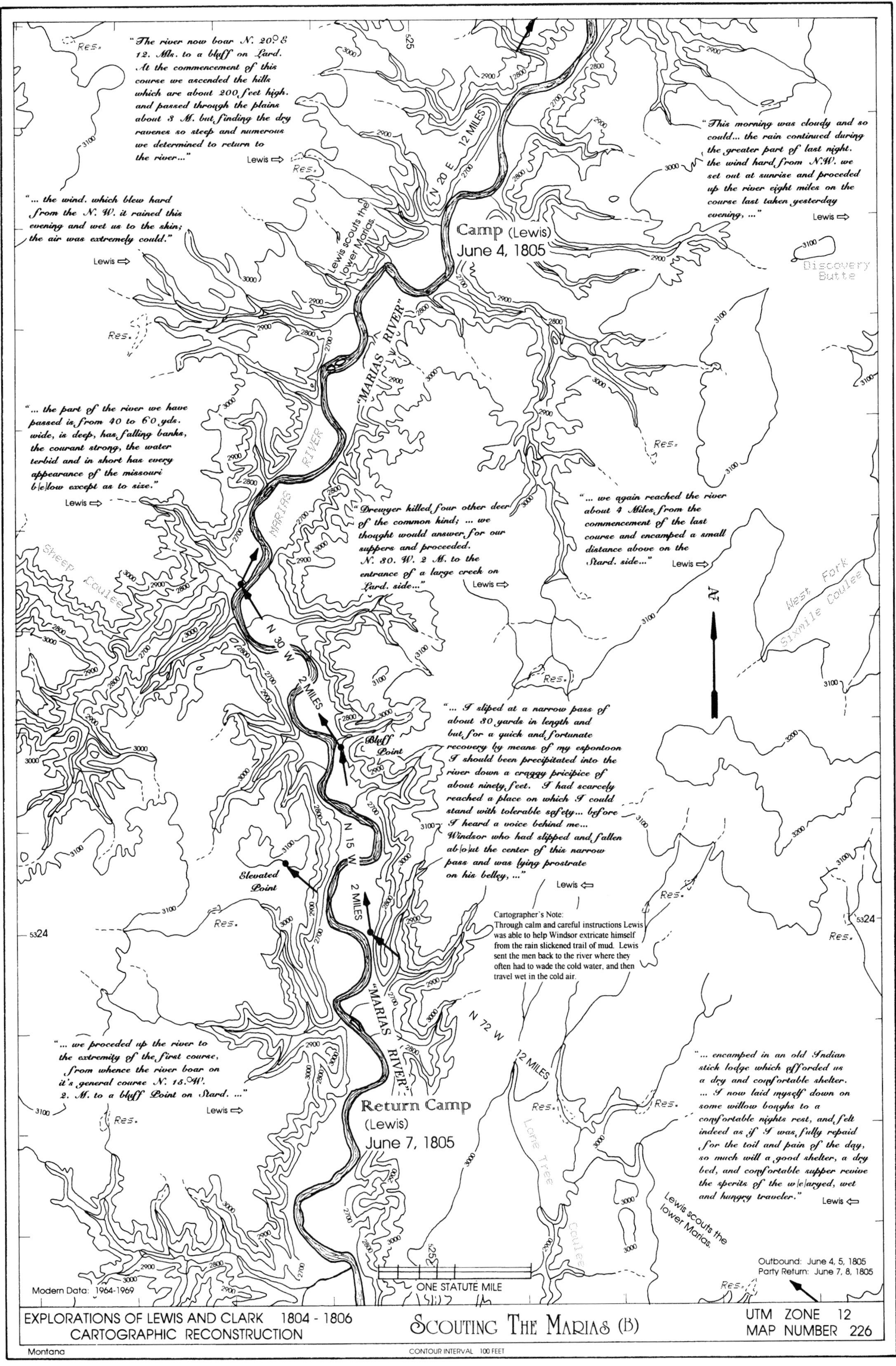
"The river now boar N. 20° E 12. Mls. to a bluff on Lard. At the commencement of this course we ascended the hills which are about 200 feet high. and passed through the plains about 3 M. but finding the dry ravenes so steep and numerous we determined to return to the river..."
Lewis ⇨
"... the wind. which blew hard from the N. W. it rained this evening and wet us to the skin; the air was extremely could."
Lewis ⇨
"This morning was cloudy and so could... the rain continued during the greater part of last night. the wind hard from N.W. we set out at sunrise and proceeded up the river eight miles on the course last taken yesterday evening, ..."
Lewis ⇨
N 20 E 12 MILES
Lewis scouts the lower Marias.
Camp (Lewis)
June 4, 1805
Discovery Butte
Res.
"MARIAS RIVER"
MARIAS RIVER
"... the part of the river we have passed is from 40 to 60 yds. wide, is deep, has falling banks, the courant strong, the water terbid and in short has every appearance of the missouri b[e]low except as to size."
Lewis ⇨
Sheep Coulee
"Drewyer killed four other deer of the common kind; ... we thought would answer for our suppers and proceeded. N. 30. W. 2 M. to the entrance of a large creek on Lard. side..."
Lewis ⇨
"... we again reached the river about 4 Miles from the commencement of the last course and encamped a small distance above on the Stard. side..."
Lewis ⇨
West Fork Sixmile Coulee
N
N 30 W 2 MILES
Bluff Point
"... I sliped at a narrow pass of about 30 yards in length and but for a quick and fortunate recovery by means of my espontoon I should been precipitated into the river down a craggy pricipice of about ninety feet. I had scarcely reached a place on which I could stand with tolerable safety... before I heard a voice behind me... Windsor who had slipped and fallen ab[o]ut the center of this narrow pass and was lying prostrate on his belley, ..."
Lewis ⇦
N 15 W 2 MILES
Elevated Point
Cartographer's Note:
Through calm and careful instructions Lewis was able to help Windsor extricate himself from the rain slickened trail of mud. Lewis sent the men back to the river where they often had to wade the cold water, and then travel wet in the cold air.
"MARIAS RIVER"
N 72 W 12 MILES
"... we proceeded up the river to the extremity of the first course, from whence the river boar on it's general course N. 15.° W. 2. M. to a bluff Point on Stard. ..."
Lewis ⇨
Return Camp (Lewis)
June 7, 1805
Lone Tree Coulee
"... encamped in an old Indian stick lodge which afforded us a dry and comfortable shelter. ... I now laid myself down on some willow boughs to a comfortable nights rest, and felt indeed as if I was fully repaid for the toil and pain of the day, so much will a good shelter, a dry bed, and comfortable supper revive the sperits of the w[e]aryed, wet and hungry traveler."
Lewis ⇦
Lewis scouts the lower Marias.
Outbound: June 4, 5, 1805
Party Return: June 7, 8, 1805
Modern Data: 1964-1969
ONE STATUTE MILE
EXPLORATIONS OF LEWIS AND CLARK 1804 - 1806
CARTOGRAPHIC RECONSTRUCTION
SCOUTING THE MARIAS (B)
UTM ZONE 12
MAP NUMBER 226
Montana
CONTOUR INTERVAL 100 FEET

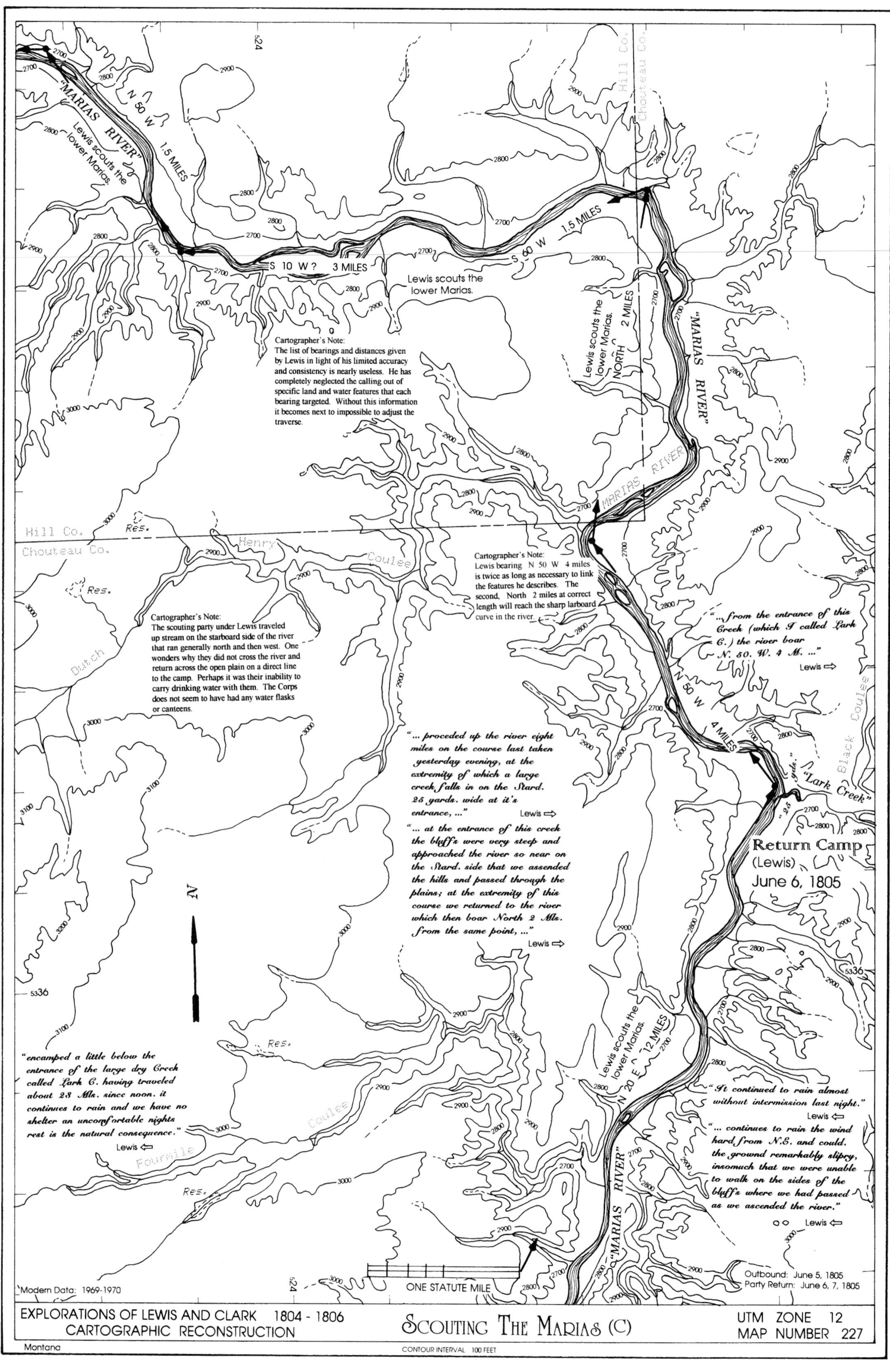
"MARIAS RIVER"
Lewis scouts the lower Marias.
N 50 W
1.5 MILES
S 10 W ? 3 MILES
S 60 W 1.5 MILES
Lewis scouts the lower Marias.
Hill Co.
Chouteau Co.
Lewis scouts the lower Marias. NORTH 2 MILES
"MARIAS RIVER"
MARIAS RIVER
Cartographer's Note:
The list of bearings and distances given by Lewis in light of his limited accuracy and consistency is nearly useless. He has completely neglected the calling out of specific land and water features that each bearing targeted. Without this information it becomes next to impossible to adjust the traverse.
Res.
Henry Coulee
Res.
Dutch
Cartographer's Note:
Lewis bearing N 50 W 4 miles is twice as long as necessary to link the features he describes. The second, North 2 miles at correct length will reach the sharp larboard curve in the river.
Cartographer's Note:
The scouting party under Lewis traveled up stream on the starboard side of the river that ran generally north and then west. One wonders why they did not cross the river and return across the open plain on a direct line to the camp. Perhaps it was their inability to carry drinking water with them. The Corps does not seem to have had any water flasks or canteens.
"...from the entrance of this Creek (which I called Lark C.) the river boar N. 50. W. 4 M. ..."
Lewis ⇨
N 50 W
4 MILES
Black Coulee
"Lark Creek"
"25 yds."
"... proceded up the river eight miles on the course last taken yesterday evening, at the extremity of which a large creek falls in on the Stard. 25 yards. wide at it's entrance, ..."
Lewis ⇨
"... at the entrance of this creek the bluff's were very steep and approached the river so near on the Stard. side that we assended the hills and passed through the plains; at the extremity of this course we returned to the river which then boar North 2 Mls. from the same point, ..."
Lewis ⇨
Return Camp
(Lewis)
June 6, 1805
N
Lewis scouts the lower Marias.
N 20 E 12 MILES
Res.
"encamped a little below the entrance of the large dry Creek called Lark C. having traveled about 23 Mls. since noon. it continues to rain and we have no shelter an uncomfortable nights rest is the natural consequence."
Lewis ⇦
Coulee
Fourmile
Res.
"It continued to rain almost without intermission last night."
Lewis ⇦
"... continues to rain the wind hard from N.E. and could. the ground remarkably slipry, insomuch that we were unable to walk on the sides of the bluff's where we had passed as we ascended the river."
Lewis ⇦
"MARIAS RIVER"
ONE STATUTE MILE
Modern Data: 1969-1970
Outbound: June 5, 1805
Party Return: June 6, 7, 1805
EXPLORATIONS OF LEWIS AND CLARK 1804 - 1806
CARTOGRAPHIC RECONSTRUCTION
SCOUTING THE MARIAS (C)
UTM ZONE 12
MAP NUMBER 227
Montana
CONTOUR INTERVAL 100 FEET

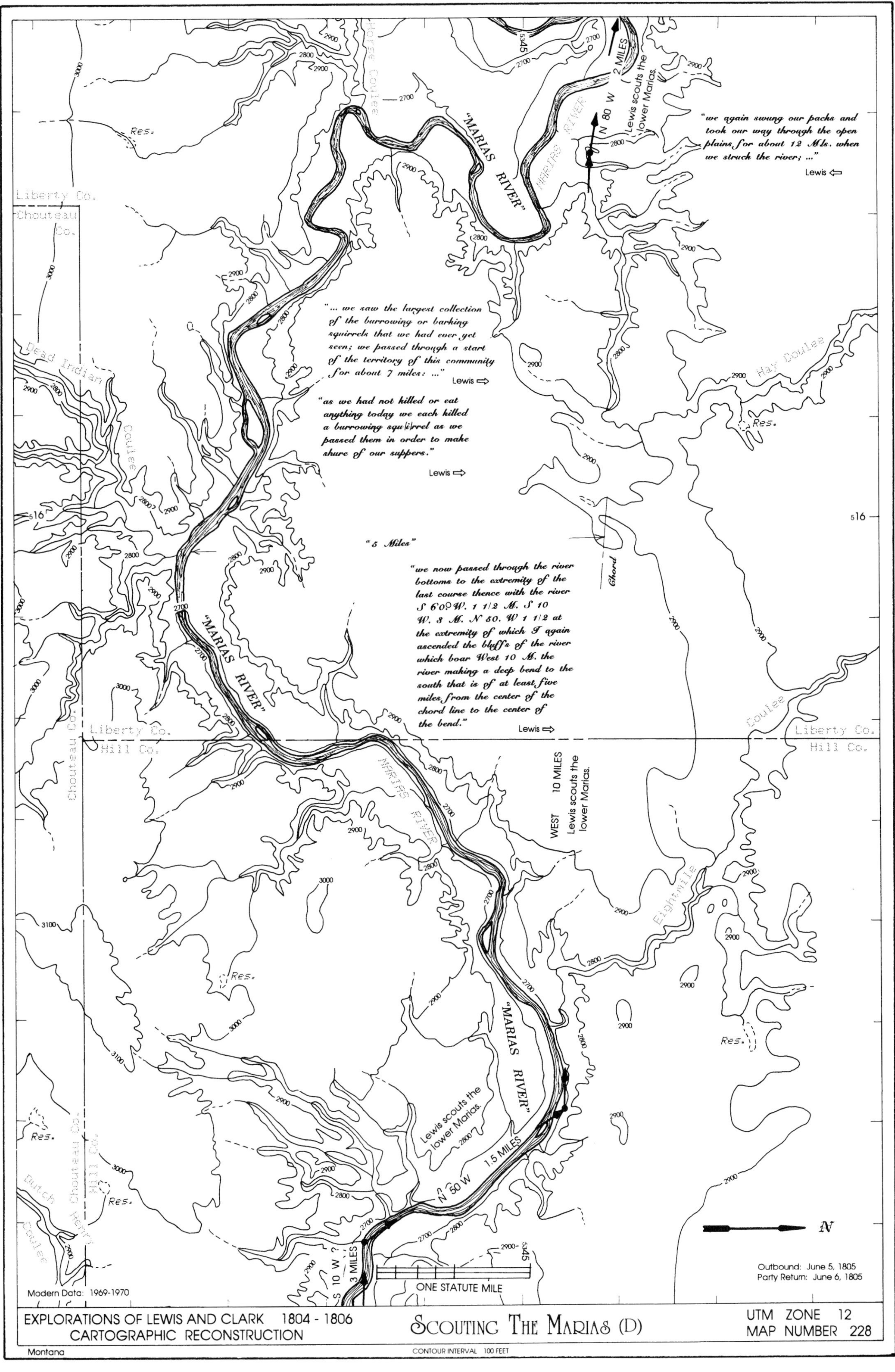
"we again swung our packs and took our way through the open plains for about 12 Mls. when we struck the river; ..."
Lewis ⇦
"... we saw the largest collection of the burrowing or barking squirrels that we had ever yet seen; we passed through a start of the territory of this community for about 7 miles: ..."
Lewis ⇨
"as we had not killed or eat anything today we each killed a burrowing squ[i]rrel as we passed them in order to make shure of our suppers."
Lewis ⇨
"5 Miles"
"we now passed through the river bottoms to the extremity of the last course thence with the river S 60° W. 1 1/2 M. S 10 W. 3 M. N 50. W 1 1/2 at the extremity of which I again ascended the bluffs of the river which boar West 10 M. the river making a deep bend to the south that is of at least five miles from the center of the chord line to the center of the bend."
Lewis ⇨
"MARIAS RIVER"
MARIAS RIVER
N 80 W
2 MILES
Lewis scouts the lower Marias.
WEST 10 MILES
Chord
N 50 W
1.5 MILES
S 10 W ?
3 MILES
Horse Coulee
Dead Indian Coulee
Hay Coulee
Coulee
Eightmile
Dutch Henry Coulee
Liberty Co.
Chouteau Co.
Hill Co.
Res.
N
ONE STATUTE MILE
Modern Data: 1969-1970
Outbound: June 5, 1805
Party Return: June 6, 1805
EXPLORATIONS OF LEWIS AND CLARK 1804 - 1806
CARTOGRAPHIC RECONSTRUCTION
SCOUTING THE MARIAS (D)
UTM ZONE 12
MAP NUMBER 228
Montana
CONTOUR INTERVAL 100 FEET

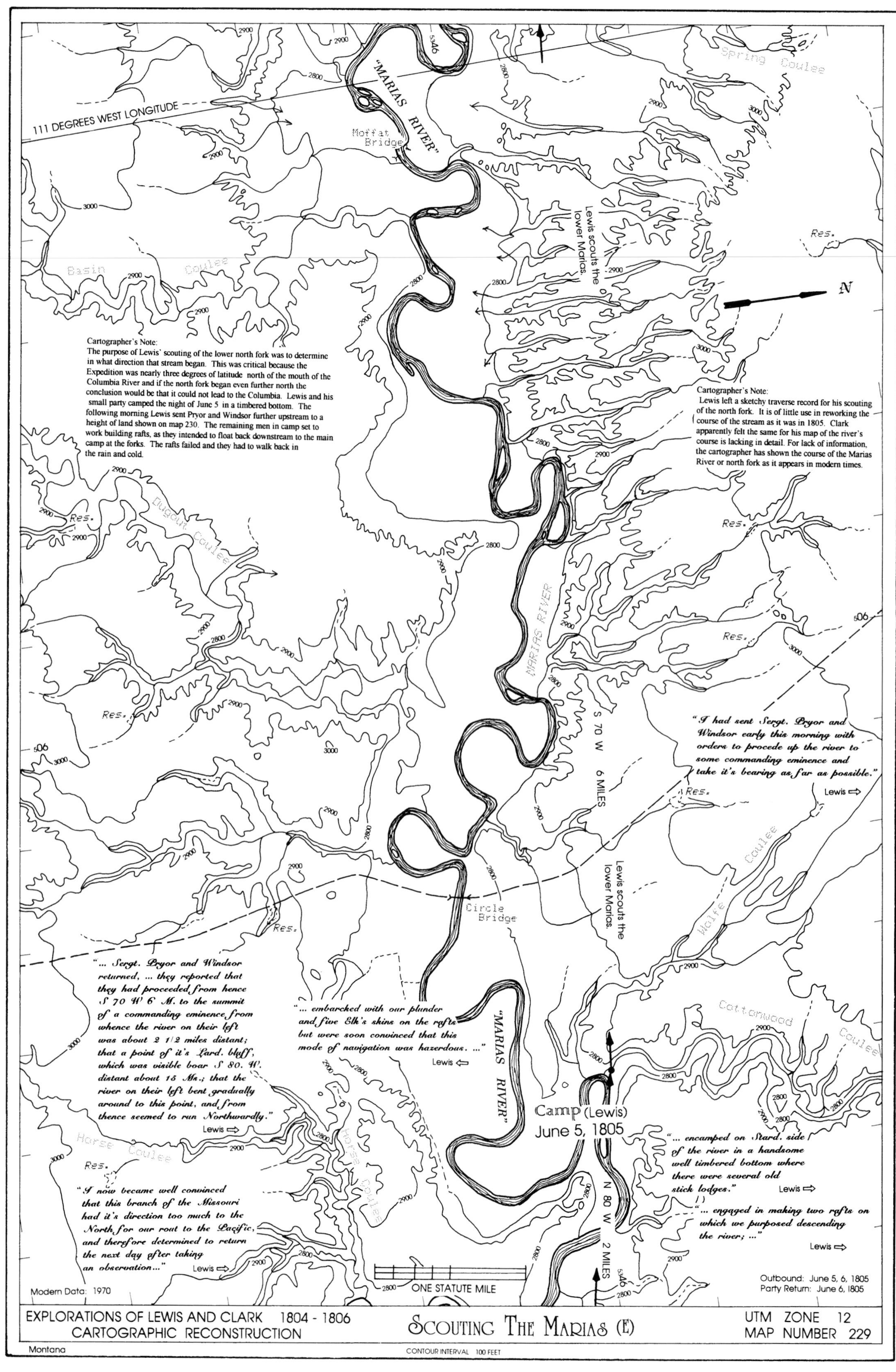
111 DEGREES WEST LONGITUDE
"MARIAS RIVER"
Moffat Bridge
Spring Coulee
Basin Coulee
Lewis scouts the lower Marias.
N
Cartographer's Note:
The purpose of Lewis' scouting of the lower north fork was to determine in what direction that stream began. This was critical because the Expedition was nearly three degrees of latitude north of the mouth of the Columbia River and if the north fork began even further north the conclusion would be that it could not lead to the Columbia. Lewis and his small party camped the night of June 5 in a timbered bottom. The following morning Lewis sent Pryor and Windsor further upstream to a height of land shown on map 230. The remaining men in camp set to work building rafts, as they intended to float back downstream to the main camp at the forks. The rafts failed and they had to walk back in the rain and cold.
Cartographer's Note:
Lewis left a sketchy traverse record for his scouting of the north fork. It is of little use in reworking the course of the stream as it was in 1805. Clark apparently felt the same for his map of the river's course is lacking in detail. For lack of information, the cartographer has shown the course of the Marias River or north fork as it appears in modern times.
Dugout Coulee
Res.
MARIAS RIVER
S 70 W 6 MILES
"I had sent Sergt. Pryor and Windsor early this morning with orders to procede up the river to some commanding eminence and take it's bearing as far as possible."
Lewis ⇨
Lewis scouts the lower Marias.
Circle Bridge
Wolfe Coulee
"... Sergt. Pryor and Windsor returned, ... they reported that they had proceeded from hence S 70 W 6 M. to the summit of a commanding eminence from whence the river on their left was about 2 1/2 miles distant; that a point of it's Lard. bluff, which was visible boar S 80. W. distant about 15 Ms.; that the river on their left bent gradually around to this point, and from thence seemed to run Northwardly."
Lewis ⇨
"... embarcked with our plunder and five Elk's skins on the rafts but were soon convinced that this mode of navigation was hazerdous. ..."
Lewis ⇦
"MARIAS RIVER"
Cottonwood Coulee
Camp (Lewis) June 5, 1805
"... encamped on Stard. side of the river in a handsome well timbered bottom where there were several old stick lodges."
Lewis ⇨
"... engaged in making two rafts on which we purposed descending the river; ..."
Lewis ⇨
Horse Coulee
"I now became well convinced that this branch of the Missouri had it's direction too much to the North for our rout to the Pacific, and therefore determined to return the next day after taking an observation..."
Lewis ⇨
N 80 W 2 MILES
ONE STATUTE MILE
Modern Data: 1970
Outbound: June 5, 6, 1805
Party Return: June 6, 1805
EXPLORATIONS OF LEWIS AND CLARK 1804 - 1806
CARTOGRAPHIC RECONSTRUCTION
SCOUTING THE MARIAS (E)
UTM ZONE 12
MAP NUMBER 229
Montana
CONTOUR INTERVAL 100 FEET

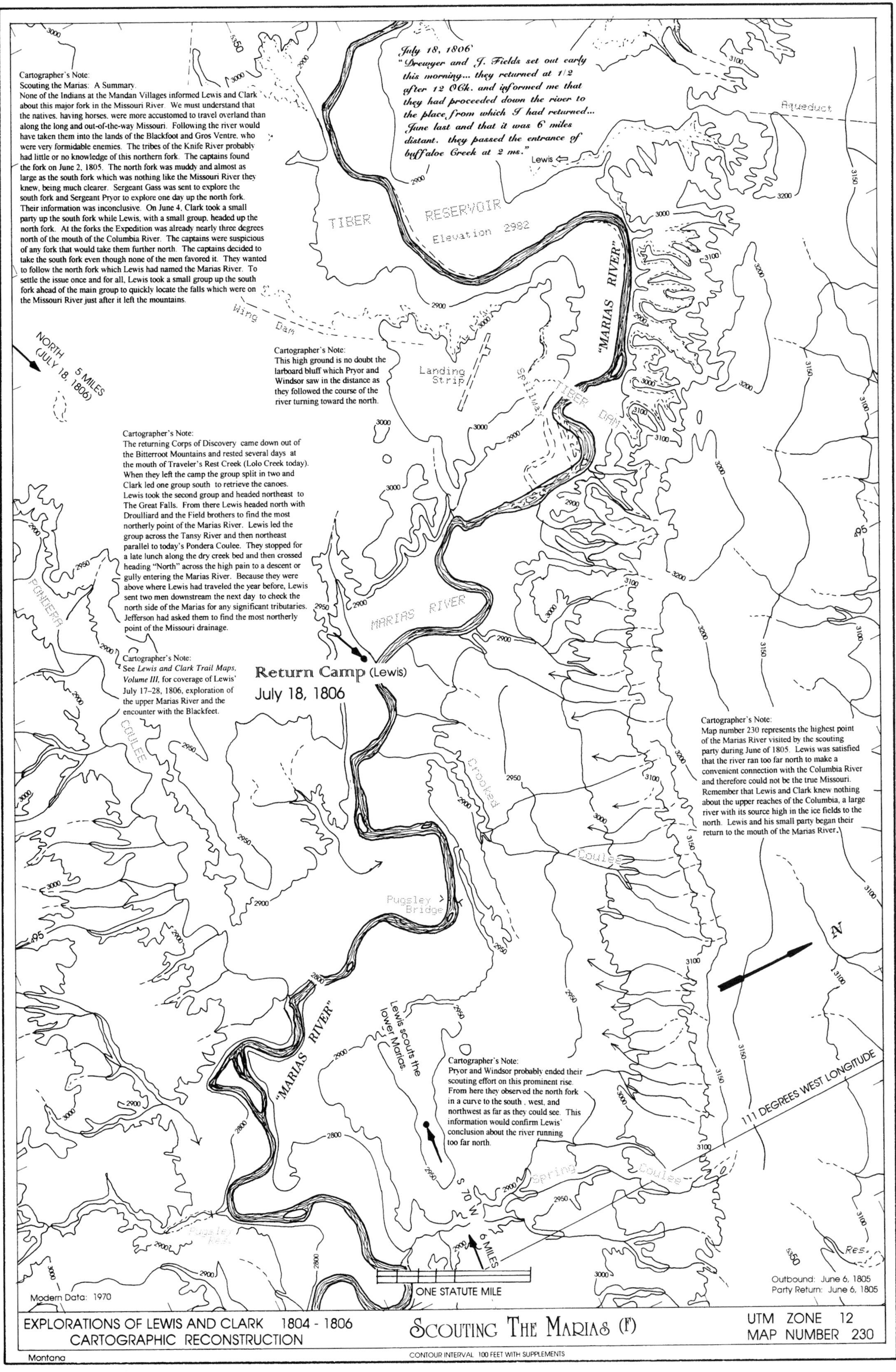
Cartographer's Note:
Scouting the Marias: A Summary.
None of the Indians at the Mandan Villages informed Lewis and Clark about this major fork in the Missouri River. We must understand that the natives, having horses, were more accustomed to travel overland than along the long and out-of-the-way Missouri. Following the river would have taken them into the lands of the Blackfoot and Gros Ventre, who were very formidable enemies. The tribes of the Knife River probably had little or no knowledge of this northern fork. The captains found the fork on June 2, 1805. The north fork was muddy and almost as large as the south fork which was nothing like the Missouri River they knew, being much clearer. Sergeant Gass was sent to explore the south fork and Sergeant Pryor to explore one day up the north fork. Their information was inconclusive. On June 4, Clark took a small party up the south fork while Lewis, with a small group, headed up the north fork. At the forks the Expedition was already nearly three degrees north of the mouth of the Columbia River. The captains were suspicious of any fork that would take them further north. The captains decided to take the south fork even though none of the men favored it. They wanted to follow the north fork which Lewis had named the Marias River. To settle the issue once and for all, Lewis took a small group up the south fork ahead of the main group to quickly locate the falls which were on the Missouri River just after it left the mountains.
July 18, 1806
"Drewyer and J. Fields set out early this morning... they returned at 1/2 after 12 OCk. and informed me that they had proceeded down the river to the place from which I had returned... June last and that it was 6 miles distant. they passed the entrance of buffaloe Creek at 2 ms."
Lewis ⇦
Aqueduct
TIBER RESERVOIR
Elevation 2982
"MARIAS RIVER"
Wing Dam
NORTH 5 MILES (JULY 18, 1806)
Cartographer's Note:
This high ground is no doubt the larboard bluff which Pryor and Windsor saw in the distance as they followed the course of the river turning toward the north.
Landing Strip
Spillway
TIBER DAM
Cartographer's Note:
The returning Corps of Discovery came down out of the Bitterroot Mountains and rested several days at the mouth of Traveler's Rest Creek (Lolo Creek today). When they left the camp the group split in two and Clark led one group south to retrieve the canoes. Lewis took the second group and headed northeast to The Great Falls. From there Lewis headed north with Droulliard and the Field brothers to find the most northerly point of the Marias River. Lewis led the group across the Tansy River and then northeast parallel to today's Pondera Coulee. They stopped for a late lunch along the dry creek bed and then crossed heading "North" across the high pain to a descent or gully entering the Marias River. Because they were above where Lewis had traveled the year before, Lewis sent two men downstream the next day to check the north side of the Marias for any significant tributaries. Jefferson had asked them to find the most northerly point of the Missouri drainage.
PONDERA
COULEE
MARIAS RIVER
Cartographer's Note:
See Lewis and Clark Trail Maps, Volume III, for coverage of Lewis' July 17–28, 1806, exploration of the upper Marias River and the encounter with the Blackfeet.
Return Camp (Lewis)
July 18, 1806
Crooked
Coulee
Cartographer's Note:
Map number 230 represents the highest point of the Marias River visited by the scouting party during June of 1805. Lewis was satisfied that the river ran too far north to make a convenient connection with the Columbia River and therefore could not be the true Missouri. Remember that Lewis and Clark knew nothing about the upper reaches of the Columbia, a large river with its source high in the ice fields to the north. Lewis and his small party began their return to the mouth of the Marias River.
Pugsley Bridge
N
"MARIAS RIVER"
Lewis scouts the lower Marias.
Cartographer's Note:
Pryor and Windsor probably ended their scouting effort on this prominent rise. From here they observed the north fork in a curve to the south, west, and northwest as far as they could see. This information would confirm Lewis' conclusion about the river running too far north.
111 DEGREES WEST LONGITUDE
Spring Coulee
S 70 W 6 MILES
Pugsley Res.
Res.
ONE STATUTE MILE
Modern Data: 1970
Outbound: June 6, 1805
Party Return: June 6, 1805
EXPLORATIONS OF LEWIS AND CLARK 1804 - 1806
CARTOGRAPHIC RECONSTRUCTION
SCOUTING THE MARIAS (F)
UTM ZONE 12
MAP NUMBER 230
Montana
CONTOUR INTERVAL 100 FEET WITH SUPPLEMENTS

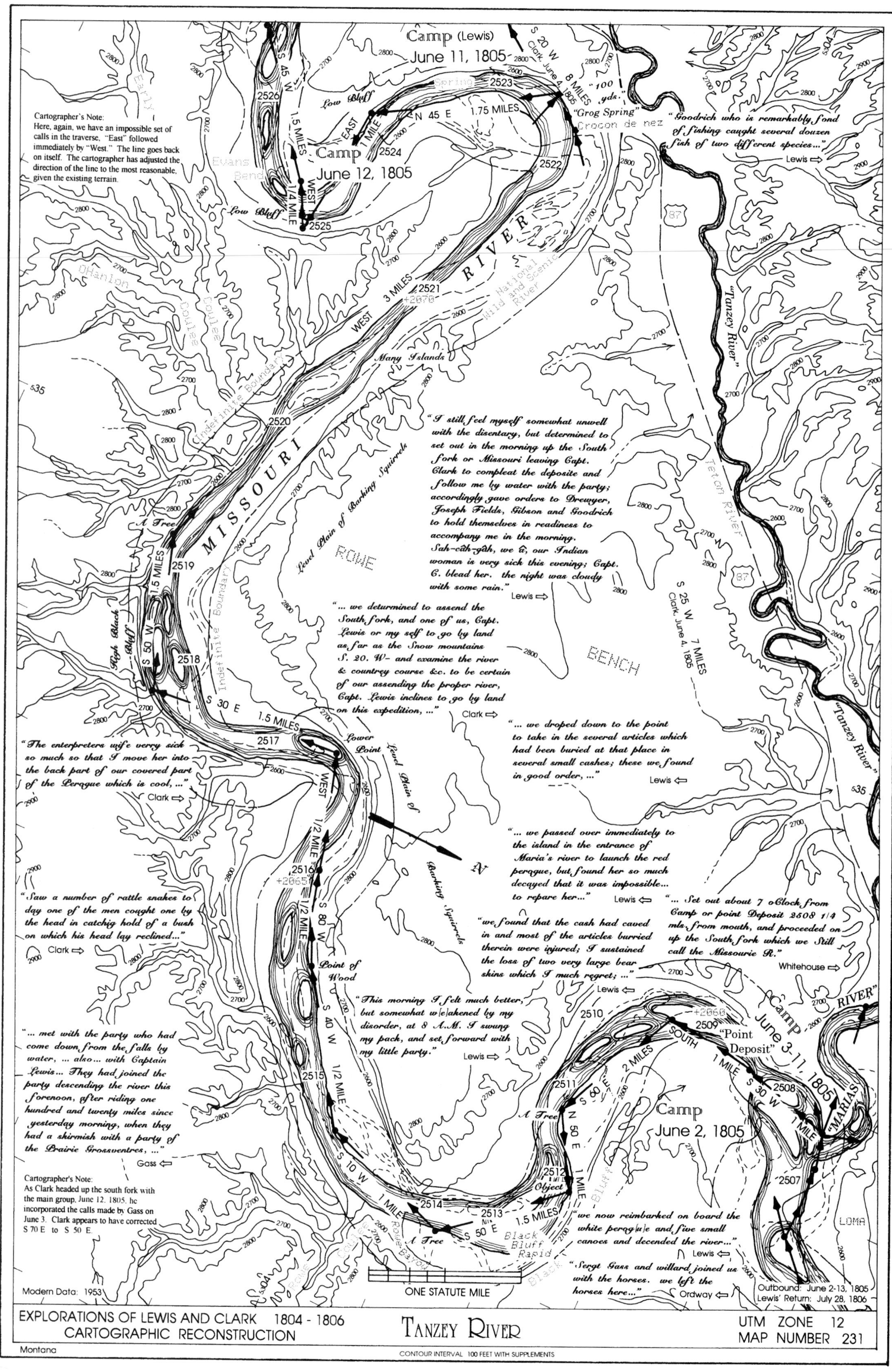
Camp (Lewis)
June 11, 1805
S 20 W
8 MILES
Clark, June 4, 1805
"100 yds."
"Grog Spring"
Crocon de nez
"Goodrich who is remarkably fond of fishing caught several douzen fish of two different species..."
Lewis ⇨
Cartographer's Note:
Here, again, we have an impossible set of calls in the traverse. "East" followed immediately by "West." The line goes back on itself. The cartographer has adjusted the direction of the line to the most reasonable, given the existing terrain.
Early
S 45 W
2526
1.5 MILES
Low Bluff
EAST
1 MILE
N 45 E
1.75 MILES
Spring
2523
Camp
June 12, 1805
2524
Evans Bend
2522
1/4 MILE
WEST
Low Bluff
2525
RIVER
87
OHanlon
Coulee
Coulee
WEST
3 MILES
2521
+2070
National Wild and Scenic River
"Tanzey River"
Many Islands
535
Indefinite Boundary
2520
MISSOURI
Level Plain of Barking Squirrels
"I still feel myself somewhat unwell with the disentary, but determined to set out in the morning up the South fork or Missouri leaving Capt. Clark to compleat the deposite and follow me by water with the party; accordingly gave orders to Drewyer, Joseph Fields, Gibson and Goodrich to hold themselves in readiness to accompany me in the morning. Sah-cāh-gāh, we â, our Indian woman is very sick this evening; Capt. C. blead her. the night was cloudy with some rain."
Lewis ⇨
Teton River
A Tree
1.5 MILES
2519
ROWE
Indefinite Boundary
"... we determined to assend the South fork, and one of us, Capt. Lewis or my self to go by land as far as the Snow mountains S. 20. W- and examine the river & countrey course &c. to be certain of our assending the proper river, Capt. Lewis inclines to go by land on this expedition, ..."
Clark ⇨
S 25 W
7 MILES
Clark, June 4, 1805
BENCH
High Black Bluff
S 50 W
2518
S 30 E
1.5 MILES
2517
Lower Point
Level Plain of Barking Squirrels
"The enterpreters wife verry sick so much so that I move her into the back part of our covered part of the Perogue which is cool, ..."
Clark ⇨
"... we droped down to the point to take in the several articles which had been buried at that place in several small cashes; these we found in good order, ..."
Lewis ⇦
"Tanzey River"
WEST
1/2 MILE
N
2516
+2065
1/2 MILE
S 80 W
"... we passed over immediately to the island in the entrance of Maria's river to launch the red perogue, but found her so much decayed that it was impossible... to repare her..."
Lewis ⇦
"Saw a number of rattle snakes to day one of the men cought one by the head in catchig hold of a bush on which his head lay reclined..."
Clark ⇨
"we found that the cash had caved in and most of the articles burried therein were injured; I sustained the loss of two very large bear skins which I much regret; ..."
Lewis ⇦
"... Set out about 7 oClock from Camp or point Deposit 2508 1/4 mls. from mouth, and proceeded on up the South fork which we Still call the Missourie R."
Whitehouse ⇨
Point of Wood
S 40 W
"This morning I felt much better, but somewhat w[e]akened by my disorder, at 8 A.M. I swung my pack, and set forward with my little party."
Lewis ⇨
2510
+2060
2509
SOUTH
"Point Deposit"
Camp
June 3-11, 1805
"RIVER"
"... met with the party who had come down from the falls by water, ... also... with Captain Lewis... They had joined the party descending the river this forenoon, after riding one hundred and twenty miles since yesterday morning, when they had a shirmish with a party of the Prairie Grossventres, ..."
Gass ⇦
2515
1/2 MILE
2 MILES
2511
S 60 W
1 MILE
S 30 W
2508
1 MILE
MARIAS
Camp
June 2, 1805
A Tree
N 50 E
S 10 W
2512
Object
1 MILE
Bluff
2507
Cartographer's Note:
As Clark headed up the south fork with the main group, June 12, 1805, he incorporated the calls made by Gass on June 3. Clark appears to have corrected S 70 E to S 50 E.
1 MILE
2514
2513
1.5 MILES
S 50 E
A Tree
Black Bluff Rapid
Rowe Coulee
Rowe Bayou
Black
"we now reimbarked on board the white perog[u]e and five small canoes and decended the river..."
Lewis ⇦
"Sergt Gass and willard joined us with the horses. we left the horses here..."
Ordway ⇦
LOMA
Outbound: June 2-13, 1805
Lewis' Return: July 28, 1806
Modern Data: 1953
ONE STATUTE MILE
EXPLORATIONS OF LEWIS AND CLARK 1804 - 1806
CARTOGRAPHIC RECONSTRUCTION
TANZEY RIVER
UTM ZONE 12
MAP NUMBER 231
Montana
CONTOUR INTERVAL 100 FEET WITH SUPPLEMENTS

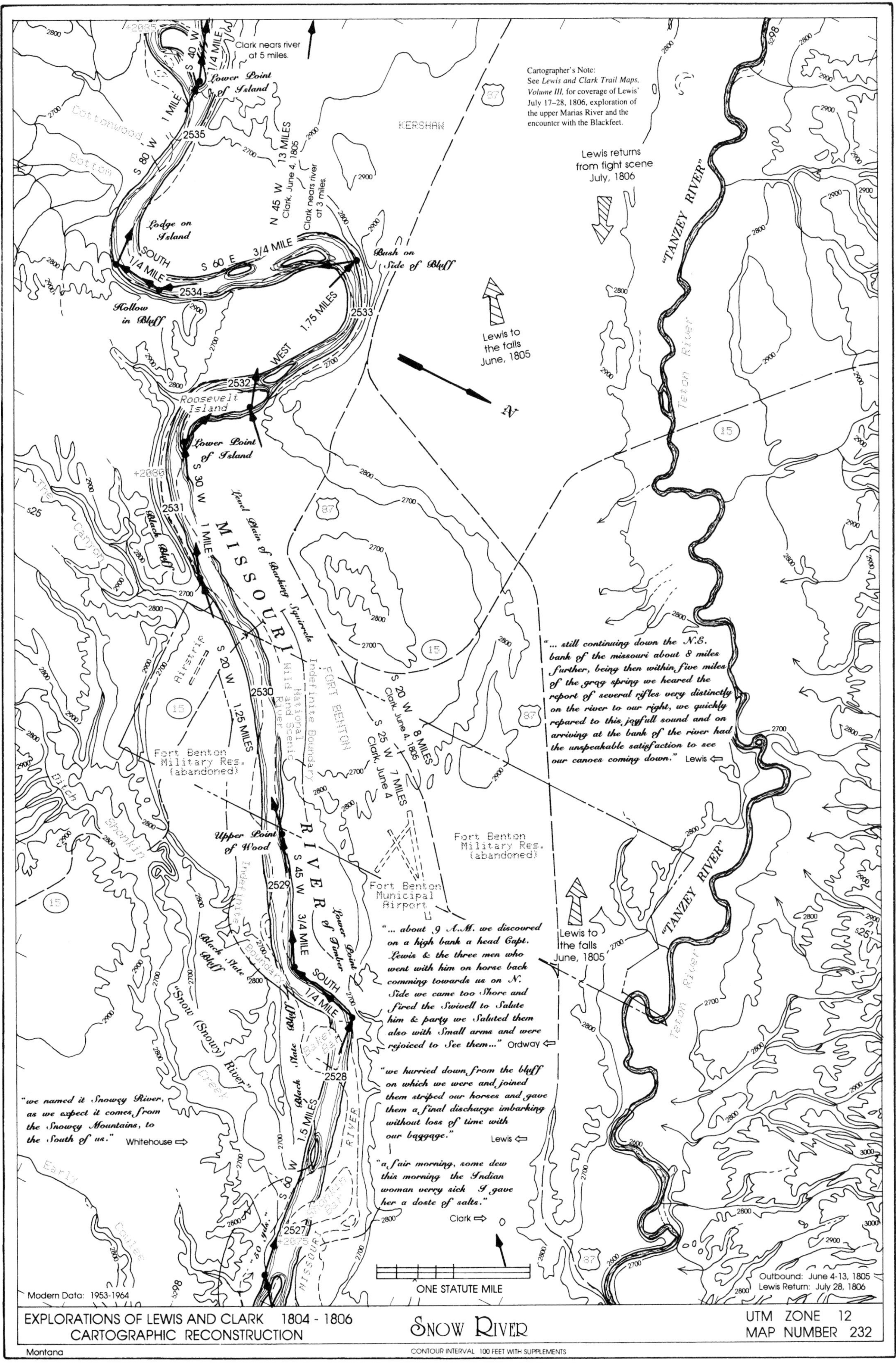
Cartographer's Note:
See *Lewis and Clark Trail Maps, Volume III*, for coverage of Lewis' July 17–28, 1806, exploration of the upper Marias River and the encounter with the Blackfeet.
Clark nears river at 5 miles.
Lower Point of Island
Cottonwood Bottom
KERSHAW
Clark nears river at 3 miles.
Clark, June 4, 1805
Lewis returns from fight scene July, 1806
Lodge on Island
Bush on Side of Bluff
Hollow in Bluff
Lewis to the falls June, 1805
"TANZEY RIVER"
Teton River
Roosevelt Island
Lower Point of Island
MISSOURI RIVER
Level Plain of Barking Squirrels
Black Bluff
Airstrip
Fort Benton Military Res. (abandoned)
FORT BENTON
Indefinite Boundary
Wild and Scenic National River
Shonkin
Upper Point of Wood
Lower Point of Timber
Fort Benton Municipal Airport
Black Slate Bluff
"Snow (Snowy) River"
"… still continuing down the N.E. bank of the missouri about 8 miles further, being then within five miles of the grog spring we heared the report of several rifles very distinctly on the river to our right, we quickly repared to this joyfull sound and on arriving at the bank of the river had the unspeakable satisfaction to see our canoes coming down." Lewis
"… about 9 A.M. we discoured on a high bank a head Capt. Lewis & the three men who went with him on horse back comming towards us on N. Side we came too Shore and fired the Swivell to Salute him & party we Saluted them also with Small arms and were rejoiced to See them…" Ordway
"we hurried down from the bluff on which we were and joined them striped our horses and gave them a final discharge imbarking without loss of time with our baggage." Lewis
"a fair morning, some dew this morning the Indian woman verry sick I gave her a doste of salts." Clark
"we named it Snowey River, as we expect it comes from the Snowey Mountains, to the South of us." Whitehouse
Early Coulee
ONE STATUTE MILE
Modern Data: 1953-1964
Outbound: June 4-13, 1805
Lewis Return: July 28, 1806
EXPLORATIONS OF LEWIS AND CLARK 1804 - 1806
CARTOGRAPHIC RECONSTRUCTION
SNOW RIVER
UTM ZONE 12
MAP NUMBER 232
Montana
CONTOUR INTERVAL 100 FEET WITH SUPPLEMENTS

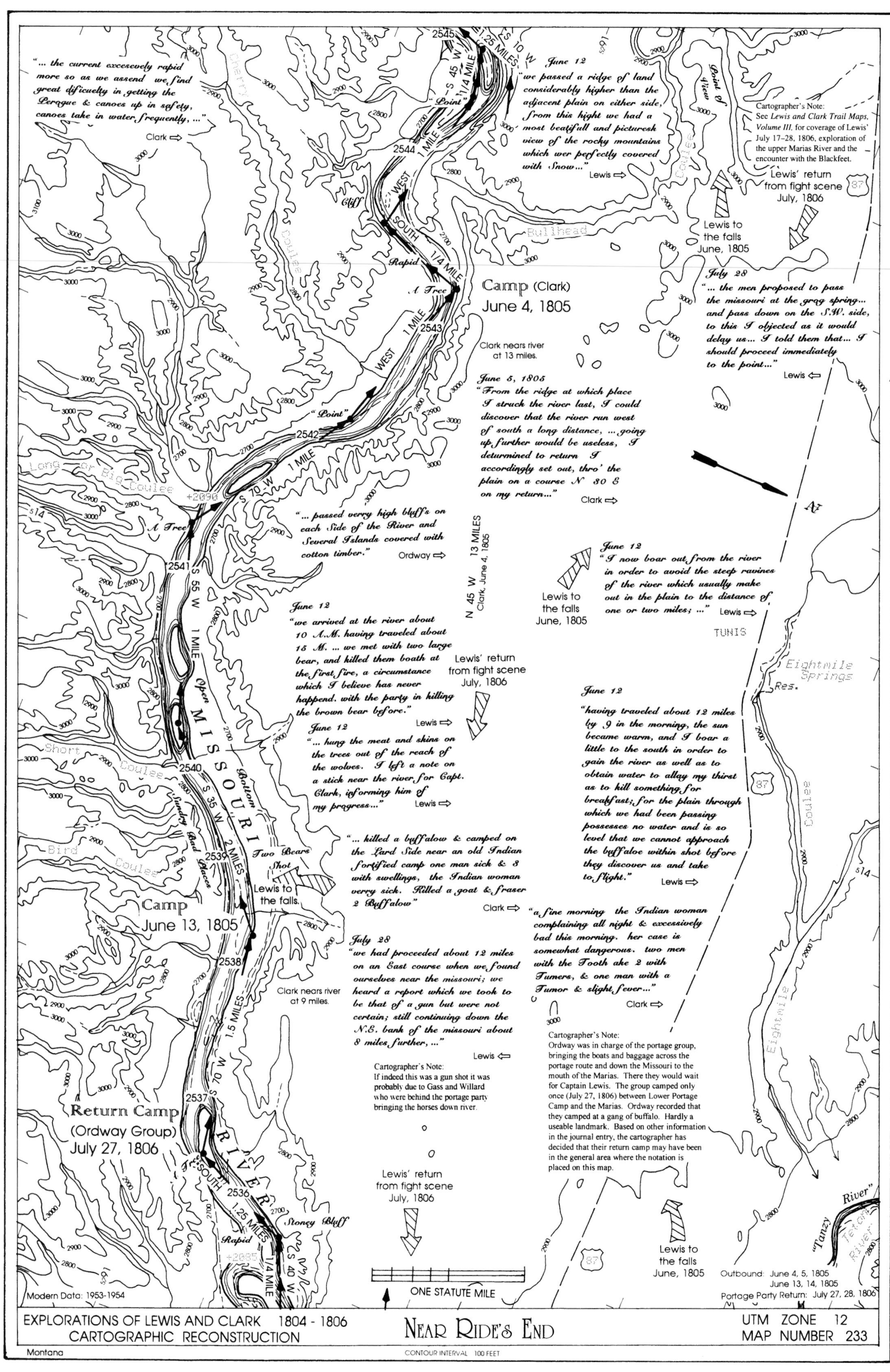

"... the current excesevely rapid more so as we assend we find great dificulty in getting the Perogue & canoes up in safety, canoes take in water frequently, ..."
Clark ⇨
June 12
"we passed a ridge of land considerably higher than the adjacent plain on either side, from this hight we had a most beatifull and picturesk view of the rocky mountains which wer perfectly covered with Snow..."
Lewis ⇨
Cartographer's Note:
See Lewis and Clark Trail Maps, Volume III, for coverage of Lewis' July 17–28, 1806, exploration of the upper Marias River and the encounter with the Blackfeet.
Lewis' return from fight scene July, 1806
Lewis to the falls June, 1805
Camp (Clark) June 4, 1805
July 28
"... the men proposed to pass the missouri at the grog spring... and pass down on the S.W. side, to this I objected as it would delay us... I told them that... I should proceed immediately to the point..."
Lewis ⇦
Clark nears river at 13 miles.
June 5, 1805
"From the ridge at which place I struck the river last, I could discover that the river run west of south a long distance, ...going up further would be useless, I deturmined to return I accordingly set out, thro' the plain on a course N 30 E on my return..."
Clark ⇨
"... passed very high bluffs on each Side of the River and Several Islands covered with cotton timber."
Ordway ⇨
N 45 W 13 MILES Clark, June 4, 1805
June 12
"I now boar out from the river in order to avoid the steep ravines of the river which usually make out in the plain to the distance of one or two miles; ..."
Lewis ⇨
Lewis to the falls June, 1805
June 12
"we arrived at the river about 10 A.M. having traveled about 15 M. ... we met with two large bear, and killed them boath at the first fire, a circumstance which I believe has never happend. with the party in killing the brown bear before."
Lewis ⇨
Lewis' return from fight scene July, 1806
June 12
"... hung the meat and skins on the trees out of the reach of the wolves. I left a note on a stick near the river for Capt. Clark, informing him of my progress..."
Lewis ⇨
June 12
"having traveled about 12 miles by 9 in the morning, the sun became warm, and I boar a little to the south in order to gain the river as well as to obtain water to allay my thirst as to kill something for breakfast; for the plain through which we had been passing possesses no water and is so level that we cannot approach the buffaloe within shot before they discover us and take to flight."
Lewis ⇨
"... killed a buffalow & camped on the Lard Side near an old Indian fortified camp one man sick & 3 with swellings, the Indian woman verry sick. Killed a goat & fraser 2 Buffalow"
Clark ⇨
Two Bears Shot
Lewis to the falls.
Camp June 13, 1805
"a fine morning the Indian woman complaining all night & excessively bad this morning. her case is somewhat dangerous. two men with the Tooth ake 2 with Tumers, & one man with a Tumor & slight fever..."
Clark ⇨
July 28
"we had proceeded about 12 miles on an East course when we found ourselves near the missouri; we heard a report which we took to be that of a gun but were not certain; still continuing down the N.E. bank of the missouri about 8 miles further, ..."
Lewis ⇦
Clark nears river at 9 miles.
Cartographer's Note:
If indeed this was a gun shot it was probably due to Gass and Willard who were behind the portage party bringing the horses down river.
Cartographer's Note:
Ordway was in charge of the portage group, bringing the boats and baggage across the portage route and down the Missouri to the mouth of the Marias. There they would wait for Captain Lewis. The group camped only once (July 27, 1806) between Lower Portage Camp and the Marias. Ordway recorded that they camped at a gang of buffalo. Hardly a useable landmark. Based on other information in the journal entry, the cartographer has decided that their return camp may have been in the general area where the notation is placed on this map.
Return Camp (Ordway Group) July 27, 1806
Lewis' return from fight scene July, 1806
Lewis to the falls June, 1805
MISSOURI RIVER
Open Bottom
Sandy Bad Places
Stoney Bluff
Rapid
Cliff
"Point"
A Tree
Long or Big Coulee
Short Coulee
Bird Coulee
Bullhead
Chatty
Point of View
Eightmile Springs
Eightmile Coulee
TUNIS
Res.
"Tanzy River"
Teton River
Modern Data: 1953-1954
ONE STATUTE MILE
Outbound: June 4, 5, 1805
June 13, 14, 1805
Portage Party Return: July 27, 28, 1806
EXPLORATIONS OF LEWIS AND CLARK 1804 - 1806
CARTOGRAPHIC RECONSTRUCTION
NEAR RIDE'S END
UTM ZONE 12
MAP NUMBER 233
Montana
CONTOUR INTERVAL 100 FEET

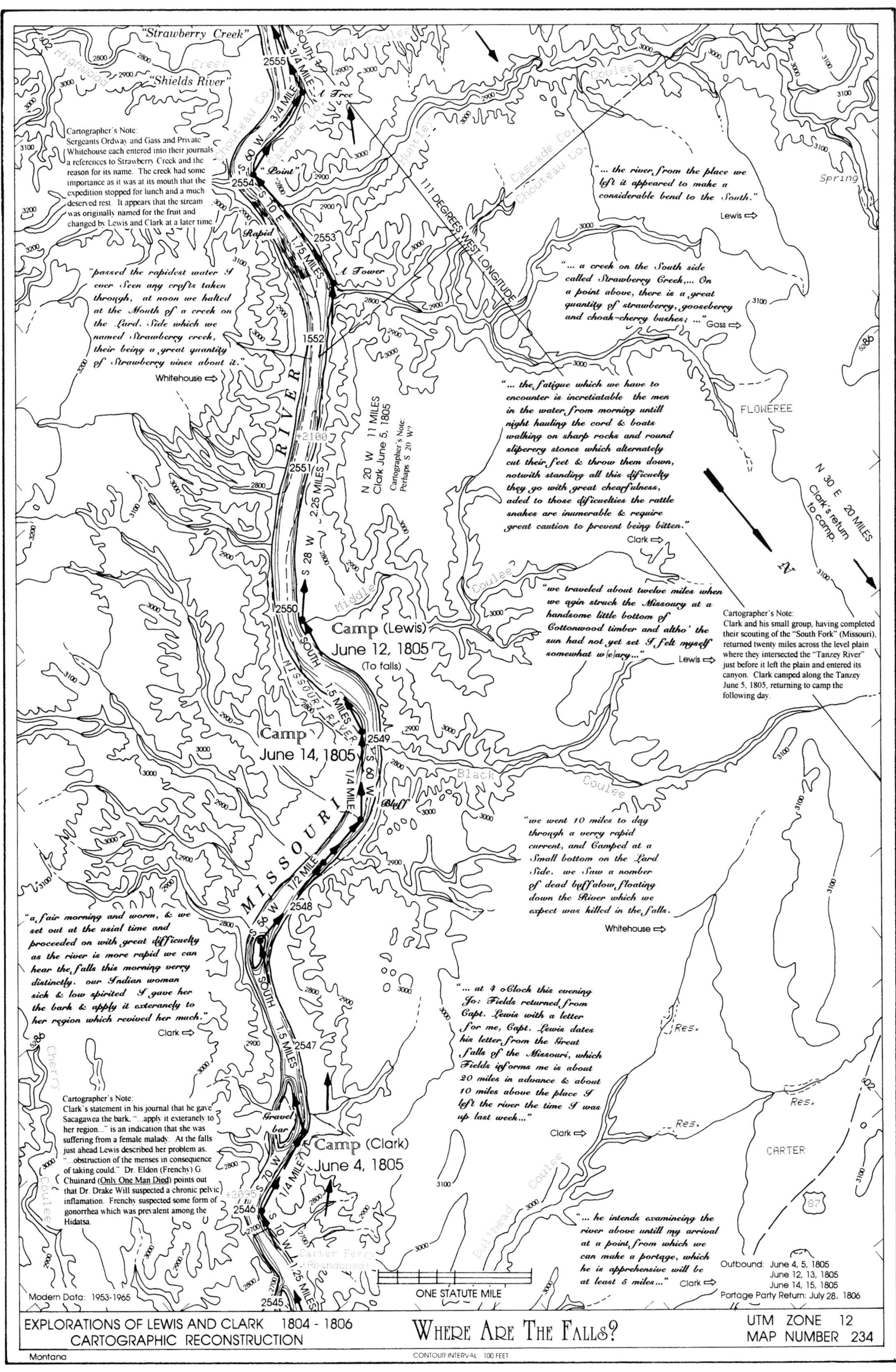

"Strawberry Creek"
"Shields River"
Highwood
Creek
Ryan Coulee
Coulee
Cascade Co.
Chouteau Co.
Huntley
Spring
Cartographer's Note:
Sergeants Ordway and Gass and Private Whitehouse each entered into their journals a references to Strawberry Creek and the reason for its name. The creek had some importance as it was at its mouth that the expedition stopped for lunch and a much deserved rest. It appears that the stream was originally named for the fruit and changed by Lewis and Clark at a later time.
SOUTH
3/4 MILE
S 80 W 3/4 MILE
A Tree
"Point"
S 10 E
Rapid
1.75 MILES
A Tower
111 DEGREES WEST LONGITUDE
"... the river from the place we left it appeared to make a considerable bend to the South."
Lewis ⇨
"... a creek on the South side called Strawberry Creek,... On a point above, there is a great quantity of strawberry, gooseberry and choak-cherry bushes; ..."
Gass ⇨
"passed the rapidest water I ever Seen any crafts taken through, at noon we halted at the Mouth of a creek on the Lard. Side which we named Strawberry creek, their being a great quantity of Strawberry vines about it."
Whitehouse ⇨
"... the fatigue which we have to encounter is incretiatable the men in the water from morning untill night hauling the cord & boats walking on sharp rocks and round sliperery stones which alternately cut their feet & throw them down, notwith standing all this dificuelty they go with great cheerfulness, aded to those dificuelties the rattle snakes are inumerable & require great caution to prevent being bitten."
Clark ⇨
FLOWEREE
N 20 W 11 MILES
Clark June 5, 1805
Cartographer's Note: Perhaps S 20 W?
RIVER
2.25 MILES
S 28 W
N 30 E 20 MILES
Clark's return to camp.
N
Middle
Coulee
"we traveled about twelve miles when we agin struck the Missoury at a handsome little bottom of Cottonwood timber and altho' the sun had not yet set I felt myself somewhat w[e]ary..."
Lewis ⇨
Cartographer's Note:
Clark and his small group, having completed their scouting of the "South Fork" (Missouri), returned twenty miles across the level plain where they intersected the "Tanzey River" just before it left the plain and entered its canyon. Clark camped along the Tanzey June 5, 1805, returning to camp the following day.
Camp (Lewis)
June 12, 1805
(To falls)
SOUTH
MISSOURI RIVER
1.5 MILES
Camp
June 14, 1805
S 60 W
1/4 MILE
Bluff
Black Coulee
MISSOURI
1/2 MILE
S 56 W
"we went 10 miles to day through a verry rapid current, and Camped at a Small bottom on the Lard Side. we Saw a nomber of dead buffalow floating down the River which we expect was killed in the falls."
Whitehouse ⇨
"a fair morning and worm, & we set out at the usial time and proceeded on with great difficuelty as the river is more rapid we can hear the falls this morning verry distinctly. our Indian woman sick & low spirited I gave her the bark & apply it externely to her region which revived her much."
Clark ⇨
SOUTH
1.5 MILES
"... at 4 oClock this evening Jo: Fields returned from Capt. Lewis with a letter for me, Capt. Lewis dates his letter from the Great falls of the Missouri, which Fields informs me is about 20 miles in advance & about 10 miles above the place I left the river the time I was up last week..."
Clark ⇨
Res.
Cherry
Coulee
Cartographer's Note:
Clark's statement in his journal that he gave Sacagawea the bark, "...apply it exteranely to her region..." is an indication that she was suffering from a female malady. At the falls just ahead Lewis described her problem as. "...obstruction of the menses in consequence of taking could." Dr. Eldon (Frenchy) G. Chuinard (Only One Man Died) points out that Dr. Drake Will suspected a chronic pelvic inflamation. Frenchy suspected some form of gonorrhea which was prevalent among the Hidatsa.
Gravel bar
Camp (Clark)
June 4, 1805
1/4 MILE
S 70 W
S 10 W
1.25 MILES
CARTER
Bullhead Coulee
Carter Ferry (Abandoned)
"... he intends examineing the river above untill my arrival at a point from which we can make a portage, which he is apprehensive will be at least 5 miles..."
Clark ⇨
ONE STATUTE MILE
Outbound: June 4, 5, 1805
June 12, 13, 1805
June 14, 15, 1805
Portage Party Return: July 28, 1806
Modern Data: 1953-1965
EXPLORATIONS OF LEWIS AND CLARK 1804 - 1806
CARTOGRAPHIC RECONSTRUCTION
WHERE ARE THE FALLS?
UTM ZONE 12
MAP NUMBER 234
Montana
CONTOUR INTERVAL 100 FEET

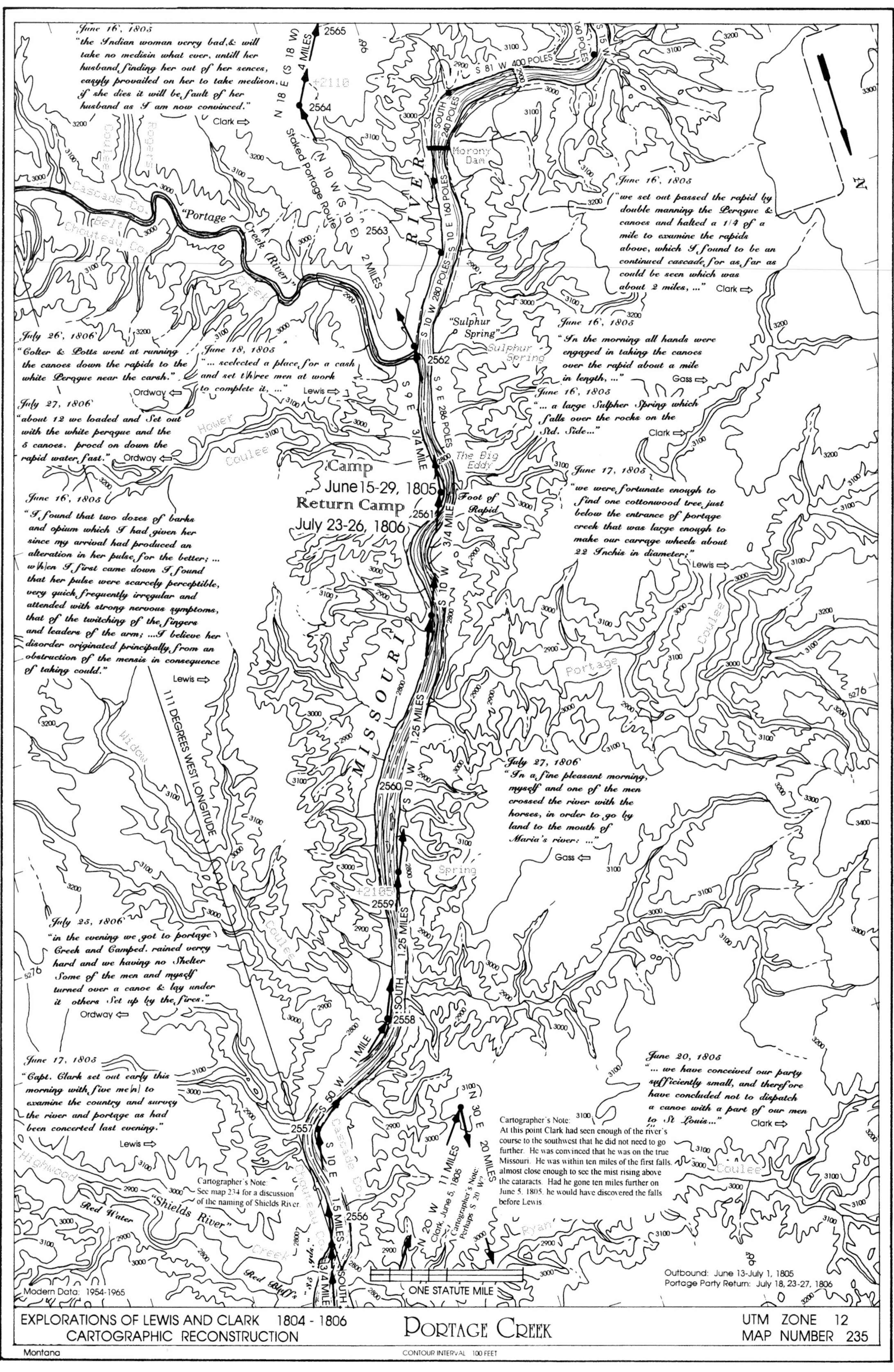

June 16, 1805
"the Indian woman verry bad,& will take no medisin what ever, untill her husband finding her out of her sences, easyly provailed on her to take medison, if she dies it will be fault of her husband as I am now convinced."
Clark ⇨
June 16, 1805
"we set out passed the rapid by double manning the Perogue & canoes and halted a 1/4 of a mile to examine the rapids above, which I found to be an continued cascade for as far as could be seen which was about 2 miles, ..."
Clark ⇨
July 26, 1806
"Colter & Potts went at running the canoes down the rapids to the white Perogue near the carsh."
Ordway ⇦
June 18, 1805
"... scelected a place for a cash and set th[r]ee men at work to complete it, ..."
Lewis ⇨
June 16, 1805
"In the morning all hands were engaged in taking the canoes over the rapid about a mile in length, ..."
Gass ⇨
June 16, 1805
"... a large Sulpher Spring which falls over the rocks on the Std. Side..."
Clark ⇨
July 27, 1806
"about 12 we loaded and Set out with the white perogue and the 5 canoes. procd on down the rapid water fast."
Ordway ⇦
June 17, 1805
"we were fortunate enough to find one cottonwood tree just below the entrance of portage creek that was large enough to make our carrage wheels about 22 Inchis in diameter;"
Lewis ⇨
June 16, 1805
"I found that two dozes of barks and opium which I had given her since my arrival had produced an alteration in her pulse for the better; ... w[h]en I first came down I found that her pulse were scarcely perceptible, very quick frequently irregular and attended with strong nervous symptoms, that of the twitching of the fingers and leaders of the arm; ...I believe her disorder originated principally from an obstruction of the mensis in consequence of taking could."
Lewis ⇨
Camp
June 15-29, 1805
Return Camp
July 23-26, 1806
July 27, 1806
"In a fine pleasant morning, myself and one of the men crossed the river with the horses, in order to go by land to the mouth of Maria's river: ..."
Gass ⇦
July 25, 1806
"in the evening we got to portage Creek and Camped. rained verry hard and we having no Shelter Some of the men and myself turned over a canoe & lay under it others Set up by the fires."
Ordway ⇦
June 17, 1805
"Capt. Clark set out early this morning with five me[n] to examine the country and survey the river and portage as had been concerted last evening."
Lewis ⇨
June 20, 1805
"... we have conceived our party sufficiently small, and therfore have concluded not to dispatch a canoe with a part of our men to St Louis..."
Clark ⇨
Cartographer's Note:
At this point Clark had seen enough of the river's course to the southwest that he did not need to go further. He was convinced that he was on the true Missouri. He was within ten miles of the first falls, almost close enough to see the mist rising above the cataracts. Had he gone ten miles further on June 5, 1805, he would have discovered the falls before Lewis.
Cartographer's Note:
See map 234 for a discussion of the naming of Shields River.
Cartographer's Note: Perhaps S. 20 W.
Clark, June 5, 1805
N 20 W 11 MILES
N 30 E 20 MILES
MISSOURI RIVER
"Portage Creek (River)"
"Shields River"
"Sulphur Spring"
Sulphur Spring
The Big Eddy
Foot of Rapid
Morony Dam
Staked Portage Route
111 DEGREES WEST LONGITUDE
Cascade Co.
Chouteau Co.
Belt Creek
Rogers Coulee
Hower Coulee
Widow Coulee
Portage Coulee
Highwood Creek
Red Water
Red Bluff's
Ryan Coulee
Spring
2555 2556 2557 2558 2559 2560 2561 2562 2563 2564 2565
+2110 +2185
N 18 E (S 18 W) 4 MILES
(N 10 W (S 10 E) 2 MILES
S 15 W 160 POLES
S 81 W 400 POLES
SOUTH 240 POLES
S 10 E 160 POLES
S 10 W 280 POLES
S 9 E 286 POLES
S 9 E 3/4 MILE
S 10 W 3/4 MILE
S 10 W 1.25 MILES
SOUTH 1.25 MILES
S 50 W 1 MILE
S 10 E 1.5 MILES
SOUTH 3/4 MILE
ONE STATUTE MILE
Modern Data: 1954-1965
Outbound: June 13-July 1, 1805
Portage Party Return: July 18, 23-27, 1806
EXPLORATIONS OF LEWIS AND CLARK 1804 - 1806
CARTOGRAPHIC RECONSTRUCTION
PORTAGE CREEK
UTM ZONE 12
MAP NUMBER 235
Montana
CONTOUR INTERVAL 100 FEET

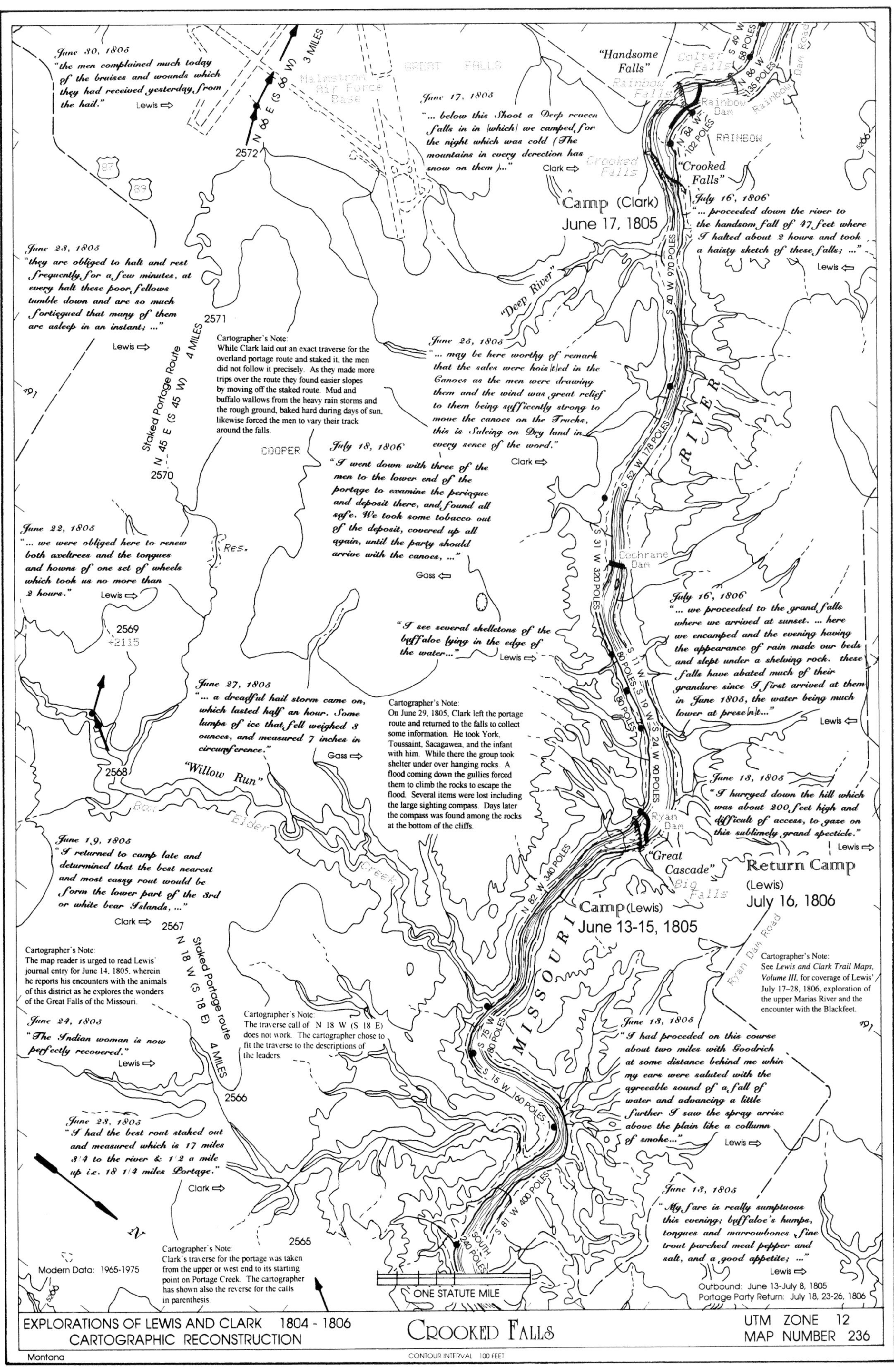
June 30, 1805
"the men complained much today of the bruises and wounds which they had received yesterday from the hail."
Lewis ⇨
N 66 E (S 66 W) 3 MILES
2572
87
89
Malmstrom Air Force Base
GREAT FALLS
June 17, 1805
"... below this Shoot a Deep reveen falls in in [which] we camped for the night which was cold (The mountains in every derection has snow on them)..."
Clark ⇨
Crooked Falls
"Handsome Falls"
Colter Falls
Rainbow Falls
S 49 W 58 POLES
N 86 W 135 POLES
Rainbow Dam
Rainbow Dam Road
N 84 W 102 POLES
RAINBOW
"Crooked Falls"
Camp (Clark)
June 17, 1805
July 16, 1806
"... proceeded down the river to the handsom fall of 47 feet where I halted about 2 hours and took a haisty sketch of these falls; ..."
Lewis ⇦
June 28, 1805
"they are obliged to halt and rest frequently for a few minutes, at every halt these poor fellows tumble down and are so much fortiegued that many of them are asleep in an instant; ..."
Lewis ⇨
2571
Staked Portage Route
N 45 E (S 45 W) 4 MILES
"Deep River"
S 40 W 970 POLES
Cartographer's Note:
While Clark laid out an exact traverse for the overland portage route and staked it, the men did not follow it precisely. As they made more trips over the route they found easier slopes by moving off the staked route. Mud and buffalo wallows from the heavy rain storms and the rough ground, baked hard during days of sun, likewise forced the men to vary their track around the falls.
June 25, 1805
"... may be here worthy of remark that the sales were hois[t]ed in the Canoes as the men were drawing them and the wind was great relief to them being sufficently strong to move the canoes on the Trucks, this is Saleing on Dry land in every sence of the word."
Clark ⇨
RIVER
2570
COOPER
July 18, 1806
"I went down with three of the men to the lower end of the portage to examine the perique and deposit there, and found all safe. We took some tobacco out of the deposit, covered up all again, until the party should arrive with the canoes, ..."
Gass ⇦
S 52 W 178 POLES
June 22, 1805
"... we were obliged here to renew both axeltrees and the tongues and howns of one set of wheels which took us no more than 2 hours."
Lewis ⇨
Res.
S 31 W 320 POLES
Cochrane Dam
July 16, 1806
"... we proceeded to the grand falls where we arrived at sunset. ... here we encamped and the evening having the appearance of rain made our beds and slept under a shelving rock. these falls have abated much of their grandure since I first arrived at them in June 1805, the water being much lower at prese[n]t..."
Lewis ⇦
2569
+2115
"I see several skelletons of the buffaloe lying in the edge of the water..."
Lewis ⇨
S 11 W 80 POLES
S 19 W 80 POLES
S 24 W 90 POLES
June 27, 1805
"... a dreadful hail storm came on, which lasted half an hour. Some lumps of ice that fell weighed 3 ounces, and measured 7 inches in circumference."
Gass ⇨
Cartographer's Note:
On June 29, 1805, Clark left the portage route and returned to the falls to collect some information. He took York, Toussaint, Sacagawea, and the infant with him. While there the group took shelter under over hanging rocks. A flood coming down the gullies forced them to climb the rocks to escape the flood. Several items were lost including the large sighting compass. Days later the compass was found among the rocks at the bottom of the cliffs.
2568
"Willow Run"
Box Elder Creek
June 18, 1805
"I hurryed down the hill which was about 200 feet high and difficult of access, to gaze on this sublimely grand specticle."
Lewis ⇨
Ryan Dam
"Great Cascade"
Big Falls
Return Camp (Lewis)
July 16, 1806
June 19, 1805
"I returned to camp late and determined that the best nearest and most easey rout would be form the lower part of the 3rd or white bear Islands, ..."
Clark ⇨
2567
N 82 W 340 POLES
Camp (Lewis)
June 13-15, 1805
MISSOURI
Ryan Dam Road
Staked Portage route
N 18 W (S 18 E) 4 MILES
Cartographer's Note:
The map reader is urged to read Lewis' journal entry for June 14, 1805, wherein he reports his encounters with the animals of this district as he explores the wonders of the Great Falls of the Missouri.
Cartographer's Note:
See Lewis and Clark Trail Maps, Volume III, for coverage of Lewis' July 17–28, 1806, exploration of the upper Marias River and the encounter with the Blackfeet.
June 24, 1805
"The Indian woman is now perfectly recovered."
Lewis ⇨
Cartographer's Note:
The traverse call of N 18 W (S 18 E) does not work. The cartographer chose to fit the traverse to the descriptions of the leaders.
S 75 W 80 POLES
June 18, 1805
"I had proceded on this course about two miles with Goodrich at some distance behind me whin my ears were saluted with the agreeable sound of a fall of water and advancing a little further I saw the spray arrise above the plain like a collumn of smoke..."
Lewis ⇨
2566
S 15 W 160 POLES
June 28, 1805
"I had the best rout staked out and measured which is 17 miles 3/4 to the river & 1/2 a mile up i.e. 18 1/4 miles Portage."
Clark ⇨
S 81 W 400 POLES
SOUTH 240 POLES
June 18, 1805
"My fare is really sumptuous this evening; buffaloe's humps, tongues and marrowbones, fine trout parched meal pepper and salt, and a good appetite; ..."
Lewis ⇨
N
2565
Cartographer's Note:
Clark's traverse for the portage was taken from the upper or west end to its starting point on Portage Creek. The cartographer has shown also the reverse for the calls in parenthesis.
Modern Data: 1965-1975
ONE STATUTE MILE
Outbound: June 13-July 8, 1805
Portage Party Return: July 18, 23-26, 1806
EXPLORATIONS OF LEWIS AND CLARK 1804 - 1806
CARTOGRAPHIC RECONSTRUCTION
CROOKED FALLS
UTM ZONE 12
MAP NUMBER 236
Montana
CONTOUR INTERVAL 100 FEET

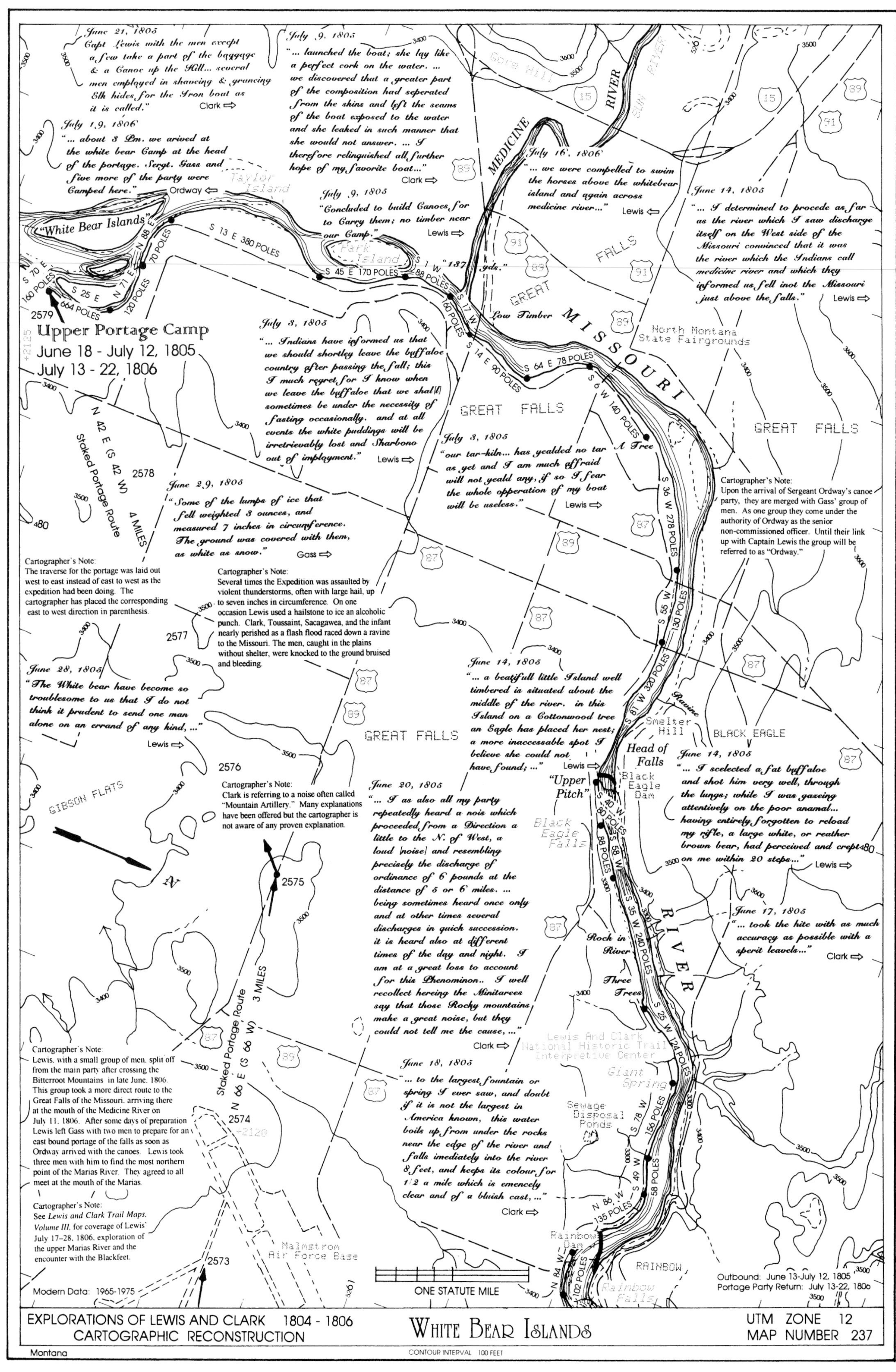
June 21, 1805
"Capt Lewis with the men except a few take a part of the baggage & a Canoe up the Hill... several men employed in shaveing & graineing Elk hides for the Iron boat as it is called." Clark
July 9, 1805
"... launched the boat; she lay like a perfect cork on the water. ... we discovered that a greater part of the composition had seperated from the skins and left the seams of the boat exposed to the water and she leaked in such manner that she would not answer. ... I therefore relinquished all further hope of my favorite boat..." Clark
July 19, 1806
"... about 3 Pm. we arived at the white bear Camp at the head of the portage. Sergt. Gass and five more of the party were Camped here." Ordway
July 9, 1805
"Concluded to build Canoes for to Carry them; no timber near our Camp." Lewis
July 16, 1806
"... we were compelled to swim the horses above the whitebear island and again across medicine river..." Lewis
June 14, 1805
"... I determined to procede as far as the river which I saw discharge itself on the West side of the Missouri convinced that it was the river which the Indians call medicine river and which they informed us fell inot the Missouri just above the falls." Lewis
Gore Hill
MEDICINE
RIVER
SUN RIVER
Taylor Island
"White Bear Islands"
Park Island
S 13 E 380 POLES
S 45 E 170 POLES
S 1 W 88 POLES
"137 yds."
N 88 E 70 POLES
N 71 E 120 POLES
S 70 E 160 POLES
S 25 E 664 POLES
2579
Upper Portage Camp
June 18 - July 12, 1805
July 13 - 22, 1806
July 3, 1805
"... Indians have informed us that we should shortley leave the buffaloe country after passing the fall; this I much regret for I know when we leave the buffaloe that we shall sometimes be under the necessity of fasting occasionally. and at all events the white puddings will be irretrievably lost and Sharbono out of imployment." Lewis
Low Timber
S 17 W 160 POLES
S 14 E 90 POLES
S 64 E 78 POLES
S 6 W 140 POLES
GREAT FALLS
MISSOURI
North Montana State Fairgrounds
N 42 E (S 42 W)
Staked Portage Route
4 MILES
2578
July 3, 1805
"our tar-kiln... has yealded no tar as yet and I am much affraid will not yeald any, if so I fear the whole opperation of my boat will be useless." Lewis
A Tree
S 36 W 278 POLES
Cartographer's Note:
Upon the arrival of Sergeant Ordway's canoe party, they are merged with Gass' group of men. As one group they come under the authority of Ordway as the senior non-commissioned officer. Until their link up with Captain Lewis the group will be referred to as "Ordway."
June 29, 1805
"Some of the lumps of ice that fell weighted 3 ounces, and measured 7 inches in circumference. The ground was covered with them, as white as snow." Gass
Cartographer's Note:
The traverse for the portage was laid out west to east instead of east to west as the expedition had been doing. The cartographer has placed the corresponding east to west direction in parenthesis.
Cartographer's Note:
Several times the Expedition was assaulted by violent thunderstorms, often with large hail, up to seven inches in circumference. On one occasion Lewis used a hailstone to ice an alcoholic punch. Clark, Toussaint, Sacagawea, and the infant nearly perished as a flash flood raced down a ravine to the Missouri. The men, caught in the plains without shelter, were knocked to the ground bruised and bleeding.
2577
S 55 W 130 POLES
June 14, 1805
"... a beatifull little Island well timbered is situated about the middle of the river. in this Island on a Cottonwood tree an Eagle has placed her nest; a more inaccessable spot I believe she could not have found; ..." Lewis
S 81 W 320 POLES
Ravine
Smelter Hill
BLACK EAGLE
June 28, 1805
"The White bear have become so troublesome to us that I do not think it prudent to send one man alone on an errand of any kind, ..." Lewis
GREAT FALLS
Head of Falls
"Upper Pitch"
Black Eagle Dam
Black Eagle Falls
June 14, 1805
"... I selected a fat buffaloe and shot him very well, through the lungs; while I was gazeing attentively on the poor anamal... having entirely forgotten to reload my rifle, a large white, or reather brown bear, had perceived and crept on me within 20 steps..." Lewis
2576
GIBSON FLATS
N
Cartographer's Note:
Clark is referring to a noise often called "Mountain Artillery." Many explanations have been offered but the cartographer is not aware of any proven explanation.
2575
June 20, 1805
"... I as also all my party repeatedly heard a nois which proceeded from a Direction a little to the N. of West, a loud [noise] and resembling precisely the discharge of ordinance of 6 pounds at the distance of 5 or 6 miles. ... being sometimes heard once only and at other times several discharges in quick succession. it is heard also at different times of the day and night. I am at a great loss to account for this Phenominon.. I well recollect hereing the Minitarees say that those Rocky mountains make a great noise, but they could not tell me the cause, ..." Clark
S 40 W 90 POLES
S 58 W 88 POLES
S 35 W 240 POLES
Rock in River
Three Trees
RIVER
June 17, 1805
"... took the hite with as much accuracy as possible with a sperit leavels..." Clark
Staked Portage Route
N 66 E (S 66 W)
3 MILES
Lewis And Clark National Historic Trail Interpretive Center
Giant Spring
S 25 W 124 POLES
Cartographer's Note:
Lewis, with a small group of men, split off from the main party after crossing the Bitterroot Mountains in late June, 1806. This group took a more direct route to the Great Falls of the Missouri, arriving there at the mouth of the Medicine River on July 11, 1806. After some days of preparation Lewis left Gass with two men to prepare for an east bound portage of the falls as soon as Ordway arrived with the canoes. Lewis took three men with him to find the most northern point of the Marias River. They agreed to all meet at the mouth of the Marias.
2574
June 18, 1805
"... to the largest fountain or spring I ever saw, and doubt if it is not the largest in America known, this water boils up from under the rocks near the edge of the river and falls imediately into the river 8 feet, and keeps its colour for 1/2 a mile which is emencely clear and of a bluish cast, ..." Clark
Sewage Disposal Ponds
S 78 W 156 POLES
S 49 W 58 POLES
N 86 W 135 POLES
Cartographer's Note:
See Lewis and Clark Trail Maps, Volume III, for coverage of Lewis' July 17-28, 1806, exploration of the upper Marias River and the encounter with the Blackfeet.
Malmstrom Air Force Base
2573
Rainbow Dam
N 84 W 102 POLES
RAINBOW
Rainbow Falls
ONE STATUTE MILE
Modern Data: 1965-1975
Outbound: June 13-July 12, 1805
Portage Party Return: July 13-22, 1806
EXPLORATIONS OF LEWIS AND CLARK 1804 - 1806
CARTOGRAPHIC RECONSTRUCTION
WHITE BEAR ISLANDS
UTM ZONE 12
MAP NUMBER 237
Montana
CONTOUR INTERVAL 100 FEET

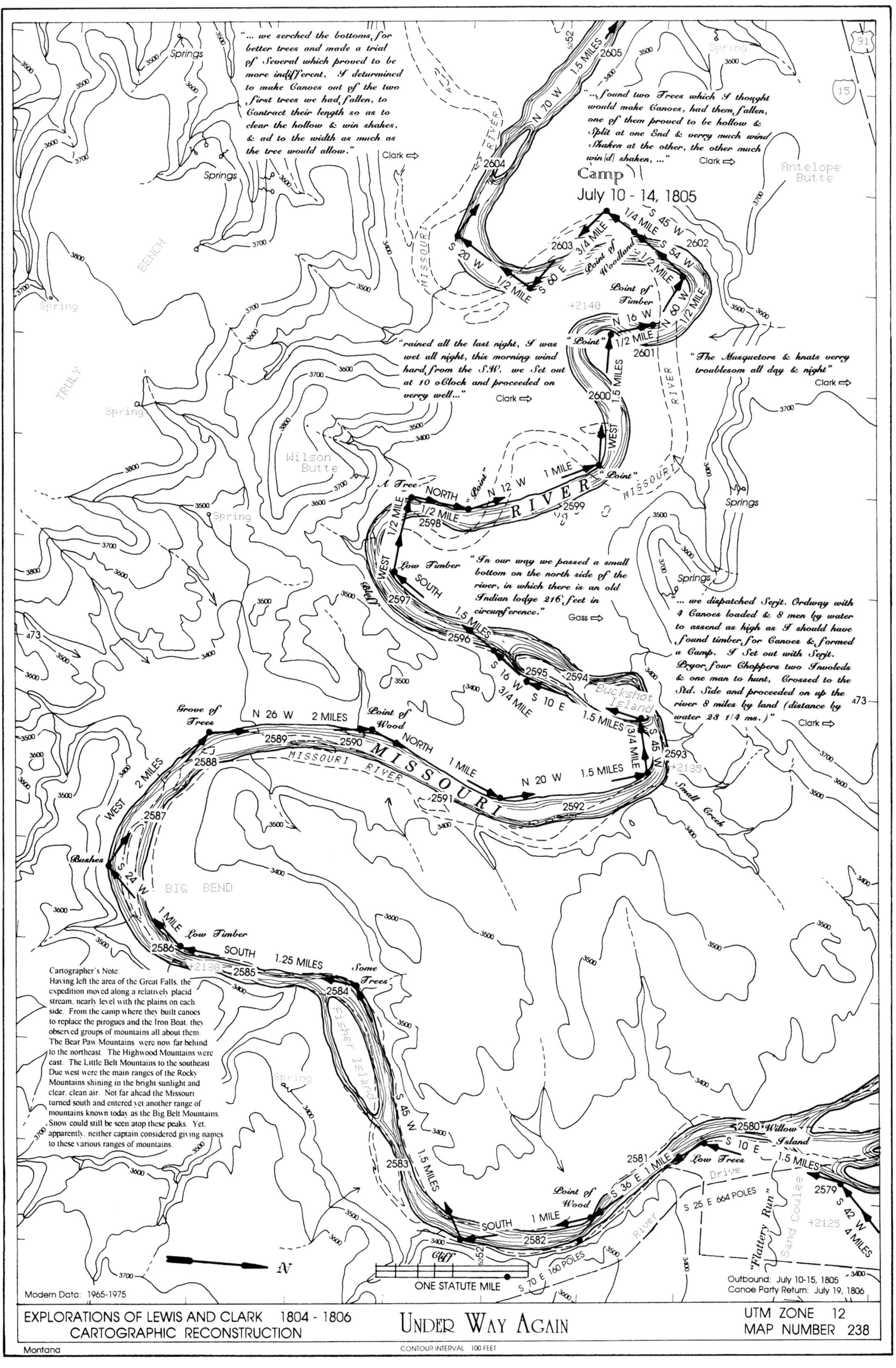
"... we serched the bottoms for better trees and made a trial of Several which proved to be more indifferent. I deturmined to make Canoes out of the two first trees we had fallen, to Contract their length so as to clear the hollow & win shakes, & ad to the width as much as the tree would allow." Clark ⇨
"...found two Trees which I thought would make Canoes, had them fallen, one of them proved to be hollow & Split at one End & verry much wind Shaken at the other, the other much win[d] shaken, ..." Clark ⇨
Camp
July 10 - 14, 1805
Antelope Butte
"rained all the last night, I was wet all night, this morning wind hard from the S.W. we Set out at 10 oClock and proceeded on verry well..." Clark ⇨
"The Musquetors & knats very troublesom all day & night" Clark ⇨
Wilson Butte
"In our way we passed a small bottom on the north side of the river, in which there is an old Indian lodge 216 feet in circumference." Gass ⇨
"... we dispatched Sergt. Ordway with 4 Canoes loaded & 8 men by water to assend as high as I should have found timber for Canoes & formed a Camp. I Set out with Sergt. Pryor four Choppers two Involeds & one man to hunt, Crossed to the Std. Side and proceeded on up the river 8 miles by land (distance by water 28 1/4 ms.)" Clark ⇨
Buckshot Island
Small Creek
MISSOURI RIVER
BIG BEND
Fisher Island
Willow Island
"Flattery Run"
Sand Coulee
BENCH
TRULY
Cartographer's Note:
Having left the area of the Great Falls, the expedition moved along a relatively placid stream, nearly level with the plains on each side. From the camp where they built canoes to replace the pirogues and the Iron Boat, they observed groups of mountains all about them. The Bear Paw Mountains were now far behind to the northeast. The Highwood Mountains were east. The Little Belt Mountains to the southeast. Due west were the main ranges of the Rocky Mountains shining in the bright sunlight and clear, clean air. Not far ahead the Missouri turned south and entered yet another range of mountains known today as the Big Belt Mountains. Snow could still be seen atop these peaks. Yet, apparently, neither captain considered giving names to these various ranges of mountains.
N
ONE STATUTE MILE
Modern Data: 1965-1975
Outbound: July 10-15, 1805
Canoe Party Return: July 19, 1806
EXPLORATIONS OF LEWIS AND CLARK 1804 - 1806
CARTOGRAPHIC RECONSTRUCTION
UNDER WAY AGAIN
UTM ZONE 12
MAP NUMBER 238
Montana
CONTOUR INTERVAL 100 FEET

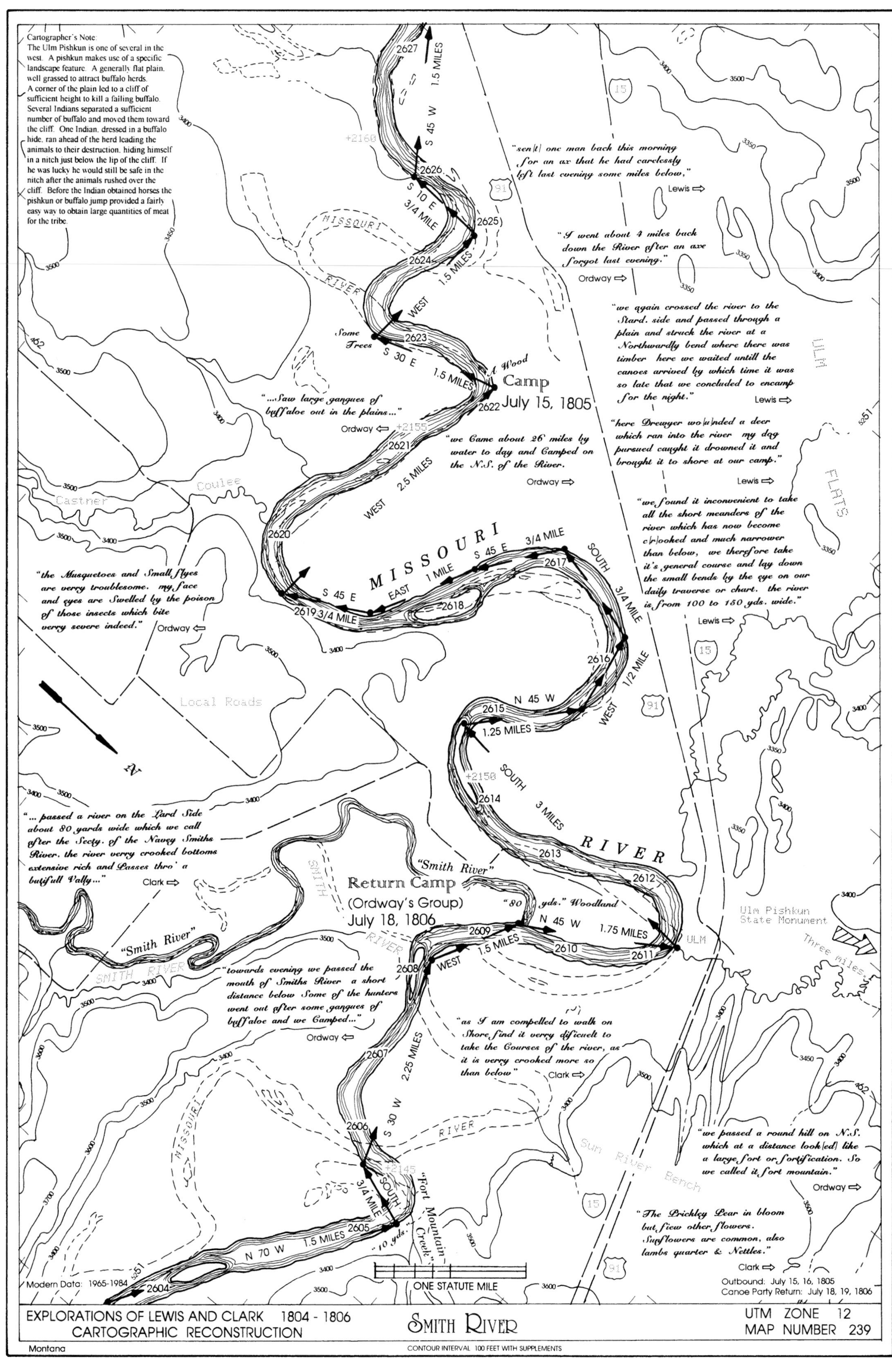

Cartographer's Note:
The Ulm Pishkun is one of several in the west. A pishkun makes use of a specific landscape feature. A generally flat plain, well grassed to attract buffalo herds. A corner of the plain led to a cliff of sufficient height to kill a failing buffalo. Several Indians separated a sufficient number of buffalo and moved them toward the cliff. One Indian, dressed in a buffalo hide, ran ahead of the herd leading the animals to their destruction, hiding himself in a nitch just below the lip of the cliff. If he was lucky he would still be safe in the nitch after the animals rushed over the cliff. Before the Indian obtained horses the pishkun or buffalo jump provided a fairly easy way to obtain large quantities of meat for the tribe.
"sen[t] one man back this morning for an ax that he had carelessly left last evening some miles below," Lewis
"I went about 4 miles back down the River after an axe forgot last evening." Ordway
"we again crossed the river to the Stard. side and passed through a plain and struck the river at a Northwardly bend where there was timber here we waited untill the canoes arrived by which time it was so late that we concluded to encamp for the night." Lewis
"here Drewyer wo[u]nded a deer which ran into the river my dog pursued caught it drowned it and brought it to shore at our camp." Lewis
"we found it inconvenient to take all the short meanders of the river which has now become c[r]ooked and much narrower than below, we therefore take it's general course and lay down the small bends by the eye on our daily traverse or chart. the river is from 100 to 150 yds. wide." Lewis
"...Saw large gangues of buffaloe out in the plains..." Ordway
"we Came about 26 miles by water to day and Camped on the N.S. of the River." Ordway
A Wood
Camp
July 15, 1805
Some Trees
"the Musquetoes and Small flyes are verry troublesome. my face and eyes are Swelled by the poison of those insects which bite verry severe indeed." Ordway
"... passed a river on the Lard Side about 80 yards wide which we call after the Secty. of the Navey Smiths River. the river verry crooked bottoms extensive rich and Passes thro' a butifull Vally..." Clark
"Smith River"
Return Camp
(Ordway's Group)
July 18, 1806
"80 yds." Woodland
"towards evening we passed the mouth of Smiths River a short distance below Some of the hunters went out after some gangues of buffaloe and we Camped..." Ordway
"as I am compelled to walk on Shore find it verry dificuelt to take the Courses of the river, as it is verry crooked more so than below" Clark
"we passed a round hill on N.S. which at a distance look[ed] like a large fort or fortification. So we called it fort mountain." Ordway
"The Prickley Pear in bloom but few other flowers. Sunflowers are common, also lambs quarter & Nettles." Clark
"Fort Mountain Creek"
"10 yds."
MISSOURI RIVER
SMITH RIVER
Castner Coulee
Local Roads
ULM FLATS
Ulm Pishkun State Monument
Three miles
Sun River Bench
ULM
N
ONE STATUTE MILE
Modern Data: 1965-1984
Outbound: July 15, 16, 1805
Canoe Party Return: July 18, 19, 1806
EXPLORATIONS OF LEWIS AND CLARK 1804 - 1806
CARTOGRAPHIC RECONSTRUCTION
SMITH RIVER
UTM ZONE 12
MAP NUMBER 239
Montana
CONTOUR INTERVAL 100 FEET WITH SUPPLEMENTS

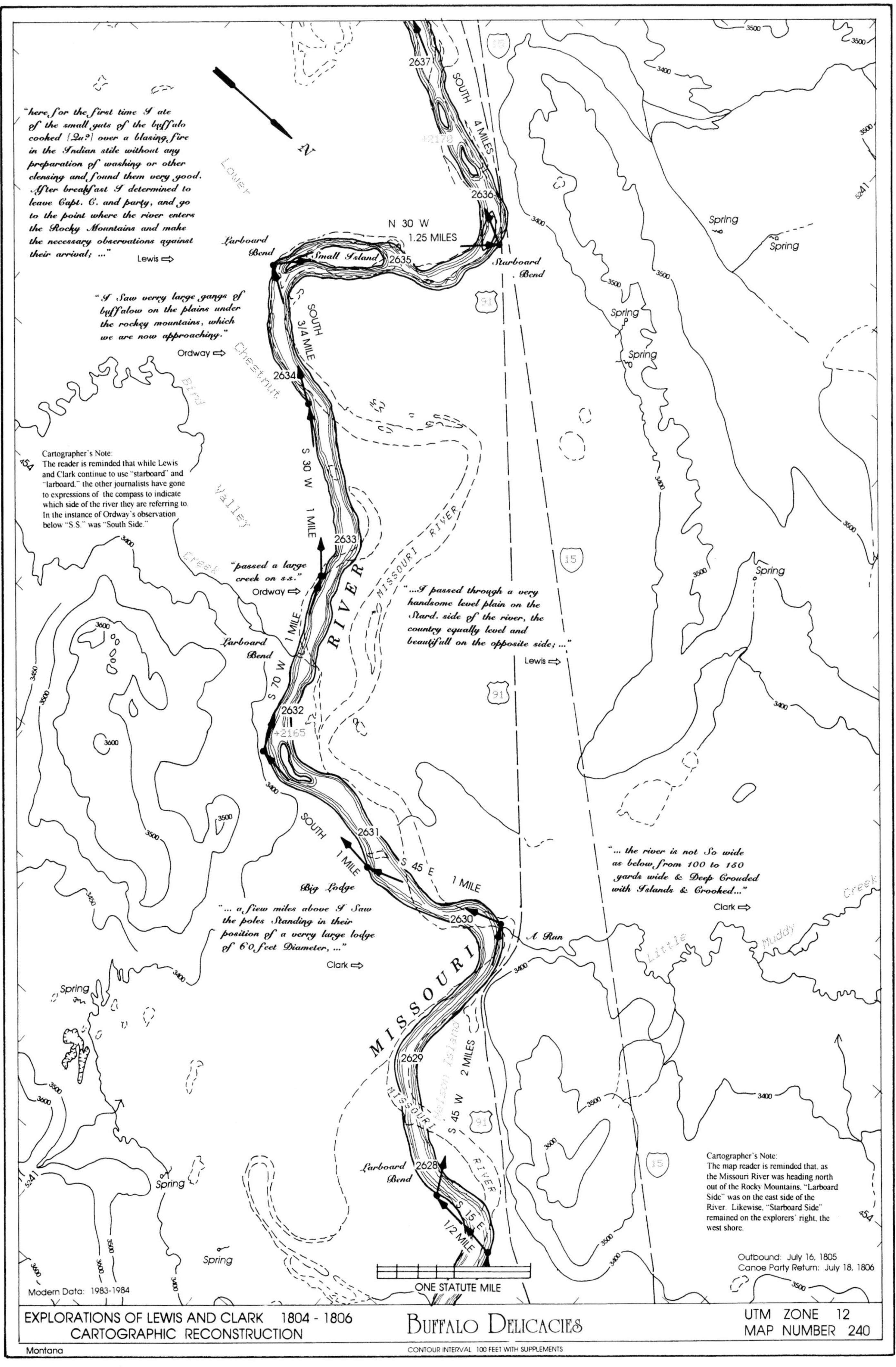
"here for the first time I ate of the small guts of the buffalo cooked [Qu?] over a blasing fire in the Indian stile without any preparation of washing or other clensing and found them very good. After breakfast I determined to leave Capt. C. and party, and go to the point where the river enters the Rocky Mountains and make the necessary observations against their arrival; ..."
Lewis ⇨
"I Saw very large gangs of buffalow on the plains under the rockey mountains, which we are now approaching."
Ordway ⇨
Cartographer's Note:
The reader is reminded that while Lewis and Clark continue to use "starboard" and "larboard," the other journalists have gone to expressions of the compass to indicate which side of the river they are referring to. In the instance of Ordway's observation below "S.S." was "South Side."
"passed a large creek on s.s."
Ordway ⇨
"...I passed through a very handsome level plain on the Stard. side of the river, the country equally level and beautifull on the opposite side; ..."
Lewis ⇨
"... the river is not So wide as below from 100 to 150 yards wide & Deep Crouded with Islands & Crooked..."
Clark ⇨
"... a fiew miles above I Saw the poles Standing in their position of a very large lodge of 60 feet Diameter, ..."
Clark ⇨
Big Lodge
A Run
Larboard Bend
Starboard Bend
Small Island
N 30 W
1.25 MILES
SOUTH
4 MILES
SOUTH
3/4 MILE
S 30 W
1 MILE
S 70 W
1 MILE
SOUTH
1 MILE
S 45 E
1 MILE
S 45 W
2 MILES
S 15 E
1/2 MILE
2637
2636
2635
2634
2633
2632
2631
2630
2629
2628
+2170
+2165
MISSOURI RIVER
Lower
Chestnut
Bird
Valley
Creek
Little
Muddy
Creek
Nelson Island
Spring
N
Cartographer's Note:
The map reader is reminded that, as the Missouri River was heading north out of the Rocky Mountains, "Larboard Side" was on the east side of the River. Likewise, "Starboard Side" remained on the explorers' right, the west shore.
Outbound: July 16, 1805
Canoe Party Return: July 18, 1806
ONE STATUTE MILE
Modern Data: 1983-1984
EXPLORATIONS OF LEWIS AND CLARK 1804 - 1806
CARTOGRAPHIC RECONSTRUCTION
BUFFALO DELICACIES
UTM ZONE 12
MAP NUMBER 240
Montana
CONTOUR INTERVAL 100 FEET WITH SUPPLEMENTS

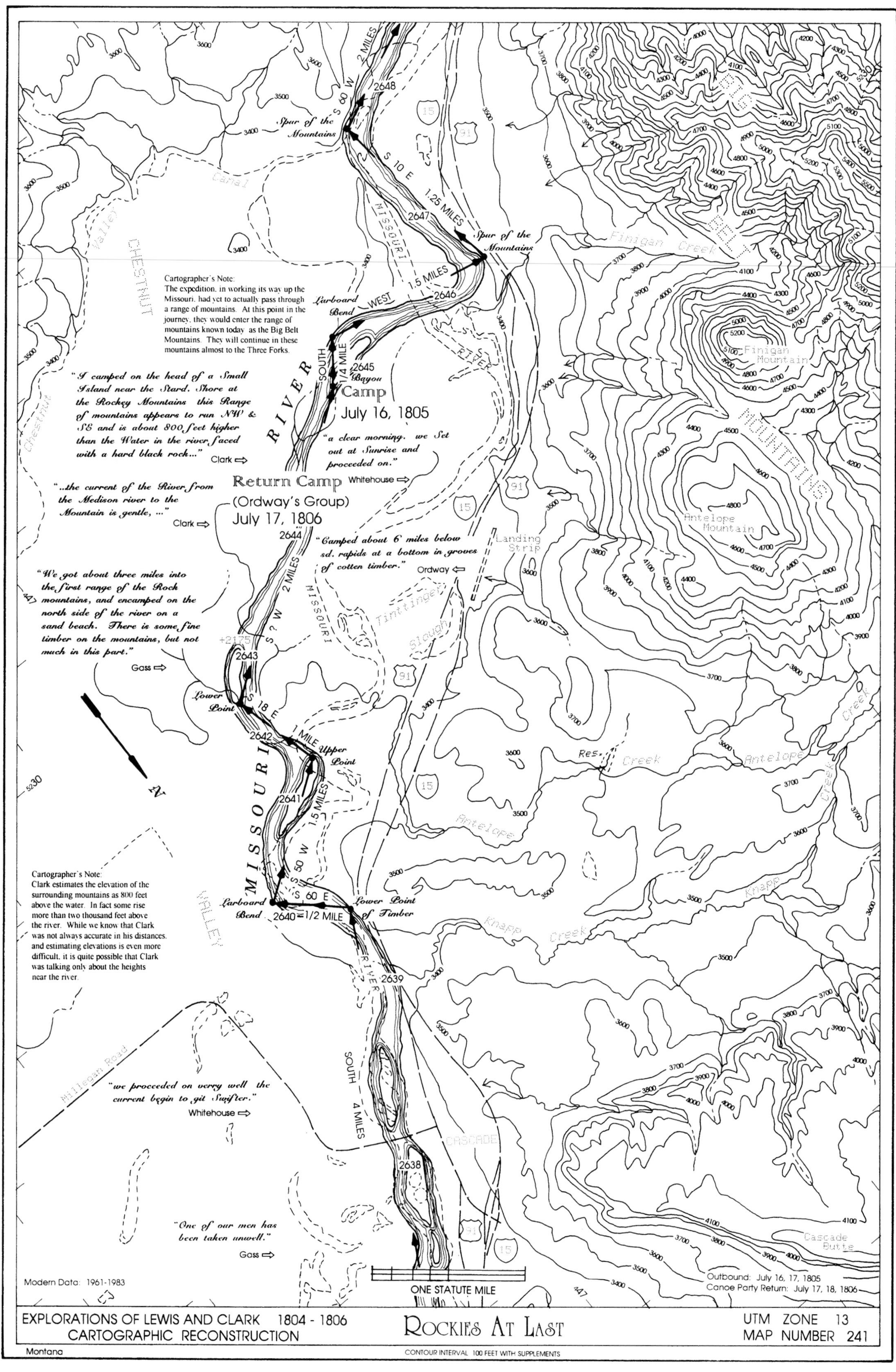
Cartographer's Note:
The expedition, in working its way up the Missouri, had yet to actually pass through a range of mountains. At this point in the journey, they would enter the range of mountains known today as the Big Belt Mountains. They will continue in these mountains almost to the Three Forks.
"I camped on the head of a Small Island near the Stard. Shore at the Rockey Mountains this Range of mountains appears to run NW & SE and is about 800 feet higher than the Water in the river faced with a hard black rock..."
Clark ⇨
"...the current of the River from the Medison river to the Mountain is gentle, ..."
Clark ⇨
"We got about three miles into the first range of the Rock mountains, and encamped on the north side of the river on a sand beach. There is some fine timber on the mountains, but not much in this part."
Gass ⇨
Camp
July 16, 1805
"a clear morning. we Set out at Sunrise and proceeded on."
Whitehouse ⇨
Return Camp
(Ordway's Group)
July 17, 1806
"Camped about 6 miles below sd. rapids at a bottom in groves of cotten timber."
Ordway ⇦
Cartographer's Note:
Clark estimates the elevation of the surrounding mountains as 800 feet above the water. In fact some rise more than two thousand feet above the river. While we know that Clark was not always accurate in his distances, and estimating elevations is even more difficult, it is quite possible that Clark was talking only about the heights near the river.
"we proceeded on verry well the current begin to git Swifter."
Whitehouse ⇨
"One of our men has been taken unwell."
Gass ⇨
Spur of the Mountains
Larboard Bend
Bayou
Lower Point
Upper Point
Lower Point of Timber
MISSOURI RIVER
BIG BELT MOUNTAINS
Finigan Creek
Finigan Mountain
Antelope Mountain
Antelope Creek
Knapp Creek
Tintinger Slough
Landing Strip
Chestnut Valley
Milligan Road
Cascade Butte
CASCADE
Canal
Res.
ONE STATUTE MILE
Modern Data: 1961-1983
Outbound: July 16, 17, 1805
Canoe Party Return: July 17, 18, 1806
EXPLORATIONS OF LEWIS AND CLARK 1804 - 1806
CARTOGRAPHIC RECONSTRUCTION
ROCKIES AT LAST
UTM ZONE 13
MAP NUMBER 241
Montana
CONTOUR INTERVAL 100 FEET WITH SUPPLEMENTS

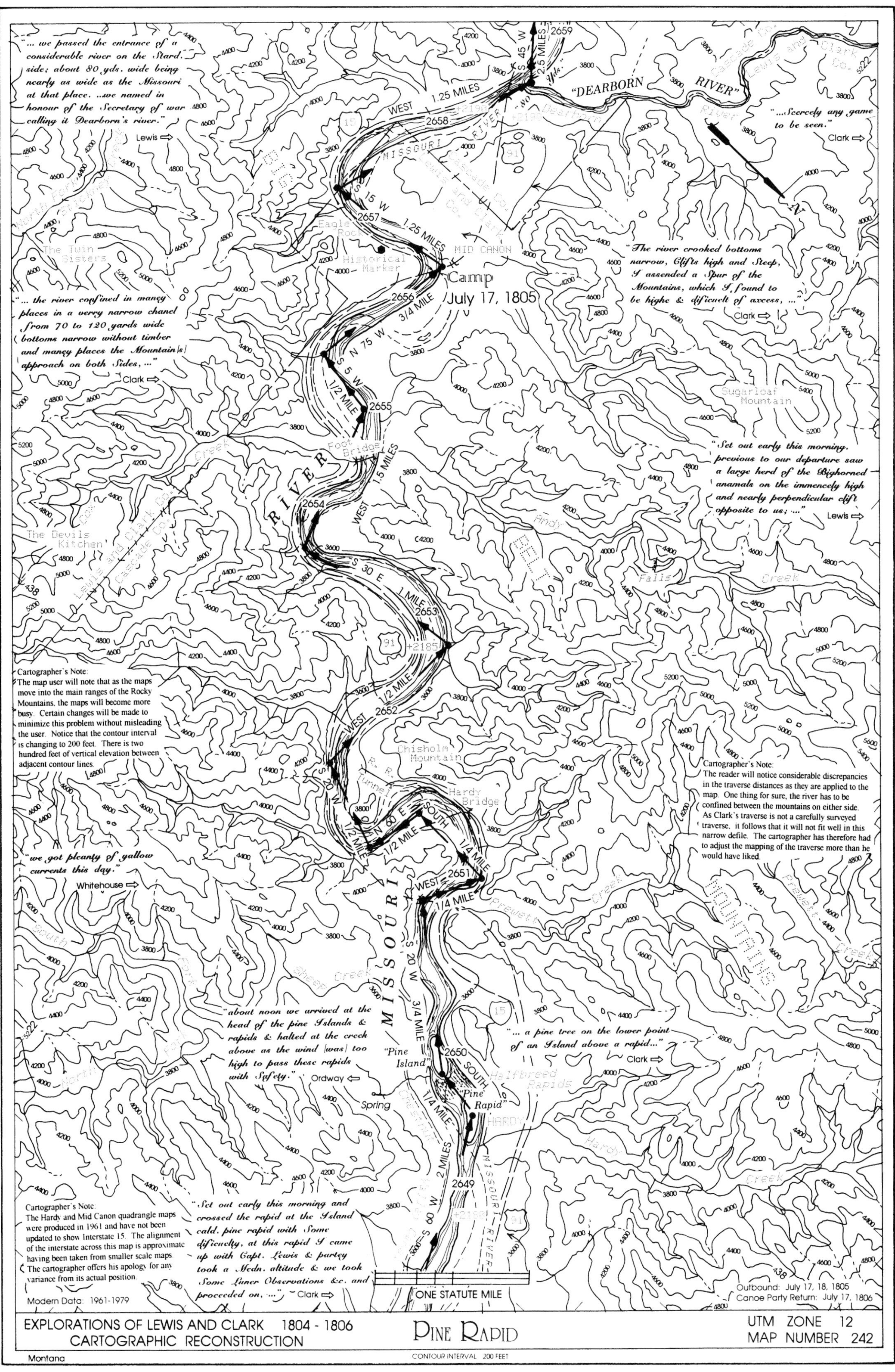
"... we passed the entrance of a considerable river on the Stard. side; about 80 yds. wide being nearly as wide as the Missouri at that place. ..we named in honour of the Secretary of war calling it Dearborn's river."
Lewis ⇨
"DEARBORN RIVER"
"...Scercely any game to be seen."
Clark ⇨
"The river crooked bottoms narrow, Clifts high and Steep, I assended a Spur of the Mountains, which I found to be highe & dificult of axcess, ..."
Clark ⇨
"... the river confined in maney places in a very narrow chanel from 70 to 120 yards wide bottoms narrow without timber and maney places the Mountain[s] approach on both Sides, ..."
Clark ⇨
Camp
July 17, 1805
MID CANON
Eagle Rock
Historical Marker
The Twin Sisters
Sugarloaf Mountain
"Set out early this morning. previous to our departure saw a large herd of the Bighorned anamals on the immencely high and nearly perpendicular clift opposite to us; ..."
Lewis ⇨
Foot Bridge
The Devils Kitchen
BELT MOUNTAINS
MISSOURI RIVER
Chisholm Mountain
R. R. Tunnel
Hardy Bridge
Cartographer's Note:
The map user will note that as the maps move into the main ranges of the Rocky Mountains, the maps will become more busy. Certain changes will be made to minimize this problem without misleading the user. Notice that the contour interval is changing to 200 feet. There is two hundred feet of vertical elevation between adjacent contour lines.
Cartographer's Note:
The reader will notice considerable discrepancies in the traverse distances as they are applied to the map. One thing for sure, the river has to be confined between the mountains on either side. As Clark's traverse is not a carefully surveyed traverse, it follows that it will not fit well in this narrow defile. The cartographer has therefore had to adjust the mapping of the traverse more than he would have liked.
"we got pleanty of yallow currents this day."
Whitehouse ⇨
"about noon we arrived at the head of the pine Islands & rapids & halted at the creek above as the wind [was] too high to pass these rapids with Safety."
Ordway ⇦
"... a pine tree on the lower point of an Island above a rapid..."
Clark ⇨
"Pine Island"
"Pine Rapid"
Halfbreed Rapids
HARDY
Spring
Cartographer's Note:
The Hardy and Mid Canon quadrangle maps were produced in 1961 and have not been updated to show Interstate 15. The alignment of the interstate across this map is approximate having been taken from smaller scale maps. The cartographer offers his apology for any variance from its actual position.
"Set out early this morning and crossed the rapid at the Island cald. pine rapid with Some dificulty, at this rapid I came up with Capt. Lewis & partey took a Medn. altitude & we took Some Luner Observations &c. and proceeded on, ..."
Clark ⇨
ONE STATUTE MILE
Modern Data: 1961-1979
Outbound: July 17, 18, 1805
Canoe Party Return: July 17, 1806
EXPLORATIONS OF LEWIS AND CLARK 1804 - 1806
CARTOGRAPHIC RECONSTRUCTION
PINE RAPID
UTM ZONE 12
MAP NUMBER 242
Montana
CONTOUR INTERVAL 200 FEET

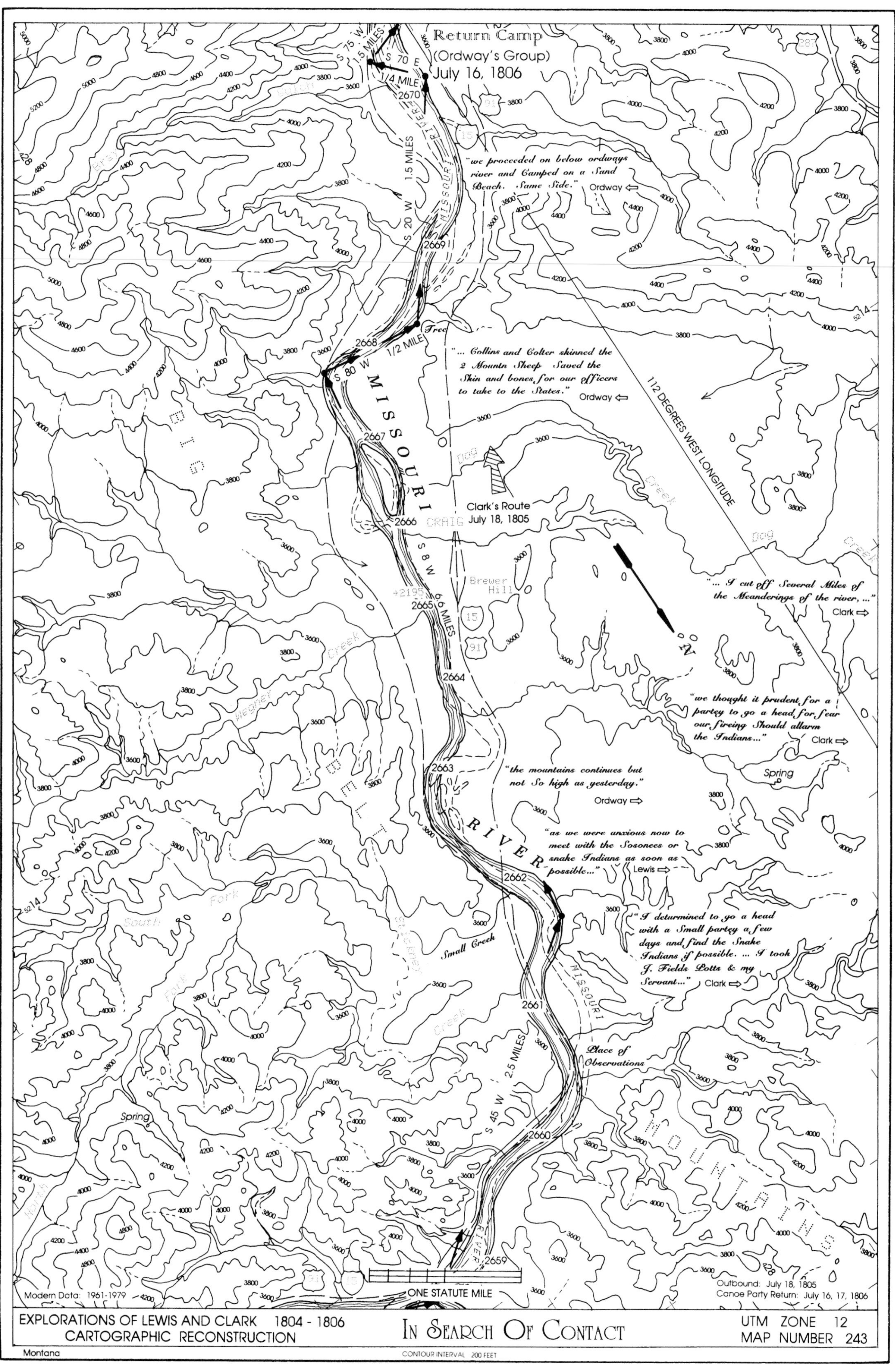
Return Camp
(Ordway's Group)
July 16, 1806
"we proceeded on below ordways river and Camped on a Sand Beach. Same Side." Ordway
"... Collins and Colter skinned the 2 Mountn Sheep Saved the Skin and bones, for our officers to take to the States." Ordway
112 DEGREES WEST LONGITUDE
Clark's Route
July 18, 1805
MISSOURI
BIG BELT
Brewer Hill
Dog Creek
"... I cut off Several Miles of the Meanderings of the river, ..." Clark
"we thought it prudent for a partey to go a head for fear our fireing Should allarm the Indians..." Clark
Spring
"the mountains continues but not So high as yesterday." Ordway
"as we were anxious now to meet with the Sosonees or snake Indians as soon as possible..." Lewis
RIVER
"I determined to go a head with a Small partey a few days and find the Snake Indians if possible. ... I took J. Fields Potts & my Servant..." Clark
Small Creek
Stickney Creek
South Fork
Place of Observations
MOUNTAINS
S 45 W 2.5 MILES
S 8 W 6.6 MILES
S 20 W 1.5 MILES
S 80 W
1/2 MILE
S 75 W 1.5 MILES
S 70 E 1/4 MILE
ONE STATUTE MILE
Modern Data: 1961-1979
Outbound: July 18, 1805
Canoe Party Return: July 16, 17, 1806
EXPLORATIONS OF LEWIS AND CLARK 1804 - 1806
CARTOGRAPHIC RECONSTRUCTION
IN SEARCH OF CONTACT
UTM ZONE 12
MAP NUMBER 243
Montana
CONTOUR INTERVAL 200 FEET

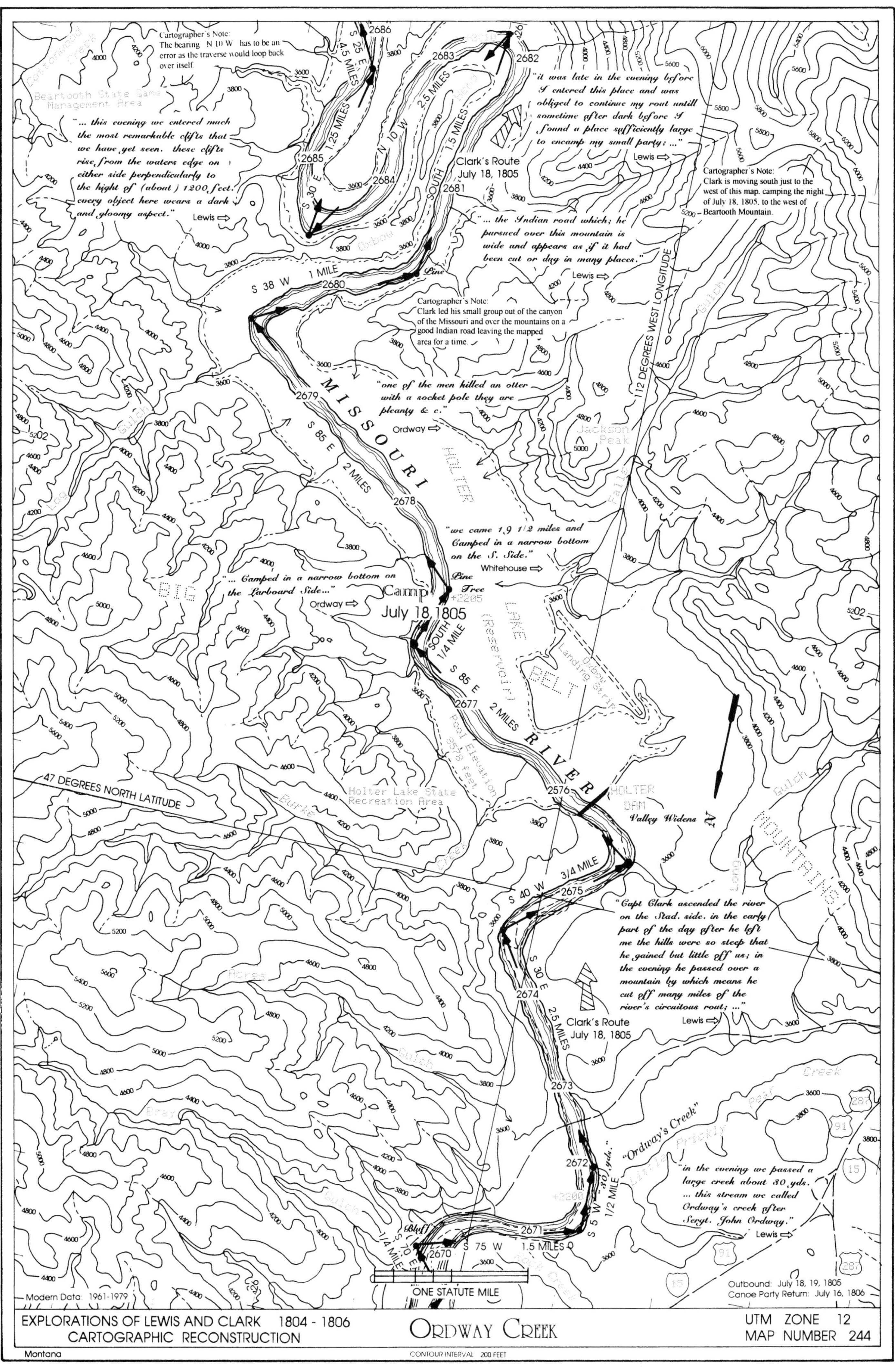
Cartographer's Note: The bearing N 10 W has to be an error as the traverse would loop back over itself.
"... this evening we entered much the most remarkable clifts that we have yet seen. these clifts rise from the waters edge on either side perpendicularly to the hight of (about) 1200 feet. every object here wears a dark and gloomy aspect." Lewis ⇨
"it was late in the evening before I entered this place and was obliged to continue my rout untill sometime after dark before I found a place sufficiently large to encamp my small party; ..." Lewis ⇨
Cartographer's Note: Clark is moving south just to the west of this map, camping the night of July 18, 1805, to the west of Beartooth Mountain.
Clark's Route July 18, 1805
"... the Indian road which; he pursued over this mountain is wide and appears as if it had been cut or dug in many places." Lewis ⇨
Cartographer's Note: Clark led his small group out of the canyon of the Missouri and over the mountains on a good Indian road leaving the mapped area for a time.
"one of the men killed an otter with a socket pole they are pleanty & c." Ordway ⇨
"we came 1,9 1/2 miles and Camped in a narrow bottom on the S. Side." Whitehouse ⇨
"... Camped in a narrow bottom on the Larboard Side..." Ordway ⇨
Camp July 18 1805
Pine Tree
MISSOURI RIVER
HOLTER LAKE (Reservoir)
BIG BELT MOUNTAINS
Beartooth State Game Management Area
Jackson Peak
Oxbow Landing Strip
Pool Elevation 3578 feet
Holter Lake State Recreation Area
HOLTER DAM
Valley Widens
47 DEGREES NORTH LATITUDE
112 DEGREES WEST LONGITUDE
"Capt Clark ascended the river on the Stad. side. in the early part of the day after he left me the hills were so steep that he gained but little off us; in the evening he passed over a mountain by which means he cut off many miles of the river's circuitous rout; ..." Lewis ⇨
Clark's Route July 18, 1805
"Ordway's Creek"
Little Prickly Pear Creek
"in the evening we passed a large creek about 30 yds. ... this stream we called Ordway's creek after Sergt. John Ordway." Lewis ⇨
Bluff
ONE STATUTE MILE
Modern Data: 1961-1979
Outbound: July 18, 19, 1805
Canoe Party Return: July 16, 1806
EXPLORATIONS OF LEWIS AND CLARK 1804 - 1806
CARTOGRAPHIC RECONSTRUCTION
ORDWAY CREEK
UTM ZONE 12
MAP NUMBER 244
Montana
CONTOUR INTERVAL 200 FEET

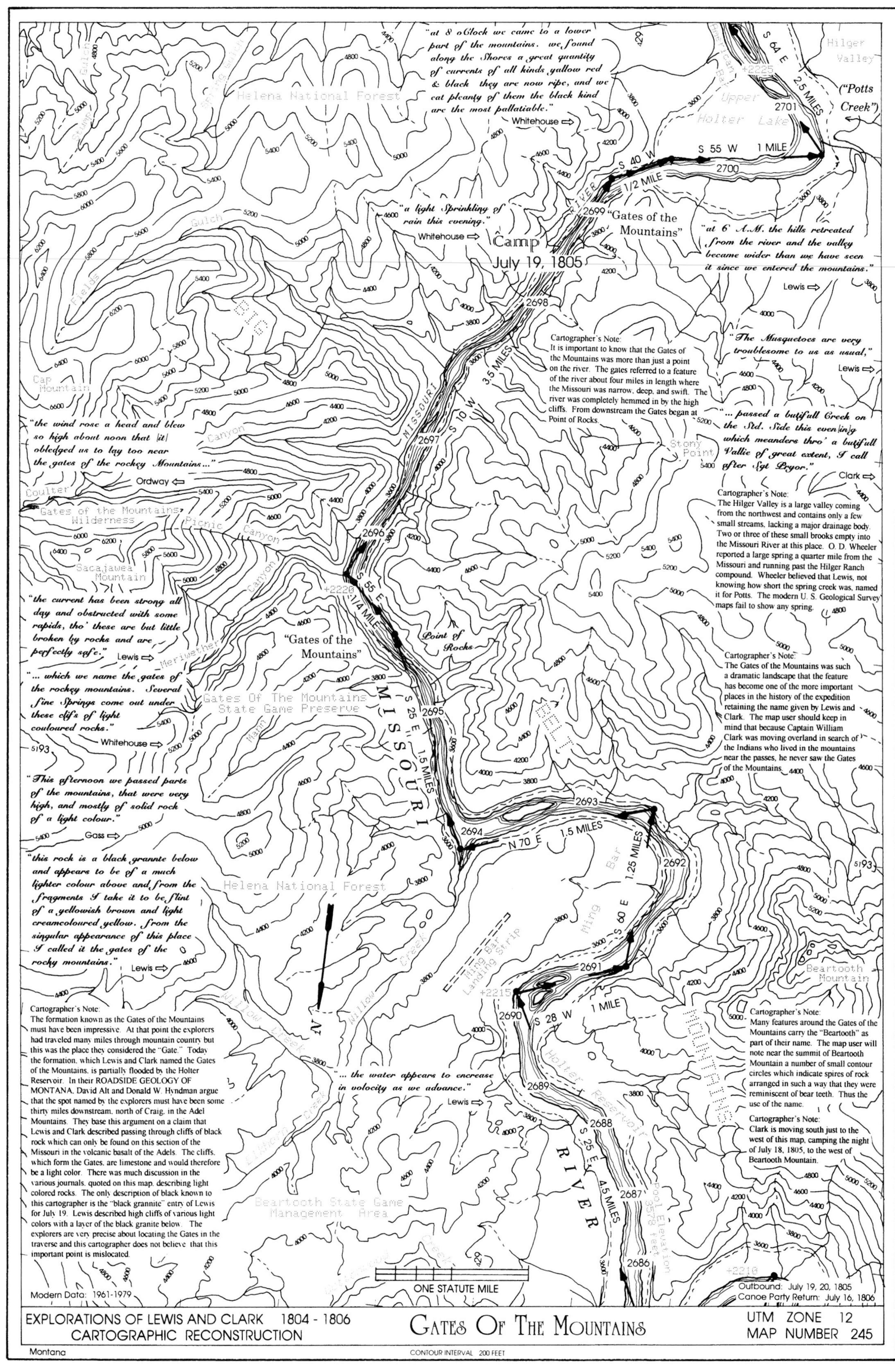
"at 8 oClock we came to a lower part of the mountains. we found along the Shores a great quantity of currents of all kinds yallow red & black they are now ripe, and we eat pleanty of them the black kind are the most pallatiable."
Whitehouse ⇨
Helena National Forest
Upper Holter Lake
Hilger Valley
("Potts Creek")
S 64 E
2.5 MILES
2701
S 40 W
S 55 W
1 MILE
2700
1/2 MILE
RIVER
"a light Sprinkling of rain this evening."
Whitehouse ⇨
2699
"Gates of the Mountains"
Camp July 19, 1805
"at 6 A.M. the hills retreated from the river and the valley became wider than we have seen it since we entered the mountains."
Lewis ⇨
2698
Cartographer's Note:
It is important to know that the Gates of the Mountains was more than just a point on the river. The gates referred to a feature of the river about four miles in length where the Missouri was narrow, deep, and swift. The river was completely hemmed in by the high cliffs. From downstream the Gates began at Point of Rocks.
"The Musquetoes are very troublesome to us as usual,"
Lewis ⇨
3.5 MILES
S 10 W
MISSOURI
2697
Cap Mountain
BIG
Fields
Gulch
"the wind rose a head and blew so high about noon that [it] obledged us to lay too near the gates of the rockey Mountains..."
Ordway ⇦
Coulter
Gates of the Mountains Wilderness
Picnic
Canyon
Sacajawea Mountain
"... passed a butifull Creek on the Std. Side this even[in]g which meanders thro' a butifull Vallie of great extent, I call after Sgt Pryor."
Clark ⇨
Stony Point
Cartographer's Note:
The Hilger Valley is a large valley coming from the northwest and contains only a few small streams, lacking a major drainage body. Two or three of these small brooks empty into the Missouri River at this place. O. D. Wheeler reported a large spring a quarter mile from the Missouri and running past the Hilger Ranch compound. Wheeler believed that Lewis, not knowing how short the spring creek was, named it for Potts. The modern U. S. Geological Survey maps fail to show any spring.
2696
+2220
S 55 E
1/4 MILE
"the current has been strong all day and obstructed with some rapids, tho' these are but little broken by rocks and are perfectly safe."
Lewis ⇨
Meriwether
"Gates of the Mountains"
Point of Rocks
"... which we name the gates of the rockey mountains. Several fine Springs come out under these clifs of light coloured rocks."
Whitehouse ⇨
Gates Of The Mountains State Game Preserve
MISSOURI
S 25 E
1.5 MILES
2695
BELT
Cartographer's Note:
The Gates of the Mountains was such a dramatic landscape that the feature has become one of the more important places in the history of the expedition retaining the name given by Lewis and Clark. The map user should keep in mind that because Captain William Clark was moving overland in search of the Indians who lived in the mountains near the passes, he never saw the Gates of the Mountains.
"This afternoon we passed parts of the mountains, that were very high, and mostly of solid rock of a light colour."
Gass ⇨
2693
2694
N 70 E
1.5 MILES
1.25 MILES
2692
"this rock is a black grannte below and appears to be of a much lighter colour above and from the fragments I take it to be flint of a yellowish brown and light creamcoloured yellow. from the singular appearance of this place I called it the gates of the rocky mountains."
Lewis ⇨
Helena National Forest
Ming Bar
S 60 E
Ming Bar Landing Strip
2691
+2215
2690
S 28 W
1 MILE
Beartooth Mountain
MOUNTAINS
N
Willow Creek
Cartographer's Note:
The formation known as the Gates of the Mountains must have been impressive. At that point the explorers had traveled many miles through mountain country but this was the place they considered the "Gate." Today the formation, which Lewis and Clark named the Gates of the Mountains, is partially flooded by the Holter Reservoir. In their ROADSIDE GEOLOGY OF MONTANA, David Alt and Donald W. Hyndman argue that the spot named by the explorers must have been some thirty miles downstream, north of Craig, in the Adel Mountains. They base this argument on a claim that Lewis and Clark described passing through cliffs of black rock which can only be found on this section of the Missouri in the volcanic basalt of the Adels. The cliffs, which form the Gates, are limestone and would therefore be a light color. There was much discussion in the various journals, quoted on this map, describing light colored rocks. The only description of black known to this cartographer is the "black grannite" entry of Lewis for July 19. Lewis described high cliffs of various light colors with a layer of the black granite below. The explorers are very precise about locating the Gates in the traverse and this cartographer does not believe that this important point is mislocated.
"... the water appears to encrease in velocity as we advance."
Lewis ⇨
2689
Holter Reservoir
2688
S 25 E
RIVER
Cartographer's Note:
Many features around the Gates of the Mountains carry the "Beartooth" as part of their name. The map user will note near the summit of Beartooth Mountain a number of small contour circles which indicate spires of rock arranged in such a way that they were reminiscent of bear teeth. Thus the use of the name.
Cartographer's Note:
Clark is moving south just to the west of this map, camping the night of July 18, 1805, to the west of Beartooth Mountain.
4.5 MILES
2687
Pool Elevation 3578 feet
Beartooth State Game Management Area
2686
+2210
ONE STATUTE MILE
Modern Data: 1961-1979
Outbound: July 19, 20, 1805
Canoe Party Return: July 16, 1806
EXPLORATIONS OF LEWIS AND CLARK 1804 - 1806
CARTOGRAPHIC RECONSTRUCTION
GATES OF THE MOUNTAINS
UTM ZONE 12
MAP NUMBER 245
Montana
CONTOUR INTERVAL 200 FEET

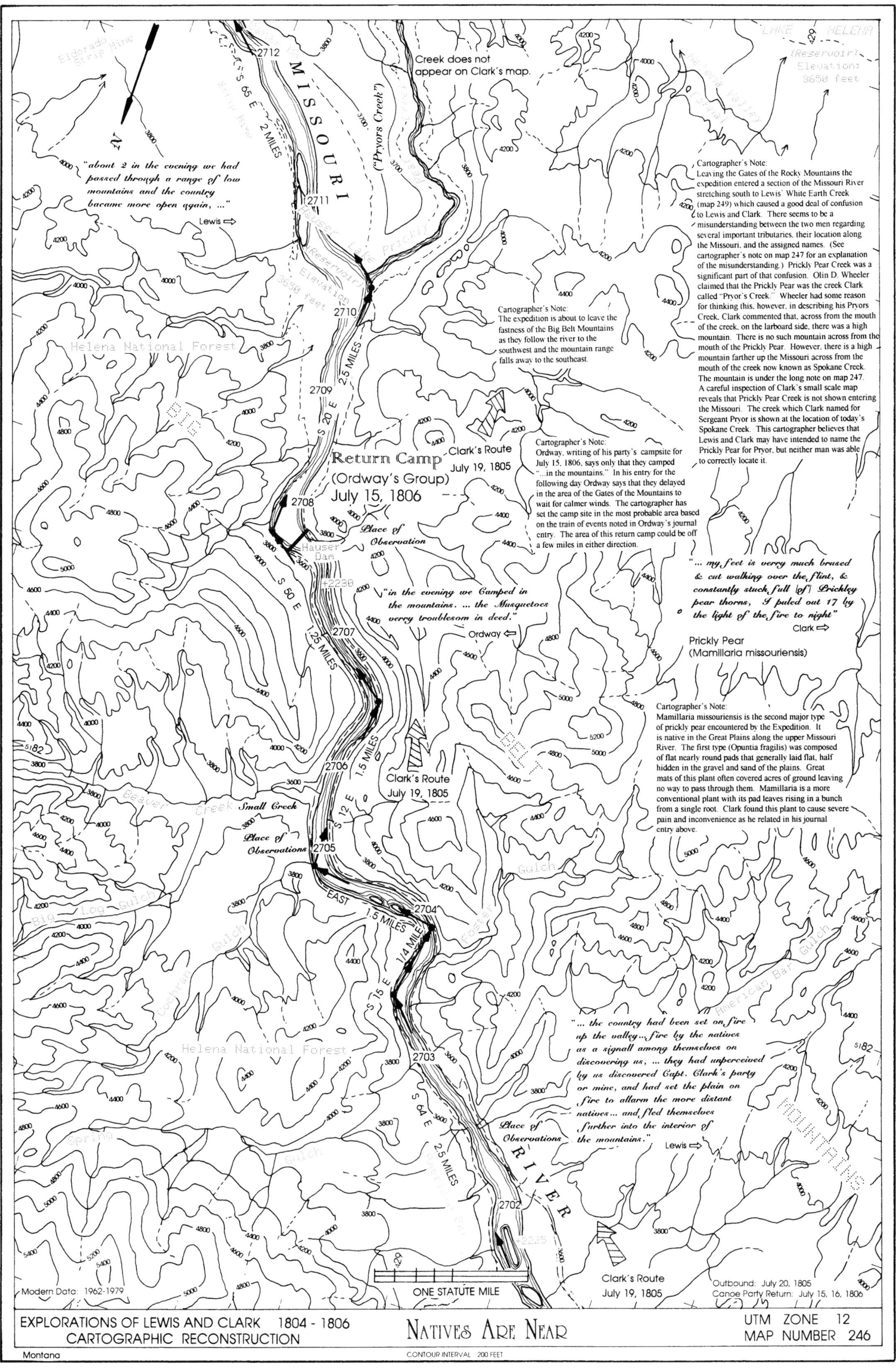

MISSOURI
RIVER
Creek does not appear on Clark's map.
("Pryors Creek")
"about 2 in the evening we had passed through a range of low mountains and the country bacame more open agian, ..."
Lewis
Cartographer's Note:
Leaving the Gates of the Rocky Mountains the expedition entered a section of the Missouri River stretching south to Lewis' White Earth Creek (map 249) which caused a good deal of confusion to Lewis and Clark. There seems to be a misunderstanding between the two men regarding several important tributaries, their location along the Missouri, and the assigned names. (See cartographer's note on map 247 for an explanation of the misunderstanding.) Prickly Pear Creek was a significant part of that confusion. Olin D. Wheeler claimed that the Prickly Pear was the creek Clark called "Pryor's Creek." Wheeler had some reason for thinking this, however, in describing his Pryors Creek, Clark commented that, across from the mouth of the creek, on the larboard side, there was a high mountain. There is no such mountain across from the mouth of the Prickly Pear. However, there is a high mountain farther up the Missouri across from the mouth of the creek now known as Spokane Creek. The mountain is under the long note on map 247. A careful inspection of Clark's small scale map reveals that Prickly Pear Creek is not shown entering the Missouri. The creek which Clark named for Sergeant Pryor is shown at the location of today's Spokane Creek. This cartographer believes that Lewis and Clark may have intended to name the Prickly Pear for Pryor, but neither man was able to correctly locate it.
Cartographer's Note:
The expedition is about to leave the fastness of the Big Belt Mountains as they follow the river to the southwest and the mountain range falls away to the southeast.
Return Camp
(Ordway's Group)
July 15, 1806
Clark's Route
July 19, 1805
Cartographer's Note:
Ordway, writing of his party's campsite for July 15, 1806, says only that they camped "...in the mountains." In his entry for the following day Ordway says that they delayed in the area of the Gates of the Mountains to wait for calmer winds. The cartographer has set the camp site in the most probable area based on the train of events noted in Ordway's journal entry. The area of this return camp could be off a few miles in either direction.
Place of Observation
Hauser Dam
"in the evening we Camped in the mountains. ... the Musquetoes verry troublesom in deed."
Ordway
"... my feet is verry much brused & cut walking over the flint, & constantly stuck full [of] Prickley pear thorns, I puled out 17 by the light of the fire to night"
Clark
Prickly Pear
(Mamillaria missouriensis)
Cartographer's Note:
Mamillaria missouriensis is the second major type of prickly pear encountered by the Expedition. It is native in the Great Plains along the upper Missouri River. The first type (Opuntia fragilis) was composed of flat nearly round pads that generally laid flat, half hidden in the gravel and sand of the plains. Great mats of this plant often covered acres of ground leaving no way to pass through them. Mamillaria is a more conventional plant with its pad leaves rising in a bunch from a single root. Clark found this plant to cause severe pain and inconvenience as he related in his journal entry above.
Clark's Route
July 19, 1805
Small Creek
Place of Observations
"... the country had been set on fire up the valley...fire by the natives as a signall among themselves on discovering us, ... they had unperceived by us discovered Capt. Clark's party or mine, and had set the plain on fire to allarm the more distant natives... and fled themselves further into the interior of the mountains."
Lewis
Place of Observations
S 65 E 2 MILES
S 20 E 2.5 MILES
S 50 E
1.25 MILES
1.5 MILES
S 12 E
EAST 1.5 MILES
1/4 MILE
S 15 E
S 64 E 2.5 MILES
ONE STATUTE MILE
Clark's Route
July 19, 1805
Outbound: July 20, 1805
Canoe Party Return: July 15, 16, 1806
Modern Data: 1962-1979
EXPLORATIONS OF LEWIS AND CLARK 1804 - 1806
CARTOGRAPHIC RECONSTRUCTION
Montana
NATIVES ARE NEAR
CONTOUR INTERVAL 200 FEET
UTM ZONE 12
MAP NUMBER 246

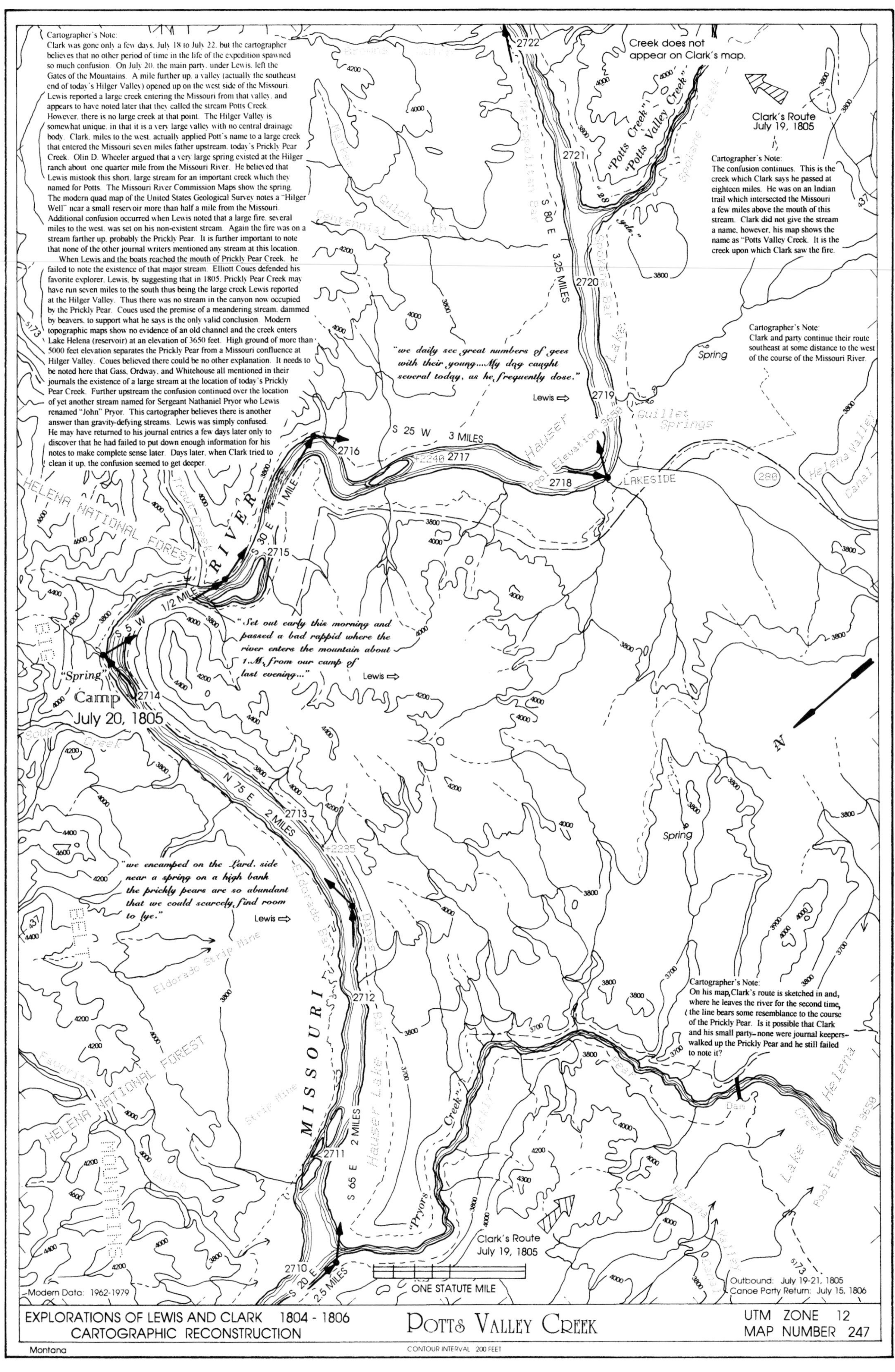

Cartographer's Note:
Clark was gone only a few days, July 18 to July 22, but the cartographer believes that no other period of time in the life of the expedition spawned so much confusion. On July 20, the main party, under Lewis, left the Gates of the Mountains. A mile further up, a valley (actually the southeast end of today's Hilger Valley) opened up on the west side of the Missouri. Lewis reported a large creek entering the Missouri from that valley, and appears to have noted later that they called the stream Potts Creek. However, there is no large creek at that point. The Hilger Valley is somewhat unique, in that it is a very large valley with no central drainage body. Clark, miles to the west, actually applied Pott's name to a large creek that entered the Missouri seven miles father upstream, today's Prickly Pear Creek. Olin D. Wheeler argued that a very large spring existed at the Hilger ranch about one quarter mile from the Missouri River. He believed that Lewis mistook this short, large stream for an important creek which they named for Potts. The Missouri River Commission Maps show the spring. The modern quad map of the United States Geological Survey notes a "Hilger Well" near a small reservoir more than half a mile from the Missouri. Additional confusion occurred when Lewis noted that a large fire, several miles to the west, was set on his non-existent stream. Again the fire was on a stream farther up, probably the Prickly Pear. It is further important to note that none of the other journal writers mentioned any stream at this location.
When Lewis and the boats reached the mouth of Prickly Pear Creek, he failed to note the existence of that major stream. Elliott Coues defended his favorite explorer, Lewis, by suggesting that in 1805, Prickly Pear Creek may have run seven miles to the south thus being the large creek Lewis reported at the Hilger Valley. Thus there was no stream in the canyon now occupied by the Prickly Pear. Coues used the premise of a meandering stream, dammed by beavers, to support what he says is the only valid conclusion. Modern topographic maps show no evidence of an old channel and the creek enters Lake Helena (reservoir) at an elevation of 3650 feet. High ground of more than 5000 feet elevation separates the Prickly Pear from a Missouri confluence at Hilger Valley. Coues believed there could be no other explanation. It needs to be noted here that Gass, Ordway, and Whitehouse all mentioned in their journals the existence of a large stream at the location of today's Prickly Pear Creek. Further upstream the confusion continued over the location of yet another stream named for Sergeant Nathaniel Pryor who Lewis renamed "John" Pryor. This cartographer believes there is another answer than gravity-defying streams. Lewis was simply confused. He may have returned to his journal entries a few days later only to discover that he had failed to put down enough information for his notes to make complete sense later. Days later, when Clark tried to clean it up, the confusion seemed to get deeper.
Creek does not appear on Clark's map.
"Potts Creek"
"Potts Valley Creek"
"28 yds."
Clark's Route July 19, 1805
Cartographer's Note:
The confusion continues. This is the creek which Clark says he passed at eighteen miles. He was on an Indian trail which intersected the Missouri a few miles above the mouth of this stream. Clark did not give the stream a name, however, his map shows the name as "Potts Valley Creek." It is the creek upon which Clark saw the fire.
Cartographer's Note:
Clark and party continue their route southeast at some distance to the west of the course of the Missouri River.
"we daily see great numbers of gees with their young...My dog caught several today, as he frequently dose."
Lewis ⇨
S 25 W 3 MILES
S 80 E 3.25 MILES
S 30 E 1 MILE
1/2 MILE
S 5 W
LAKESIDE
Spring
Guillet Springs
"Set out early this morning and passed a bad rappid where the river enters the mountain about 1.M. from our camp of last evening..."
Lewis ⇨
"Spring"
Camp July 20, 1805
N 75 E 2 MILES
"we encamped on the Lard. side near a spring on a high bank the prickly pears are so abundant that we could scarcely find room to lye."
Lewis ⇨
Cartographer's Note:
On his map, Clark's route is sketched in and, where he leaves the river for the second time, the line bears some resemblance to the course of the Prickly Pear. Is it possible that Clark and his small party- none were journal keepers- walked up the Prickly Pear and he still failed to note it?
MISSOURI RIVER
HELENA NATIONAL FOREST
BIG BELT MOUNTAINS
Hauser Lake
Lake Helena
"Pryors Creek"
S 65 E 2 MILES
S 20 E 2.5 MILES
Clark's Route July 19, 1805
ONE STATUTE MILE
N
Modern Data: 1962-1979
Outbound: July 19-21, 1805
Canoe Party Return: July 15, 1806
EXPLORATIONS OF LEWIS AND CLARK 1804 - 1806
CARTOGRAPHIC RECONSTRUCTION
POTTS VALLEY CREEK
UTM ZONE 12
MAP NUMBER 247
Montana
CONTOUR INTERVAL 200 FEET

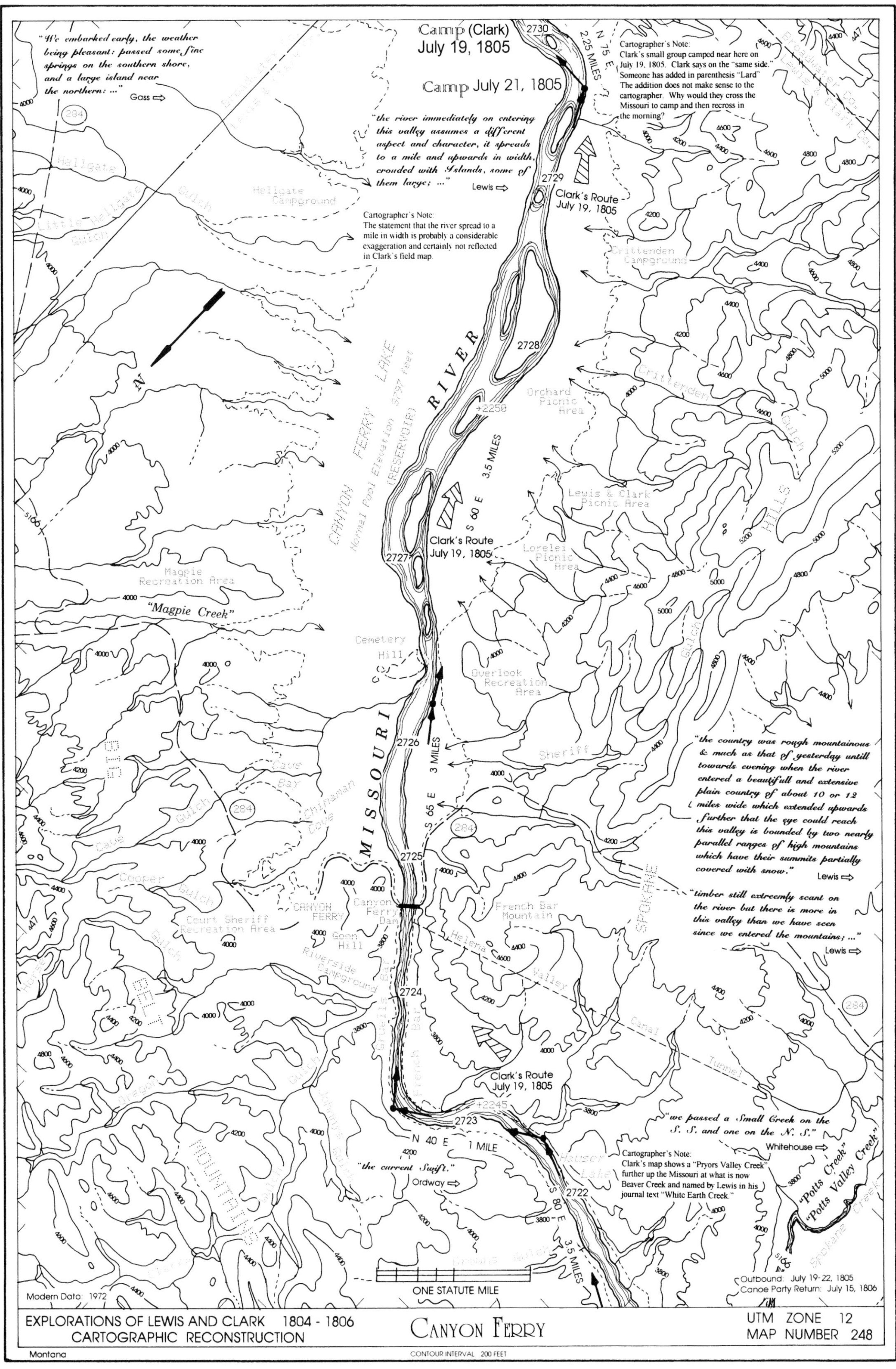
"We embarked early, the weather being pleasant: passed some fine springs on the southern shore, and a large island near the northern: ..."
Gass
Camp (Clark) July 19, 1805
Camp July 21, 1805
Cartographer's Note: Clark's small group camped near here on July 19, 1805. Clark says on the "same side." Someone has added in parenthesis "Lard" The addition does not make sense to the cartographer. Why would they cross the Missouri to camp and then recross in the morning?
"the river immediately on entering this valley assumes a different aspect and character, it spreads to a mile and upwards in width, crouded with Islands, some of them large; ..."
Lewis
Cartographer's Note: The statement that the river spread to a mile in width is probably a considerable exaggeration and certainly not reflected in Clark's field map.
Clark's Route July 19, 1805
N 75 E 2.25 MILES
S 60 E 3.5 MILES
S 65 E 3 MILES
N 40 E 1 MILE
S 80 E 3.5 MILES
MISSOURI RIVER
CANYON FERRY LAKE
Normal Pool Elevation 3797 feet (RESERVOIR)
"Magpie Creek"
Magpie Recreation Area
Hellgate Campground
Crittenden Campground
Orchard Picnic Area
Lewis & Clark Picnic Area
Lorelei Picnic Area
Cemetery Hill
Overlook Recreation Area
Canyon Ferry Dam
Court Sheriff Recreation Area
Riverside Campground
French Bar Mountain
Hauser Lake
BIG BELT MOUNTAINS
SPOKANE HILLS
"the country was rough mountainous & much as that of yesterday untill towards evening when the river entered a beautifull and extensive plain country of about 10 or 12 miles wide which extended upwards further that the eye could reach this valley is bounded by two nearly parallel ranges of high mountains which have their summits partially covered with snow."
Lewis
"timber still extreemly scant on the river but there is more in this valley than we have seen since we entered the mountains; ..."
Lewis
"we passed a Small Creek on the S. S. and one on the N. S."
Whitehouse
"the current Swift."
Ordway
Cartographer's Note: Clark's map shows a "Pryors Valley Creek" further up the Missouri at what is now Beaver Creek and named by Lewis in his journal text "White Earth Creek."
"Potts Creek"
"Potts Valley Creek"
ONE STATUTE MILE
Modern Data: 1972
Outbound: July 19-22, 1805
Canoe Party Return: July 15, 1806
EXPLORATIONS OF LEWIS AND CLARK 1804 - 1806
CARTOGRAPHIC RECONSTRUCTION
CANYON FERRY
UTM ZONE 12
MAP NUMBER 248
Montana
CONTOUR INTERVAL 200 FEET

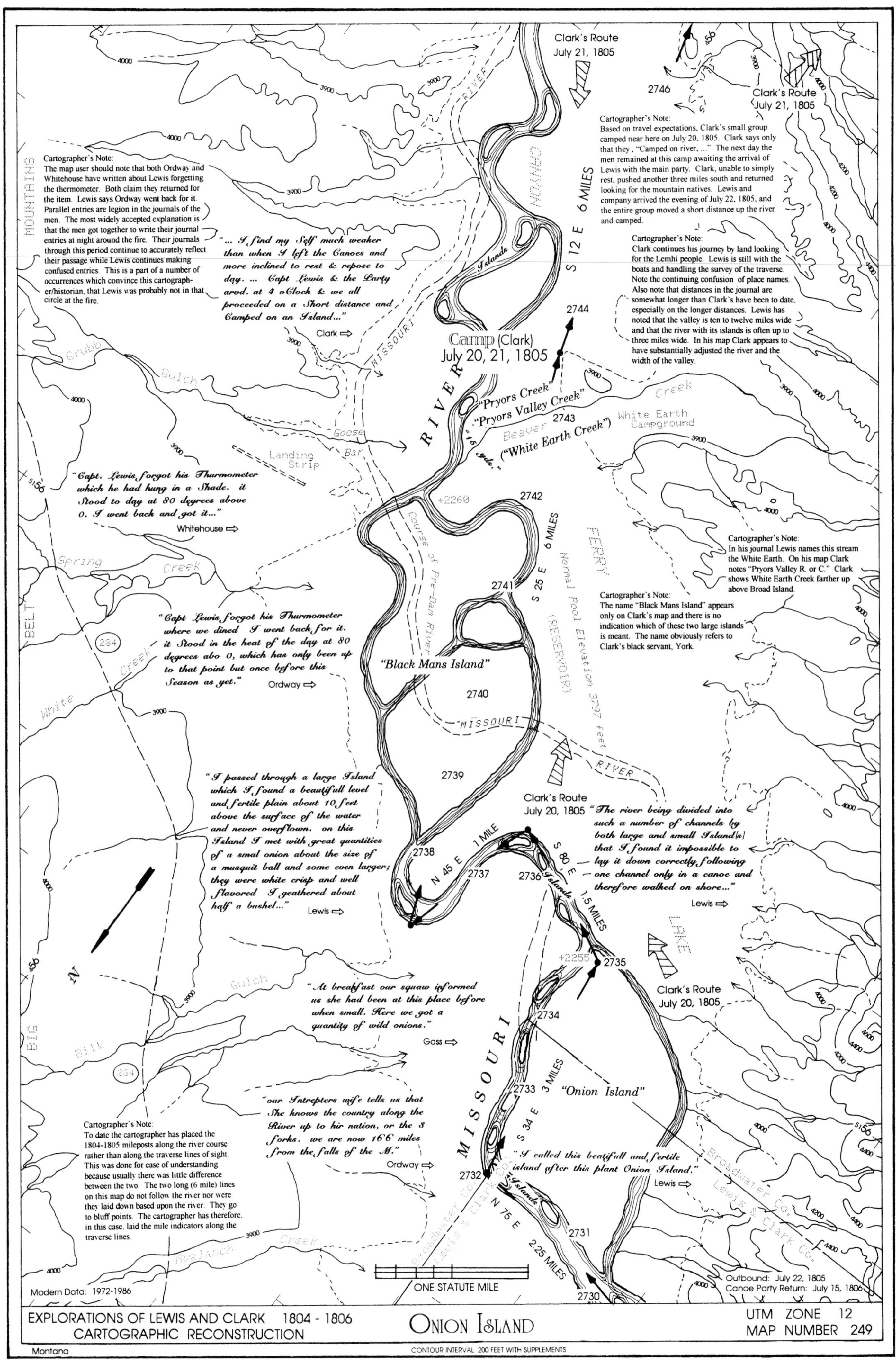
Clark's Route
July 21, 1805
Clark's Route
July 21, 1805
Cartographer's Note:
Based on travel expectations, Clark's small group camped near here on July 20, 1805. Clark says only that they , "Camped on river, ..." The next day the men remained at this camp awaiting the arrival of Lewis with the main party. Clark, unable to simply rest, pushed another three miles south and returned looking for the mountain natives. Lewis and company arrived the evening of July 22, 1805, and the entire group moved a short distance up the river and camped.
Cartographer's Note:
The map user should note that both Ordway and Whitehouse have written about Lewis forgetting the thermometer. Both claim they returned for the item. Lewis says Ordway went back for it. Parallel entries are legion in the journals of the men. The most widely accepted explanation is that the men got together to write their journal entries at night around the fire. Their journals through this period continue to accurately reflect their passage while Lewis continues making confused entries. This is a part of a number of occurrences which convince this cartographer/historian, that Lewis was probably not in that circle at the fire.
"... I find my Self much weaker than when I left the Canoes and more inclined to rest & repose to day. ... Capt Lewis & the Party arod. at 4 oClock & we all proceeded on a Short distance and Camped on an Island..."
Clark
Cartographer's Note:
Clark continues his journey by land looking for the Lemhi people. Lewis is still with the boats and handling the survey of the traverse. Note the continuing confusion of place names. Also note that distances in the journal are somewhat longer than Clark's have been to date, especially on the longer distances. Lewis has noted that the valley is ten to twelve miles wide and that the river with its islands is often up to three miles wide. In his map Clark appears to have substantially adjusted the river and the width of the valley.
Camp (Clark)
July 20, 21, 1805
"Pryors Creek"
"Pryors Valley Creek"
("White Earth Creek")
White Earth Campground
"Capt. Lewis forgot his Thurmometer which he had hung in a Shade. it Stood to day at 80 degrees above 0. I went back and got it..."
Whitehouse
Cartographer's Note:
In his journal Lewis names this stream the White Earth. On his map Clark notes "Pryors Valley R. or C." Clark shows White Earth Creek farther up above Broad Island.
Cartographer's Note:
The name "Black Mans Island" appears only on Clark's map and there is no indication which of these two large islands is meant. The name obviously refers to Clark's black servant, York.
"Capt Lewis forgot his Thurmometer where we dined I went back for it. it Stood in the heat of the day at 80 degrees abo 0, which has only been up to that point but once before this Season as yet."
Ordway
"Black Mans Island"
Course of Pre-Dam River
Normal Pool Elevation 3797 feet
(RESERVOIR)
FERRY
MISSOURI RIVER
CANYON
"I passed through a large Island which I found a beautifull level and fertile plain about 10 feet above the surface of the water and never overflown. on this Island I met with great quantities of a smal onion about the size of a musquit ball and some even larger; they were white crisp and well flavored I geathered about half a bushel..."
Lewis
Clark's Route
July 20, 1805
"The river being divided into such a number of channels by both large and small Island[s] that I found it impossible to lay it down correctly following one channel only in a canoe and therefore walked on shore..."
Lewis
Clark's Route
July 20, 1805
LAKE
"At breakfast our squaw informed us she had been at this place before when small. Here we got a quantity of wild onions."
Gass
"Onion Island"
"our Intrepters wife tells us that She knows the country along the River up to hir nation, or the 3 forks. we are now 166 miles from the falls of the M."
Ordway
"I called this beatifull and fertile island after this plant Onion Island."
Lewis
Cartographer's Note:
To date the cartographer has placed the 1804-1805 mileposts along the river course rather than along the traverse lines of sight. This was done for ease of understanding because usually there was little difference between the two. The two long (6 mile) lines on this map do not follow the river nor were they laid down based upon the river. They go to bluff points. The cartographer has therefore, in this case, laid the mile indicators along the traverse lines.
BELT MOUNTAINS
BIG BELT
Grubb Gulch
Spring Creek
White Creek
Goose Bar
Landing Strip
Beaver Creek
Gulch
Bilk
Avalanch Creek
S 12 E 6 MILES
S 25 E 6 MILES
N 45 E 1 MILE
S 80 E
1.5 MILES
S 34 E 3 MILES
N 75 E
2.25 MILES
Islands
Broadwater Co.
Lewis & Clark Co.
ONE STATUTE MILE
Modern Data: 1972-1986
Outbound: July 22, 1805
Canoe Party Return: July 15, 1806
EXPLORATIONS OF LEWIS AND CLARK 1804 - 1806
CARTOGRAPHIC RECONSTRUCTION
ONION ISLAND
UTM ZONE 12
MAP NUMBER 249
Montana
CONTOUR INTERVAL 200 FEET WITH SUPPLEMENTS

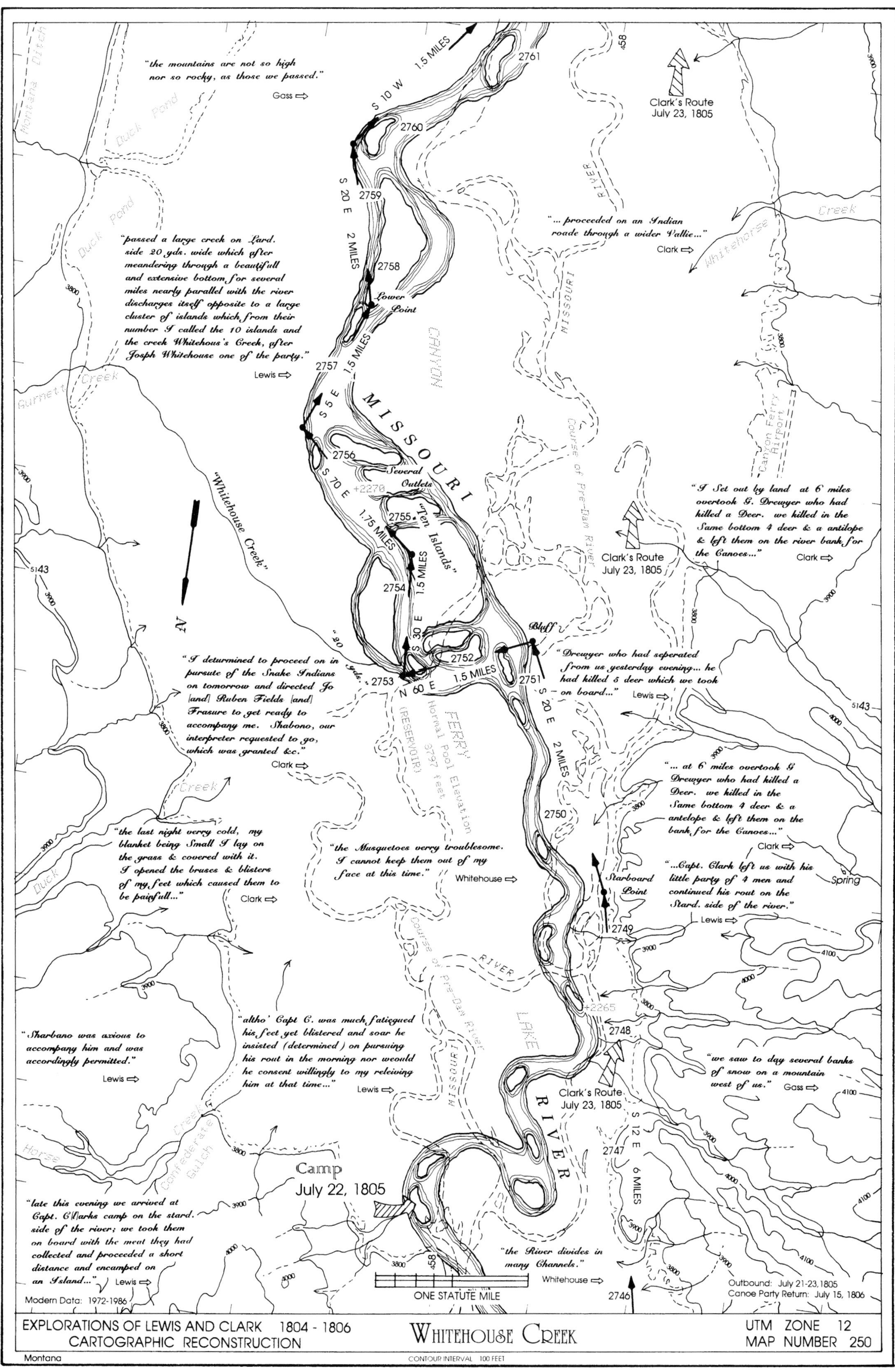
"the mountains are not so high nor so rocky, as those we passed."
Gass ⇨
S 10 W 1.5 MILES
2761
2760
Clark's Route July 23, 1805
Montana Ditch
Duck Pond
S 20 E 2 MILES
2759
RIVER
"... proceeded on an Indian roade through a wider Vallie..."
Clark ⇨
Creek
Whitehouse
"passed a large creek on Lard. side 20 yds. wide which after meandering through a beautifull and extensive bottom for several miles nearly parallel with the river discharges itself opposite to a large cluster of islands which from their number I called the 10 islands and the creek Whitehous's Creek, after Joseph Whitehouse one of the party."
Lewis ⇨
2758
Lower Point
CANYON
MISSOURI
2757
1.5 MILES
S 5 E
Gurnett Creek
Canyon Ferry Airport
Course of Pre-Dam River
2756
Several Outlets
S 70 E
+2270
"Whitehouse Creek"
2755
"Ten Islands"
1.75 MILES
"I Set out by land at 6 miles overtook G. Drewyer who had killed a Deer. we killed in the Same bottom 4 deer & a antilope & left them on the river bank for the Canoes..."
Clark ⇨
Clark's Route July 23, 1805
2754
1.5 MILES
5143
N
S 30 E
Bluff
2752
"I determined to proceed on in pursute of the Snake Indians on tomorrow and directed Jo [and] Ruben Fields [and] Frasure to get ready to accompany me. Shabono, our interpreter requested to go, which was granted &c."
Clark ⇨
"20 yds."
2753
N 60 E
1.5 MILES
2751
"Drewyer who had seperated from us yesterday evening... he had killed 5 deer which we took on board..."
Lewis ⇨
S 20 E
2 MILES
FERRY
(RESERVOIR)
Normal Pool Elevation 3797 feet
Creek
"... at 6 miles overtook G Drewyer who had killed a Deer. we killed in the Same bottom 4 deer & a antelope & left them on the bank for the Canoes..."
Clark ⇨
2750
"the last night verry cold, my blanket being Small I lay on the grass & covered with it. I opened the bruses & blisters of my feet which caused them to be painfull..."
Clark ⇨
"the Musquetoes verry troublesome. I cannot keep them out of my face at this time."
Whitehouse ⇨
Starboard Point
"...Capt. Clark left us with his little party of 4 men and continued his rout on the Stard. side of the river."
Lewis ⇨
Spring
Duck
2749
RIVER
Course of Pre-Dam River
+2265
"altho' Capt C. was much fatiegued his feet yet blistered and soar he insisted (determined) on pursuing his rout in the morning nor weould he consent willingly to my releiving him at that time..."
Lewis ⇨
"Sharbano was axious to accompany him and was accordingly permitted."
Lewis ⇨
LAKE
2748
MISSOURI
"we saw to day several banks of snow on a mountain west of us."
Gass ⇨
Clark's Route July 23, 1805
RIVER
S 12 E 6 MILES
Horse Creek
Confederate Gulch
2747
Camp July 22, 1805
"late this evening we arrived at Capt. C[l]arks camp on the stard. side of the river; we took them on board with the meat they had collected and proceeded a short distance and encamped on an Island..."
Lewis ⇨
"the River divides in many Channels."
Whitehouse ⇨
ONE STATUTE MILE
2746
Outbound: July 21-23, 1805
Canoe Party Return: July 15, 1806
Modern Data: 1972-1986
EXPLORATIONS OF LEWIS AND CLARK 1804 - 1806
CARTOGRAPHIC RECONSTRUCTION
WHITEHOUSE CREEK
UTM ZONE 12
MAP NUMBER 250
Montana
CONTOUR INTERVAL 100 FEET

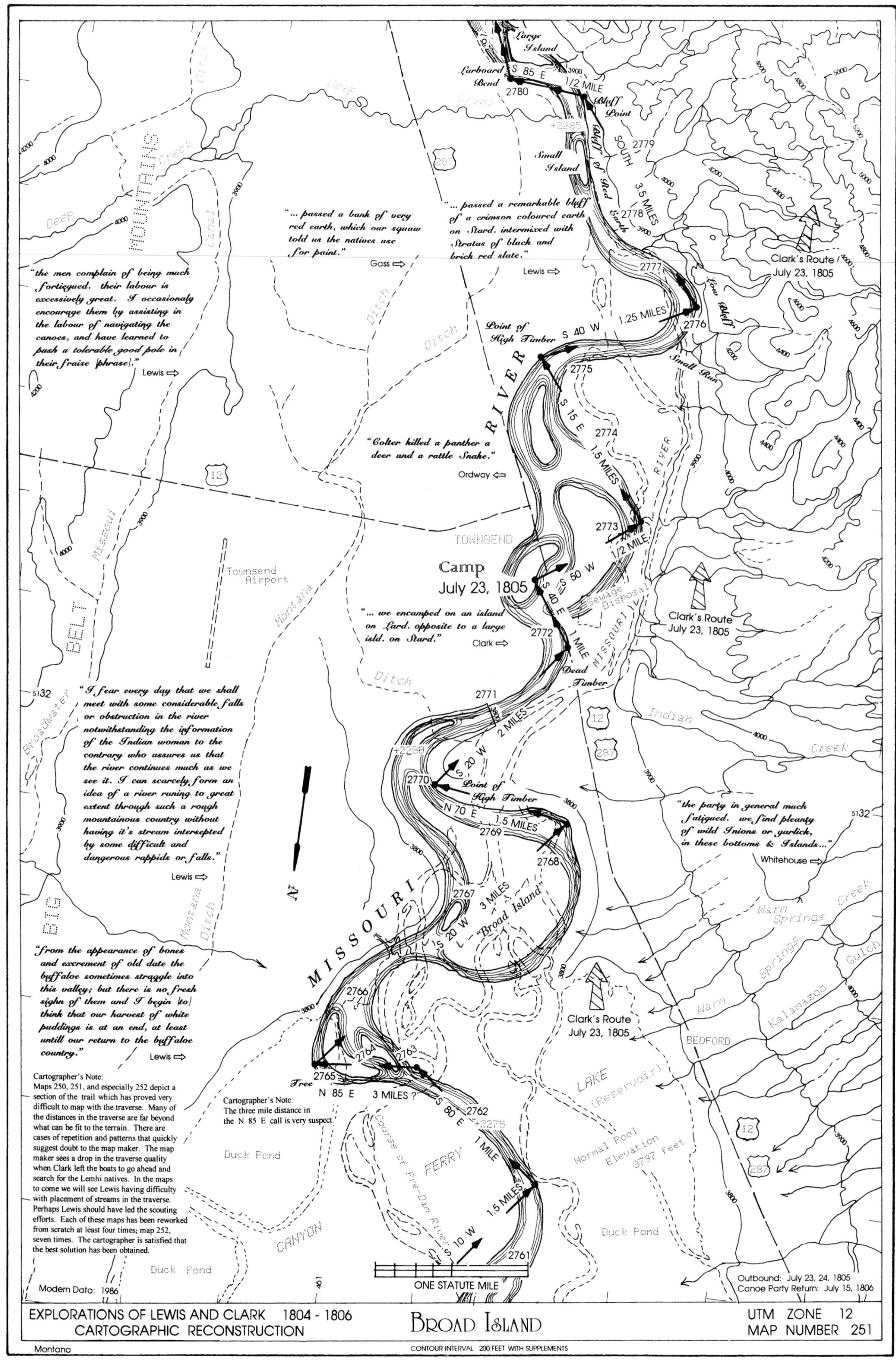

"... passed a bank of very red earth, which our squaw told us the natives use for paint."
Gass
"... passed a remarkable bluff of a crimson coloured earth on Stard. intermixed with Stratas of black and brick red slate."
Lewis
"the men complain of being much fortigued. their labour is excessively great. I occasionaly encourage them by assisting in the labour of navigating the canoes, and have learned to push a tolerable good pole in their fraize [phrase]."
Lewis
"Colter killed a panther a deer and a rattle Snake."
Ordway
Camp
July 23, 1805
"... we encamped on an island on Lard. opposite to a large isld. on Stard."
Clark
"I fear every day that we shall meet with some considerable falls or obstruction in the river notwithstanding the information of the Indian woman to the contrary who assures us that the river continues much as we see it. I can scarcely form an idea of a river runing to great extent through such a rough mountainous country without having it's stream intersepted by some difficult and dangerous rappids or falls."
Lewis
"the party in general much fatigued. we find pleanty of wild Onions or garlick, in these bottoms & Islands..."
Whitehouse
"from the appearance of bones and excrement of old date the buffaloe sometimes straggle into this valley; but there is no fresh sighn of them and I begin [to] think that our harvest of white puddings is at an end, at least untill our return to the buffaloe country."
Lewis
Cartographer's Note:
Maps 250, 251, and especially 252 depict a section of the trail which has proved very difficult to map with the traverse. Many of the distances in the traverse are far beyond what can be fit to the terrain. There are cases of repetition and patterns that quickly suggest doubt to the map maker. The map maker sees a drop in the traverse quality when Clark left the boats to go ahead and search for the Lemhi natives. In the maps to come we will see Lewis having difficulty with placement of streams in the traverse. Perhaps Lewis should have led the scouting efforts. Each of these maps has been reworked from scratch at least four times; map 252, seven times. The cartographer is satisfied that the best solution has been obtained.
Cartographer's Note:
The three mile distance in the N 85 E call is very suspect.
Large Island
Larboard Bend
Bluff Point
Small Island
Bluff of Red Earth
Low Bluff
Small Run
Point of High Timber
Dead Timber
Point of High Timber
"Broad Island"
Tree
SOUTH
RIVER
MISSOURI
RIVER
MISSOURI
BIG BELT MOUNTAINS
Deep Creek
Indian Creek
Warm Springs Creek
Kalamazoo Gulch
Broadwater
Montana Ditch
Townsend Airport
TOWNSEND
BEDFORD
Sewage Disposal
LAKE (Reservoir)
Normal Pool Elevation 3797 feet
Course of Pre-Dam River
FERRY
CANYON
Duck Pond
Clark's Route July 23, 1805
N
ONE STATUTE MILE
Modern Data: 1986
Outbound: July 23, 24, 1805
Canoe Party Return: July 15, 1806
EXPLORATIONS OF LEWIS AND CLARK 1804 - 1806
CARTOGRAPHIC RECONSTRUCTION
BROAD ISLAND
UTM ZONE 12
MAP NUMBER 251
Montana
CONTOUR INTERVAL 200 FEET WITH SUPPLEMENTS

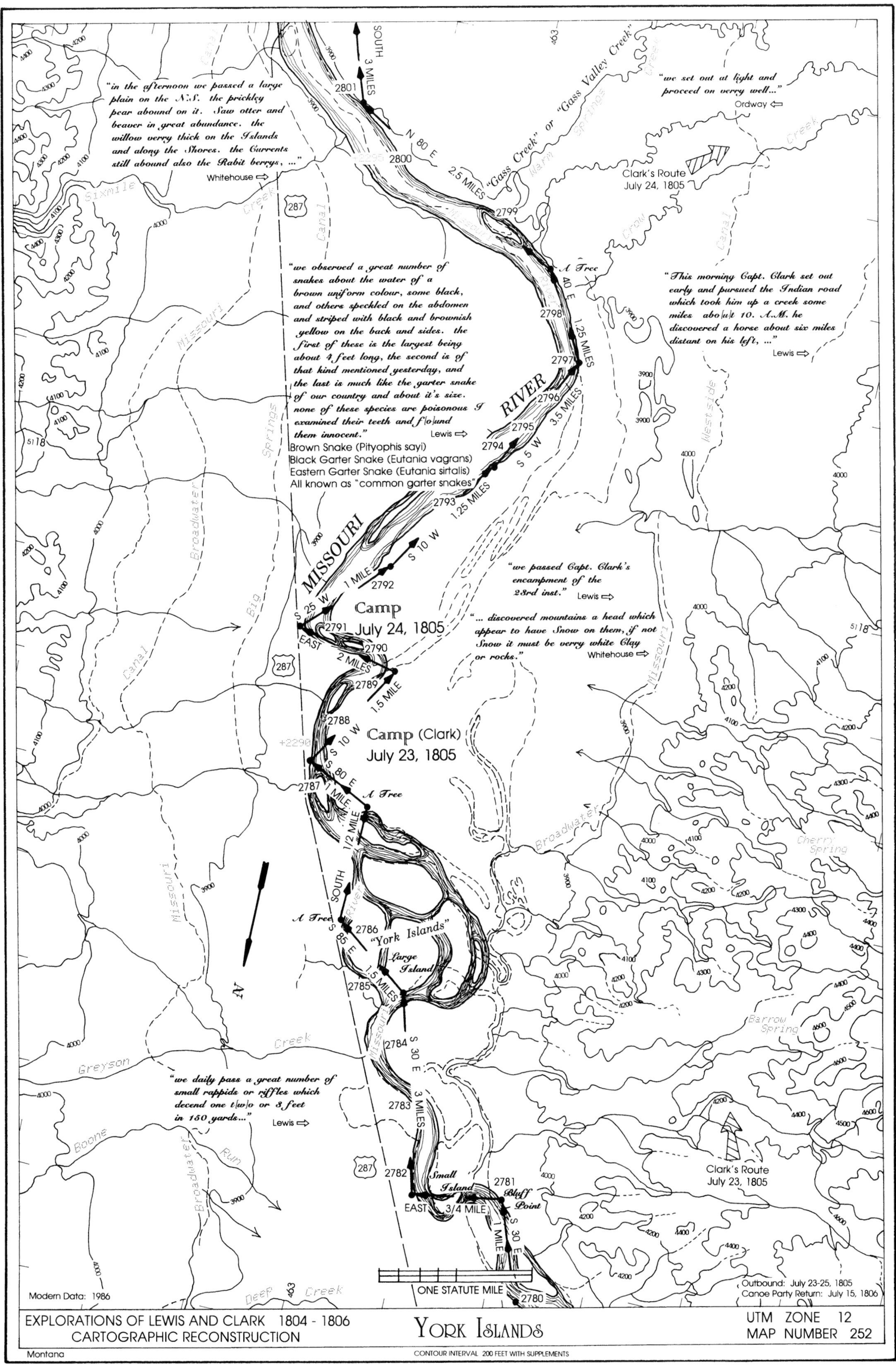
"in the afternoon we passed a large plain on the N.S. the prickley pear abound on it. Saw otter and beaver in great abundance. the willow verry thick on the Islands and along the Shores. the Currents still abound also the Rabit berrys, ..."
Whitehouse ⇨
"we set out at light and proceed on verry well..."
Ordway ⇦
Clark's Route July 24, 1805
"we observed a great number of snakes about the water of a brown uniform colour, some black, and others speckled on the abdomen and striped with black and brownish yellow on the back and sides. the first of these is the largest being about 4 feet long, the second is of that kind mentioned yesterday, and the last is much like the garter snake of our country and about it's size. none of these species are poisonous I examined their teeth and f[o]und them innocent."
Lewis ⇨
Brown Snake (Pityophis sayi)
Black Garter Snake (Eutania vagrans)
Eastern Garter Snake (Eutania sirtalis)
All known as "common garter snakes"
"This morning Capt. Clark set out early and pursued the Indian road which took him up a creek some miles abo[u]t 10. A.M. he discovered a horse about six miles distant on his left, ..."
Lewis ⇨
"we passed Capt. Clark's encampment of the 23rd inst."
Lewis ⇨
"... discovered mountains a head which appear to have Snow on them, if not Snow it must be verry white Clay or rocks."
Whitehouse ⇨
Camp July 24, 1805
Camp (Clark) July 23, 1805
MISSOURI RIVER
"Gass Creek" or "Gass Valley Creek"
"York Islands"
Large Island
Small Island
Bluff Point
A Tree
"we daily pass a great number of small rappids or riffles which decend one t[w]o or 3 feet in 150 yards..."
Lewis ⇨
Clark's Route July 23, 1805
Outbound: July 23-25, 1805
Canoe Party Return: July 15, 1806
ONE STATUTE MILE
Modern Data: 1986
EXPLORATIONS OF LEWIS AND CLARK 1804 - 1806
CARTOGRAPHIC RECONSTRUCTION
YORK ISLANDS
UTM ZONE 12
MAP NUMBER 252
Montana
CONTOUR INTERVAL 200 FEET WITH SUPPLEMENTS

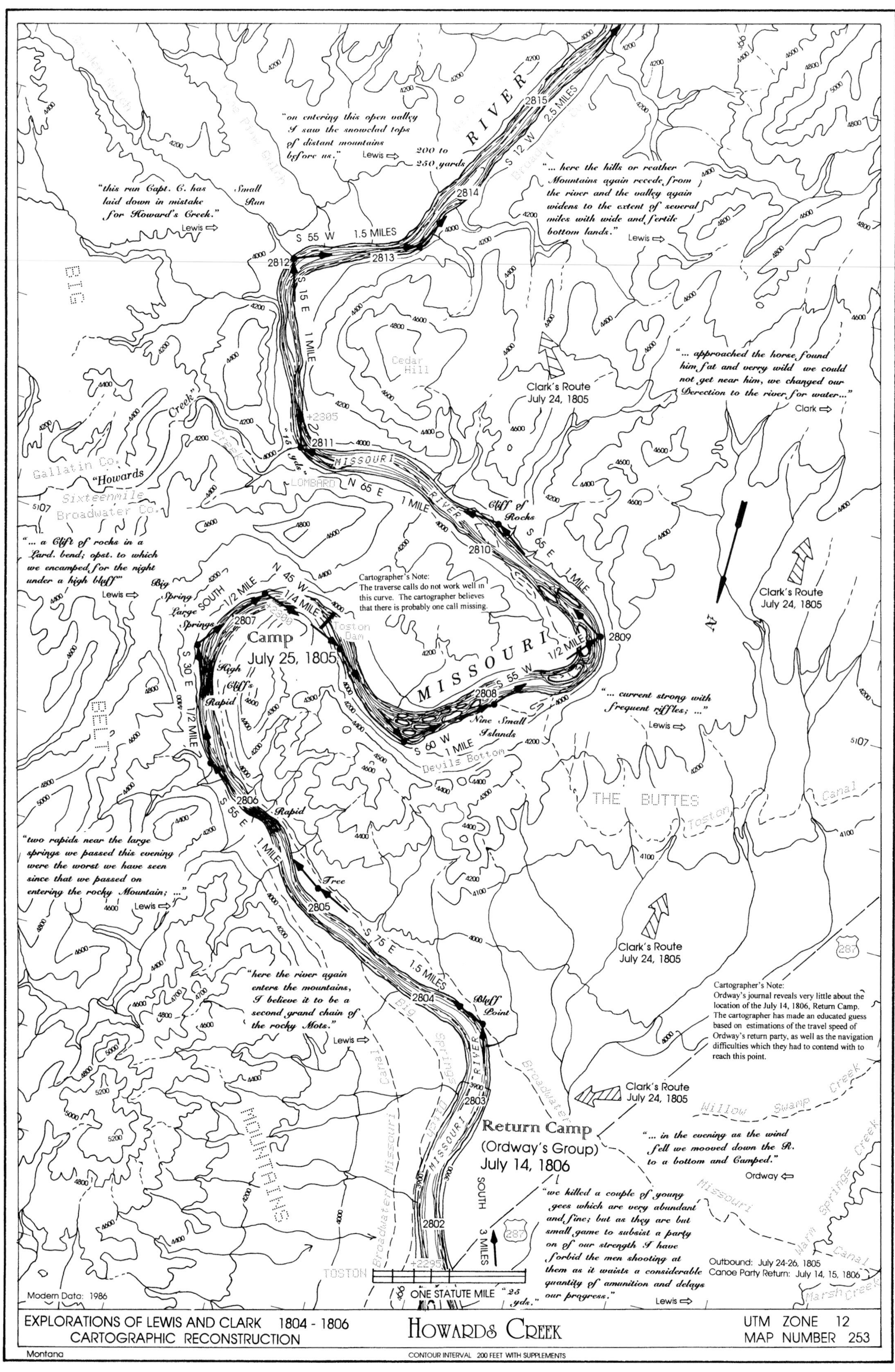
"on entering this open valley I saw the snowclad tops of distant mountains before us." Lewis ⇨
200 to 250 yards
RIVER
"this run Capt. C. has laid down in mistake for Howard's Creek." Lewis ⇨
Small Run
"... here the hills or reather Mountains again recede from the river and the valley again widens to the extent of several miles with wide and fertile bottom lands." Lewis ⇨
S 12 W 2.5 MILES
S 55 W 1.5 MILES
2815
2814
2813
2812
S 15 E 1 MILE
BIG
Cedar Hill
Clark's Route July 24, 1805
"... approached the horse found him fat and verry wild we could not get near him, we changed our Derection to the river for water..." Clark ⇨
2811
MISSOURI
RIVER
"Howards Creek"
Gallatin Co.
Broadwater Co.
Sixteenmile Creek
LOMBARD
N 65 E 1 MILE
Cliff of Rocks
S 65 E 1 MILE
2810
"... a Clift of rocks in a Lard. bend; opst. to which we encamped for the night under a high bluff" Lewis ⇨
Big Spring
Large Springs
SOUTH 1/2 MILE
N 45 W 1/4 MILE
Cartographer's Note: The traverse calls do not work well in this curve. The cartographer believes that there is probably one call missing.
Toston Dam
2807
Camp July 25, 1805
2809
1/2 MILE
MISSOURI
S 55 W
2808
S 30 E 1/2 MILE
High Cliffs
Rapid
BELT
"... current strong with frequent riffles; ..." Lewis ⇨
Nine Small Islands
S 60 W 1 MILE
Devils Bottom
THE BUTTES
Toston
Canal
2806
S 55 E 1 MILE
Rapid
Clark's Route July 24, 1805
"two rapids near the large springs we passed this evening were the worst we have seen since that we passed on entering the rocky Mountain; ..." Lewis ⇨
Tree
2805
S 75 E 1.5 MILES
Clark's Route July 24, 1805
"here the river again enters the mountains, I believe it to be a second grand chain of the rocky Mots." Lewis ⇨
2804
Bluff Point
Cartographer's Note: Ordway's journal reveals very little about the location of the July 14, 1806, Return Camp. The cartographer has made an educated guess based on estimations of the travel speed of Ordway's return party, as well as the navigation difficulties which they had to contend with to reach this point.
Broadwater
Clark's Route July 24, 1805
Willow Swamp Creek
2803
MOUNTAINS
Return Camp (Ordway's Group) July 14, 1806
"... in the evening as the wind fell we mooved down the R. to a bottom and Camped." Ordway ⇦
Missouri
Warm Springs Creek
SOUTH 3 MILES
2802
"we killed a couple of young gees which are very abundant and fine; but as they are but small game to subsist a party on of our strength I have forbid the men shooting at them as it waists a considerable quantity of amunition and delays our progress." Lewis ⇨
Broadwater Missouri Canal
Big Springs
TOSTON
ONE STATUTE MILE
"25 yds."
Outbound: July 24-26, 1805
Canoe Party Return: July 14, 15, 1806
Canal
Marsh Creek
Modern Data: 1986
EXPLORATIONS OF LEWIS AND CLARK 1804 - 1806
CARTOGRAPHIC RECONSTRUCTION
HOWARDS CREEK
UTM ZONE 12
MAP NUMBER 253
Montana
CONTOUR INTERVAL 200 FEET WITH SUPPLEMENTS

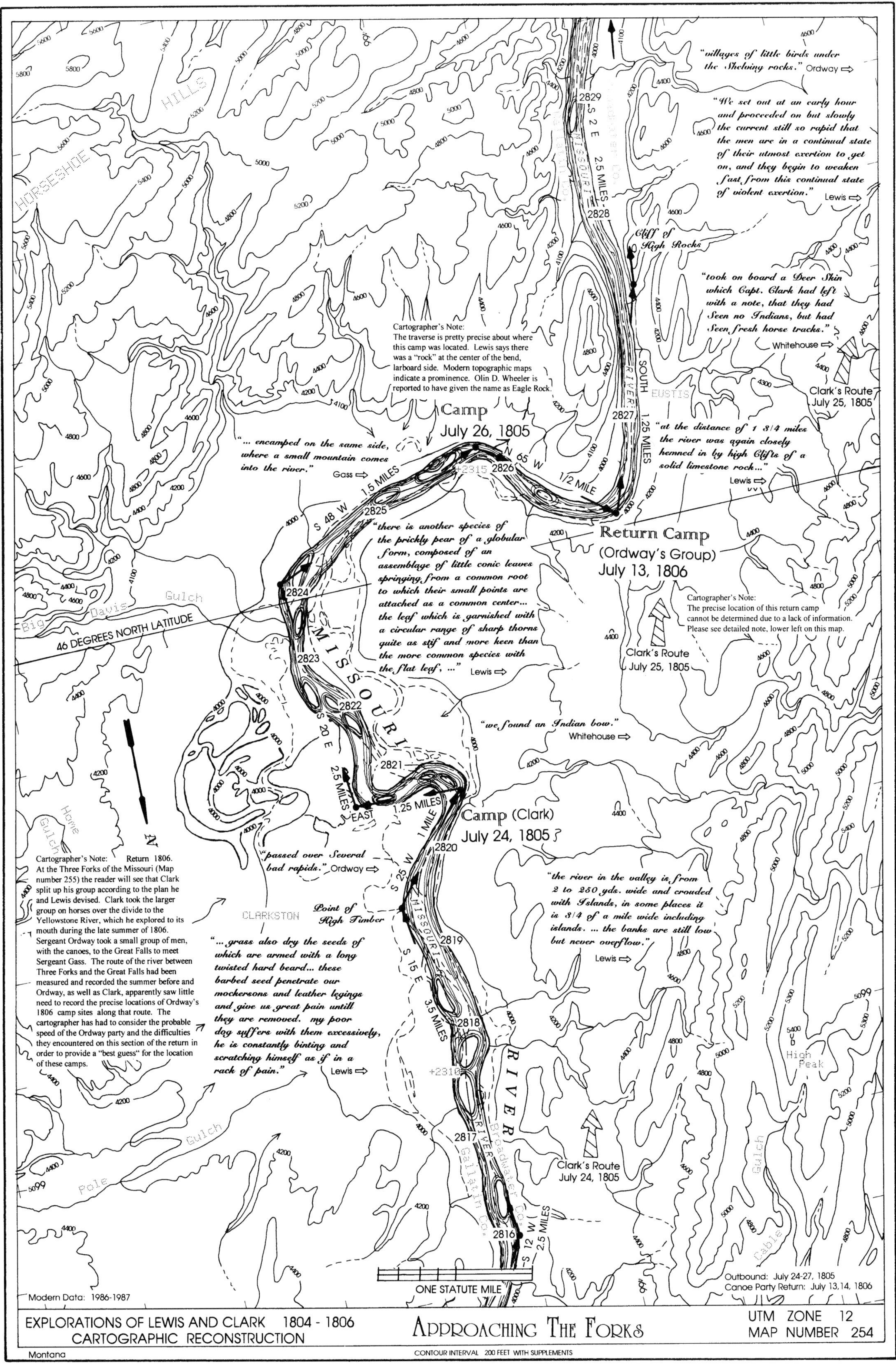

"villages of little birds under the Shelving rocks." Ordway ⇨
"We set out at an early hour and proceeded on but slowly the current still so rapid that the men are in a continual state of their utmost exertion to get on, and they begin to weaken fast from this continual state of violent exertion." Lewis ⇨
Cliff of High Rocks
"took on board a Deer Skin which Capt. Clark had left with a note, that they had Seen no Indians, but had Seen fresh horse tracks." Whitehouse ⇨
Clark's Route July 25, 1805
Cartographer's Note:
The traverse is pretty precise about where this camp was located. Lewis says there was a "rock" at the center of the bend, larboard side. Modern topographic maps indicate a prominence. Olin D. Wheeler is reported to have given the name as Eagle Rock.
Camp
July 26, 1805
"... encamped on the same side, where a small mountain comes into the river." Gass ⇨
"at the distance of 1 3/4 miles the river was again closely hemmed in by high Cliffs of a solid limestone rock..." Lewis ⇨
HORSESHOE HILLS
MISSOURI
S 2 E 2.5 MILES
SOUTH RIVER
EUSTIS
1.25 MILES
N 65 W
1/2 MILE
1.5 MILES
S 48 W
"there is another species of the prickly pear of a globular form, composed of an assemblage of little conic leaves springing from a common root to which their small points are attached as a common center... the leaf which is garnished with a circular range of sharp thorns quite as stif and more keen than the more common species with the flat leaf, ..." Lewis ⇨
Return Camp
(Ordway's Group)
July 13, 1806
Cartographer's Note:
The precise location of this return camp cannot be determined due to a lack of information. Please see detailed note, lower left on this map.
Clark's Route
July 25, 1805
Big Davis Gulch
46 DEGREES NORTH LATITUDE
MISSOURI
"we found an Indian bow." Whitehouse ⇨
S 20 E
2.5 MILES
EAST
1.25 MILES
1 MILE
Camp (Clark)
July 24, 1805
Home Gulch
N
Cartographer's Note: Return 1806.
At the Three Forks of the Missouri (Map number 255) the reader will see that Clark split up his group according to the plan he and Lewis devised. Clark took the larger group on horses over the divide to the Yellowstone River, which he explored to its mouth during the late summer of 1806. Sergeant Ordway took a small group of men, with the canoes, to the Great Falls to meet Sergeant Gass. The route of the river between Three Forks and the Great Falls had been measured and recorded the summer before and Ordway, as well as Clark, apparently saw little need to record the precise locations of Ordway's 1806 camp sites along that route. The cartographer has had to consider the probable speed of the Ordway party and the difficulties they encountered on this section of the return in order to provide a "best guess" for the location of these camps.
"passed over Several bad rapids." Ordway ⇨
S 25 W
CLARKSTON
Point of High Timber
"the river in the valley is from 2 to 250 yds. wide and crouded with Islands, in some places it is 3/4 of a mile wide including islands. ... the banks are still low but never overflow." Lewis ⇨
"... grass also dry the seeds of which are armed with a long twisted hard beard... these barbed seed penetrate our mockersons and leather legings and give us great pain untill they are removed. my poor dog suffers with them excessively, he is constantly binting and scratching himself as if in a rack of pain." Lewis ⇨
S 15 E
3.5 MILES
RIVER
High Peak
Pole Gulch
Clark's Route
July 24, 1805
Broadwater Co.
Gallatin Co.
S 12 W
2.5 MILES
Cable Gulch
ONE STATUTE MILE
Modern Data: 1986-1987
Outbound: July 24-27, 1805
Canoe Party Return: July 13,14, 1806
EXPLORATIONS OF LEWIS AND CLARK 1804 - 1806
CARTOGRAPHIC RECONSTRUCTION
APPROACHING THE FORKS
UTM ZONE 12
MAP NUMBER 254
Montana
CONTOUR INTERVAL 200 FEET WITH SUPPLEMENTS

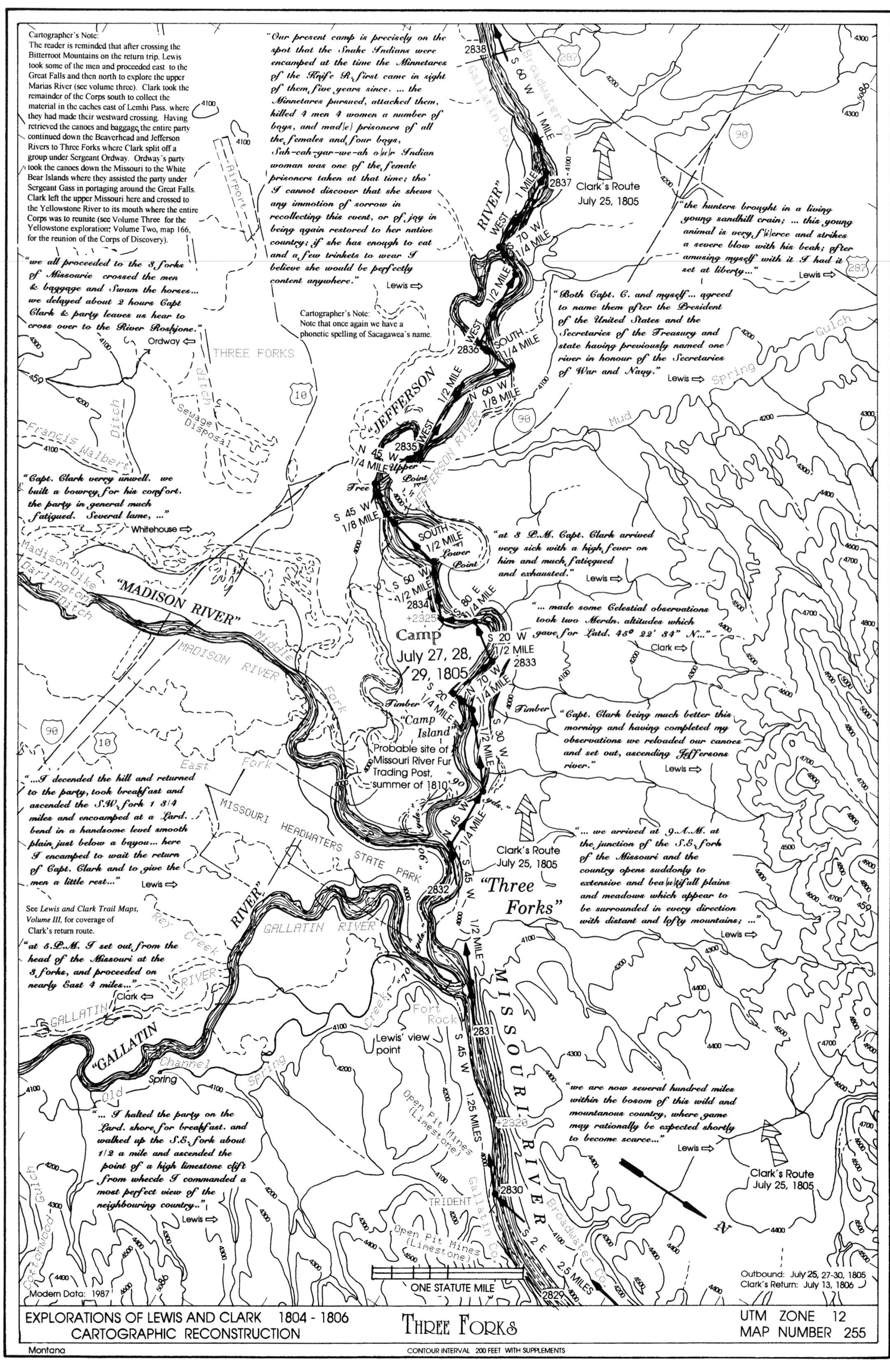
Cartographer's Note:
The reader is reminded that after crossing the Bitterroot Mountains on the return trip, Lewis took some of the men and proceeded east to the Great Falls and then north to explore the upper Marias River (see volume three). Clark took the remainder of the Corps south to collect the material in the caches east of Lemhi Pass, where they had made their westward crossing. Having retrieved the canoes and baggage the entire party continued down the Beaverhead and Jefferson Rivers to Three Forks where Clark split off a group under Sergeant Ordway. Ordway's party took the canoes down the Missouri to the White Bear Islands where they assisted the party under Sergeant Gass in portaging around the Great Falls. Clark left the upper Missouri here and crossed to the Yellowstone River to its mouth where the entire Corps was to reunite (see Volume Three for the Yellowstone exploration; Volume Two, map 166, for the reunion of the Corps of Discovery).
"Our present camp is precisely on the spot that the Snake Indians were encamped at the time the Minnetares of the Knife R. first came in sight of them five years since. ... the Minnetares pursued, attacked them, killed 4 men 4 women a number of boys, and mad[e] prisoners of all the females and four boys, Sah-cah-gar-we-ah o[u]r Indian woman was one of the female prisoners taken at that time; tho' I cannot discover that she shews any immotion of sorrow in recollecting this event, or of joy in being again restored to her native country; if she has enough to eat and a few trinkets to wear I believe she would be perfectly content anywhere."
Lewis ⇨
Cartographer's Note:
Note that once again we have a phonetic spelling of Sacagawea's name.
"we all proceeded to the 3 forks of Missourie crossed the men & baggage and Swam the horses... we delayed about 2 hours Capt Clark & party leaves us hear to cross over to the River Roshjone."
Ordway ⇦
"the hunters brought in a living young sandhill crain; ... this young animal is very f[i]erce and strikes a severe blow with his beak; after amusing myself with it I had it set at liberty..."
Lewis ⇨
"Both Capt. C. and myself... agreed to name them after the President of the United States and the Secretaries of the Treasury and state having previously named one river in honour of the Secretaries of War and Navy."
Lewis ⇨
Clark's Route
July 25, 1805
"Capt. Clark very unwell. we built a bowrey for his comfort. the party in general much fatigued. Several lame, ..."
Whitehouse ⇨
"at 3 P.M. Capt. Clark arrived very sick with a high fever on him and much fatiegued and exhausted."
Lewis ⇨
"... made some Celestial observations took two Merdn. altitudes which gave for Latd. 45° 22' 34" N..."
Clark ⇨
"JEFFERSON
RIVER"
"MADISON RIVER"
Camp
July 27, 28, 29, 1805
"Camp Island"
Probable site of Missouri River Fur Trading Post, summer of 1810
"Capt. Clark being much better this morning and having completed my observations we reloaded our canoes and set out, ascending Jeffersons river."
Lewis ⇨
"...I decended the hill and returned to the party, took breakfast and ascended the S.W. fork 1 3/4 miles and encoamped at a Lard. bend in a handsome level smooth plain just below a bayou... here I encamped to wait the return of Capt. Clark and to give the men a little rest..."
Lewis ⇨
"... we arrived at 9 A.M. at the junction of the S.E. fork of the Missouri and the country opens suddenly to extensive and bea[u]tifull plains and meadows which appear to be surrounded in every direction with distant and lofty mountains; ..."
Lewis ⇨
Clark's Route
July 25, 1805
"Three Forks"
MISSOURI HEADWATERS STATE PARK
See Lewis and Clark Trail Maps, Volume III, for coverage of Clark's return route.
"at 5 P.M. I set out from the head of the Missouri at the 3 forks, and proceeded on nearly East 4 miles..."
Clark ⇦
"GALLATIN
RIVER"
MISSOURI RIVER
"we are now several hundred miles within the bosom of this wild and mountanous country, where game may rationally be expected shortly to become scarce..."
Lewis ⇨
Lewis' view point
"... I halted the party on the Lard. shore for breakfast. and walked up the S.E. fork about 1/2 a mile and ascended the point of a high limestone clift from whence I commanded a most perfect view of the neighbouring country.."
Lewis ⇨
Clark's Route
July 25, 1805
THREE FORKS
TRIDENT
Gallatin Co.
Broadwater Co.
ONE STATUTE MILE
Modern Data: 1987
Outbound: July 25, 27-30, 1805
Clark's Return: July 13, 1806
EXPLORATIONS OF LEWIS AND CLARK 1804 - 1806
CARTOGRAPHIC RECONSTRUCTION
THREE FORKS
UTM ZONE 12
MAP NUMBER 255
Montana
CONTOUR INTERVAL 200 FEET WITH SUPPLEMENTS

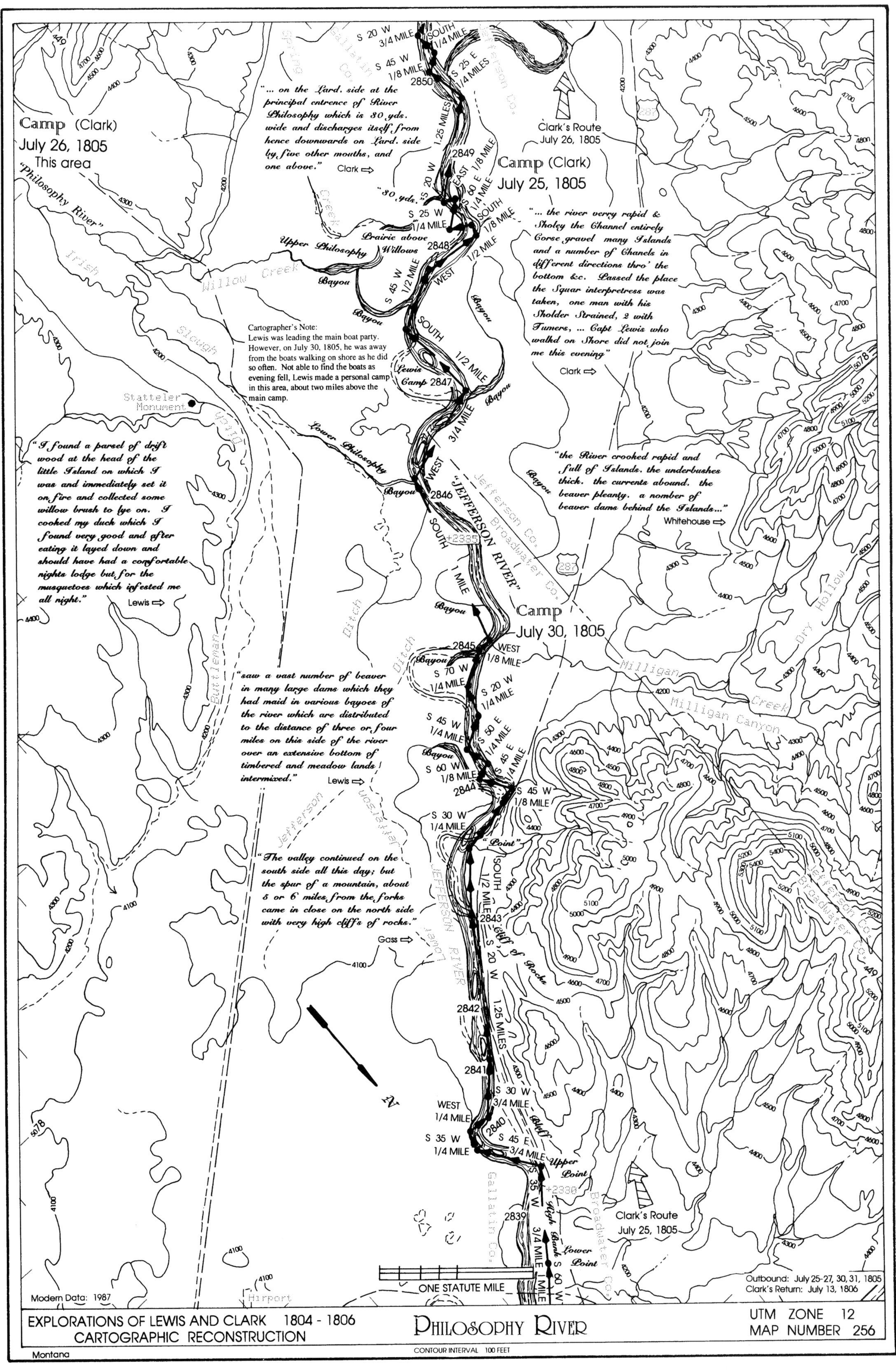

Camp (Clark)
July 26, 1805
This area
"Philosophy River"
"... on the Lard. side at the principal entrence of River Philosophy which is 30 yds. wide and discharges itself from hence downwards on Lard. side by five other mouths, and one above."
Clark ⇨
"30 yds."
Clark's Route
July 26, 1805
Camp (Clark)
July 25, 1805
"... the river verry rapid & Sholey the Channel entirely Corse gravel many Islands and a number of Chanels in different directions thro' the bottom &c. Passed the place the Squar interpretress was taken, one man with his Sholder Strained, 2 with Tumers, ... Capt Lewis who walkd on Shore did not join me this evening"
Clark ⇨
Prairie above Willows
Upper Philosophy
Bayou
Willow Creek
Irish
Slough
Spring Creek
Gallatin Co.
Jefferson Co.
287
Cartographer's Note:
Lewis was leading the main boat party. However, on July 30, 1805, he was away from the boats walking on shore as he did so often. Not able to find the boats as evening fell, Lewis made a personal camp in this area, about two miles above the main camp.
Lewis Camp 2847
Statteler Monument
Lower Philosophy
Bayou
"I found a parsel of drift wood at the head of the little Island on which I was and immediately set it on fire and collected some willow brush to lye on. I cooked my duck which I found very good and after eating it layed down and should have had a comfortable nights lodge but for the musquetoes which infested me all night."
Lewis ⇨
"the River crooked rapid and full of Islands. the underbushes thick. the currents abound. the beaver pleanty. a nomber of beaver dams behind the Islands..."
Whitehouse ⇨
"JEFFERSON RIVER"
Jefferson Co.
Broadwater Co.
Camp
July 30, 1805
Milligan Creek
Milligan Canyon
Dry Hollow
Ditch
Buttleman
"saw a vast number of beaver in many large dams which they had maid in various bayoes of the river which are distributed to the distance of three or four miles on this side of the river over an extensive bottom of timbered and meadow lands intermixed."
Lewis ⇨
Jefferson
"Point"
"The valley continued on the south side all this day; but the spur of a mountain, about 5 or 6 miles from the forks came in close on the north side with very high cliffs of rocks."
Gass ⇨
JEFFERSON RIVER
Cliff of Rocks
Bluff
Upper Point
High Bank
Lower Point
Clark's Route
July 25, 1805
Gallatin Co.
Broadwater Co.
Jefferson Co.
Broadwater Co.
2850
2849
2848
2846
2845
2844
2843
2842
2841
2840
2839
+2335
+2330
S 20 W 3/4 MILE
SOUTH 1/4 MILE
S 45 W 1/8 MILE
S 25 E 1/4 MILES
1.25 MILES
S 20 W
EAST 1/8 MILE
S 60 E 1/4 MILE
SOUTH 1/8 MILE
S 25 W 1/4 MILE
1/2 MILE
S 45 W 1/2 MILE
WEST
SOUTH
1/2 MILE
3/4 MILE
WEST
SOUTH
1 MILE
WEST 1/8 MILE
S 70 W 1/4 MILE
S 20 W 1/4 MILE
S 45 W 1/4 MILE
S 50 E 1/4 MILE
S 45 E 1/4 MILE
S 60 W 1/8 MILE
S 45 W 1/8 MILE
S 30 W 1/4 MILE
SOUTH 1/2 MILE
S 20 W
1.25 MILES
S 30 W 3/4 MILE
WEST 1/4 MILE
S 35 W 1/4 MILE
S 45 E 3/4 MILE
S 35 W
3/4 MILE
S 60 W 1 MILE
N
ONE STATUTE MILE
Airport
Modern Data: 1987
Outbound: July 25-27, 30, 31, 1805
Clark's Return: July 13, 1806
EXPLORATIONS OF LEWIS AND CLARK 1804 - 1806
CARTOGRAPHIC RECONSTRUCTION
PHILOSOPHY RIVER
UTM ZONE 12
MAP NUMBER 256
Montana
CONTOUR INTERVAL 100 FEET

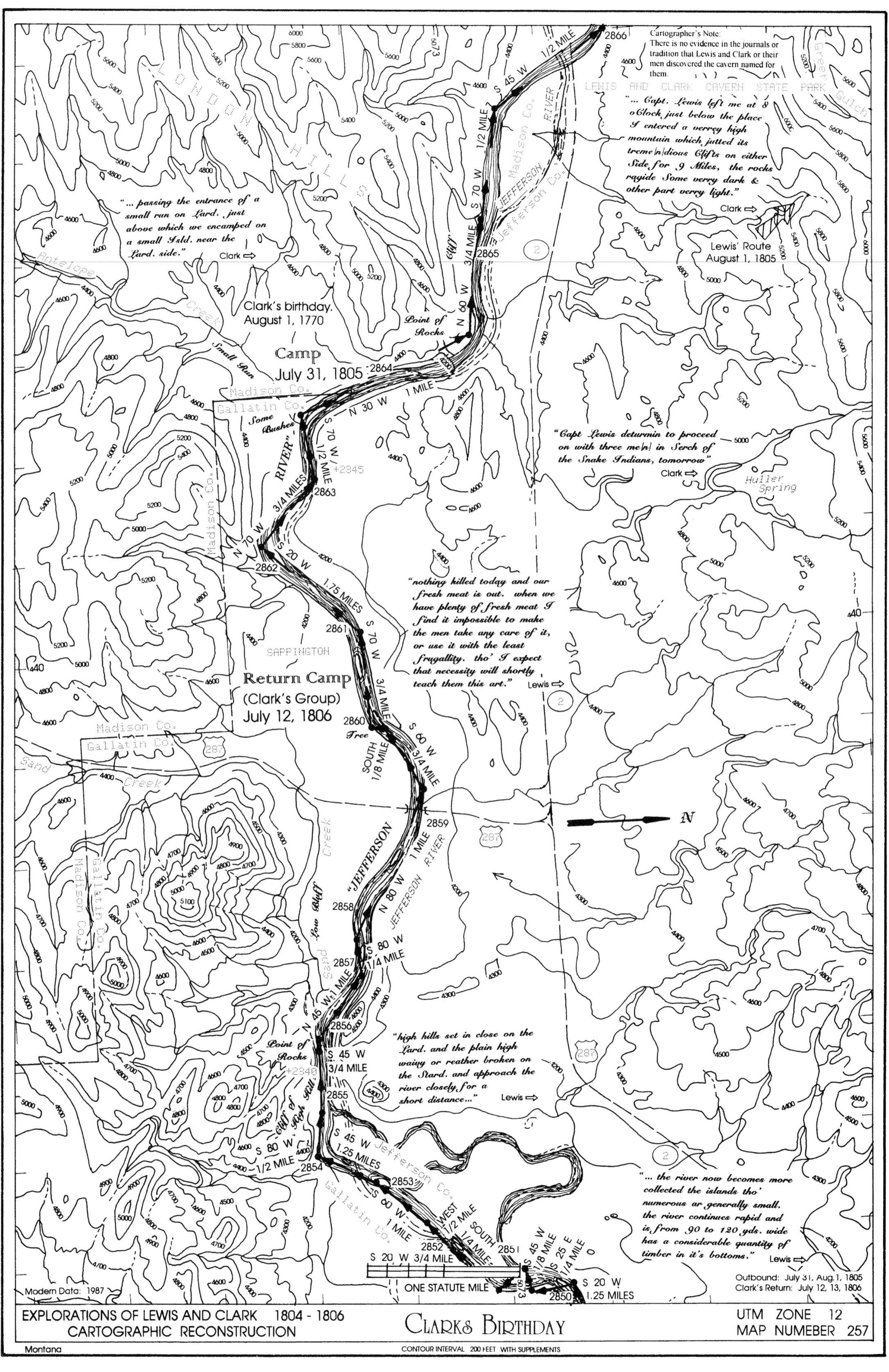

Cartographer's Note:
There is no evidence in the journals or tradition that Lewis and Clark or their men discovered the cavern named for them.
LEWIS AND CLARK CAVERN STATE PARK
"... Capt. Lewis left me at 8 oClock just below the place I entered a verrey high mountain which jutted its treme[n]dious Clifts on either Side for 9 Miles, the rocks rayide Some verry dark & other part verry light."
Clark
Lewis' Route
August 1, 1805
"... passing the entrance of a small run on Lard. just above which we encamped on a small Isld. near the Lard. side."
Clark
LONDON HILLS
Antelope Creek
Small Run
Clark's birthday.
August 1, 1770
Point of Rocks
Cliff
Camp
July 31, 1805
Some Bushes
"RIVER"
JEFFERSON RIVER
Madison Co.
Jefferson Co.
Gallatin Co.
"Capt Lewis deturmin to proceed on with three me[n] in Serch of the Snake Indians, tomorrow"
Clark
Huller Spring
"nothing killed today and our fresh meat is out. when we have plenty of fresh meat I find it impossible to make the men take any care of it, or use it with the least frugallity. tho' I expect that necessity will shortly teach them this art."
Lewis
SAPPINGTON
Return Camp
(Clark's Group)
July 12, 1806
Tree
Sand Creek
"JEFFERSON"
Low Bluff
Point of Rocks
Cliff of High Hill
N
"high hills set in close on the Lard. and the plain high waivy or reather broken on the Stard. and approach the river closely for a short distance..."
Lewis
"... the river now becomes more collected the islands tho' numerous ar generally small. the river continues rapid and is from 90 to 120 yds. wide has a considerable quantity of timber in it's bottoms."
Lewis
ONE STATUTE MILE
Outbound: July 31, Aug. 1, 1805
Clark's Return: July 12, 13, 1806
Modern Data: 1987
EXPLORATIONS OF LEWIS AND CLARK 1804 - 1806
CARTOGRAPHIC RECONSTRUCTION
CLARKS BIRTHDAY
UTM ZONE 12
MAP NUMEBER 257
Montana
CONTOUR INTERVAL 200 FEET WITH SUPPLEMENTS

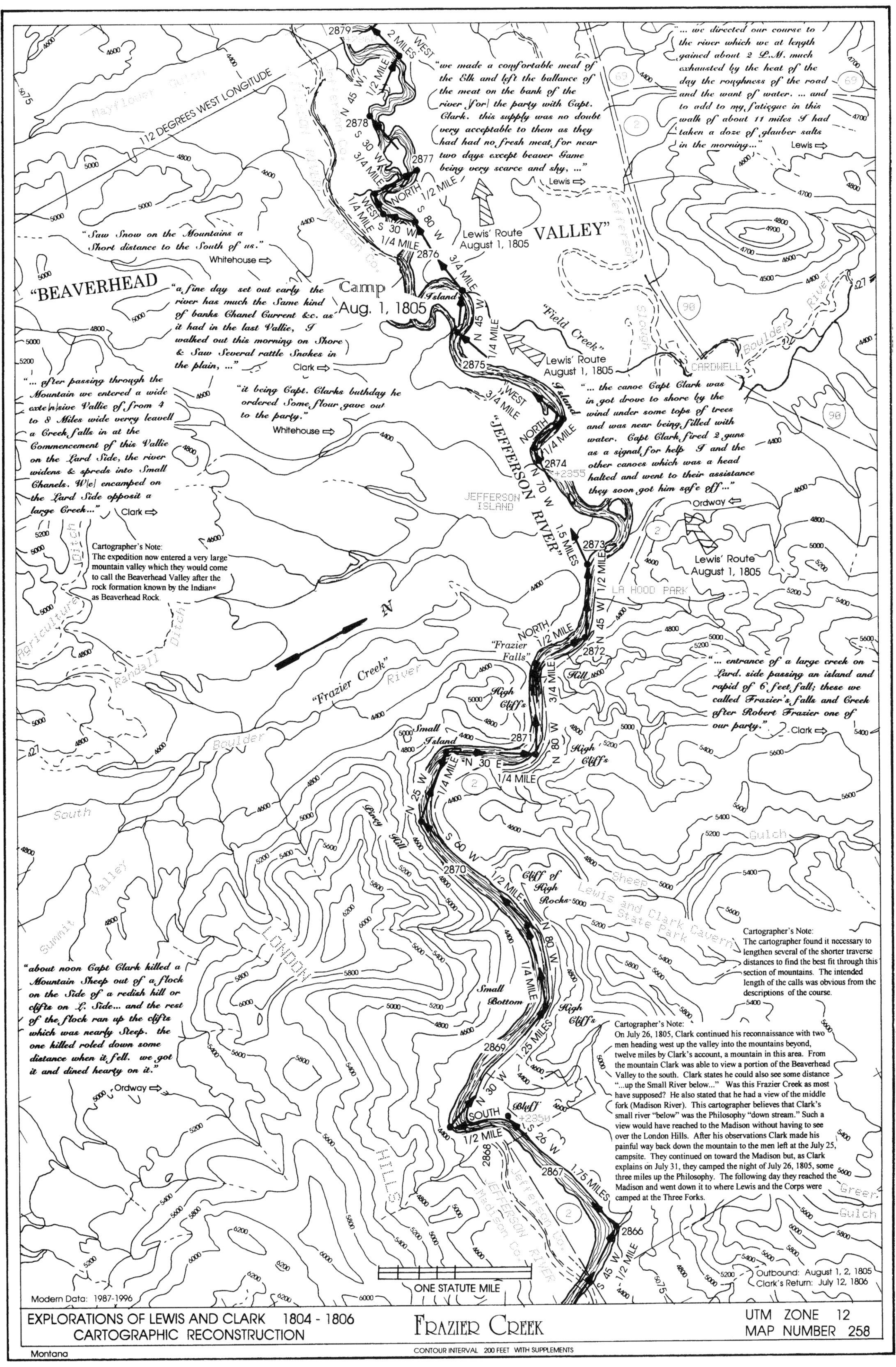
"we made a confortable meal of the Elk and left the ballance of the meat on the bank of the river [for] the party with Capt. Clark. this supply was no doubt very acceptable to them as they had had no fresh meat for near two days except beaver Game being very scarce and shy, ..."
Lewis ⇨
"... we directed our course to the river which we at length gained about 2 P.M. much exhausted by the heat of the day the roughness of the road and the want of water. ... and to add to my fatigue in this walk of about 11 miles I had taken a doze of glauber salts in the morning..."
Lewis ⇨
112 DEGREES WEST LONGITUDE
"Saw Snow on the Mountains a Short distance to the South of us."
Whitehouse ⇨
Lewis' Route August 1, 1805
VALLEY"
"BEAVERHEAD
"a fine day set out early the river has much the Same kind of banks Chanel Current &c. as it had in the last Vallie, I walked out this morning on Shore & Saw Several rattle Snokes in the plain, ..."
Clark ⇨
Camp Aug. 1, 1805
"Field Creek"
Lewis' Route August 1, 1805
"... after passing through the Mountain we entered a wide exte[n]sive Vallie of from 4 to 8 Miles wide verry leavell a Creek falls in at the Commencement of this Vallie on the Lard Side, the river widens & spreds into Small Chanels. W[e] encamped on the Lard Side opposit a large Creek..."
Clark ⇨
"it being Capt. Clarks buthday he ordered Some flour gave out to the party."
Whitehouse ⇨
"... the canoe Capt Clark was in got drove to shore by the wind under some tops of trees and was near being filled with water. Capt Clark fired 2 guns as a signal for help I and the other canoes which was a head halted and went to their assistance they soon got him safe off..."
Ordway ⇦
"JEFFERSON RIVER"
JEFFERSON ISLAND
CARDWELL
LA HOOD PARK
Lewis' Route August 1, 1805
Cartographer's Note:
The expedition now entered a very large mountain valley which they would come to call the Beaverhead Valley after the rock formation known by the Indians as Beaverhead Rock.
N
"Frazier Falls"
"Frazier Creek"
"... entrance of a large creek on Lard. side passing an island and rapid of 6 feet fall; these we called Frazier's falls and Creek after Robert Frazier one of our party."
Clark ⇨
High Cliffs
Small Island
Cliff of High Rocks
Lewis and Clark Cavern State Park
LONDON HILLS
Cartographer's Note:
The cartographer found it necessary to lengthen several of the shorter traverse distances to find the best fit through this section of mountains. The intended length of the calls was obvious from the descriptions of the course.
"about noon Capt Clark killed a Mountain Sheep out of a flock on the Side of a redish hill or clifts on L. Side... and the rest of the flock ran up the clifts which was nearly Steep. the one killed roled down some distance when it fell. we got it and dined hearty on it."
Ordway ⇨
Small Bottom
Bluff
Cartographer's Note:
On July 26, 1805, Clark continued his reconnaissance with two men heading west up the valley into the mountains beyond, twelve miles by Clark's account, a mountain in this area. From the mountain Clark was able to view a portion of the Beaverhead Valley to the south. Clark states he could also see some distance "...up the Small River below..." Was this Frazier Creek as most have supposed? He also stated that he had a view of the middle fork (Madison River). This cartographer believes that Clark's small river "below" was the Philosophy "down stream." Such a view would have reached to the Madison without having to see over the London Hills. After his observations Clark made his painful way back down the mountain to the men left at the July 25, campsite. They continued on toward the Madison but, as Clark explains on July 31, they camped the night of July 26, 1805, some three miles up the Philosophy. The following day they reached the Madison and went down it to where Lewis and the Corps were camped at the Three Forks.
ONE STATUTE MILE
Outbound: August 1, 2, 1805
Clark's Return: July 12, 1806
Modern Data: 1987-1996
EXPLORATIONS OF LEWIS AND CLARK 1804 - 1806
CARTOGRAPHIC RECONSTRUCTION
FRAZIER CREEK
UTM ZONE 12
MAP NUMBER 258
Montana
CONTOUR INTERVAL 200 FEET WITH SUPPLEMENTS

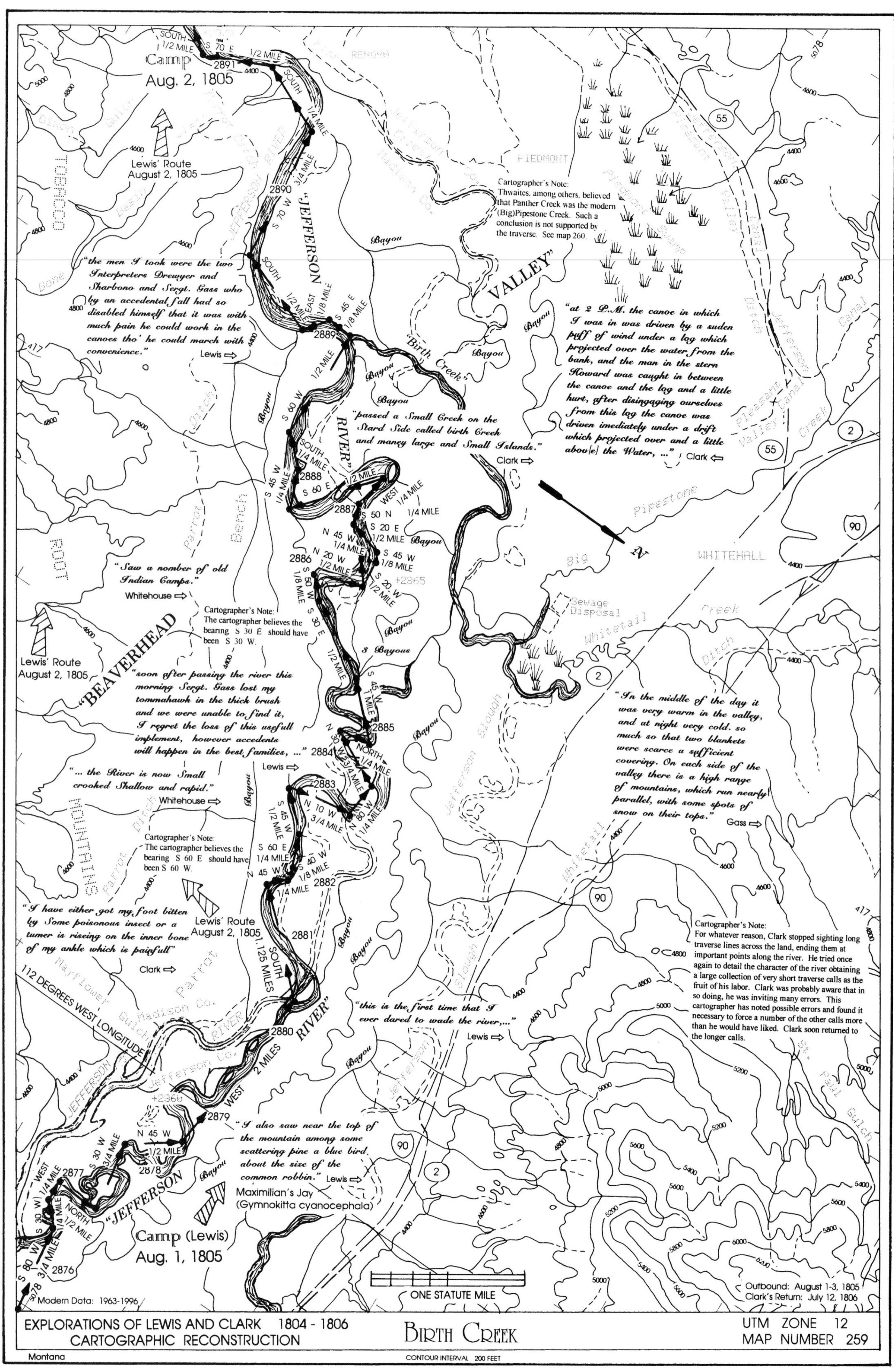
Camp
Aug. 2, 1805
Lewis' Route
August 2, 1805
"JEFFERSON
VALLEY"
Cartographer's Note:
Thwaites, among others, believed that Panther Creek was the modern (Big)Pipestone Creek. Such a conclusion is not supported by the traverse. See map 260.
"the men I took were the two Interpreters Drewyer and Sharbono and Sergt. Gass who by an accedental fall had so disabled himself that it was with much pain he could work in the canoes tho' he could march with convenience."
Lewis ⇨
"at 2 P.M. the canoe in which I was in was driven by a suden puff of wind under a log which projected over the water from the bank, and the man in the stern Howard was caught in between the canoe and the log and a little hurt, after disingaging ourselves from this log the canoe was driven imediately under a drift which projected over and a little abov[e] the Water, ..."
Clark ⇦
"Birth Creek"
"passed a Small Creek on the Stard Side called birth Creek and maney large and Small Islands."
Clark ⇨
RIVER"
"Saw a nomber of old Indian Camps."
Whitehouse ⇨
Cartographer's Note:
The cartographer believes the bearing S 30 E should have been S 30 W.
Lewis' Route
August 2, 1805
"BEAVERHEAD
"soon after passing the river this morning Sergt. Gass lost my tommahawk in the thick brush and we were unable to find it, I regret the loss of this usefull implement, however accedents will happen in the best families, ..."
Lewis ⇨
"... the River is now Small crooked Shallow and rapid."
Whitehouse ⇨
MOUNTAINS
Cartographer's Note:
The cartographer believes the bearing S 60 E should have been S 60 W.
"In the middle of the day it was very warm in the valley, and at night very cold. so much so that two blankets were scarce a sufficient covering. On each side of the valley there is a high range of mountains, which run nearly parallel, with some spots of snow on their tops."
Gass ⇨
"I have either got my foot bitten by Some poisonous insect or a tumer is riseing on the inner bone of my ankle which is painfull"
Clark ⇨
Lewis' Route
August 2, 1805
Cartographer's Note:
For whatever reason, Clark stopped sighting long traverse lines across the land, ending them at important points along the river. He tried once again to detail the character of the river obtaining a large collection of very short traverse calls as the fruit of his labor. Clark was probably aware that in so doing, he was inviting many errors. This cartographer has noted possible errors and found it necessary to force a number of the other calls more than he would have liked. Clark soon returned to the longer calls.
112 DEGREES WEST LONGITUDE
"this is the first time that I ever dared to wade the river,..."
Lewis ⇨
"I also saw near the top of the mountain among some scattering pine a blue bird, about the size of the common robbin."
Lewis ⇨
Maximilian's Jay
(Gymnokitta cyanocephala)
"JEFFERSON
Camp (Lewis)
Aug. 1, 1805
Modern Data: 1963-1996
ONE STATUTE MILE
Outbound: August 1-3, 1805
Clark's Return: July 12, 1806
EXPLORATIONS OF LEWIS AND CLARK 1804 - 1806
CARTOGRAPHIC RECONSTRUCTION
BIRTH CREEK
UTM ZONE 12
MAP NUMBER 259
Montana
CONTOUR INTERVAL 200 FEET

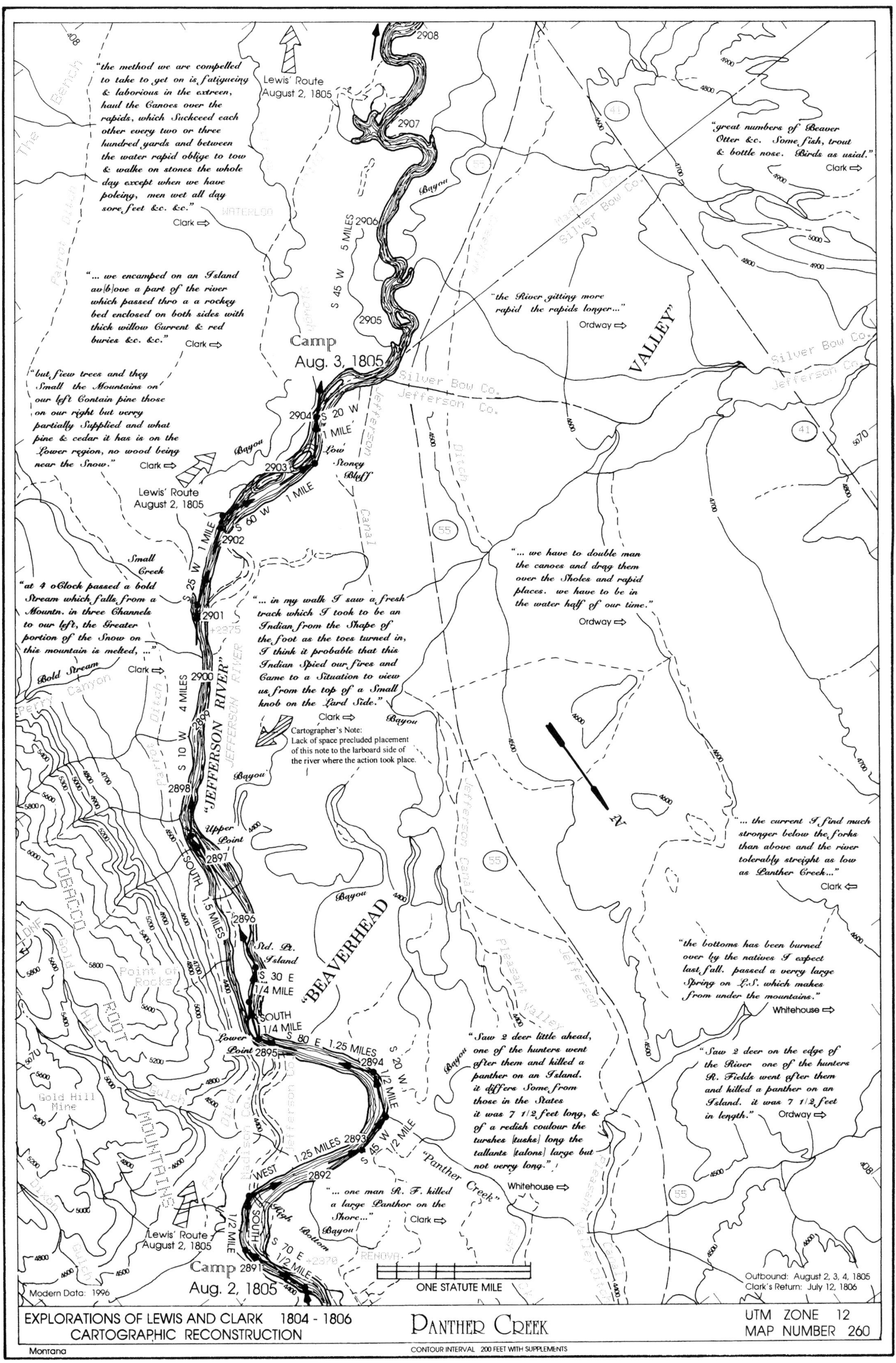
"the method we are compelled to take to get on is fatigueing & laborious in the extreen, haul the Canoes over the rapids, which Suckceed each other every two or three hundred yards and between the water rapid oblige to tow & walke on stones the whole day except when we have poleing, men wet all day sore feet &c. &c."
Clark ⇨
Lewis' Route August 2, 1805
"great numbers of Beaver Otter &c. Some fish, trout & bottle nose. Birds as usial."
Clark ⇨
"... we encamped on an Island av[b]ove a part of the river which passed thro a a rockey bed enclosed on both sides with thick willow Current & red buries &c. &c."
Clark ⇨
"the River gitting more rapid the rapids longer..."
Ordway ⇨
Camp
Aug. 3, 1805
"but fiew trees and they Small the Mountains on our left Contain pine those on our right but verry partially Supplied and what pine & cedar it has is on the Lower region, no wood being near the Snow."
Clark ⇨
Lewis' Route August 2, 1805
"VALLEY"
Silver Bow Co.
Jefferson Co.
Madison Co.
Low Stoney Bluff
Bayou
S 45 W 5 MILES
S 20 W 1 MILE
S 60 W 1 MILE
S 25 W 1 MILE
Small Creek
"at 4 oClock passed a bold Stream which falls from a Mountn. in three Channels to our left, the Greater portion of the Snow on this mountain is melted, ..."
Clark ⇨
"... in my walk I saw a fresh track which I took to be an Indian from the Shape of the foot as the toes turned in, I think it probable that this Indian Spied our fires and Came to a Situation to view us from the top of a Small knob on the Lard Side."
Clark ⇨
"... we have to double man the canoes and drag them over the Sholes and rapid places. we have to be in the water half of our time."
Ordway ⇨
Bold Stream
Perry Canyon
S 10 W 4 MILES
"JEFFERSON RIVER"
Cartographer's Note:
Lack of space precluded placement of this note to the larboard side of the river where the action took place.
"... the current I find much stronger below the forks than above and the river tolerably streight as low as Panther Creek..."
Clark ⇦
N
Upper Point
SOUTH 1.5 MILES
Std. Pt. Island
S 30 E 1/4 MILE
SOUTH 1/4 MILE
"BEAVERHEAD
TOBACCO ROOT MOUNTAINS
Gold Hill
Point of Rocks
Gold Hill Mine
Pleasant Valley
"the bottoms has been burned over by the natives I expect last fall. passed a very large Spring on L.S. which makes from under the mountains."
Whitehouse ⇨
Lower Point
S 80 E 1.25 MILES
S 20 W 1/2 MILE
S 45 W 1/2 MILE
WEST 1.25 MILES
"Saw 2 deer little ahead, one of the hunters went after them and killed a panther on an Island. it differs Some from those in the States it was 7 1/2 feet long, & of a redish coulour the turshes [tusks] long the tallants [talons] large but not verry long."
Whitehouse ⇨
"Saw 2 deer on the edge of the River one of the hunters R. Fields went after them and killed a panther on an Island. it was 7 1/2 feet in length."
Ordway ⇨
"Panther Creek"
"... one man R. F. killed a large Panthor on the Shore..."
Clark ⇨
High Bottom
SOUTH 1/2 MILE
S 70 E 1/2 MILE
Lewis' Route August 2, 1805
Camp
Aug. 2, 1805
ONE STATUTE MILE
Modern Data: 1996
Outbound: August 2, 3, 4, 1805
Clark's Return: July 12, 1806
EXPLORATIONS OF LEWIS AND CLARK 1804 - 1806
CARTOGRAPHIC RECONSTRUCTION
PANTHER CREEK
UTM ZONE 12
MAP NUMBER 260
Montana
CONTOUR INTERVAL 200 FEET WITH SUPPLEMENTS

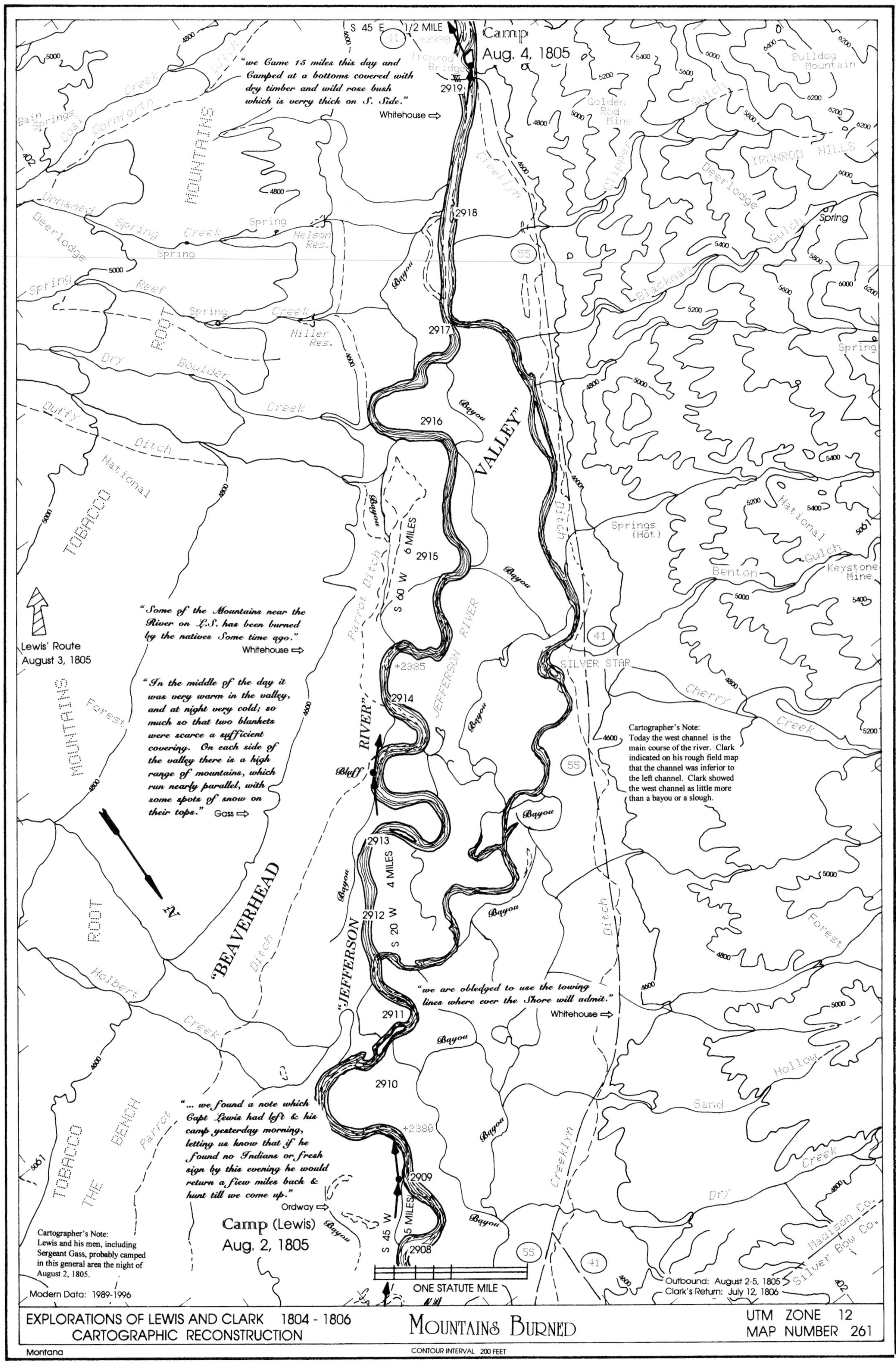

Camp
Aug. 4, 1805
"we Came 15 miles this day and Camped at a bottoms covered with dry timber and wild rose bush which is very thick on S. Side."
Whitehouse
S 45 E 1/2 MILE
Ironrod Bridge
Bulldog Mountain
Golden Rod Mine
IRONROD HILLS
Coal Cornforth Creek Ditch
Bain Springs
ROOT MOUNTAINS
Unnamed
Deerlodge
Spring Creek
Nelson Res.
Reef Spring Creek
Miller Res.
Dry Boulder Creek
Duffy Ditch
Clipper
Deerlodge Gulch
Blackman
Creeklyn
Spring
Bayou
VALLEY"
National Forest
TOBACCO ROOT MOUNTAINS
S 60 W 6 MILES
Parrot Ditch
Springs (Hot)
Benton
Keystone Mine
National Gulch
Lewis' Route
August 3, 1805
"Some of the Mountains near the River on L.S. has been burned by the natives Some time ago."
Whitehouse
"In the middle of the day it was very warm in the valley, and at night very cold; so much so that two blankets were scarce a sufficient covering. On each side of the valley there is a high range of mountains, which run nearly parallel, with some spots of snow on their tops."
Gass
JEFFERSON RIVER
SILVER STAR
Cherry Creek
Cartographer's Note:
Today the west channel is the main course of the river. Clark indicated on his rough field map that the channel was inferior to the left channel. Clark showed the west channel as little more than a bayou or a slough.
Bluff
"JEFFERSON RIVER"
"BEAVERHEAD
S 20 W 4 MILES
Holbert Creek
Ditch
"we are obledged to use the towing lines where ever the Shore will admit."
Whitehouse
Hollow
Sand
Dry Creek
TOBACCO ROOT
THE BENCH
Parrot
"... we found a note which Capt Lewis had left & his camp yesterday morning, letting us know that if he found no Indians or fresh sign by this evening he would return a fiew miles back & hunt till we come up."
Ordway
Camp (Lewis)
Aug. 2, 1805
S 45 W 5 MILES
Madison Co.
Silver Bow Co.
Cartographer's Note:
Lewis and his men, including Sergeant Gass, probably camped in this general area the night of August 2, 1805.
Modern Data: 1989-1996
ONE STATUTE MILE
Outbound: August 2-5, 1805
Clark's Return: July 12, 1806
EXPLORATIONS OF LEWIS AND CLARK 1804 - 1806
CARTOGRAPHIC RECONSTRUCTION
MOUNTAINS BURNED
UTM ZONE 12
MAP NUMBER 261
Montana
CONTOUR INTERVAL 200 FEET

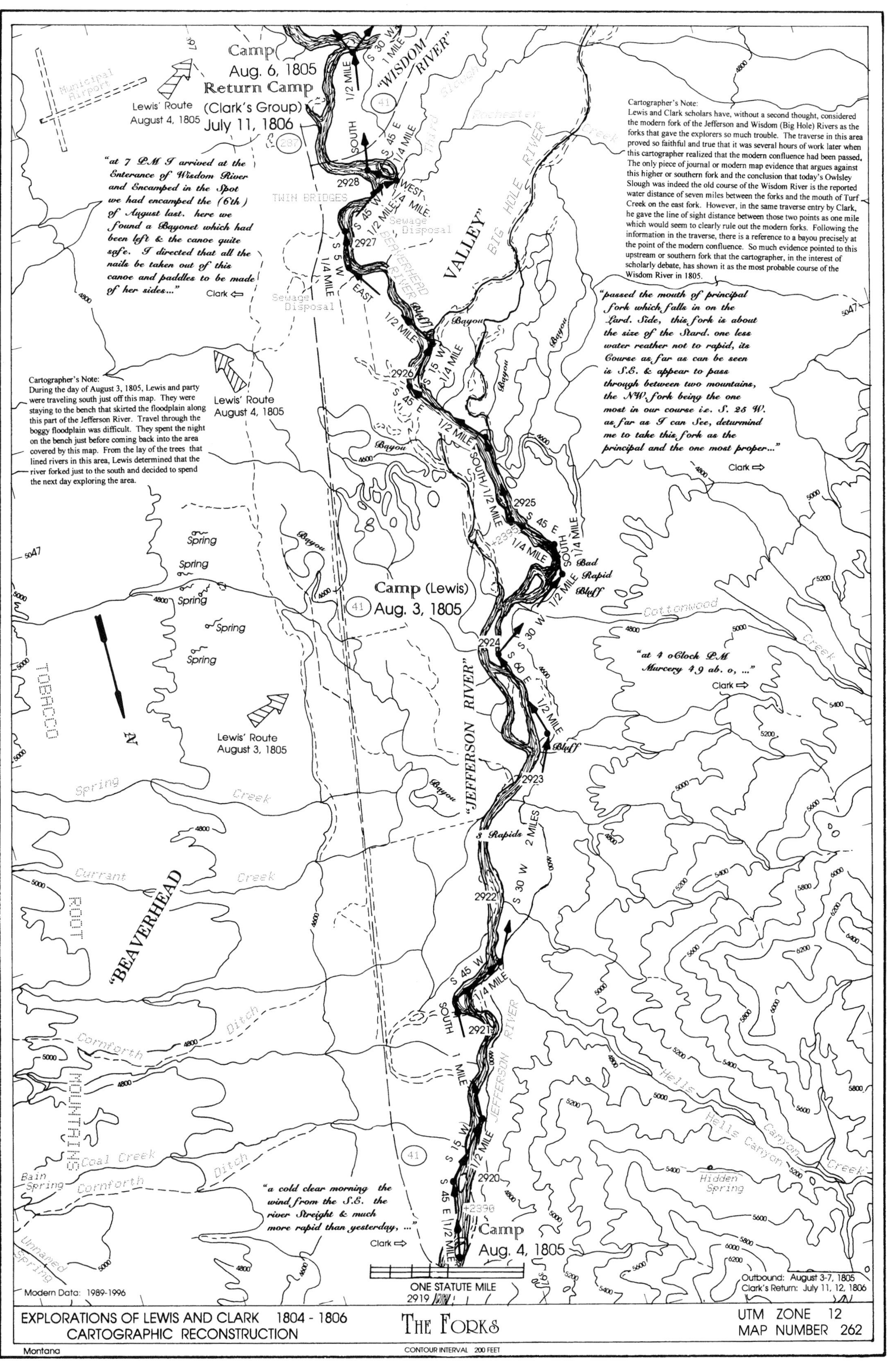
Camp
Aug. 6, 1805
Return Camp
(Clark's Group)
July 11, 1806
Lewis' Route
August 4, 1805
Municipal Airport
"WISDOM RIVER"
Rochester
Creek
"at 7 P.M. I arrived at the Entrance of Wisdom River and Encamped in the Spot we had encamped the (6th) of August last. here we found a Bayonet which had been left & the canoe quite safe. I directed that all the nails be taken out of this canoe and paddles to be made of her sides..."
Clark ⇦
TWIN BRIDGES
Sewage Disposal
VALLEY
BIG HOLE RIVER
BEAVERHEAD RIVER
Cartographer's Note:
Lewis and Clark scholars have, without a second thought, considered the modern fork of the Jefferson and Wisdom (Big Hole) Rivers as the forks that gave the explorers so much trouble. The traverse in this area proved so faithful and true that it was several hours of work later when this cartographer realized that the modern confluence had been passed. The only piece of journal or modern map evidence that argues against this higher or southern fork and the conclusion that today's Owlsley Slough was indeed the old course of the Wisdom River is the reported water distance of seven miles between the forks and the mouth of Turf Creek on the east fork. However, in the same traverse entry by Clark, he gave the line of sight distance between those two points as one mile which would seem to clearly rule out the modern forks. Following the information in the traverse, there is a reference to a bayou precisely at the point of the modern confluence. So much evidence pointed to this upstream or southern fork that the cartographer, in the interest of scholarly debate, has shown it as the most probable course of the Wisdom River in 1805.
"passed the mouth of principal fork which falls in on the Lard. Side, this fork is about the size of the Stard. one less water reather not to rapid, its Course as far as can be seen is S.E. & appear to pass through between two mountains, the NW. fork being the one most in our course i.e. S. 25 W. as far as I can See, deturmind me to take this fork as the principal and the one most proper..."
Clark ⇨
Cartographer's Note:
During the day of August 3, 1805, Lewis and party were traveling south just off this map. They were staying to the bench that skirted the floodplain along this part of the Jefferson River. Travel through the boggy floodplain was difficult. They spent the night on the bench just before coming back into the area covered by this map. From the lay of the trees that lined rivers in this area, Lewis determined that the river forked just to the south and decided to spend the next day exploring the area.
Lewis' Route
August 4, 1805
Bayou
Spring
Camp (Lewis)
Aug. 3, 1805
Bad Rapid Bluff
Cottonwood
Creek
"at 4 oClock P.M Murcery 4.9 ab. o, ..."
Clark ⇨
TOBACCO
N
Lewis' Route
August 3, 1805
"JEFFERSON RIVER"
Bluff
Spring
Creek
3 Rapids
Currant
Creek
"BEAVERHEAD
ROOT
Ditch
Cornforth
MOUNTAINS
JEFFERSON RIVER
Hells
Hells Canyon
Creek
Bain Spring
Coal Creek
Cornforth
Ditch
Hidden Spring
Unnamed Spring
"a cold clear morning the wind from the S.E. the river Streight & much more rapid than yesterday, ..."
Clark ⇨
Camp
Aug. 4, 1805
ONE STATUTE MILE
Modern Data: 1989-1996
Outbound: August 3-7, 1805
Clark's Return: July 11, 12, 1806
EXPLORATIONS OF LEWIS AND CLARK 1804 - 1806
CARTOGRAPHIC RECONSTRUCTION
THE FORKS
UTM ZONE 12
MAP NUMBER 262
Montana
CONTOUR INTERVAL 200 FEET

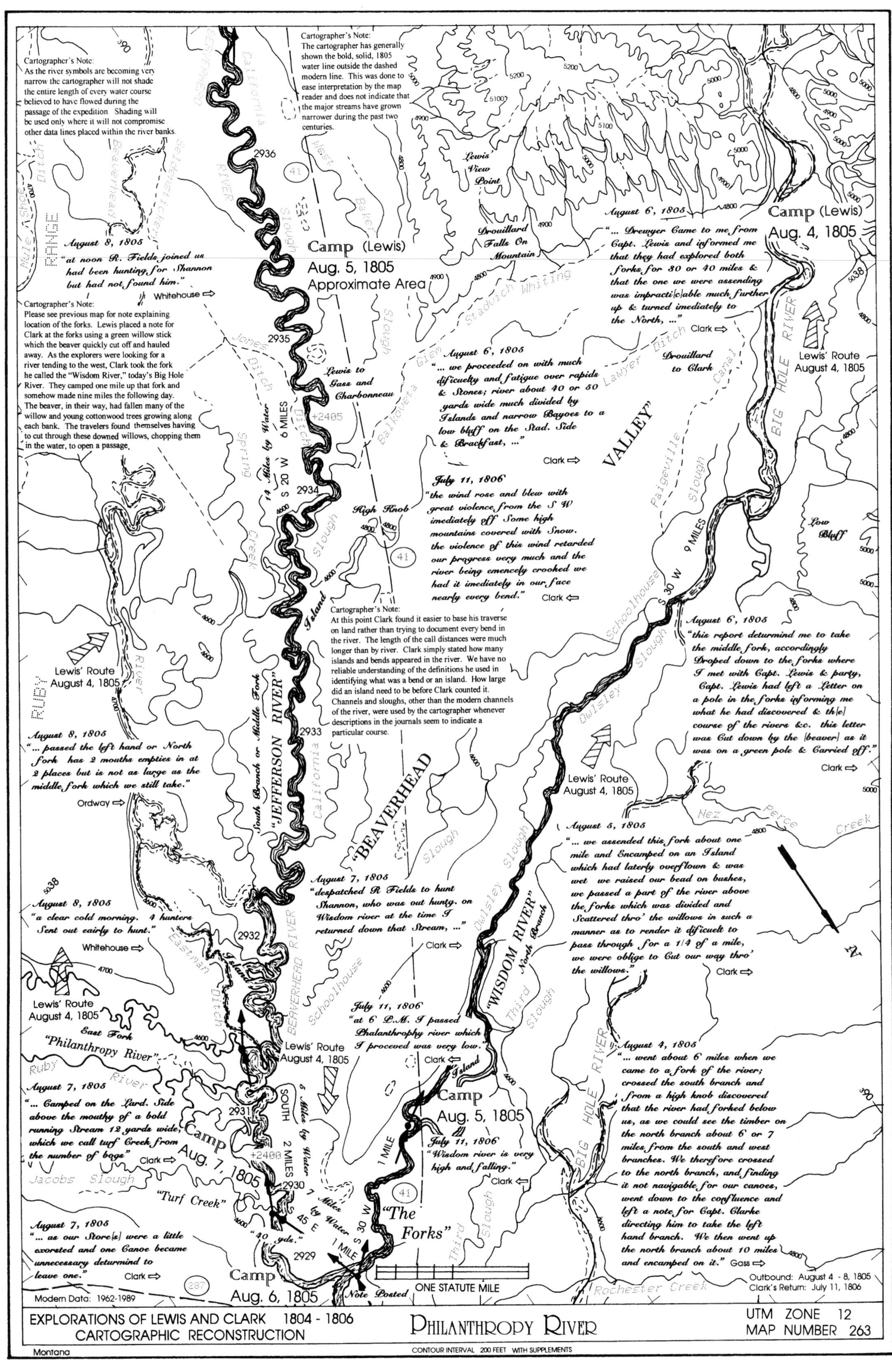

Cartographer's Note:
As the river symbols are becoming very narrow the cartographer will not shade the entire length of every water course believed to have flowed during the passage of the expedition. Shading will be used only where it will not compromise other data lines placed within the river banks.
Cartographer's Note:
The cartographer has generally shown the bold, solid, 1805 water line outside the dashed modern line. This was done to ease interpretation by the map reader and does not indicate that the major streams have grown narrower during the past two centuries.
Lewis View Point
Camp (Lewis) Aug. 4, 1805
August 6, 1805
"... Drewyer Came to me from Capt. Lewis and informed me that they had explored both forks for 30 or 40 miles & that the one we were assending was impracti[c]able much further up & turned imediately to the North, ..."
Clark ⇨
Drouillard Falls On Mountain
Camp (Lewis) Aug. 5, 1805 Approximate Area
August 8, 1805
"at noon R. Fields joined us had been hunting for Shannon but had not found him."
Whitehouse ⇨
Cartographer's Note:
Please see previous map for note explaining location of the forks. Lewis placed a note for Clark at the forks using a green willow stick which the beaver quickly cut off and hauled away. As the explorers were looking for a river tending to the west, Clark took the fork he called the "Wisdom River," today's Big Hole River. They camped one mile up that fork and somehow made nine miles the following day. The beaver, in their way, had fallen many of the willow and young cottonwood trees growing along each bank. The travelers found themselves having to cut through these downed willows, chopping them in the water, to open a passage.
Lewis to Gass and Charbonneau
August 6, 1805
"... we proceeded on with much dificuelty and fatigue over rapids & Stones; river about 40 or 50 yards wide much divided by Islands and narrow Bayoes to a low bluff on the Stad. Side & Brackfast, ..."
Clark ⇨
Drouillard to Clark
Lewis' Route August 4, 1805
BIG HOLE RIVER
VALLEY
14 Miles by Water 6 MILES S 20 W
High Knob
July 11, 1806
"the wind rose and blew with great violence from the S W imediately off Some high mountains covered with Snow. the violence of this wind retarded our progress very much and the river being emencely crooked we had it imediately in our face nearly every bend."
Clark ⇦
Low Bluff
9 MILES S 30 W
Cartographer's Note:
At this point Clark found it easier to base his traverse on land rather than trying to document every bend in the river. The length of the call distances were much longer than by river. Clark simply stated how many islands and bends appeared in the river. We have no reliable understanding of the definitions he used in identifying what was a bend or an island. How large did an island need to be before Clark counted it. Channels and sloughs, other than the modern channels of the river, were used by the cartographer whenever descriptions in the journals seem to indicate a particular course.
August 6, 1805
"this report deturmind me to take the middle fork, accordingly Droped down to the forks where I met with Capt. Lewis & party, Capt. Lewis had left a Letter on a pole in the forks informing me what he had discovered & th[e] course of the rivers &c. this letter was Cut down by the [beaver] as it was on a green pole & Carried off."
Clark ⇨
Lewis' Route August 4, 1805
RUBY RANGE
South Branch or Middle Fork
"JEFFERSON RIVER"
Island
August 8, 1805
"... passed the left hand or North fork has 2 mouths empties in at 2 places but is not as large as the middle fork which we still take."
Ordway ⇨
"BEAVERHEAD"
Lewis' Route August 4, 1805
August 5, 1805
"... we assended this fork about one mile and Encamped on an Island which had laterly overflown & was wet we raised our bead on bushes, we passed a part of the river above the forks which was divided and Scattered thro' the willows in such a manner as to render it dificult to pass through for a 1/4 of a mile, we were oblige to Cut our way thro' the willows."
Clark ⇨
August 7, 1805
"despatched R Fields to hunt Shannon, who was out huntg. on Wisdom river at the time I returned down that Stream, ..."
Clark ⇨
August 8, 1805
"a clear cold morning. 4 hunters Sent out eairly to hunt."
Whitehouse ⇨
"WISDOM RIVER" North Branch
Lewis' Route August 4, 1805
East Fork
"Philanthropy River"
July 11, 1806
"at 6 P.M. I passed Phalanthrophy river which I proceved was very low."
Lewis' Route August 4, 1805
Clark ⇦
Island
Camp Aug. 5, 1805
August 4, 1805
"... went about 6 miles when we came to a fork of the river; crossed the south branch and from a high knob discovered that the river had forked below us, as we could see the timber on the north branch about 6 or 7 miles from the south and west branches. We therfore crossed to the north branch, and finding it not navigable for our canoes, went down to the confluence and left a note for Capt. Clarke directing him to take the left hand branch. We then went up the north branch about 10 miles and encamped on it."
Gass ⇨
August 7, 1805
"... Camped on the Lard. Side above the mouthy of a bold running Stream 12 yards wide, which we call turf Creek from the number of bogs"
Clark ⇨
Camp Aug. 7, 1805
SOUTH 2 MILES 5 Miles by Water
1 MILE
July 11, 1806
"Wisdom river is very high and falling."
Clark ⇦
"Turf Creek"
7 Miles by Water S 45 E
"40 yds."
1 MILE S 30 W
"The Forks"
August 7, 1805
"... as our Store[s] were a little exorated and one Canoe became unnecessary deturmind to leave one."
Clark ⇨
Camp Aug. 6, 1805
Note Posted
ONE STATUTE MILE
Outbound: August 4 - 8, 1805
Clark's Return: July 11, 1806
Modern Data: 1962-1989
EXPLORATIONS OF LEWIS AND CLARK 1804 - 1806
CARTOGRAPHIC RECONSTRUCTION
PHILANTHROPY RIVER
UTM ZONE 12
MAP NUMBER 263
Montana
CONTOUR INTERVAL 200 FEET WITH SUPPLEMENTS

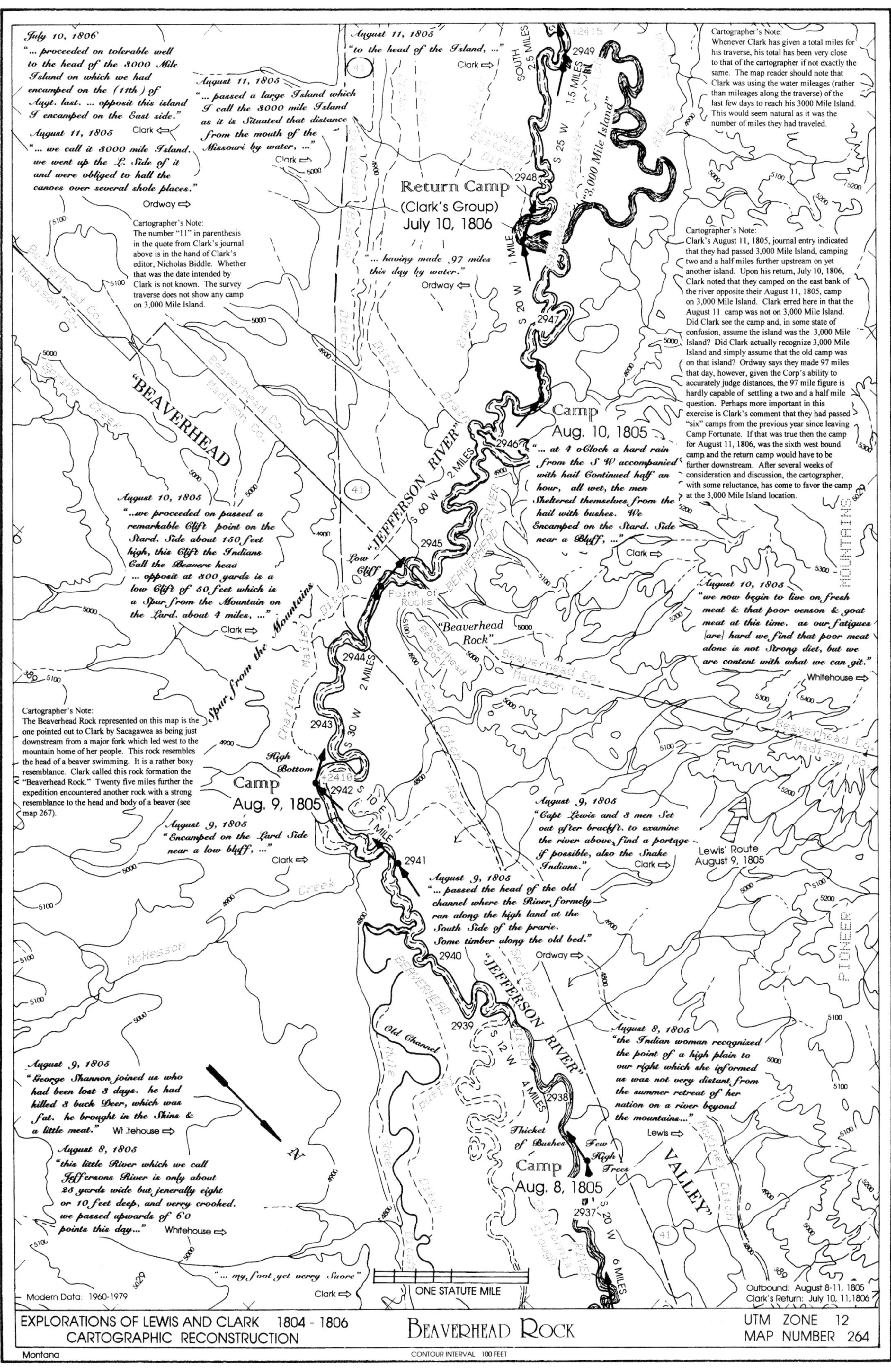
July 10, 1806
"... proceeded on tolerable well to the head of the 3000 Mile Island on which we had encamped on the (11th) of Augt. last. ... opposit this island I encamped on the East side."
August 11, 1805
"... we call it 3000 mile Island. we went up the L. Side of it and were obliged to hall the canoes over several shole places."
Ordway
August 11, 1805
"... passed a large Island which I call the 3000 mile Island as it is Situated that distance from the mouth of the Missouri by water, ..."
Clark
August 11, 1805
"to the head of the Island, ..."
Clark
Cartographer's Note:
Whenever Clark has given a total miles for his traverse, his total has been very close to that of the cartographer if not exactly the same. The map reader should note that Clark was using the water mileages (rather than mileages along the traverse) of the last few days to reach his 3000 Mile Island. This would seem natural as it was the number of miles they had traveled.
Return Camp
(Clark's Group)
July 10, 1806
"... having made 97 miles this day by water."
Ordway
"3,000 Mile Island"
Cartographer's Note:
The number "11" in parenthesis in the quote from Clark's journal above is in the hand of Clark's editor, Nicholas Biddle. Whether that was the date intended by Clark is not known. The survey traverse does not show any camp on 3,000 Mile Island.
Cartographer's Note:
Clark's August 11, 1805, journal entry indicated that they had passed 3,000 Mile Island, camping two and a half miles further upstream on yet another island. Upon his return, July 10, 1806, Clark noted that they camped on the east bank of the river opposite their August 11, 1805, camp on 3,000 Mile Island. Clark erred here in that the August 11 camp was not on 3,000 Mile Island. Did Clark see the camp and, in some state of confusion, assume the island was the 3,000 Mile Island? Did Clark actually recognize 3,000 Mile Island and simply assume that the old camp was on that island? Ordway says they made 97 miles that day, however, given the Corp's ability to accurately judge distances, the 97 mile figure is hardly capable of settling a two and a half mile question. Perhaps more important in this exercise is Clark's comment that they had passed "six" camps from the previous year since leaving Camp Fortunate. If that was true then the camp for August 11, 1806, was the sixth west bound camp and the return camp would have to be further downstream. After several weeks of consideration and discussion, the cartographer, with some reluctance, has come to favor the camp at the 3,000 Mile Island location.
"BEAVERHEAD
Camp
Aug. 10, 1805
"... at 4 oClock a hard rain from the S W accompanied with hail Continued half an hour, all wet, the men Sheltered themselves from the hail with bushes. We Encamped on the Stard. Side near a Bluff, ..."
Clark
"JEFFERSON RIVER"
August 10, 1805
"..we proceeded on passed a remarkable Clift point on the Stard. Side about 150 feet high, this Clift the Indians Call the Beavers head ... opposit at 300 yards is a low Clift of 50 feet which is a Spur from the Mountain on the Lard. about 4 miles, ..."
Clark
Low Cliff
Point of Rocks
"Beaverhead Rock"
Spur from the Mountains
August 10, 1805
"we now begin to live on fresh meat & that poor venson & goat meat at this time. as our fatigues [are] hard we find that poor meat alone is not Strong diet, but we are content with what we can git."
Whitehouse
MOUNTAINS
Cartographer's Note:
The Beaverhead Rock represented on this map is the one pointed out to Clark by Sacagawea as being just downstream from a major fork which led west to the mountain home of her people. This rock resembles the head of a beaver swimming. It is a rather boxy resemblance. Clark called this rock formation the "Beaverhead Rock." Twenty five miles further the expedition encountered another rock with a strong resemblance to the head and body of a beaver (see map 267).
High Bottom
Camp
Aug. 9, 1805
August 9, 1805
"Encamped on the Lard Side near a low bluff, ..."
Clark
August 9, 1805
"Capt Lewis and 3 men Set out after brackft. to examine the river above, find a portage if possible, also the Snake Indians."
Clark
Lewis' Route
August 9, 1805
August 9, 1805
"... passed the head of the old channel where the River formely ran along the high land at the South Side of the prarie. Some timber along the old bed."
Ordway
"JEFFERSON RIVER"
PIONEER
Old Channel
August 9, 1805
"George Shannon joined us who had been lost 3 days. he had killed 3 buck Deer, which was fat. he brought in the Skins & a little meat."
Whitehouse
N
August 8, 1805
"this little River which we call Jeffersons River is only about 25 yards wide but jenerally eight or 10 feet deep, and verry crooked. we passed upwards of 60 points this day..."
Whitehouse
August 8, 1805
"the Indian woman recognized the point of a high plain to our right which she informed us was not very distant from the summer retreat of her nation on a river beyond the mountains..."
Lewis
Thicket of Bushes
Few High Trees
Camp
Aug. 8, 1805
VALLEY"
"... my foot get verry Sore"
Clark
ONE STATUTE MILE
Modern Data: 1960-1979
Outbound: August 8-11, 1805
Clark's Return: July 10, 11, 1806
EXPLORATIONS OF LEWIS AND CLARK 1804 - 1806
CARTOGRAPHIC RECONSTRUCTION
BEAVERHEAD ROCK
UTM ZONE 12
MAP NUMBER 264
Montana
CONTOUR INTERVAL 100 FEET

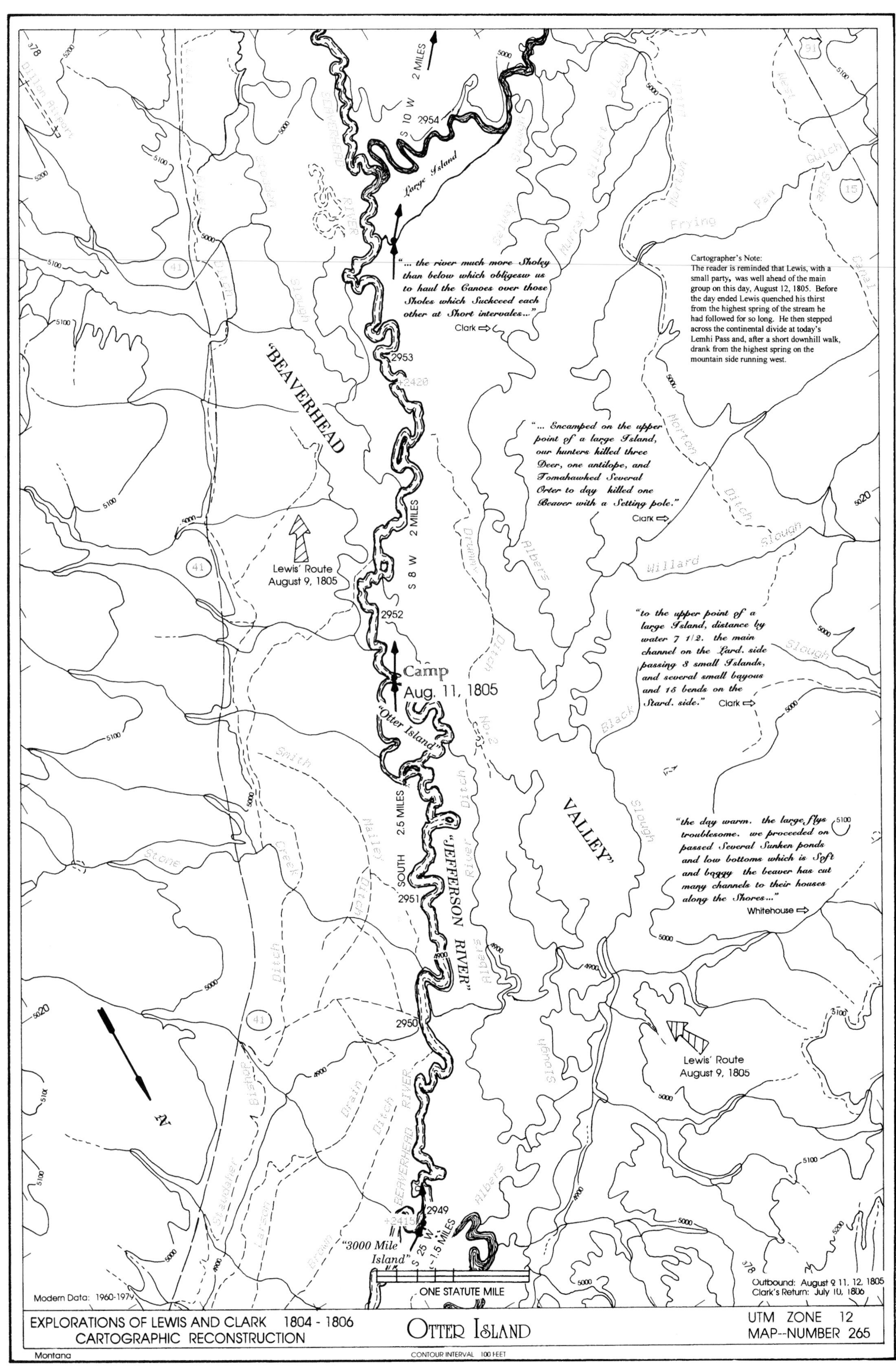
"... the river much more Sholey than below which obligesw us to haul the Canoes over those Sholes which Suckceed each other at Short intervales..."
Clark
Cartographer's Note:
The reader is reminded that Lewis, with a small party, was well ahead of the main group on this day, August 12, 1805. Before the day ended Lewis quenched his thirst from the highest spring of the stream he had followed for so long. He then stepped across the continental divide at today's Lemhi Pass and, after a short downhill walk, drank from the highest spring on the mountain side running west.
"... Encamped on the upper point of a large Island, our hunters killed three Deer, one antilope, and Tomahawked Several Orter to day killed one Beaver with a Setting pole."
Clark
"BEAVERHEAD VALLEY"
Lewis' Route August 9, 1805
"to the upper point of a large Island, distance by water 7 1/2. the main channel on the Lard. side passing 3 small Islands, and several small bayous and 15 bends on the Stard. side."
Clark
Camp Aug. 11, 1805
"Otter Island"
"JEFFERSON RIVER"
"the day warm. the large flys troublesome. we proceeded on passed Several Sunken ponds and low bottoms which is Soft and boggy the beaver has cut many channels to their houses along the Shores..."
Whitehouse
Large Island
BEAVERHEAD RIVER
S 10 W 2 MILES
S 8 W 2 MILES
SOUTH 2.5 MILES
S 25 W 1.5 MILES
"3000 Mile Island"
Frying Pan Gulch
Willard Slough
Black Slough
Albers
Smith
Stone Creek
Bishop
Staudaher
Drain Ditch
N
Outbound: August 9, 11, 12, 1805
Clark's Return: July 10, 1806
Modern Data: 1960-1979
ONE STATUTE MILE
EXPLORATIONS OF LEWIS AND CLARK 1804 - 1806
CARTOGRAPHIC RECONSTRUCTION
OTTER ISLAND
UTM ZONE 12
MAP--NUMBER 265
Montana
CONTOUR INTERVAL 100 FEET

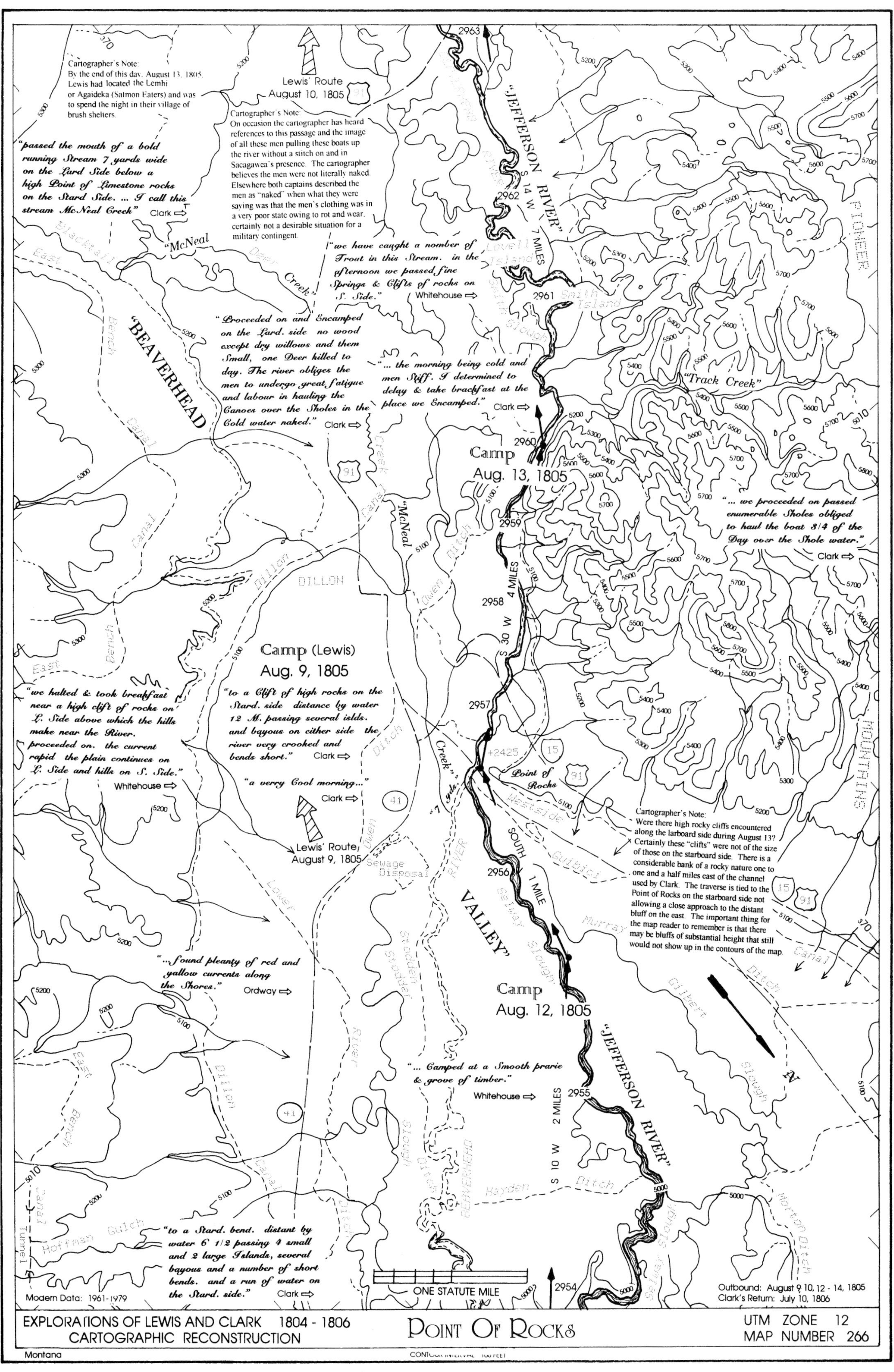

Cartographer's Note:
By the end of this day, August 13, 1805, Lewis had located the Lemhi or Agaideka (Salmon Eaters) and was to spend the night in their village of brush shelters.
Lewis' Route
August 10, 1805
Cartographer's Note:
On occasion the cartographer has heard references to this passage and the image of all these men pulling these boats up the river without a stitch on and in Sacagawea's presence. The cartographer believes the men were not literally naked. Elsewhere both captains described the men as "naked" when what they were saying was that the men's clothing was in a very poor state owing to rot and wear, certainly not a desirable situation for a military contingent.
"passed the mouth of a bold running Stream 7 yards wide on the Lard Side below a high Point of Limestone rocks on the Stard Side. ... I call this stream McNeal Creek" Clark ⇨
"JEFFERSON RIVER"
"McNeal
Deer Creek"
Blacktail
East
"we have caught a nomber of Trout in this Stream. in the afternoon we passed fine Springs & Clifts of rocks on S. Side." Whitehouse ⇨
Lovell Island
Smith Island
Smith Slough
PIONEER
"BEAVERHEAD
Bench
Canal
"Proceeded on and Encamped on the Lard. side no wood except dry willows and them Small, one Deer killed to day. The river obliges the men to undergo great fatigue and labour in hauling the Canoes over the Sholes in the Cold water naked." Clark ⇨
"... the morning being cold and men Stiff. I determined to delay & take brackfast at the place we Encamped." Clark ⇨
"Track Creek"
Camp
Aug. 13, 1805
"... we proceeded on passed enumerable Sholes obliged to haul the boat 3/4 of the Day over the Shole water." Clark ⇨
"McNeal
Creek"
Owen Ditch
Dillon
DILLON
Camp (Lewis)
Aug. 9, 1805
"we halted & took breakfast near a high clift of rocks on L. Side above which the hills make near the River. proceeded on. the current rapid the plain continues on L. Side and hills on S. Side." Whitehouse ⇨
"to a Clift of high rocks on the Stard. side distance by water 12 M. passing several islds. and bayous on either side the river very crooked and bends short." Clark ⇨
"a verry Cool morning..." Clark ⇨
Point of Rocks
Westside
Guibici
MOUNTAINS
Cartographer's Note:
Were there high rocky cliffs encountered along the larboard side during August 13? Certainly these "clifts" were not of the size of those on the starboard side. There is a considerable bank of a rocky nature one to one and a half miles east of the channel used by Clark. The traverse is tied to the Point of Rocks on the starboard side not allowing a close approach to the distant bluff on the east. The important thing for the map reader to remember is that there may be bluffs of substantial height that still would not show up in the contours of the map.
Lewis' Route
August 9, 1805
Sewage Disposal
RIVER
VALLEY"
Selway Slough
Murray
Canal
Ditch
Gilbert Slough
N
Camp
Aug. 12, 1805
"...found pleanty of red and yallow currents along the Shores." Ordway ⇨
Stodden
Lower
River
"... Camped at a Smooth prarie & grove of timber." Whitehouse ⇨
"JEFFERSON RIVER"
East Bench
BEAVERHEAD
Hayden Ditch
Morton Ditch
Tunnel
Hoffman Gulch
"to a Stard. bend. distant by water 6 1/2 passing 4 small and 2 large Islands, several bayous and a number of short bends. and a run of water on the Stard. side." Clark ⇨
ONE STATUTE MILE
Modern Data: 1961-1979
Outbound: August 9 10, 12 - 14, 1805
Clark's Return: July 10, 1806
EXPLORATIONS OF LEWIS AND CLARK 1804 - 1806
CARTOGRAPHIC RECONSTRUCTION
POINT OF ROCKS
UTM ZONE 12
MAP NUMBER 266
Montana

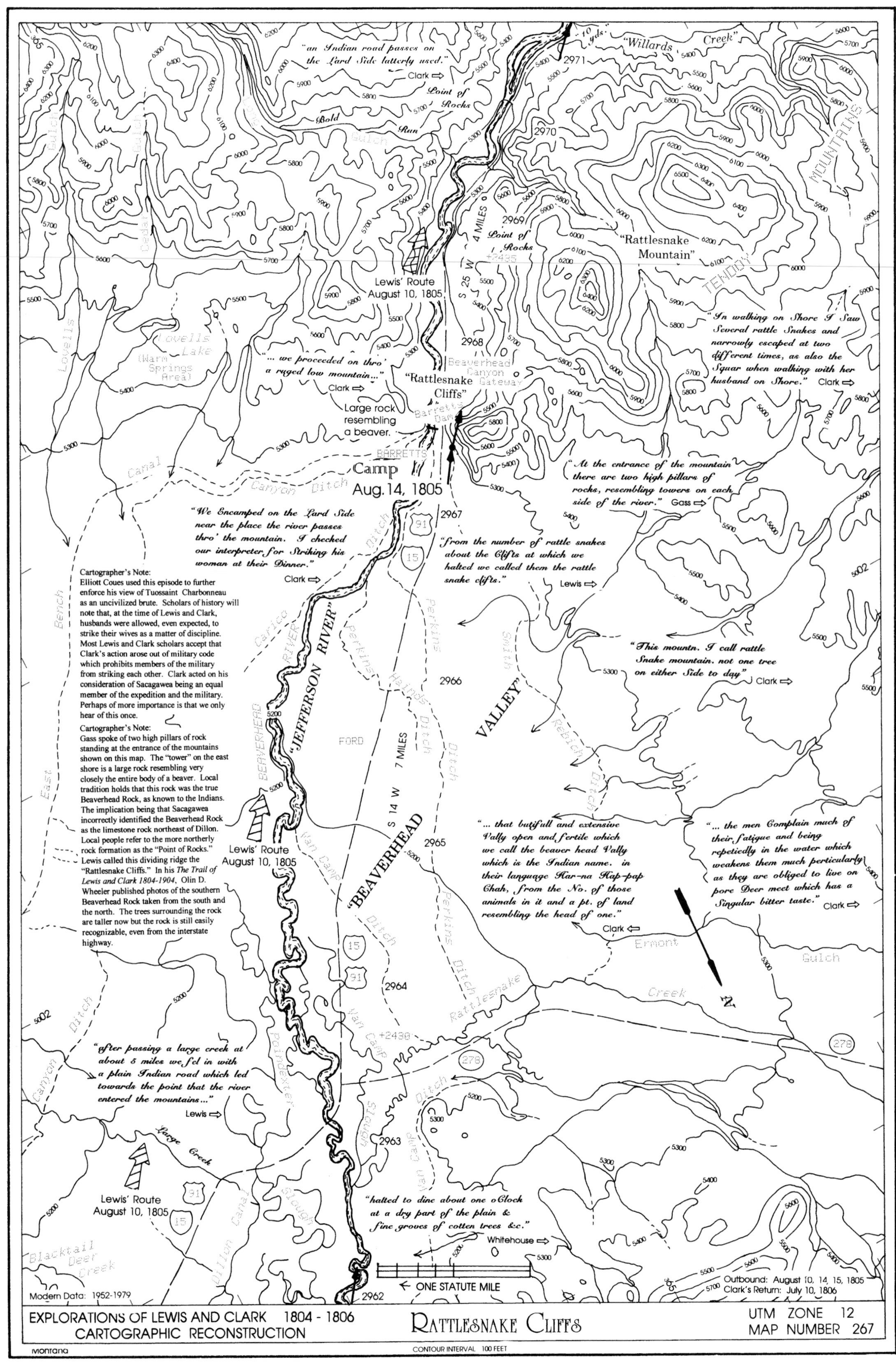

"an Indian road passes on the Lard Side latterly used." Clark ⇨
Point of Rocks
Bold Run
"Willards Creek"
"10 yds."
2971
2970
2969
2968
2967
2966
2965
2964
2963
2962
MOUNTAINS
TENDOY
"Rattlesnake Mountain"
Point of Rocks
S 25 W 4 MILES
Lewis' Route August 10, 1805
Lovells Lake
(Warm Springs Area)
"... we proceeded on thro' a ruged low mountain..." Clark ⇨
"Rattlesnake Cliffs"
Beaverhead Canyon Gateway
Large rock resembling a beaver.
Barretts Dam
BARRETTS
Camp Aug. 14, 1805
Canal
Canyon Ditch
"In walking on Shore I Saw Several rattle Snakes and narrowly escaped at two different times, as also the Squar when walking with her husband on Shore." Clark ⇨
"At the entrance of the mountain there are two high pillars of rocks, resembling towers on each side of the river." Gass ⇨
"We Encamped on the Lard Side near the place the river passes thro' the mountain. I checked our interpreter for Striking his woman at their Dinner." Clark ⇨
"from the number of rattle snakes about the Clifts at which we halted we called them the rattle snake clifts." Lewis ⇨
Cartographer's Note:
Elliott Coues used this episode to further enforce his view of Tuossaint Charbonneau as an uncivilized brute. Scholars of history will note that, at the time of Lewis and Clark, husbands were allowed, even expected, to strike their wives as a matter of discipline. Most Lewis and Clark scholars accept that Clark's action arose out of military code which prohibits members of the military from striking each other. Clark acted on his consideration of Sacagawea being an equal member of the expedition and the military. Perhaps of more importance is that we only hear of this once.
Cartographer's Note:
Gass spoke of two high pillars of rock standing at the entrance of the mountains shown on this map. The "tower" on the east shore is a large rock resembling very closely the entire body of a beaver. Local tradition holds that this rock was the true Beaverhead Rock, as known to the Indians. The implication being that Sacagawea incorrectly identified the Beaverhead Rock as the limestone rock northeast of Dillon. Local people refer to the more northerly rock formation as the "Point of Rocks." Lewis called this dividing ridge the "Rattlesnake Cliffs." In his The Trail of Lewis and Clark 1804-1904, Olin D. Wheeler published photos of the southern Beaverhead Rock taken from the south and the north. The trees surrounding the rock are taller now but the rock is still easily recognizable, even from the interstate highway.
Carico Ditch
"JEFFERSON RIVER"
BEAVERHEAD RIVER
Perkins
Perkins Ditch
Haynds Ditch
Smith
VALLEY
"This mountn. I call rattle Snake mountain. not one tree on either Side to day" Clark ⇨
Rebich Ditch
FORD
S 14 W 7 MILES
"BEAVERHEAD"
Bench
East Bench
Lewis' Route August 10, 1805
Van Camp
"... that butifull and extensive Vally open and fertile which we call the beaver head Vally which is the Indian name. in their language Har-na Hap-pap Chah, from the No. of those animals in it and a pt. of land resembling the head of one." Clark ⇦
"... the men Complain much of their fatigue and being repetiedly in the water which weakens them much perticularly as they are obliged to live on pore Deer meet which has a Singular bitter taste." Clark ⇨
Ermont Gulch
Creek
Rattlesnake
N
Canyon Ditch
Poindexter
Slough
"after passing a large creek at about 5 miles we fel in with a plain Indian road which led towards the point that the river entered the mountains..." Lewis ⇨
Large Creek
Lewis' Route August 10, 1805
Dillon Canal
Blacktail Deer Creek
"halted to dine about one oClock at a dry part of the plain & fine groves of cotten trees &c." Whitehouse ⇨
ONE STATUTE MILE
Modern Data: 1952-1979
Outbound: August 10, 14, 15, 1805
Clark's Return: July 10, 1806
EXPLORATIONS OF LEWIS AND CLARK 1804 - 1806
CARTOGRAPHIC RECONSTRUCTION
RATTLESNAKE CLIFFS
UTM ZONE 12
MAP NUMBER 267
Montana
CONTOUR INTERVAL 100 FEET

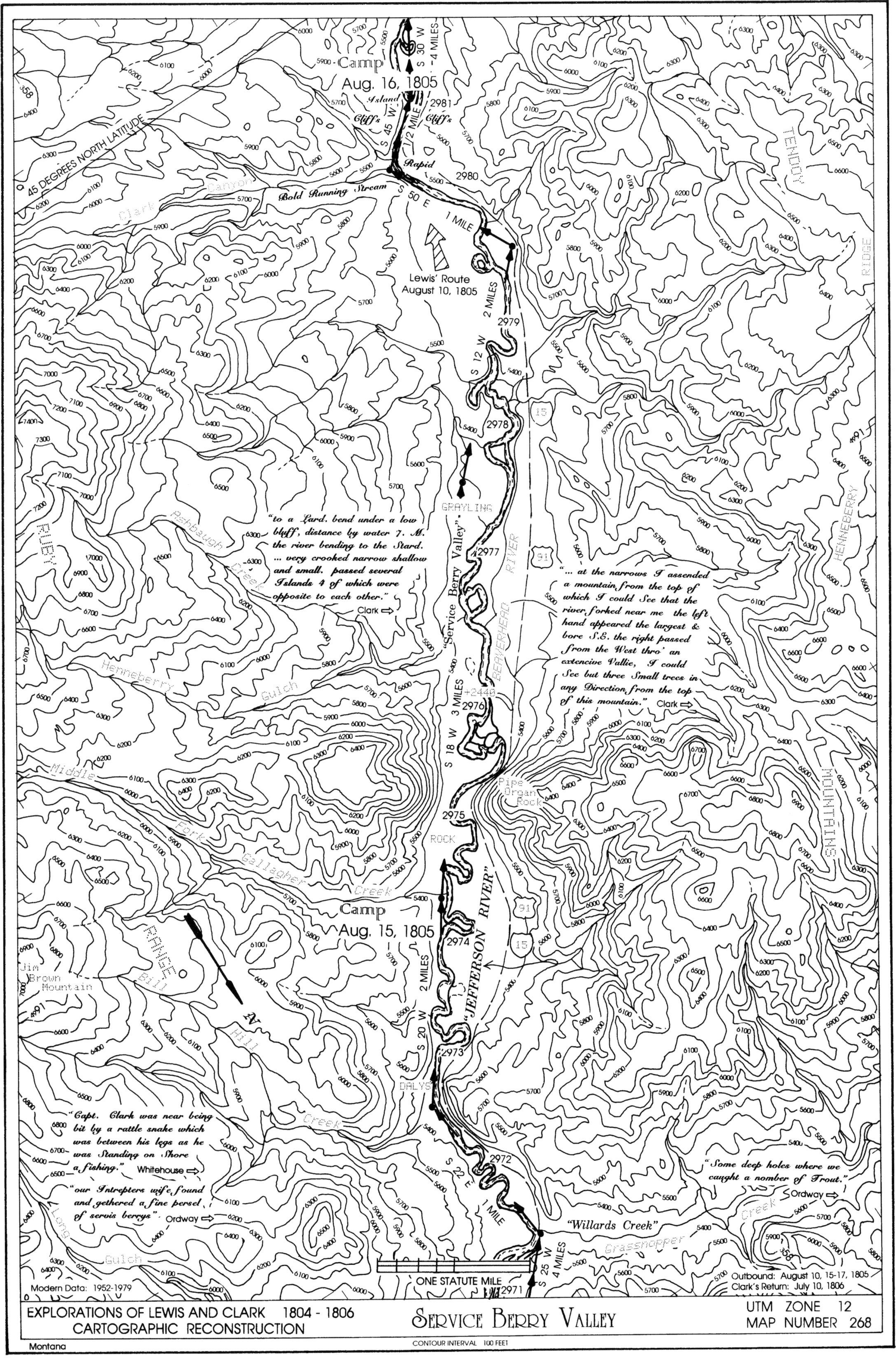

Camp
Aug. 16, 1805
Island
Cliffs
Cliffs
Rapid
Bold Running Stream
45 DEGREES NORTH LATITUDE
Clark
Canyon
Lewis' Route
August 10, 1805
TENDOY
RIDGE
GRAYLING
"Service Berry Valley"
BEAVERHEAD RIVER
"to a Lard. bend under a low bluff, distance by water 7. M. the river bending to the Stard. ... very crooked narrow shallow and small. passed several Islands 4 of which were opposite to each other." Clark ⇨
"... at the narrows I assended a mountain from the top of which I could See that the river forked near me the left hand appeared the largest & bore S.E. the right passed from the West thro' an extencive Vallie, I could See but three Small trees in any Direction from the top of this mountain." Clark ⇨
Ashbaugh Creek
RUBY
HENNEBERRY
Henneberry Gulch
Middle Fork
Gallagher Creek
Pipe Organ Rock
ROCK
MOUNTAINS
Camp
Aug. 15, 1805
"JEFFERSON RIVER"
RANGE
Jim Brown Mountain
Bill Hill
N
DALYS
Creek
"Capt. Clark was near being bit by a rattle snake which was between his legs as he was Standing on Shore a fishing." Whitehouse ⇨
"our Intrepters wife found and gethered a fine persel of servis berrys". Ordway ⇨
Long Gulch
"Some deep holes where we caught a nomber of Trout." Ordway ⇨
"Willards Creek"
Grasshopper Creek
ONE STATUTE MILE
Modern Data: 1952-1979
Outbound: August 10, 15-17, 1805
Clark's Return: July 10, 1806
EXPLORATIONS OF LEWIS AND CLARK 1804 - 1806
CARTOGRAPHIC RECONSTRUCTION
SERVICE BERRY VALLEY
UTM ZONE 12
MAP NUMBER 268
Montana
CONTOUR INTERVAL 100 FEET

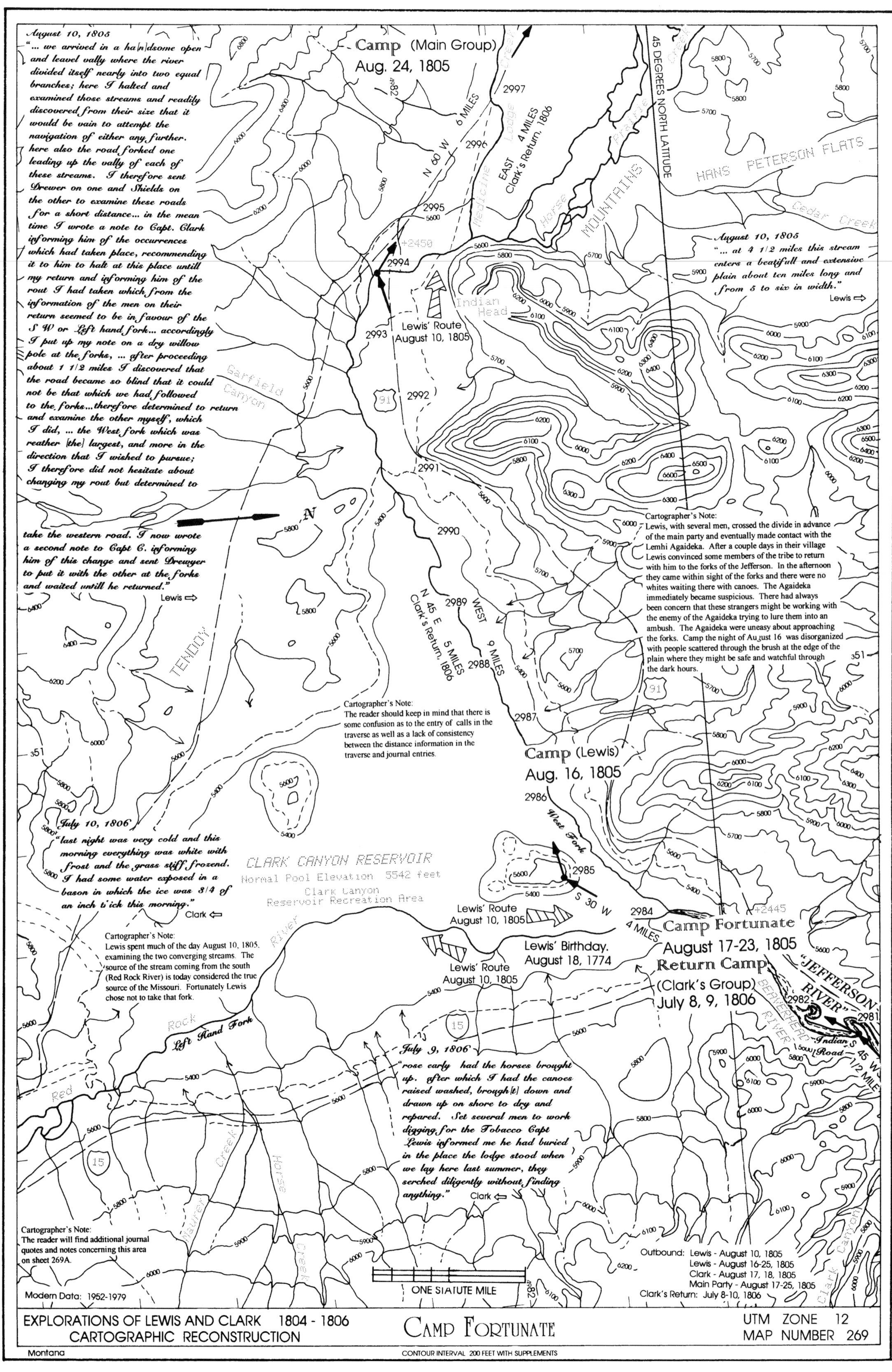

August 10, 1805
"... we arrived in a ha[n]dsome open and leavel vally where the river divided itself nearly into two equal branches; here I halted and examined those streams and readily discovered from their size that it would be vain to attempt the navigation of either any further. here also the road forked one leading up the vally of each of these streams. I therfore sent Drewer on one and Shields on the other to examine these roads for a short distance... in the mean time I wrote a note to Capt. Clark informing him of the occurrences which had taken place, recommending it to him to halt at this place untill my return and informing him of the rout I had taken which from the information of the men on their return seemed to be in favour of the S W or Left hand fork... accordingly I put up my note on a dry willow pole at the forks, ... after proceeding about 1 1/2 miles I discovered that the road became so blind that it could not be that which we had followed to the forks...therfore determined to return and examine the other myself, which I did, ... the West fork which was reather [the] largest, and more in the direction that I wished to pursue; I therefore did not hesitate about changing my rout but determined to take the western road. I now wrote a second note to Capt C. informing him of this change and sent Drewyer to put it with the other at the forks and waited untill he returned."
Lewis ⇨
Camp (Main Group)
Aug. 24, 1805
N 60 W 6 MILES
EAST 4 MILES
Clark's Return, 1806
Medicine Lodge Creek
Horse Prairie Creek
MOUNTAINS
45 DEGREES NORTH LATITUDE
HANS PETERSON FLATS
Cedar Creek
August 10, 1805
"... at 4 1/2 miles this stream enters a beatifull and extensive plain about ten miles long and from 5 to six in width."
Lewis ⇨
Indian Head
Lewis' Route
August 10, 1805
Garfield Canyon
TENDOY
N
Cartographer's Note:
Lewis, with several men, crossed the divide in advance of the main party and eventually made contact with the Lemhi Agaideka. After a couple days in their village Lewis convinced some members of the tribe to return with him to the forks of the Jefferson. In the afternoon they came within sight of the forks and there were no whites waiting there with canoes. The Agaideka immediately became suspicious. There had always been concern that these strangers might be working with the enemy of the Agaideka trying to lure them into an ambush. The Agaideka were uneasy about approaching the forks. Camp the night of August 16 was disorganized with people scattered through the brush at the edge of the plain where they might be safe and watchful through the dark hours.
N 45 E 5 MILES
Clark's Return, 1806
WEST 9 MILES
Cartographer's Note:
The reader should keep in mind that there is some confusion as to the entry of calls in the traverse as well as a lack of consistency between the distance information in the traverse and journal entries.
Camp (Lewis)
Aug. 16, 1805
West Fork
S 30 W
4 MILES
July 10, 1806
"last night was very cold and this morning everything was white with frost and the grass stiff frozend. I had some water exposed in a bason in which the ice was 3/4 of an inch ti'ick this morning."
Clark ⇦
CLARK CANYON RESERVOIR
Normal Pool Elevation 5542 feet
Clark Canyon
Reservoir Recreation Area
Lewis' Route
August 10, 1805
Camp Fortunate
August 17-23, 1805
Return Camp
(Clark's Group)
July 8, 9, 1806
Lewis' Birthday.
August 18, 1774
Lewis' Route
August 10, 1805
"JEFFERSON RIVER"
BEAVERHEAD RIVER
Indian Road
S 45 W 1/2 MILE
Cartographer's Note:
Lewis spent much of the day August 10, 1805, examining the two converging streams. The source of the stream coming from the south (Red Rock River) is today considered the true source of the Missouri. Fortunately Lewis chose not to take that fork.
Red Rock River
Left Hand Fork
July 9, 1806
"rose early had the horses brought up. after which I had the canoes raised washed, brough[t] down and drawn up on shore to dry and repared. Set several men to work digging for the Tobacco Capt Lewis informed me he had buried in the place the lodge stood when we lay here last summer, they serched diligently without finding anything."
Clark ⇦
Horse Creek
Cartographer's Note:
The reader will find additional journal quotes and notes concerning this area on sheet 269A.
Clark Canyon
ONE STATUTE MILE
Outbound: Lewis - August 10, 1805
Lewis - August 16-25, 1805
Clark - August 17, 18, 1805
Main Party - August 17-25, 1805
Clark's Return: July 8-10, 1806
Modern Data: 1952-1979
EXPLORATIONS OF LEWIS AND CLARK 1804 - 1806
CARTOGRAPHIC RECONSTRUCTION
CAMP FORTUNATE
UTM ZONE 12
MAP NUMBER 269
Montana
CONTOUR INTERVAL 200 FEET WITH SUPPLEMENTS

August 12, 1805

"... a stout stream which is a principal fork of the ma[i]n stream and falls into it just above the narrow pass between the two clifts before mentioned and which we now saw below us. here we halted and breakfasted on the last of our venison, having yet a small peice of pork in reserve." Lewis ⇨

August 12, 1805

"... the main stream now after discarding two stream[s] on the left in this valley turns abruptly to the West through a narrow bottom betwe[e]n the mountains. the road was still plain, I therefore did not dispair of shortly finding a passage over the mountains and of taisting the waters of the great Columbia this evening." Lewis ⇨

August 12, 1805

"we saw an animal which we took to be of the fox kind as large or reather larger than the small wolf of the plains. it's colours were a curious mixture of black, redis[h] brown and yellow. Drewyer shot at him about 180 yards and knocked him dow[n] bet [but] he recovered and got out of our reach. it is certainly a different animal from any that we have yet seen." Lewis ⇨

Wolverene
(Gulo luscus)

August 12, 1805

"we also saw several of the heath cock with a long pointed tail and an uniform dark brown colour but could not kill one of them." Lewis ⇨

Heath Cock
(Centrocercus urophasianus)

August 16, 1805

"after the hunters had been gone about an hour we set out. we had just passed through the narrows when we saw one of the spies comeing up the level plain underwhip, the chief pawsed a little and seemed under whip, the chief I felt a good deel so myself and began to suspect that by some unfortunate accedent that perhaps some of their enimies had straggled hither at this unlucky moment; but we were all agreeably disappointed on the arrival of the young man to learn that he had come to inform us that one of the whitemen had killed a deer." Lewis ⇨

August 16, 1805

"when they arrived where the deer was which was in view of me they dismounted and ran in tumbling over each other like a parcel of famished dogs each seizing and tearing away a part of the intestens which had been previously thrown out by Drewyer who killed it; the seen was such when I arrived that had I not have had a pretty keen appetite myself I am confident I should not have taisted any part of the venison shortly."

Lewis ⇨

August 16, 1805

"after eating and suffering the horses to graize about 2 hours we renued our march..."

Lewis ⇨

August 19, 1805

"... the beaver has Damed up the River in maney places we proceeded on up the main branch with a gradial assent..."

Clark ⇨

August 26, 1805

"passed a nomber of fine large Springs and drank at the head Spring of the Missoure."

Whitehouse ⇨

August 25, 1805

"Charbono mentioned to me with apparent unconcern that he expected to meet all the Indians from the camp on the Columbia tomorrow on their way to the Missouri. allarmed at this information I asked why he expected to meet them. he then informed me that the 1st. Cheif had dispatched some of his young men this morning to this camp requesting the Indians to meet them tomorrow and that himself and those with him would go on with them down the Missouri, and consequently leave me and my baggage on the mountain... he had been in possession of this information since early in the morning... yet he never mentioned it untill the after noon. ... I saw that there was no time to be lost in having those orders countermanded, ... I therefore Called the three Cheifs together... I then asked them why they had requested their people... to meet them tomorrow... the two inferior cheifs said... they had not sent for their people, that it was the first Chief who had done so. ... Cameahwait remained silent for some time, ... he told me that he knew he had done wrong but that he had been induced to that measure from seeing all his people hungry, ..." Lewis ⇨

August 26, 1805

"This morning was excessively cold; there was ice on the vessels of water which stood exposed to the air nearly a quarter of an inch thick. we collected our horses and set out at sunrise. we soon arrived at the extreem source of the Missouri; here I halted a few minutes, the men drank of the water and consoled themselves with the idea of having at length arrived at this long wished for point. from hence we proceeded to a fine spring on the side of the mountain where I had lain the evening before I first arrived at the Shoshone Camp. here I halted to dine and graize our horses, ..."

Lewis ⇨

August 26, 1805

"one of the women... halted at a little run about a mile behind us, ... I enquired of Cameahwait the cause of her detention, and was informed by him in an unconcerned manner that she had halted to bring fourth a child and would soon overtake us; in about an hour the woman arrived with her newborn babe and passed us on her way to the camp apparently as well as she ever was. It appears to me that the facility and ease with which the women of the aborigines of North America bring fourth their children is reather a gift of nature than depending as some have supposed on the habitude of carrying heavy burthens on their backs while in a state of pregnacy. if a pure and dry air, an elivated and cold country is unfavourable to childbirth, we might expect every difficult incident to that operation of nature in this part of the continent; again as the snake Indians possess an abundance of horses, their women are seldom compelled like those in other parts of the continent to carry burthens on their backs, yet they have their children with equal convenience, and it is a rare occurrence for any of them to experience difficulty in childbirth. I have been several times informed by those who were conversent with the fact, that the indian women who are pregnant by whitemen experience more difficulty in childbnirth than when pregnant by an Indian. if this be true it would go far in suport of the opinion I have advanced."

Lewis ⇨

Council with the Lemhi Shoshone (Agaideka)

August 17, 1805

"This morning I arrose very early and dispatched Drewyer and the Indian down the river. ... Drewyer had been gone about 2 hours when an Indian who had straggled some little distance down the river returned and reported that the whitemen were coming, that he had seen them just below. they all appeared transported with joy, & the ch[i]ef repeated his fraturnal hug. I felt quite as much gratifyed at this information as the Indians appeared to be. Shortly after Capt. Clark arrived with the Interpreter Charbono, and the Indian woman, who proved to be a sister of the Chief Cameahwait. the meeting of those people was really affecting, particularly between Sah-cah-gar-we-ah and an Indian woman, who had been taken prisoner at the same time with her and who, had afterwards escaped from the Minnetares and rejoined her nation. At noon the Canoes arrived, and we had the satisfaction once more to find ourselves all together, with a flattering prospect of being able to obtain as many horses shortly as would enable us to prosicute our voyage by land should that by water be deemed unadvisable.

"We now formed our camp just below the junction of the forks on the Lard. side... formed a canopy of one of our large sails and planted some willow brush in the ground to form a shade for the Indians to set under while we spoke to them, which we thought it best to do this evening. acordingly about 4.P.M. we called them together and through the medium of Labuish, Charbono and Sah-cah-gar-weah, we communicated to them fully the objects which had brought us into this distant part of the country, in which we took care to make them a conspicuous object of our own good wishes and the care of our government. we made them sensible of their dependance on the will of our government for every species of merchandize as well for their defence & comfort; and apprized them of the strength of our government and it's friendly dispositions towards them." Lewis ⇨

August 17, 1805

"... as the Canoes were proceeding on nearly opposit me, I turned those people & Joined Capt Lewis who had Camped with 16 of those Snake Indians at the forks 2 miles in advance. those Indians Sung all the way to their Camp where the others had provd a cind [kind] of Shade of Willows Stuck up in a Circle the Three Chiefs with Capt. Lewis met me with great cordiallity embraced and took a Seat on a white robe, the Main Chief imediately tied to my hair Six Small pieces of Shells resembling perl which is highly Valued by those people and is pr[o]cured from the nations resideing near the Sea Coast. we then Smoked in their fassion without Shoes and without much ceremoey and form.

"Capt Lewis informed me he found those people on the Columbia River about 40 miles from the forks at that place there was a large camp of them, he had purswaded those with him to Come and see that what he said was the truth, they had been under great apprehension all the way, for fear of their being deceived. The Great Chief of this nation proved to be the brother of the woman with us and is a man of Influence Sence & easey & reserved manners, appears to possess a great deel of Cincerity. The Canoes arrived & unloaded. every thing appeared to astonish those people. the appearance of the men, their arms, the Canoes, the Clothing my black Servent & the Segassity of Capt Lewis's Dog."

Clark ⇨

Cartographer's Note:
There is a strong tradition of a dramatic scene during the council when Sacagawea realized that Cameahwait was her brother. Tradition tells us that Sacagawea had been seated for a few moments when she recognized her brother. As she broke into tears, it is reported, she threw her blanket about Cameahwait, covering them both from stares as they renewed a family bond. Another few moments passed before Sacagawea returned, with her blanket, to her place in the circle and Cameahwait appeared shaken. If the scene took place, it was not related in any of the known journals.

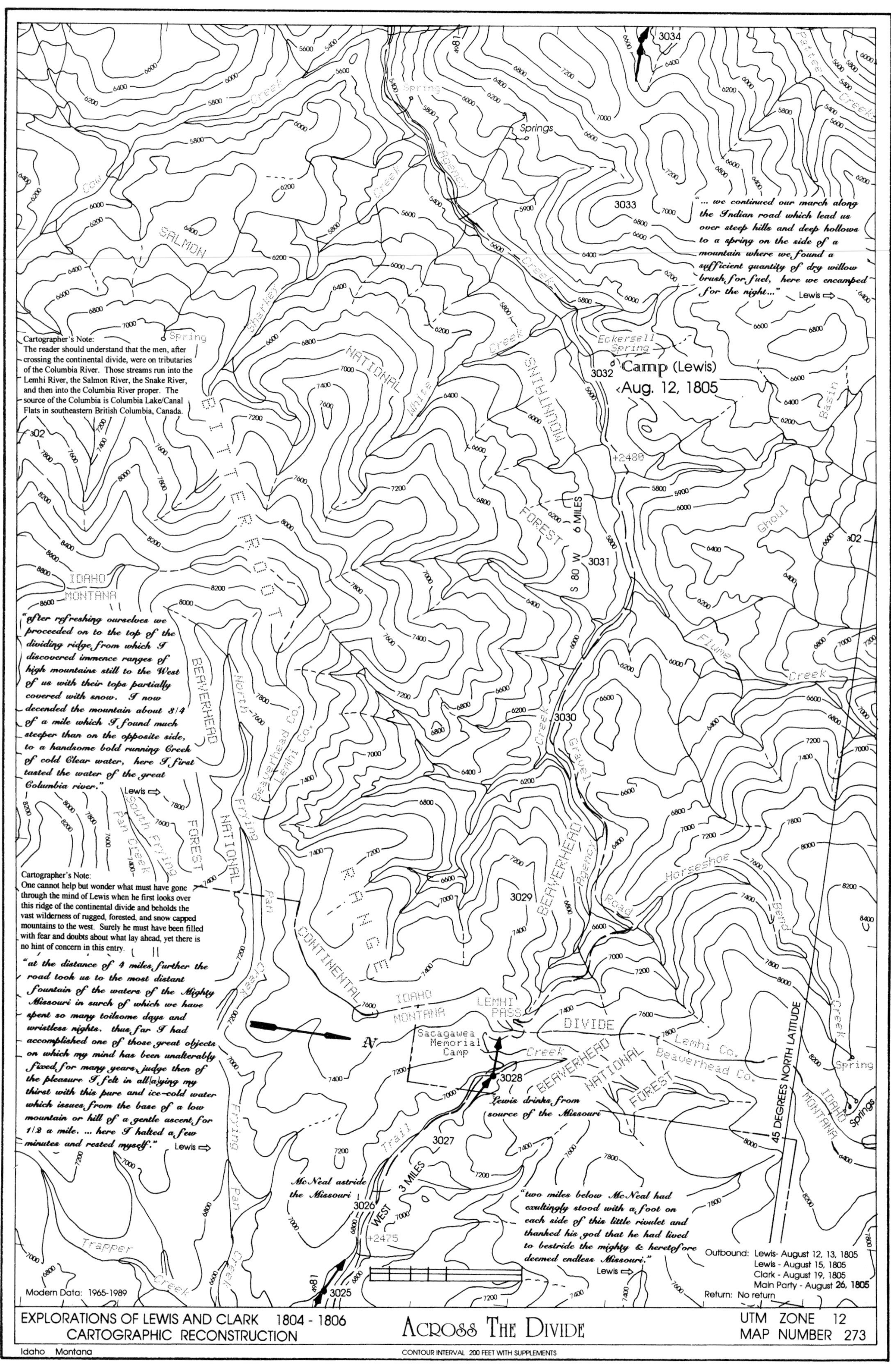
"... we continued our march along the Indian road which lead us over steep hills and deep hollows to a spring on the side of a mountain where we found a sufficient quantity of dry willow brush for fuel, here we encamped for the night..." Lewis ⇨
Camp (Lewis) Aug. 12, 1805
Eckersell Spring
Cartographer's Note:
The reader should understand that the men, after crossing the continental divide, were on tributaries of the Columbia River. Those streams run into the Lemhi River, the Salmon River, the Snake River, and then into the Columbia River proper. The source of the Columbia is Columbia Lake/Canal Flats in southeastern British Columbia, Canada.
"after refreshing ourselves we proceeded on to the top of the dividing ridge from which I discovered immence ranges of high mountains still to the West of us with their tops partially covered with snow. I now decended the mountain about 3/4 of a mile which I found much steeper than on the opposite side, to a handsome bold running Creek of cold Clear water, here I first tasted the water of the great Columbia river." Lewis ⇨
Cartographer's Note:
One cannot help but wonder what must have gone through the mind of Lewis when he first looks over this ridge of the continental divide and beholds the vast wilderness of rugged, forested, and snow capped mountains to the west. Surely he must have been filled with fear and doubts about what lay ahead, yet there is no hint of concern in this entry.
"at the distance of 4 miles further the road took us to the most distant fountain of the waters of the Mighty Missouri in surch of which we have spent so many toilsome days and wristless nights. thus far I had accomplished one of those great objects on which my mind has been unalterably fixed for many years, judge then of the pleasure I felt in all(a)ying my thirst with this pure and ice-cold water which issues from the base of a low mountain or hill of a gentle ascent for 1/2 a mile. ... here I halted a few minutes and rested myself." Lewis ⇨
Lewis drinks from source of the Missouri
McNeal astride the Missouri
"two miles below McNeal had exultingly stood with a foot on each side of this little rivulet and thanked his god that he had lived to bestride the mighty & heretofore deemed endless Missouri." Lewis ⇨
Sacagawea Memorial Camp
LEMHI PASS
IDAHO
MONTANA
DIVIDE
CONTINENTAL
BITTERROOT RANGE
BEAVERHEAD NATIONAL FOREST
SALMON NATIONAL FOREST
BEAVERHEAD MOUNTAINS
Agency Creek
Lemhi Co.
Beaverhead Co.
45 DEGREES NORTH LATITUDE
S 80 W 6 MILES
WEST 3 MILES
Trail Creek
Outbound: Lewis- August 12, 13, 1805
Lewis - August 15, 1805
Clark - August 19, 1805
Main Party - August 26, 1805
Return: No return
Modern Data: 1965-1989
EXPLORATIONS OF LEWIS AND CLARK 1804 - 1806
CARTOGRAPHIC RECONSTRUCTION
ACROSS THE DIVIDE
UTM ZONE 12
MAP NUMBER 273
Idaho Montana
CONTOUR INTERVAL 200 FEET WITH SUPPLEMENTS

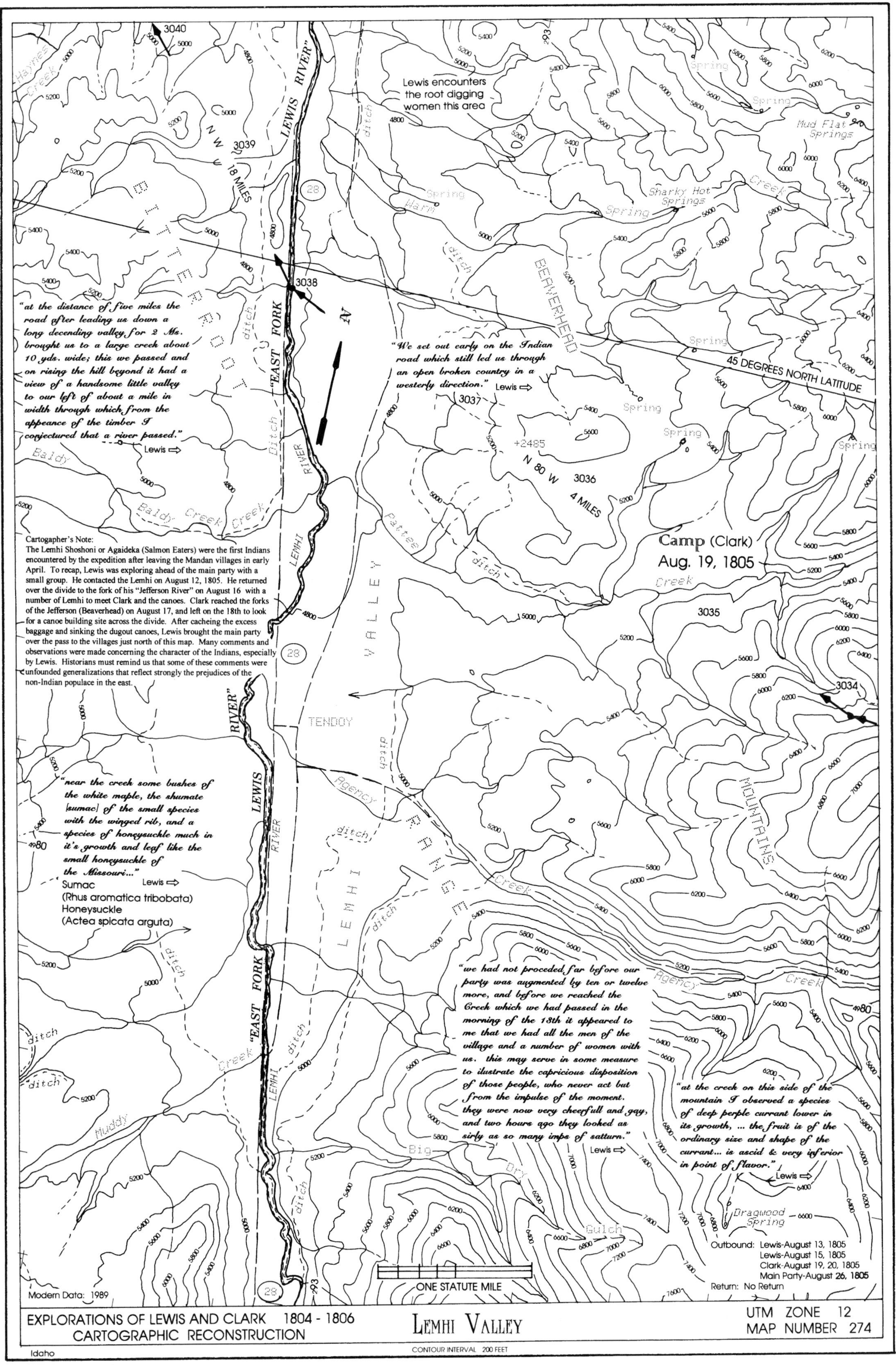

Lewis encounters the root digging women this area
N W 18 MILES
3040
3039
3038
3037
3036
3035
3034
BITTERROOT
LEWIS RIVER
"EAST FORK
Haynes Creek
Warm Spring
Sharky Hot Springs
Mud Flat Springs
Spring
BEAVERHEAD
45 DEGREES NORTH LATITUDE
"at the distance of five miles the road after leading us down a long decending valley for 2 Ms. brought us to a large creek about 10 yds. wide; this we passed and on rising the hill beyond it had a view of a handsome little valley to our left of about a mile in width through which from the appeance of the timber I conjectured that a river passed."
Lewis ⇨
"We set out early on the Indian road which still led us through an open broken country in a westerly direction."
Lewis ⇨
+2485
N 80 W 4 MILES
Baldy Creek
Camp (Clark) Aug. 19, 1805
Pattee ditch
Creek
Cartographer's Note:
The Lemhi Shoshoni or Agaideka (Salmon Eaters) were the first Indians encountered by the expedition after leaving the Mandan villages in early April. To recap, Lewis was exploring ahead of the main party with a small group. He contacted the Lemhi on August 12, 1805. He returned over the divide to the fork of his "Jefferson River" on August 16 with a number of Lemhi to meet Clark and the canoes. Clark reached the forks of the Jefferson (Beaverhead) on August 17, and left on the 18th to look for a canoe building site across the divide. After cacheing the excess baggage and sinking the dugout canoes, Lewis brought the main party over the pass to the villages just north of this map. Many comments and observations were made concerning the character of the Indians, especially by Lewis. Historians must remind us that some of these comments were unfounded generalizations that reflect strongly the prejudices of the non-Indian populace in the east.
LEMHI RIVER
LEMHI VALLEY
TENDOY
MOUNTAINS
LEMHI RANGE
Agency Creek
"near the creek some bushes of the white maple, the shumate [sumac] of the small species with the winged rib, and a species of honeysuckle much in it's growth and leaf like the small honeysuckle of the Missouri..."
Lewis ⇨
Sumac
(Rhus aromatica tribobata)
Honeysuckle
(Actea spicata arguta)
"we had not proceeded far before our party was augmented by ten or twelve more, and before we reached the Creek which we had passed in the morning of the 18th it appeared to me that we had all the men of the village and a number of women with us. this may serve in some measure to illustrate the capricious disposition of those people, who never act but from the impulse of the moment. they were now very cheerfull and gay, and two hours ago they looked as sirly as so many imps of satturn."
Lewis ⇨
"at the creek on this side of the mountain I observed a species of deep perple currant lower in its growth, ... the fruit is of the ordinary size and shape of the currant... is ascid & very inferior in point of flavor."
Lewis ⇨
Muddy Creek
Big Dry Gulch
Dragwood Spring
Outbound: Lewis-August 13, 1805
Lewis-August 15, 1805
Clark-August 19, 20, 1805
Main Party-August 26, 1805
Return: No Return
ONE STATUTE MILE
Modern Data: 1989
EXPLORATIONS OF LEWIS AND CLARK 1804 - 1806
CARTOGRAPHIC RECONSTRUCTION
LEMHI VALLEY
UTM ZONE 12
MAP NUMBER 274
Idaho
CONTOUR INTERVAL 200 FEET

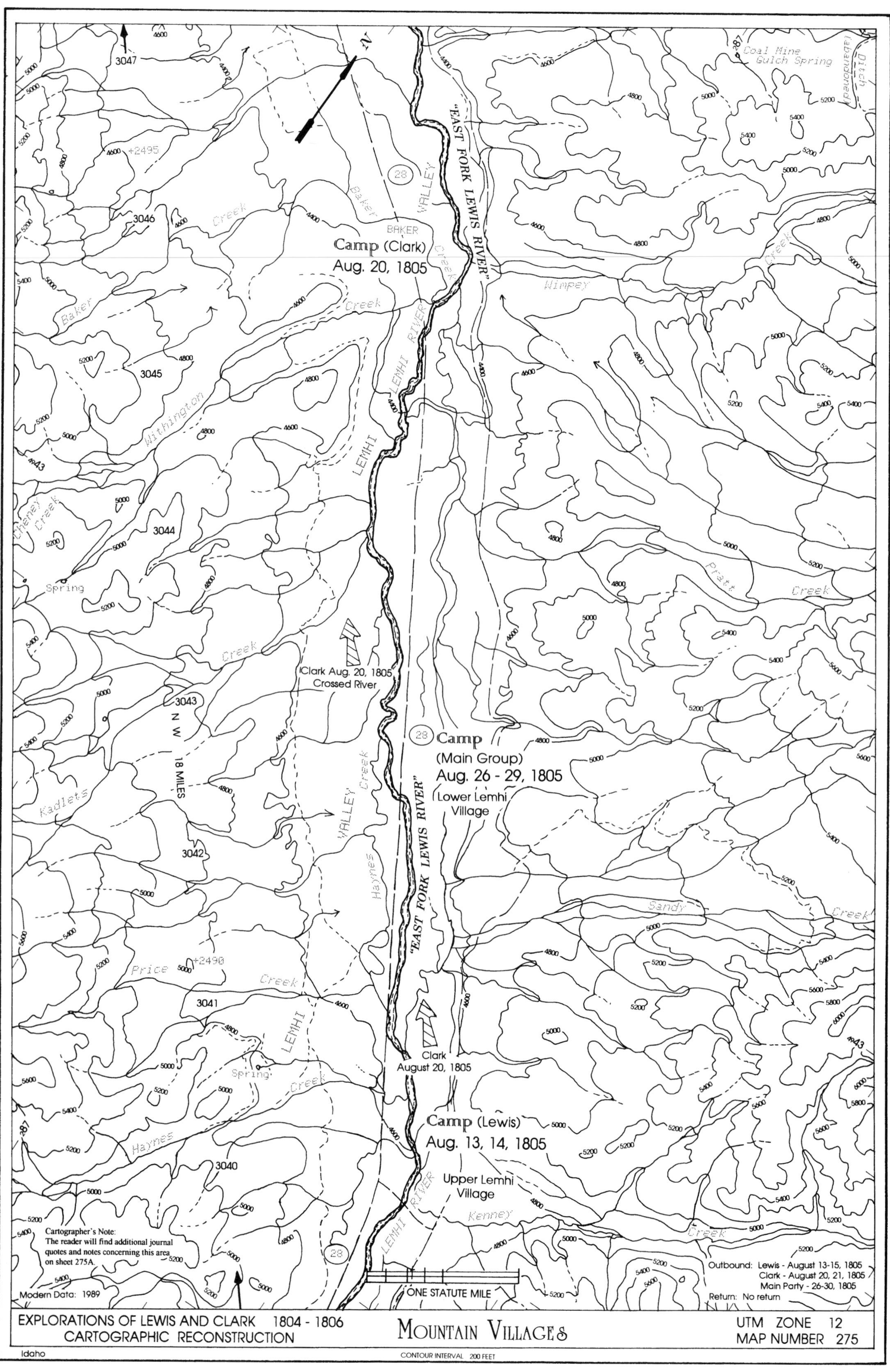

Camp (Clark)
Aug. 20, 1805
"EAST FORK LEWIS RIVER"
LEMHI RIVER
LEMHI
VALLEY
Baker Creek
Withington Creek
Wimpey Creek
Pratt Creek
Cheney Creek
Coal Mine Gulch Spring
Ditch (abandoned)
Clark Aug. 20, 1805
Crossed River
Camp
(Main Group)
Aug. 26 - 29, 1805
Lower Lemhi
Village
Kadletz Creek
Haynes Creek
Sandy Creek
Price Creek
Spring
18 MILES
N W
Clark
August 20, 1805
Camp (Lewis)
Aug. 13, 14, 1805
Upper Lemhi
Village
Kenney Creek
Cartographer's Note:
The reader will find additional journal quotes and notes concerning this area on sheet 275A.
Modern Data: 1989
ONE STATUTE MILE
Outbound: Lewis - August 13-15, 1805
Clark - August 20, 21, 1805
Main Party - 26-30, 1805
Return: No return
EXPLORATIONS OF LEWIS AND CLARK 1804 - 1806
CARTOGRAPHIC RECONSTRUCTION
MOUNTAIN VILLAGES
UTM ZONE 12
MAP NUMBER 275
Idaho
CONTOUR INTERVAL 200 FEET

Cartographer's Note:
The following quotes are from Lewis' first visit to the village of the Lemhi people. Lewis needed to have the use of enough horses to carry the expedition's baggage from the forks of his Jefferson (today's Beaverhead) River over the divide to, hopefully, a site where they could make canoes to take them down the waters of the Columbia River system. Fearing that Clark was still struggling up to the forks with the canoes, Lewis delayed at the upper village before explaining his need. The village could not have been very impressive. These Lemhi had been attacked by the Blackfeet in the spring. The powerful Blackfeet had burned all of the leather tepee shelters of the Lemhi, save the one the Lemhi set up for Lewis and his men. The Lemhi were sheltered in small huts made of sticks and covered with brush. Even in mid August, the high mountain valley was clothed nearly every morning in frost and ice.

August 13, 1805

"... proceeded about four miles through a wavy plain parallel to the valley or river bottom when at the distance of about a mile we saw two women, a man and some dogs on an eminence immediately before us. ... two of them after a few minutes set down as if to wait our arrival we continued our usual pace towards them. ... the women soon disappeared behind the hill, the man continued untill I arrived within a hundred yards of him and then likewise absconded."

Lewis ⇨

August 13, 1805

"the prickley pear are of three species that with a broad leaf common to the missouri; ... a 3rd peculiar to this country. it consists of small circular thick leaves with a much greater number of thorns. these thorns are stronger and appear to be barbed. the leaves... are so slightly attached that when the thorn touches your mockerson it adheres and brings with it the leaf covered in every direction with many others."

Lewis ⇨

Cartographer's Note:
The cartographer grows a number of plants significant to the expedition and attests that this prickly pear is every bit as nasty as Lewis claims. Excellent as a foundation planting to keep burglars from windows. The plant has two types of thorns. The large stiff thorns are one to one and a half inches in length and scattered over the pads. The second is about a quarter of an inch or less, light brown in color, and is scattered over the pads in tight tufts of a dozen or more thorns. They almost seem to jump at any person or animal that comes close. They, usually the entire tuft, burrow into the skin and are hard to remove intact. They will pass through heavy leather gloves in seconds. The cartographer has found that a very few of these thorns in the skin can cause a mild poison like effect lasting several hours.

August 13, 1805

"... we were so fortunate as to meet with three female savages. the short and steep ravines which we passed concealed us from each other untill we arrived within 30 paces. a young woman immediately took to flight, an Elderly woman and a girl of about 12 years old remained. ... they appeared much allarmed but saw that we were to near for them to escape by flight they therefore seated themselves on the ground, holding down their heads as if reconciled to die which the[y] expected..."

Lewis ⇨

August 13, 1805

"I wished them to conduct us to their camp... we set out, still pursuing the road... met a party of about 60 warriors mounted on excellent horses who came in nearly full speed, ... the chief and two others who were a little in advance of the main body spoke to the women, and they informed them who we were and exultingly shewed the presents which had been given them these men then advanced and embraced me very affectionately in their way..."

Lewis ⇨

August 13, 1805

"... walked to the river, which I found about 40 yards wide very rapid clear and about 3 feet deep. ...Cameahwait informed me... that the river was confined between inacessable mountains, was very rapid and rocky insomuch that it was impossible for us to pass either by land or water down this river to the great lake where the white men lived..."

Lewis ⇨

August 13, 1805

"these people had been attacked by the Minetares of Fort de prarie this spring and about 20 of them killed and taken prisoners. on this occasion they lost a great part of their horses and all their lodges..."

Lewis ⇨

August 13, 1805

"this was the first salmon I had seen and perfectly convinced me that we were on the waters of the Pacific Ocean."

Lewis ⇨

August 14, 1805

"In order to give Capt. Clark time to reach the forks of Jefferson's river I concluded to spend this day at the Shoshone Camp..."

Lewis ⇨

August 14, 1805

"I directed Drewyer and Shields to hunt a few hours and try to kill something, the Indians furnished them with horses and most of their young men also turned out to hunt. the game which they principally hunt is the Antelope which they pursue on horseback and shoot with their arrows. this animal is so extreemly fleet and dureable that a single horse has no possible chance to overtake them or run them down. the Indians are therefore obliged to have recorce to strategem when they discover a herd of the Antelope they seperate and scatter themselves to the distance of five or six miles in different directions arround them generally scelecting some commanding eminence for a stand; some one or two now pursue the herd at full speed over the hills vallies gullies and the sides of precipices that are tremendious to view. thus after runing them from five to six or seven miles the fresh horses that were in waiting head them and drive them back persuing them as far or perhaps further quite to the other extreem of the hunters who now in turn pursue on their fresh horses thus worrying the poor animal down and finally killing them with their arrows. forty or fifty hunters will be engaged for half a day in this manner and perhaps not kill more than two or three Antelopes."

Lewis ⇨

August 14, 1805

"I was very much entertained with a view of this indian chase; it was after a herd of about 10 Antelope and about 20 hunters. it lasted about 2 hours and considerable part of the chase in view from my tent. about 1.A.M. the hunters returned had not killed a single Antelope, and their horses foaming with sweat. my hunters returned soon after and had been equally unsuccessfull."

Lewis ⇨

August 14, 1805

"The means I had of communicating with these people was by way of Drewyer who understood perfectly the common language of jesticulation or signs which seems to be universally understood by all the Nations we have yet seen."

Lewis ⇨

August 14, 1805

"I now told Cameahwait that I wished him to speak to his people and engage them to go with me tomorrow to the forks of Jeffersons river where our baggage was by this time arrived with another Chief and a large party of whitemen..."

Lewis ⇨

August 14, 1805

"notwithstanding the extreem poverty of those poor people they are very merry they danced again this evening untill midnight. each warrior keep[s] one or more horses tyed by a cord to a stake near his lodge both day and night and are always prepared for action at a moments warning. they fight on horseback altogether. I observe that the large flies are extreemly troublesome to the horses as well as ourselves."

Lewis ⇨

August 15, 1805

"I found on enquiry of McNeal that we had only about two pounds of flour remaining. this I directed him to divide into two equal parts and to cook the one half this morning in a kind of pudding with the burries as he had done yesterday and reserve the ballance for the evening. on this new fashoned pudding four of us breakfasted, giving a pretty good allowance also to the Chief who declared it the best thing he had taisted for a long time."

Lewis ⇨

August 15, 1805

"the Chief addressed them several times before they would move they seemed very reluctant to accompany me. I at length asked the reason and he told me that some foolish persons among them had suggested the idea that we were in league with the Pahkees and had come on in order to decoy them into an ambuscade where their enimies were waiting to receive them. ... I readily perceived that our situation was not enterely free from danger as the transicion from suspicion to the confermation of the fact would not be very difficult in the minds of these ignorant people who have been accustomed from their infancy to view every stranger as an enimy. I told Cameahwait that I was sorry to find that they had put so little confidence in us, that I knew they were not acquainted with whitemen and therefore could forgive them. that among whitemen it was considered disgracefull to lye or entrap an enimy by falsehood."

Lewis ⇨

August 20, 1805

"... to the Camp of the Indians on a branch of the Columbia River, ..."

Clark ⇨

August 20, 1805

"Those pore people Could only raise a Sammon & a little dried Choke Cherries for us..."

Clark ⇨

August 20, 1805

"... at 8 oClock... I set out accompanied by an old man as a Guide..."

Clark ⇨

Cartographer's Note:
Clark was leading a small party of men to examine the Lewis River, today's Salmon, to determine if canoes could be constructed and navigated downstream.

August 26, 1805

"we were conducted to a large lodge which had been prepared for me in the center of their encampment which was situated in a beautifull level smooth and extensive bottom near the river about 3 miles above the place I had first found them encamped."

Lewis ⇨

August 26, 1805

"I found Colter here who had just arrived with a letter from Capt. Clark in which Capt. C. had given me an account of his perigrination and the description of the river and country as before detailed [advised the purchase of horses and the pursute of a rout he had learned from his guide who had promised to pilot ous to a road. to the North &c.] from this view of the subject I found it a folly to think of attemp[t]ing to decend this river in canoes and therefore determined to commence the purchase of horses in the morning..."

Lewis ⇨

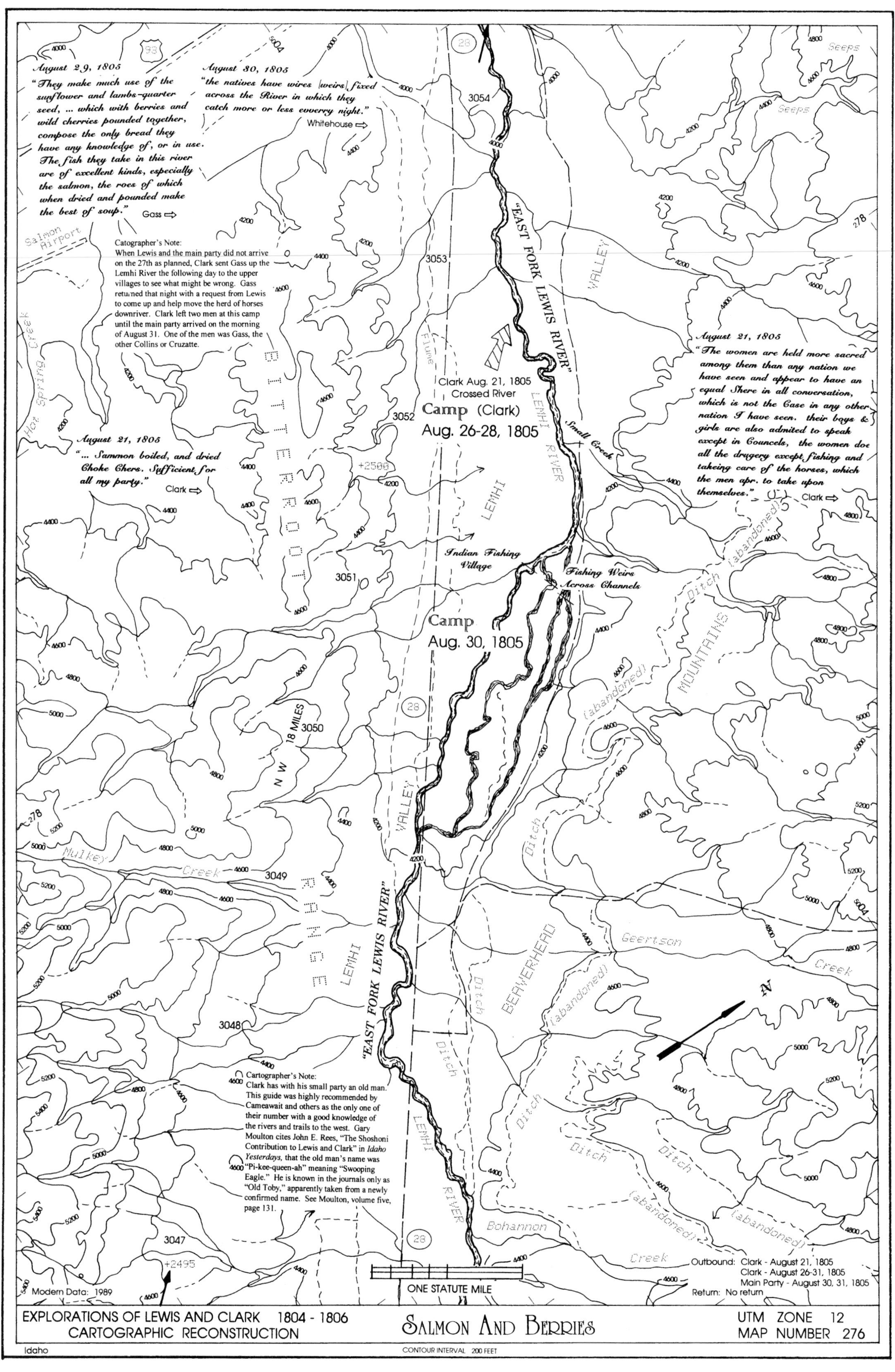
August 29, 1805
"They make much use of the sunflower and lambs-quarter seed, ... which with berries and wild cherries pounded together, compose the only bread they have any knowledge of, or in use. The fish they take in this river are of excellent kinds, especially the salmon, the roes of which when dried and pounded make the best of soup."
Gass ⇨
August 30, 1805
"the natives have wires [weirs] fixed across the River in which they catch more or less evverry night."
Whitehouse ⇨
Catographer's Note:
When Lewis and the main party did not arrive on the 27th as planned, Clark sent Gass up the Lemhi River the following day to the upper villages to see what might be wrong. Gass returned that night with a request from Lewis to come up and help move the herd of horses downriver. Clark left two men at this camp until the main party arrived on the morning of August 31. One of the men was Gass, the other Collins or Cruzatte.
August 21, 1805
"... Sammon boiled, and dried Choke Chers. Sufficient for all my party."
Clark ⇨
August 21, 1805
"The women are held more sacred among them than any nation we have seen and appear to have an equal Shere in all conversation, which is not the Case in any other nation I have seen. their boys & girls are also admited to speak except in Councels, the women doe all the drugery except fishing and takeing care of the horses, which the men apr. to take upon themselves."
Clark ⇨
Salmon Airport
Hot Spring Creek
BITTERROOT
RANGE
"EAST FORK LEWIS RIVER"
LEMHI RIVER
LEMHI VALLEY
Small Creek
Clark Aug. 21, 1805
Crossed River
Camp (Clark)
Aug. 26-28, 1805
Indian Fishing Village
Fishing Weirs Across Channels
Camp
Aug. 30, 1805
18 MILES
Flume
Seeps
MOUNTAINS
Ditch (abandoned)
Mulkey Creek
Geertson Creek
BEAVERHEAD
Bohannon Creek
Cartographer's Note:
Clark has with his small party an old man. This guide was highly recommended by Cameawait and others as the only one of their number with a good knowledge of the rivers and trails to the west. Gary Moulton cites John E. Rees, "The Shoshoni Contribution to Lewis and Clark" in Idaho Yesterdays, that the old man's name was "Pi-kee-queen-ah" meaning "Swooping Eagle." He is known in the journals only as "Old Toby," apparently taken from a newly confirmed name. See Moulton, volume five, page 131.
N
Modern Data: 1989
ONE STATUTE MILE
Outbound: Clark - August 21, 1805
Clark - August 26-31, 1805
Main Party - August 30, 31, 1805
Return: No return
EXPLORATIONS OF LEWIS AND CLARK 1804 - 1806
CARTOGRAPHIC RECONSTRUCTION
SALMON AND BERRIES
UTM ZONE 12
MAP NUMBER 276
Idaho
CONTOUR INTERVAL 200 FEET

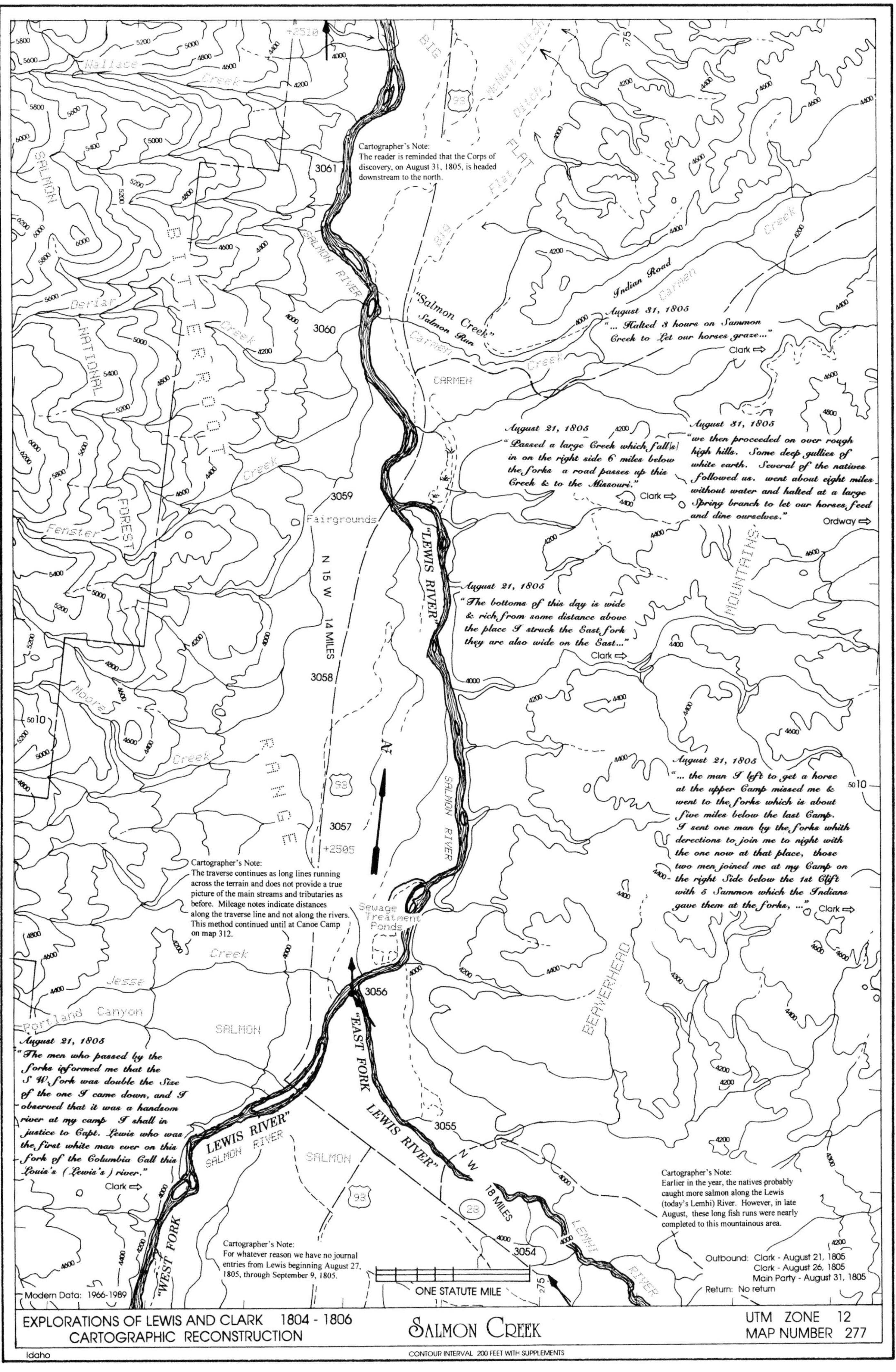
Cartographer's Note:
The reader is reminded that the Corps of discovery, on August 31, 1805, is headed downstream to the north.
"Salmon Creek"
Salmon Run
August 31, 1805
"... Halted 3 hours on Sammon Creek to Let our horses graze..."
Clark ⇨
Indian Road
August 21, 1805
"Passed a large Creek which fall[s] in on the right side 6 miles below the forks a road passes up this Creek & to the Missouri."
Clark ⇨
August 31, 1805
"we then proceeded on over rough high hills. Some deep gullies of white earth. Several of the natives followed us. went about eight miles without water and halted at a large Spring branch to let our horses feed and dine ourselves."
Ordway ⇨
August 21, 1805
"The bottoms of this day is wide & rich from some distance above the place I struck the East fork they are also wide on the East..."
Clark ⇨
August 21, 1805
"... the man I left to get a horse at the upper Camp missed me & went to the forks which is about five miles below the last Camp. I sent one man by the forks whith derections to join me to night with the one now at that place, those two men joined me at my Camp on the right Side below the 1st Clift with 5 Sammon which the Indians gave them at the forks, ..."
Clark ⇨
Cartographer's Note:
The traverse continues as long lines running across the terrain and does not provide a true picture of the main streams and tributaries as before. Mileage notes indicate distances along the traverse line and not along the rivers. This method continued until at Canoe Camp on map 312.
August 21, 1805
"The men who passed by the forks informed me that the S W fork was double the Size of the one I came down, and I observed that it was a handsom river at my camp I shall in justice to Capt. Lewis who was the first white man ever on this fork of the Columbia Call this Louis's (Lewis's) river."
Clark ⇨
Cartographer's Note:
Earlier in the year, the natives probably caught more salmon along the Lewis (today's Lemhi) River. However, in late August, these long fish runs were nearly completed to this mountainous area.
Cartographer's Note:
For whatever reason we have no journal entries from Lewis beginning August 27, 1805, through September 9, 1805.
Outbound: Clark - August 21, 1805
Clark - August 26, 1805
Main Party - August 31, 1805
Return: No return
SALMON NATIONAL FOREST
BITTERROOT RANGE
BEAVERHEAD MOUNTAINS
SALMON RIVER
"LEWIS RIVER"
"EAST FORK LEWIS RIVER"
"WEST FORK"
LEMHI RIVER
Wallace Creek
Deriar Creek
Fenster Creek
Moore Creek
Jesse Creek
Portland Canyon
Carmen Creek
CARMEN
SALMON
Big Flat Ditch
McNutt Ditch
Fairgrounds
Sewage Treatment Ponds
N 15 W 14 MILES
N W 18 MILES
3061
3060
3059
3058
3057
3056
3055
3054
93
28
ONE STATUTE MILE
Modern Data: 1966-1989
EXPLORATIONS OF LEWIS AND CLARK 1804 - 1806
CARTOGRAPHIC RECONSTRUCTION
SALMON CREEK
UTM ZONE 12
MAP NUMBER 277
Idaho
CONTOUR INTERVAL 200 FEET WITH SUPPLEMENTS

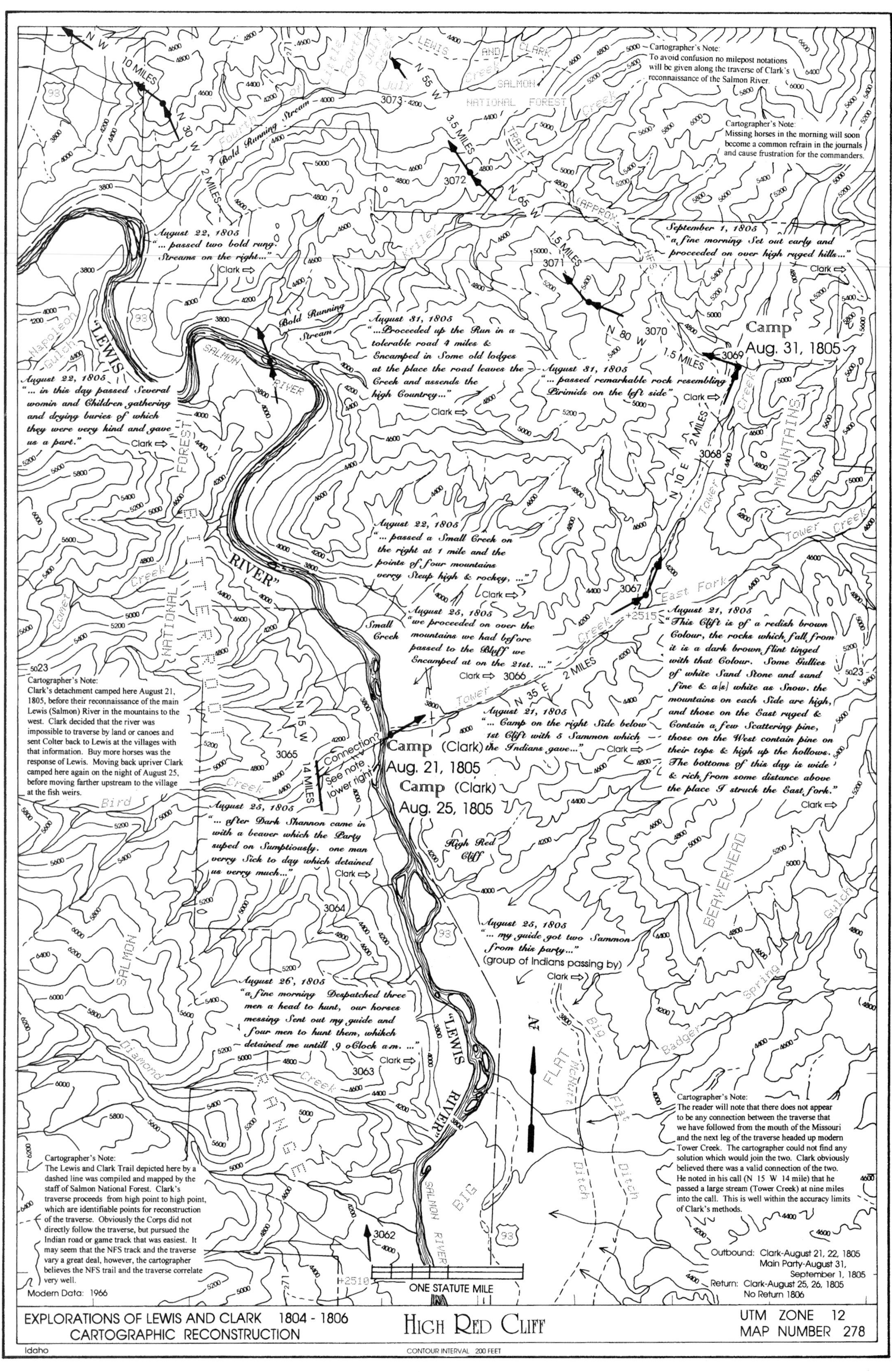
Cartographer's Note:
To avoid confusion no milepost notations will be given along the traverse of Clark's reconnaissance of the Salmon River.
Cartographer's Note:
Missing horses in the morning will soon become a common refrain in the journals and cause frustration for the commanders.
LEWIS AND CLARK TRAIL
SALMON NATIONAL FOREST
Fourth of July Creek
Little Fourth of July Creek
Bold Running Stream
10 MILES
N 30 W
2 MILES
N 55 W
3.5 MILES
N 65 W
(APPROX.)
1.5 MILES
N 80 W
1.5 MILES
N 10 E
2 MILES
N 35 E
2 MILES
N 15 W
14 MILES
Connection? See note lower right
August 22, 1805
"... passed two bold rung. Streams on the right..."
Clark ⇨
September 1, 1805
"a fine morning Set out early and proceeded on over high ruged hills..."
Clark ⇨
Camp
Aug. 31, 1805
August 31, 1805
"...Proceeded up the Run in a tolerable road 4 miles & Encamped in Some old lodges at the place the road leaves the Creek and assends the high Countrey..."
Clark ⇨
August 31, 1805
"... passed remarkable rock resembling Pirimids on the left side"
Clark ⇨
August 22, 1805
"... in this day passed Several womin and Children gathering and drying buries of which they were very kind and gave us a part."
Clark ⇨
"LEWIS RIVER"
SALMON RIVER
Napoleon Gulch
Kriley
BITTERROOT
NATIONAL FOREST
MOUNTAINS
Tower Creek
East Fork
August 22, 1805
"... passed a Small Creek on the right at 1 mile and the points of four mountains verry Steup high & rockey, ..."
Clark ⇨
Small Creek
August 25, 1805
"we proceeded on over the mountains we had before passed to the Bluff we Encamped at on the 21st. ..."
Clark ⇨
August 21, 1805
"This Clift is of a redish brown Colour, the rocks which fall from it is a dark brown flint tinged with that Colour. Some Gullies of white Sand Stone and sand fine & a[s] white as Snow. the mountains on each Side are high, and those on the East ruged & Contain a few Scattering pine, those on the West contain pine on their tops & high up the hollows. The bottoms of this day is wide & rich from some distance above the place I struck the East fork."
Clark ⇨
August 21, 1805
"... Camp on the right Side below 1st Clift with 5 Sammon which the Indians gave..."
Clark ⇨
Cartographer's Note:
Clark's detachment camped here August 21, 1805, before their reconnaissance of the main Lewis (Salmon) River in the mountains to the west. Clark decided that the river was impossible to traverse by land or canoes and sent Colter back to Lewis at the villages with that information. Buy more horses was the response of Lewis. Moving back upriver Clark camped here again on the night of August 25, before moving farther upstream to the village at the fish weirs.
Camp (Clark)
Aug. 21, 1805
Camp (Clark)
Aug. 25, 1805
Comet Creek
Bird Creek
August 25, 1805
"... after Dark Shannon came in with a beaver which the Party suped on Sumptiously. one man verry Sick to day which detained us verry much..."
Clark ⇨
High Red Cliff
August 25, 1805
"... my guide got two Sammon from this party..."
(group of Indians passing by)
Clark ⇨
BEAVERHEAD
Spring Gulch
Badger
August 26, 1805
"a fine morning Despatched three men a head to hunt, our horses messing Sent out my guide and four men to hunt them, whikch detained me untill 9 oClock a.m. ..."
Clark ⇨
SALMON RIVER RANGE
Diamond Creek
"LEWIS RIVER"
FLAT
McNUTT
Big Flat Ditch
BIG
SALMON RIVER
Cartographer's Note:
The reader will note that there does not appear to be any connection between the traverse that we have followed from the mouth of the Missouri and the next leg of the traverse headed up modern Tower Creek. The cartographer could not find any solution which would join the two. Clark obviously believed there was a valid connection of the two. He noted in his call (N 15 W 14 mile) that he passed a large stream (Tower Creek) at nine miles into the call. This is well within the accuracy limits of Clark's methods.
Cartographer's Note:
The Lewis and Clark Trail depicted here by a dashed line was compiled and mapped by the staff of Salmon National Forest. Clark's traverse proceeds from high point to high point, which are identifiable points for reconstruction of the traverse. Obviously the Corps did not directly follow the traverse, but pursued the Indian road or game track that was easiest. It may seem that the NFS track and the traverse vary a great deal, however, the cartographer believes the NFS trail and the traverse correlate very well.
Modern Data: 1966
ONE STATUTE MILE
Outbound: Clark-August 21, 22, 1805
Main Party-August 31, September 1, 1805
Return: Clark-August 25, 26, 1805
No Return 1806
EXPLORATIONS OF LEWIS AND CLARK 1804 - 1806
CARTOGRAPHIC RECONSTRUCTION
HIGH RED CLIFF
UTM ZONE 12
MAP NUMBER 278
Idaho
CONTOUR INTERVAL 200 FEET

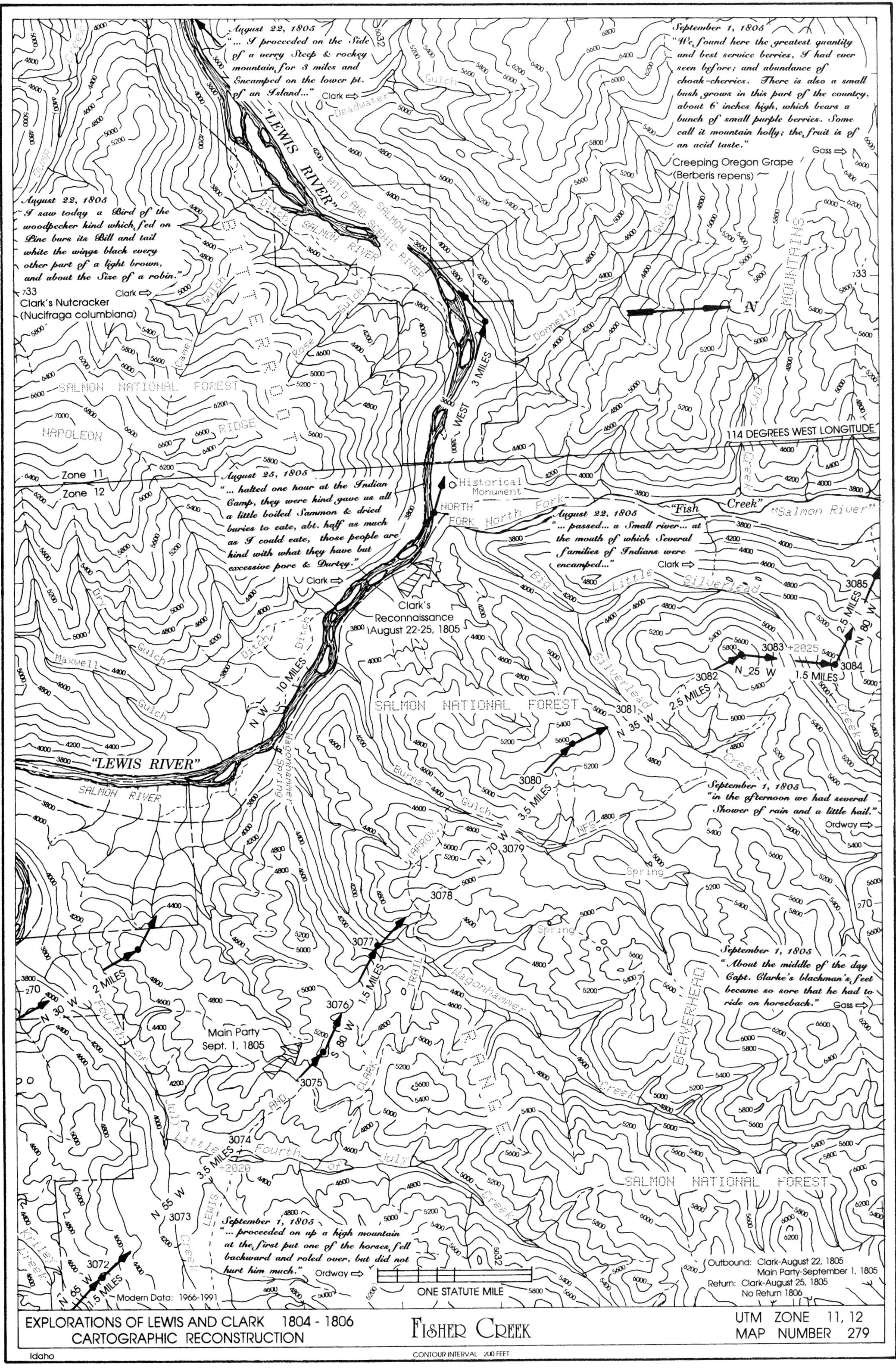

August 22, 1805
"... I proceeded on the Side of a verry Steep & rockey mountain for 3 miles and Encamped on the lower pt. of an Island..."
Clark
September 1, 1805
"We found here the greatest quantity and best service berries, I had ever seen before; and abundance of choak-cherries. There is also a small bush grows in this part of the country, about 6' inches high, which bears a bunch of small purple berries. Some call it mountain holly; the fruit is of an acid taste."
Gass
Creeping Oregon Grape
(Berberis repens)
August 22, 1805
"I saw today a Bird of the woodpecker kind which fed on Pine burs its Bill and tail white the wings black every other part of a light brown, and about the Size of a robin."
Clark
Clark's Nutcracker
(Nucifraga columbiana)
"LEWIS RIVER"
SALMON RIVER
WILD AND SCENIC RIVER
SALMON NATIONAL FOREST
NAPOLEON
RIDGE
BITTERROOT
MOUNTAINS
WEST 3 MILES
114 DEGREES WEST LONGITUDE
Zone 11
Zone 12
August 25, 1805
"... halted one hour at the Indian Camp, they were kind gave us all a little boiled Sammon & dried buries to eate, abt. half as much as I could eate, those people are kind with what they have but excessive pore & Durtey."
Clark
Historical Monument
NORTH FORK
North Fork
August 22, 1805
"... passed... a Small river... at the mouth of which Several families of Indians were encamped..."
Clark
"Fish Creek"
"Salmon River"
Clark's Reconnaissance
August 22-25, 1805
NW 10 MILES
SALMON NATIONAL FOREST
N 35 W 2.5 MILES
N 25 W
1.5 MILES
2.5 MILES N 80 W
September 1, 1805
"in the afternoon we had several Shower of rain and a little hail."
Ordway
N 70 W 3.5 MILES
September 1, 1805
"About the middle of the day Capt. Clarke's blackman's feet became so sore that he had to ride on horseback."
Gass
N 30 W 2 MILES
1.5 MILES
S 80 W
Main Party
Sept. 1, 1805
LEWIS AND CLARK TRAIL
RANGE
BEAVERHEAD
3.5 MILES
N 55 W
N 65 W 1.5 MILES
SALMON NATIONAL FOREST
September 1, 1805
"... proceeded on up a high mountain at the first put one of the horses fell backward and roled over, but did not hurt him much."
Ordway
ONE STATUTE MILE
Modern Data: 1966-1991
Outbound: Clark-August 22, 1805
Main Party-September 1, 1805
Return: Clark-August 25, 1805
No Return 1806
EXPLORATIONS OF LEWIS AND CLARK 1804 - 1806
CARTOGRAPHIC RECONSTRUCTION
FISHER CREEK
UTM ZONE 11, 12
MAP NUMBER 279
Idaho
CONTOUR INTERVAL 200 FEET

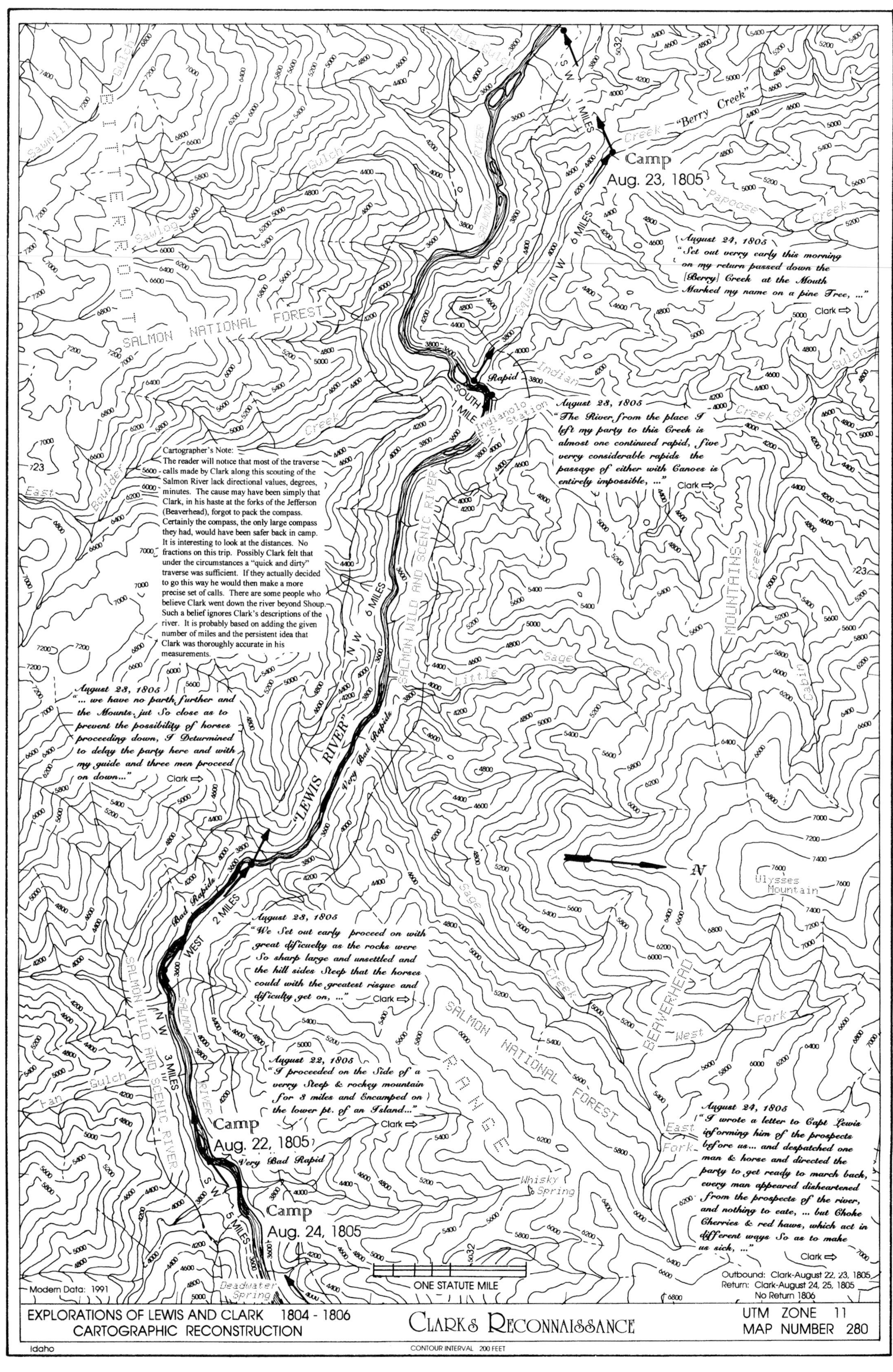
Camp
Aug. 23, 1805
"Berry Creek"
Papoose Creek
Hale Gulch
SALMON RIVER
Squaw
Indian
Rapid
SOUTH
MILE
Indianola F.S. Station
BITTERROOT
SALMON NATIONAL FOREST
Sawmill Gulch
Sawlog
Boulder
East
Creek
Cow Creek
Gulch
MOUNTAINS
Little Sage Creek
Cabin
S W MILES
N W 6 MILES
N W 6 MILES
SALMON WILD AND SCENIC RIVER
"LEWIS RIVER"
Very Bad Rapids
Bad Rapids
WEST 2 MILES
N W 3 MILES
SALMON RIVER
Gulch
Fan
Camp
Aug. 22, 1805
Very Bad Rapid
Camp
Aug. 24, 1805
S W 5 MILES
Deadwater Spring
Whisky Spring
Sage Creek
SALMON RIVER RANGE
SALMON NATIONAL FOREST
BEAVERHEAD
West Fork
East Fork
Ulysses Mountain
N
August 24, 1805
"Set out verry early this morning on my return passed down the [Berry] Creek at the Mouth Marked my name on a pine Tree, ..."
Clark ⇨
August 23, 1805
"The River from the place I left my party to this Creek is almost one continued rapid, five verry considerable rapids the passage of either with Canoes is entirely impossible, ..."
Clark ⇨
Cartographer's Note:
The reader will notice that most of the traverse calls made by Clark along this scouting of the Salmon River lack directional values, degrees, minutes. The cause may have been simply that Clark, in his haste at the forks of the Jefferson (Beaverhead), forgot to pack the compass. Certainly the compass, the only large compass they had, would have been safer back in camp. It is interesting to look at the distances. No fractions on this trip. Possibly Clark felt that under the circumstances a "quick and dirty" traverse was sufficient. If they actually decided to go this way he would then make a more precise set of calls. There are some people who believe Clark went down the river beyond Shoup. Such a belief ignores Clark's descriptions of the river. It is probably based on adding the given number of miles and the persistent idea that Clark was thoroughly accurate in his measurements.
August 23, 1805
"... we have no parth further and the Mounts. jut So close as to prevent the possibility of horses proceeding down, I Deturmined to delay the party here and with my guide and three men proceed on down..."
Clark ⇨
August 23, 1805
"We Set out early proceed on with great dificuelty as the rocks were So sharp large and unsettled and the hill sides Steep that the horses could with the greatest risque and dificulty get on, ..."
Clark ⇨
August 22, 1805
"I proceeded on the Side of a verry Steep & rockey mountain for 3 miles and Encamped on the lower pt. of an Island..."
Clark ⇨
August 24, 1805
"I wrote a letter to Capt Lewis informing him of the prospects before us... and despatched one man & horse and directed the party to get ready to march back, every man appeared disheartened from the prospects of the river, and nothing to eate, ... but Choke Cherries & red haws, which act in different ways So as to make us sick, ..."
Clark ⇨
ONE STATUTE MILE
Modern Data: 1991
Outbound: Clark-August 22, 23, 1805
Return: Clark-August 24, 25, 1805
No Return 1806
EXPLORATIONS OF LEWIS AND CLARK 1804 - 1806
CARTOGRAPHIC RECONSTRUCTION
CLARKS RECONNAISSANCE
UTM ZONE 11
MAP NUMBER 280
Idaho
CONTOUR INTERVAL 200 FEET

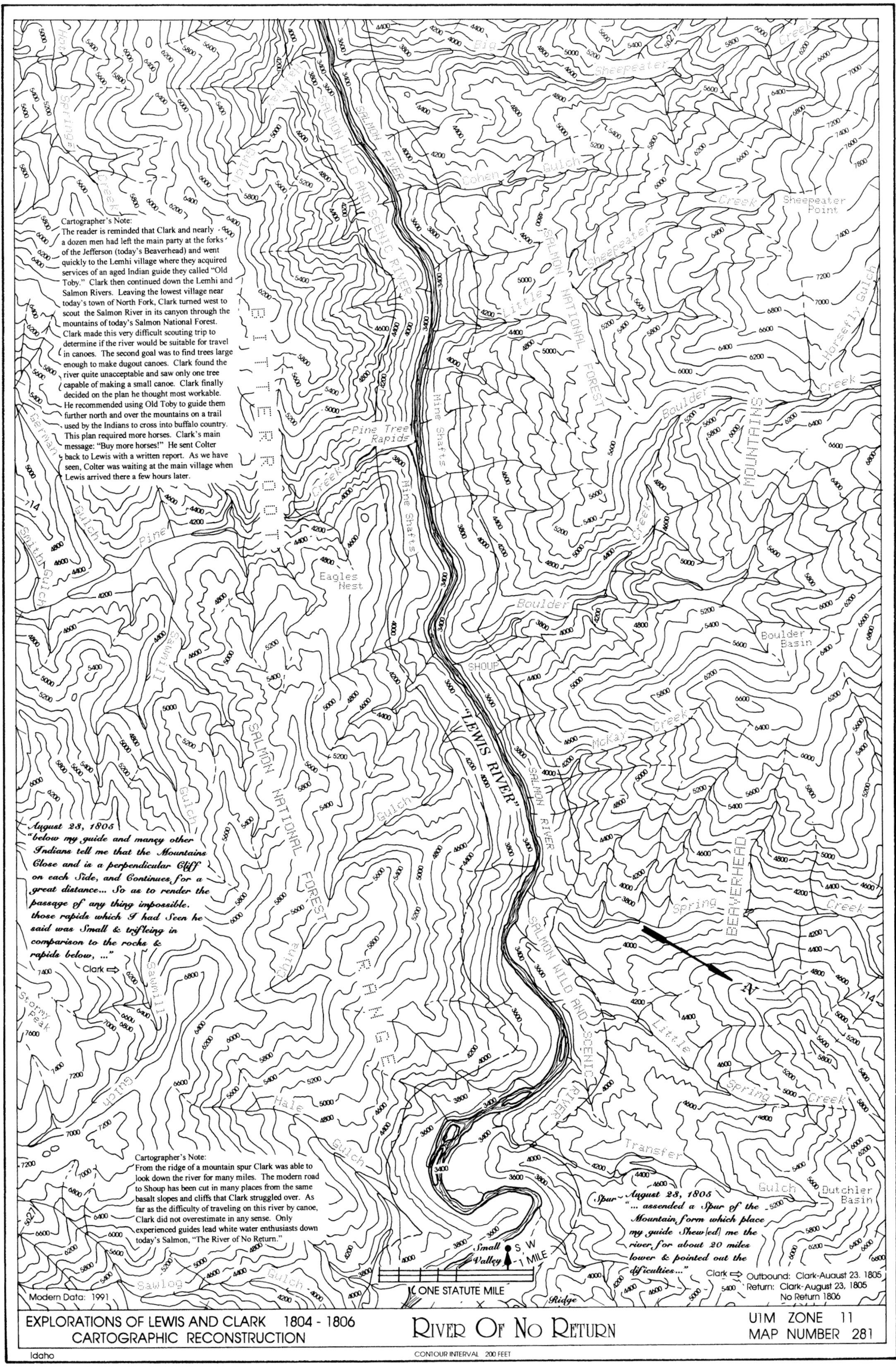
Cartographer's Note:
The reader is reminded that Clark and nearly a dozen men had left the main party at the forks of the Jefferson (today's Beaverhead) and went quickly to the Lemhi village where they acquired services of an aged Indian guide they called "Old Toby." Clark then continued down the Lemhi and Salmon Rivers. Leaving the lowest village near today's town of North Fork, Clark turned west to scout the Salmon River in its canyon through the mountains of today's Salmon National Forest. Clark made this very difficult scouting trip to determine if the river would be suitable for travel in canoes. The second goal was to find trees large enough to make dugout canoes. Clark found the river quite unacceptable and saw only one tree capable of making a small canoe. Clark finally decided on the plan he thought most workable. He recommended using Old Toby to guide them further north and over the mountains on a trail used by the Indians to cross into buffalo country. This plan required more horses. Clark's main message: "Buy more horses!" He sent Colter back to Lewis with a written report. As we have seen, Colter was waiting at the main village when Lewis arrived there a few hours later.
August 28, 1805
"below my guide and maney other Indians tell me that the Mountains Close and is a perpendicular Cliff on each Side, and Continues for a great distance... So as to render the passage of any thing impossible. those rapids which I had Seen he said was Small & trifleing in comparison to the rocks & rapids below, ..."
Clark ⇨
Cartographer's Note:
From the ridge of a mountain spur Clark was able to look down the river for many miles. The modern road to Shoup has been cut in many places from the same basalt slopes and cliffs that Clark struggled over. As far as the difficulty of traveling on this river by canoe, Clark did not overestimate in any sense. Only experienced guides lead white water enthusiasts down today's Salmon, "The River of No Return."
Spur
August 28, 1805
"... assended a Spur of the Mountain form which place my guide Shew[ed] me the river for about 20 miles lower & pointed out the dificulties..."
Clark ⇨ Outbound: Clark-Auaust 23. 1805
Return: Clark-August 23, 1805
No Return 1806
SALMON WILD AND SCENIC RIVER
SALMON RIVER
"LEWIS RIVER"
SALMON NATIONAL FOREST
BITTERROOT RANGE
BEAVERHEAD MOUNTAINS
Big Sheepeater Creek
Cohen Gulch
Sheepeater Creek
Sheepeater Point
Little Sheepeater
Horsefly Gulch
Boulder Creek
Boulder Basin
Pine Tree Rapids
Mine Shafts
Eagles Nest
Pine Creek
Smith Gulch
Sawmill Gulch
Hale Gulch
China
SHOUP
McKay Creek
Spring Creek
Little Spring Creek
Transfer Gulch
Dutchler Basin
Stormy Peak
Sawlog Gulch
Small Valley
S. W 1 MILE
ONE STATUTE MILE
Ridge
N
Modern Data: 1991
EXPLORATIONS OF LEWIS AND CLARK 1804 - 1806
CARTOGRAPHIC RECONSTRUCTION
RIVER OF NO RETURN
UTM ZONE 11
MAP NUMBER 281
Idaho
CONTOUR INTERVAL 200 FEET

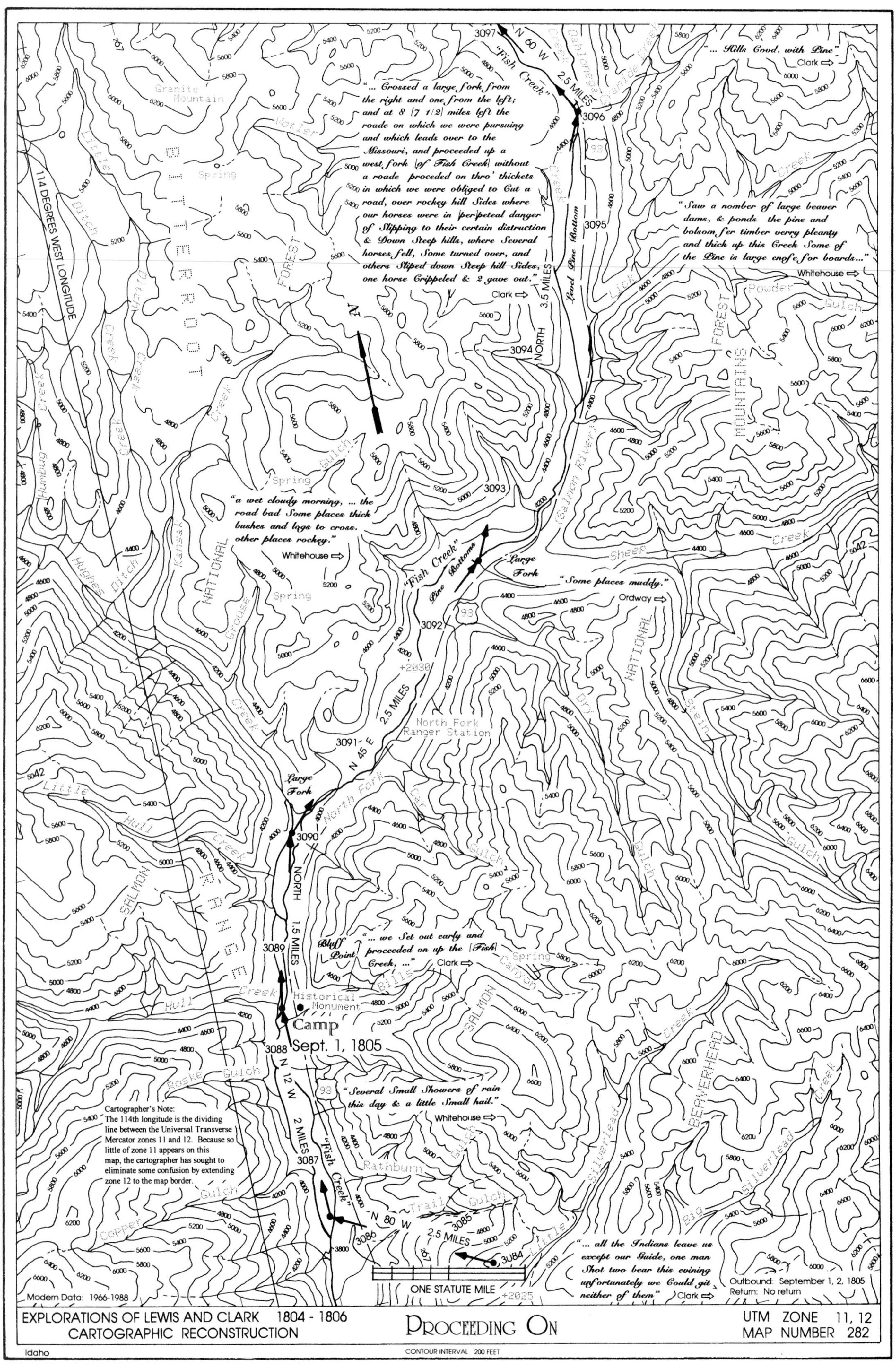
"... Crossed a large fork from the right and one from the left; and at 8 [7 1/2] miles left the roade on which we were pursuing and which leads over to the Missouri, and proceeded up a west fork [of Fish Creek] without a roade proceded on thro' thickets in which we were obliged to Cut a road, over rockey hill Sides where our horses were in [per]peteal danger of Slipping to their certain distruction & Down Steep hills, where Several horses fell, Some turned over, and others Sliped down Steep hill Sides, one horse Crippeled & 2 gave out."
Clark ⇨
"... Hills Covd. with Pine"
Clark ⇨
"Saw a nomber of large beaver dams, & ponds the pine and bolsom fer timber verry pleanty and thick up this Creek Some of the Pine is large enofe for boards..."
Whitehouse ⇨
"a wet cloudy morning, ... the road bad Some places thick bushes and logs to cross. other places rockey."
Whitehouse ⇨
"Some places muddy."
Ordway ⇨
"... we Set out early and proceeded on up the [Fish] Creek, ..."
Clark ⇨
"Several Small Showers of rain this day & a little Small hail."
Whitehouse ⇨
"... all the Indians leave us except our Guide, one man Shot two bear this evining unfortunately we Could git neither of them"
Clark ⇨
Camp
Sept. 1, 1805
Historical Monument
North Fork Ranger Station
Large Fork
Bluff Point
Pine Bottom
Level Pine Bottom
Fish Creek
Salmon River
BITTERROOT RANGE
SALMON NATIONAL FOREST
BEAVERHEAD NATIONAL FOREST
114 DEGREES WEST LONGITUDE
N 60 W 2.5 MILES
NORTH 3.5 MILES
2.5 MILES N 45 E
NORTH 1.5 MILES
N 12 W 2 MILES
N 80 W 2.5 MILES
Cartographer's Note:
The 114th longitude is the dividing line between the Universal Transverse Mercator zones 11 and 12. Because so little of zone 11 appears on this map, the cartographer has sought to eliminate some confusion by extending zone 12 to the map border.
ONE STATUTE MILE
Modern Data: 1966-1988
Outbound: September 1, 2, 1805
Return: No return
EXPLORATIONS OF LEWIS AND CLARK 1804 - 1806
CARTOGRAPHIC RECONSTRUCTION
PROCEEDING ON
UTM ZONE 11, 12
MAP NUMBER 282
Idaho
CONTOUR INTERVAL 200 FEET

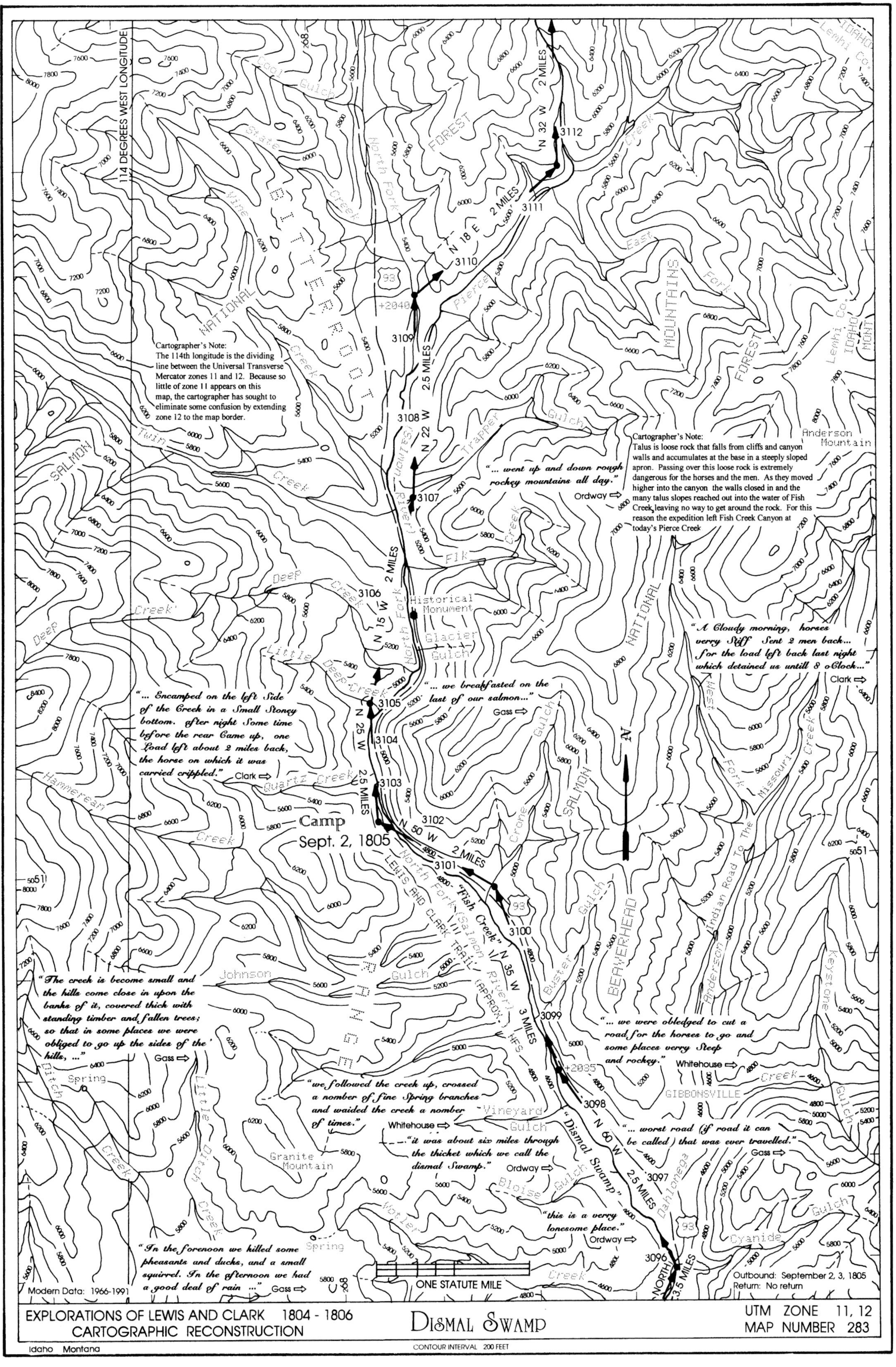

114 DEGREES WEST LONGITUDE
Cartographer's Note:
The 114th longitude is the dividing line between the Universal Transverse Mercator zones 11 and 12. Because so little of zone 11 appears on this map, the cartographer has sought to eliminate some confusion by extending zone 12 to the map border.
Cartographer's Note:
Talus is loose rock that falls from cliffs and canyon walls and accumulates at the base in a steeply sloped apron. Passing over this loose rock is extremely dangerous for the horses and the men. As they moved higher into the canyon the walls closed in and the many talus slopes reached out into the water of Fish Creek, leaving no way to get around the rock. For this reason the expedition left Fish Creek Canyon at today's Pierce Creek
"... went up and down rough rockey mountains all day."
Ordway
"A Cloudy morning, horses verry Stiff Sent 2 men back... for the load left back last night which detained us untill 8 oClock..."
Clark
"... we breakfasted on the last of our salmon..."
Gass
"... Encamped on the left Side of the Creek in a Small Stoney bottom. after night Some time before the rear Came up, one Load left about 2 miles back, the horse on which it was carried crippled."
Clark
Camp
Sept. 2, 1805
"The creek is become small and the hills come close in upon the banks of it, covered thick with standing timber and fallen trees; so that in some places we were obliged to go up the sides of the hills, ..."
Gass
"we followed the creek up, crossed a nomber of fine Spring branches and waided the creek a nomber of times."
Whitehouse
"it was about six miles through the thicket which we call the dismal Swamp."
Ordway
"... we were obledged to cut a road for the horses to go and some places verry Steep and rockey."
Whitehouse
"... worst road (if road it can be called) that was ever travelled."
Gass
"this is a very lonesome place."
Ordway
"In the forenoon we killed some pheasants and ducks, and a small squirrel. In the afternoon we had a good deal of rain ..."
Gass
BITTERROOT
NATIONAL
FOREST
SALMON
RANGE
MOUNTAINS
BEAVERHEAD
IDAHO
MONT
Lemhi Co.
Anderson Mountain
Granite Mountain
Historical Monument
GIBBONSVILLE
LEWIS AND CLARK TRAIL (APPROX.)
Indian Road To The Missouri
"Fish Creek"
"Dismal Swamp"
N 32 W 2 MILES
N 18 E 2 MILES
2.5 MILES
N 22 W
N 15 W 2 MILES
N 25 W
2.5 MILES
N 50 W 2 MILES
N 35 W 3 MILES
N 60 W 2.5 MILES
NORTH 3.5 MILES
ONE STATUTE MILE
Modern Data: 1966-1991
Outbound: September 2, 3, 1805
Return: No return
EXPLORATIONS OF LEWIS AND CLARK 1804 - 1806
CARTOGRAPHIC RECONSTRUCTION
DISMAL SWAMP
UTM ZONE 11, 12
MAP NUMBER 283
Idaho Montana
CONTOUR INTERVAL 200 FEET

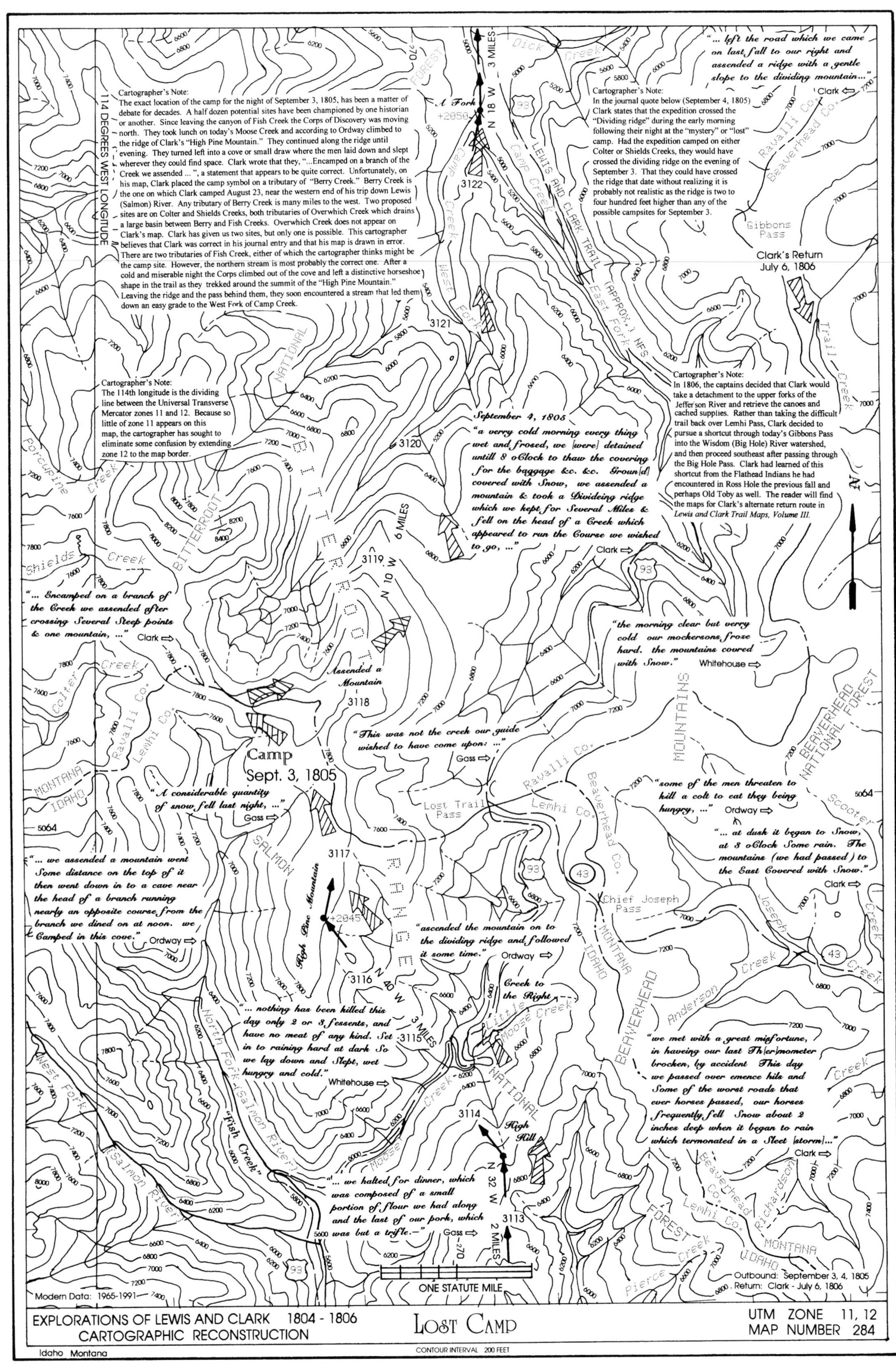

Cartographer's Note:
The exact location of the camp for the night of September 3, 1805, has been a matter of debate for decades. A half dozen potential sites have been championed by one historian or another. Since leaving the canyon of Fish Creek the Corps of Discovery was moving north. They took lunch on today's Moose Creek and according to Ordway climbed to the ridge of Clark's "High Pine Mountain." They continued along the ridge until evening. They turned left into a cove or small draw where the men laid down and slept wherever they could find space. Clark wrote that they, "...Encamped on a branch of the Creek we assended ... ", a statement that appears to be quite correct. Unfortunately, on his map, Clark placed the camp symbol on a tributary of "Berry Creek." Berry Creek is the one on which Clark camped August 23, near the western end of his trip down Lewis (Salmon) River. Any tributary of Berry Creek is many miles to the west. Two proposed sites are on Colter and Shields Creeks, both tributaries of Overwhich Creek which drains a large basin between Berry and Fish Creeks. Overwhich Creek does not appear on Clark's map. Clark has given us two sites, but only one is possible. This cartographer believes that Clark was correct in his journal entry and that his map is drawn in error. There are two tributaries of Fish Creek, either of which the cartographer thinks might be the camp site. However, the northern stream is most probably the correct one. After a cold and miserable night the Corps climbed out of the cove and left a distinctive horseshoe shape in the trail as they trekked around the summit of the "High Pine Mountain." Leaving the ridge and the pass behind them, they soon encountered a stream that led them down an easy grade to the West Fork of Camp Creek.
"... left the road which we came on last fall to our right and assended a ridge with a gentle slope to the dividing mountain..." Clark
Cartographer's Note:
In the journal quote below (September 4, 1805) Clark states that the expedition crossed the "Dividing ridge" during the early morning following their night at the "mystery" or "lost" camp. Had the expedition camped on either Colter or Shields Creeks, they would have crossed the dividing ridge on the evening of September 3. That they could have crossed the ridge that date without realizing it is probably not realistic as the ridge is two to four hundred feet higher than any of the possible campsites for September 3.
114 DEGREES WEST LONGITUDE
A Fork +2050
N 18 W 3 MILES
Dick Creek
Camp Creek
LEWIS AND CLARK TRAIL (APPROX.) NFS
West Fork
East Fork
Ravalli Co.
Beaverhead Co.
Gibbons Pass
Clark's Return July 6, 1806
Trail Creek
Cartographer's Note:
The 114th longitude is the dividing line between the Universal Transverse Mercator zones 11 and 12. Because so little of zone 11 appears on this map, the cartographer has sought to eliminate some confusion by extending zone 12 to the map border.
Cartographer's Note:
In 1806, the captains decided that Clark would take a detachment to the upper forks of the Jefferson River and retrieve the canoes and cached supplies. Rather than taking the difficult trail back over Lemhi Pass, Clark decided to pursue a shortcut through today's Gibbons Pass into the Wisdom (Big Hole) River watershed, and then proceed southeast after passing through the Big Hole Pass. Clark had learned of this shortcut from the Flathead Indians he had encountered in Ross Hole the previous fall and perhaps Old Toby as well. The reader will find the maps for Clark's alternate return route in Lewis and Clark Trail Maps, Volume III.
September 4, 1805
"a verry cold morning every thing wet and frosed, we [were] detained untill 8 oClock to thaw the covering for the baggage &c. &c. Groun[d] covered with Snow, we assended a mountain & took a Divideing ridge which we kept for Several Miles & fell on the head of a Creek which appeared to run the Course we wished to go, ..." Clark
NATIONAL
BITTERROOT
Porcupine Creek
Shields Creek
N 10 W 6 MILES
"... Encamped on a branch of the Creek we assended after crossing Several Steep points & one mountain, ..." Clark
"the morning clear but verry cold our mockersons froze hard. the mountains coverd with Snow." Whitehouse
Colter Creek
Assended a Mountain
MOUNTAINS
BEAVERHEAD NATIONAL FOREST
"This was not the creek our guide wished to have come upon: ..." Gass
Camp Sept. 3, 1805
MONTANA IDAHO
"A considerable quantity of snow fell last night, ..." Gass
Lost Trail Pass
Ravalli Co.
Lemhi Co.
Beaverhead Co.
"some of the men threaten to kill a colt to eat they being hungry, ..." Ordway
Scooter
"... at dusk it began to Snow, at 3 oClock Some rain. The mountains (we had passed) to the East Covered with Snow." Clark
"... we assended a mountain went Some distance on the top of it then went down in to a cave near the head of a branch running nearly an opposite course from the branch we dined on at noon. we Camped in this cove." Ordway
SALMON
RANGE
High Pine Mountain +2045
Chief Joseph Pass
"ascended the mountain on to the dividing ridge and followed it some time." Ordway
Creek to the Right
Joseph Creek
Anderson Creek
IDAHO MONTANA
N 40 W 3 MILES
"... nothing has been killed this day only 2 or 3 fessents, and have no meat of any kind. Set in to raining hard at dark So we lay down and Slept, wet hungry and cold." Whitehouse
Little Moose Creek
"we met with a great misfortune, in haveing our last Th[er]mometer brocken, by accident This day we passed over emence hils and Some of the worst roads that ever horses passed, our horses frequently fell Snow about 2 inches deep when it began to rain which termonated in a Sleet [storm]..." Clark
North Fork (Salmon River)
West Fork
Fish Creek
Moose Creek
NATIONAL
High Hill
N 32 W 2 MILES
"... we halted for dinner, which was composed of a small portion of flour we had along and the last of our pork, which was but a trifle.-" Gass
(Salmon River)
FOREST
Pierce Creek
Richardson
MONTANA IDAHO
ONE STATUTE MILE
Outbound: September 3, 4, 1805
Return: Clark - July 6, 1806
Modern Data: 1965-1991
EXPLORATIONS OF LEWIS AND CLARK 1804 - 1806
CARTOGRAPHIC RECONSTRUCTION
LOST CAMP
UTM ZONE 11, 12
MAP NUMBER 284
Idaho Montana
CONTOUR INTERVAL 200 FEET

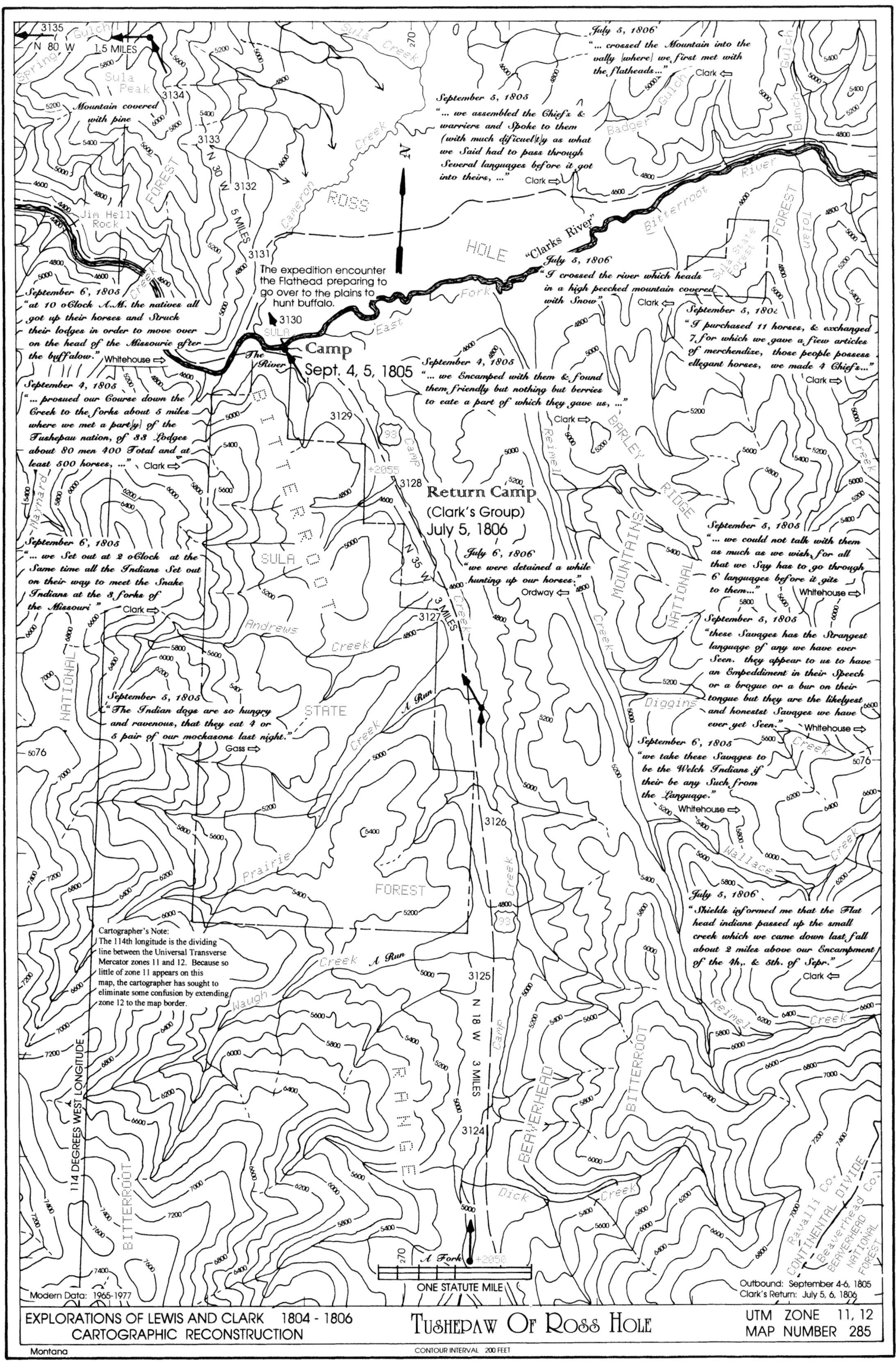

September 6, 1805
"at 10 oClock A.M. the natives all got up their horses and Struck their lodges in order to move over on the head of the Missourie after the buffalow."
Whitehouse ⇨
September 4, 1805
"... prosued our Course down the Creek to the forks about 5 miles where we met a part[y] of the Tushepau nation, of 33 Lodges about 80 men 400 Total and at least 500 horses, ..."
Clark ⇨
September 6, 1805
"... we Set out at 2 oClock at the Same time all the Indians Set out on their way to meet the Snake Indians at the 3 forks of the Missouri"
Clark ⇨
September 5, 1805
"The Indian dogs are so hungry and ravenous, that they eat 4 or 5 pair of our mockasons last night."
Gass ⇨
The expedition encounter the Flathead preparing to go over to the plains to hunt buffalo.
Camp
Sept. 4, 5, 1805
September 5, 1805
"... we assembled the Chiefs & warriers and Spoke to them (with much dificuel[t]y as what we Said had to pass through Several languages before it got into theirs, ..."
Clark ⇨
July 5, 1806
"... crossed the Mountain into the vally [where] we first met with the flatheads..."
Clark ⇦
"Clarks River"
July 5, 1806
"I crossed the river which heads in a high pecked mountain covered with Snow"
Clark ⇦
September 4, 1805
"... we Encamped with them & found them friendly but nothing but berries to eate a part of which they gave us, ..."
Clark ⇨
September 5, 1805
"I purchased 11 horses, & exchanged 7 for which we gave a fiew articles of merchendize, those people possess ellegant horses, we made 4 Chiefs..."
Clark ⇨
Return Camp
(Clark's Group)
July 5, 1806
July 6, 1806
"we were detained a while hunting up our horses."
Ordway ⇦
September 5, 1805
"... we could not talk with them as much as we wish for all that we Say has to go through 6 languages before it gits to them..."
Whitehouse ⇨
September 5, 1805
"these Savages has the Strangest language of any we have ever Seen. they appear to us to have an Empeddiment in their Speech or a brogue or a bur on their tongue but they are the likelyest and honestst Savages we have ever yet Seen."
Whitehouse ⇨
September 6, 1805
"we take these Savages to be the Welch Indians if their be any Such from the Language."
Whitehouse ⇨
July 5, 1806
"Shields informed me that the Flat head indians passed up the small creek which we came down last fall about 2 miles above our Encampment of the 4th,. & 5th. of Sepr."
Clark ⇦
Mountain covered with pine
Jim Hell Rock
Sula Peak
N 80 W 1.5 MILES
N 30 W 5 MILES
N 35 W 3 MILES
N 18 W 3 MILES
ROSS HOLE
BITTERROOT
SULA
STATE
FOREST
RANGE
BARLEY RIDGE
MOUNTAINS
NATIONAL
BEAVERHEAD
Cartographer's Note:
The 114th longitude is the dividing line between the Universal Transverse Mercator zones 11 and 12. Because so little of zone 11 appears on this map, the cartographer has sought to eliminate some confusion by extending zone 12 to the map border.
114 DEGREES WEST LONGITUDE
CONTINENTAL DIVIDE
Ravalli Co.
Beaverhead Co.
BEAVERHEAD NATIONAL FOREST
ONE STATUTE MILE
Modern Data: 1965-1977
Outbound: September 4-6, 1805
Clark's Return: July 5, 6, 1806
EXPLORATIONS OF LEWIS AND CLARK 1804 - 1806
CARTOGRAPHIC RECONSTRUCTION
TUSHEPAW OF ROSS HOLE
UTM ZONE 11, 12
MAP NUMBER 285
Montana
CONTOUR INTERVAL 200 FEET

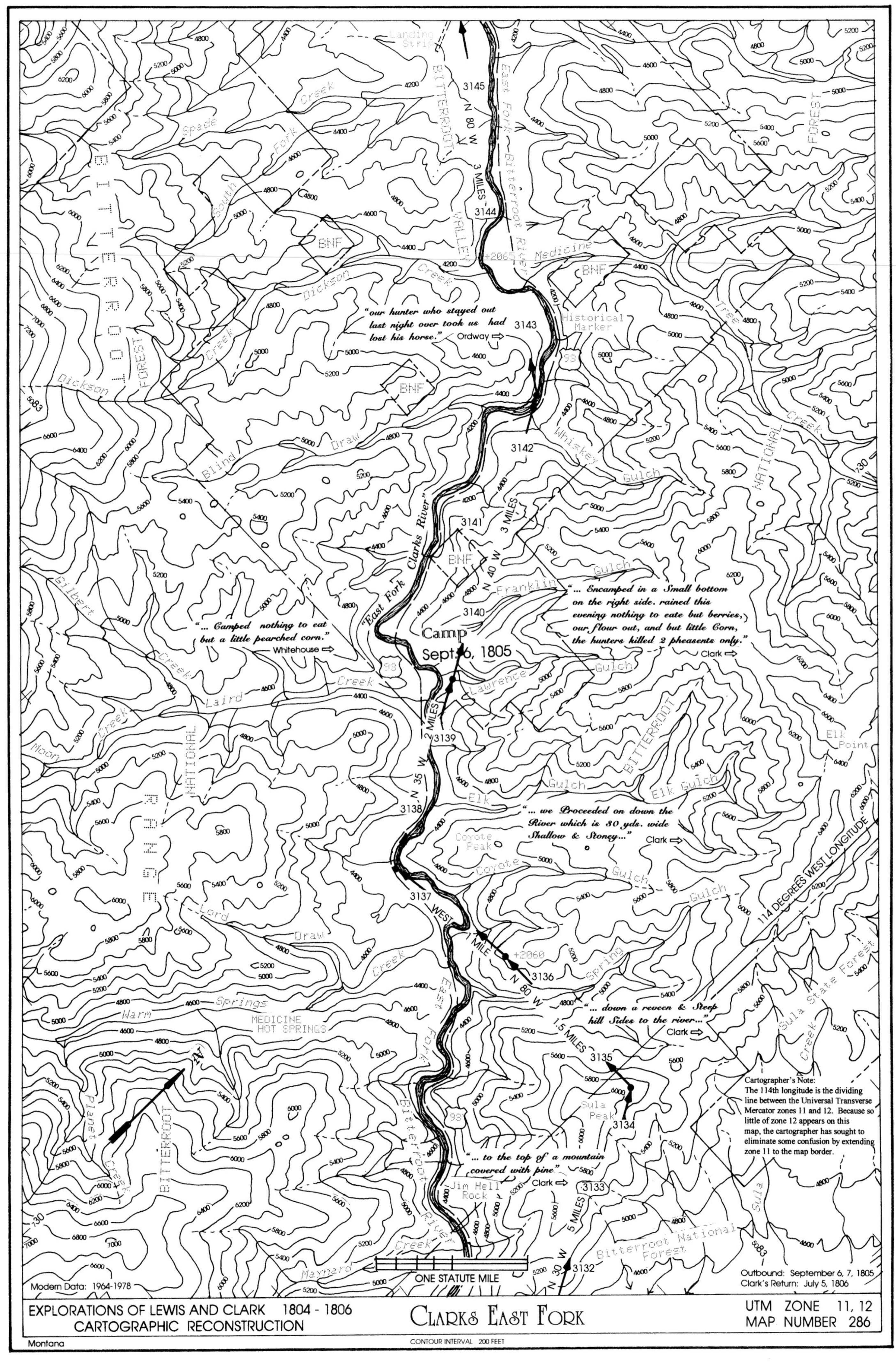
EXPLORATIONS OF LEWIS AND CLARK 1804 - 1806
CARTOGRAPHIC RECONSTRUCTION
CLARKS EAST FORK
UTM ZONE 11, 12
MAP NUMBER 286
Montana
CONTOUR INTERVAL 200 FEET
Modern Data: 1964-1978
ONE STATUTE MILE
Outbound: September 6, 7, 1805
Clark's Return: July 5, 1806
Cartographer's Note:
The 114th longitude is the dividing line between the Universal Transverse Mercator zones 11 and 12. Because so little of zone 12 appears on this map, the cartographer has sought to eliminate some confusion by extending zone 11 to the map border.
"our hunter who stayed out last night over took us had lost his horse." Ordway ⇨
"... Camped nothing to eat but a little pearched corn." Whitehouse ⇨
"... Encamped in a Small bottom on the right side. rained this evening nothing to eat but berries, our flour out, and but little Corn, the hunters killed 2 pheasents only." Clark ⇨
Camp
Sept. 6, 1805
"... we Proceeded on down the River which is 80 yds. wide Shallow & Stoney..." Clark ⇨
"... down a reveen & Steep hill Sides to the river..." Clark ⇨
"... to the top of a mountain covered with pine." Clark ⇨
"East Fork Clarks River"
114 DEGREES WEST LONGITUDE
BITTERROOT VALLEY
BITTERROOT NATIONAL FOREST
BITTERROOT RANGE
East Fork Bitterroot River
Medicine Tree Creek
Historical Marker
Landing Strip
Spade Creek
South Fork
Dickson Creek
Blind Draw
Whiskey Gulch
Franklin Gulch
Lawrence Gulch
Laird Creek
Moon Creek
Gilbert Creek
Elk Gulch
Elk Point
Coyote Peak
Coyote Gulch
Lord Draw
Spring Gulch
Warm Springs Creek
MEDICINE HOT SPRINGS
Planet Creek
Sula Peak
Sula State Forest
Jim Hell Rock
Maynard Creek
Sula
Bitterroot National Forest
3 MILES
N 80 W
N 40 W
2 MILES
N 35 W
1 MILE
WEST
1.5 MILES
.5 MILES
N 30 W
3145
3144
3143
3142
3141
3140
3139
3138
3137
3136
3135
3134
3133
3132
+2065
+2060
BNF
93

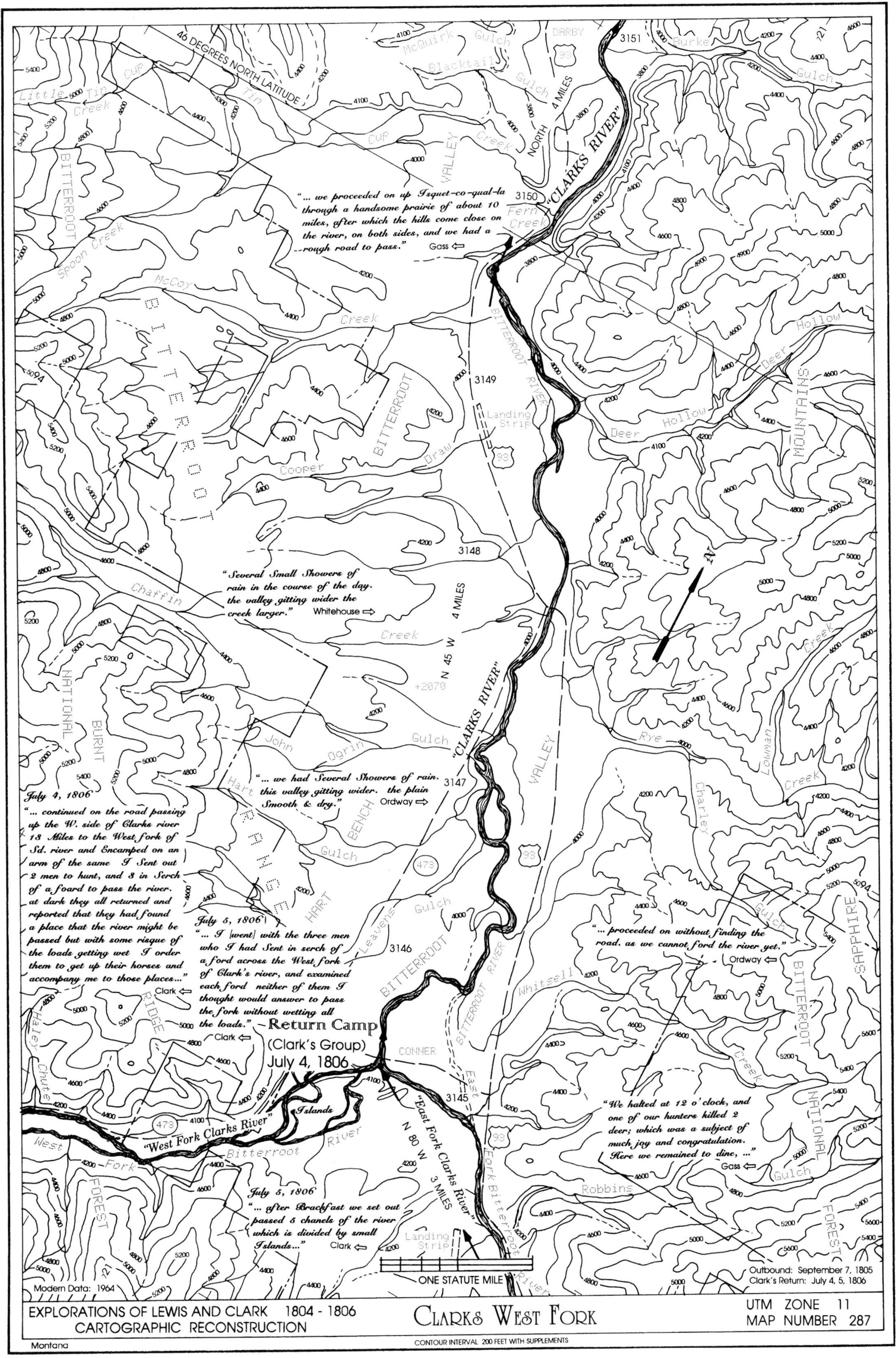
46 DEGREES NORTH LATITUDE
DARBY
3151
NORTH 4 MILES
"CLARKS RIVER"
3150
"... we proceeded on up Isquet-co-qual-la through a handsome prairie of about 10 miles, after which the hills come close on the river, on both sides, and we had a rough road to pass." Gass
McQuirk Gulch
Blacktail Gulch
Burke Gulch
Little Tin Creek
Tin Cup Creek
Fern Creek
Spoon Creek
McCoy Creek
BITTERROOT
BITTERROOT RIVER
3149
Landing Strip
Deer Hollow
SAPPHIRE MOUNTAINS
Cooper Draw
3148
"Several Small Showers of rain in the course of the day. the valley gitting wider the creek larger." Whitehouse
Chaffin Creek
N 45 W 4 MILES
"CLARKS RIVER"
NATIONAL
BURNT
John Ogrin Gulch
Hart Bench Gulch
VALLEY
Rye Creek
Lowman
Charley
"... we had Several Showers of rain. this valley gitting wider. the plain Smooth & dry." Ordway
3147
July 4, 1806
"... continued on the road passing up the W. side of Clarks river 18 Miles to the West fork of Sd. river and Encamped on an arm of the same I Sent out 2 men to hunt, and 3 in Serch of a foard to pass the river. at dark they all returned and reported that they had found a place that the river might be passed but with some risque of the loads getting wet I order them to get up their horses and accompany me to those places..." Clark
RANGE
HART
July 5, 1806
"... I [went] with the three men who I had Sent in serch of a ford across the West fork of Clark's river, and examined each ford neither of them I thought would answer to pass the fork without wetting all the loads." Clark
Leavens Gulch
3146
"... proceeded on without finding the road. as we cannot ford the river yet." Ordway
Whitsell Creek
RIDGE
Haley Chute
Return Camp
(Clark's Group)
July 4, 1806
CONNER
3145
Islands
"West Fork Clarks River"
West Fork Bitterroot River
"East Fork Clarks River"
N 80 W 3 MILES
East Fork Bitterroot River
"We halted at 12 o'clock, and one of our hunters killed 2 deer; which was a subject of much joy and congratulation. Here we remained to dine, ..." Gass
Robbins Gulch
FOREST
July 5, 1806
"... after Brackfast we set out passed 5 chanels of the river which is divided by small Islands..." Clark
Landing Strip
ONE STATUTE MILE
Outbound: September 7, 1805
Clark's Return: July 4, 5, 1806
Modern Data: 1964
EXPLORATIONS OF LEWIS AND CLARK 1804 - 1806
CARTOGRAPHIC RECONSTRUCTION
CLARKS WEST FORK
UTM ZONE 11
MAP NUMBER 287
Montana
CONTOUR INTERVAL 200 FEET WITH SUPPLEMENTS

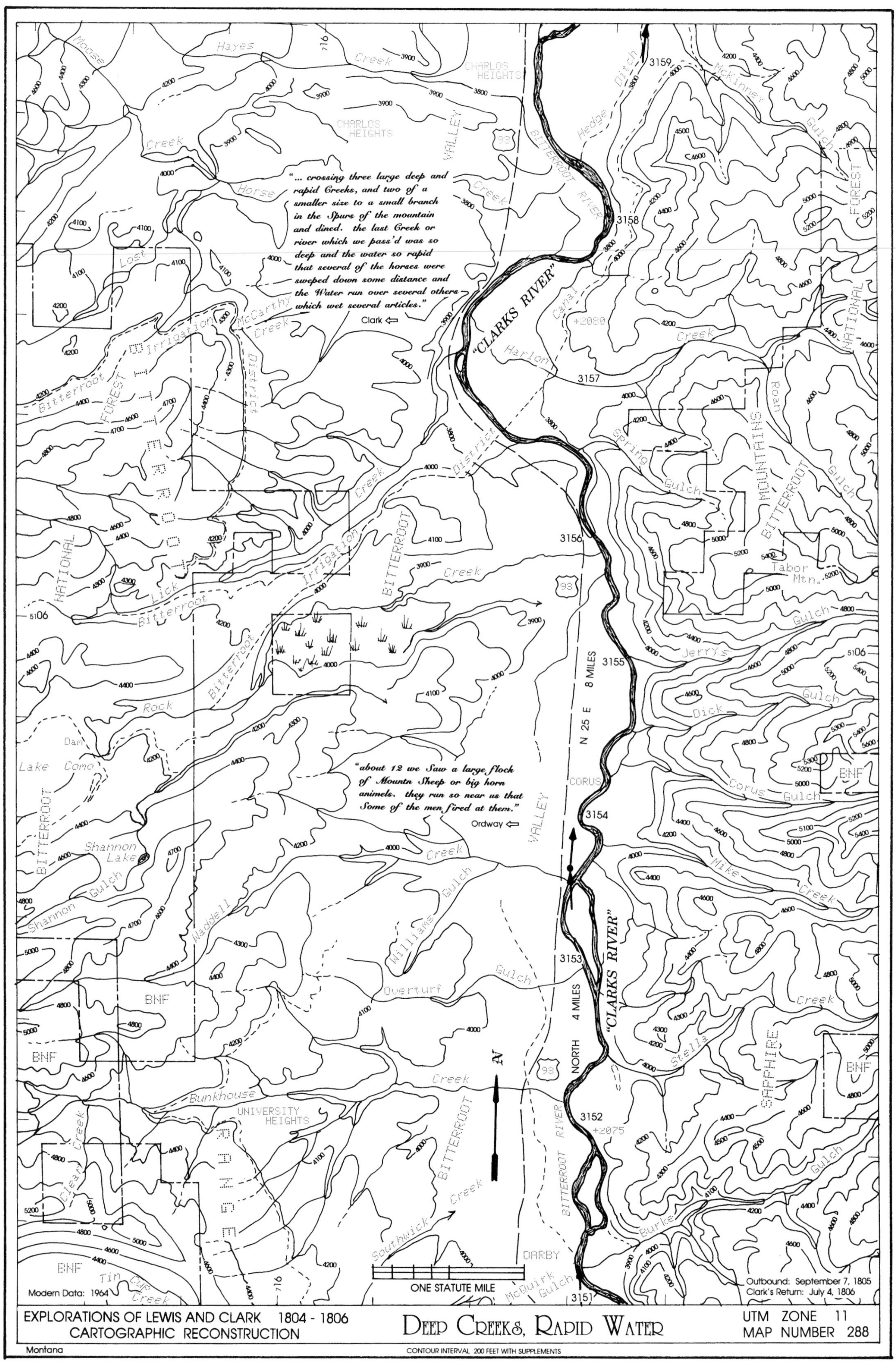

"... crossing three large deep and rapid Greeks, and two of a smaller size to a small branch in the Spurs of the mountain and dined. the last Creek or river which we pass'd was so deep and the water so rapid that several of the horses were sweped down some distance and the Water run over several others which wet several articles."
Clark ⇦
"about 12 we Saw a large flock of Mountn Sheep or big horn animels. they run so near us that Some of the men fired at them."
Ordway ⇦
"CLARKS RIVER"
"CLARKS RIVER"
BITTERROOT RIVER
BITTERROOT VALLEY
BITTERROOT RANGE
BITTERROOT FOREST
BITTERROOT NATIONAL FOREST
SAPPHIRE
BITTERROOT MOUNTAINS
CHARLOS HEIGHTS
UNIVERSITY HEIGHTS
CORUS
DARBY
Hayes Creek
Moose Creek
Horse Creek
Lost Horse Creek
McCarthy Creek
Bitterroot Irrigation District
Lick Creek
Rock Creek
Lake Como
Dam
Shannon Lake
Shannon Gulch
Waddell Creek
Williams Gulch
Overturf Gulch
Bunkhouse Creek
Clear Creek
Tin Cup Creek
Southwick Creek
McQuirk Gulch
Hedge Ditch
McKinney Gulch
Canal
Harlan Creek
Spring Gulch
Roan Gulch
Tabor Mtn.
Jerry's Gulch
Dick Gulch
Corus Gulch
Mike Creek
Stella Creek
Burke Gulch
BNF
N 25 E 8 MILES
NORTH 4 MILES
ONE STATUTE MILE
Modern Data: 1964
Outbound: September 7, 1805
Clark's Return: July 4, 1806
EXPLORATIONS OF LEWIS AND CLARK 1804 - 1806
CARTOGRAPHIC RECONSTRUCTION
DEEP CREEKS, RAPID WATER
UTM ZONE 11
MAP NUMBER 288
Montana
CONTOUR INTERVAL 200 FEET WITH SUPPLEMENTS

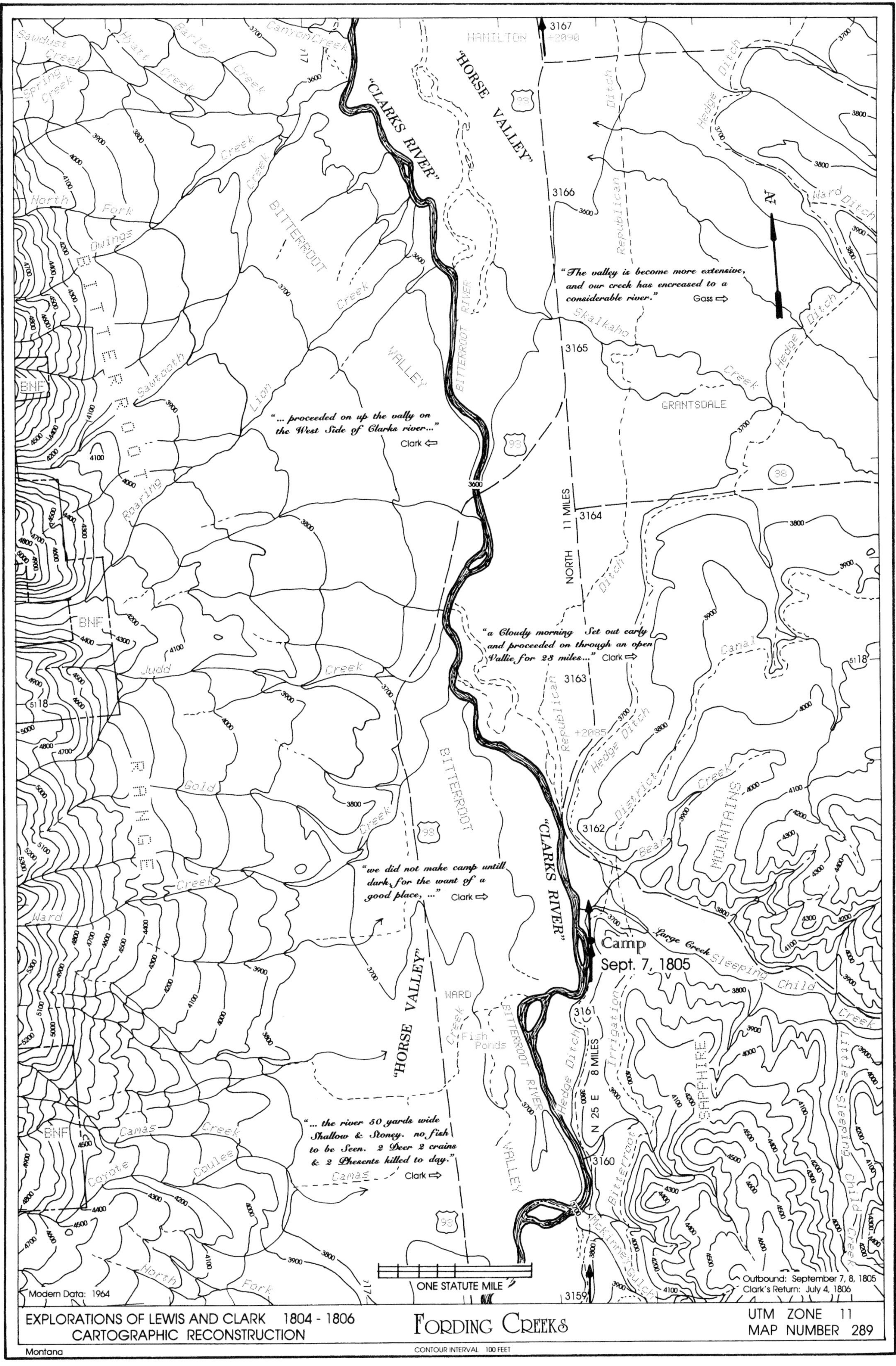
"CLARKS RIVER"
"HORSE VALLEY"
HAMILTON
BITTERROOT VALLEY
BITTERROOT RANGE
"The valley is become more extensive, and our creek has encreased to a considerable river." Gass ⇨
"... proceeded on up the vally on the West Side of Clarks river..." Clark ⇦
"a Cloudy morning Set out early and proceeded on through an open Vallie for 28 miles..." Clark ⇨
"we did not make camp untill dark, for the want of a good place, ..." Clark ⇨
"... the river 50 yards wide Shallow & Stoney. no fish to be Seen. 2 Deer 2 crains & 2 Phesents killed to day." Clark ⇨
Camp
Sept. 7, 1805
GRANTSDALE
SAPPHIRE MOUNTAINS
NORTH 11 MILES
N 25 E 8 MILES
ONE STATUTE MILE
Modern Data: 1964
Outbound: September 7, 8, 1805
Clark's Return: July 4, 1806
EXPLORATIONS OF LEWIS AND CLARK 1804 - 1806
CARTOGRAPHIC RECONSTRUCTION
FORDING CREEKS
UTM ZONE 11
MAP NUMBER 289
Montana
CONTOUR INTERVAL 100 FEET

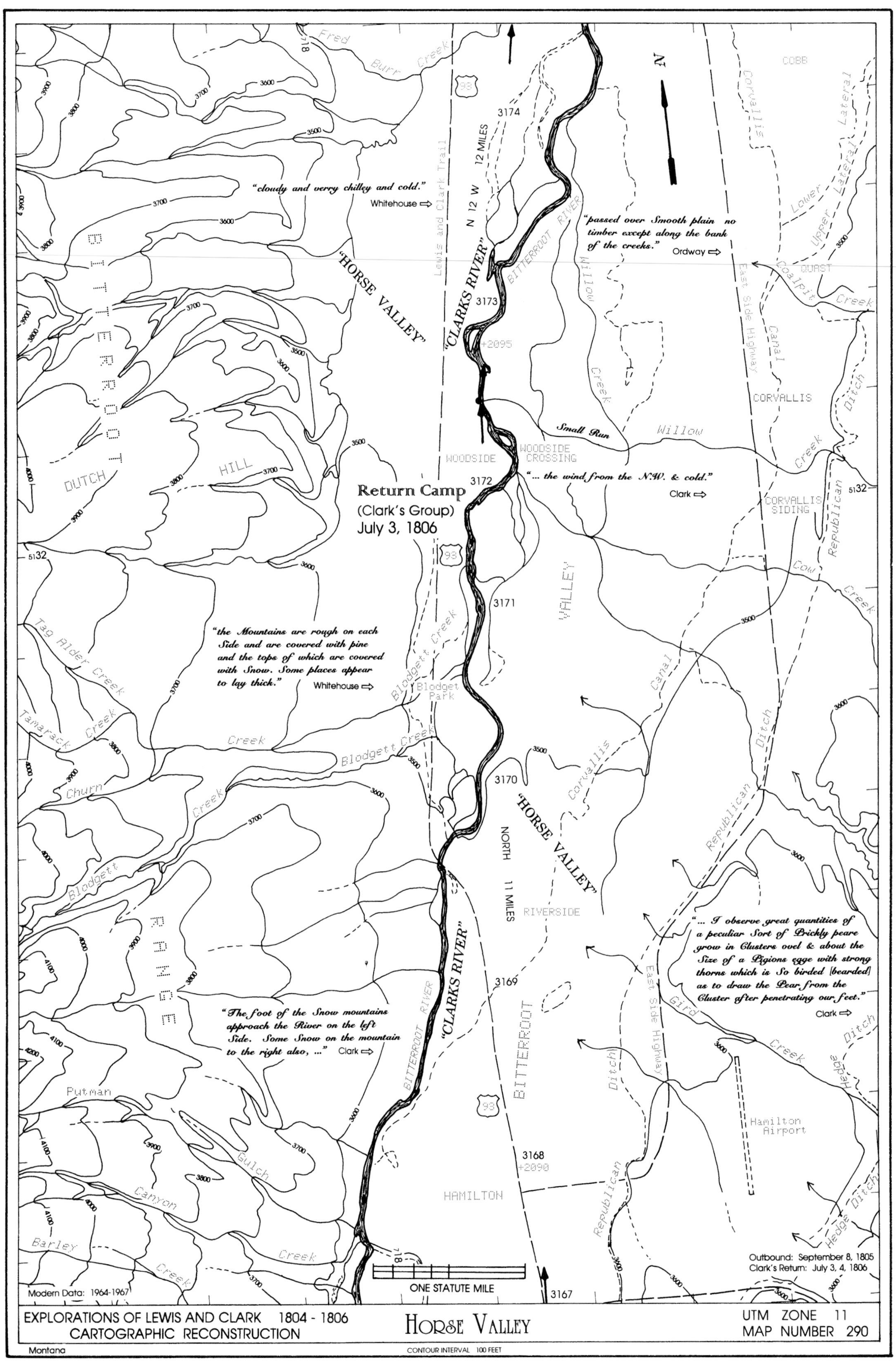
"cloudy and very chilley and cold."
Whitehouse ⇨
"passed over Smooth plain no timber except along the bank of the creeks."
Ordway ⇨
"HORSE VALLEY"
"CLARKS RIVER"
BITTERROOT RIVER
BITTERROOT RANGE
DUTCH HILL
Lewis and Clark Trail
N 12 W 12 MILES
Return Camp
(Clark's Group)
July 3, 1806
"... the wind from the N.W. & cold."
Clark ⇨
Small Run
Willow Creek
WOODSIDE
WOODSIDE CROSSING
CORVALLIS
CORVALLIS SIDING
COBB
QUAST
Corvallis Canal
East Side Highway
Lower Lateral
Upper Lateral
Coalpit Creek
Republican Ditch
Cow Creek
"the Mountains are rough on each Side and are covered with pine and the tops of which are covered with Snow. Some places appear to lay thick."
Whitehouse ⇨
Tag Alder Creek
Tamarack Creek
Blodgett Creek
Blodgett Park
Churn Creek
NORTH 11 MILES
RIVERSIDE
BITTERROOT VALLEY
"... I observe great quantities of a peculiar Sort of Prickly peare grow in Clusters ovel & about the Size of a Pigions egge with strong thorns which is So birded [bearded] as to draw the Pear from the Cluster after penetrating our feet."
Clark ⇨
"The foot of the Snow mountains approach the River on the left Side. Some Snow on the mountain to the right also, ..."
Clark ⇨
Gird Creek
Hedge Ditch
Hamilton Airport
Putman
Gulch
Canyon
Barley Creek
HAMILTON
Outbound: September 8, 1805
Clark's Return: July 3, 4, 1806
ONE STATUTE MILE
Modern Data: 1964-1967
EXPLORATIONS OF LEWIS AND CLARK 1804 - 1806
CARTOGRAPHIC RECONSTRUCTION
HORSE VALLEY
UTM ZONE 11
MAP NUMBER 290
Montana
CONTOUR INTERVAL 100 FEET

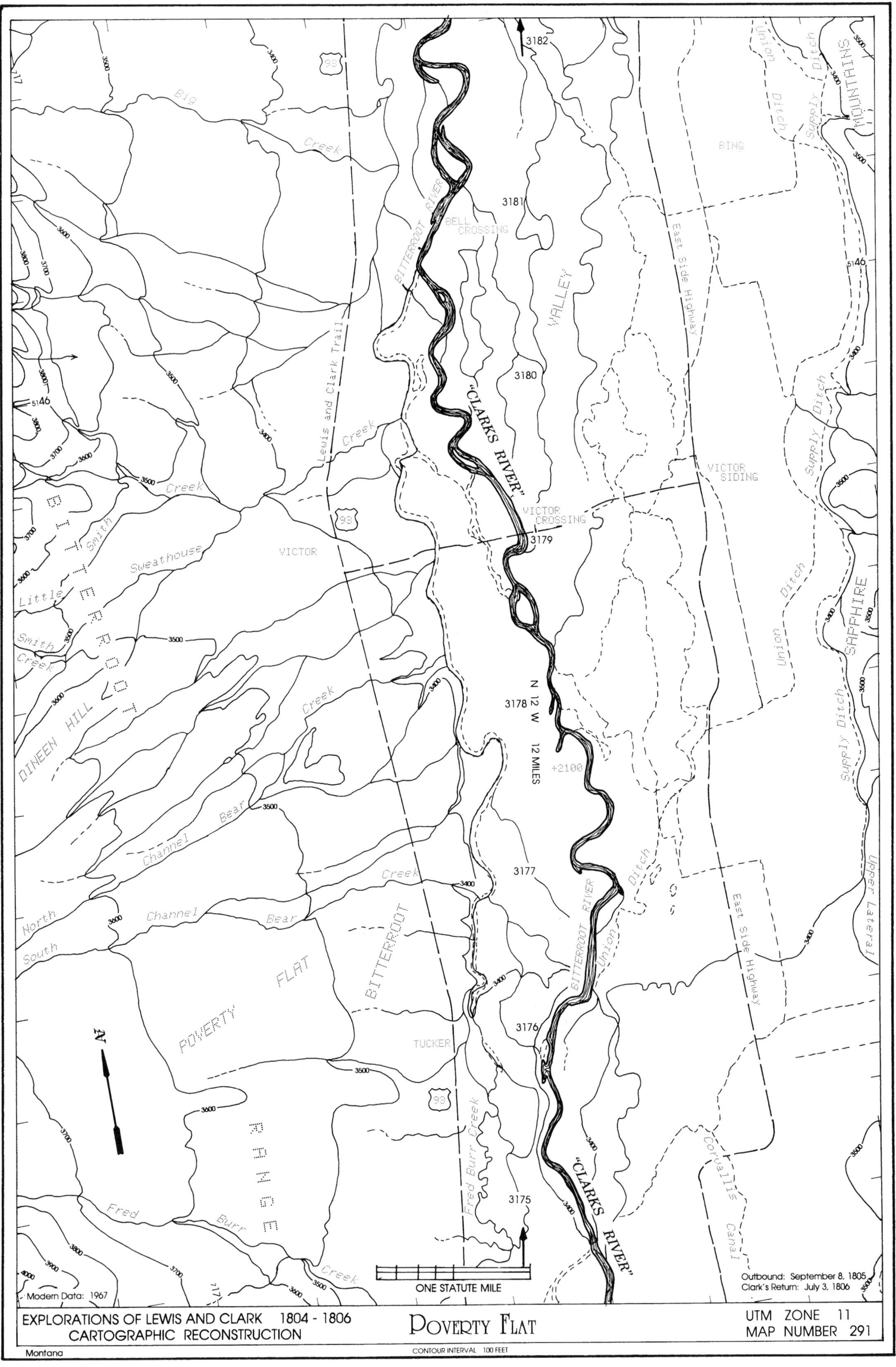

EXPLORATIONS OF LEWIS AND CLARK 1804 - 1806
CARTOGRAPHIC RECONSTRUCTION
POVERTY FLAT
UTM ZONE 11
MAP NUMBER 291
Montana
CONTOUR INTERVAL 100 FEET
ONE STATUTE MILE
Modern Data: 1967
Outbound: September 8, 1805
Clark's Return: July 3, 1806
"CLARKS RIVER"
BITTERROOT RIVER
BELL CROSSING
VICTOR CROSSING
VICTOR SIDING
VICTOR
BING
TUCKER
VALLEY
BITTERROOT
POVERTY FLAT
BITTERROOT RANGE
DINEEN HILL
SAPPHIRE MOUNTAINS
Lewis and Clark Trail
East Side Highway
Union Ditch
Supply Ditch
Upper Lateral
Corvallis Canal
Big Creek
Sweathouse Creek
Little Smith Creek
Smith Creek
North Channel Bear Creek
South Channel Bear Creek
Fred Burr Creek
N 12 W 12 MILES
+2100
3182
3181
3180
3179
3178
3177
3176
3175

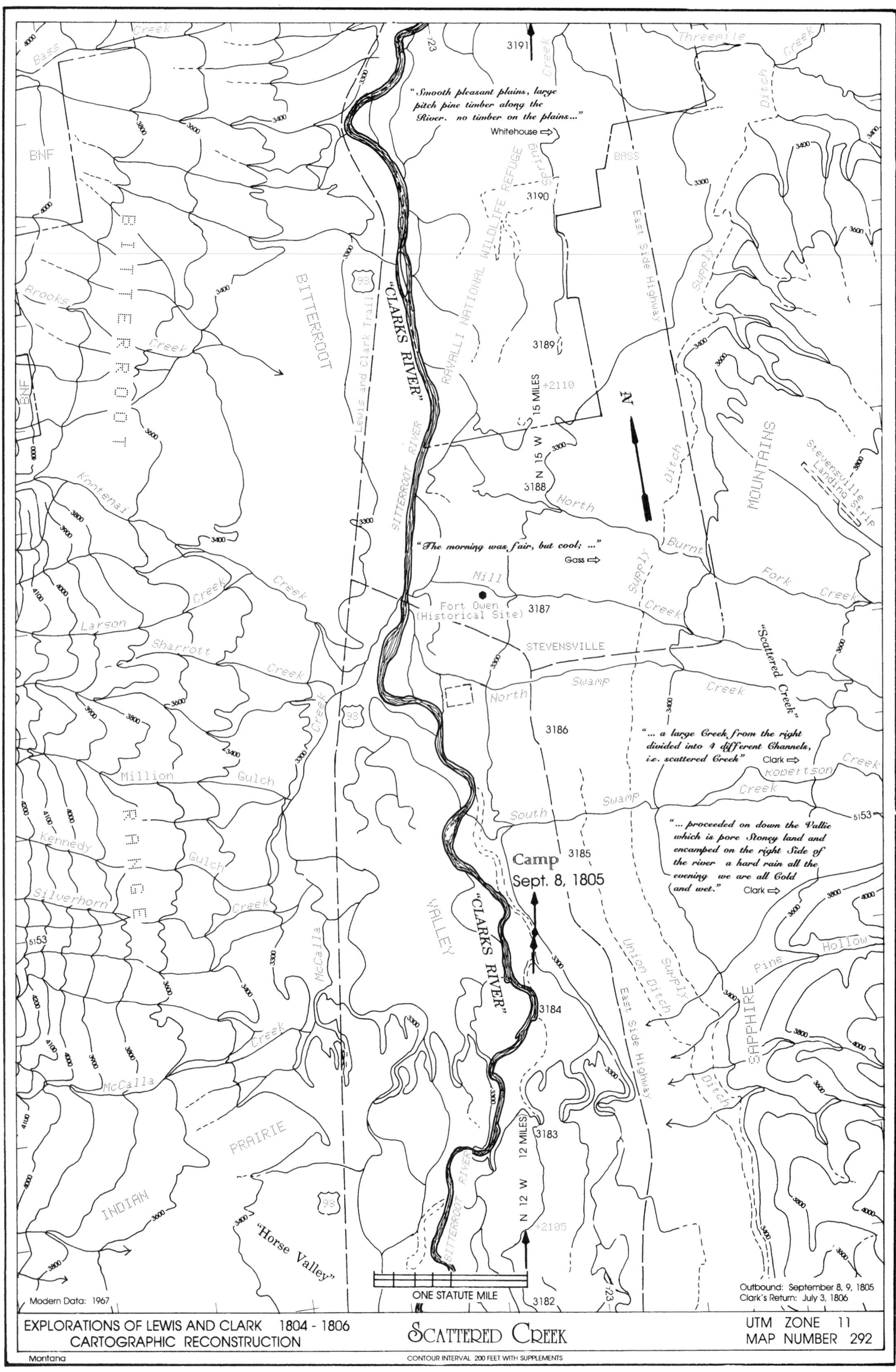

"Smooth pleasant plains, large pitch pine timber along the River. no timber on the plains..."
Whitehouse
"The morning was fair, but cool; ..."
Gass
"... a large Creek from the right divided into 4 different Channels, i.e. scattered Creek"
Clark
"... proceeded on down the Vallie which is pore Stoney land and encamped on the right Side of the river a hard rain all the evening we are all Cold and wet."
Clark
Camp
Sept. 8, 1805
"CLARKS RIVER"
"Scattered Creek"
"Horse Valley"
Fort Owen
(Historical Site)
STEVENSVILLE
BITTERROOT RANGE
BITTERROOT VALLEY
SAPPHIRE MOUNTAINS
RAVALLI NATIONAL WILDLIFE REFUGE
Lewis and Clark Trail
East Side Highway
Stevensville Landing Strip
INDIAN PRAIRIE
T 10 N R 20 W
Modern Data: 1967
ONE STATUTE MILE
Outbound: September 8, 9, 1805
Clark's Return: July 3, 1806
EXPLORATIONS OF LEWIS AND CLARK 1804 - 1806
CARTOGRAPHIC RECONSTRUCTION
SCATTERED CREEK
UTM ZONE 11
MAP NUMBER 292
Montana
CONTOUR INTERVAL 200 FEET WITH SUPPLEMENTS

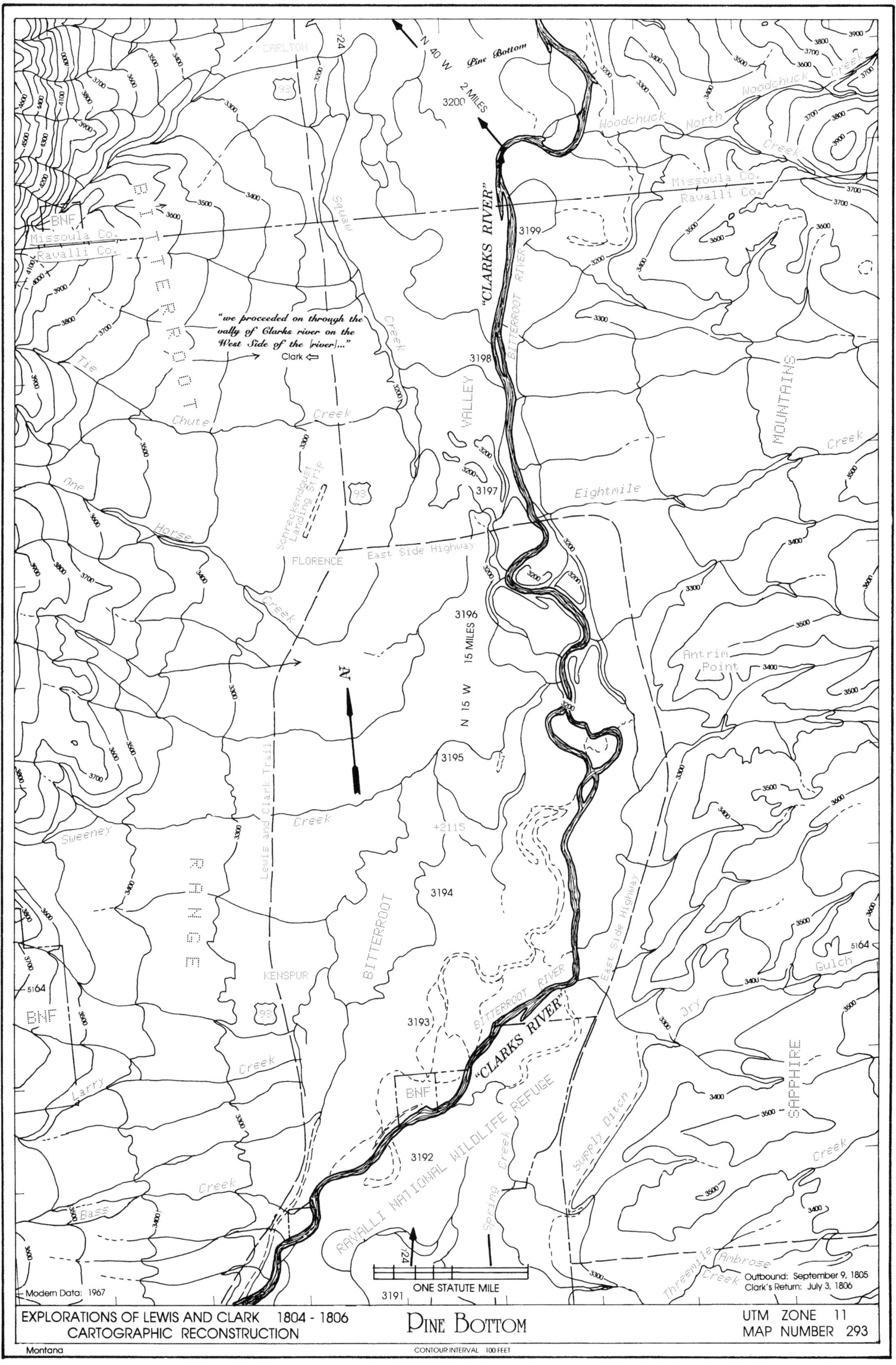
Pine Bottom
N 40 W
2 MILES
"CLARKS RIVER"
"we proceeded on through the vally of Clarks river on the West Side of the [river]..."
Clark
N 15 W 15 MILES
"CLARKS RIVER"
BITTERROOT RANGE
BITTERROOT VALLEY
SAPPHIRE MOUNTAINS
RAVALLI NATIONAL WILDLIFE REFUGE
Outbound: September 9, 1805
Clark's Return: July 3, 1806
ONE STATUTE MILE
Modern Data: 1967
EXPLORATIONS OF LEWIS AND CLARK 1804 - 1806
CARTOGRAPHIC RECONSTRUCTION
PINE BOTTOM
UTM ZONE 11
MAP NUMBER 293
Montana
CONTOUR INTERVAL 100 FEET

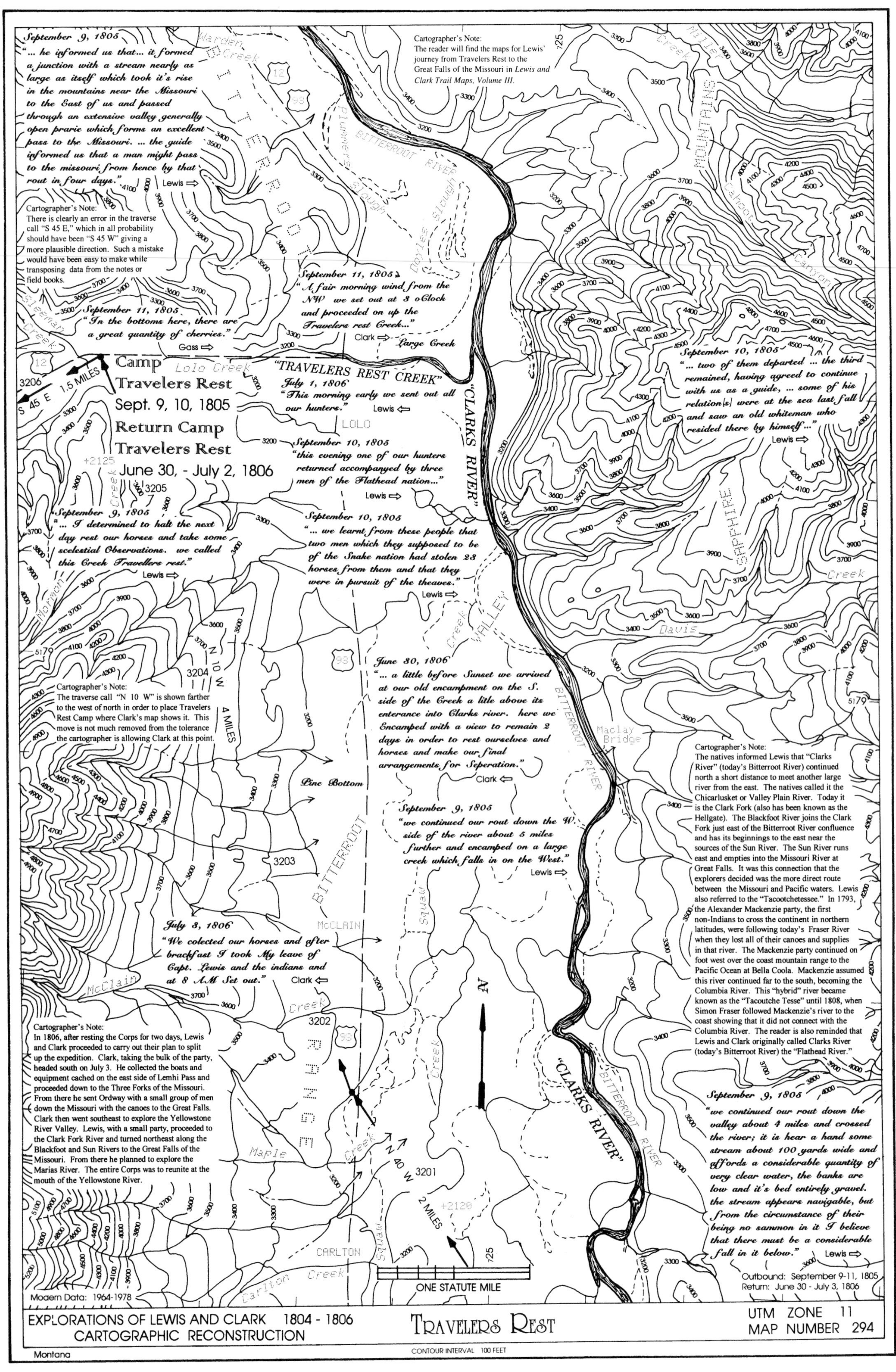

September 9, 1805
"... he informed us that... it formed a junction with a stream nearly as large as itself which took it's rise in the mountains near the Missouri to the East of us and passed through an extensive valley generally open prarie which forms an excellent pass to the Missouri. ... the guide informed us that a man might pass to the missouri from hence by that rout in four days."
Lewis ⇨
Cartographer's Note:
The reader will find the maps for Lewis' journey from Travelers Rest to the Great Falls of the Missouri in Lewis and Clark Trail Maps, Volume III.
Cartographer's Note:
There is clearly an error in the traverse call "S 45 E," which in all probability should have been "S 45 W" giving a more plausible direction. Such a mistake would have been easy to make while transposing data from the notes or field books.
September 11, 1805
"In the bottoms here, there are a great quantity of cherries."
Gass ⇨
September 11, 1805
"A fair morning wind from the NW we set out at 3 oClock and proceeded on up the Travelers rest Creek..."
Clark ⇨
Large Creek
Camp
Travelers Rest
Sept. 9, 10, 1805
Return Camp
Travelers Rest
June 30, - July 2, 1806
S 45 E 1.5 MILES
"TRAVELERS REST CREEK"
July 1, 1806
"This morning early we sent out all our hunters."
Lewis ⇦
September 10, 1805
"this evening one of our hunters returned accompanyed by three men of the Flathead nation..."
Lewis ⇨
September 9, 1805
"... I determined to halt the next day rest our horses and take some scelestial Observations. we called this Creek Travellers rest."
Lewis ⇨
September 10, 1805
"... we learnt from these people that two men which they supposed to be of the Snake nation had stolen 23 horses from them and that they were in pursuit of the theaves."
Lewis ⇨
September 10, 1805
"... two of them departed ... the third remained, having agreed to continue with us as a guide, ... some of his relation[s] were at the sea last fall and saw an old whiteman who resided there by himself..."
Lewis ⇨
"CLARKS RIVER"
BITTERROOT RIVER
Lolo Creek
LOLO
MOUNTAINS
SAPPHIRE
Davis
Creek
Miller Creek
Cahoon Canyon
Sleeman Creek
Mormon Creek
Warden Creek
Plummers Slough
Doyles Slough
VALLEY
Maclay Bridge
N 10 W
4 MILES
Cartographer's Note:
The traverse call "N 10 W" is shown farther to the west of north in order to place Travelers Rest Camp where Clark's map shows it. This move is not much removed from the tolerance the cartographer is allowing Clark at this point.
June 30, 1806
"... a little before Sunset we arrived at our old encampment on the S. side of the Creek a little above its enterance into Clarks river. here we Encamped with a view to remain 2 days in order to rest ourselves and horses and make our final arrangements for Seperation."
Clark ⇦
Pine Bottom
September 9, 1805
"we continued our rout down the W. side of the river about 5 miles further and encamped on a large creek which falls in on the West."
Lewis ⇨
Cartographer's Note:
The natives informed Lewis that "Clarks River" (today's Bitterroot River) continued north a short distance to meet another large river from the east. The natives called it the Chicarlusket or Valley Plain River. Today it is the Clark Fork (also has been known as the Hellgate). The Blackfoot River joins the Clark Fork just east of the Bitterroot River confluence and has its beginnings to the east near the sources of the Sun River. The Sun River runs east and empties into the Missouri River at Great Falls. It was this connection that the explorers decided was the more direct route between the Missouri and Pacific waters. Lewis also referred to the "Tacootchetessee." In 1793, the Alexander Mackenzie party, the first non-Indians to cross the continent in northern latitudes, were following today's Fraser River when they lost all of their canoes and supplies in that river. The Mackenzie party continued on foot west over the coast mountain range to the Pacific Ocean at Bella Coola. Mackenzie assumed this river continued far to the south, becoming the Columbia River. This "hybrid" river became known as the "Tacoutche Tesse" until 1808, when Simon Fraser followed Mackenzie's river to the coast showing that it did not connect with the Columbia River. The reader is also reminded that Lewis and Clark originally called Clarks River (today's Bitterroot River) the "Flathead River."
BITTERROOT
McCLAIN
McClain
Squaw
July 3, 1806
"We colected our horses and after brackfast I took My leave of Capt. Lewis and the indians and at 8 AM Set out."
Clark ⇦
Cartographer's Note:
In 1806, after resting the Corps for two days, Lewis and Clark proceeded to carry out their plan to split up the expedition. Clark, taking the bulk of the party, headed south on July 3. He collected the boats and equipment cached on the east side of Lemhi Pass and proceeded down to the Three Forks of the Missouri. From there he sent Ordway with a small group of men down the Missouri with the canoes to the Great Falls. Clark then went southeast to explore the Yellowstone River Valley. Lewis, with a small party, proceeded to the Clark Fork River and turned northeast along the Blackfoot and Sun Rivers to the Great Falls of the Missouri. From there he planned to explore the Marias River. The entire Corps was to reunite at the mouth of the Yellowstone River.
RANGE
Maple
Creek
N 40 W
2 MILES
"CLARKS RIVER"
BITTERROOT RIVER
September 9, 1805
"we continued our rout down the valley about 4 miles and crossed the river; it is hear a hand some stream about 100 yards wide and affords a considerable quantity of very clear water, the banks are low and it's bed entirely gravel. the stream appears navigable, but from the circumstance of their being no sammon in it I believe that there must be a considerable fall in it below."
Lewis ⇨
CARLTON
Carlton Creek
ONE STATUTE MILE
Outbound: September 9-11, 1805
Return: June 30 - July 3, 1806
Modern Data: 1964-1978
EXPLORATIONS OF LEWIS AND CLARK 1804 - 1806
CARTOGRAPHIC RECONSTRUCTION
TRAVELERS REST
UTM ZONE 11
MAP NUMBER 294
Montana
CONTOUR INTERVAL 100 FEET

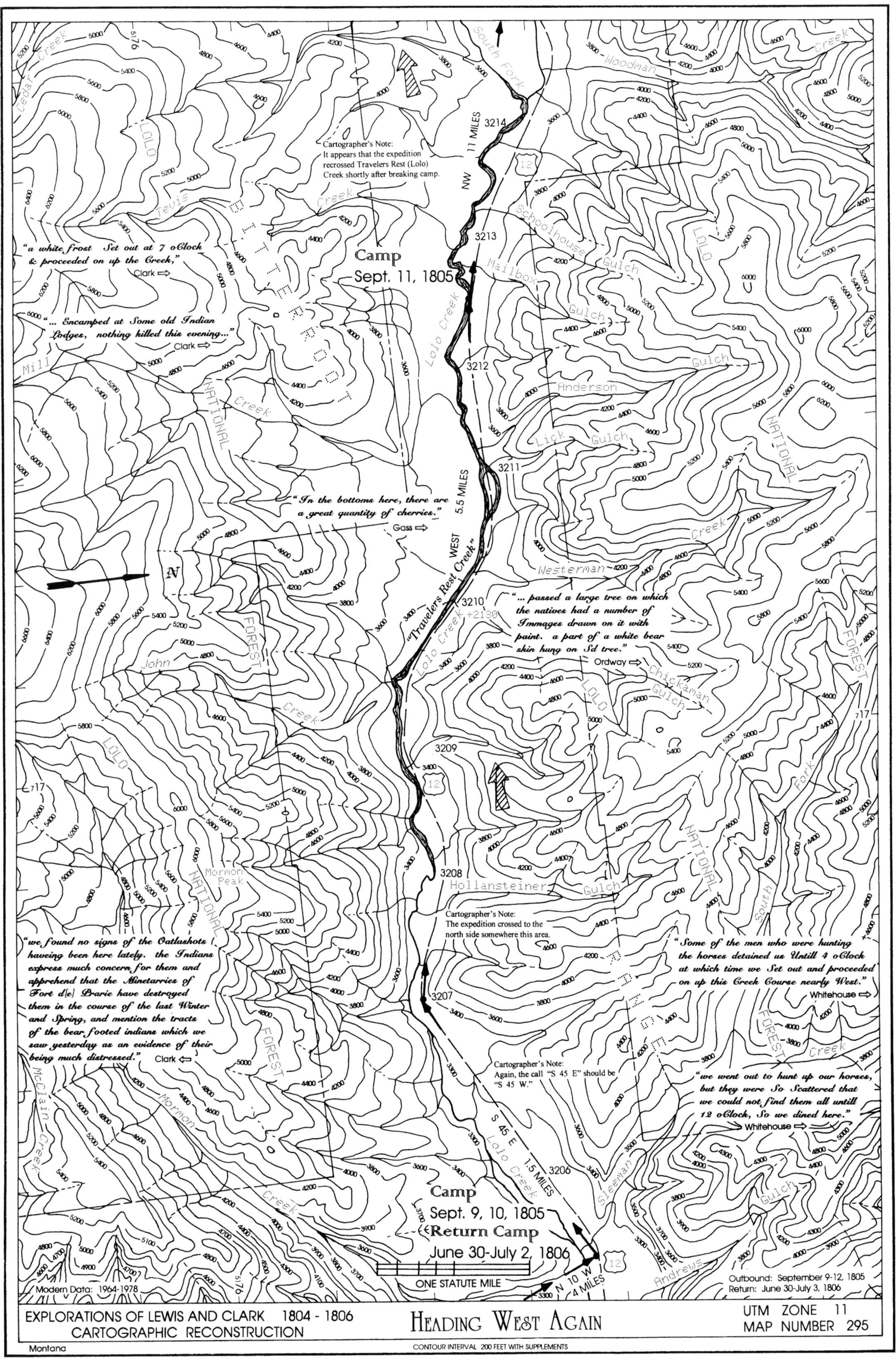
Cartographer's Note:
It appears that the expedition recrossed Travelers Rest (Lolo) Creek shortly after breaking camp.
NW 11 MILES
"a white frost Set out at 7 oClock & proceeded on up the Creek,"
Clark ⇨
Camp
Sept. 11, 1805
"... Encamped at Some old Indian Lodges, nothing killed this evening..."
Clark ⇨
"In the bottoms here, there are a great quantity of cherries."
Gass ⇨
WEST 5.5 MILES
"Travelers Rest Creek"
"... passed a large tree on which the natives had a number of Immages drawn on it with paint. a part of a white bear skin hung on Sd tree."
Ordway ⇨
Cartographer's Note:
The expedition crossed to the north side somewhere this area.
"we found no signs of the Oatlashots haveing been here lately. the Indians express much concern for them and apprehend that the Minetarries of Fort d[e] Prarie have destroyed them in the course of the last Winter and Spring, and mention the tracts of the bear footed indians which we saw yesterday as an evidence of their being much distressed."
Clark ⇦
"Some of the men who were hunting the horses detained us Untill 4 oClock at which time we Set out and proceeded on up this Creek Course nearly West."
Whitehouse ⇨
Cartographer's Note:
Again, the call "S 45 E" should be "S 45 W."
"we went out to hunt up our horses, but they were So Scattered that we could not find them all untill 12 oClock, So we dined here."
Whitehouse ⇨
S 45 E 1.5 MILES
Camp
Sept. 9, 10, 1805
Return Camp
June 30-July 2, 1806
N 10 W 4 MILES
ONE STATUTE MILE
Modern Data: 1964-1978
Outbound: September 9-12, 1805
Return: June 30-July 3, 1806
EXPLORATIONS OF LEWIS AND CLARK 1804 - 1806
CARTOGRAPHIC RECONSTRUCTION
HEADING WEST AGAIN
UTM ZONE 11
MAP NUMBER 295
Montana
CONTOUR INTERVAL 200 FEET WITH SUPPLEMENTS

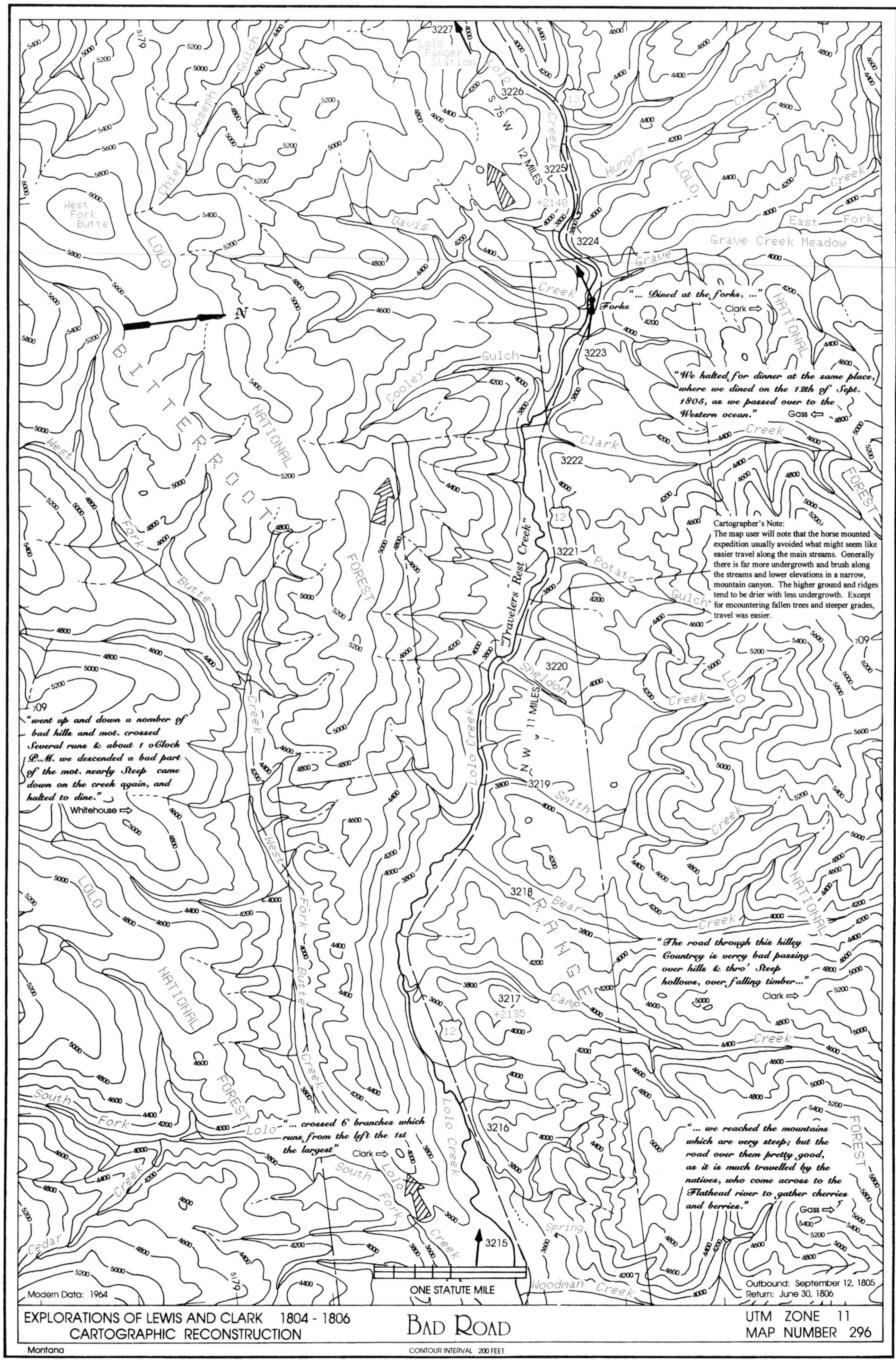
"... Dined at the forks, ..." Clark ⇨
"We halted for dinner at the same place, where we dined on the 12th of Sept. 1805, as we passed over to the Western ocean." Gass ⇦
Cartographer's Note:
The map user will note that the horse mounted expedition usually avoided what might seem like easier travel along the main streams. Generally there is far more undergrowth and brush along the streams and lower elevations in a narrow, mountain canyon. The higher ground and ridges tend to be drier with less undergrowth. Except for encountering fallen trees and steeper grades, travel was easier.
"went up and down a nomber of bad hills and mot. crossed Several runs & about 1 oClock P.M. we descended a bad part of the mot. nearly Steep came down on the creek again, and halted to dine." Whitehouse ⇨
"The road through this hilley Countrey is very bad passing over hills & thro' Steep hollows, over falling timber..." Clark ⇨
"... crossed 6 branches which runs from the left the 1st the largest" Clark ⇨
"... we reached the mountains which are very steep; but the road over them pretty good, as it is much travelled by the natives, who come across to the Flathead river to gather cherries and berries." Gass ⇨
Lolo Ranger Station
West Fork Butte
Forks
Travelers' Rest Creek
Grave Creek Meadow
BITTERROOT RANGE
LOLO NATIONAL FOREST
12 MILES
11 MILES
ONE STATUTE MILE
Modern Data: 1964
Outbound: September 12, 1805
Return: June 30, 1806
EXPLORATIONS OF LEWIS AND CLARK 1804 - 1806
CARTOGRAPHIC RECONSTRUCTION
BAD ROAD
UTM ZONE 11
MAP NUMBER 296
Montana
CONTOUR INTERVAL 200 FEET

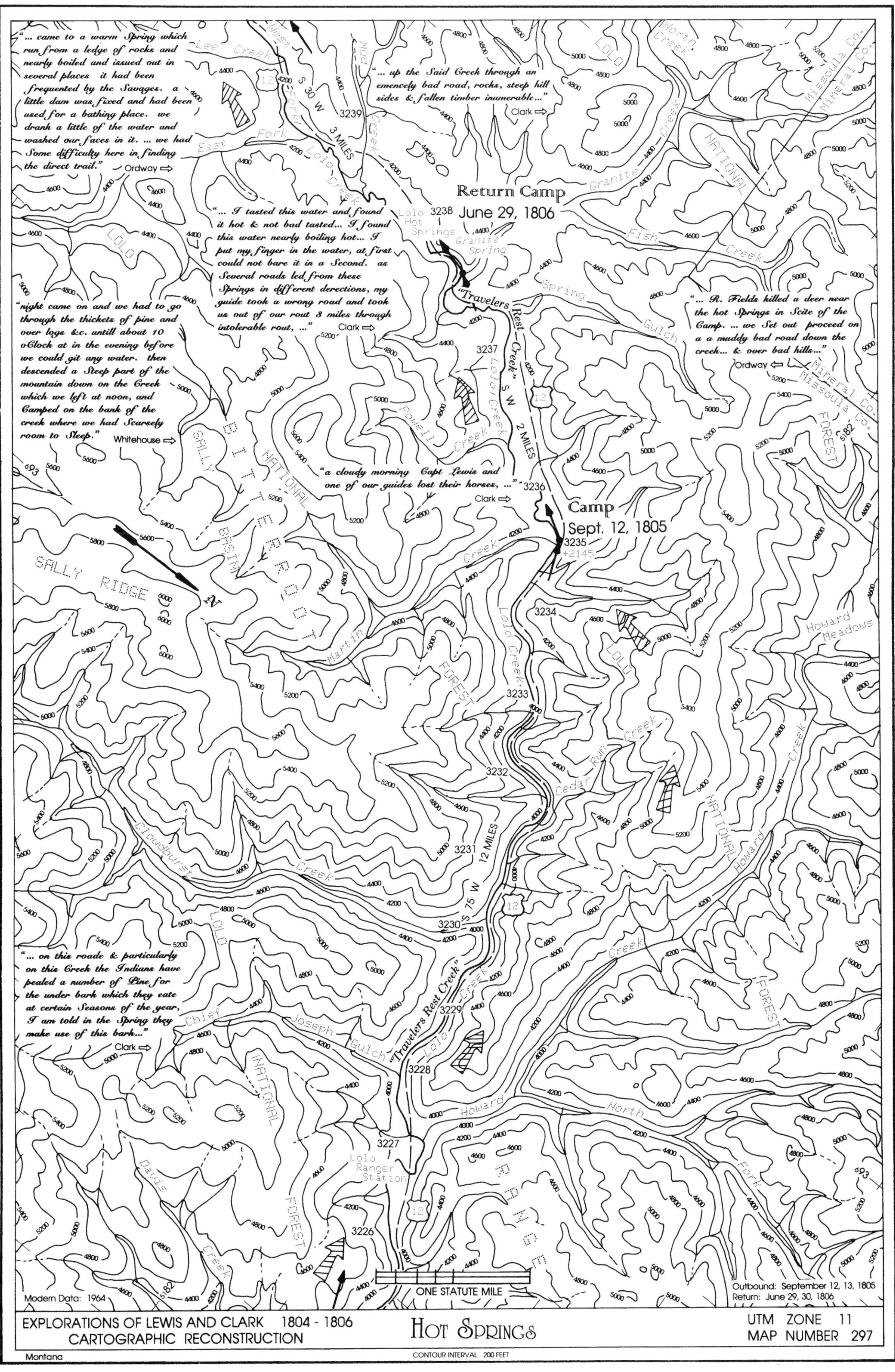
"... came to a warm Spring which run from a ledge of rocks and nearly boiled and issued out in several places it had been frequented by the Savages. a little dam was fixed and had been used for a bathing place. we drank a little of the water and washed our faces in it. ... we had Some difficulty here in finding the direct trail." Ordway
"... up the Said Creek through an emencely bad road, rocks, steep hill sides & fallen timber inumerable..." Clark
Return Camp
June 29, 1806
"... I tasted this water and found it hot & not bad tasted... I found this water nearly boiling hot... I put my finger in the water, at first could not bare it in a Second. as Several roads led from these Springs in different derections, my guide took a wrong road and took us out of our rout 3 miles through intolerable rout, ..." Clark
"... R. Fields killed a deer near the hot Springs in Scite of the Camp. ... we Set out proceed on a a muddy bad road down the creek... & over bad hills..." Ordway
"night came on and we had to go through the thickets of pine and over logs &c. untill about 10 oClock at in the evening before we could git any water. then descended a Steep part of the mountain down on the Creek which we left at noon, and Camped on the bank of the creek where we had Scarsely room to Sleep." Whitehouse
"a cloudy morning Capt Lewis and one of our guides lost their horses, ..." Clark
Camp
Sept. 12, 1805
"Travelers Rest Creek"
"... on this roade & particularly on this Creek the Indians have pealed a number of Pine for the under bark which they eate at certain Seasons of the year, I am told in the Spring they make use of this bark..." Clark
Lolo Hot Springs
Granite Spring
Lolo Ranger Station
SALLY RIDGE
BITTERROOT NATIONAL FOREST
LOLO NATIONAL FOREST
S 30 W 3 MILES
SW 2 MILES
S 75 W 12 MILES
ONE STATUTE MILE
Modern Data: 1964
Outbound: September 12, 13, 1805
Return: June 29, 30, 1806
EXPLORATIONS OF LEWIS AND CLARK 1804 - 1806
CARTOGRAPHIC RECONSTRUCTION
HOT SPRINGS
UTM ZONE 11
MAP NUMBER 297
Montana
CONTOUR INTERVAL 200 FEET

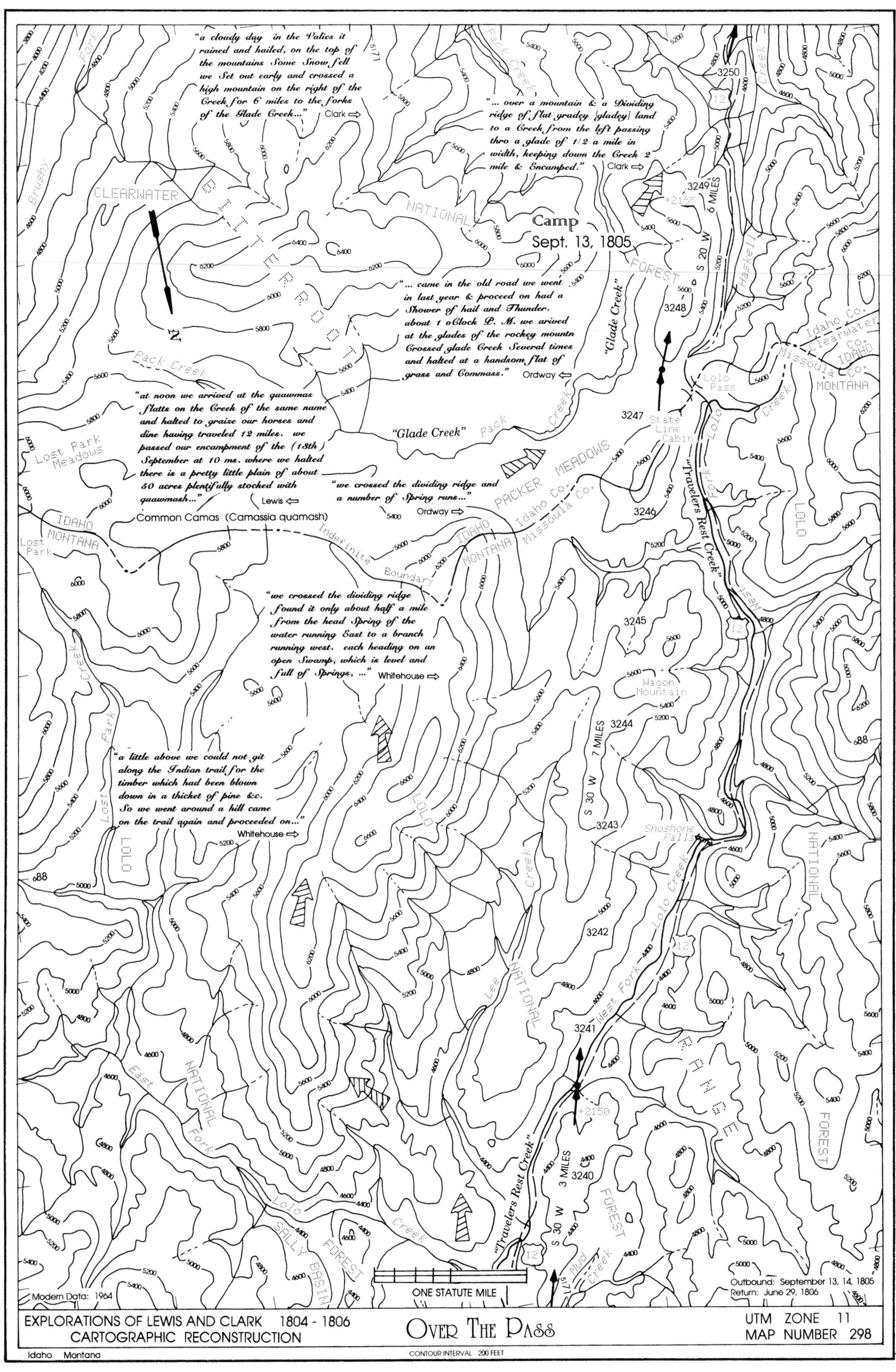
"a cloudy day in the Valies it rained and hailed, on the top of the mountains Some Snow fell we Set out early and crossed a high mountain on the right of the Creek for 6 miles to the forks of the Glade Creek..." Clark ⇨
"... over a mountain & a Dividing ridge of flat gradey [gladey] land to a Creek from the left passing thro a glade of 1/2 a mile in width, keeping down the Creek 2 mile & Encamped." Clark ⇨
Camp
Sept. 13, 1805
"... came in the old road we went in last year & proceed on had a Shower of hail and Thunder. about 1 oClock P. M. we arived at the glades of the rockey mountn Crossed glade Creek Several times and halted at a handsom flat of grass and Commass." Ordway ⇦
"at noon we arrived at the quawmas flatts on the Creek of the same name and halted to graize our horses and dine having traveled 12 miles. we passed our encampment of the (13th) September at 10 ms. where we halted there is a pretty little plain of about 50 acres plentifully stocked with quawmash..." Lewis ⇦
"we crossed the dividing ridge and a number of Spring runs..." Ordway ⇨
Common Camas (Camassia quamash)
"we crossed the dividing ridge found it only about half a mile from the head Spring of the water running East to a branch running west. each heading on an open Swamp, which is level and full of Springs, ..." Whitehouse ⇨
"a little above we could not git along the Indian trail for the timber which had been blown down in a thicket of pine &c. So we went around a hill came on the trail again and proceeded on..." Whitehouse ⇨
CLEARWATER
BITTERROOT
NATIONAL
FOREST
"Glade Creek"
Pack Creek
Brushy Fork
Lost Park Meadows
Lost Park
IDAHO
MONTANA
Indefinite Boundary
PACKER MEADOWS
Idaho Co.
Missoula Co.
Clearwater Co.
Lolo Pass
State Line Cabin
"Travelers Rest Creek"
Haskell Creek
Lolo Creek
Lolo Fork
Wagon Mountain
Shoshone Falls
Lost Park Creek
LOLO
Lee Creek
West Fork
East Fork
Sally Basin
Mud Creek
RANGE
S 20 W 6 MILES
S 30 W 7 MILES
S 30 W 3 MILES
+2155
+2150
3250
3249
3248
3247
3246
3245
3244
3243
3242
3241
3240
12
ONE STATUTE MILE
Modern Data: 1964
Outbound: September 13, 14, 1805
Return: June 29, 1806
EXPLORATIONS OF LEWIS AND CLARK 1804 - 1806
CARTOGRAPHIC RECONSTRUCTION
OVER THE PASS
UTM ZONE 11
MAP NUMBER 298
Idaho Montana
CONTOUR INTERVAL 200 FEET

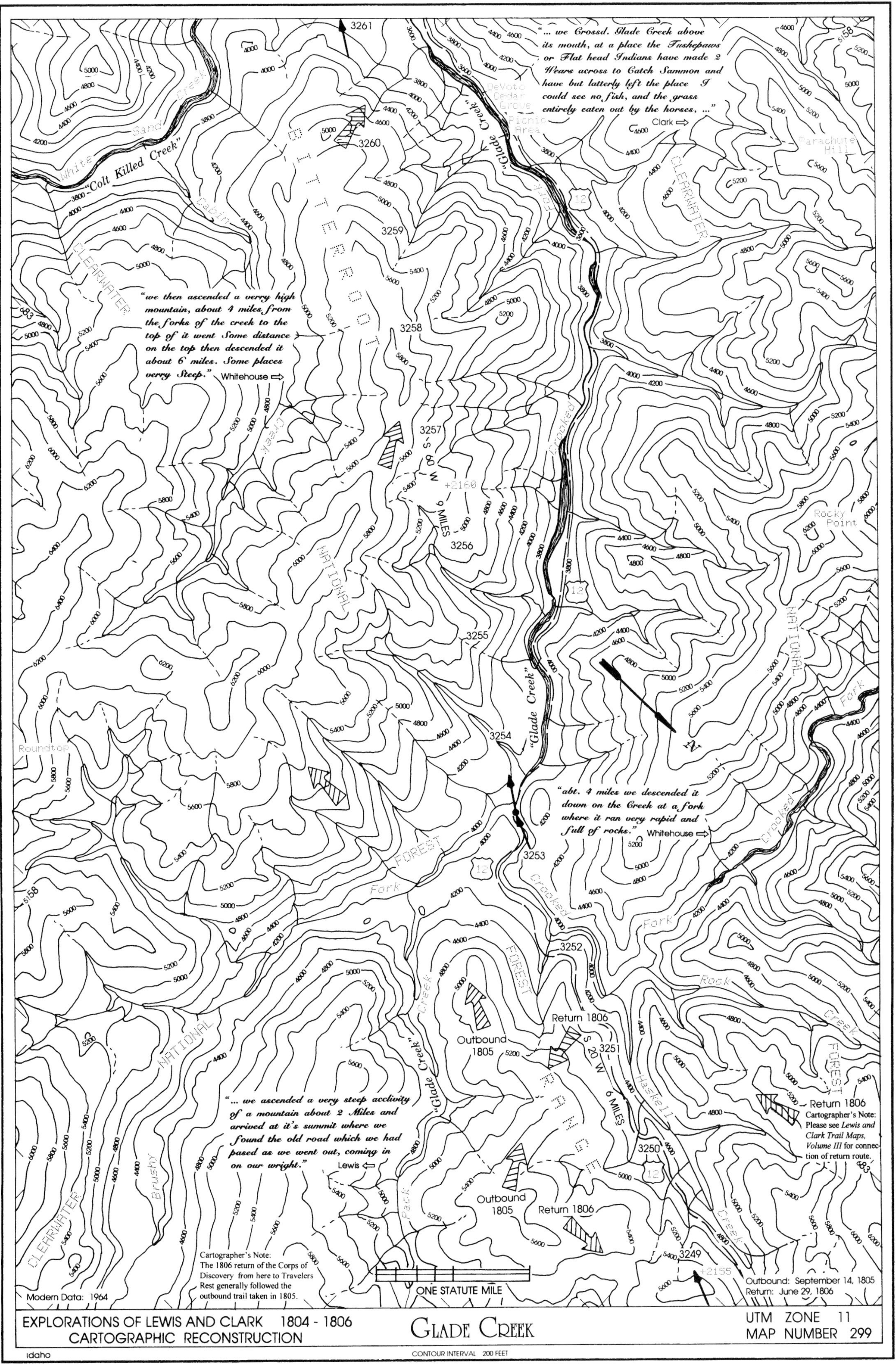

"... we Crossd. Glade Creek above its mouth, at a place the Tushepaws or Flat head Indians have made 2 Wears across to Catch Sammon and have but latterly left the place I could see no fish, and the grass entirely eaten out by the horses, ..."
Clark
"we then ascended a verry high mountain, about 4 miles from the forks of the creek to the top of it went Some distance on the top then descended it about 6 miles. Some places verry Steep."
Whitehouse
"abt. 4 miles we descended it down on the Creek at a fork where it ran very rapid and full of rocks."
Whitehouse
"... we ascended a very steep acclivity of a mountain about 2 Miles and arrived at it's summit where we found the old road which we had pased as we went out, coming in on our wright."
Lewis
"Colt Killed Creek"
"Glade Creek"
White Sand Creek
DeVoto Cedar Grove
Picnic Area
Parachute Hill
Rocky Point
Roundtop
BITTERROOT NATIONAL FOREST
RANGE
CLEARWATER NATIONAL FOREST
Crooked Fork
Rock Creek
Haskell Creek
Brushy Fork
Pack Creek
Cabin Creek
N
N 60° W 9 MILES
S 20° W 6 MILES
+2160
+2155
Outbound 1805
Return 1806
Cartographer's Note: Please see Lewis and Clark Trail Maps, Volume III for connection of return route.
Cartographer's Note: The 1806 return of the Corps of Discovery from here to Travelers Rest generally followed the outbound trail taken in 1805.
Outbound: September 14, 1805
Return: June 29, 1806
ONE STATUTE MILE
Modern Data: 1964
EXPLORATIONS OF LEWIS AND CLARK 1804 - 1806
CARTOGRAPHIC RECONSTRUCTION
GLADE CREEK
UTM ZONE 11
MAP NUMBER 299
Idaho
CONTOUR INTERVAL 200 FEET

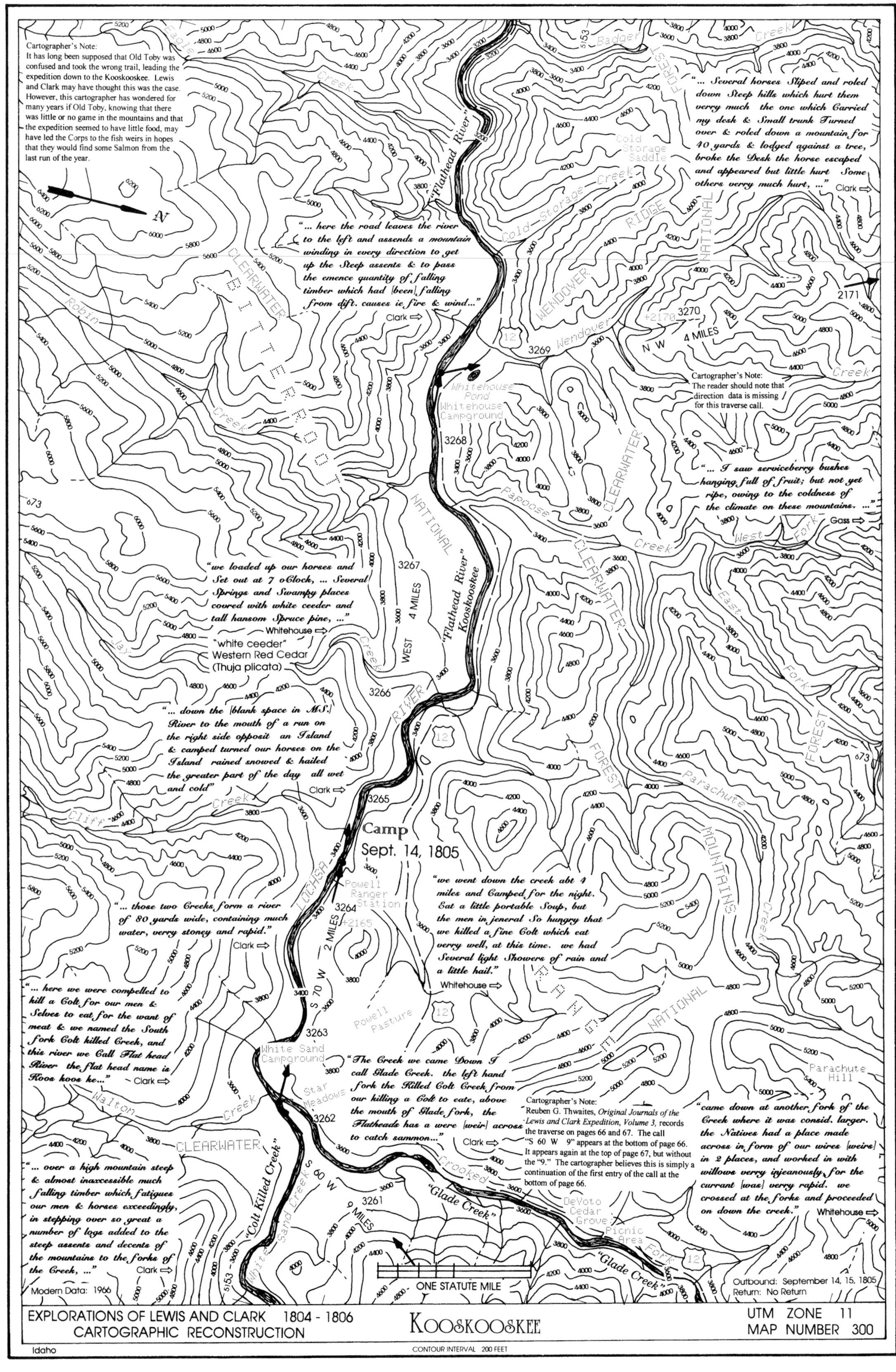

Cartographer's Note:
It has long been supposed that Old Toby was confused and took the wrong trail, leading the expedition down to the Kooskooskee. Lewis and Clark may have thought this was the case. However, this cartographer has wondered for many years if Old Toby, knowing that there was little or no game in the mountains and that the expedition seemed to have little food, may have led the Corps to the fish weirs in hopes that they would find some Salmon from the last run of the year.
"... Several horses Sliped and roled down Steep hills which hurt them verry much the one which Carried my desk & Small trunk Turned over & roled down a mountain for 40 yards & lodged against a tree, broke the Desk the horse escaped and appeared but little hurt Some others verry much hurt, ..." Clark ⇨
"... here the road leaves the river to the left and assends a mountain winding in every direction to get up the Steep assents & to pass the emence quantity of falling timber which had [been] falling from dift. causes ie, fire & wind..." Clark ⇨
Cartographer's Note:
The reader should note that direction data is missing for this traverse call.
"... I saw serviceberry bushes hanging full of fruit; but not yet ripe, owing to the coldness of the climate on these mountains. ..." Gass ⇨
"we loaded up our horses and Set out at 7 oClock, ... Several Springs and Swampy places coured with white ceeder and tall hansom Spruce pine, ..." Whitehouse ⇨
"white ceeder"
Western Red Cedar
(Thuja plicata)
"... down the [blank space in MS.] River to the mouth of a run on the right side opposit an Island & camped turned our horses on the Island rained snowed & hailed the greater part of the day all wet and cold" Clark ⇨
Camp
Sept. 14, 1805
"... those two Creeks form a river of 80 yards wide, containing much water, verry stoney and rapid." Clark ⇨
"we went down the creek abt 4 miles and Camped for the night. Eat a little portable Soup, but the men in jeneral So hungry that we killed a fine Colt which eat verry well, at this time. we had Several light Showers of rain and a little hail." Whitehouse ⇨
"... here we were compelled to kill a Colt for our men & Selves to eat for the want of meat & we named the South fork Colt killed Creek, and this river we Call Flat head River the flat head name is Koos koos ke..." Clark ⇨
"The Creek we came Down I call Glade Creek. the left hand fork the Killed Colt Creek from our killing a Colt to eate, above the mouth of Glade fork, the Flatheads has a were [weir] across to catch sammon..." Clark ⇨
Cartographer's Note:
Reuben G. Thwaites, Original Journals of the Lewis and Clark Expedition, Volume 3, records the traverse on pages 66 and 67. The call "S 60 W 9" appears at the bottom of page 66. It appears again at the top of page 67, but without the "9." The cartographer believes this is simply a continuation of the first entry of the call at the bottom of page 66.
"came down at another fork of the Creek where it was consid. larger. the Natives had a place made across in form of our wires [weirs] in 2 places, and worked in with willows verry injeanously for the currant [was] verry rapid. we crossed at the forks and proceeded on down the creek." Whitehouse ⇨
"... over a high mountain steep & almost inaxcessible much falling timber which fatigues our men & horses exceedingly, in stepping over so great a number of logs added to the steep assents and decents of the mountains to the forks of the Creek, ..." Clark ⇨
"Flathead River"
"Flathead River" Kooskooskee
"Colt Killed Creek"
"Glade Creek"
BITTERROOT
CLEARWATER
NATIONAL
FOREST
MOUNTAINS
LOCHSA RIVER
WENDOVER RIDGE
Whitehouse Pond
Whitehouse Campground
Powell Ranger Station
Powell Pasture
White Sand Campground
Star Meadows
DeVoto Cedar Grove
Picnic Area
Parachute Hill
Cold Storage Saddle
N W 4 MILES
WEST 4 MILES
S 70 W 2 MILES
S 60 W 9 MILES
ONE STATUTE MILE
Modern Data: 1966
Outbound: September 14, 15, 1805
Return: No Return
EXPLORATIONS OF LEWIS AND CLARK 1804 - 1806
CARTOGRAPHIC RECONSTRUCTION
KOOSKOOSKEE
UTM ZONE 11
MAP NUMBER 300
Idaho
CONTOUR INTERVAL 200 FEET

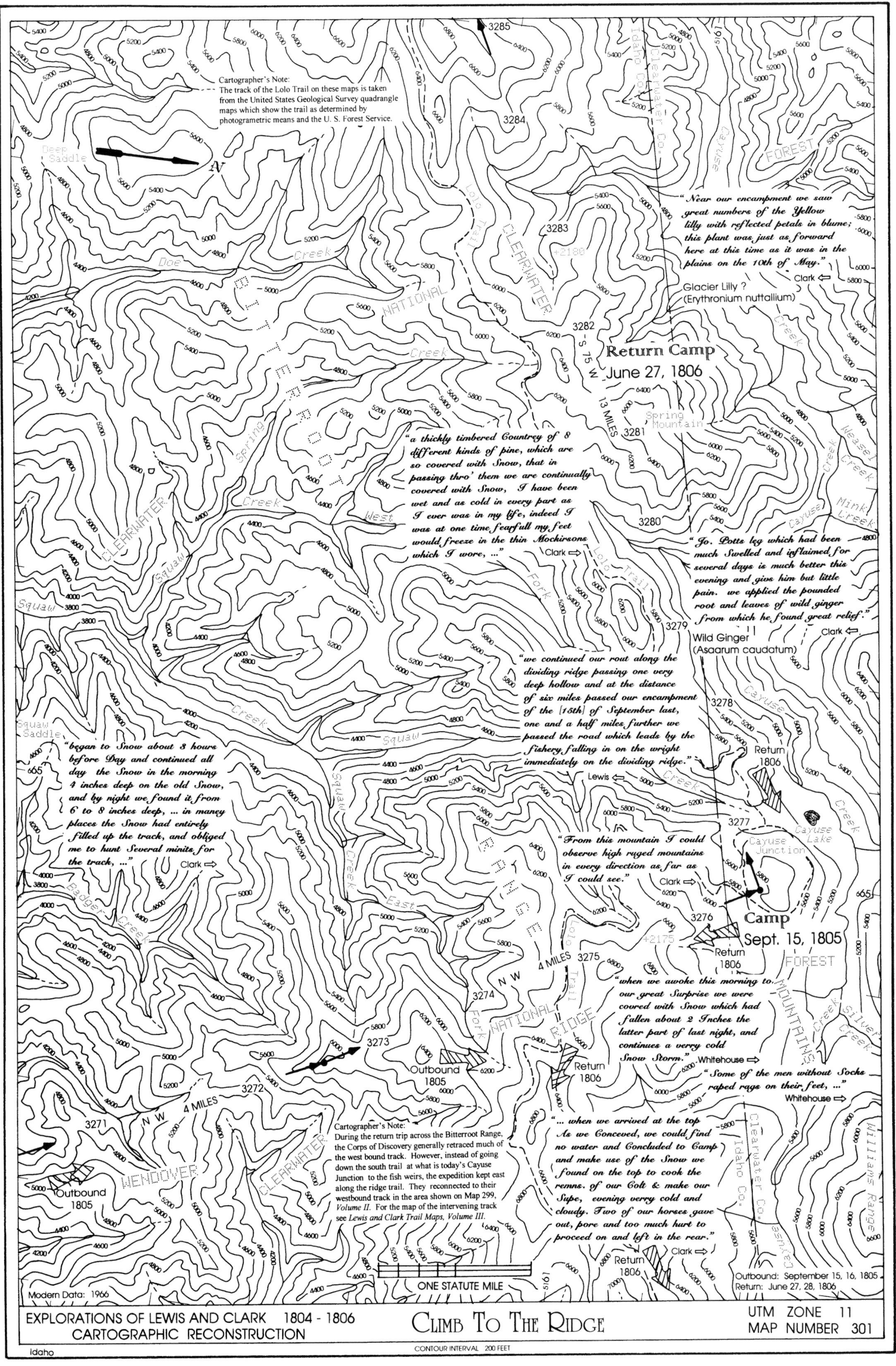

Cartographer's Note:
The track of the Lolo Trail on these maps is taken from the United States Geological Survey quadrangle maps which show the trail as determined by photogrametric means and the U. S. Forest Service.
"Near our encampment we saw great numbers of the Yellow lilly with reflected petals in blume; this plant was just as forward here at this time as it was in the plains on the 10th of May."
Clark ⇦
Glacier Lilly ?
(Erythronium nuttallium)
Return Camp
June 27, 1806
S 75 W
13 MILES
"a thickly timbered Countrey of 8 different kinds of pine, which are so covered with Snow, that in passing thro' them we are continually covered with Snow, I have been wet and as cold in every part as I ever was in my life, indeed I was at one time fearfull my feet would freeze in the thin Mockirsons which I wore, ..."
Clark ⇨
"Jo. Potts leg which had been much Swelled and inflaimed for several days is much better this evening and gives him but little pain. we applied the pounded root and leaves of wild ginger from which he found great relief."
Clark ⇦
Wild Ginger
(Asaarum caudatum)
"we continued our rout along the dividing ridge passing one very deep hollow and at the distance of six miles passed our encampment of the [15th] of September last, one and a half miles further we passed the road which leads by the fishery falling in on the wright immediately on the dividing ridge."
Lewis ⇦
"began to Snow about 3 hours before Day and continued all day the Snow in the morning 4 inches deep on the old Snow, and by night we found it from 6 to 8 inches deep, ... in maney places the Snow had entirely filled up the track, and obliged me to hunt Several minits for the track, ..."
Clark ⇨
"From this mountain I could observe high ruged mountains in every direction as far as I could see."
Clark ⇨
Camp
Sept. 15, 1805
Cayuse Junction
Cayuse Lake
Return 1806
"when we awoke this morning to our great Surprise we were covered with Snow which had fallen about 2 Inches the latter part of last night, and continues a verry cold Snow Storm."
Whitehouse ⇨
"Some of the men without Socks raped rags on their feet, ..."
Whitehouse ⇨
NW 4 MILES
Outbound 1805
Cartographer's Note:
During the return trip across the Bitterroot Range, the Corps of Discovery generally retraced much of the west bound track. However, instead of going down the south trail at what is today's Cayuse Junction to the fish weirs, the expedition kept east along the ridge trail. They reconnected to their westbound track in the area shown on Map 299, Volume II. For the map of the intervening track see Lewis and Clark Trail Maps, Volume III.
"... when we arrived at the top As we Conceved, we could find no water and Concluded to Camp and make use of the Snow we found on the top to cook the remns. of our Colt & make our Supe, evening verry cold and cloudy. Two of our horses gave out, pore and too much hurt to proceed on and left in the rear."
Clark ⇨
Outbound: September 15, 16, 1805
Return: June 27, 28, 1806
ONE STATUTE MILE
Modern Data: 1966
BITTERROOT RANGE
CLEARWATER NATIONAL FOREST
Lolo Trail
Idaho Co.
Clearwater Co.
EXPLORATIONS OF LEWIS AND CLARK 1804 - 1806
CARTOGRAPHIC RECONSTRUCTION
CLIMB TO THE RIDGE
UTM ZONE 11
MAP NUMBER 301
Idaho
CONTOUR INTERVAL 200 FEET

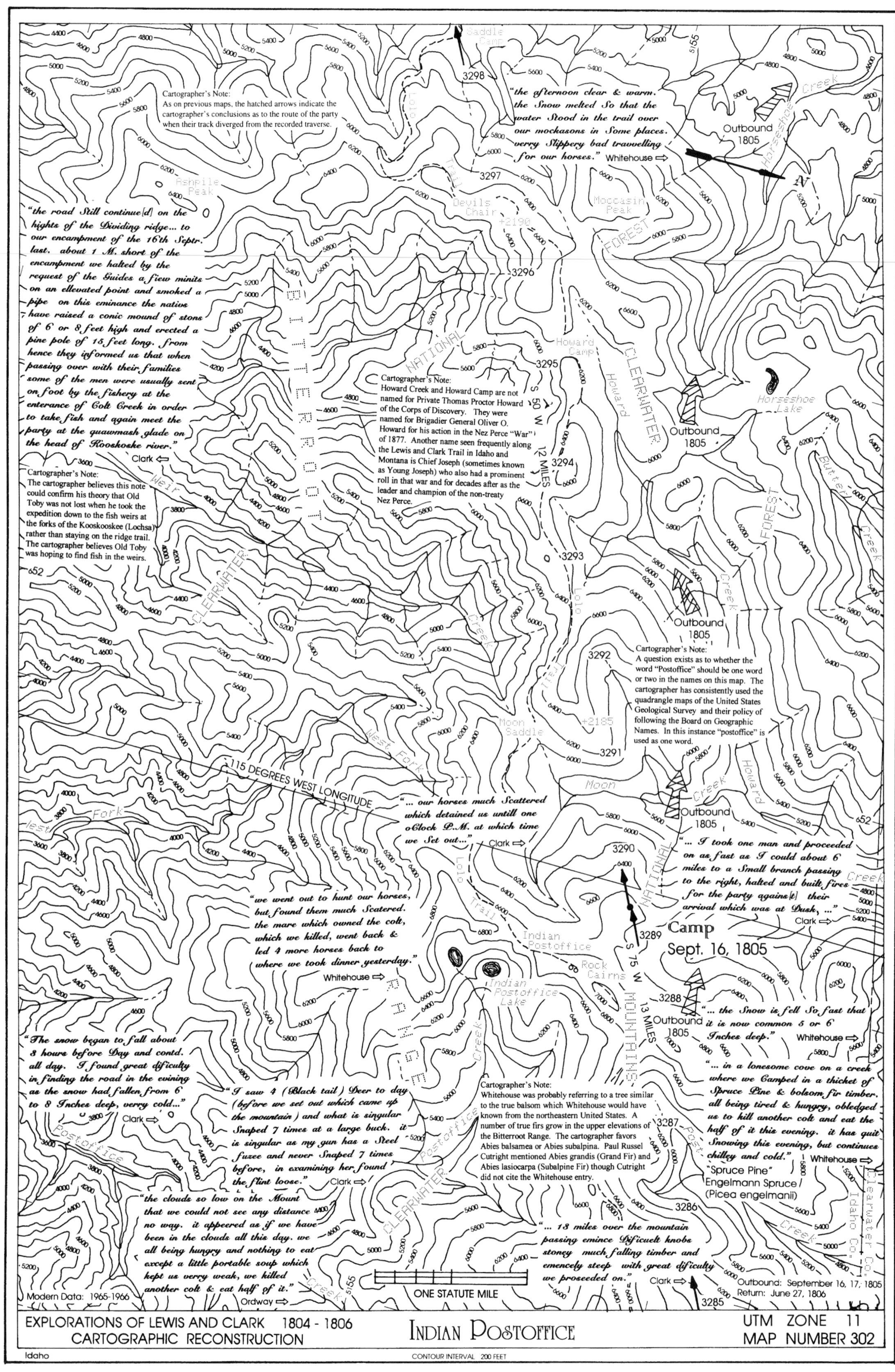
Cartographer's Note:
As on previous maps, the hatched arrows indicate the cartographer's conclusions as to the route of the party when their track diverged from the recorded traverse.
Saddle Camp
3298
"the afternoon clear & warm. the Snow melted So that the water Stood in the trail over our mockasons in Some places. verry Slippery bad travelling for our horses." Whitehouse ⇨
Outbound 1805
Horseshoe
Creek
N
Lolo
Trail
3297
Ashpile Peak
Devils Chair
+2190
Moccasin Peak
FOREST
"the road Still continue[d] on the hights of the Dividing ridge... to our encampment of the 16th Septr. last. about 1 M. short of the encampment we halted by the request of the Guides a fiew minits on an ellevated point and smoked a pipe on this eminance the natives have raised a conic mound of stons of 6 or 8 feet high and erected a pine pole of 15 feet long. from hence they informed us that when passing over with their families some of the men were usually sent on foot by the fishery at the enterance of Colt Creek in order to take fish and again meet the party at the quawmash glade on the head of Kooskoske river." Clark ⇦
3296
BITTERROOT
NATIONAL
Howard Camp
3295
CLEARWATER
Howard
Horseshoe Lake
Outbound 1805
Cartographer's Note:
Howard Creek and Howard Camp are not named for Private Thomas Proctor Howard of the Corps of Discovery. They were named for Brigadier General Oliver O. Howard for his action in the Nez Perce "War" of 1877. Another name seen frequently along the Lewis and Clark Trail in Idaho and Montana is Chief Joseph (sometimes known as Young Joseph) who also had a prominent roll in that war and for decades after as the leader and champion of the non-treaty Nez Perce.
S 50 W
12 MILES
3294
Butter
Creek
FOREST
Cartographer's Note:
The cartographer believes this note could confirm his theory that Old Toby was not lost when he took the expedition down to the fish weirs at the forks of the Kooskooskee (Lochsa) rather than staying on the ridge trail. The cartographer believes Old Toby was hoping to find fish in the weirs.
Weir
3293
Lolo
Creek
Outbound 1805
652
CLEARWATER
Creek
3292
Cartographer's Note:
A question exists as to whether the word "Postoffice" should be one word or two in the names on this map. The cartographer has consistently used the quadrangle maps of the United States Geological Survey and their policy of following the Board on Geographic Names. In this instance "postoffice" is used as one word.
Trail
Moon Saddle
+2185
3291
West Fork
115 DEGREES WEST LONGITUDE
Moon
Creek
Howard
Outbound 1805
652
Fork
West
"... our horses much Scattered which detained us untill one oClock P.M. at which time we Set out..." Clark ⇨
3290
NATIONAL
"... I took one man and proceeded on as fast as I could about 6 miles to a Small branch passing to the right, halted and built fires for the party agains[t] their arrival which was at Dusk, ..." Clark ⇨
Creek
Lolo
Trail
"we went out to hunt our horses, but found them much Scatered. the mare which owned the colt, which we killed, went back & led 4 more horses back to where we took dinner yesterday." Whitehouse ⇨
Indian Postoffice
3289
S 75 W
Camp
Sept. 16, 1805
Rock Cairns
Indian Postoffice Lake
RANGE
3288
MOUNTAINS
13 MILES
Outbound 1805
"... the Snow is fell So fast that it is now common 5 or 6 Inches deep." Whitehouse ⇨
"The snow began to fall about 3 hours before Day and contd. all day. I found great dificulty in finding the road in the evining as the snow had fallen from 6 to 8 Inches deep, verry cold..." Clark ⇨
"I saw 4 (Black tail) Deer to day (before we set out which came up the mountain) and what is singular Snaped 7 times at a large buck. it is singular as my gun has a Steel fuzee and never Snaped 7 times before, in examining her found the flint loose." Clark ⇨
Creek
Cartographer's Note:
Whitehouse was probably referring to a tree similar to the true balsom which Whitehouse would have known from the northeastern United States. A number of true firs grow in the upper elevations of the Bitterroot Range. The cartographer favors Abies balsamea or Abies subalpina. Paul Russel Cutright mentioned Abies grandis (Grand Fir) and Abies lasiocarpa (Subalpine Fir) though Cutright did not cite the Whitehouse entry.
3287
Post
"... in a lonesome cove on a creek where we Camped in a thicket of Spruce Pine & bolsom fir timber. all being tired & hungry, obledged us to kill another colt and eat the half of it this evening. it has quit Snowing this evening, but continues chilley and cold." Whitehouse ⇨
"Spruce Pine"
Engelmann Spruce / (Picea engelmanii)
Postoffice
Postoffice
CLEARWATER
Clearwater Co.
Idaho Co.
"the clouds so low on the Mount that we could not see any distance no way. it appeered as if we have been in the clouds all this day. we all being hungry and nothing to eat except a little portable soup which kept us verry weak, we killed another colt & eat half of it." Ordway ⇨
3286
"... 13 miles over the mountain passing emince Dificuelt knobs stoney much falling timber and emencely steep with great dificulty we proseeded on." Clark ⇨
Creek
Creek
ONE STATUTE MILE
Modern Data: 1965-1966
Outbound: September 16, 17, 1805
Return: June 27, 1806
3285
EXPLORATIONS OF LEWIS AND CLARK 1804 - 1806
CARTOGRAPHIC RECONSTRUCTION
INDIAN POSTOFFICE
UTM ZONE 11
MAP NUMBER 302
Idaho
CONTOUR INTERVAL 200 FEET

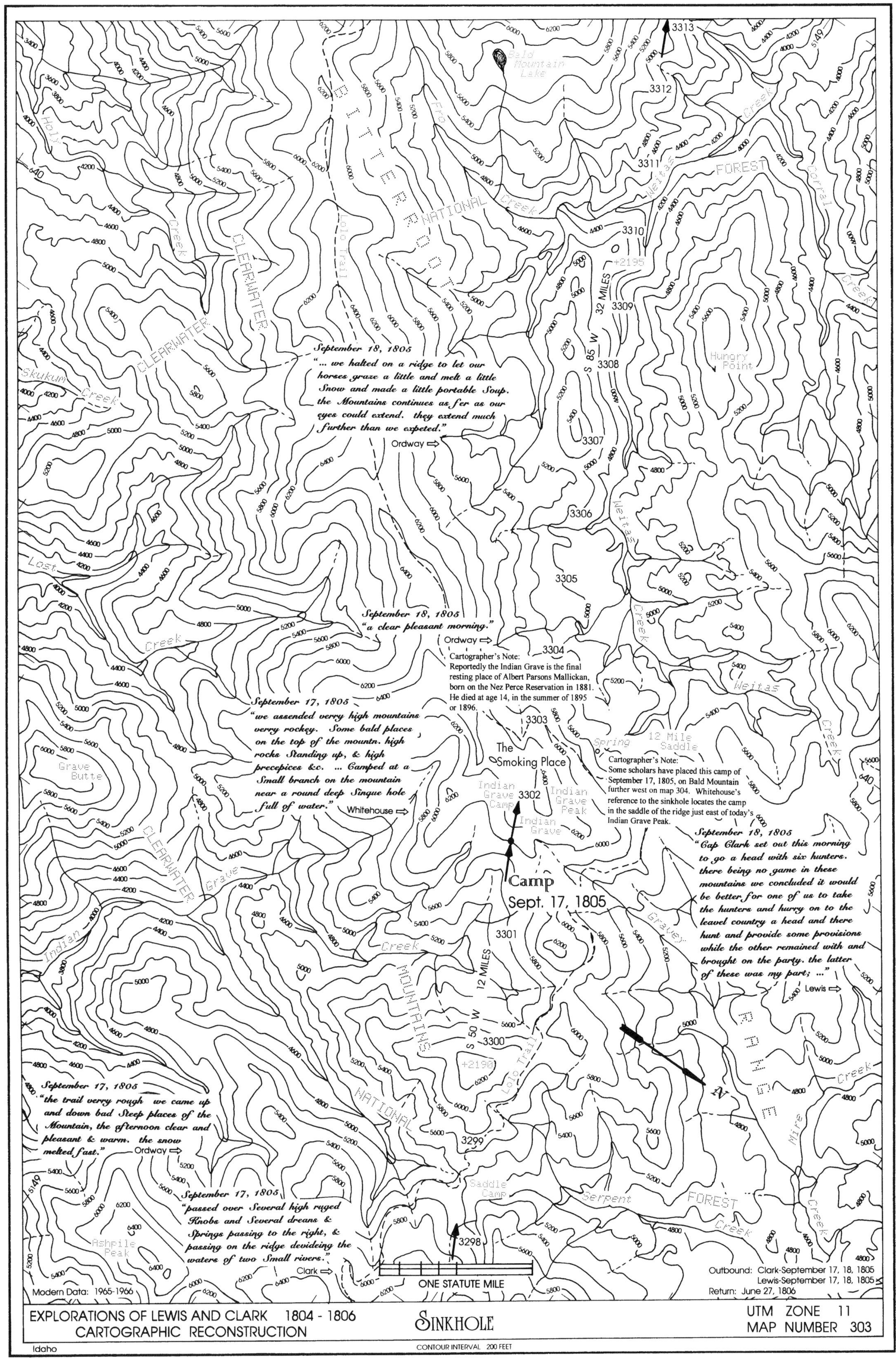

Bald Mountain Lake
BITTERROOT
NATIONAL
FOREST
Lolo Trail
Fro Creek
Weitas Creek
Corral Creek
Holly
Creek
CLEARWATER
CLEARWATER
Skukum Creek
Lost Creek
Hungry Point
3313
3312
3311
3310
+2195
3309
32 MILES
S 85 W
3308
3307
3306
3305
3304
3303
3302
3301
3300
3299
3298
September 18, 1805
"... we halted on a ridge to let our horses graze a little and melt a little Snow and made a little portable Soup. the Mountains continues as fer as our eyes could extend. they extend much further than we expeted."
Ordway ⇨
September 18, 1805
"a clear pleasant morning."
Ordway ⇨
Cartographer's Note:
Reportedly the Indian Grave is the final resting place of Albert Parsons Mallickan, born on the Nez Perce Reservation in 1881. He died at age 14, in the summer of 1895 or 1896.
September 17, 1805
"we assended verry high mountains verry rockey. Some bald places on the top of the mountn. high rocks Standing up, & high precepices &c. ... Camped at a Small branch on the mountain near a round deep Sinque hole full of water."
Whitehouse ⇨
The Smoking Place
Spring
12 Mile Saddle
Cartographer's Note:
Some scholars have placed this camp of September 17, 1805, on Bald Mountain further west on map 304. Whitehouse's reference to the sinkhole locates the camp in the saddle of the ridge just east of today's Indian Grave Peak.
Indian Grave Camp
Indian Grave Peak
Indian Grave
Camp
Sept. 17, 1805
Grave Butte
Grave Creek
Indian
Gravey
September 18, 1805
"Cap Clark set out this morning to go a head with six hunters. there being no game in these mountains we concluded it would be better for one of us to take the hunters and hurry on to the leavel country a head and there hunt and provide some provisions while the other remained with and brought on the party. the latter of these was my part; ..."
Lewis ⇨
MOUNTAINS
RANGE
12 MILES
S 50 W
+2190
Lolo Trail
NATIONAL
N
Creek
Mire
September 17, 1805
"the trail verry rough we came up and down bad Steep places of the Mountain, the afternoon clear and pleasant & warm. the snow melted fast."
Ordway ⇨
September 17, 1805
"passed over Several high ruged Knobs and Several dreans & Springs passing to the right, & passing on the ridge devideing the waters of two Small rivers."
Clark ⇨
Saddle Camp
Serpent
FOREST
Creek
Ashpile Peak
ONE STATUTE MILE
Modern Data: 1965-1966
Outbound: Clark-September 17, 18, 1805
Lewis-September 17, 18, 1805
Return: June 27, 1806
EXPLORATIONS OF LEWIS AND CLARK 1804 - 1806
CARTOGRAPHIC RECONSTRUCTION
SINKHOLE
UTM ZONE 11
MAP NUMBER 303
Idaho
CONTOUR INTERVAL 200 FEET

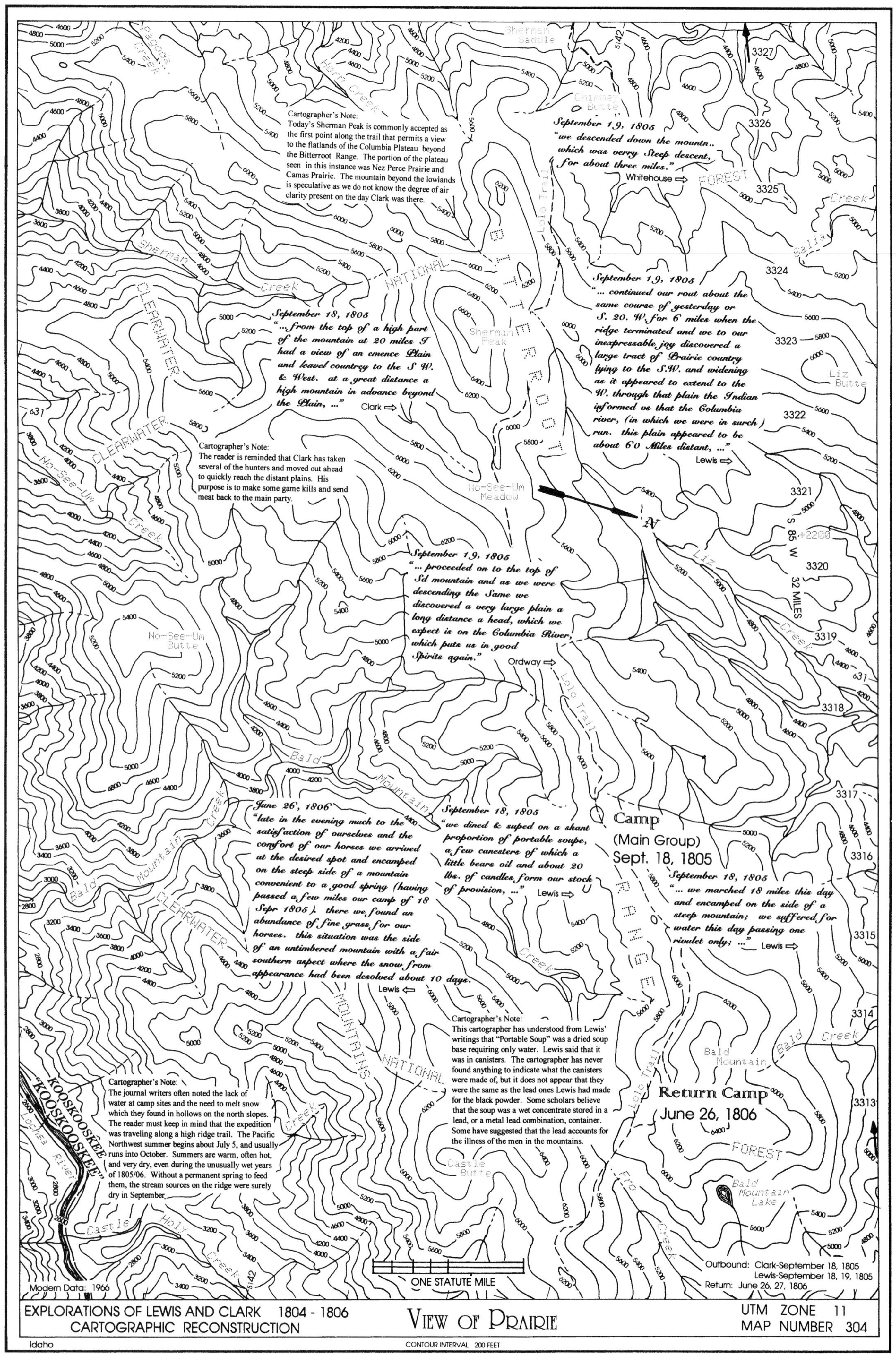

Cartographer's Note:
Today's Sherman Peak is commonly accepted as the first point along the trail that permits a view to the flatlands of the Columbia Plateau beyond the Bitterroot Range. The portion of the plateau seen in this instance was Nez Perce Prairie and Camas Prairie. The mountain beyond the lowlands is speculative as we do not know the degree of air clarity present on the day Clark was there.
September 19, 1805
"we descended down the mountn.. which was verry Steep descent, for about three miles."
Whitehouse ⇨
September 19, 1805
"... continued our rout about the same course of yesterday or S. 20. W. for 6 miles when the ridge terminated and we to our inexpressable joy discovered a large tract of Prairie country lying to the S.W. and widening as it appeared to extend to the W. through that plain the Indian informed us that the Columbia river, (in which we were in surch) run. this plain appeared to be about 60 Miles distant, ..."
Lewis ⇨
September 18, 1805
"...from the top of a high part of the mountain at 20 miles I had a view of an emence Plain and leavel countrey to the S W. & West. at a great distance a high mountain in advance beyond the Plain, ..."
Clark ⇨
Cartographer's Note:
The reader is reminded that Clark has taken several of the hunters and moved out ahead to quickly reach the distant plains. His purpose is to make some game kills and send meat back to the main party.
September 19, 1805
"... proceeded on to the top of Sd mountain and as we were descending the Same we discovered a very large plain a long distance a head, which we expect is on the Columbia River, which puts us in good Spirits again."
Ordway ⇨
June 26, 1806
"late in the evening much to the satisfaction of ourselves and the comfort of our horses we arrived at the desired spot and encamped on the steep side of a mountain convenient to a good spring (having passed a few miles our camp of 18 Sepr 1805). there we found an abundance of fine grass for our horses. this situation was the side of an untimbered mountain with a fair southern aspect where the snow from appearance had been desolved about 10 days."
Lewis ⇦
September 18, 1805
"we dined & suped on a skant proportion of portable soupe, a few canesters of which a little bears oil and about 20 lbs. of candles form our stock of provision, ..."
Lewis ⇨
Camp
(Main Group)
Sept. 18, 1805
September 18, 1805
"... we marched 18 miles this day and encamped on the side of a steep mountain; we suffered for water this day passing one rivulet only; ..."
Lewis ⇨
Cartographer's Note:
This cartographer has understood from Lewis' writings that "Portable Soup" was a dried soup base requiring only water. Lewis said that it was in canisters. The cartographer has never found anything to indicate what the canisters were made of, but it does not appear that they were the same as the lead ones Lewis had made for the black powder. Some scholars believe that the soup was a wet concentrate stored in a lead, or a metal lead combination, container. Some have suggested that the lead accounts for the illness of the men in the mountains.
Cartographer's Note:
The journal writers often noted the lack of water at camp sites and the need to melt snow which they found in hollows on the north slopes. The reader must keep in mind that the expedition was traveling along a high ridge trail. The Pacific Northwest summer begins about July 5, and usually runs into October. Summers are warm, often hot, and very dry, even during the unusually wet years of 1805/06. Without a permanent spring to feed them, the stream sources on the ridge were surely dry in September.
Return Camp
June 26, 1806
Sherman Saddle
Chimney Butte
Pagoda Creek
Horn Creek
Sherman Creek
Sherman Peak
Lolo Trail
BITTERROOT
RANGE
NATIONAL
FOREST
CLEARWATER
No-See-Um Creek
No-See-Um Meadow
No-See-Um Butte
Bald Mountain
Bald Mountain Creek
Liz Butte
Liz Creek
Salia Creek
Castle Butte
Castle Creek
Holy Creek
Fro Creek
Bald Mountain Lake
MOUNTAINS
KOOSKOOSKEE
"KOOSKOOSKEE"
Lochsa River
S 85 W 32 MILES
N
ONE STATUTE MILE
Modern Data: 1966
Outbound: Clark-September 18, 1805
Lewis-September 18, 19, 1805
Return: June 26, 27, 1806
EXPLORATIONS OF LEWIS AND CLARK 1804 - 1806
CARTOGRAPHIC RECONSTRUCTION
VIEW OF PRAIRIE
UTM ZONE 11
MAP NUMBER 304
Idaho
CONTOUR INTERVAL 200 FEET

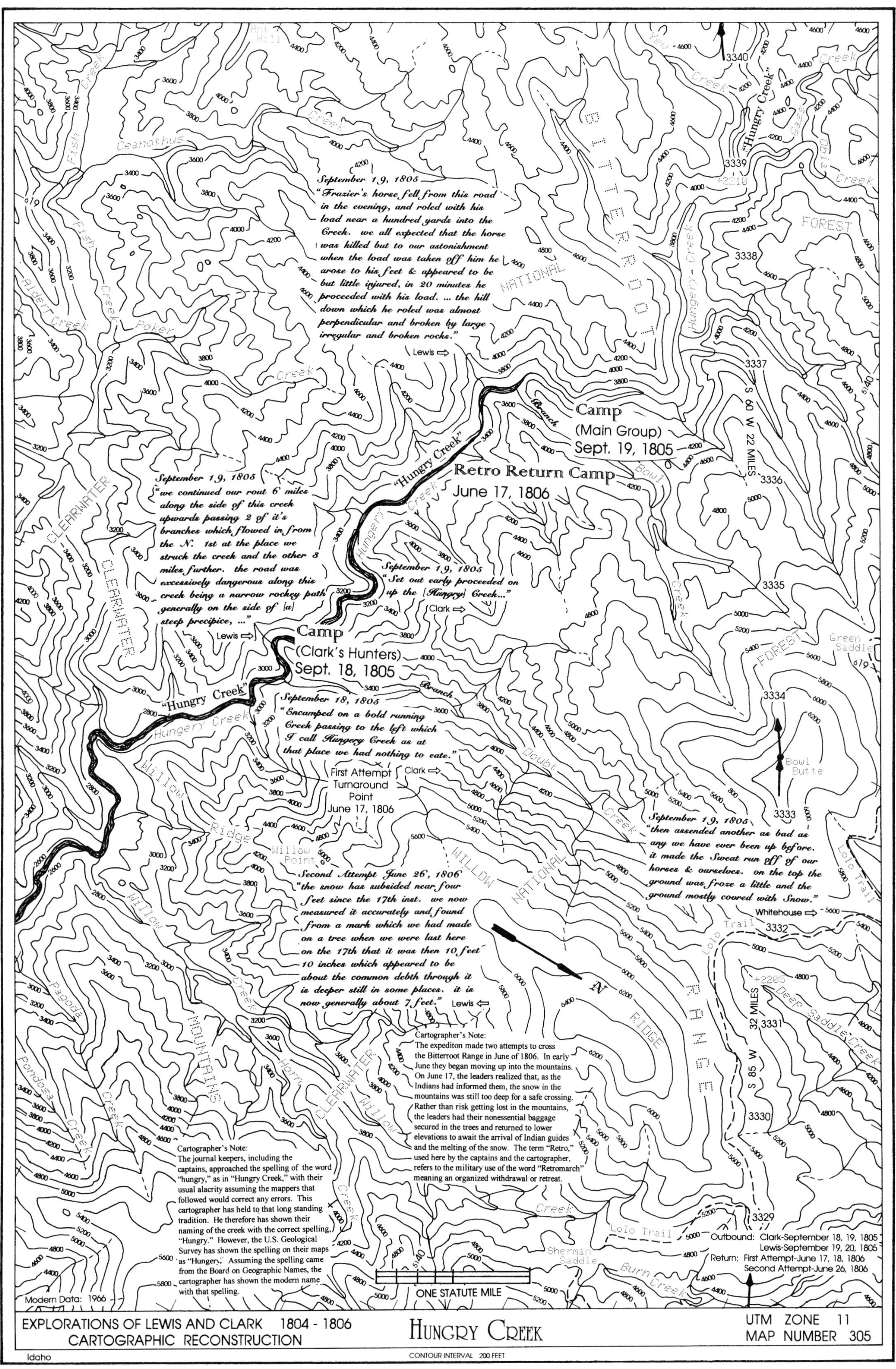

September 19, 1805
"Frazier's horse fell from this road in the evening, and roled with his load near a hundred yards into the Creek. we all expected that the horse was killed but to our astonishment when the load was taken off him he arose to his feet & appeared to be but little injured, in 20 minutes he proceeded with his load. ... the hill down which he roled was almost perpendicular and broken by large irregular and broken rocks."
Lewis ⇨
Camp
(Main Group)
Sept. 19, 1805
Retro Return Camp
June 17, 1806
"Hungry Creek"
September 19, 1805
"we continued our rout 6 miles along the side of this creek upwards passing 2 of it's branches which flowed in from the N. 1st at the place we struck the creek and the other 3 miles further. the road was excessively dangerous along this creek being a narrow rockey path generally on the side of [a] steep precipice, ..."
Lewis ⇨
September 19, 1805
"Set out early proceeded on up the [Hungry] Creek..."
Clark ⇨
Camp
(Clark's Hunters)
Sept. 18, 1805
"Hungry Creek"
September 18, 1805
"Encamped on a bold running Creek passing to the left which I call Hungery Creek as at that place we had nothing to eate."
First Attempt
Turnaround
Point
June 17, 1806
Clark ⇨
September 19, 1805
"then assended another as bad as any we have ever been up before. it made the Sweat run off of our horses & ourselves. on the top the ground was froze a little and the ground mostly coured with Snow."
Whitehouse ⇨
Second Attempt June 26, 1806
"the snow has subsided near four feet since the 17th inst. we now measured it accurately and found from a mark which we had made on a tree when we were last here on the 17th that it was then 10 feet 10 inches which appeared to be about the common debth through it is deeper still in some places. it is now generally about 7 feet."
Lewis ⇦
Cartographer's Note:
The expediton made two attempts to cross the Bitterroot Range in June of 1806. In early June they began moving up into the mountains. On June 17, the leaders realized that, as the Indians had informed them, the snow in the mountains was still too deep for a safe crossing. Rather than risk getting lost in the mountains, the leaders had their nonessential baggage secured in the trees and returned to lower elevations to await the arrival of Indian guides and the melting of the snow. The term "Retro," used here by the captains and the cartographer, refers to the military use of the word "Retromarch" meaning an organized withdrawal or retreat.
Cartographer's Note:
The journal keepers, including the captains, approached the spelling of the word "hungry," as in "Hungry Creek," with their usual alacrity assuming the mappers that followed would correct any errors. This cartographer has held to that long standing tradition. He therefore has shown their naming of the creek with the correct spelling, "Hungry." However, the U.S. Geological Survey has shown the spelling on their maps as "Hungery." Assuming the spelling came from the Board on Geographic Names, the cartographer has shown the modern name with that spelling.
BITTERROOT NATIONAL FOREST
CLEARWATER NATIONAL FOREST
WILLOW RIDGE
RANGE
S 60 W 22 MILES
S 85 W 32 MILES
Outbound: Clark-September 18, 19, 1805
Lewis-September 19, 20, 1805
Return: First Attempt-June 17, 18, 1806
Second Attempt-June 26, 1806
ONE STATUTE MILE
Modern Data: 1966
EXPLORATIONS OF LEWIS AND CLARK 1804 - 1806
CARTOGRAPHIC RECONSTRUCTION
HUNGRY CREEK
UTM ZONE 11
MAP NUMBER 305
Idaho
CONTOUR INTERVAL 200 FEET

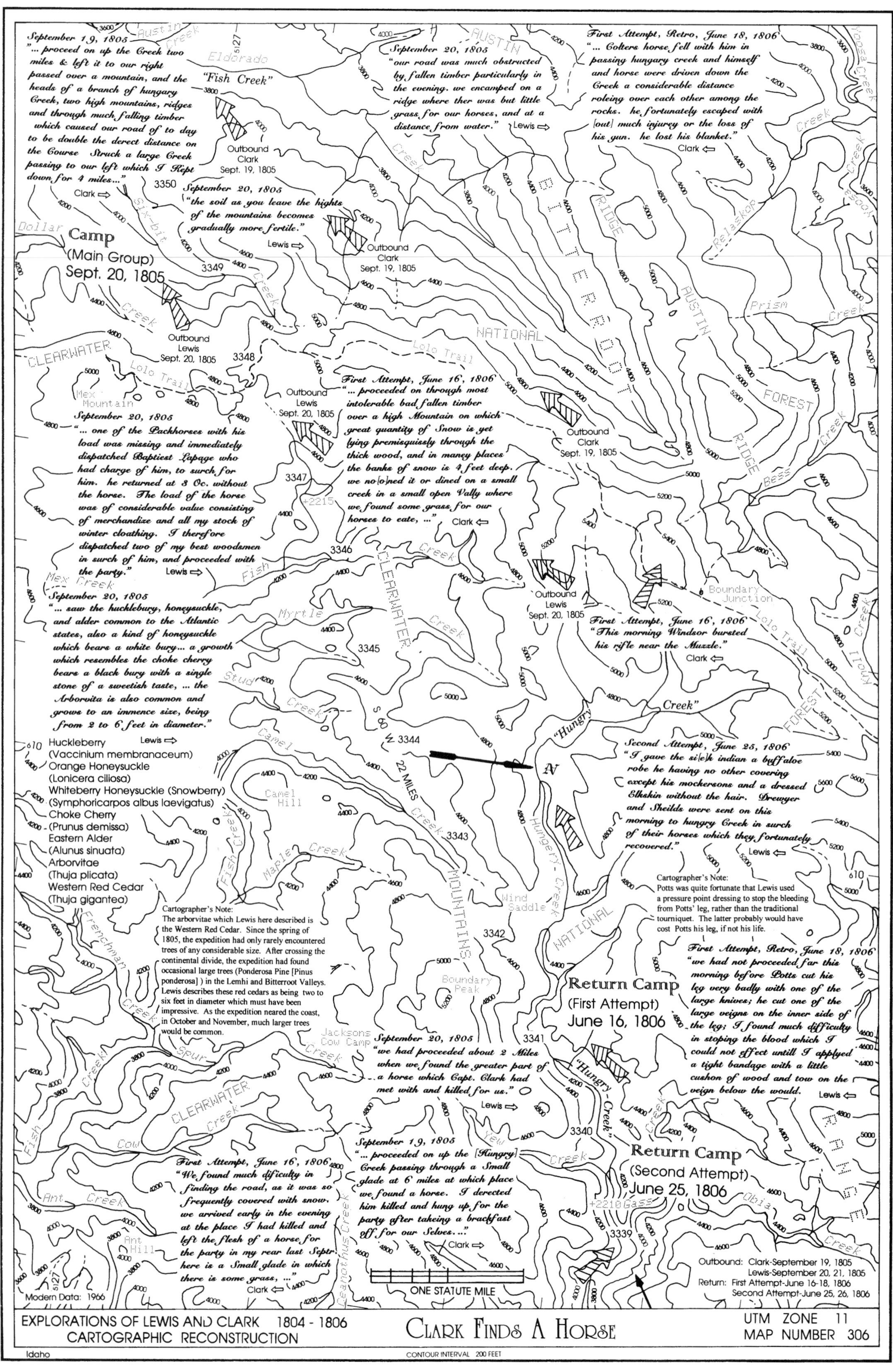
September 19, 1805
"... proceed on up the Creek two miles & left it to our right passed over a mountain, and the heads of a branch of hungary Creek, two high mountains, ridges and through much falling timber which caused our road of to day to be double the derect distance on the Course Struck a large Creek passing to our left which I Kept down for 4 miles..."
Clark ⇨
"Fish Creek"
Outbound Clark Sept. 19, 1805
September 20, 1805
"our road was much obstructed by fallen timber particularly in the evening. we encamped on a ridge where ther was but little grass for our horses, and at a distance from water."
Lewis ⇨
First Attempt, Retro, June 18, 1806
"... Colters horse fell with him in passing hungary creek and himself and horse were driven down the Creek a considerable distance roleing over each other among the rocks. he fortunately escaped with [out] much injurey or the loss of his gun. he lost his blanket."
Clark ⇦
September 20, 1805
"the soil as you leave the hights of the mountains becomes gradually more fertile."
Lewis ⇨
Outbound Clark Sept. 19, 1805
Camp
(Main Group)
Sept. 20, 1805
Outbound Lewis Sept. 20, 1805
Outbound Lewis Sept. 20, 1805
Outbound Clark Sept. 19, 1805
First Attempt, June 16, 1806
"... proceeded on through most intolerable bad fallen timber over a high Mountain on which great quantity of Snow is yet lying premisquissly through the thick wood, and in maney places the banks of snow is 4 feet deep. we no[o]ned it or dined on a small creek in a small open Vally where we found some grass for our horses to eate, ..."
Clark ⇦
September 20, 1805
"... one of the Packhorses with his load was missing and immediately dispatched Baptiest Lapage who had charge of him, to surch for him. he returned at 3 Oc. without the horse. The load of the horse was of considerable value consisting of merchandize and all my stock of winter cloathing. I therefore dispatched two of my best woodsmen in surch of him, and proceeded with the party."
Lewis ⇨
September 20, 1805
"... saw the huckleburry, honeysuckle, and alder common to the Atlantic states, also a kind of honeysuckle which bears a white bury... a growth which resembles the choke cherry bears a black bury with a single stone of a sweetish taste, ... the Arborvita is also common and grows to an immence size, being from 2 to 6 feet in diameter."
Lewis ⇨
Huckleberry
(Vaccinium membranaceum)
Orange Honeysuckle
(Lonicera ciliosa)
Whiteberry Honeysuckle (Snowberry)
(Symphoricarpos albus laevigatus)
Choke Cherry
(Prunus demissa)
Eastern Alder
(Alunus sinuata)
Arborvitae
(Thuja plicata)
Western Red Cedar
(Thuja gigantea)
Outbound Lewis Sept. 20, 1805
First Attempt, June 16, 1806
"This morning Windsor bursted his rifle near the Muzzle."
Clark ⇦
Second Attempt, June 25, 1806
"I gave the si[c]k indian a buffaloe robe he having no other covering except his mockersons and a dressed Elkskin without the hair. Drewyer and Sheilds were sent on this morning to hungry Creek in surch of their horses which they fortunately recovered."
Lewis ⇦
Cartographer's Note:
Potts was quite fortunate that Lewis used a pressure point dressing to stop the bleeding from Potts' leg, rather than the traditional tourniquet. The latter probably would have cost Potts his leg, if not his life.
Cartographer's Note:
The arborvitae which Lewis here described is the Western Red Cedar. Since the spring of 1805, the expedition had only rarely encountered trees of any considerable size. After crossing the continental divide, the expedition had found occasional large trees (Ponderosa Pine [Pinus ponderosa]) in the Lemhi and Bitterroot Valleys. Lewis describes these red cedars as being two to six feet in diameter which must have been impressive. As the expedition neared the coast, in October and November, much larger trees would be common.
First Attempt, Retro, June 18, 1806
"we had not proceeded far this morning before Potts cut his leg very badly with one of the large knives; he cut one of the large veigns on the inner side of the leg; I found much difficulty in stoping the blood which I could not effect untill I applyed a tight bandage with a little cushon of wood and tow on the veign below the would."
Lewis ⇦
Return Camp
(First Attempt)
June 16, 1806
September 20, 1805
"we had proceeded about 2 Miles when we found the greater part of a horse which Capt. Clark had met with and killed for us."
Lewis ⇨
Return Camp
(Second Attempt)
June 25, 1806
September 19, 1805
"... proceed on up the [Hungry] Creek passing through a Small glade at 6 miles at which place we found a horse. I derected him killed and hung up for the party after takeing a brackfast off for our Selves..."
Clark ⇨
First Attempt, June 16, 1806
"We found much dificulty in finding the road, as it was so frequently covered with snow. we arrived early in the evening at the place I had killed and left the flesh of a horse for the party in my rear last Septr. here is a Small glade in which there is some grass, ..."
Clark ⇦
Outbound: Clark-September 19, 1805
Lewis-September 20, 21, 1805
Return: First Attempt-June 16-18, 1806
Second Attempt-June 25, 26, 1806
ONE STATUTE MILE
Modern Data: 1966
S 60 W 22 MILES
N
Eldorado
Austin Creek
AUSTIN
BITTERROOT
RIDGE
AUSTIN
RIDGE
NATIONAL
FOREST
Lolo Trail
Lolo Trail
Lolo Trail
CLEARWATER
Mex Mountain
Mex Creek
Dollar
Six-bit Creek
Creek
Fish Creek
Myrtle
Creek
Stud Creek
Camel
Camel Hill
CLEARWATER
MOUNTAINS
Maple Creek
Fish Creek
Frenchman Creek
Wind Saddle
Hungry Creek
"Hungry Creek"
"Hungry-Creek"
Boundary Peak
Boundary Junction
Jacksons Cow Camp
Spur Creek
Fish Creek
CLEARWATER
Creek
Cow
Ant Creek
Ant Hill
Ceanothus Creek
Yew Creek
Gass
Obia Creek
Relaskop
Prism Creek
Bess
Creek
Yoosa Creek
Esock
IDAHO
NATIONAL
RANGE
3350
3349
3348
3347
3346
3345
3344
3343
3342
3341
3340
3339
+2215
+2210
EXPLORATIONS OF LEWIS AND CLARK 1804 - 1806
CARTOGRAPHIC RECONSTRUCTION
CLARK FINDS A HORSE
UTM ZONE 11
MAP NUMBER 306
Idaho
CONTOUR INTERVAL 200 FEET

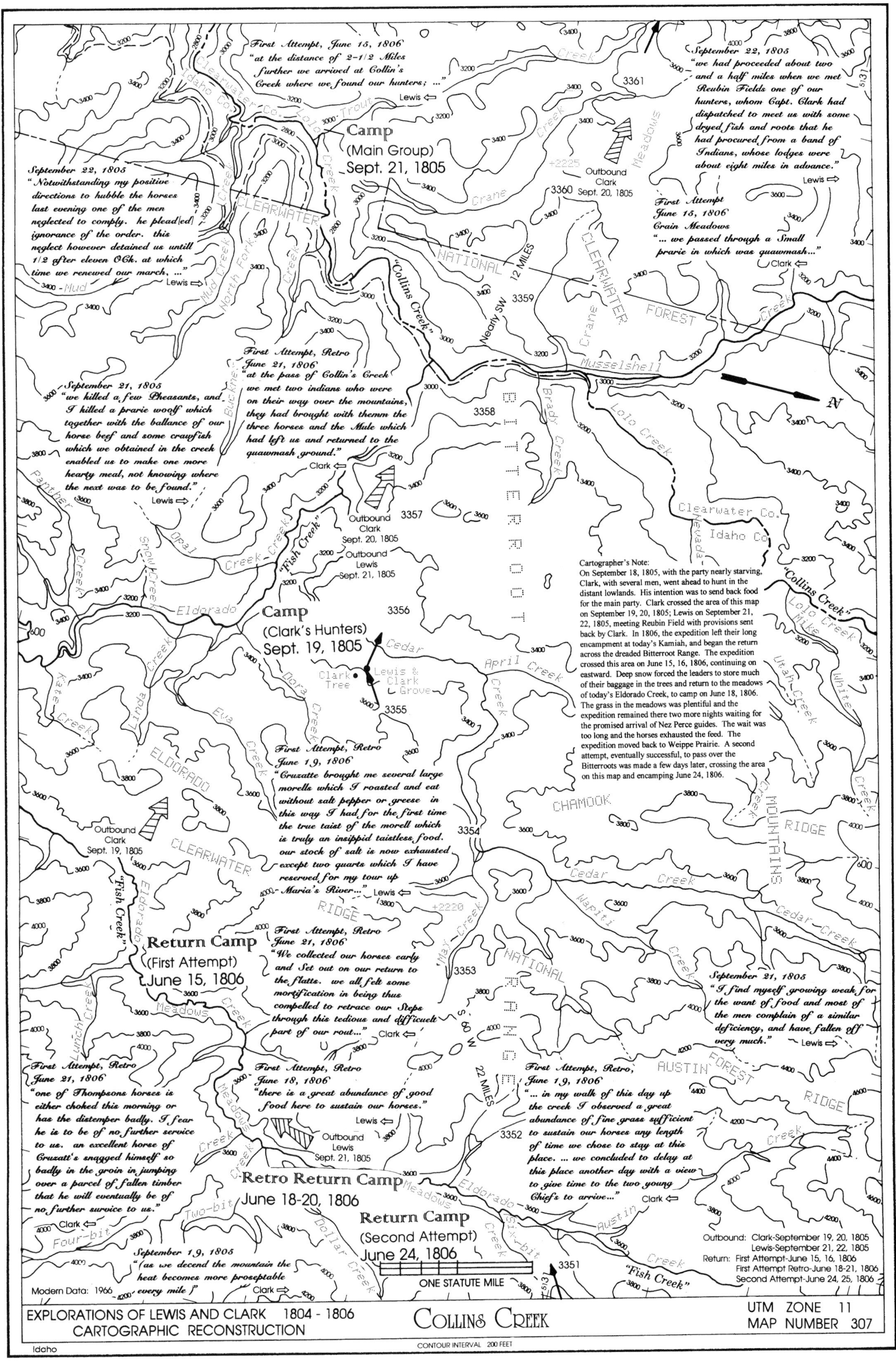
First Attempt, June 15, 1806
"at the distance of 2-1/2 Miles further we arrived at Collin's Creek where we found our hunters; ..."
Lewis ⇦
September 22, 1805
"we had proceeded about two and a half miles when we met Reubin Fields one of our hunters, whom Capt. Clark had dispatched to meet us with some dryed fish and roots that he had procured from a band of Indians, whose lodges were about eight miles in advance."
Lewis ⇨
Camp
(Main Group)
Sept. 21, 1805
September 22, 1805
"Notwithstanding my positive directions to hubble the horses last evening one of the men neglected to comply. he plead[ed] ignorance of the order. this neglect however detained us untill 1/2 after eleven OCk. at which time we renewed our march, ..."
Lewis ⇨
Outbound
Clark
Sept. 20, 1805
First Attempt
June 15, 1806
Crain Meadows
"... we passed through a Small prarie in which was quawmash..."
Clark ⇦
"Collins Creek"
12 MILES
Nearly SW
First Attempt, Retro
June 21, 1806
"at the pass of Collin's Creek we met two indians who were on their way over the mountains, they had brought with themm the three horses and the Mule which had left us and returned to the quawmash ground."
Clark ⇦
September 21, 1805
"we killed a few Pheasants, and I killed a prarie woolf which together with the ballance of our horse beef and some crawfish which we obtained in the creek enabled us to make one more hearty meal, not knowing where the next was to be found."
Lewis ⇨
Outbound
Clark
Sept. 20, 1805
Outbound
Lewis
Sept. 21, 1805
"Fish Creek"
Camp
(Clark's Hunters)
Sept. 19, 1805
Clark Tree
Lewis & Clark Grove
BITTERROOT
CLEARWATER
NATIONAL
FOREST
Cartographer's Note:
On September 18, 1805, with the party nearly starving, Clark, with several men, went ahead to hunt in the distant lowlands. His intention was to send back food for the main party. Clark crossed the area of this map on September 19, 20, 1805; Lewis on September 21, 22, 1805, meeting Reubin Field with provisions sent back by Clark. In 1806, the expedition left their long encampment at today's Kamiah, and began the return across the dreaded Bitterroot Range. The expedition crossed this area on June 15, 16, 1806, continuing on eastward. Deep snow forced the leaders to store much of their baggage in the trees and return to the meadows of today's Eldorado Creek, to camp on June 18, 1806. The grass in the meadows was plentiful and the expedition remained there two more nights waiting for the promised arrival of Nez Perce guides. The wait was too long and the horses exhausted the feed. The expedition moved back to Weippe Prairie. A second attempt, eventually successful, to pass over the Bitterroots was made a few days later, crossing the area on this map and encamping June 24, 1806.
"Collins Creek"
First Attempt, Retro
June 19, 1806
"Cruzatte brought me several large morells which I roasted and eat without salt pepper or greese in this way I had for the first time the true taist of the morell which is truly an insippid taistless food. our stock of salt is now exhausted except two quarts which I have reserved for my tour up Maria's River..."
Lewis ⇦
Outbound
Clark
Sept. 19, 1805
CHAMOOK
MOUNTAINS
RIDGE
ELDORADO
CLEARWATER
RIDGE
"Fish Creek"
Return Camp
(First Attempt)
June 15, 1806
First Attempt, Retro
June 21, 1806
"We collected our horses early and Set out on our return to the flatts. we all felt some mortification in being thus compelled to retrace our Steps through this tedious and difficult part of our rout..."
Clark ⇦
NATIONAL
RANGE
S 60 W
22 MILES
September 21, 1805
"I find myself growing weak for the want of food and most of the men complain of a similar deficiency, and have fallen off very much."
Lewis ⇨
AUSTIN
FOREST
RIDGE
First Attempt, Retro
June 21, 1806
"one of Thompsons horses is either choked this morning or has the distemper badly. I fear he is to be of no further service to us. an excellent horse of Cruzatt's snagged himself so badly in the groin in jumping over a parcel of fallen timber that he will eventually be of no further survice to us."
Clark ⇦
First Attempt, Retro
June 18, 1806
"there is a great abundance of good food here to sustain our horses."
Lewis ⇨
Outbound
Lewis
Sept. 21, 1805
First Attempt, Retro,
June 19, 1806
"... in my walk of this day up the creek I observed a great abundance of fine grass sufficient to sustain our horses any length of time we chose to stay at this place. ... we concluded to delay at this place another day with a view to give time to the two young Chiefs to arrive..."
Clark ⇦
Retro Return Camp
June 18-20, 1806
Return Camp
(Second Attempt)
June 24, 1806
September 19, 1805
"(as we decend the mountain the heat becomes more proseptable every mile)"
Clark ⇨
ONE STATUTE MILE
Outbound: Clark-September 19, 20, 1805
Lewis-September 21, 22, 1805
Return: First Attempt-June 15, 16, 1806
First Attempt Retro-June 18-21, 1806
Second Attempt-June 24, 25, 1806
"Fish Creek"
N
Modern Data: 1966
EXPLORATIONS OF LEWIS AND CLARK 1804 - 1806
CARTOGRAPHIC RECONSTRUCTION
COLLINS CREEK
UTM ZONE 11
MAP NUMBER 307
Idaho
CONTOUR INTERVAL 200 FEET

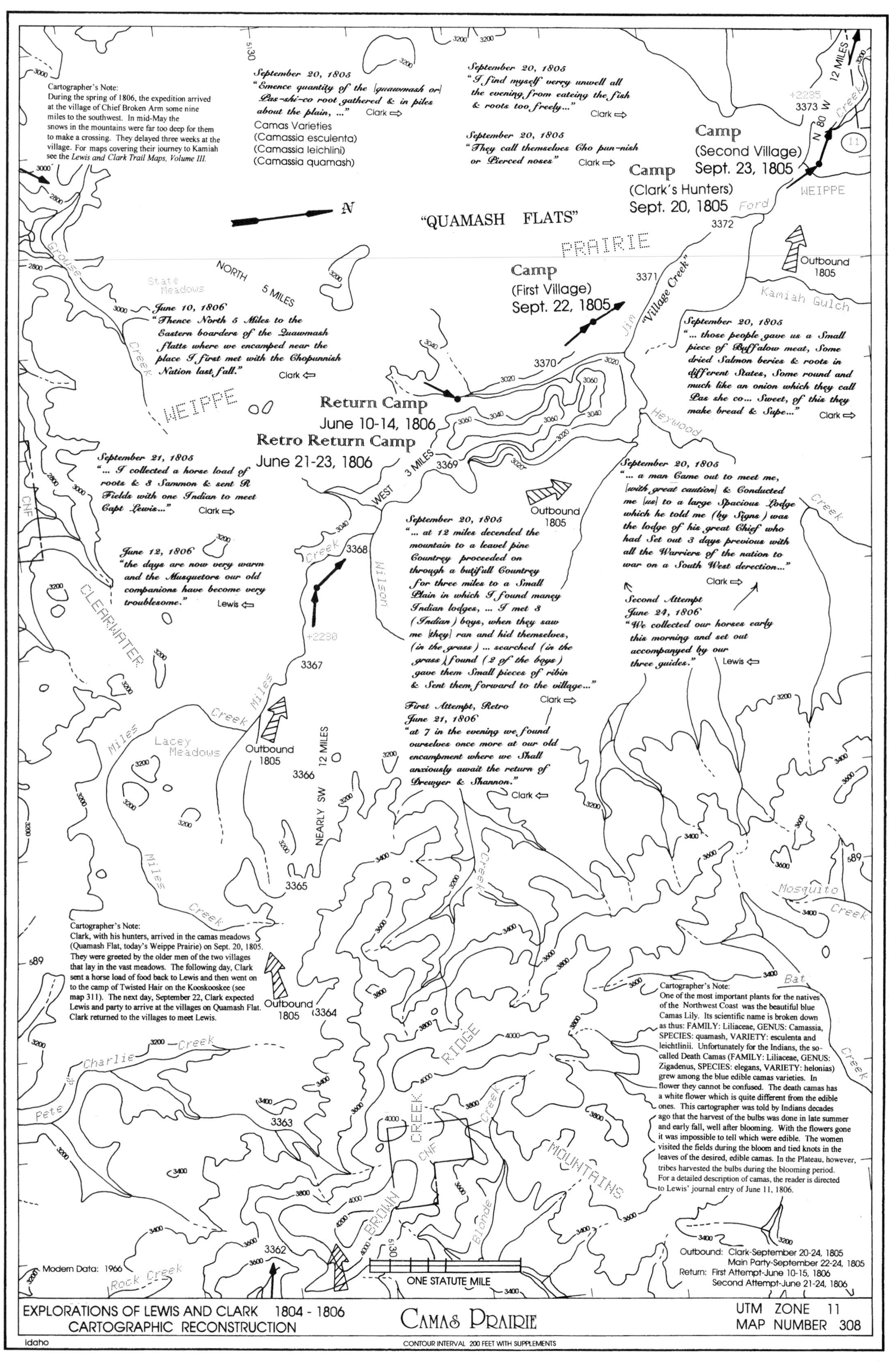

Cartographer's Note:
During the spring of 1806, the expedition arrived at the village of Chief Broken Arm some nine miles to the southwest. In mid-May the snows in the mountains were far too deep for them to make a crossing. They delayed three weeks at the village. For maps covering their journey to Kamiah see the Lewis and Clark Trail Maps, Volume III.
September 20, 1805
"Emence quantity of the [quawmash or] Pas-shi-co root gathered & in piles about the plain, ..." Clark ⇨
Camas Varieties
(Camassia esculenta)
(Camassia leichlini)
(Camassia quamash)
September 20, 1805
"I find myself verry unwell all the evening from eateing the fish & roots too freely..." Clark ⇨
September 20, 1805
"They call themselves Cho pun-nish or Pierced noses" Clark ⇨
12 MILES
N 80 W
3373 W
+2235
Creek
11
Camp
(Second Village)
Sept. 23, 1805
WEIPPE
Camp
(Clark's Hunters)
Sept. 20, 1805
Ford
3372
N
"QUAMASH FLATS"
PRAIRIE
Outbound
1805
Kamiah Gulch
Grouse
State
Meadows
NORTH
5 MILES
Camp
(First Village)
Sept. 22, 1805
3371
Jim
"Village Creek"
June 10, 1806
"Thence North 5 Miles to the Eastern boarders of the Quawmash flatts where we encamped near the place I first met with the Chopunnish Nation last fall." Clark ⇦
Creek
3370
September 20, 1805
"... those people gave us a Small piece of Buffalow meat, Some dried Salmon beries & roots in different States, Some round and much like an onion which they call Pas she co... Sweet, of this they make bread & Supe..." Clark ⇨
WEIPPE
Return Camp
June 10-14, 1806
Retro Return Camp
June 21-23, 1806
Heywood
3 MILES
WEST
3369
September 21, 1805
"... I collected a horse load of roots & 3 Sammon & sent R Fields with one Indian to meet Capt Lewis..." Clark ⇨
CNF
Outbound
1805
September 20, 1805
"... a man Came out to meet me, [with great caution] & Conducted me [us] to a large Spacious Lodge which he told me (by Signs) was the lodge of his great Chief who had Set out 3 days previous with all the Warriers of the nation to war on a South West derection..." Clark ⇨
Creek
September 20, 1805
"... at 12 miles decended the mountain to a leavel pine Countrey proceeded on through a butifull Countrey for three miles to a Small Plain in which I found maney Indian lodges, ... I met 3 (Indian) boys, when they saw me [they] ran and hid themselves, (in the grass) ... searched (in the grass) found (2 of the boys) gave them Small pieces of ribin & Sent them forward to the village..." Clark ⇨
June 12, 1806
"the days are now very warm and the Musquetors our old companions have become very troublesome." Lewis ⇦
Creek
3368
Wilson
CLEARWATER
+2230
Second Attempt
June 24, 1806
"We collected our horses early this morning and set out accompanyed by our three guides." Lewis ⇦
3367
Miles
Creek
First Attempt, Retro
June 21, 1806
"at 7 in the evening we found ourselves once more at our old encampment where we Shall anxiously await the return of Drewyer & Shannon." Clark ⇦
Miles
Lacey
Meadows
Outbound
1805
12 MILES
3366
NEARLY SW
589
Miles
Mosquito
Creek
3365
Creek
Creek
Cartographer's Note:
Clark, with his hunters, arrived in the camas meadows (Quamash Flat, today's Weippe Prairie) on Sept. 20, 1805. They were greeted by the older men of the two villages that lay in the vast meadows. The following day, Clark sent a horse load of food back to Lewis and then went on to the camp of Twisted Hair on the Kooskooskee (see map 311). The next day, September 22, Clark expected Lewis and party to arrive at the villages on Quamash Flat. Clark returned to the villages to meet Lewis.
589
Outbound
1805
3364
Bat
Cartographer's Note:
One of the most important plants for the natives of the Northwest Coast was the beautiful blue Camas Lily. Its scientific name is broken down as thus: FAMILY: Liliaceae, GENUS: Camassia, SPECIES: quamash, VARIETY: esculenta and leichtlinii. Unfortunately for the Indians, the so-called Death Camas (FAMILY: Liliaceae, GENUS: Zigadenus, SPECIES: elegans, VARIETY: helonias) grew among the blue edible camas varieties. In flower they cannot be confused. The death camas has a white flower which is quite different from the edible ones. This cartographer was told by Indians decades ago that the harvest of the bulbs was done in late summer and early fall, well after blooming. With the flowers gone it was impossible to tell which were edible. The women visited the fields during the bloom and tied knots in the leaves of the desired, edible camas. In the Plateau, however, tribes harvested the bulbs during the blooming period. For a detailed description of camas, the reader is directed to Lewis' journal entry of June 11, 1806.
Charlie
Creek
RIDGE
Creek
Pete
3363
CREEK
CNF
Creek
MOUNTAINS
BROWN
Blonde
3362
Modern Data: 1966
Rock Creek
ONE STATUTE MILE
Outbound: Clark-September 20-24, 1805
Main Party-September 22-24, 1805
Return: First Attempt-June 10-15, 1806
Second Attempt-June 21-24, 1806
EXPLORATIONS OF LEWIS AND CLARK 1804 - 1806
CARTOGRAPHIC RECONSTRUCTION
CAMAS PRAIRIE
UTM ZONE 11
MAP NUMBER 308
Idaho
CONTOUR INTERVAL 200 FEET WITH SUPPLEMENTS

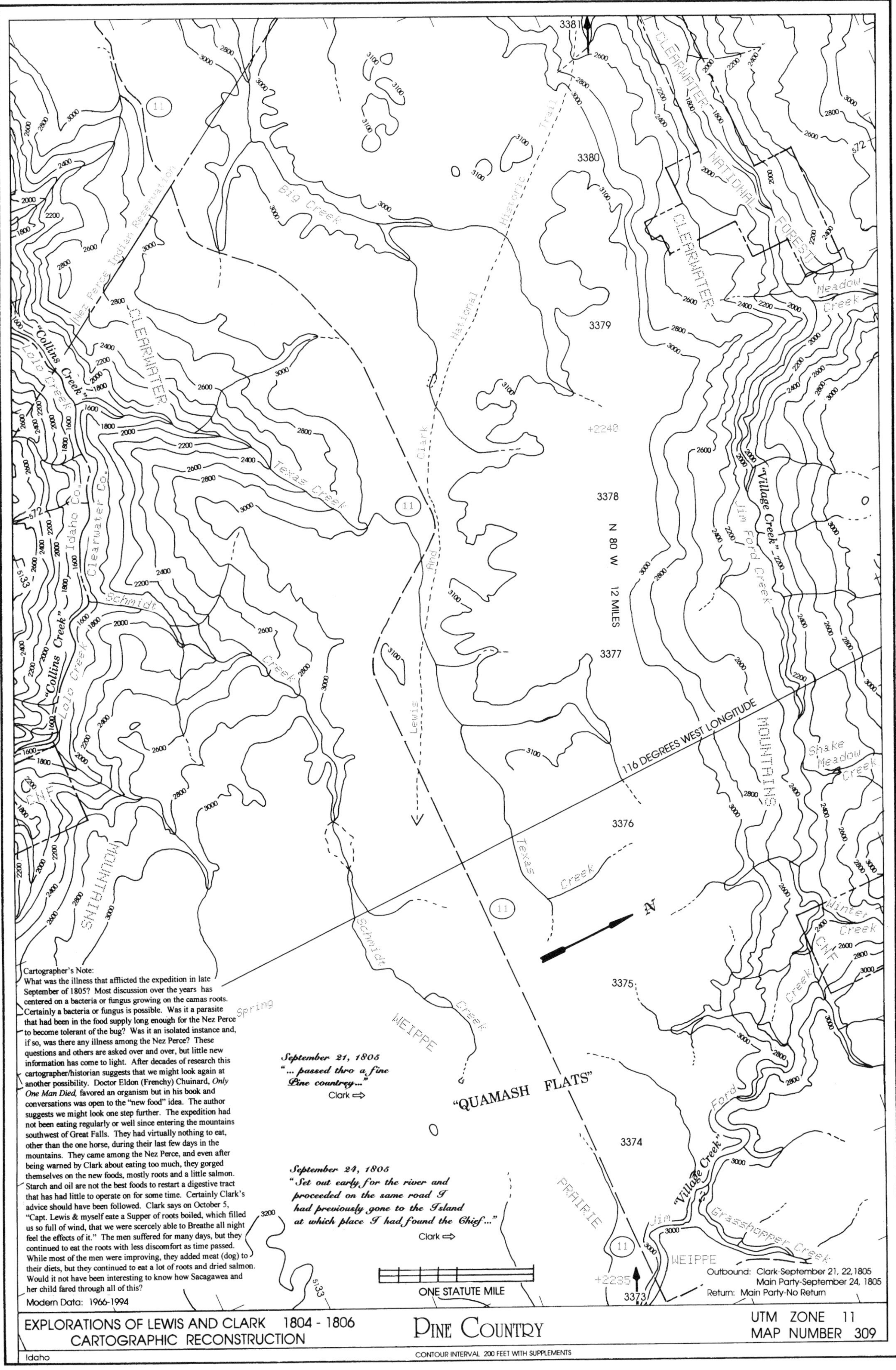

Cartographer's Note:
What was the illness that afflicted the expedition in late September of 1805? Most discussion over the years has centered on a bacteria or fungus growing on the camas roots. Certainly a bacteria or fungus is possible. Was it a parasite that had been in the food supply long enough for the Nez Perce to become tolerant of the bug? Was it an isolated instance and, if so, was there any illness among the Nez Perce? These questions and others are asked over and over, but little new information has come to light. After decades of research this cartographer/historian suggests that we might look again at another possibility. Doctor Eldon (Frenchy) Chuinard, *Only One Man Died,* favored an organism but in his book and conversations was open to the "new food" idea. The author suggests we might look one step further. The expedition had not been eating regularly or well since entering the mountains southwest of Great Falls. They had virtually nothing to eat, other than the one horse, during their last few days in the mountains. They came among the Nez Perce, and even after being warned by Clark about eating too much, they gorged themselves on the new foods, mostly roots and a little salmon. Starch and oil are not the best foods to restart a digestive tract that has had little to operate on for some time. Certainly Clark's advice should have been followed. Clark says on October 5, "Capt. Lewis & myself eate a Supper of roots boiled, which filled us so full of wind, that we were scercely able to Breathe all night feel the effects of it." The men suffered for many days, but they continued to eat the roots with less discomfort as time passed. While most of the men were improving, they added meat (dog) to their diets, but they continued to eat a lot of roots and dried salmon. Would it not have been interesting to know how Sacagawea and her child fared through all of this?
Modern Data: 1966-1994
September 21, 1805
"... passed thro a fine Pine countrey..."
Clark ⇨
September 24, 1805
"Set out early for the river and proceeded on the same road I had previously gone to the Island at which place I had found the Chief..."
Clark ⇨
"QUAMASH FLATS"
WEIPPE
PRAIRIE
ONE STATUTE MILE
Outbound: Clark-September 21, 22, 1805
Main Party-September 24, 1805
Return: Main Party-No Return
116 DEGREES WEST LONGITUDE
N 80 W 12 MILES
N
Lewis And Clark National Historic Trail
Nez Perce Indian Reservation
CLEARWATER NATIONAL FOREST
CLEARWATER MOUNTAINS
"Collins Creek"
Lolo Creek
"Village Creek"
Jim Ford Creek
Big Creek
Texas Creek
Schmidt Creek
Spring Creek
Meadow Creek
Shake Meadow Creek
Winter Creek
Grasshopper Creek
Idaho Co.
Clearwater Co.
CNF
WEIPPE
+2240
+2235
3381
3380
3379
3378
3377
3376
3375
3374
3373
572
533
11
EXPLORATIONS OF LEWIS AND CLARK 1804 - 1806
CARTOGRAPHIC RECONSTRUCTION
PINE COUNTRY
UTM ZONE 11
MAP NUMBER 309
Idaho
CONTOUR INTERVAL 200 FEET WITH SUPPLEMENTS

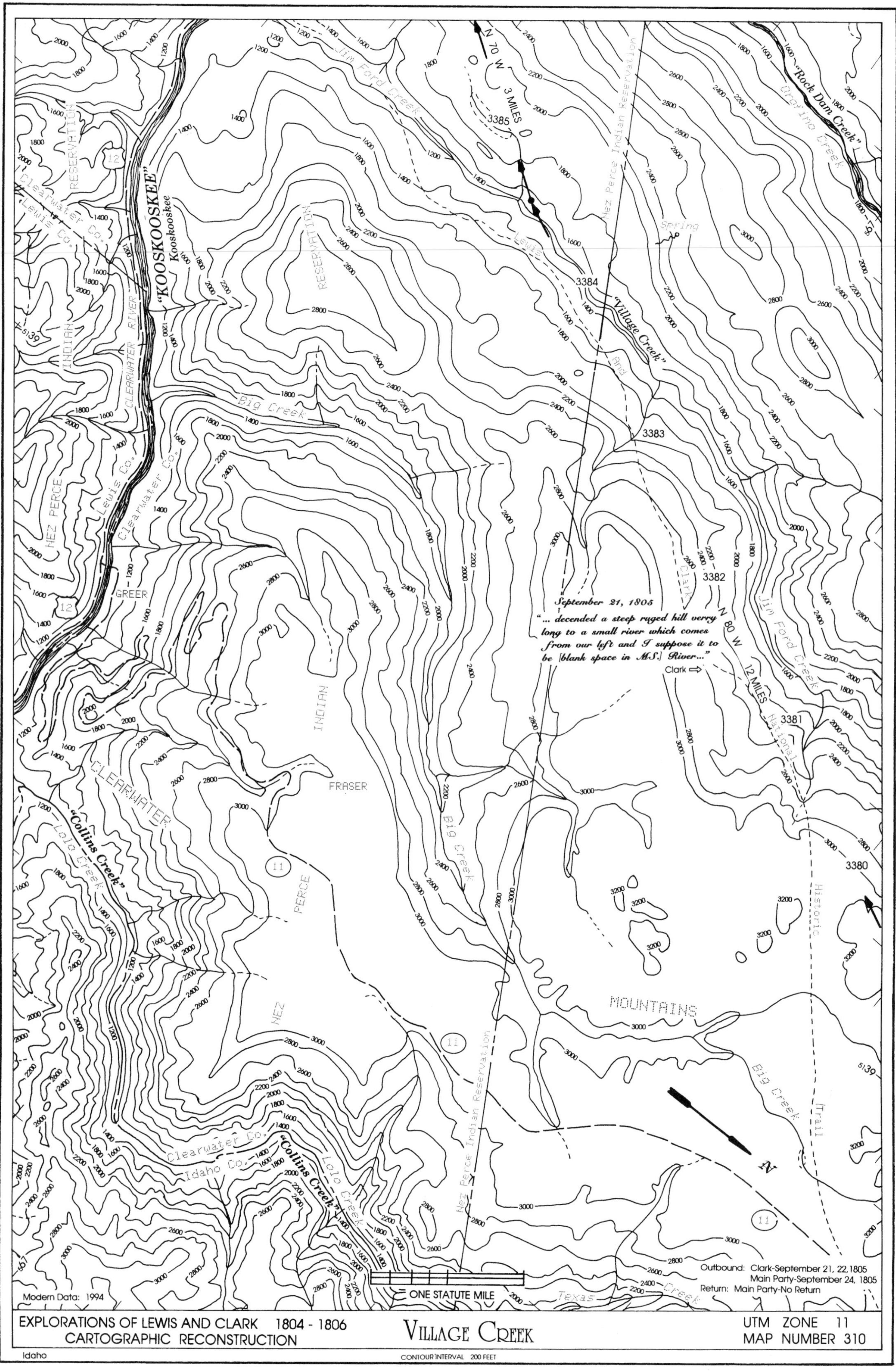

EXPLORATIONS OF LEWIS AND CLARK 1804 - 1806
CARTOGRAPHIC RECONSTRUCTION
VILLAGE CREEK
UTM ZONE 11
MAP NUMBER 310
Idaho
CONTOUR INTERVAL 200 FEET
Modern Data: 1994
ONE STATUTE MILE
Outbound: Clark-September 21, 22, 1805
Main Party-September 24, 1805
Return: Main Party-No Return
September 21, 1805
"... decended a steep ruged hill verry long to a small river which comes from our left and I suppose it to be [blank space in MS.] River..."
Clark
"KOOSKOOSKEE"
Kooskooskee
"Village Creek"
"Rock Dam Creek"
"Collins Creek"
Lolo Creek
Jim Ford Creek
Orofino Creek
Big Creek
Nez Perce Indian Reservation
NEZ PERCE INDIAN RESERVATION
CLEARWATER RIVER
CLEARWATER MOUNTAINS
Clearwater Co.
Lewis Co.
Idaho Co.
Lewis and Clark
Historic National Trail
GREER
FRASER
Spring
Texas Creek
N 70 W 3 MILES
N 80 W 12 MILES
3385
3384
3383
3382
3381
3380

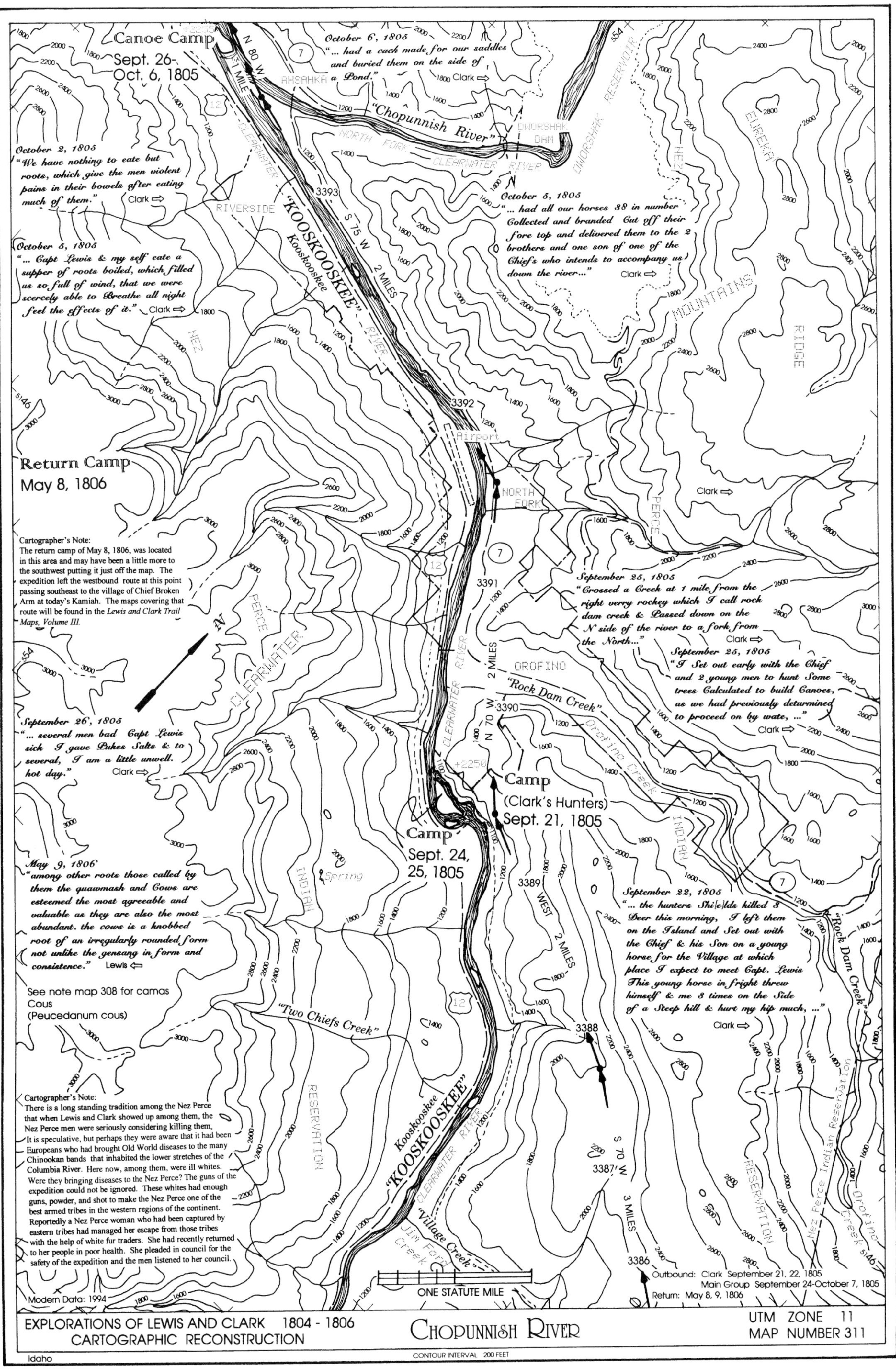

Canoe Camp
Sept. 26-Oct. 6, 1805
October 6, 1805
"... had a cach made for our saddles and buried them on the side of a Pond."
Clark ⇨
AHSAHKA
"Chopunnish River"
NORTH FORK
CLEARWATER RIVER
DWORSHAK DAM
DWORSHAK RESERVOIR
October 2, 1805
"We have nothing to eate but roots, which give the men violent pains in their bowels after eating much of them."
Clark ⇨
RIVERSIDE
October 5, 1805
"... had all our horses 38 in number Collected and branded Cut off their fore top and delivered them to the 2 brothers and one son of one of the Chiefs who intends to accompany us down the river..."
Clark ⇨
October 5, 1805
"... Capt Lewis & my self eate a supper of roots boiled, which filled us so full of wind, that we were scercely able to Breathe all night feel the effects of it."
Clark ⇨
"KOOSKOOSKEE"
Kooskooskee
RIVER
S 75 W
2 MILES
N 80 W
MOUNTAINS
RIDGE
EUREKA
NEZ
PERCE
Airport
NORTH FORK
Return Camp
May 8, 1806
Cartographer's Note:
The return camp of May 8, 1806, was located in this area and may have been a little more to the southwest putting it just off the map. The expedition left the westbound route at this point passing southeast to the village of Chief Broken Arm at today's Kamiah. The maps covering that route will be found in the Lewis and Clark Trail Maps, Volume III.
Clark ⇨
September 25, 1805
"Crossed a Creek at 1 mile from the right verry rockey which I call rock dam creek & Passed down on the N side of the river to a fork from the North..."
Clark ⇨
September 25, 1805
"I Set out early with the Chief and 2 young men to hunt Some trees Calculated to build Canoes, as we had previously deturmined to proceed on by wate, ..."
Clark ⇨
OROFINO
"Rock Dam Creek"
Orofino Creek
CLEARWATER
CLEARWATER RIVER
N 70 W
2 MILES
September 26, 1805
"... several men bad Capt Lewis sick I gave Pukes Salts & to several, I am a little unwell. hot day."
Clark ⇨
Camp
(Clark's Hunters)
Sept. 21, 1805
Camp
Sept. 24, 25, 1805
INDIAN
Spring
May 9, 1806
"among other roots those called by them the quawmash and Cows are esteemed the most agreeable and valuable as they are also the most abundant. the cows is a knobbed root of an irregularly rounded form not unlike the gensang in form and consistence."
Lewis ⇦
See note map 308 for camas
Cous
(Peucedanum cous)
September 22, 1805
"... the hunters Shi[e]lds killed 3 Deer this morning, I left them on the Island and Set out with the Chief & his Son on a young horse for the Village at which place I expect to meet Capt. Lewis This young horse in fright threw himself & me 3 times on the Side of a Steep hill & hurt my hip much, ..."
Clark ⇨
WEST
2 MILES
"Rock Dam Creek"
"Two Chiefs Creek"
RESERVATION
Nez Perce Indian Reservation
Orofino Creek
Cartographer's Note:
There is a long standing tradition among the Nez Perce that when Lewis and Clark showed up among them, the Nez Perce men were seriously considering killing them. It is speculative, but perhaps they were aware that it had been Europeans who had brought Old World diseases to the many Chinookan bands that inhabited the lower stretches of the Columbia River. Here now, among them, were ill whites. Were they bringing diseases to the Nez Perce? The guns of the expedition could not be ignored. These whites had enough guns, powder, and shot to make the Nez Perce one of the best armed tribes in the western regions of the continent. Reportedly a Nez Perce woman who had been captured by eastern tribes had managed her escape from those tribes with the help of white fur traders. She had recently returned to her people in poor health. She pleaded in council for the safety of the expedition and the men listened to her council.
Kooskooskee
"KOOSKOOSKEE"
CLEARWATER RIVER
"Village Creek"
Jim Ford Creek
S 70 W
3 MILES
3393
3392
3391
3390
3389
3388
3387
3386
Outbound: Clark September 21, 22, 1805
Main Group September 24-October 7, 1805
Return: May 8, 9, 1806
ONE STATUTE MILE
Modern Data: 1994
EXPLORATIONS OF LEWIS AND CLARK 1804 - 1806
CARTOGRAPHIC RECONSTRUCTION
CHOPUNNISH RIVER
UTM ZONE 11
MAP NUMBER 311
Idaho
CONTOUR INTERVAL 200 FEET

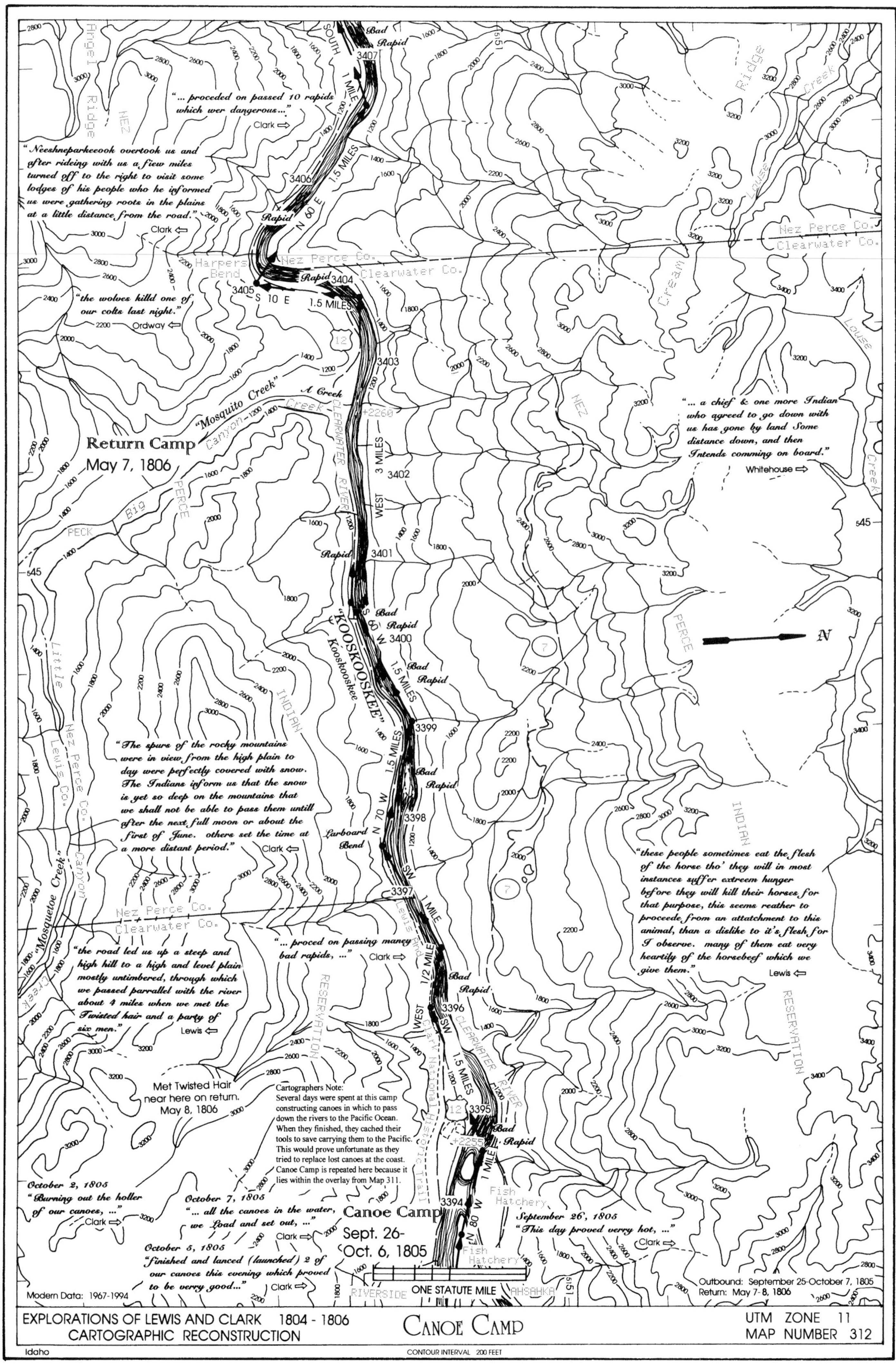

Bad Rapid
"... proceded on passed 10 rapids which wer dangerous..."
Clark ⇨
"Neeshneparkeeook overtook us and after rideing with us a fiew miles turned off to the right to visit some lodges of his people who he informed us were gathering roots in the plains at a little distance from the road."
Clark ⇦
Angel Ridge
Harpers Bend
Nez Perce Co.
Clearwater Co.
"the wolves killd one of our colts last night."
Ordway ⇦
S 10 E 1.5 MILES
N 60 E 1.5 MILES
"Mosquito Creek"
Canyon Creek
A Creek
Return Camp
May 7, 1806
CLEARWATER RIVER
WEST 3 MILES
"... a chief & one more Indian who agreed to go down with us has gone by land Some distance down, and then Intends comming on board."
Whitehouse ⇨
Big
PECK
Rapid
Bad Rapid
"KOOSKOOSKEE"
Kooskooskee
S 80 W 1.5 MILES
N
Little
"The spurs of the rocky mountains were in view from the high plain to day were perfectly covered with snow. The Indians inform us that the snow is yet so deep on the mountains that we shall not be able to pass them untill after the next full moon or about the first of June. others set the time at a more distant period."
Clark ⇦
Larboard Bend
N 70 W 1.5 MILES
"these people sometimes eat the flesh of the horse tho' they will in most instances suffer extreem hunger before they will kill their horses for that purpose, this seems reather to proceede from an attatchment to this animal, than a dislike to it's flesh for I observe. many of them eat very heartily of the horsebeef which we give them."
Lewis ⇦
"Mosquetoe Creek"
Canyon
"the road led us up a steep and high hill to a high and level plain mostly untimbered, through which we passed parrallel with the river about 4 miles when we met the Twisted hair and a party of six men."
Lewis ⇦
"... proced on passing maney bad rapids, ..."
Clark ⇨
INDIAN RESERVATION
Met Twisted Hair near here on return. May 8, 1806
Cartographers Note: Several days were spent at this camp constructing canoes in which to pass down the rivers to the Pacific Ocean. When they finished, they cached their tools to save carrying them to the Pacific. This would prove unfortunate as they tried to replace lost canoes at the coast. Canoe Camp is repeated here because it lies within the overlay from Map 311.
Lewis and Clark National Historic Trail
October 2, 1805 "Burning out the holler of our canoes, ..."
Clark ⇨
October 7, 1805 "... all the canoes in the water, we Load and set out, ..."
Clark ⇨
Canoe Camp
Sept. 26- Oct. 6, 1805
Fish Hatchery
September 26, 1805 "This day proved verry hot, ..."
Clark ⇨
October 5, 1805 "finished and lanced (launched) 2 of our canoes this evening which proved to be verry good..."
Clark ⇨
Modern Data: 1967-1994
ONE STATUTE MILE
RIVERSIDE
AHSAHKA
Outbound: September 25-October 7, 1805
Return: May 7-8, 1806
EXPLORATIONS OF LEWIS AND CLARK 1804 - 1806
CARTOGRAPHIC RECONSTRUCTION
CANOE CAMP
UTM ZONE 11
MAP NUMBER 312
Idaho
CONTOUR INTERVAL 200 FEET

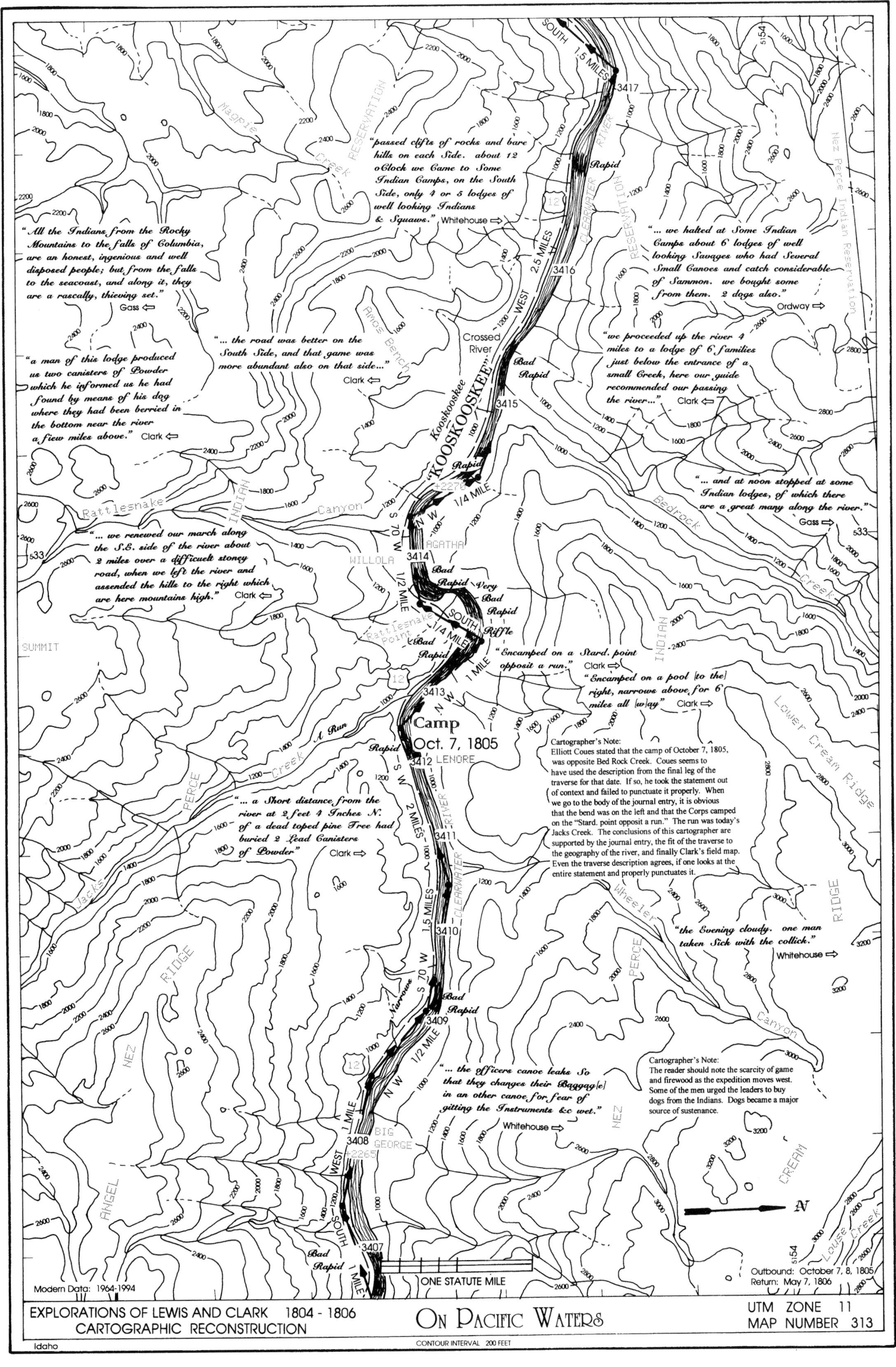

"passed clifts of rocks and bare hills on each Side. about 12 oClock we Came to Some Indian Camps, on the South Side, only 4 or 5 lodges of well looking Indians & Squaws." Whitehouse ⇨
"All the Indians from the Rocky Mountains to the falls of Columbia, are an honest, ingenious and well disposed people; but from the falls to the seacoast, and along it, they are a rascally, thieving set." Gass ⇦
"... we halted at Some Indian Camps about 6 lodges of well looking Savages who had Several Small Canoes and catch considerable of Sammon. we bought some from them. 2 dogs also." Ordway ⇨
"... the road was better on the South Side, and that game was more abundant also on that side..." Clark ⇦
"a man of this lodge produced us two canisters of Powder which he informed us he had found by means of his dog where they had been berried in the bottom near the river a fiew miles above." Clark ⇦
"we proceeded up the river 4 miles to a lodge of 6 families just below the entrance of a small Creek, here our guide recommended our passing the river..." Clark ⇦
"... and at noon stopped at some Indian lodges, of which there are a great many along the river." Gass ⇨
"... we renewed our march along the S.E. side of the river about 2 miles over a difficult stoney road, when we left the river and assended the hills to the right which are here mountains high." Clark ⇨
"Encamped on a Stard. point opposit a run." Clark ⇨
"Encamped on a pool [to the] right, narrows above for 6 miles all [w]ay" Clark ⇨
Camp
Oct. 7, 1805
Cartographer's Note:
Elliott Coues stated that the camp of October 7, 1805, was opposite Bed Rock Creek. Coues seems to have used the description from the final leg of the traverse for that date. If so, he took the statement out of context and failed to punctuate it properly. When we go to the body of the journal entry, it is obvious that the bend was on the left and that the Corps camped on the "Stard. point opposit a run." The run was today's Jacks Creek. The conclusions of this cartographer are supported by the journal entry, the fit of the traverse to the geography of the river, and finally Clark's field map. Even the traverse description agrees, if one looks at the entire statement and properly punctuates it.
"... a Short distance from the river at 2 feet 4 Inches N. of a dead toped pine Tree had buried 2 Lead Canisters of Powder" Clark ⇨
"the Evening cloudy. one man taken Sick with the collick." Whitehouse ⇨
"... the officers canoe leaks So that they changes their Baggag[e] in an other canoe for fear of gitting the Instruments &c wet." Whitehouse ⇨
Cartographer's Note:
The reader should note the scarcity of game and firewood as the expedition moves west. Some of the men urged the leaders to buy dogs from the Indians. Dogs became a major source of sustenance.
"KOOSKOOSKEE"
Kooskooskee
CLEARWATER RIVER
Crossed River
Rattlesnake Canyon
Bedrock Creek
Lower Cream Ridge
Jacks Creek
Wheeler Canyon
Louse Creek
Magpie Creek
Amos Bench
Rattlesnake Point
A Run
WILLOLA
AGATHA
LENORE
BIG GEORGE
SUMMIT
NEZ PERCE RESERVATION
Nez Perce Indian Reservation
SOUTH 1.5 MILES
WEST 2.5 MILES
S 70 W
N W 1/4 MILE
1/2 MILE
SOUTH 1/4 MILE
N W 1 MILE
S W 2 MILES
1.5 MILES
S 70 W
N W 1/2 MILE
WEST 1 MILE
SOUTH 1 MILE
Rapid
Bad Rapid
Very Bad Rapid
Riffle
Narrows
ONE STATUTE MILE
N
Modern Data: 1964-1994
Outbound: October 7, 8, 1805
Return: May 7, 1806
EXPLORATIONS OF LEWIS AND CLARK 1804 - 1806
CARTOGRAPHIC RECONSTRUCTION
ON PACIFIC WATERS
UTM ZONE 11
MAP NUMBER 313
Idaho
CONTOUR INTERVAL 200 FEET

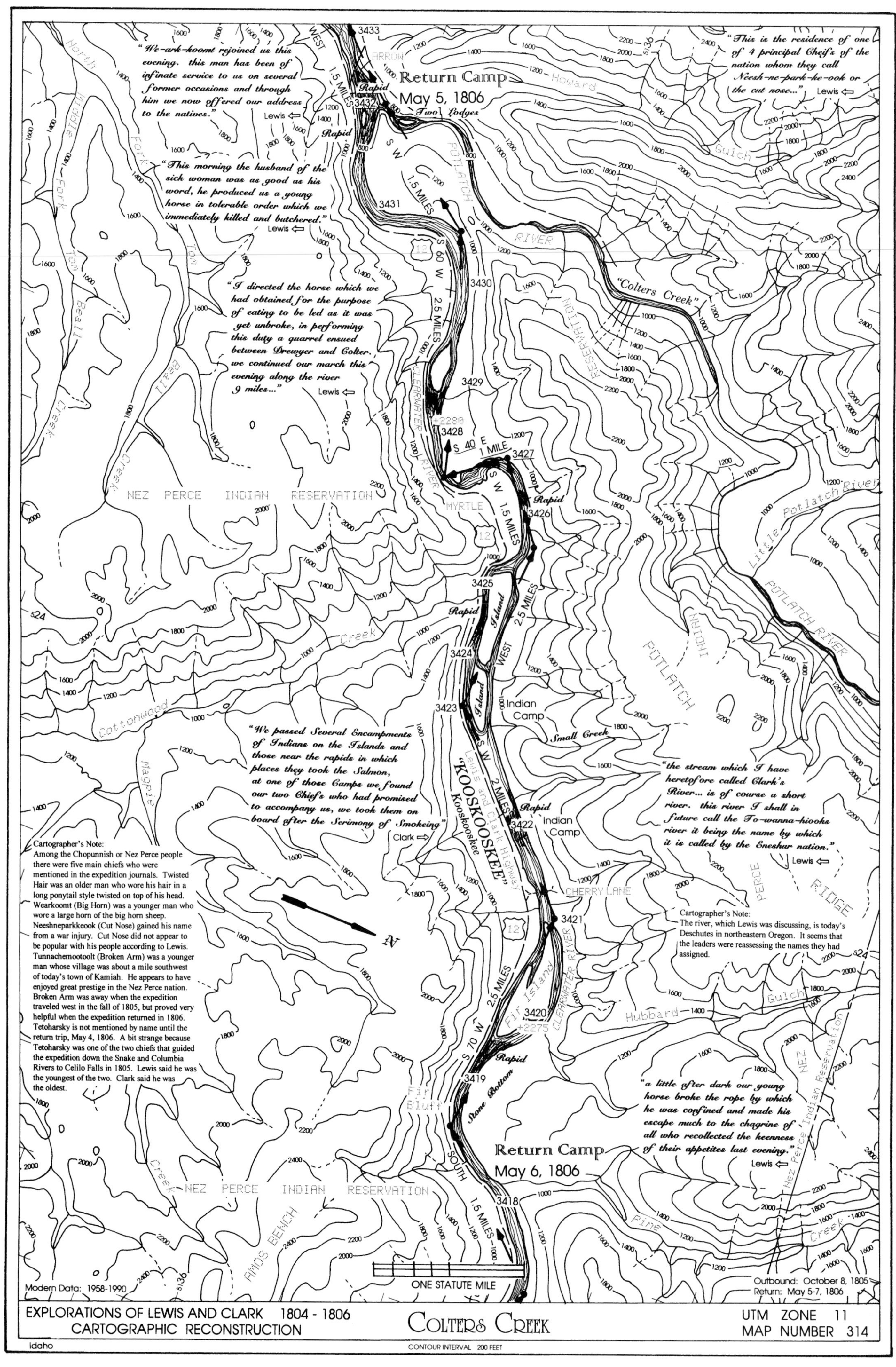

"We-ark-koomt rejoined us this evening. this man has been of infinate service to us on several former occasions and through him we now offered our address to the natives." Lewis
Return Camp
May 5, 1806
Two Lodges
Rapid
"This is the residence of one of 4 principal Cheifs of the nation whom they call Neesh-ne-park-ke-ook or the cut nose..." Lewis
"This morning the husband of the sick woman was as good as his word, he produced us a young horse in tolerable order which we immediately killed and butchered." Lewis
POTLATCH RIVER
"Colters Creek"
"I directed the horse which we had obtained for the purpose of eating to be led as it was yet unbroke, in performing this duty a quarrel ensued between Drewyer and Colter. we continued our march this evening along the river 9 miles..." Lewis
CLEARWATER RIVER
NEZ PERCE INDIAN RESERVATION
MYRTLE
Little Potlatch River
POTLATCH RIVER
POTLATCH INDIAN RESERVATION
Island
Indian Camp
Small Creek
Cottonwood Creek
"We passed Several Encampments of Indians on the Islands and those near the rapids in which places they took the Salmon, at one of those Camps we found our two Chiefs who had promised to accompany us, we took them on board after the Serimony of Smokeing" Clark
"KOOSKOOSKEE"
Kooskooskee
Lewis and Clark Highway
"the stream which I have heretofore called Clark's River... is of course a short river. this river I shall in future call the To-wanna-hiooks river it being the name by which it is called by the Eneshur nation." Lewis
CHERRY LANE
PERCE RIDGE
Cartographer's Note:
Among the Chopunnish or Nez Perce people there were five main chiefs who were mentioned in the expedition journals. Twisted Hair was an older man who wore his hair in a long ponytail style twisted on top of his head. Wearkoomt (Big Horn) was a younger man who wore a large horn of the big horn sheep. Neeshneparkkeook (Cut Nose) gained his name from a war injury. Cut Nose did not appear to be popular with his people according to Lewis. Tunnachemootoolt (Broken Arm) was a younger man whose village was about a mile southwest of today's town of Kamiah. He appears to have enjoyed great prestige in the Nez Perce nation. Broken Arm was away when the expedition traveled west in the fall of 1805, but proved very helpful when the expedition returned in 1806. Tetoharsky is not mentioned by name until the return trip, May 4, 1806. A bit strange because Tetoharsky was one of the two chiefs that guided the expedition down the Snake and Columbia Rivers to Celilo Falls in 1805. Lewis said he was the youngest of the two. Clark said he was the oldest.
Cartographer's Note:
The river, which Lewis was discussing, is today's Deschutes in northeastern Oregon. It seems that the leaders were reassessing the names they had assigned.
Fir Island
Hubbard Gulch
Nez Perce Indian Reservation
Fir Bluff
Stone Bottom
"a little after dark our young horse broke the rope by which he was confined and made his escape much to the chagrine of all who recollected the keenness of their appetites last evening." Lewis
Return Camp
May 6, 1806
NEZ PERCE INDIAN RESERVATION
AMOS BENCH
Pine Creek
ONE STATUTE MILE
Modern Data: 1958-1990
Outbound: October 8, 1805
Return: May 5-7, 1806
EXPLORATIONS OF LEWIS AND CLARK 1804 - 1806
CARTOGRAPHIC RECONSTRUCTION
COLTERS CREEK
UTM ZONE 11
MAP NUMBER 314
Idaho
CONTOUR INTERVAL 200 FEET

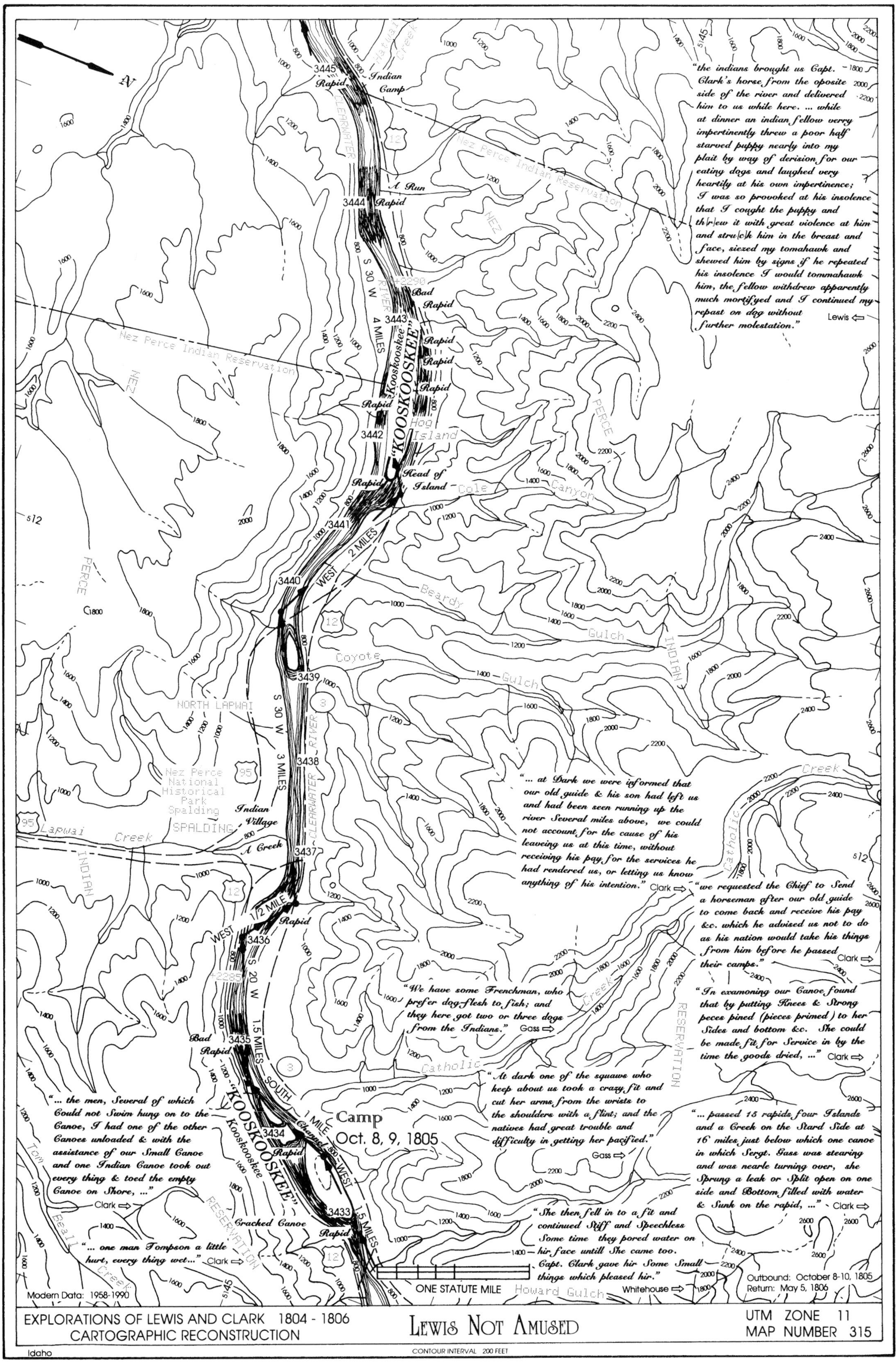

"the indians brought us Capt. Clark's horse from the oposite side of the river and delivered him to us while here. ... while at dinner an indian fellow verry impertinently threw a poor half starved puppy nearly into my plait by way of derision for our eating dogs and laughed very heartily at his own impertinence; I was so provoked at his insolence that I cought the puppy and th[r]ew it with great violence at him and stru[c]k him in the breast and face, siezed my tomahawk and shewed him by signs if he repeated his insolence I would tommahawk him, the fellow withdrew apparently much mortifyed and I continued my repast on dog without further molestation." Lewis ⇦
"... at Dark we were informed that our old guide & his son had left us and had been seen running up the river Several miles above, we could not account for the cause of his leaveing us at this time, without receiving his pay for the services he had rendered us, or letting us know anything of his intention." Clark ⇨
"we requested the Chief to Send a horseman after our old guide to come back and receive his pay &c. which he advised us not to do as his nation would take his things from him before he passed their camps." Clark ⇨
"We have some Frenchman, who prefer dog-flesh to fish; and they here got two or three dogs from the Indians." Gass ⇨
"In examoning our Canoe found that by putting Knees & Strong peces pined (pieces primed) to her Sides and bottom &c. She could be made fit for Service in by the time the goods dried, ..." Clark ⇨
"At dark one of the squaws who keep about us took a crazy fit and cut her arms from the wrists to the shoulders with a flint; and the natives had great trouble and difficulty in getting her pacified." Gass ⇨
"... the men, Several of which Could not Swim hung on to the Canoe, I had one of the other Canoes unloaded & with the assistance of our Small Canoe and one Indian Canoe took out every thing & toed the empty Canoe on Shore, ..." Clark ⇨
"... passed 15 rapids four Islands and a Creek on the Stard Side at 16 miles just below which one canoe in which Sergt. Gass was stearing and was nearle turning over, she Sprung a leak or Split open on one side and Bottom filled with water & Sunk on the rapid, ..." Clark ⇨
"... one man Tompson a little hurt, every thing wet..." Clark ⇨
"She then fell in to a fit and continued Stiff and Speechless Some time they pored water on hir face untill She came too. Capt. Clark gave hir Some Small things which pleased hir." Whitehouse ⇨
N
Indian Camp
3445 Rapid
A Run
3444 Rapid
Bad Rapid
3443
Rapid
Rapid
Rapid
Rapid
3442
Head of Island
Rapid
3441
3440
3439
3438
Indian Village
A Creek
3437
Rapid
3436
Bad Rapid
3435 Rapid
3434
Rapid
Camp
Oct. 8, 9, 1805
Channel
Cracked Canoe
3433 Rapid
"KOOSKOOSKEE"
Kooskooskee
CLEARWATER RIVER
S 30 W 4 MILES
WEST 2 MILES
S 30 W 3 MILES
WEST 1/2 MILE
S 20 W 1.5 MILES
SOUTH 1 MILE
WEST 1.5 MILES
Hog Island
Cole Canyon
Beardy Gulch
Coyote Gulch
Catholic Creek
Nez Perce Indian Reservation
NORTH LAPWAI
Nez Perce National Historical Park Spalding
SPALDING
Lapwai Creek
Tom Beall Creek
Howard Gulch
ONE STATUTE MILE
Modern Data: 1958-1990
Outbound: October 8-10, 1805
Return: May 5, 1806
EXPLORATIONS OF LEWIS AND CLARK 1804 - 1806
CARTOGRAPHIC RECONSTRUCTION
LEWIS NOT AMUSED
UTM ZONE 11
MAP NUMBER 315
Idaho
CONTOUR INTERVAL 200 FEET

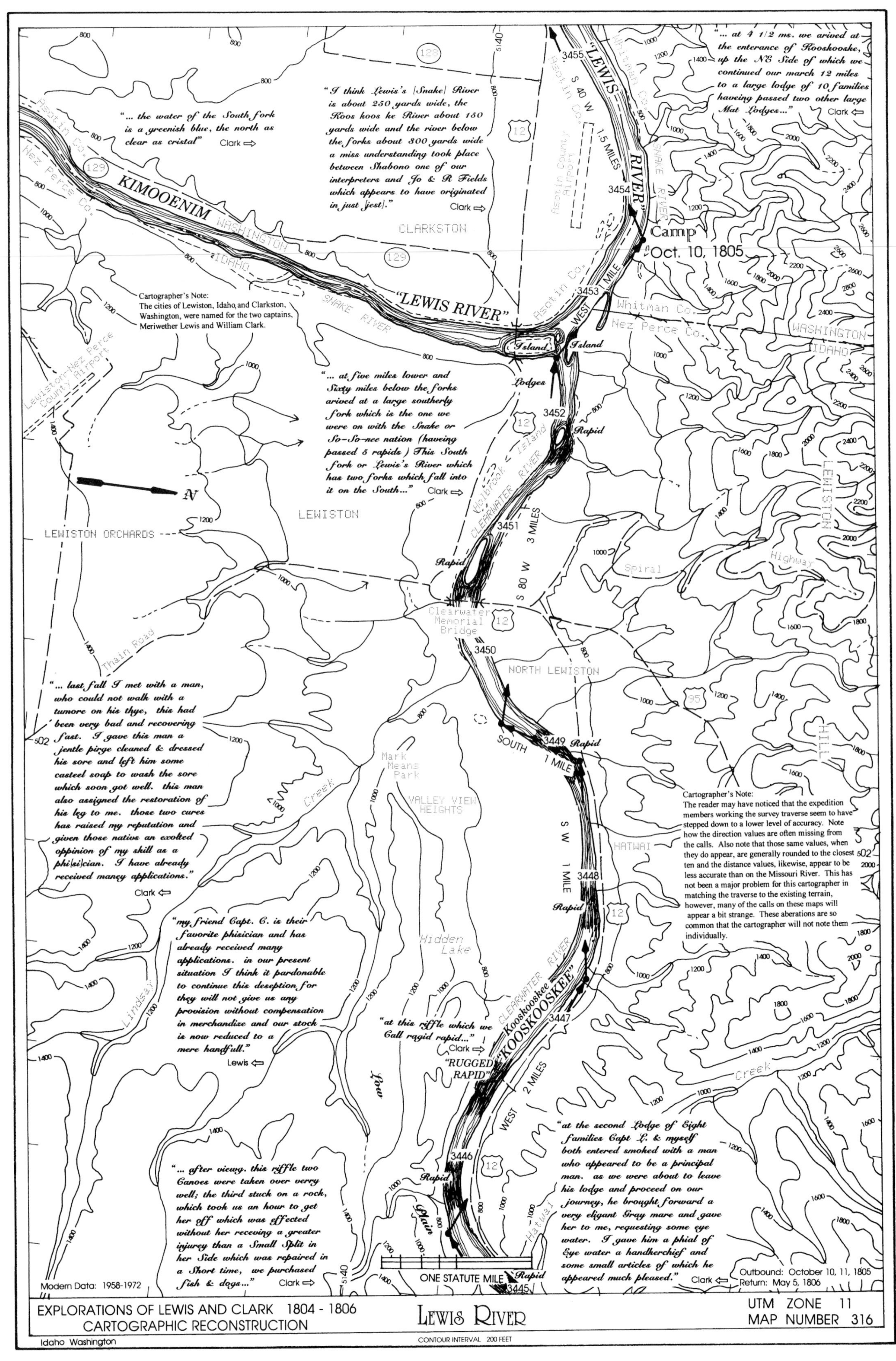
"... the water of the South fork is a greenish blue, the north as clear as cristal" Clark
"I think Lewis's [Snake] River is about 250 yards wide, the Koos koos ke River about 150 yards wide and the river below the forks about 300 yards wide a miss understanding took place between Shabono one of our interpreters and Jo & R Fields which appears to have originated in just [jest]." Clark
"... at 4 1/2 ms. we arived at the enterance of Kooskooske, up the NE Side of which we continued our march 12 miles to a large lodge of 10 families haveing passed two other large Mat Lodges..." Clark
KIMOOENIM
WASHINGTON
IDAHO
CLARKSTON
"LEWIS RIVER"
SNAKE RIVER
Asotin Co.
Nez Perce Co.
Whitman Co.
Asotin County Airport
Camp Oct. 10, 1805
S 40 W 1.5 MILES
WEST 1 MILE
Island
Island
Lodges
Rapid
Cartographer's Note:
The cities of Lewiston, Idaho and Clarkston, Washington, were named for the two captains, Meriwether Lewis and William Clark.
Lewiston-Nez Perce County Airport
"... at five miles lower and Sixty miles below the forks arived at a large southerly fork which is the one we were on with the Snake or So-So-nee nation (haveing passed 5 rapids) This South fork or Lewis's River which has two forks which fall into it on the South..." Clark
N
LEWISTON
LEWISTON ORCHARDS
CLEARWATER RIVER
Holbrook Island
S 80 W 3 MILES
Clearwater Memorial Bridge
Spiral Highway
LEWISTON HILL
Thain Road
NORTH LEWISTON
"... last fall I met with a man, who could not walk with a tumore on his thye, this had been very bad and recovering fast. I gave this man a jentle pirge cleaned & dressed his sore and left him some casteel soap to wash the sore which soon got well. this man also assigned the restoration of his leg to me. those two cures has raised my reputation and given those natives an exalted oppinion of my skill as a phi[si]cian. I have already received maney applications." Clark
SOUTH 1 MILE
Mark Means Park
VALLEY VIEW HEIGHTS
Creek
S W 1 MILE
HATWAI
Cartographer's Note:
The reader may have noticed that the expedition members working the survey traverse seem to have stepped down to a lower level of accuracy. Note how the direction values are often missing from the calls. Also note that those same values, when they do appear, are generally rounded to the closest ten and the distance values, likewise, appear to be less accurate than on the Missouri River. This has not been a major problem for this cartographer in matching the traverse to the existing terrain, however, many of the calls on these maps will appear a bit strange. These aberations are so common that the cartographer will not note them individually.
"my friend Capt. C. is their favorite phisician and has already received many applications. in our present situation I think it pardonable to continue this deception for they will not give us any provision without compensation in merchandize and our stock is now reduced to a mere handfull." Lewis
Hidden Lake
Lindsay
"at this riffle which we Call ragid rapid..." Clark
"RUGGED RAPID"
CLEARWATER RIVER
Kooskooskee
"KOOSKOOSKEE"
WEST 2 MILES
Creek
Low
"at the second Lodge of Eight families Capt L. & myself both entered smoked with a man who appeared to be a principal man. as we were about to leave his lodge and proceed on our journey, he brought forward a very eligant Gray mare and gave her to me, requesting some eye water. I gave him a phial of Eye water a handkerchief and some small articles of which he appeared much pleased." Clark
"... after viewg. this riffle two Canoes were taken over very well; the third stuck on a rock, which took us an hour to get her off which was effected without her receving a greater injurey than a Small Split in her Side which was repaired in a Short time, we purchased fish & dogs..." Clark
Plain
Hatwai
ONE STATUTE MILE
Rapid
Modern Data: 1958-1972
Outbound: October 10, 11, 1805
Return: May 5, 1806
EXPLORATIONS OF LEWIS AND CLARK 1804 - 1806
CARTOGRAPHIC RECONSTRUCTION
LEWIS RIVER
UTM ZONE 11
MAP NUMBER 316
Idaho Washington
CONTOUR INTERVAL 200 FEET

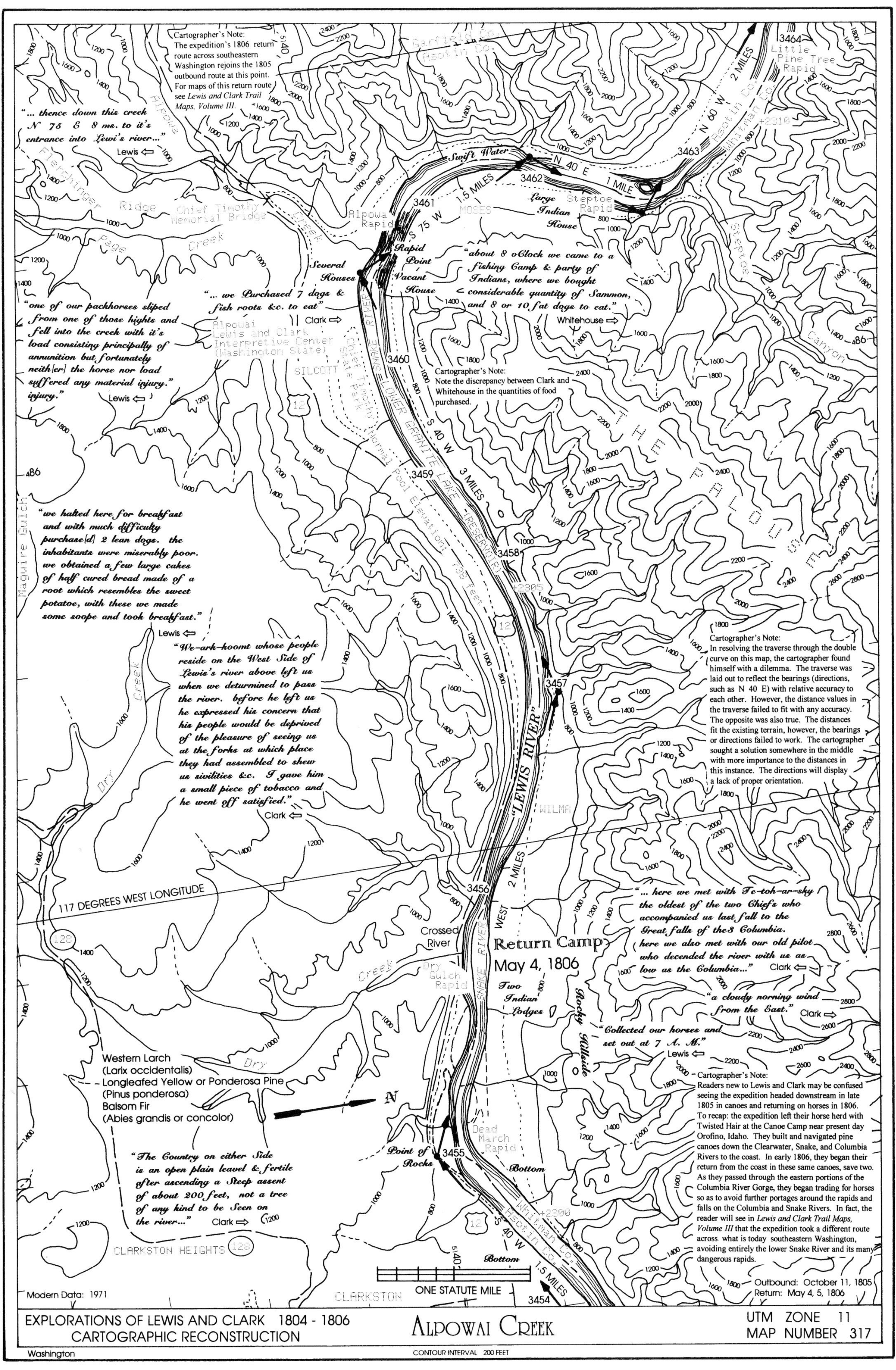

Cartographer's Note:
The expedition's 1806 return route across southeastern Washington rejoins the 1805 outbound route at this point. For maps of this return route see Lewis and Clark Trail Maps, Volume III.
"... thence down this creek N 75 E 8 ms. to it's entrance into Lewi's river..."
Lewis
Garfield Co.
Asotin Co.
3464
Little Pine Tree Rapid
2 MILES
N 60 W
Asotin Co.
Whitman Co.
+2310
3463
Swift Water
N 40 E
1 MILE
3462
Large Indian House
Steptoe Rapid
Fletchinger Ridge
Chief Timothy Memorial Bridge
Alpowa Creek
Page Creek
3461
1.5 MILES
MOSES
Alpowa Rapid
S 75 W
Rapid Point
Vacant House
Several Houses
"about 8 oClock we came to a fishing Camp & party of Indians, where we bought considerable quantity of Sammon, and 8 or 10 fat dogs to eat."
Whitehouse
"... we Purchased 7 dogs & fish roots &c. to eat"
Clark
"one of our packhorses sliped from one of those hights and fell into the creek with it's load consisting principally of annunition but fortunately neith[er] the horse nor load suffered any material injury."
Lewis
Alpowai Lewis and Clark Interpretive Center (Washington State)
SILCOTT
Chief Timothy State Park
SNAKE RIVER
3460
LOWER GRANITE LAKE
Cartographer's Note:
Note the discrepancy between Clark and Whitehouse in the quantities of food purchased.
Steptoe Canyon
THE PALOUSE
S 40 W
3 MILES
3459
Normal Pool Elevation: 738 feet
(RESERVOIR)
3458
+2305
Maguire Gulch
"we halted here for breakfast and with much difficulty purchase[d] 2 lean dogs. the inhabitants were miserably poor. we obtained a few large cakes of half cured bread made of a root which resembles the sweet potatoe, with these we made some soope and took breakfast."
Lewis
"We-ark-koomt whose people reside on the West Side of Lewis's river above left us when we deturmined to pass the river. before he left us he expressed his concern that his people would be deprived of the pleasure of seeing us at the forks at which place they had assembled to shew us sivilities &c. I gave him a small piece of tobacco and he went off satisfied."
Clark
Cartographer's Note:
In resolving the traverse through the double curve on this map, the cartographer found himself with a dilemma. The traverse was laid out to reflect the bearings (directions, such as N 40 E) with relative accuracy to each other. However, the distance values in the traverse failed to fit with any accuracy. The opposite was also true. The distances fit the existing terrain, however, the bearings or directions failed to work. The cartographer sought a solution somewhere in the middle with more importance to the distances in this instance. The directions will display a lack of proper orientation.
3457
"LEWIS RIVER"
Dry Creek
WILMA
2 MILES
117 DEGREES WEST LONGITUDE
3456
WEST
"... here we met with Te-toh-ar-sky the oldest of the two Chief's who accompanied us last fall to the Great falls of the 3 Columbia. here we also met with our old pilot who decended the river with us as low as the Columbia..."
Clark
Crossed River
Return Camp
May 4, 1806
Dry Gulch Rapid
Two Indian Lodges
Rocky Hillside
"a cloudy norning wind from the East."
Clark
"Collected our horses and set out at 7 A. M."
Lewis
Western Larch
(Larix occidentalis)
Longleafed Yellow or Ponderosa Pine
(Pinus ponderosa)
Balsom Fir
(Abies grandis or concolor)
N
Cartographer's Note:
Readers new to Lewis and Clark may be confused seeing the expedition headed downstream in late 1805 in canoes and returning on horses in 1806. To recap: the expedition left their horse herd with Twisted Hair at the Canoe Camp near present day Orofino, Idaho. They built and navigated pine canoes down the Clearwater, Snake, and Columbia Rivers to the coast. In early 1806, they began their return from the coast in these same canoes, save two. As they passed through the eastern portions of the Columbia River Gorge, they began trading for horses so as to avoid further portages around the rapids and falls on the Columbia and Snake Rivers. In fact, the reader will see in Lewis and Clark Trail Maps, Volume III that the expedition took a different route across what is today southeastern Washington, avoiding entirely the lower Snake River and its many dangerous rapids.
Dead March Rapid
Point of Rocks
3455
Bottom
"The Country on either Side is an open plain leavel & fertile after ascending a Steep assent of about 200 feet, not a tree of any kind to be Seen on the river..."
Clark
Whitman Co.
Asotin Co.
+2300
CLARKSTON HEIGHTS
S 40 W
Bottom
1.5 MILES
ONE STATUTE MILE
3454
Modern Data: 1971
CLARKSTON
Outbound: October 11, 1805
Return: May 4, 5, 1806
EXPLORATIONS OF LEWIS AND CLARK 1804 - 1806
CARTOGRAPHIC RECONSTRUCTION
ALPOWAI CREEK
UTM ZONE 11
MAP NUMBER 317
Washington
CONTOUR INTERVAL 200 FEET

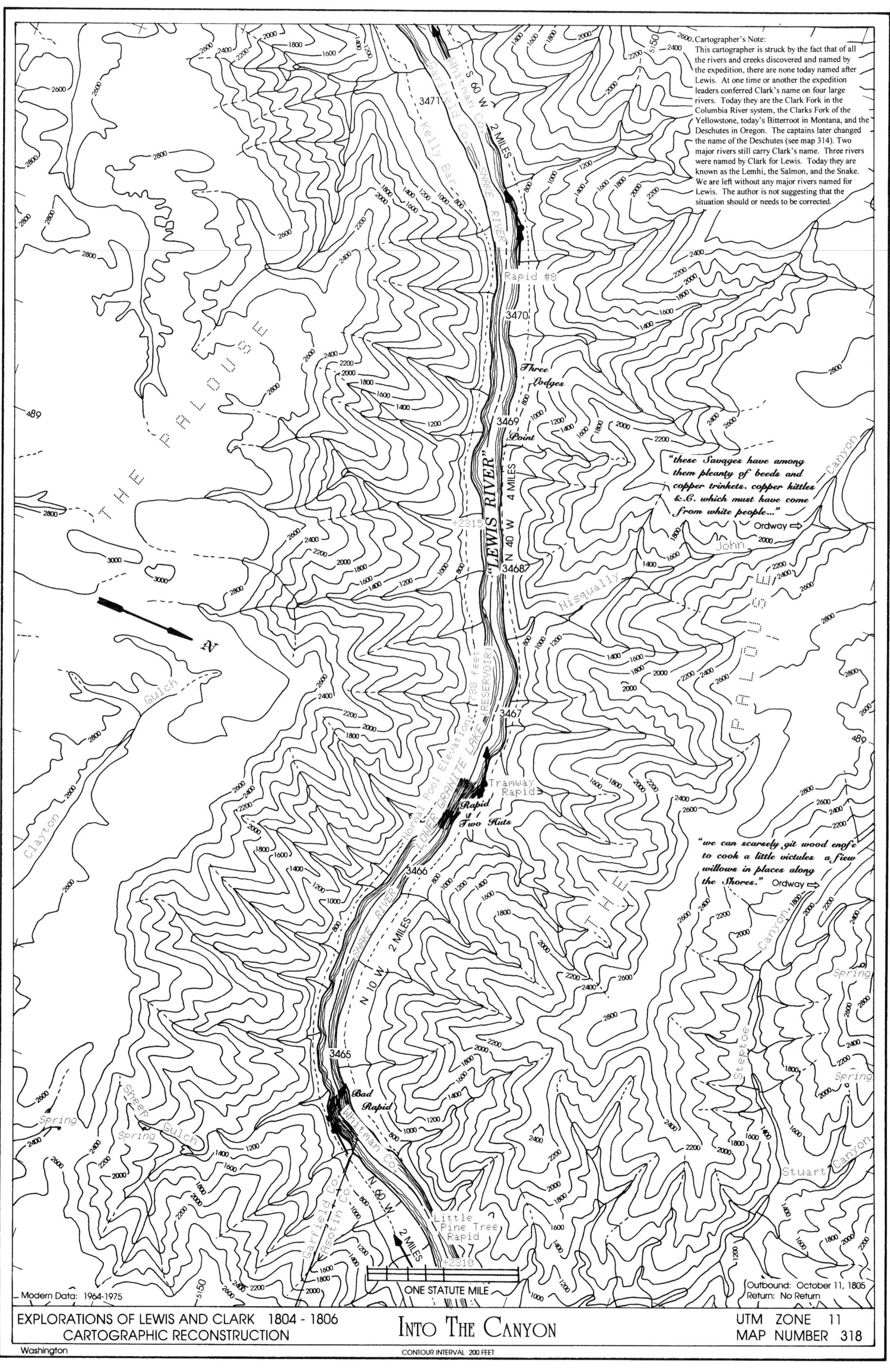
Cartographer's Note:
This cartographer is struck by the fact that of all the rivers and creeks discovered and named by the expedition, there are none today named after Lewis. At one time or another the expedition leaders conferred Clark's name on four large rivers. Today they are the Clark Fork in the Columbia River system, the Clarks Fork of the Yellowstone, today's Bitterroot in Montana, and the Deschutes in Oregon. The captains later changed the name of the Deschutes (see map 314). Two major rivers still carry Clark's name. Three rivers were named by Clark for Lewis. Today they are known as the Lemhi, the Salmon, and the Snake. We are left without any major rivers named for Lewis. The author is not suggesting that the situation should or needs to be corrected.
"these Savages have among them pleanty of beeds and copper trinkets. copper kittles &.C. which must have come from white people..." Ordway
"we can scarsely git wood enofe to cook a little victules a fiew willows in places along the Shores." Ordway
"LEWIS RIVER"
SNAKE RIVER
LOWER GRANITE LAKE (RESERVOIR)
Normal Pool Elevation: 738 feet
THE PALOUSE
THE PALOUSE
Whitman Co.
Garfield Co.
Asotin Co.
Kelly Bar
Rapid #8
Three Lodges
Point
Tramway Rapid
Rapid
Two Huts
Bad Rapid
Little Pine Tree Rapid
S 60 W 2 MILES
N 40 W 4 MILES
N 10 W 2 MILES
N 60 W 2 MILES
John
Hisqually
Canyon
Gulch
Clayton
Sheep Gulch
Spring
Steptoe Canyon
Stuart Canyon
Outbound: October 11, 1805
Return: No Return
Modern Data: 1964-1975
ONE STATUTE MILE
EXPLORATIONS OF LEWIS AND CLARK 1804 - 1806
CARTOGRAPHIC RECONSTRUCTION
INTO THE CANYON
UTM ZONE 11
MAP NUMBER 318
Washington
CONTOUR INTERVAL 200 FEET

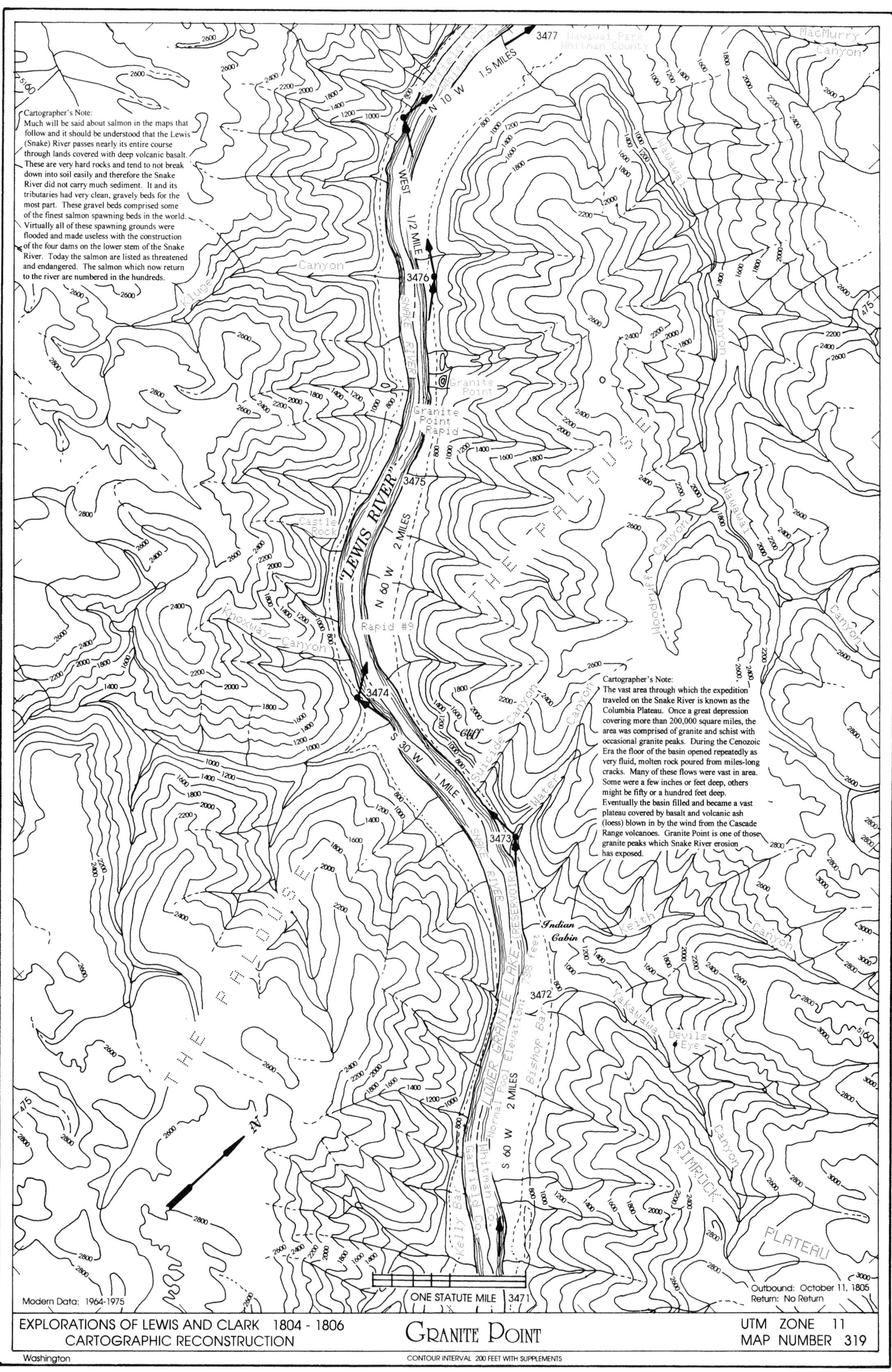
Cartographer's Note:
Much will be said about salmon in the maps that follow and it should be understood that the Lewis (Snake) River passes nearly its entire course through lands covered with deep volcanic basalt. These are very hard rocks and tend to not break down into soil easily and therefore the Snake River did not carry much sediment. It and its tributaries had very clean, gravely beds for the most part. These gravel beds comprised some of the finest salmon spawning beds in the world. Virtually all of these spawning grounds were flooded and made useless with the construction of the four dams on the lower stem of the Snake River. Today the salmon are listed as threatened and endangered. The salmon which now return to the river are numbered in the hundreds.
Cartographer's Note:
The vast area through which the expedition traveled on the Snake River is known as the Columbia Plateau. Once a great depression covering more than 200,000 square miles, the area was comprised of granite and schist with occasional granite peaks. During the Cenozoic Era the floor of the basin opened repeatedly as very fluid, molten rock poured from miles-long cracks. Many of these flows were vast in area. Some were a few inches or feet deep, others might be fifty or a hundred feet deep. Eventually the basin filled and became a vast plateau covered by basalt and volcanic ash (loess) blown in by the wind from the Cascade Range volcanoes. Granite Point is one of those granite peaks which Snake River erosion has exposed.
3477
Wawawai Park
Whitman County
MacMurry Canyon
1.5 MILES
N 10 W
WEST
1/2 MILE
3476
Canyon
Kluge
SNAKE RIVER
Granite Point
Granite Point Rapid
3475
"LEWIS RIVER"
2 MILES
N 60 W
Castle Rock
Knoxway Canyon
Rapid #9
3474
S 30 W
1 MILE
Cliff
Suicide Canyon
Water Canyon
3473
Wawawai Canyon
Woodruff Canyon
Canyon
THE PALOUSE
THE PALOUSE
SNAKE RIVER
LOWER GRANITE LAKE (RESERVOIR)
Normal Pool Elevation: 738 feet
Indian Cabin
Keith Canyon
Yakawawa
3472
Devils Eye
Bishop Bar
2 MILES
S 60 W
Kelly Bar
Garfield Co.
Whitman Co.
RIMROCK Canyon
PLATEAU
N
ONE STATUTE MILE
3471
Modern Data: 1964-1975
Outbound: October 11, 1805
Return: No Return
EXPLORATIONS OF LEWIS AND CLARK 1804 - 1806
CARTOGRAPHIC RECONSTRUCTION
GRANITE POINT
UTM ZONE 11
MAP NUMBER 319
Washington
CONTOUR INTERVAL 200 FEET WITH SUPPLEMENTS

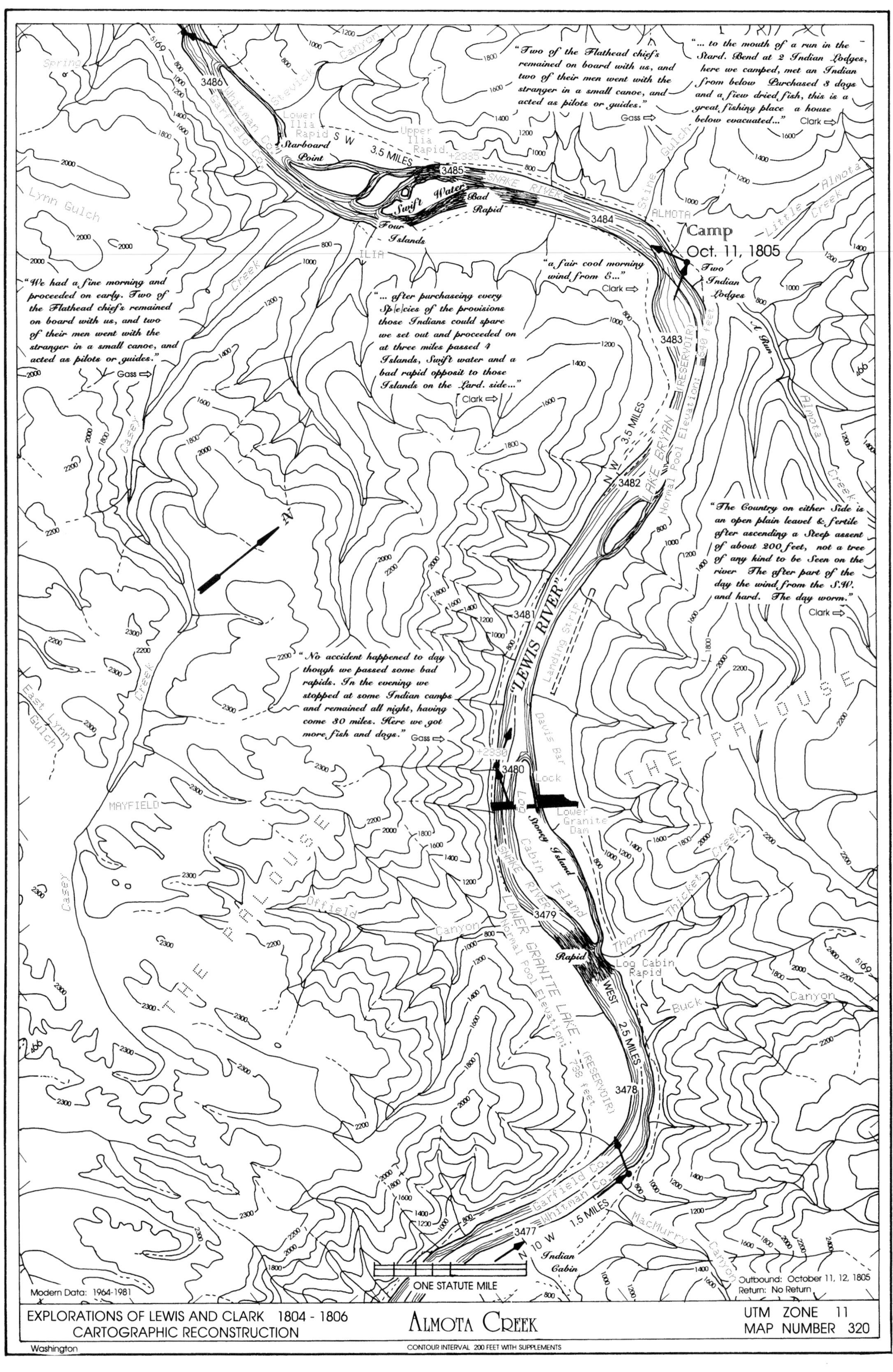
"Two of the Flathead chiefs remained on board with us, and two of their men went with the stranger in a small canoe, and acted as pilots or guides."
Gass
"... to the mouth of a run in the Stard. Bend at 2 Indian Lodges, here we camped, met an Indian from below Purchased 3 dogs and a fiew dried fish, this is a great fishing place a house below evacuated..."
Clark
Lower Ilia Rapid
Upper Ilia Rapid
Starboard Point
3.5 MILES
SNAKE RIVER
Swift Water
Bad Rapid
Four Islands
Lynn Gulch
ILIA
ALMOTA
Stine Gulch
Little Almota Creek
Camp Oct. 11, 1805
Two Indian Lodges
"a fair cool morning wind from E..."
Clark
"We had a fine morning and proceeded on early. Two of the Flathead chiefs remained on board with us, and two of their men went with the stranger in a small canoe, and acted as pilots or guides."
Gass
"... after purchaseing every Sp[e]cies of the provisions those Indians could spare we set out and proceeded on at three miles passed 4 Islands, Swift water and a bad rapid opposit to those Islands on the Lard. side..."
Clark
LAKE BRYAN (RESERVOIR)
Normal Pool Elevation: 640 feet
3.5 MILES
Almota Creek
Casey Creek
"The Country on either Side is an open plain leavel & fertile after ascending a Steep assent of about 200 feet, not a tree of any kind to be Seen on the river The after part of the day the wind from the S.W. and hard. The day worm."
Clark
"LEWIS RIVER"
Landing Strip
"No accident happened to day though we passed some bad rapids. In the evening we stopped at some Indian camps and remained all night, having come 30 miles. Here we got more fish and dogs."
Gass
East Lynn Gulch
Davis Bar
THE PALOUSE
Lock
Lower Granite Dam
MAYFIELD
Log Cabin Island
Stoney Island
SNAKE RIVER
Offield Canyon
Thorn Thicket Creek
Rapid
Log Cabin Rapid
LOWER GRANITE LAKE (RESERVOIR)
Normal Pool Elevation: 738 feet
WEST
2.5 MILES
Buck Canyon
Garfield Co.
Whitman Co.
1.5 MILES
MacMurry Canyon
Indian Cabin
ONE STATUTE MILE
Modern Data: 1964-1981
Outbound: October 11, 12, 1805
Return: No Return
EXPLORATIONS OF LEWIS AND CLARK 1804 - 1806
CARTOGRAPHIC RECONSTRUCTION
ALMOTA CREEK
UTM ZONE 11
MAP NUMBER 320
Washington
CONTOUR INTERVAL 200 FEET WITH SUPPLEMENTS

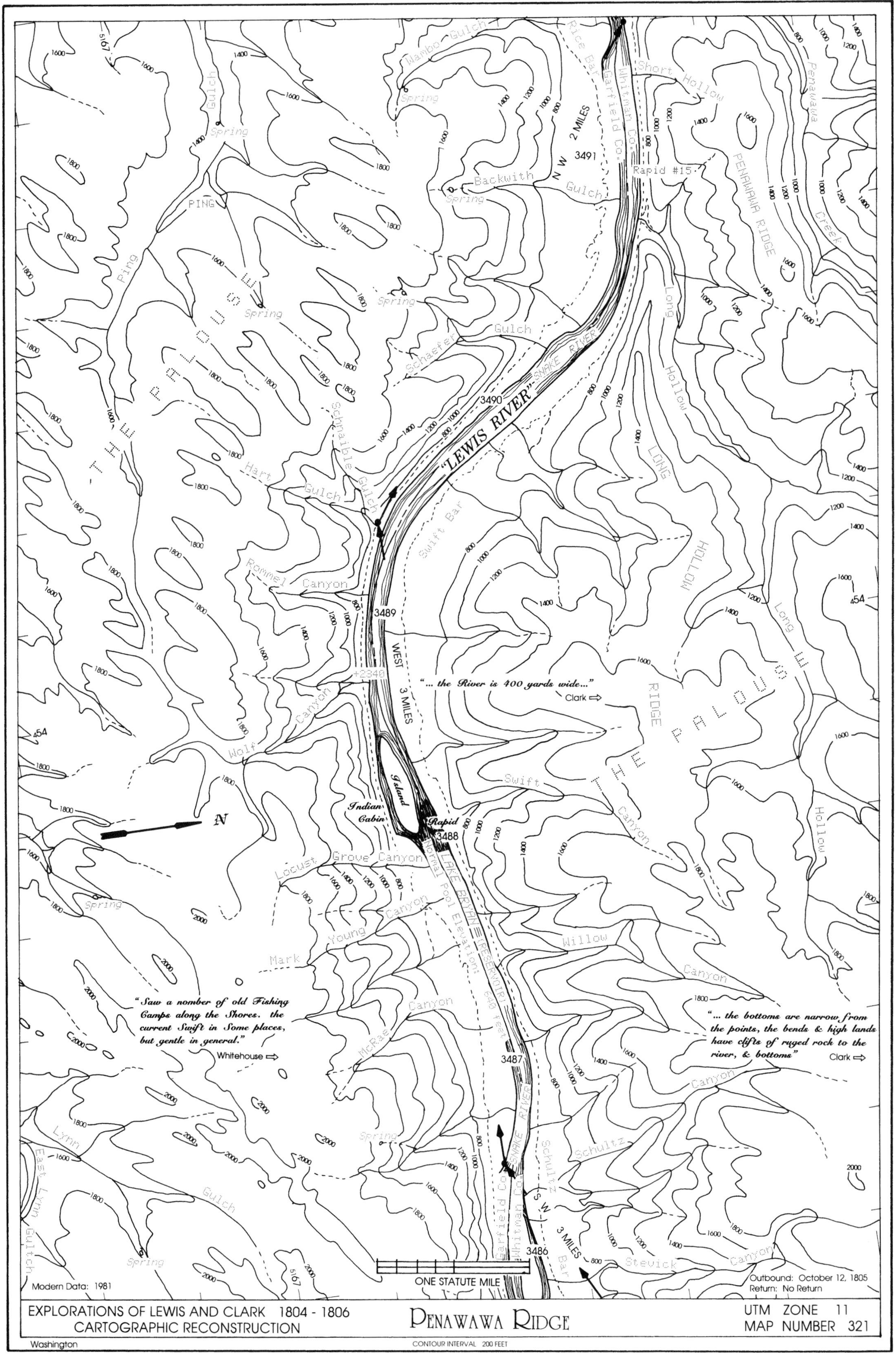
"LEWIS RIVER"
SNAKE RIVER
Rapid #15
Rapid
Island
Indian Cabin
LAKE BRYAN (RESERVOIR)
Normal Pool Elevation: 540 feet
NW 2 MILES
WEST 3 MILES
SW 3 MILES
THE PALOUSE
PENAWAWA RIDGE
Penawawa Creek
LONG HOLLOW RIDGE
Long Hollow
Short Hollow
Whitman Co.
Garfield Co.
"... the River is 400 yards wide..."
Clark ⇨
"Saw a nomber of old Fishing Camps along the Shores. the current Swift in Some places, but gentle in general."
Whitehouse ⇨
"... the bottoms are narrow from the points, the bends & high lands have clifts of ruged rock to the river, & bottoms"
Clark ⇨
N
ONE STATUTE MILE
Modern Data: 1981
Outbound: October 12, 1805
Return: No Return
EXPLORATIONS OF LEWIS AND CLARK 1804 - 1806
CARTOGRAPHIC RECONSTRUCTION
PENAWAWA RIDGE
UTM ZONE 11
MAP NUMBER 321
Washington
CONTOUR INTERVAL 200 FEET

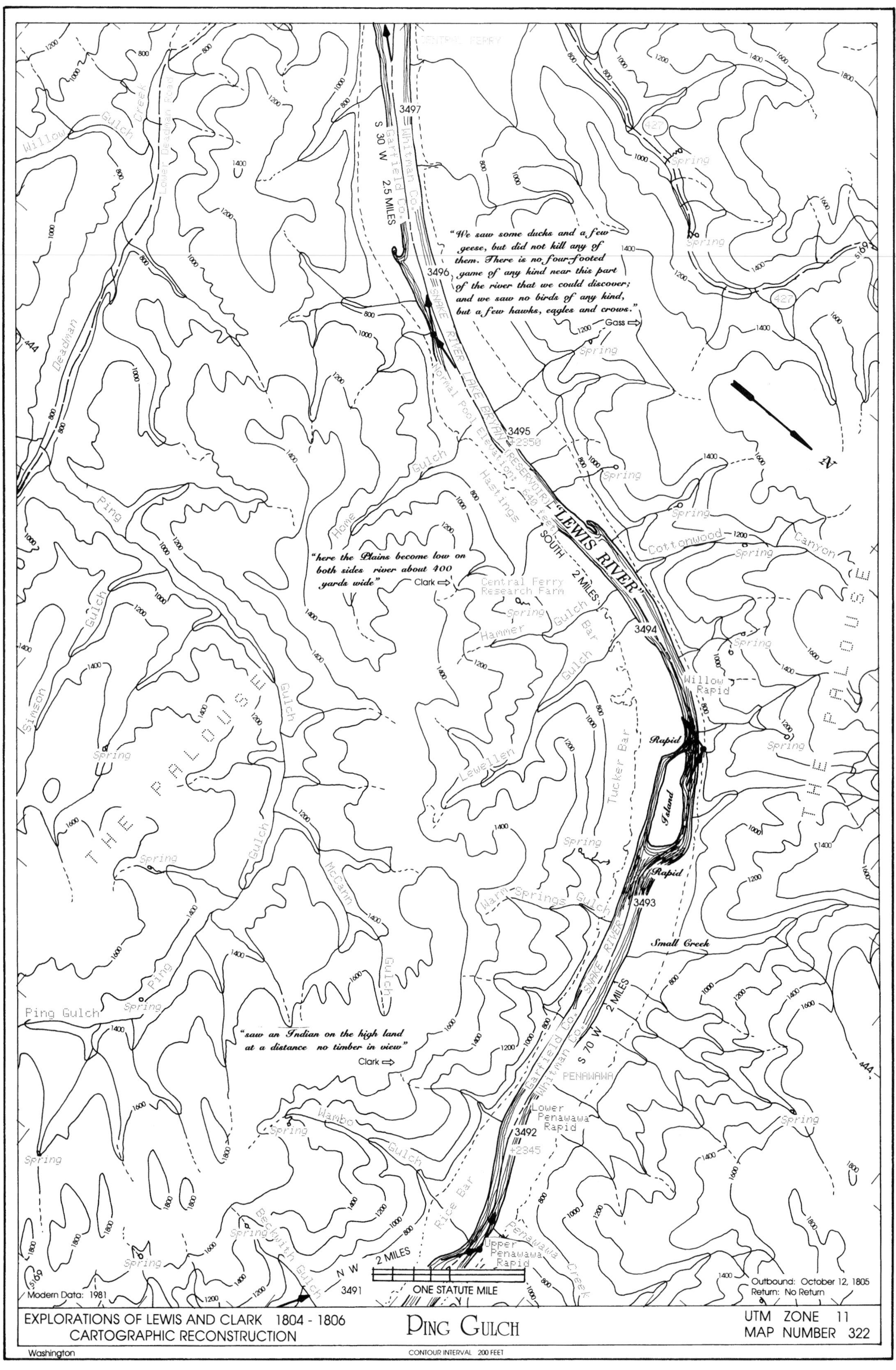
"We saw some ducks and a few geese, but did not kill any of them. There is no four-footed game of any kind near this part of the river that we could discover; and we saw no birds of any kind, but a few hawks, eagles and crows."
Gass
"here the Plains become low on both sides river about 400 yards wide"
Clark
"saw an Indian on the high land at a distance no timber in view"
Clark
"LEWIS RIVER"
SNAKE RIVER
LAKE BRYAN RESERVOIR
Normal Pool Elevation: 640 feet
Central Ferry Research Farm
THE PALOUSE
Island
Rapid
Small Creek
Willow Rapid
Lower Penawawa Rapid
Upper Penawawa Rapid
PENAWAWA
Ping Gulch
S 30 W 2.5 MILES
SOUTH 2 MILES
S 70 W 2 MILES
N W 2 MILES
ONE STATUTE MILE
Modern Data: 1981
Outbound: October 12, 1805
Return: No Return
EXPLORATIONS OF LEWIS AND CLARK 1804 - 1806
CARTOGRAPHIC RECONSTRUCTION
PING GULCH
UTM ZONE 11
MAP NUMBER 322
Washington
CONTOUR INTERVAL 200 FEET

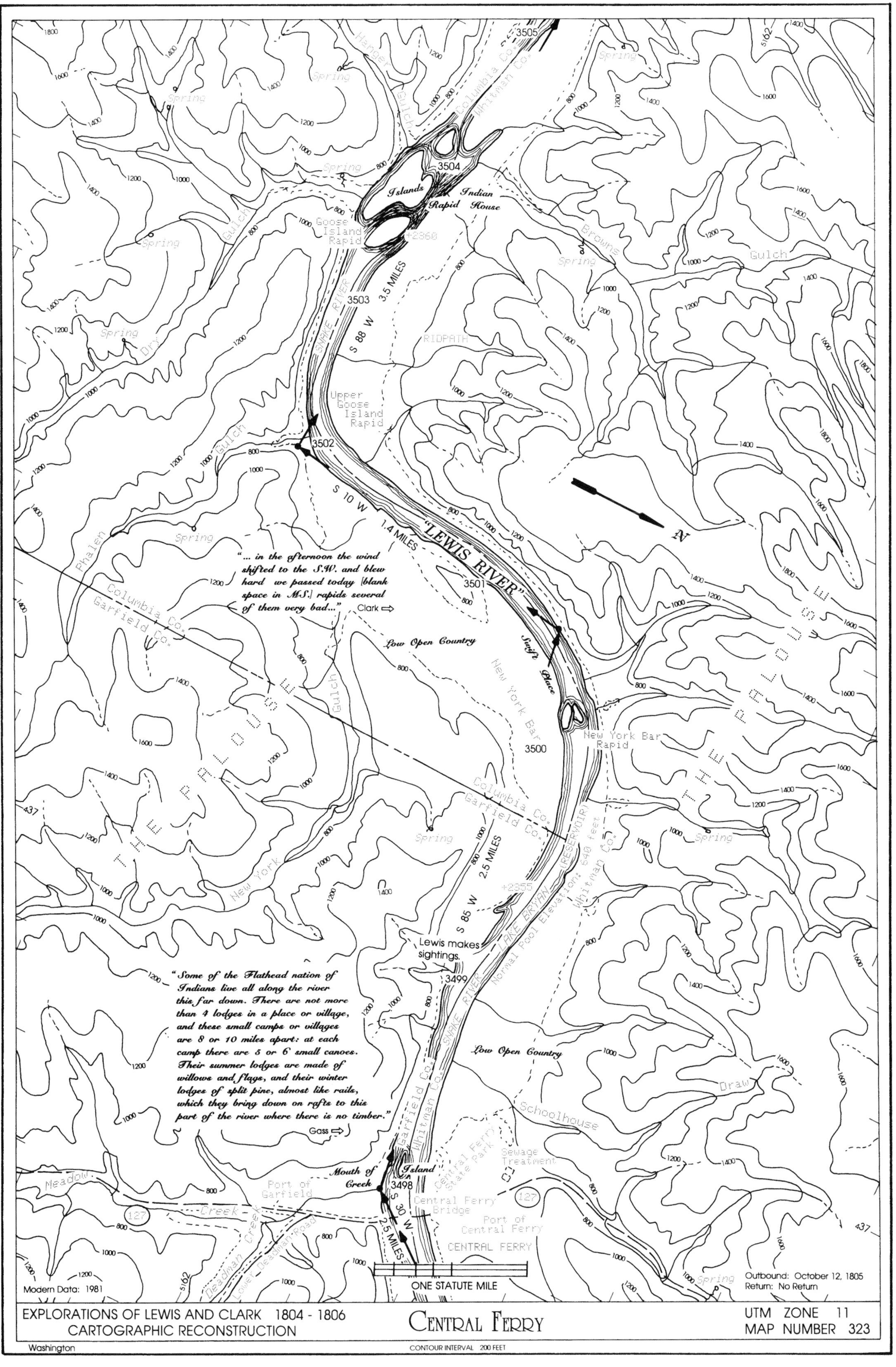
"... in the afternoon the wind shifted to the S.W. and blew hard we passed today [blank space in M.S.] rapids several of them very bad..." Clark
"Some of the Flathead nation of Indians live all along the river this far down. There are not more than 4 lodges in a place or village, and these small camps or villages are 8 or 10 miles apart: at each camp there are 5 or 6 small canoes. Their summer lodges are made of willows and flags, and their winter lodges of split pine, almost like rails, which they bring down on rafts to this part of the river where there is no timber." Gass
"LEWIS RIVER"
SNAKE RIVER
Islands
Indian House
Rapid
Goose Island Rapid
Upper Goose Island Rapid
New York Bar Rapid
Swift Place
Low Open Country
Lewis makes sightings.
Mouth of Creek
Island
S 88 W 3.5 MILES
S 10 W 1.4 MILES
S 85 W 2.5 MILES
S 30 W 2.5 MILES
LAKE BRYAN (RESERVOIR) Normal Pool Elevation: 640 feet
Columbia Co.
Whitman Co.
Garfield Co.
THE PALOUSE
Central Ferry State Park
Central Ferry Bridge
Port of Garfield
Port of Central Ferry
CENTRAL FERRY
Meadow Creek
Deadman Creek
Lower Deadman Road
Schoolhouse
Sewage Treatment
RIDPATH
New York Bar
N
ONE STATUTE MILE
Modern Data: 1981
Outbound: October 12, 1805
Return: No Return
EXPLORATIONS OF LEWIS AND CLARK 1804 - 1806
CARTOGRAPHIC RECONSTRUCTION
CENTRAL FERRY
UTM ZONE 11
MAP NUMBER 323
Washington
CONTOUR INTERVAL 200 FEET

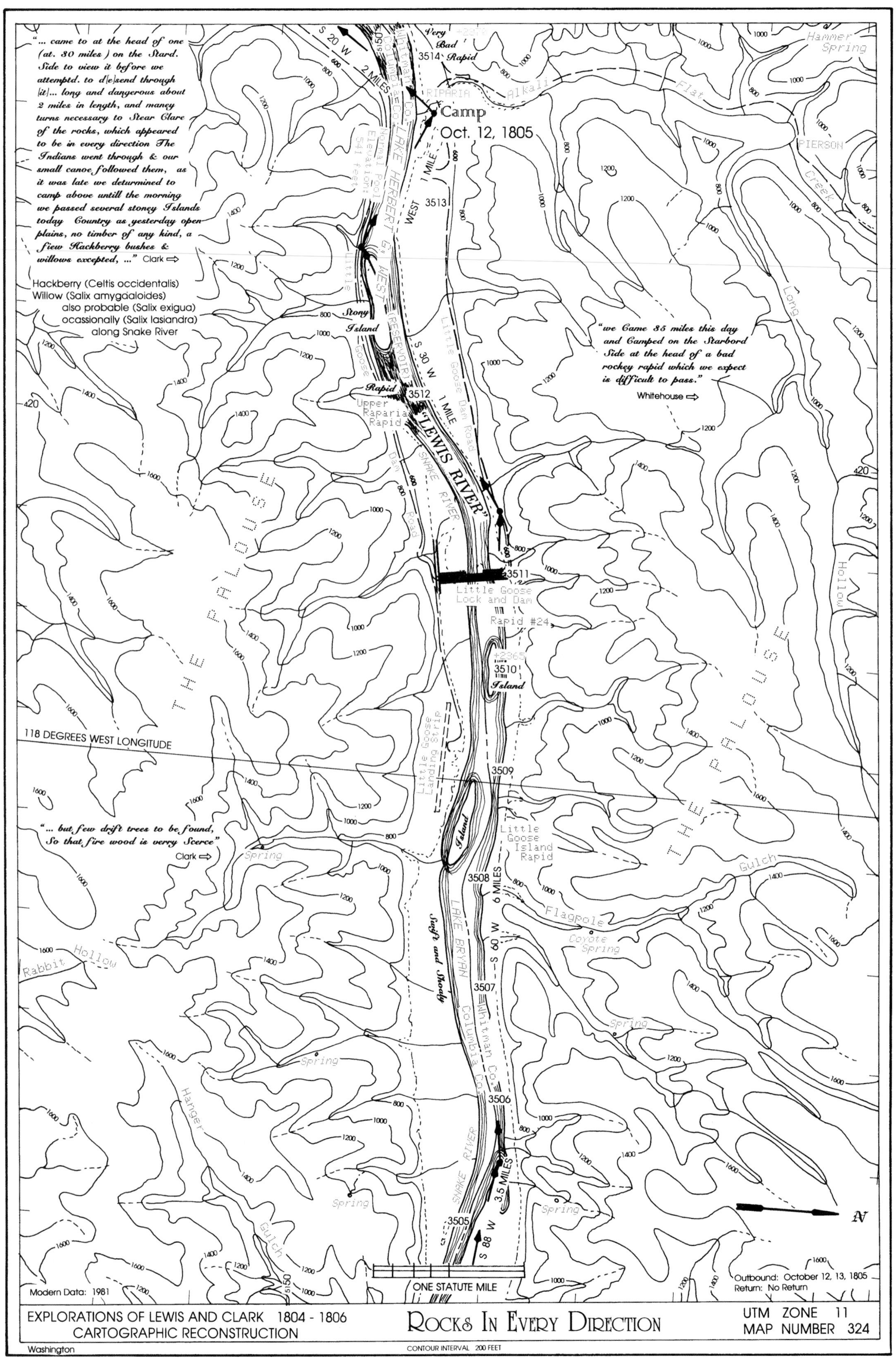
"... came to at the head of one (at. 30 miles) on the Stard. Side to view it before we attemptd. to d[e]send through [it]... long and dangerous about 2 miles in length, and maney turns necessary to Stear Clare of the rocks, which appeared to be in every direction The Indians went through & our small canoe followed them, as it was late we deturmined to camp above untill the morning we passed several stoney Islands today Country as yesterday open plains, no timber of any kind, a fiew Hackberry bushes & willows excepted, ..." Clark ⇨
Hackberry (Celtis occidentalis)
Willow (Salix amygdaloides)
also probable (Salix exigua)
ocassionally (Salix lasiandra)
along Snake River
"we Came 35 miles this day and Camped on the Starbord Side at the head of a bad rockey rapid which we expect is difficult to pass."
Whitehouse ⇨
"... but few drift trees to be found, So that fire wood is verry Scerce"
Clark ⇨
Very Bad Rapid
3514
Camp
Oct. 12, 1805
RIPARIA
Alkali Flat
Hammer Spring
PIERSON
Creek
S 20 W
2 MILES
1 MILE
WEST
3513
Stony Island
Rapid
3512
Upper Raparia Rapid
S 30 W
1 MILE
"LEWIS RIVER"
SNAKE RIVER
Little Goose Dam Road
Dam Road
3511
Little Goose Lock and Dam
Rapid #24
3510
Island
THE PALOUSE
Long Hollow
118 DEGREES WEST LONGITUDE
Little Goose Landing Strip
3509
Island
Little Goose Island Rapid
3508
6 MILES
S 60 W
Swift and Shoaly
LAKE BRYAN
Flagpole Gulch
Coyote Spring
Rabbit Hollow
Spring
3507
Columbia Co.
Whitman Co.
3506
Hanger Gulch
3.5 MILES
3505
S 88 W
N
ONE STATUTE MILE
Modern Data: 1981
Outbound: October 12, 13, 1805
Return: No Return
EXPLORATIONS OF LEWIS AND CLARK 1804 - 1806
CARTOGRAPHIC RECONSTRUCTION
Rocks In Every Direction
UTM ZONE 11
MAP NUMBER 324
Washington
CONTOUR INTERVAL 200 FEET

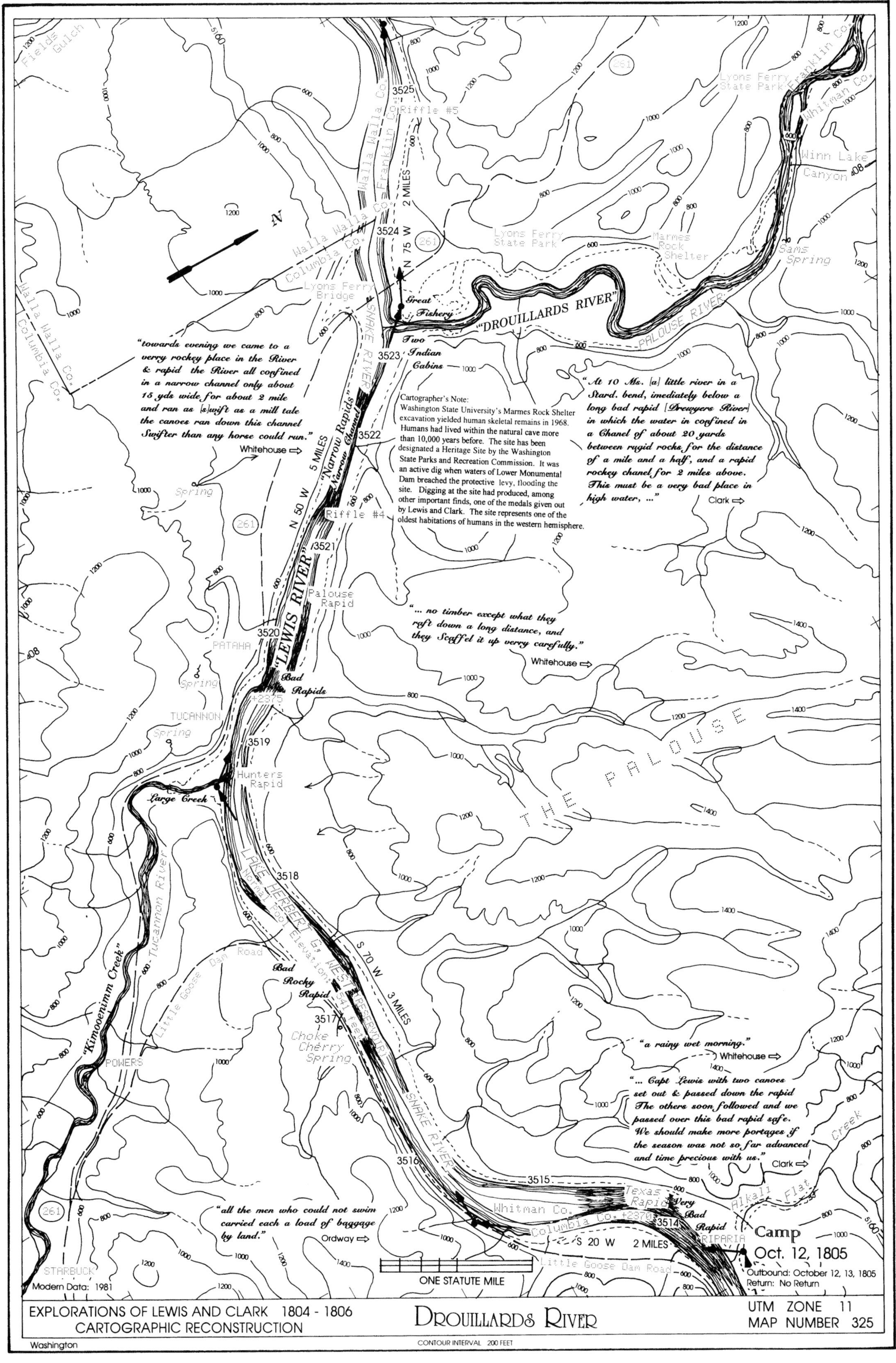
"towards evening we came to a verry rockey place in the River & rapid the River all confined in a narrow channel only about 15 yds wide for about 2 mile and ran as [s]wift as a mill tale the canoes ran down this channel Swifter than any horse could run."
Whitehouse ⇨
"At 10 Ms. [a] little river in a Stard. bend, imediately below a long bad rapid [Drewyers River] in which the water in confined in a Chanel of about 20 yards between rugid rocks for the distance of a mile and a half, and a rapid rockey chanel for 2 miles above. This must be a very bad place in high water, ..."
Clark ⇨
Cartographer's Note:
Washington State University's Marmes Rock Shelter excavation yielded human skeletal remains in 1968. Humans had lived within the natural cave more than 10,000 years before. The site has been designated a Heritage Site by the Washington State Parks and Recreation Commission. It was an active dig when waters of Lower Monumental Dam breached the protective levy, flooding the site. Digging at the site had produced, among other important finds, one of the medals given out by Lewis and Clark. The site represents one of the oldest habitations of humans in the western hemisphere.
"... no timber except what they raft down a long distance, and they Scaffel it up verry carefully."
Whitehouse ⇨
"a rainy wet morning."
Whitehouse ⇨
"... Capt Lewis with two canoes set out & passed down the rapid The others soon followed and we passed over this bad rapid safe. We should make more portages if the season was not so far advanced and time precious with us."
Clark ⇨
"all the men who could not swim carried each a load of baggage by land."
Ordway ⇨
"DROUILLARDS RIVER"
"LEWIS RIVER"
SNAKE RIVER
PALOUSE RIVER
THE PALOUSE
"Narrow Rapids"
Narrow Channel
Great Fishery
Two Indian Cabins
Bad Rapids
Large Creek
Bad Rocky Rapid
Very Bad Rapid
"Kimooenimm Creek"
Tucannon River
Lyons Ferry State Park
Lyons Ferry Bridge
Marmes Rock Shelter
Sams Spring
Winn Lake Canyon
Riffle #5
Riffle #4
Palouse Rapid
Hunters Rapid
Texas Rapid
Choke Cherry Spring
LAKE HERBERT G. WEST (RESERVOIR)
Normal Pool Elevation 541 feet
Little Goose Dam Road
Alkali Flat Creek
Walla Walla Co.
Columbia Co.
Franklin Co.
Whitman Co.
PATAHA
TUCANNON
POWERS
STARBUCK
RIPARIA
N 75 W 2 MILES
N 50 W 5 MILES
S 70 W 3 MILES
S 20 W 2 MILES
Camp
Oct. 12, 1805
Outbound: October 12, 13, 1805
Return: No Return
ONE STATUTE MILE
Modern Data: 1981
EXPLORATIONS OF LEWIS AND CLARK 1804 - 1806
CARTOGRAPHIC RECONSTRUCTION
DROUILLARDS RIVER
UTM ZONE 11
MAP NUMBER 325
Washington
CONTOUR INTERVAL 200 FEET

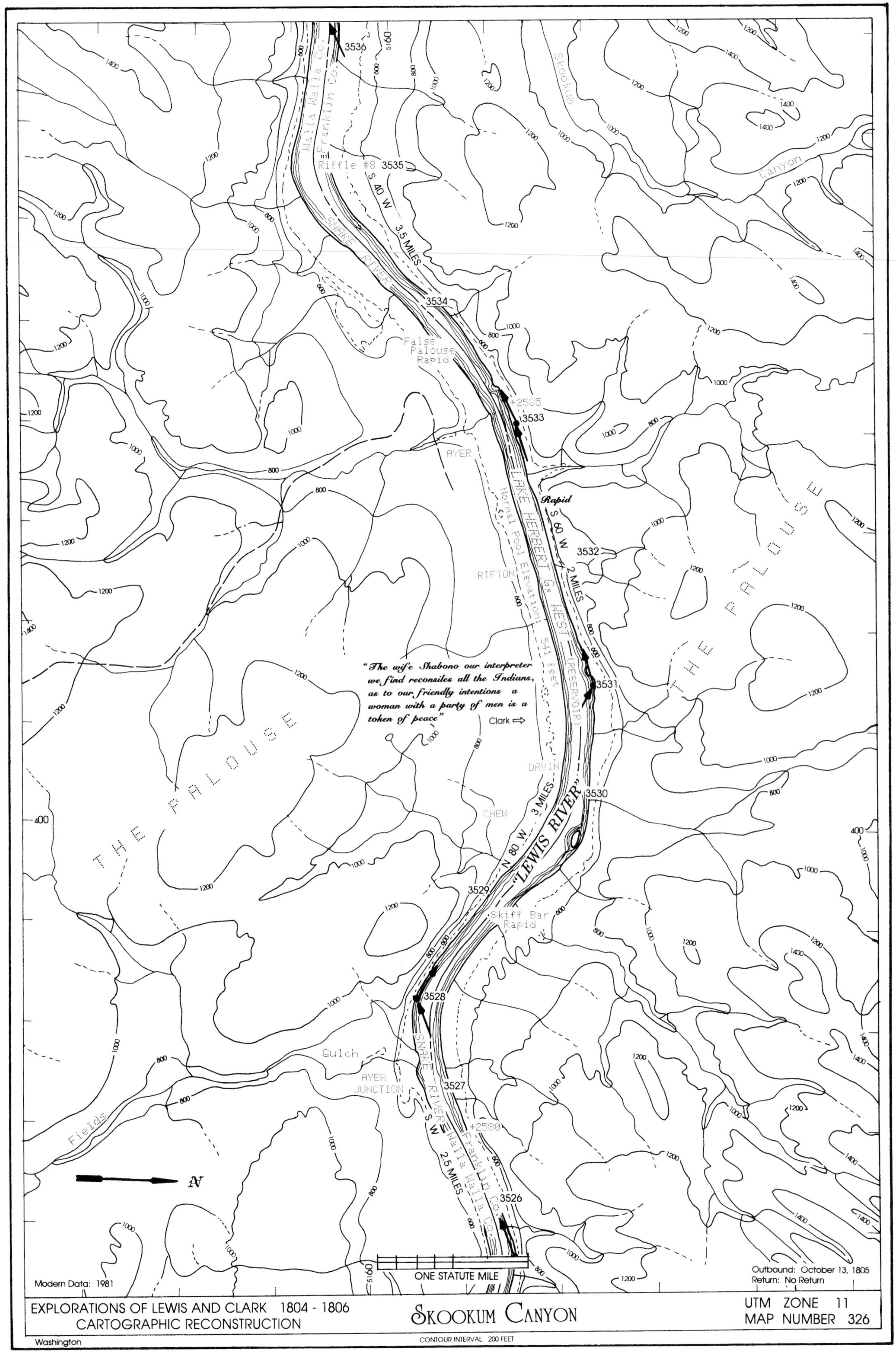

Riffle #8
S 40 W
3.5 MILES
SNAKE RIVER
Walla Walla Co.
Franklin Co.
Skookum Canyon
False Palouse Rapid
AYER
Rapid
S 60 W
2 MILES
LAKE HERBERT G. WEST (RESERVOIR)
Normal Pool Elevation: 541 feet
RIFTON
THE PALOUSE
"The wife Shabono our interpreter we find reconsiles all the Indians, as to our friendly intentions a woman with a party of men is a token of peace"
Clark ⇨
DAVIN
N 80 W
3 MILES
"LEWIS RIVER"
CHEW
THE PALOUSE
Skiff Bar Rapid
Gulch
AYER JUNCTION
Fields
S W
2.5 MILES
N
ONE STATUTE MILE
Modern Data: 1981
Outbound: October 13, 1805
Return: No Return
EXPLORATIONS OF LEWIS AND CLARK 1804 - 1806
CARTOGRAPHIC RECONSTRUCTION
SKOOKUM CANYON
UTM ZONE 11
MAP NUMBER 326
Washington
CONTOUR INTERVAL 200 FEET

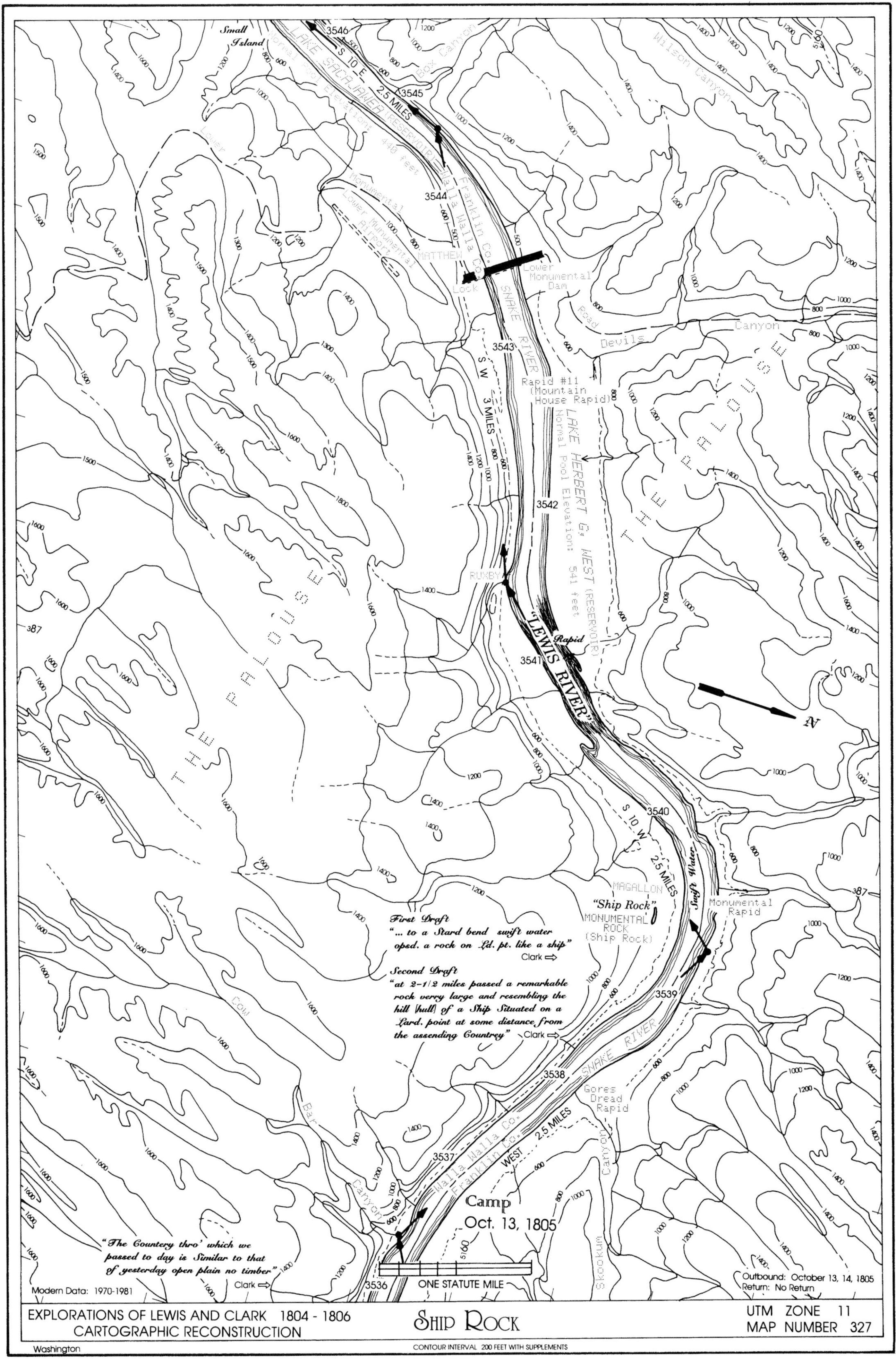
Small Island
LAKE SACAJAWEA (RESERVOIR)
Normal Pool Elevation: 440 feet
S 10 E
2.5 MILES
Box Canyon
Wilson Canyon
Lower Monumental
Lower Monumental Airport
MATTHEW
Walla Walla Co.
Franklin Co.
Lock
Lower Monumental Dam
SNAKE RIVER
Devils Canyon
Road
S W
3 MILES
Rapid #11 (Mountain House Rapid)
LAKE HERBERT G. WEST (RESERVOIR)
Normal Pool Elevation: 541 feet
THE PALOUSE
RUXBY
"LEWIS RIVER"
Rapid
N
S 10 W
2.5 MILES
Swift Water
MAGALLON
"Ship Rock"
MONUMENTAL ROCK (Ship Rock)
Monumental Rapid
First Draft
"... to a Stard bend swift water opsd. a rock on Ld. pt. like a ship"
Clark ⇨
Second Draft
"at 2-1/2 miles passed a remarkable rock verry large and resembling the hill [hull] of a Ship Situated on a Lard. point at some distance from the assending Countrey"
Clark ⇨
Cow
Bar
Canyon
Gores Dread Rapid
WEST
2.5 MILES
Camp
Oct. 13, 1805
Skookum Canyon
"The Countery thro' which we passed to day is Similar to that of yesterday open plain no timber"
Clark ⇨
Modern Data: 1970-1981
ONE STATUTE MILE
Outbound: October 13, 14, 1805
Return: No Return
EXPLORATIONS OF LEWIS AND CLARK 1804 - 1806
CARTOGRAPHIC RECONSTRUCTION
SHIP ROCK
UTM ZONE 11
MAP NUMBER 327
Washington
CONTOUR INTERVAL 200 FEET WITH SUPPLEMENTS

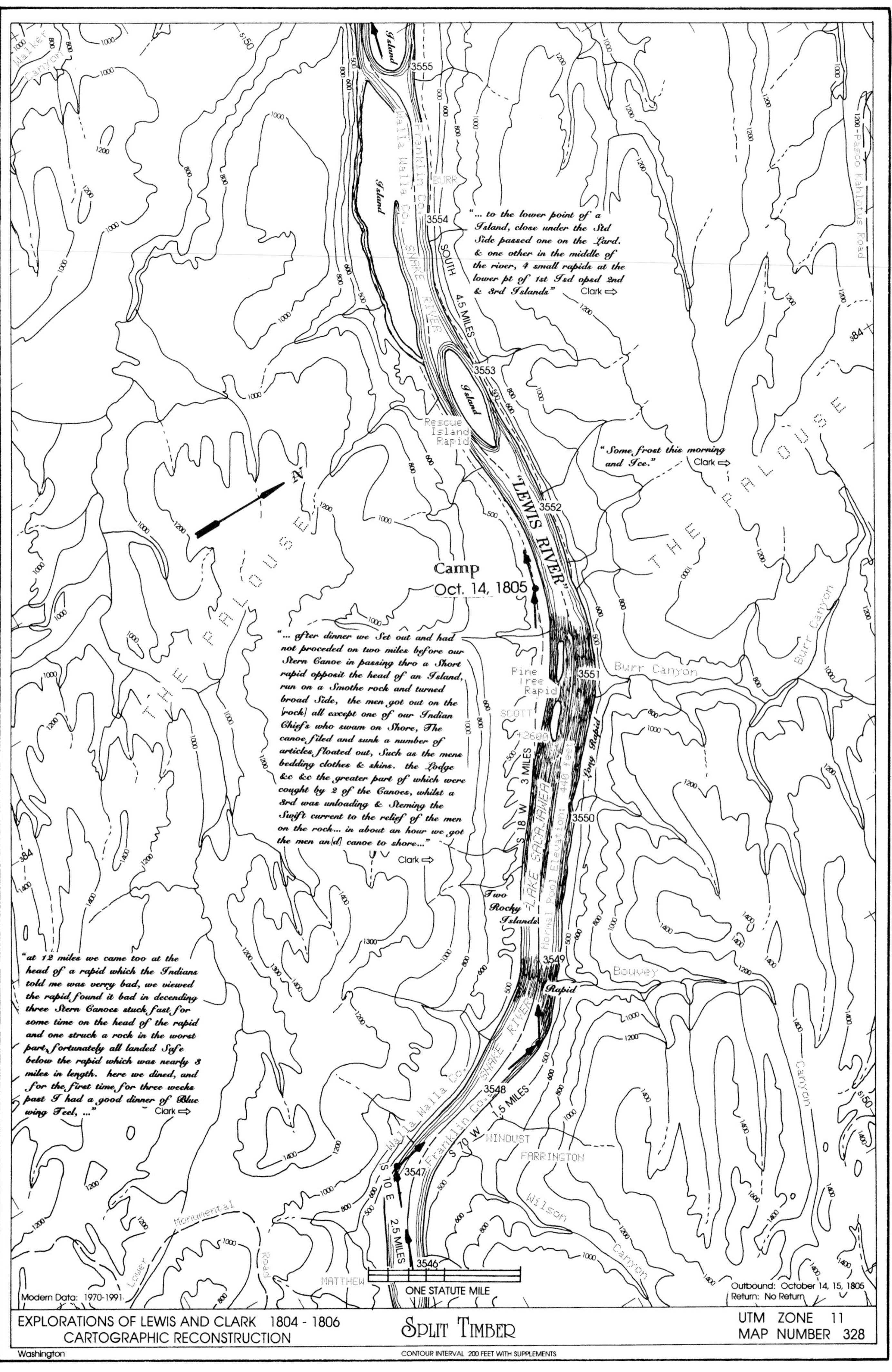

"... to the lower point of a Island, close under the Std Side passed one on the Lard. & one other in the middle of the river, 4 small rapids at the lower pt of 1st Isd opsd 2nd & 3rd Islands" Clark ⇨
"Some frost this morning and Ice." Clark ⇨
"... after dinner we Set out and had not proceded on two miles before our Stern Canoe in passing thro a Short rapid opposit the head of an Island, run on a Smothe rock and turned broad Side, the men got out on the [rock] all except one of our Indian Chiefs who swam on Shore, The canoe filed and sunk a number of articles floated out, Such as the mens bedding clothes & skins. the Lodge &c &c the greater part of which were cought by 2 of the Canoes, whilst a 3rd was unloading & Steming the Swift current to the relief of the men on the rock... in about an hour we got the men an[d] canoe to shore..." Clark ⇨
"at 12 miles we came too at the head of a rapid which the Indians told me was verry bad, we viewed the rapid found it bad in decending three Stern Canoes stuck fast for some time on the head of the rapid and one struck a rock in the worst part, fortunately all landed Safe below the rapid which was nearly 3 miles in length. here we dined, and for the first time for three weeks past I had a good dinner of Blue wing Teel, ..." Clark ⇨
Camp
Oct. 14, 1805
"LEWIS RIVER"
SNAKE RIVER
LAKE SACAJAWEA
Normal Pool Elevation: 440 feet
THE PALOUSE
THE PALOUSE
Island
Island
Island
Rescue Island Rapid
Pine Tree Rapid
Long Rapid
Two Rocky Islands
Rapid
Walla Walla Co.
Franklin Co.
SOUTH 4.5 MILES
S 18 W 3 MILES
S 70 W 1.5 MILES
S 10 E 2.5 MILES
3555
3554
3553
3552
3551
3550
3549
3548
3547
3546
BURR
SCOTT
+2600
WINDUST
FARRINGTON
MATTHEW
Burr Canyon
Bouvey
Walker Canyon
Wilson Canyon
Canyon
Lower Monumental Road
Pasco Kahlotus Road
N
ONE STATUTE MILE
Modern Data: 1970-1991
Outbound: October 14, 15, 1805
Return: No Return
EXPLORATIONS OF LEWIS AND CLARK 1804 - 1806
CARTOGRAPHIC RECONSTRUCTION
SPLIT TIMBER
UTM ZONE 11
MAP NUMBER 328
Washington
CONTOUR INTERVAL 200 FEET WITH SUPPLEMENTS

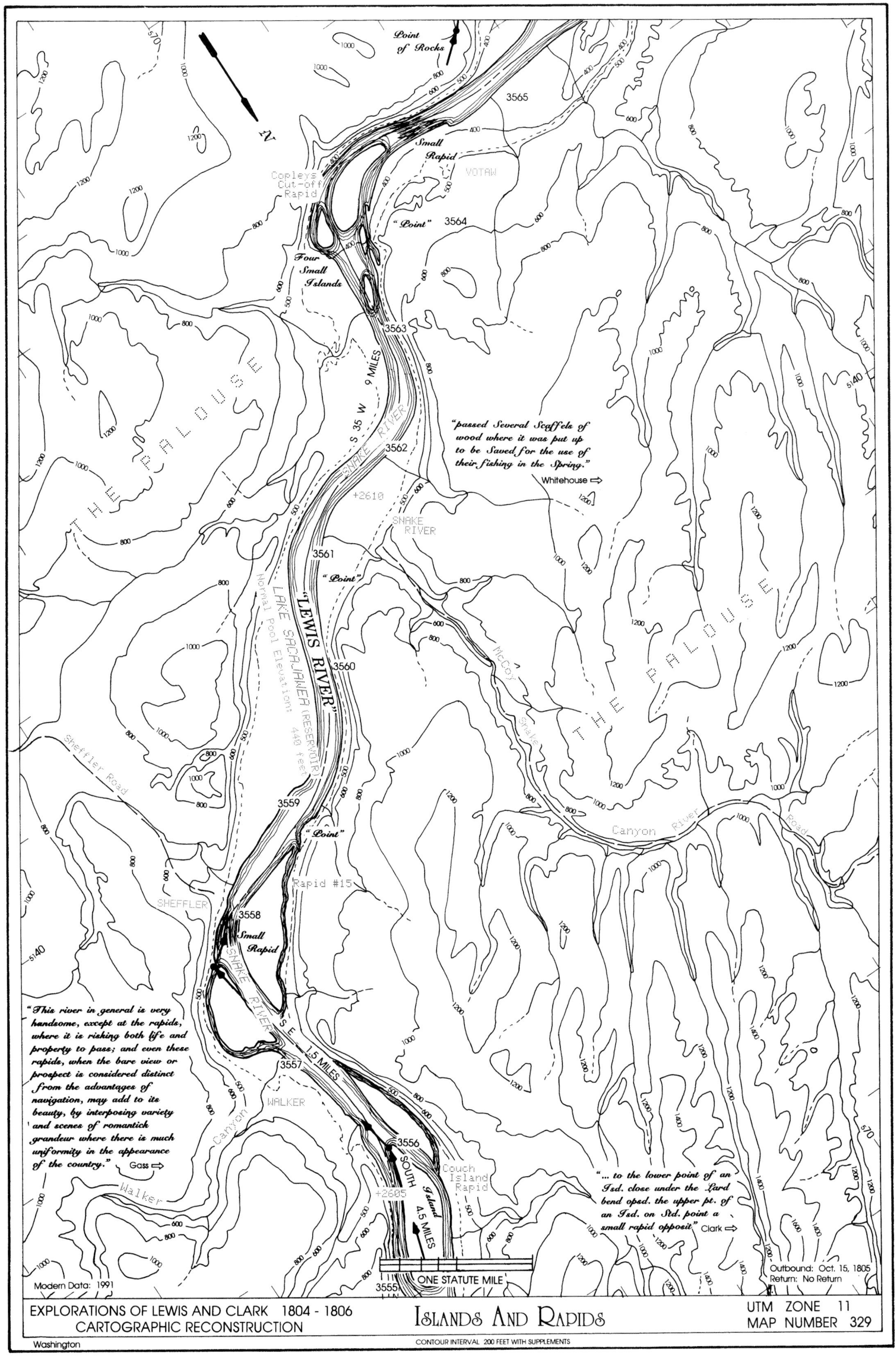

Point of Rocks
N
Small Rapid
Copleys Cut-off Rapid
VOTAW
"Point"
Four Small Islands
3565
3564
3563
3562
3561
3560
3559
3558
3557
3556
3555
S 35 W 9 MILES
SNAKE RIVER
THE PALOUSE
"passed Several Scaffels of wood where it was put up to be Saved for the use of their fishing in the Spring." Whitehouse ⇨
+2610
SNAKE RIVER
"Point"
"LEWIS RIVER"
LAKE SACAJAWEA (RESERVOIR)
Normal Pool Elevation: 440 feet
McCoy
Snake
Canyon River Road
Sheffler Road
SHEFFLER
"Point"
Rapid #15
Small Rapid
SNAKE RIVER
S E 1.5 MILES
"This river in general is very handsome, except at the rapids, where it is risking both life and property to pass; and even these rapids, when the bare view or prospect is considered distinct from the advantages of navigation, may add to its beauty, by interposing variety and scenes of romantick grandeur where there is much uniformity in the appearance of the country." Gass ⇨
WALKER
Canyon
Walker
Couch Island Rapid
+2605
SOUTH 4.5 MILES
Island
"... to the lower point of an Isd. close under the Lard bend opsd. the upper pt. of an Isd. on Std. point a small rapid opposit" Clark ⇨
ONE STATUTE MILE
Modern Data: 1991
Outbound: Oct. 15, 1805
Return: No Return
EXPLORATIONS OF LEWIS AND CLARK 1804 - 1806
CARTOGRAPHIC RECONSTRUCTION
ISLANDS AND RAPIDS
UTM ZONE 11
MAP NUMBER 329
Washington
CONTOUR INTERVAL 200 FEET WITH SUPPLEMENTS

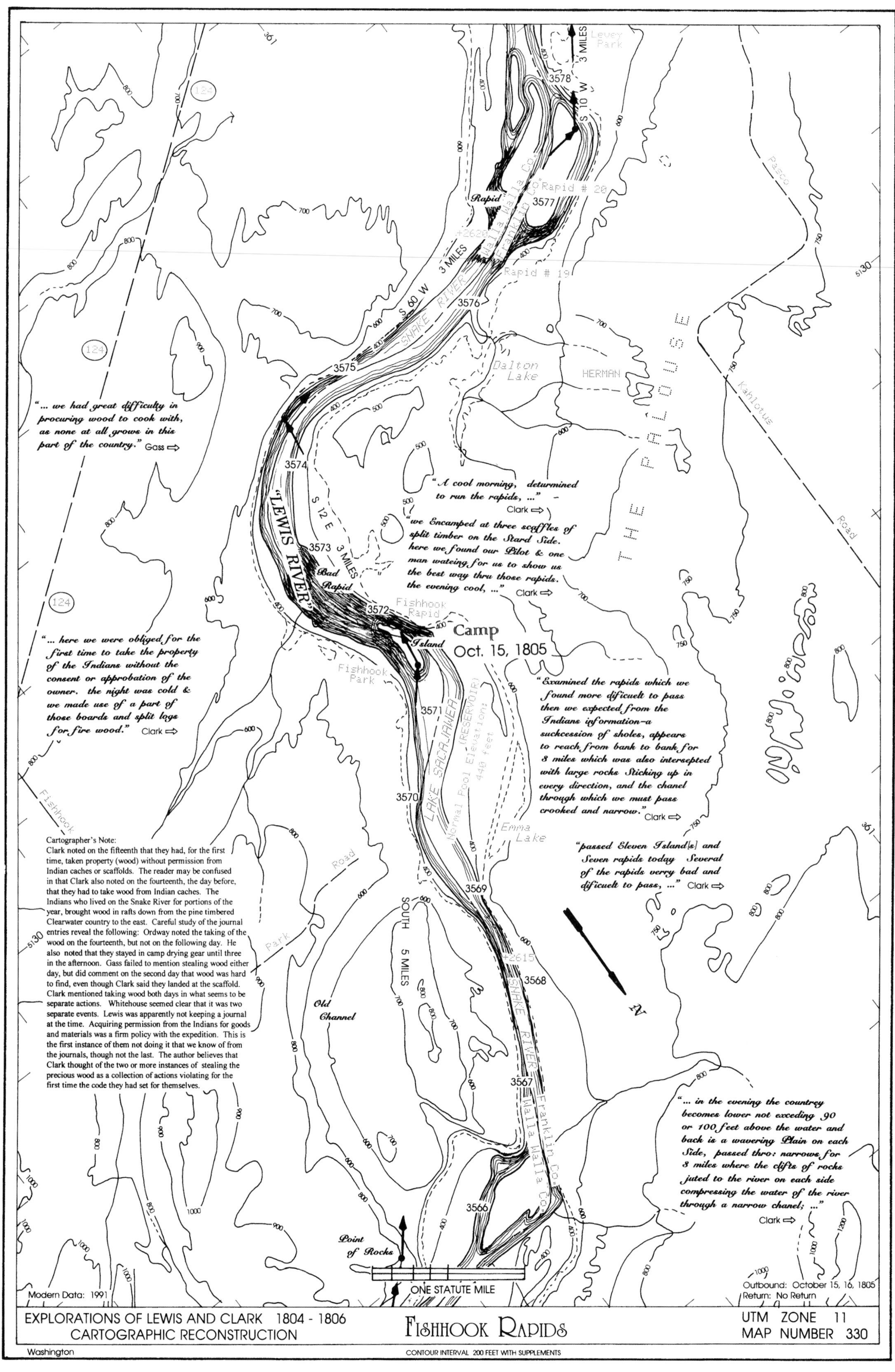

"... we had great difficulty in procuring wood to cook with, as none at all grows in this part of the country." Gass ⇨
"A cool morning, determined to run the rapids, ..." Clark ⇨
"we Encamped at three scaffles of split timber on the Stard Side. here we found our Pilot & one man wateing for us to show us the best way thru those rapids. the evening cool, ..." Clark ⇨
"... here we were obliged for the first time to take the property of the Indians without the consent or approbation of the owner. the night was cold & we made use of a part of those boards and split logs for fire wood." Clark ⇨
"Examined the rapids which we found more dificuelt to pass then we expected from the Indians information–a suckcession of sholes, appears to reach from bank to bank for 8 miles which was also intersepted with large rocks Sticking up in every direction, and the chanel through which we must pass crooked and narrow." Clark ⇨
"passed Eleven Island[s] and Seven rapids today Several of the rapids verry bad and dificuelt to pass, ..." Clark ⇨
"... in the evening the countrey becomes lower not exceding 90 or 100 feet above the water and back is a wavering Plain on each Side, passed thro: narrows for 3 miles where the clifts of rocks juted to the river on each side compressing the water of the river through a narrow chanel; ..." Clark ⇨
Cartographer's Note:
Clark noted on the fifteenth that they had, for the first time, taken property (wood) without permission from Indian caches or scaffolds. The reader may be confused in that Clark also noted on the fourteenth, the day before, that they had to take wood from Indian caches. The Indians who lived on the Snake River for portions of the year, brought wood in rafts down from the pine timbered Clearwater country to the east. Careful study of the journal entries reveal the following: Ordway noted the taking of the wood on the fourteenth, but not on the following day. He also noted that they stayed in camp drying gear until three in the afternoon. Gass failed to mention stealing wood either day, but did comment on the second day that wood was hard to find, even though Clark said they landed at the scaffold. Clark mentioned taking wood both days in what seems to be separate actions. Whitehouse seemed clear that it was two separate events. Lewis was apparently not keeping a journal at the time. Acquiring permission from the Indians for goods and materials was a firm policy with the expedition. This is the first instance of them not doing it that we know of from the journals, though not the last. The author believes that Clark thought of the two or more instances of stealing the precious wood as a collection of actions violating for the first time the code they had set for themselves.
Camp Oct. 15, 1805
Island
Fishhook Rapid
Bad Rapid
Rapid
Rapid # 20
Rapid # 19
"LEWIS RIVER"
SNAKE RIVER
LAKE SACAJAWEA (RESERVOIR)
Normal Pool Elevation: 440 feet
THE PALOUSE
Dalton Lake
HERMAN
Emma Lake
Fishhook Park
Levey Park
Walla Walla Co.
Franklin Co.
Old Channel
Point of Rocks
S 10 W 3 MILES
S 60 W 3 MILES
S 12 E 3 MILES
SOUTH 5 MILES
ONE STATUTE MILE
N
Modern Data: 1991
Outbound: October 15, 16, 1805
Return: No Return
EXPLORATIONS OF LEWIS AND CLARK 1804 - 1806
CARTOGRAPHIC RECONSTRUCTION
FISHHOOK RAPIDS
UTM ZONE 11
MAP NUMBER 330
Washington
CONTOUR INTERVAL 200 FEET WITH SUPPLEMENTS

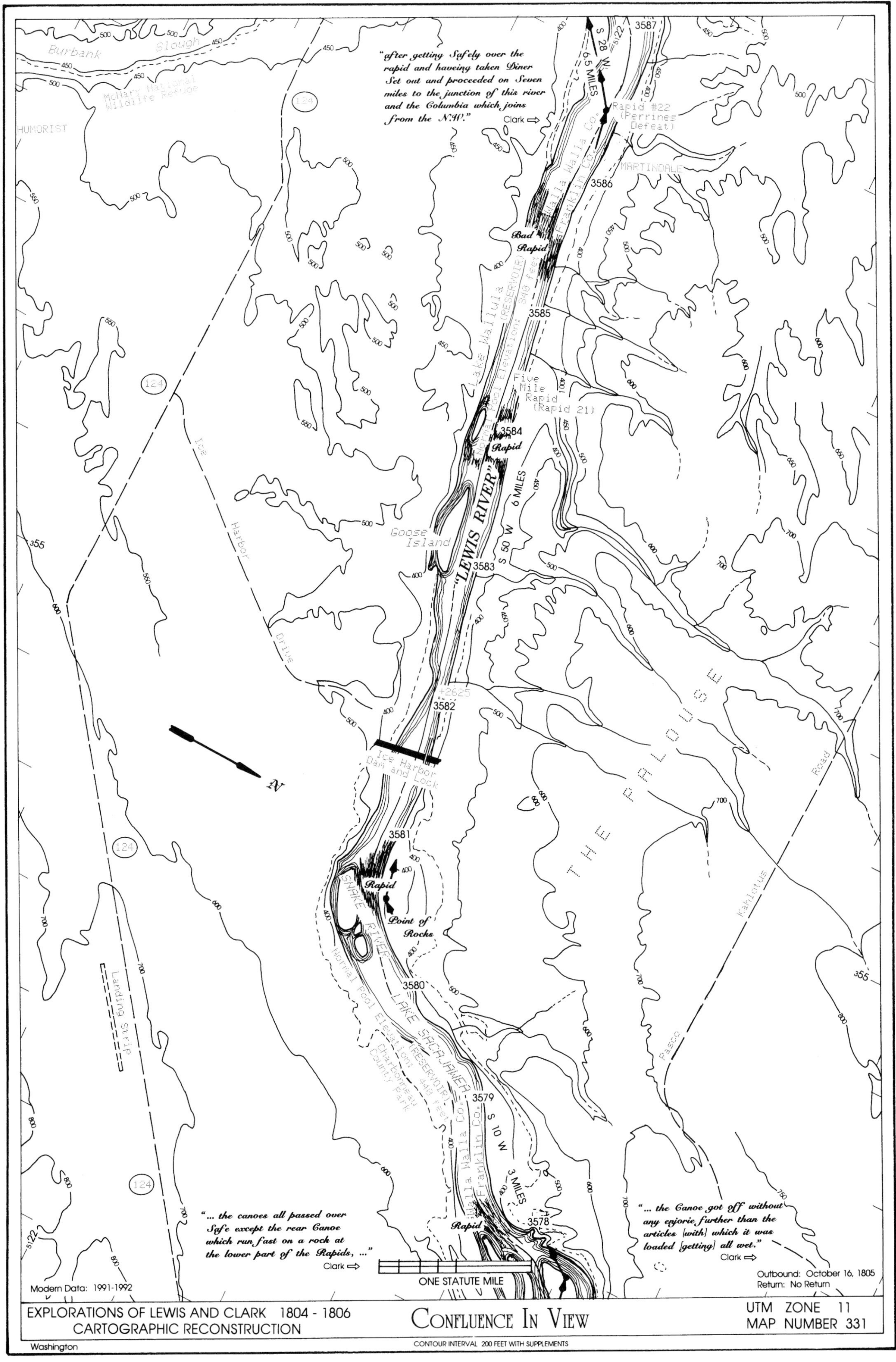

"after getting Safely over the rapid and haveing taken Diner Set out and proceeded on Seven miles to the junction of this river and the Columbia which joins from the N.W."
Clark ⇨
"... the canoes all passed over Safe except the rear Canoe which run fast on a rock at the lower part of the Rapids, ..."
Clark ⇨
"... the Canoe got off without any enjorie further than the articles [with] which it was loaded [getting] all wet."
Clark ⇨
Burbank Slough
McNary National Wildlife Refuge
HUMORIST
MARTINDALE
Rapid #22 (Perrines Defeat)
Walla Walla Co.
Franklin Co.
Bad Rapid
Lake Wallula (RESERVOIR)
Normal Pool Elevation: 340 feet
"LEWIS RIVER"
Five Mile Rapid (Rapid 21)
Rapid
Goose Island
S 28 W
6.5 MILES
S 50 W
6 MILES
S 10 W
3 MILES
Ice Harbor Drive
Ice Harbor Dam and Lock
SNAKE RIVER
Point of Rocks
LAKE SACAJAWEA (RESERVOIR)
Normal Pool Elevation: 440 feet
Charbonneau County Park
Landing Strip
THE PALOUSE
Kahlotus Road
Pasco
3587
3586
3585
3584
3583
3582
3581
3580
3579
3578
N
ONE STATUTE MILE
Modern Data: 1991-1992
Outbound: October 16, 1805
Return: No Return
EXPLORATIONS OF LEWIS AND CLARK 1804 - 1806
CARTOGRAPHIC RECONSTRUCTION
CONFLUENCE IN VIEW
UTM ZONE 11
MAP NUMBER 331
Washington
CONTOUR INTERVAL 200 FEET WITH SUPPLEMENTS

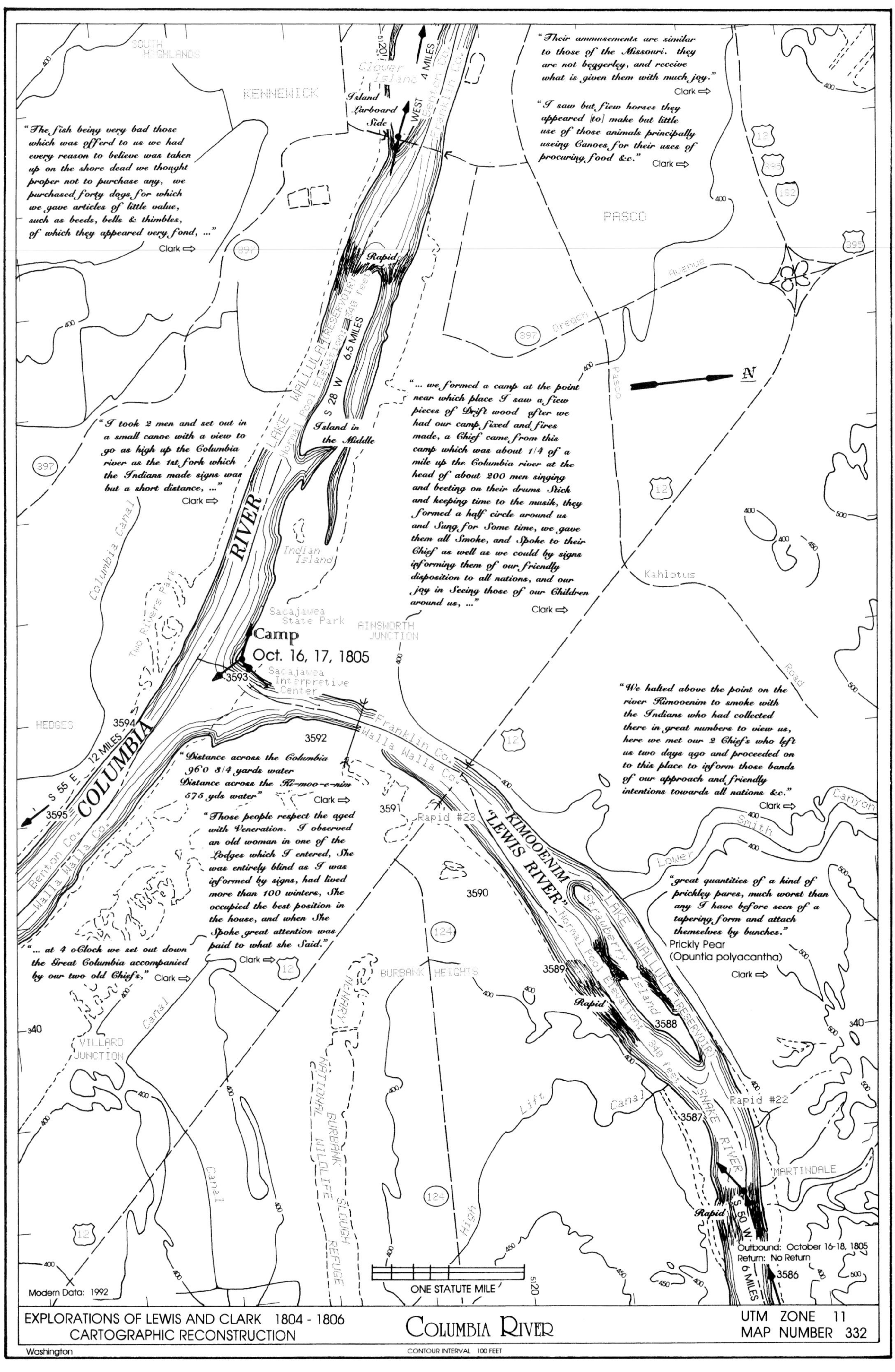

"Their amusements are similar to those of the Missouri. they are not beggerley, and receive what is given them with much joy."
Clark ⇨
"I saw but fiew horses they appeared [to] make but little use of those animals principally useing Canoes for their uses of procuring food &c."
Clark ⇨
"The fish being very bad those which was offerd to us we had every reason to believe was taken up on the shore dead we thought proper not to purchase any, we purchased forty dogs for which we gave articles of little value, such as beeds, bells & thimbles, of which they appeared very fond, ..."
Clark ⇨
"... we formed a camp at the point near which place I saw a fiew pieces of Drift wood after we had our camp fixed and fires made, a Chief came from this camp which was about 1/4 of a mile up the Columbia river at the head of about 200 men singing and beeting on their drums Stick and keeping time to the musik, they formed a half circle around us and Sung for Some time, we gave them all Smoke, and Spoke to their Chief as well as we could by signs informing them of our friendly disposition to all nations, and our joy in Seeing those of our Children around us, ..."
Clark ⇨
"I took 2 men and set out in a small canoe with a view to go as high up the Columbia river as the 1st fork which the Indians made signs was but a short distance, ..."
Clark ⇨
"We halted above the point on the river Kimooenim to smoke with the Indians who had collected there in great numbers to view us, here we met our 2 Chiefs who left us two days ago and proceeded on to this place to inform those bands of our approach and friendly intentions towards all nations &c."
Clark ⇨
"Distance across the Columbia 960 3/4 yards water Distance across the Ki-moo-e-nim 575 yds water"
Clark ⇨
"Those people respect the aged with Veneration. I observed an old woman in one of the Lodges which I entered, She was entirely blind as I was informed by signs, had lived more than 100 winters, She occupied the best position in the house, and when She Spoke great attention was paid to what she Said."
Clark ⇨
"great quantities of a kind of prickley pares, much worst than any I have before seen of a tapering form and attach themselves by bunches."
Prickly Pear
(Opuntia polyacantha)
Clark ⇨
"... at 4 oClock we set out down the Great Columbia accompanied by our two old Chiefs,"
Clark ⇨
SOUTH HIGHLANDS
KENNEWICK
Clover Island
Island Larboard Side
WEST 4 MILES
Benton Co.
Franklin Co.
PASCO
Rapid
LAKE WALLULA (RESERVOIR)
Normal Pool Elevation: 340 feet
S 28 W 6.5 MILES
Island in the Middle
Oregon Avenue
N
Pasco
Kahlotus Road
COLUMBIA RIVER
Columbia Canal
Two Rivers Park
Indian Island
Sacajawea State Park
AINSWORTH JUNCTION
Camp
Oct. 16, 17, 1805
Sacajawea Interpretive Center
HEDGES
S 55 E 12 MILES
Franklin Co.
Walla Walla Co.
Benton Co.
Walla Walla Co.
Rapid #23
KIMOOENIM "LEWIS RIVER"
Lower Smith Canyon
LAKE WALLULA (RESERVOIR)
Strawberry Island
Normal Pool Elevation: 340 feet
BURBANK HEIGHTS
McNARY NATIONAL WILDLIFE REFUGE
BURBANK SLOUGH
VILLARD JUNCTION
Canal
Lift Canal
High
Rapid #22
SNAKE RIVER
MARTINDALE
S 50 W 6 MILES
Outbound: October 16-18, 1805
Return: No Return
ONE STATUTE MILE
Modern Data: 1992
EXPLORATIONS OF LEWIS AND CLARK 1804 - 1806
CARTOGRAPHIC RECONSTRUCTION
COLUMBIA RIVER
UTM ZONE 11
MAP NUMBER 332
Washington
CONTOUR INTERVAL 100 FEET

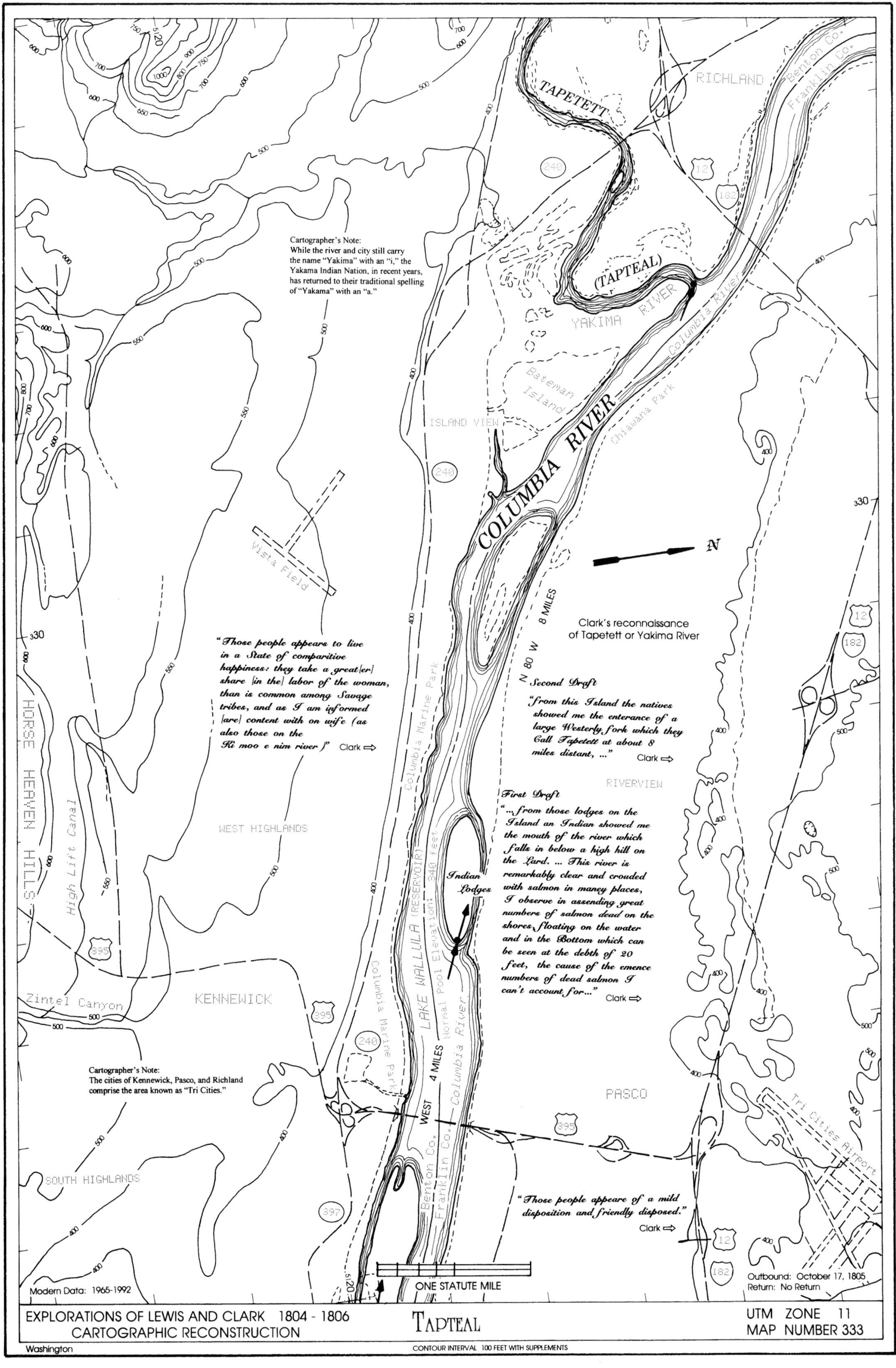
TAPETETT
RICHLAND
Benton Co.
Franklin Co.
(TAPTEAL)
YAKIMA RIVER
Columbia River
Bateman Island
ISLAND VIEW
Chiawana Park
COLUMBIA RIVER
Cartographer's Note:
While the river and city still carry the name "Yakima" with an "i," the Yakama Indian Nation, in recent years, has returned to their traditional spelling of "Yakama" with an "a."
Vista Field
N
8 MILES
N 80 W
Clark's reconnaissance of Tapetett or Yakima River
"Those people appears to live in a State of comparitive happiness: they take a great[er] share [in the] labor of the woman, than is common among Savage tribes, and as I am informed [are] content with on wife (as also those on the Ki moo e nim river)" Clark ⇨
Second Draft
"from this Island the natives showed me the enterance of a large Westerly fork which they Call Tapetett at about 8 miles distant, ..." Clark ⇨
RIVERVIEW
First Draft
"...from those lodges on the Island an Indian showed me the mouth of the river which falls in below a high hill on the Lard. ... This river is remarkably clear and crouded with salmon in maney places, I observe in assending great numbers of salmon dead on the shores, floating on the water and in the Bottom which can be seen at the debth of 20 feet, the cause of the emence numbers of dead salmon I can't account for..." Clark ⇨
Indian Lodges
HORSE HEAVEN HILLS
High Lift Canal
WEST HIGHLANDS
Columbia Marine Park
LAKE WALLULA (RESERVOIR)
Normal Pool Elevation: 340 feet
Zintel Canyon
KENNEWICK
Cartographer's Note:
The cities of Kennewick, Pasco, and Richland comprise the area known as "Tri Cities."
PASCO
Tri Cities Airport
WEST 4 MILES
SOUTH HIGHLANDS
"Those people appeare of a mild disposition and friendly disposed." Clark ⇨
ONE STATUTE MILE
Modern Data: 1965-1992
Outbound: October 17, 1805
Return: No Return
EXPLORATIONS OF LEWIS AND CLARK 1804 - 1806
CARTOGRAPHIC RECONSTRUCTION
TAPTEAL
UTM ZONE 11
MAP NUMBER 333
Washington
CONTOUR INTERVAL 100 FEET WITH SUPPLEMENTS

Indexes to the Lewis and Clark Trail Maps, Volume II

Outbound and Return Camps

Outbound and Return Dates

Selected Locations and Events

Place Names

Outbound and Return Camps

Outbound Camps (April 7 to October 17, 1805)

April 7, 1805 (left "Fort Mandan" winter encampment) [see *L&C Trail Maps, Vol. I,* Map 152]
April 8, 1805 [see *Vol. I,* Map 153]
April 9, 1805 ... Map 156
April 10, 1805 ("Little Basin") ... Map 157
April 11, 1805 ... Map 159
April 12, 1805 (Little Missouri River) ... Map 160
April 13, 1805 ... Map 162, 163
April 14, 1805 ... Map 165
April 15, 1805 ... Map 167
April 16, 1805 ("Grand Point") ... Map 169
April 17, 1805 ("Burnt Hills") ... Map 171
April 18–19, 1805 ... Map 172
April 20, 1805 ... Map 173
April 21, 1805 ... Map 174
April 22, 1805 ("Beaver Bends") ... Map 175
April 23–24, 1805 ... Map 176
April 25, 1805 ... Map 176, 177
April 26, 1805 (Yellowstone River) ... Map 177
April 27, 1805 ... Map 178
April 28, 1805 ... Map 179, 180
April 29, 1805 ("Marthas River") ... Map 182
April 30, 1805 ... Map 184
May 1, 1805 ... Map 184
May 2, 1805 ... Map 185
May 3, 1805 ... Map 186
May 4, 1805 ... Map 187
May 5, 1805 ... Map 188
May 6, 1805 ... Map 190
May 7, 1805 ... Map 191
May 8, 1805 ... Map 193
May 9, 1805 ("Warner River") ... Map 195
May 10, 1805 ... Map 195
May 11, 1805 ... Map 196
May 12, 1805 ... Map 198
May 13, 1805 ... Map 199
May 14–15, 1805 (Panther Camp) ... Map 200
May 16, 1805 ... Map 200
May 17, 1805 ... Map 202
May 18, 1805 ... Map 203
May 19, 1805 ... Map 205
May 20, 1805 (Musselshell River) ... Map 205
May 21, 1805 ... Map 206
May 22, 1805 ... Map 207
May 23, 1805 ... Map 209
May 24, 1805 ... Map 211
May 25, 1805 ("Goodrichs Island") ... Map 212
May 26, 1805 ("Elk and Fawn Riffle") ... Map 214
May 27, 1805 ... Map 215
May 28, 1805 ("Seven Valley Islands") ... Map 217
May 29, 1805 ... Map 218
May 30, 1805 ... Map 219
May 31, 1805 ("Stone Wall Creek") ... Map 221
June 1, 1805 ... Map 222
June 2, 1805 ("Marias River") ... Map 224, 231
June 3–11, 1805 (main party at "Marias") ... Map 224, 231
June 4, 1805 (Lewis on "Marias") ... Map 226
June 4, 1805, Clark on south fork) ... Map 233, 234
June 5, 1805 (Lewis on "Marias") ... Map 229
June 5, 1805 (Clark on "Tanzey" [off maps])
June 6, 1805 (Lewis return on "Marias") ... Map 227
June 6, 1805 (Clark return to main camp) ... Map 224, 231
June 7, 1805 (Lewis return on "Marias") ... Map 226
June 11, 1805 (Lewis to Great Falls) ... Map 231
June 12, 1805 (main party) ... Map 231
June 12, 1805 (Lewis to Great Falls) ... Map 234
June 13, 1805 (main party) ... Map 233
June 13, 1805 (Lewis finds Great Falls) ... Map 236
June 14, 1805 (main party) ... Map 234
June 14, 1805 (Lewis at Great Falls) ... Map 236
June 15–29, 1805 (lower portage camp) ... Map 235
June 15, 1805 (Lewis at Great Falls) ... Map 236
June 16, 1805 (Lewis rejoins main party) ... Map 235
June 17, 1805 (Clark at "Crooked Falls") ... Map 236
June 18–July 12, 1805 (upper portage camp) ... Map 237
July 10–14, 1805 (canoe building camp) ... Map 238
July 15, 1805 ... Map 239
July 16, 1805 (entering the mountains) ... Map 241
July 17, 1805 ... Map 242
July 18, 1805 (main party) ... Map 244
July 18, 1805 (Clark seeking the Lemhi) ... Map 244
July 19, 1805 ("Gates of the Mountains") ... Map 245
July 19, 1805 (Clark seeking the Lemhi) ... Map 248
July 20, 1805 (main party) ... Map 247
July 20–21, 1805 (Clark seeking the Lemhi) ... Map 249
July 21, 1805 (main party) ... Map 248
July 22, 1805 ... Map 250
July 23, 1805 (main party) ... Map 251
July 23, 1805 (Clark seeking the Lemhi) ... Map 252
July 24, 1805 (main party) ... Map 252
July 24, 1805 (Clark seeking the Lemhi) ... Map 254
July 25, 1805 (main party) ... Map 253
July 25, 1805 (Clark seeking the Lemhi) ... Map 256
July 26, 1805 (main party) ... Map 254
July 26, 1805 (Clark seeking the Lemhi) ... Map 256
July 27–29, 1805 (main party) ... Map 255
July 30, 1805 ... Map 256
July 31, 1805 ... Map 257
August 1, 1805 (main party) ... Map 258
August 1, 1805 (Lewis seeking the Lemhi) ... Map 259
August 2, 1805 (main party) ... Map 259, 260
August 2, 1805 (Lewis seeking the Lemhi) ... Map 261
August 3, 1805 (main party) ... Map 260
August 3, 1805 (Lewis seeking the Lemhi) ... Map 262
August 4, 1805 (main party) ... Map 261, 262
August 4, 1805 (Lewis seeking the Lemhi) ... Map 263
August 5, 1805 (main party) ... Map 263
August 5, 1805 (Lewis seeking the Lemhi) ... Map 263
August 6, 1805 (main party) ... Map 262, 263
August 6, 1805 (Lewis meets Clark, "Wisdom River") ... Map 262, 263
August 7, 1805 ... Map 263
August 8, 1805 ... Map 264
August 9, 1805 ("Beaverhead Rock") ... Map 264
August 9, 1805 (Lewis seeking the Lemhi) ... Map 266
August 10, 1805 (main party) ... Map 264
August 10, 1805 (Lewis seeking the Lemhi) ... Map 270
August 11, 1805 (main party) ... Map 264, 265
August 11, 1805 (Lewis approaches Lemhi Pass) ... Map 272
August 12, 1805 (main party) ... Map 266
August 12, 1805 (Lewis crosses Lemhi Pass) ... Map 273
August 13, 1805 (main party) ... Map 266
August 13, 1805 (Lewis among the Lemhi) ... Map 275
August 14, 1805 ("Rattlesnake Cliffs") ... Map 267
August 14, 1805 (Lewis among the Lemhi) ... Map 275
August 15, 1805 (main party) ... Map 268
August 15, 1805 (Lewis returns via Lemhi Pass) .. Map 271, 272
August 16, 1805 ("Service Berry Valley") ... Map 268
August 16, 1805 (Lewis returns to the forks) ... Map 269
August 17–23, 1805 ("Camp Fortunate") ... Map 269
August 18, 1805 (Clark detachment) ... Map 271
August 19, 1805 (Clark in Lemhi Valley) ... Map 274
August 20, 1805 (Clark at Lemhi villages) ... Map 275
August 21, 1805 (Clark seeks water route) ... Map 278
August 22, 1805 (Clark on Salmon River) ... Map 280
August 23, 1805 (Clark on Salmon River) ... Map 280
August 24, 1805 (main party toward Lemhi Pass) ... Map 269, 270
August 24, 1805 (Clark returns, Salmon River) ... Map 280
August 25, 1805 (main party near Lemhi Pass) ... Map 272
August 25, 1805 (Clark returns to Lemhi Valley) ... Map 278
August 26–29, 1805 (main party at Lemhi villages) ... Map 275
August 26, 1805 (Clark returns to main party) ... Map 276
August 30, 1805 (main party to northern trail) ... Map 276
August 31, 1805 ... Map 278
September 1, 1805 ... Map 282
September 2, 1805 ("Dismal Swamp") ... Map 283
September 3, 1805 (Lost Trail Pass) ... Map 284
September 4–5, 1805 (Ross Hole) ... Map 285
September 6, 1805 ... Map 286
September 7, 1805 ... Map 289
September 8, 1805 ... Map 292
September 9–10, 1805 ("Travelers Rest") ... Map 294, 295
September 11, 1805 ... Map 295
September 12, 1805 ... Map 297
September 13, 1805 (Lolo Pass) ... Map 298
September 14, 1805 ... Map 300
September 15, 1805 (Cayuse Junction) ... Map 301
September 16, 1805 (Indian Postoffice) ... Map 302
September 17, 1805 (Indian Grave Peak) ... Map 303
September 18, 1805 (main party) ... Map 304
September 18, 1805 (Clark's hunters) ... Map 305
September 19, 1805 (main party) ... Map 305
September 19, 1805 (Clark's hunters) ... Map 307
September 20, 1805 (main party) ... Map 306
September 20, 1805 (Clark among Nez Perce) ... Map 308
September 21, 1805 (main party) ... Map 307
September 21, 1805 (Clark among Nez Perce) ... Map 311
September 22, 1805 (1st Nez Perce village) ... Map 308
September 23, 1805 (2nd Nez Perce village) ... Map 308
September 24–25, 1805 (Twisted Hair camp) ... Map 311
Sept. 26–Oct. 6, 1805 (Canoe Camp) ... Map 311, 312
October 7, 1805 ... Map 313
October 8–9, 1805 ... Map 315
October 10, 1805 ("Lewis River") ... Map 316
October 11, 1805 ... Map 320
October 12, 1805 ... Map 324, 325
October 13, 1805 ... Map 327
October 14, 1805 ... Map 328
October 15, 1805 ... Map 330
October 16–17, 1805 (Snake/Columbia confluence) ... Map 332

Return Camps (May 4 to August 13, 1806)

May 4, 1806 ... Map 317
May 5, 1806 ("Colters Creek") ... Map 314
May 6, 1806 ... Map 314
May 7, 1806 ... Map 312
May 8, 1806 ... Map 311
May 9–June 9, 1806 (Long Camp) [see *L&C Trail Maps, Vol. III*]
June 10–14, 1806 ... Map 308

Outbound and Return Dates

Outbound Dates (April 7 to October 18, 1805)

Return Dates (May 4 to August 14, 1806)

Selected Locations and Events

Place Names

A

B

C

D

E

F

G

H

I

J

K

L

M

N

O

P

Q

R

S

T

U

V

W

XYZ